THE GLOBAL CHALLENGE

INTERNATIONAL HUMAN RESOURCE MANAGEMENT

Third Edition

Vladimir Pucik, Paul Evans, Ingmar Björkman and Shad Morris

CHICAGO
BUSINESS PRESS

CHICAGO
BUSINESS PRESS

THE GLOBAL CHALLENGE: INTERNATIONAL HUMAN RESOURCE MANAGEMENT,
THIRD EDITION

For product information or assistance, visit:
www.chicagobusinesspress.com

ISBN-13: 978-0-983-33249-7

THE GLOBAL CHALLENGE

INTERNATIONAL HUMAN RESOURCE MANAGEMENT

BRIEF CONTENTS

CONTENTS

PREFACE

Globalization has reshaped our world, and it will continue to do so—witness the rapidly growing presence of China, India, and other emerging countries on the world economic scene in the years since the first edition of this book in 2002. Financial markets are increasingly interdependent, with dramatic consequences for the volatility of the world economy, while advances in information technology have facilitated the globalization of knowledge. With money and other tangible assets becoming increasingly global and accessible, it is natural that companies are looking to people as a source of competitive differentiation.

Faced with ever more pressing requirements to do things better, cheaper, and faster, the ability to attract people in different regions of the world, to manage their performance, to develop and retain them, and to coordinate effectively across boundaries becomes critical. Developing future global leaders is high on nearly every CEO's agenda. The battle to grow and prosper in markets around the world is to a great extent over talent—and here multinationals face the need to accelerate the diversity and localization of management. Therefore, most business executives and scholars agree that the ability to manage human resources (HR) is crucial if multinational firms are to successfully meet the challenges they face in the dynamic and competitive global environment.

We take a *general management perspective* on these issues, since strategy, organizational capabilities, and people management are increasingly intertwined in multinational firms. Each chapter in this book is a stand-alone guide to a particular aspect of international human resource management (HRM)—from the history and overview of international HRM in the first chapter to the functional implications for HR professionals in the last, from building multinational coordination to managing the human side of cross-border acquisitions.

We build on the traditional agenda of international human resource management—how to respond to *cultural and institutional differences, manage cross-border mobility*, and *develop global leaders*. These issues were already discussed in the first two editions of this book, and we have updated the chapters with new learning from research and practice.

The structure of this book has not changed much from the second edition, but we have tried to simplify and shorten the content while updating research findings and emphasizing the experience of companies from different regions of the world, as well as learning from the new generation of high-technology firms riding the digitalization wave. We also address the increasingly critical people challenges of coordination, talent and knowledge management, and the underlying dynamics of change:

- Reflecting competitive demands, the organization of multinational companies is increasingly multidimensional. If stultifying bureaucracy is to be avoided, firms must rely on *lateral leadership* roles to create alignment. *Cross-boundary teams* in different shapes and forms become the basic unit of the multinational firm, and we devote one chapter to discussing HRM issues related to such mechanisms of horizontal coordination.

- In an increasingly networked world where talented people have many career options, the binding glue comes from social capital and organizational culture—shared values, beliefs, and norms. Global mindset also helps resolve the inevitable tensions embedded in international business. We discuss how HRM contributes to this *social architecture* of multinational firms.

- The *core global HRM processes*—from talent attraction and selection through performance management to leadership development and steering mobility—need to be redesigned to support the needs of global organizations. We summarize the latest evidence from research and corporate practice and outline the implications for HRM.

- *Implementing rapid change* in operations spread across the globe is typically a difficult challenge for complex multinationals. Line managers have to pay close attention to the hows of change, as well as the whats—and the line looks to their HR managers for guidance. We build on the experience of leading firms to present frameworks for how to manage processes of change and how to apply them.

- Knowledge management in multinational firms is largely a people game. Social networking opens up tremendous possibilities for *global knowledge sharing and the management of innovation*. Multinational corporations are learning how to capitalize on this—with new opportunities for HR to make a contribution.

- Also, companies continue to grow through *mergers and acquisitions*, where value depends greatly on the people challenges of integration; and *cross-border alliances* are part of the fabric of organizational life, along with the associated HR dimension.

- Many multinational firms are struggling with the issue of globalizing their HR practices. How can they build worldwide consistency while respecting the realities of local environments? At the same time, the HR function is undergoing a profound transformation, built around e-HR, self-help, and shared services, while deepening its business support role. We address these issues by mapping out various *configurations of global HRM*.

- Most fundamentally, how can firms be both local and global in their orientation to HRM, capable of exploiting capabilities today while developing talent for tomorrow, integrating worldwide operations while at the same time encouraging local entrepreneurship? In other words, how can firms cope with the *"both/and" dualities* that underlie international management?

Addressing these issues means that instructors, students, and practitioners have to go beyond a narrow functional perspective on international human resource management. While keeping a clear focus on HRM, we wanted to combine the leading edge of practice with the state of the art in theory, building on research in strategy, international management, organizational theory, and cross-cultural management, among other domains. Indeed we argue that what is exciting about the international HRM field is that it must be interdisciplinary in its orientation.

Our teaching, research, and consulting have taken place more or less equally over the years in North America, Europe, and Asia, and to a lesser extent in South America and Australia. Our intention has been to write a book on such issues that is genuinely international in its orientation. The cases we use to introduce each chapter cover the globe, as do our examples from corporate practice—Nestlé and KONE from Europe; GE and eBay from North America; Haier, Infosys, and CEMEX from emerging countries; as well as the World Bank.

Our intended audience is the graduate student and the reflective practitioner. The material presented in *The Global Challenge* is designed for use in advanced undergraduate, MBA, and masters-level courses, as well as executive programs at business schools and in companies. We strive to provide practical advice, built on the experience of leaders and organizations as well as research, but we aspire to do more than that. Our objective is to help people understand the mindset, the deeper set of attitudes, needed to thrive in a world that is increasingly characterized by paradox and duality.

We hope that HR professionals will find this book helpful in providing new insights and actions as they face up to the paradoxes of their field. We also hope that our academic colleagues will be stimulated by the way we have attempted to frame this area.

ABOUT THE AUTHORS

Vladimir Pucik is a Visiting Professor in the Department of Management at China Europe International Business School (CEIBS) in Shanghai. Until his retirement, he was for fifteen years a Professor of International Human Resources and Strategy at IMD, in Switzerland, where he directed a variety of executive programs. Before joining IMD, he taught at Cornell University and the University of Michigan and spent three years as a visiting scholar at Keio and Hitotsubashi Universities in Tokyo.

He was born in Prague where he studied international economics, law, and political science. After falling out with the country's repressive government, he left Czechoslovakia and received a master's degree in international affairs—specializing in East Asia—and a PhD in business administration from Columbia University.

He has published extensively in first-tier academic and professional journals, contributed to more than 30 books and monographs in the area of international business and HRM, and written numerous case studies in the field of business strategy, organization, and international HRM. His recent research interests include strategic HRM in multinational firms, cross-border M&A and strategic alliances, building organizational capabilities for global competition, and comparative management with a particular emphasis on China, Japan, and Central and Eastern Europe.

During his career, he has consulted and conducted workshops for major corporations worldwide, including ABB, Allianz, AGC, Baxter, BMW, Bosch, Canon, Daimler, GE, Hitachi, IBM, Intel, J&J, KPMG, Merck, Nokia, Oracle, Shell, and Toyota. In addition to his work as an academic and consultant/coach to senior management teams, Dr. Pucik is also a founding partner in several high-tech start-up ventures.

Paul Evans is the Shell Chaired Professor of Human Resources and Organizational Development, Emeritus, at INSEAD (Europe and Singapore). British by nationality but raised in Africa, he has a PhD in Organizational Psychology from MIT, an MBA from INSEAD, and a Danish business diploma, and he is a graduate in law from Cambridge University. He led INSEAD's activities in the field of international HRM for many years, directing many of their executive programs in this domain. He was titular professor at the European Institute for Advanced Studies in Management in Brussels, and has taught at Boston University, MIT, l'Université de Montréal, Stockholm School of Economics, Cornell University, Skolkovo Moscow, CEIBS Shanghai, as well as spending periods as visiting scholar at the University of Southern California, UC Berkeley, and London Business School.

His research interests focus on international HRM, leadership, the management of change, and matrix organization, while his long-standing intellectual interest is in the dualities that underlie human and organizational behavior. Among his books are a pioneering study of the relationship between the professional and private life of executives, *Must Success Cost so Much?* (translated into seven languages). During his career, he has been founder or board member of a number of professional associations and forums. He received an award from INSEAD's MBA students as "outstanding teacher of the year" for his course on IHRM, and he has worked as an advisor or directed/taught programs for more than 200 multinational corporations. Currently he is the founding academic director of INSEAD's *Global Talent Competitiveness Index* (GTCI), a composite model and index covering 109 countries of the world aimed at measuring talent competitiveness of countries, regions, and cities.

Ingmar Björkman is Professor of International Business and Dean of Aalto University School of Business in Finland. He has previously been Professor, Head of Department, and Vice Rector of Research at Hanken School of Economics, and has held visiting positions at Hong Kong University, ESSEC (Paris), INSEAD (Fontainebleau and Singapore), and SCANCOR (Stanford University). He has also taught at a number of other business schools in Europe and Asia.

His research interests focus on international human resource management and the management of international mergers and acquisitions. He is a winner of the *Journal of International Business Studies Decade Award* (2013, together with Dana Minbaeva, Torben Pedersen, Carl Fey, and H.-J. Park). He has coedited *The Handbook of Research in International Human Resource Management* (2012, second edition, Edward Elgar) with Günter Stahl (WU) and Shad Morris (Brigham Young University). A regular contributor to international academic journals, he works with organizations on issues related to how they manage their human resources.

Shad Morris is the Georgia White Fellow and Associate Professor of Organizational Leadership and Strategy at the Marriott School of Management, Brigham Young University, in the USA. He teaches and conducts research at the intersection of human resource management and strategy. In particular, he explores empirical problems related to how companies invest in employee competencies and social networks to build organizational capabilities in a global market. In addition to his full-time position at the Marriott School, he is a Research Fellow at Cambridge University's Centre for International Human Resource Management and has been a visiting professor at MIT's Sloan School of Management, Copenhagen Business School, and the Indian School of Business.

He has coauthored two other books: *Managing People* and *Knowledge in Professional Service Firms* and *Managing Human Resources*. He has also published in journals such as *Academy of Management Review*, *Journal of International Business Studies*, *Strategic Management Journal*, *Journal of Operations Management*, *Harvard Business Review*, *MIT Sloan Management Review*, and *Human Resource Management*. Prior to becoming an academic, he worked for the World Bank, Management Systems International, and Alcoa.

ACKNOWLEDGMENTS

A book such as this builds on the insights, experiences, and research of many people.

First, we would like to thank the executives from the numerous companies that we have worked with over the last thirty years, who have shared their experiences and views during teaching seminars, research studies, consulting projects, forums, and conferences. If we were to single out a few, they would include ABB, AGC Glass, Allianz, Canon, General Electric, Haier, Infosys, KONE, Nokia, Merck Group, Shell, Schlumberger, and Toyota. We extend particular thanks to Matti Alahuhta, Wilf Blackburn, Rick Brown, Hirata Yasutoshi, Hugh Mitchell, Christine Shih, Gary Steel, Tsuruoka Hajime, Sita Ramaswami, Kerttu Tuomas, Yamashita Yukio, and Zhang Ruimin.

We have intellectual debts to pay to many academic colleagues and friends. Some of the foundation concepts on international strategy and organization underlying this book were laid down by Chris Bartlett and the late Sumantra Ghoshal, along with Yves Doz and Charles Hampden-Turner, as well as close colleagues now deceased—Jay Galbraith, Gunnar Hedlund and C.K. Prahalad, In the human resource management field, we owe particular thanks to Dick Beatty, John Boudreau, Chris Brewster, Pawan Budwar, Peter Cappelli, Lee Dyer, Mats Ehrnrooth, Carl Fey, Paul Gooderham, Lynda Gratton, Anne-Wil Harzing, Susan Jackson, Henrik Holt Larsen, Ed Lawler, Jon Lervik, Kristiina Mäkelä, Mark Mendenhall, George Milkovich, Dana Minbaeva, H.J. Park, Randall Schuler, Adam Smale, Scott Snell, Paul Sparrow, Günter Stahl, Jennie Sumelius, Betania Tanure, Dave Ulrich, Theresa Welbourne, Denise Welch, and Pat Wright. We also benefited from interactions with Ulf Andersson, Wilhelm Barner-Rasmussen, Henri-Claude de Bettignies, Julian Birkinshaw, Michael Brimm, Dan Denison, Robert Diab, Mats Forsgren, Morten Hansen, Ludo van der Heyden, Quy Huy, Tim Judge, Peter Killing, André Laurent, Stefanie Lenway, Don Marchand, Jean-Francois Manzoni, Martha Maznevski, Tom Murtha, Maury Peiperl, Torben Pedersen, Rebecca Piekkari, Joe Santos, Ed Schein, Susan Schneider, Katherine Xin, Eero Vaara, Zhixing Xiao, Tatiana Zalan, and Udo Zander.

Thanks also for the initiative, encouragement, and patience of our able publisher Paul Ducham, as well as to Alex Antidius Arpoudam and the rest of the editing crew at Chicago Business Press.

And finally there is the deepest appreciation for the constant and loyal support of our families. For Vlado, Hoan has yet again provided invaluable encouragement and help to move this project forward—for longer than they would care to remember. For Paul, Bente has lived with and supported this ongoing venture, for which he is grateful beyond measure. For Ingmar, Anna has patiently looked forward to the completion of the third edition so that her husband can spend more time with the family. For Shad, Mindi has been very supportive and provided valuable feedback on new ideas for the book.

1

The Challenges of International Human Resource Management

SUMMARY

Challenge

Many companies struggle to implement global strategies that call for local responsiveness to capture market opportunities *and* global integration to gain from economies of scale and scope

Analysis

Successful multinationals align elements of the *HRM Wheel* to support:

- Building differentiating organizational capabilities in line with the global strategy
- Leveraging a balanced portfolio of control and coordination mechanisms

Solutions

- Recognize the importance of people management for responding to challenges of globalization
- View *HRM* from the perspective of guiding principles, practices, and functional roles and learn how they lead to superior outcomes
- Support the transnational organization through structural coordination, social architecture, and global *HRM* processes
- Avoid pendulum swings by embracing competing dualities

The International Journey of Lincoln Electric

The 120-year-old Ohio-based Lincoln Electric has long been a favorite case used by business schools to show how human resource management (HRM) can contribute to sustainable business performance. The largest manufacturer of welding equipment in the world, Lincoln motivates its American employees through a distinctive compensation system and a culture of cooperation between management and labor, based on one of the founders' fervent beliefs in self-reliance, the necessity of competition for human progress, and egalitarian treatment of managers and employees. Introduced by family management in the 1930s, the incentive system is based on piece rates and an annual bonus linked to profits that can amount to over half of employees' income. To determine the bonus, production employees are appraised on four criteria: output, quality, dependability, and ideas/cooperation.

Abroad, Lincoln Electric invested successfully in Canada (1925), Australia (1938), and France (1955), but until the late 1980s the firm still focused mostly on its domestic market. The company had enjoyed unrivaled and much-acclaimed growth and prosperity, driving its domestic competitors (including GE) out of the business. Led by a management team that had never worked outside the US, the firm then decided on a bold strategy for internationalization, spending the equivalent of over half its sales on building new plants in Japan and Latin America and on 19 acquisitions in various European countries and Mexico.[1] Senior executives envisioned opportunities to leverage Lincoln's manufacturing expertise and HRM system internationally, implementing its motivational and incentive system, which already worked well in France and other foreign operations. Combining the most productive and low-cost manufacturing operation with high quality, Lincoln seemed destined to dominate the global market.

The rapid international expansion turned out to be a failure. Lacking managers with international experience, the firm was forced to rely on acquired managers who were not familiar with Lincoln's culture and who wanted to maintain their autonomy. The only new country where its incentive system and culture took gradual hold was Mexico. In most of Europe and Japan, where piece-rate payments are viewed with deep suspicion, Lincoln's approach was rejected. In Germany, with its 35-hour working week, employees would not agree to work nearly 50 hours when necessary, as they did in the US. The tight link between sales and manufacturing—another pillar of Lincoln's success—disintegrated, and inventory ballooned while sales stagnated in the recession of the early 1990s. The control and coordination challenges associated with the rapidly internationalizing operations were of a different magnitude than the organization had handled in the past. To fix the problems, senior managers with strong international track records were recruited from outside the company. A new team then sold off or restructured most of its international acquisitions.

Lincoln's failure was in part a consequence of poor transfer of HRM practices abroad, in spite of the phenomenal success of its approach at home. When Lincoln again expanded its international operations in the late 1990s, it kept the expensive lessons from its previous internationalization attempt in mind. The company relied more on joint ventures and other alliances and, when necessary, adapted its management approach to fit local conditions.[2] It also gradually built a cadre of managers with international experience who were transferred to the foreign units. By 2015, the company came back to enjoying record sales and profits, with a third of sales from foreign operations. However, in spite of the significant progress made, Lincoln still experienced challenges in managing people in some of its overseas units. For instance, in China it was difficult to find, develop, and retain talented local professionals and managers, and the company was struggling to reach profitability in Asia Pacific.[3]

OVERVIEW

A look at the history of international business shows that the dilemmas faced by Lincoln Electric have always existed: how to build on the existing strengths of a company when going international but also be flexible and responsive to local needs, and how to control and coordinate diverse units and people as well as capture the scale advantages of international operations.

We explore first the challenges faced by companies as they internationalize their operations. We address the question of how HRM adds value in international firms, arguing that it can best contribute to firm performance when HR practices support the organizational capabilities that allow the company to compete successfully. We also review the HRM domain, represented by the segments of an HRM Wheel that ties strategy with organizational capabilities and how these capabilities are developed.

DEFYING BORDERS: WHAT'S NEW?

International business is not a recent phenomenon; nor is international HRM a product of the twentieth or twenty-first century. The Assyrians, Phoenicians, Greeks, and Romans all engaged in extensive cross-border trade. There is evidence that shortly after 2000 BC, Assyrian commercial organizations already had many of the traits of modern multinational companies, complete with head offices and branches, clear hierarchy, foreign employees, and value-adding activities in multiple regions.[4] While empire-building was the primary goal of Roman-style international expansion, commerce was a by-product of the need to clothe and feed the dispersed garrisons.[5] So when can we situate the birth of international companies?

International Operations in the Pre-Industrial Era

The real pioneers of international business were the sixteenth- and seventeenth-century trading companies—the English and Dutch East India companies, the Muscovy Company, the Hudson's Bay Company, and the Royal African Company.[6] These companies exchanged merchandise and services across continents and had a geographical spread to rival today's multinational firms. They signed on crews and chartered ships, and engaged the services of experts with skills in trade negotiations and foreign languages, capable of assessing the quality of goods and determining how they should be handled and loaded. The companies were obliged to delegate considerable responsibility to local representatives running their operations in far-away countries, which created a new challenge: how to develop control structures and systems to monitor the behavior of their scattered agents?

Distance makes control more difficult. This was particularly true in an era when the means of transport and communication were inseparable and slow.[7] Initially, companies demanded not only accounts but also written records of decisions and notification of compliance with directives from home. The high volume of transactions then led to the creation of administrative units to process receipts and accounts and to handle correspondence at the home office. By the mid-eighteenth century, the Dutch and English East India companies each employed over 350 salaried staff involved in office administration.

Establishing formal rules and procedures was one way of exercising control but other control measures were also developed, such as employment contracts stipulating that managers would work hard and in the interests of the company. Failure to do so could lead to reprimand or dismissal. Setting performance measures was the next step. These included the amount of outstanding credit on advance contracts, whether ships sailed on time, and the care taken in loading mixed cargoes.

Further, systems were installed to provide additional information about employees' behavior and activities. Ships were staffed with pursers, ships' captains were rewarded for detecting illegal goods, and private correspondence was read to minimize the risk of violations. In addition, bonds were often required from managers as insurance against private trade. However, there were also generous financial incentives, such as remuneration packages comprising a fixed cash component and a sizeable bonus. Such a mix of control approaches was not far off contemporary methods used to evaluate and reward managerial performance in large multinationals.

The Impact of Industrialization

The Industrial Revolution originated in Britain in the late eighteenth century. The emergence of the factory system had a dramatic impact both on international business and on the management of people.

The international spread of rail networks and the advent of steamships brought new speed and reliability to international travel, and the invention of the telegraph uncoupled long-distance communication from transportation. Improved communication and transportation opened up new markets and facilitated access to resources in distant locations. Cross-border manufacturing began to emerge by the mid-nineteenth century. The Great Exhibition of 1851, staged in London, was an early forum for international benchmarking and exposed visitors to a number of US products.[8] Among these products were the Singer sewing machine and the Colt repeating pistol. Not surprisingly these firms established two of the earliest recorded US manufacturing investments in Britain: Colt set up a plant in 1853 and Singer in 1867.

Still, it was difficult to exercise real control over distant operations. The rare manufacturing firms that ventured abroad often used family members to manage their international operations. For example, when Siemens set up its St Petersburg factory in 1855, a brother of the founder was put in charge. In 1863 another brother established a factory to produce sea cables in Britain. Keeping it in the family was the best guarantee that those in distant subsidiaries could be trusted not to act opportunistically.

Prelude to the Modern Era

The late nineteenth and early twentieth centuries saw a number of developments in international business, leading to a degree of internationalization that the world would not see again until it had fully recovered from the damage to the global economy created by two world wars.

By 1914, the list of companies with foreign subsidiaries was starting to have a contemporary look about it (see Table 1-1). Singer's second Scottish sewing

Company	Nationality	Product	No. of foreign factories in 1914	Location of foreign factories
Singer	US	Sewing machines	5	UK, Canada, Germany, Russia
J & P Coats	UK	Cotton thread	20	US, Canada, Russia, Austria-Hungary, Spain, Belgium, Italy, Switzerland, Portugal, Brazil, Japan
Nestlé	Swiss	Condensed milk/baby food	14	US, UK, Germany, Netherlands, Norway, Spain, Australia
Lever Brothers [today: Unilever]	UK	Soap	33	US, Canada, Germany, Switzerland, Belgium, France, Japan, Australia, South Africa
Saint-Gobain	French	Glass	8	Germany, Belgium, Netherlands, Italy, Spain, Austria-Hungary
Bayer	German	Chemicals	7	US, UK, France, Russia, Belgium
American Radiator	US	Radiators	6	Canada, UK, France, Germany, Italy, Austria-Hungary
Siemens	German	Electrical equipment	10	UK, France, Spain, Austria-Hungary, Russia
L.M. Ericsson	Swedish	Telephone equipment	8	US, UK, France, Austria-Hungary, Russia

TABLE 1-1
Large Multinational Manufacturers in 1914

Source: Adapted from G. Jones, *The Evolution of International Business* (London: Routledge, 1996), p. 106.

machine factory, opened in 1885, was actually bigger than any of its domestic factories in the US. The company went on to open plants in Canada, Austria, Germany, and Russia. The first large cross-border merger, between Britain's Shell and Royal Dutch, took place in 1907.

The growth in international manufacturing sustained a flourishing service sector, which provided the global infrastructure—finance, insurance, and transport—to permit the international flow of goods. Multinational activity had become an important element in the world economy. It was a golden age for multinationals, with foreign direct investment (FDI: assets controlled abroad) accounting for around 9 percent of world output.[9]

However, the outbreak of World War I abruptly ended the growth in international business. Furthermore, with the loss of direct investments in Russia in the wake of the 1917 Communist Revolution, firms began to think twice about foreign investment. In an environment of political uncertainty and exchange controls, this caution was reinforced by the Great Depression at the end of the 1920s, followed by the collapse of the international financial system. The adverse conditions during the interwar years encouraged firms to enter cross-border cartels rather than risk foreign direct investment. Trade barriers were erected as countries rushed to support local firms, effectively reducing international trade.

World War II reshaped the global economic system. While US firms emerged from the war in excellent shape, European competition was devastated, and the large Japanese corporations (known as *zaibatsu)* had been dismembered. Also, the war had stimulated technological innovation and American corporations had every incentive to expand their activities beyond the home market. A new era of international business had begun.

EMERGENCE OF THE MODERN MULTINATIONAL

Although Europe had a long tradition in international commerce, it was the global drive of US firms after World War II that gave birth to the multinationals as we know them today. American firms that had hardly ventured beyond their home markets before the war now began to flex their muscles abroad, and by the 1960s, US companies had built an unprecedented lead in the world economy.

Many American firms moved abroad through acquisitions, followed by investments in the acquired subsidiary.[10] This was the approach taken by Procter & Gamble (P&G), who established a presence in Continental Europe by acquiring an ailing French detergent plant in 1954.[11] An alternative strategy was to join forces with a local partner, as in the case of Xerox, which entered global markets through two joint ventures with an English and a Japanese firm in the late fifties.

American service firms followed their clients abroad, but internationalization strategies varied. The advertising agency J. Walter Thompson had an agreement with General Motors that it would open an office in every country where the car firm had an assembly operation or distributor.[12] In professional services, McKinsey scrambled to open its own offices in foreign countries through the 1950s and 1960s. Others, such as Price Waterhouse and Coopers & Lybrand,[13] built their international presence through mergers with established national practices in other countries. For most others, the route was via informal federations or networks of otherwise independent firms.

Advances in transport and communications—such as the introduction of commercial jet travel and the first transatlantic telephone link in 1956—facilitated this rapid internationalization. More significant still was the emergence of computers as business tools by the mid-1970s. Computers had become key elements in the control and information systems of industrial concerns, paving the way for later complex integration strategies. Taken together, these developments contributed to a "spectacular shrinkage of space,"[14] a process which has continued until today with the Internet and will accelerate in the future.

By the end of the 1980s, international competition was no longer the preserve of industrial giants; it was affecting everybody's business.

Deepening of Globalization

Globalization surfaced as the new buzzword at the beginning of the 1990s. Economic barriers such as national borders gradually became less relevant (but not irrelevant!) as governments dismantled the barriers to trade and investment. At the same time, deregulation and privatization opened new opportunities for international business in both developing and developed countries. The multi-national domain, long associated with the industrial company, was shifting to the service sector, which by the mid-1990s represented over half of total world FDI.[15] Problems of distance and time zones were further smoothed away as communication by fax gave way to e-mail and fixed phone networks to wireless mobile technology.

Globalization was further stimulated by the fall of communism in Russia and Eastern Europe. Together with China's adoption of market-oriented policies, huge new opportunities were opened to international business as most of the world was drawn into the integrated global economy. World trade was growing faster than world output, and global FDI was increasing even faster than trade.

International business was not just growing in volume; it was also changing in form. Most early multinationals had followed a step-by-step progression to international status;[16] now many companies were learning how to internationalize rapidly through various types of alliances, including international licensing agreements, cross-border R&D partnerships, and joint ventures that were commonly used to expand quickly into emerging markets. Cross-border acquisitions began to grow rapidly.

Multinationals increasingly located different elements of their value-adding activities in different parts of the world. Formerly hierarchical companies with clean-cut boundaries were giving way to complex arrangements and configurations, often fluctuating over time. The new buzzword from GE was "the boundaryless organization."[17] With increasing cross-border project work and mobility, the image of an organization as a network was rapidly becoming as accurate as that of hierarchy. For example, a European pharmaceutical corporation could have international R&D partnerships with competitors in the US, and manufacturing joint ventures with local partners in China, where it would outsource sales of generic products to a firm strong in distribution.

Another characteristic of the emerging competitive environment was the breakdown of historic sources of strategic advantage, leading to the search for new ways to compete. Traditionally, the only distant resources that multinationals sought were raw materials or cheap labor. Everything else was at home: sources of leading-edge technology and finance, world-class suppliers, pressure-cooker competition, the most sophisticated customers, and the best intelligence on future trends.[18] The home base advantage was so strong that multinationals could maintain their competitiveness while they gradually learned to adapt their offerings to fit better with local needs.

Global competition was now dispersing some of these capabilities around the world. India, for example, developed its software industry using a low-cost strategy as a means of entry but then quickly climbed the value chain, just as Japan had done previously in the automobile industry. The implication of such developments was that multinational firms could no longer assume that all the capabilities deemed strategic were available close to home.

The process of globalization has continued in the twenty-first century. In his influential book *The World Is Flat*, Thomas Friedman suggests that the world has become "flat" and argues that there is a more level competitive playing field for individuals, groups, and companies from all parts of a shrinking world. While the process of globalization was previously driven mostly by countries and then by corporations striving to expand their influence and integrate their activities, what Friedman calls "Globalization 3.0" is driven more by the ability of firms to collaborate and compete internationally using the tools of the increasingly virtual world.

The forces described by Friedman have contributed to many of the recent changes in the world economy. China has consistently attracted large amounts of FDI as it developed into the factory for the world,[19] while India has become an incubator of new multinationals in global businesses that did not even exist 20 years ago, in fields such as IT support and business process outsourcing. Multinationals from high-growth emerging markets have turned into major global players. International acquisitions by firms like Mittal Steel from India and Mexico's CEMEX, now two of the world's largest building materials companies, have transformed industries that were traditionally led by firms from developed countries. The US and Japan no longer dominate lists of the world's largest companies, with a large number of Chinese corporations but also Brazilian, Indian and Russian firms joining the elite club.[20] On its Internet platforms, Alibaba handles a larger volume of goods than Amazon and eBay combined.

With the erosion of traditional sources of competitive advantage, multinationals needed to change their approach to doing business around the world—including managing employees. To compete successfully, multinationals had to do more than exploit their old advantages. A new way of thinking about the multinational corporations came out of studies of how they were responding to these challenges: the concept of the transnational organization.

The Roadmap for Managing Global Tensions

If there is a single perspective that has shaped our understanding of the multinational corporation and its HRM implications, it is the concept of the dual strategic imperatives that emerged from the research on multinational strategy and the tools of control and coordination available to firms competing globally.[21] According to this perspective, multinational firms face one central problem: responding to a variety of national demands and opportunities while maintaining a clear and consistent global business strategy. This tension between strong opposing forces, dubbed local responsiveness and global integration, was captured by Sony's "think global, act local," aphorism, since then adopted by many multinationals as their guiding motto.[22]

These concepts were developed further by Bartlett and Ghoshal in their path-breaking study of nine firms in a sample of three industries (consumer electronics, branded packaged goods, and telephone switching) and three regions (North America, Europe, and Japan).[23] They discovered that these companies seemed to have followed one of three internationalization paths, which they called "administrative heritages":

- One path emphasized responsiveness to local conditions, leading to what they called a "multinational enterprise" and which we prefer to call **multidomestic** (we use the term "multinational" in its generic sense, as a firm with operations in multiple countries). This led to a decentralized federation of local units enjoying a high degree of strategic autonomy. Close to their customers and with strong links to the local infrastructure, the subsidiaries were seen almost as indigenous companies. The strength of the multidomestic approach was local responsiveness, and some European firms, such as Unilever and Philips, embodied this approach.

- A second path to internationalization was that of the "global" firm, typified by US corporations such as Ford and Japanese enterprises such as Panasonic.[24] Since the term "global" as used by Bartlett and Ghoshal is now, just like the term "multinational," commonly applied to any large firm competing globally, in this book we prefer to call such a firm the **meganational** firm. Here, worldwide facilities are typically centralized in the parent country, products are standardized, and overseas operations are considered as delivery pipelines to access international markets. The global hub maintains tight control over strategic decisions, resources, and information. The competitive strength of the meganational firm comes from efficiencies of scale and cost.

- Some companies appeared to have taken a third route, a variant on the meganational path. Like the meganational, their facilities were located at the center. But the competitive strength of these **"international"** firms[25] was their ability to transfer expertise to less advanced overseas environments, allowing local firms more discretion in adapting products and services. They were also capable of capturing learning from such local initiatives and then transferring it back to the central R&D and marketing departments, from where it was reexported to other foreign units. The "international" enterprise was thus a tightly coordinated federation of local firms, controlled by sophisticated management systems and corporate staffs. Some American and European firms such as Ericsson fitted this pattern, heralding the growing concern with global knowledge management.

Certain firms were doing well because their internationalization paths matched the requirements of their industry closely. Consumer products required local responsiveness, so Unilever thrived with its multidomestic approach, while Kao in Japan—centralized and meganational in heritage—was hardly able to move outside its Japanese borders. The situation was different in consumer electronics, where the centralized meganational heritage of Panasonic seemed to fit better than the more localized approaches of Philips and GE's consumer electronics business. And in telecommunications, the "international" strategy of Ericsson, transferring its learning from abroad, led to superior performance in comparison with the multidomestic and meganational strategies of its competitors.[26]

In all of these three industries, leading firms had to become more **transnational** in their orientation (see Figure 1-1)—more locally responsive *and* more globally integrated *and* better at sharing learning between headquarters and subsidiaries. What has been driving this change? Increasing competition was shifting the approach of these firms from *either/or* to *and*.[27] The challenge for Unilever was to maintain its local responsiveness but at the same time to increase its global efficiency by eliminating duplication and integrating manufacturing. Conversely, the challenge for Panasonic was to keep the economies of centralized product development and manufacturing but to become more responsive to differentiated niches in markets around the world.

FIGURE 1-1
The Transnational
Approach

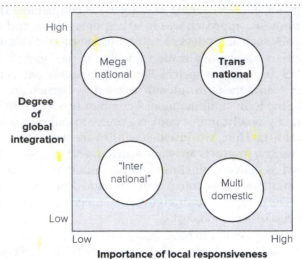

Source: Adapted from Bartlett and Ghoshal (1989), p. 438.

The Transnational Solution

The defining characteristic of the transnational enterprise is its capacity to steer between the contradictions that it confronts. As Ghoshal and Bartlett put it:

> Managers in most worldwide companies recognize the need for simultaneously achieving global efficiency, national responsiveness, and the ability to develop and exploit knowledge on a worldwide basis. Some, however, regard the goal as inherently unattainable. Perceiving irreconcilable contradictions among the three objectives, they opt to focus on one of them, at least temporarily. The transnational company is one that overcomes these contradictions.[28]

However, it is not clear that all international firms are destined to become equally "transnational." While most companies are forced to contend with the dimensions of responsiveness, efficiency, and learning, these demands are not equally salient in all industries. Transnational pressures have been strongest in industries such as pharmaceuticals and automobiles where firms must be close to local authorities and consumers, while at the same time harnessing global efficiencies in product development, marketing, and manufacturing.

The transnational tensions are not limited to corporate strategy; they also appear within the HRM domain.[29] For example, a very relevant question is the extent to which HRM policies and practices should be left to local subsidiaries and adapted to fit the local cultural context and institutional rules. If the multinational decentralizes the responsibility for HRM and adapts practices to the local environment, it could suffer from a lack of global or regional scale advantages within the HR function, forego the possibilities of inter-unit learning within the corporation, and fail to use HRM effectively to enhance global coordination.

Moreover, the pressures do not apply equally to all parts of a firm. One subsidiary may be more local in orientation, whereas another may be tightly integrated. Even within a particular function, such as marketing, pricing may be a local matter whereas distribution may be controlled from the center. In

HR, performance management systems may be more globally standardized, whereas reward systems for workers may be left to local discretion. Indeed, this differentiation is another aspect of the complexity of the transnational— one size does not fit all.

While industry characteristics influence the strategic approach of the firm[30]—multidomestic, meganational, or transnational—companies also have some degree of choice. Take the case of the brewing industry, where two neighboring firms have taken contrasting paths. Everyone has heard of the Dutch company Heineken through its global Heineken and Amstel brands. But how many had heard of InBev before it acquired the American Anheuser-Busch with its iconic Budweiser beer? Based in Belgium, InBev came about through a merger of Belgian and Brazilian brewers, and in addition to Budweiser, it now owns over 200 beer brands across the world, including Stella Artois, Corona, Becks and Skol. InBev is increasingly leveraging its top global brands but also continues to invest in its large portfolio of local and regional brews. Thus, notwithstanding industry imperatives, different models may be equally viable provided that there is good execution, consistency in implementation, and alignment between HRM and competitive strategy— expressed mainly through application of various control and coordination mechanisms.

Global Control and Coordination and the Evolution of International HRM

Since the onset of international economic activities, organizations have struggled with the problems of how to control and coordinate their cross-border operations; for a definition of the two terms see the box below. A key challenge for multinationals is how to enhance alignment and collaboration across geographically dispersed units, and people management is an important part of how global firms can respond—and the traditional control mechanisms simply cannot cope with the complexity of the transnational.[31]

Early in their internationalization, the emphasis is typically on the staffing of key positions in foreign units, often with people (expatriates) from the home country of the corporation. Individuals have to be persuaded to move abroad—those with needed technical skills as well as managers who will exercise control over foreign subsidiaries and help coordinate activities with those of other international units. It is not only a question of persuading

The Difference Between Control and Coordination

Sometimes, there is confusion between the meaning of these two terms, but in this book the term "**control**" refers to visible *hierarchical* structures (authority over decision-making, responsibilities, and reporting lines) and organizational procedures, while "**coordination**" refers to tools that facilitate alignment and collaboration through *lateral* structures, steering procedures, social architecture (social capital and shared values), and organizational processes, including HRM.

people to move abroad; the challenge is above all how to help them be successful in their roles.

Some firms have already for a long time used expatriate assignments for developmental reasons rather than just to solve an immediate job need. The assumption is that with growing internationalization, *all* senior executives need international experience, even those in domestic positions. The link between international management development and the problems of control and coordination was established in a landmark study of the expatriation policies of four multinationals, including Shell.[32] The research showed that these companies had quite different levels and patterns of international personnel transfer.[33] There were three motives for transferring managers abroad. The first and most common was to meet an immediate need for particular skills in a foreign subsidiary. The second was to develop managers through challenging international experience. However, the study of Shell revealed a third motive for international transfers—as a mechanism for control and coordination. The managers sent abroad were steeped in the policies and style of the organization, so they could be relied on to act appropriately in diverse situations. Moreover, frequent assignments abroad developed a network of personal relationships that facilitated coordination.

Shell was able to maintain a high degree of control and coordination while at the same time having a more decentralized organization than other firms. Social networks and shared global values can be built through appropriate HR practices, minimizing the necessity for centralized headquarters control or bureaucratic procedures.

These findings also lend substance to earlier research by Perlmutter, suggesting that multinationals vary in the "states of mind" characterizing their operations.[34] The first is the *ethnocentric orientation*, where subsidiaries are required to conform to parent company ways regardless of local conditions. The second is the decentralized *polycentric corporation*, where each subsidiary is given the freedom to develop with minimal interference, providing it remains profitable. The third is the *geocentric orientation*, where "subsidiaries are neither satellites nor independent city states, but parts of a whole whose focus is on worldwide objectives as well as local objectives, each making its unique contribution with its unique competence."[35] A geocentric orientation can be built when an individual's skills counts more than his or her passport, and there is a high degree of mobility not only from headquarters to subsidiaries but also from subsidiaries to headquarters and between the subsidiaries themselves, as with Shell. Perlmutter saw the route from initial ethnocentrism to geocentrism as tortuous but inevitable.

Thus, international HRM is much more than just a question of sending expatriates abroad and putting the right person in the right place in foreign environment. It plays a crucial role in the strategic and organizational development of the multinational corporation.[36] This view is at the heart of Bartlett and Ghoshal's notion of the transnational and discussed by other early writers on strategic HRM in multinational enterprises.[37]

As we have seen, the challenges of foreign assignments, adapting people management practices to foreign situations, and coordinating and controlling distant operations have existed since antiquity. The centrality of these issues has increased over time. The scope of expatriation has changed; today expatriates come not only from the multinational's home country but also from other third countries. Localization of key staff across foreign units has become a new imperative, leading to the complex task of tracking and developing a global talent pool. As globalization started to have an impact on local operations, for example in China, it also became clear that even local executives need to have international experience. With the acceleration of globalization, firms with superior international HRM capabilities are likely to have a competitive advantage. As Floris Maljers, former co-chairman of Unilever, put it: "Limited human resources—not unreliable or inadequate sources of capital—has become the biggest constraint in most globalization efforts."[38] Many scholars studying the multinational firm today, whatever their discipline or background, would agree.

However, the opportunities for HRM to impact how multinational firms tackle the challenges of globalization go well beyond supply and motivation of talent. Sustainable competitive advantage rests not only on designing smart global strategies but also on building layers of organizational capabilities supporting their execution—an area where HRM plays an increasingly critical role.

BUSINESS STRATEGY AND ORGANIZATIONAL CAPABILITIES

Since the inception of the field of strategic management, its main preoccupation has been with the question of why some firms are more successful than others. Initially, little attention was paid to the role played by human resources, and strategy meant competitive positioning based on the analysis of industry characteristics.[39] But it soon became clear that having the right strategy is not enough; what also matters is the capacity to execute that strategy. Execution is to a greater or lesser extent always a question of people—having the right leaders to implement the strategy; training and coaching people in the new skills and behaviors that are required; realigning performance management and rewards to the new strategy; and having an organization whose members share values, beliefs, and behavioral norms in line with the chosen strategy. In other words, human resource management is key to strategy implementation, closely associated with the management of change.

But short-term success is not enough. The *resource-based view of the firm* provides a complementary view of strategic management, shifting the focus to sustainable performance and turning the spotlight even more on the firm's internal resources. To prepare the basis for superior, long-term economic performance, the organization's resources should be valuable to the customer, rare, and difficult to purchase or imitate.[40] Today, this view is widely accepted in the field of strategic management, where human resources and other intangible resources, like organizational culture and reputation, have moved squarely to the center of the debate about why some firms are more successful than others. The firm's pool of human resources as well as its processes for managing them can constitute bases for long-term competitive advantage.[41] They must also be intimately linked to the firm's business model and strategy. This brings us to the concept of organizational capabilities.

Organizational Capabilities

A formal definition of organizational capability is "the ability to perform repeatedly a productive task which relates to a firm's capacity for creating value through effecting the transformation of input to output."[42] In short, organizational capabilities refer to the firm's ability to combine and leverage their resources to bring about a desired end.[43] 3M's long-term track record in innovation, Toyota's continuous improvement process in manufacturing, and the ability of Southwest Airlines to deliver excellent customer experiences at a low price are examples of such capabilities.[44]

From this perspective, the HRM elements of an organizational capability are inseparable from its business model and strategy. Such capabilities are often difficult to unravel and thus hard to imitate. The box "Organizational Capabilities of Lincoln Electric" examines the case of Lincoln from a capability perspective.

In most cases, a firm must put in place a range of capabilities to create value, although usually there are only a few that drive the company's competitive advantage. These *differentiating* capabilities must satisfy three criteria:[46]

- They must create value for the customer—doing something that does not add value to the customer, however well it is done, cannot be a source of competitive advantage.

Organizational Capabilities of Lincoln Electric

A casual observer may consider Lincoln's piece-rate incentive system as driving the business model—aggressive pay-for-performance stimulates high productivity. This is combined with a distinctive and strong employer brand that especially in the area around Cleveland, Ohio, where the center of the US operations is located, helps the firm recruit highly efficient employees attracted by promises of generous rewards in exchange for extraordinary productivity.

In addition to workforce productivity, at the core of Lincoln's successful business model is the elasticity of its cost structure—the ability to transform fixed costs into variable cost, essential in an environment with high volatility of demand. Anything that HRM at Lincoln can do to convert fixed cost to variable cost is given priority; so production workers are expected to reduce their working hours in economic downturns and increase them when demand is high.

However, there is another more intangible element in Lincoln's way to operate. Piece-rate systems of pay are often associated with adversarial relationships between employers and employees but, at Lincoln, the relationship between management and employees is characterized by a high degree of mutual trust. Without the trust that has evolved over decades in the US plant, Lincoln's capabilities would fall apart.

Its executives are conscious of this. Careful attention is paid to fixing the piece rates, which do not change unless there are unusual circumstances and full consultation. When the disastrous foreign expansion led to large corporate losses in the 1990s, Lincoln borrowed money to be able to continue to pay bonuses to its US workers since these generous bonuses were a part of the psychological contract that existed between the workforce and the company.[45] If the company had broken its side of the deal, this would have seriously jeopardized the employees' trust in management and destroyed the workers' belief in what is fair—high financial rewards in return for high productivity and flexible work practices.

- The capability has to be rare and unique—if competitors have a similar capability, it cannot be a source of competitive advantage.
- The capability has to be difficult to duplicate—otherwise it will quickly be replicated by competitors.

It should be noted that certain capabilities, even if they do not satisfy these criteria, may be essential just to participate in a business; we call them *enabling* capabilities.[47] The difference between enabling and differentiating organizational capabilities is important; only the latter contribute to competitive advantage. For example, in the pharmaceutical industry, conducting R&D in strict compliance with regulatory rules is an enabling capability, while doing it faster and more cheaply than competitors may deliver differentiation.

However, an additional perspective is critical for understanding—and building—capabilities. Focusing on the scope of capabilities, both enabling and differentiating capabilities can be also classified as *functional* capabilities or *coordination* capabilities.[48] The former (well understood in the strategic literature) allow the firm to perform the essential activities and routines within a specific function, segment of a value chain, or geography.

Less understood by both academics and industry executives are coordination capabilities that come into play when functional resources and routines need to be aligned across different parts of the organization or even across a third-party network to deliver products or services to customers. From an organizational perspective, functional capabilities are essentially "vertical"— embedded in distinct functions, units, and departments. In contrast, coordination capabilities are essentially "horizontal"—spanning and crossing multiple intra- and inter-organizational boundaries. Figure 1-2 shows the overall capability framework.

For example, in the global automotive parts and production equipment business, functional capabilities include various elements of product development from engineering design, testing, validation, and technical integration, to deploying tools like CAD, as well as applying state-of-the-art lean manufacturing concepts. Functional capabilities are often directly comparable between

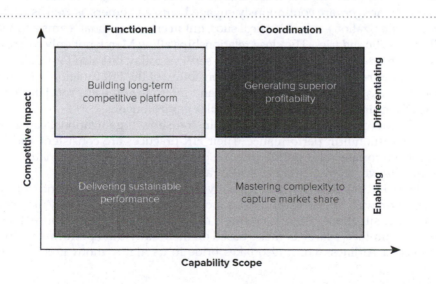

FIGURE 1-2
Organizational Capability Matrix

competitors. Typical coordination capabilities in the automotive parts business are synchronization of global product launches for multiple customers or coordinating overlapping or conflicting commercial and technical tasks.

Implementing Capabilities

Implementing a competitive and robust HR strategy that supports the business requires decision-makers to think ahead about some important questions:

- What are the essential characteristics of the business model?
- What differentiating and enabling organizational capabilities should support the business model?
- What systems will be required to drive these capabilities? And what behaviors?
- What are the implications for the desired social architecture? What people strategies will promote these desired behaviors?

Long-term success is driven far more by consistency and coherence in answering these questions than by the quest for "best practice." A number of firms have tried to copy Lincoln's compensation system but failed. What they have missed is that at Lincoln, the piece-rate system is only one of the tools that drive cost flexibility and productivity. It is the unique bundling of people management and organizational practices that produces the desired effect (see the box above).

Consider another example. Merck KGaA, the world's oldest chemical and pharmaceutical firm with a more than 300-year history, is the global leader in supplying liquid crystal materials for LCD displays.[49] While the display business is highly competitive, Merck is enjoying healthy margins—by superior "customer intimacy"—delivering not just materials but value-adding solutions addressing its customers' needs when and where required. It seems natural, but Merck's R&D and manufacturing operations and related knowledge are concentrated mainly in Germany, and all its key customers are in East Asia. How does the company do it?

Over the last two decades Merck has developed strong country organizations in each of its key markets complementing the core global functions. Key account managers are continuously engaged with customers as well as with the home organization—not in vertical silos, but in cross-sectional teams and virtually across boundaries. The close relationships allow Merck not only to provide its customers with better products and services today but also to predict what they would require in future. The responsibility of the HR function is to ensure that business leaders worldwide learn and internalize the appropriate competencies required to excel in such a complex environment.

The Merck and Lincoln examples illustrate how organizational capabilities help to sustain firm performance. Their HR practices are consistent and have played important roles in building the differentiating and coordination capabilities. However, these examples also raise two other points.

First, HR practices that have a positive impact on firm performance for a particular firm with a particular business model in a particular industry may not do so in other situations. There is no single recipe for success. For instance, Lincoln pays its employees large bonuses based on their individual performance, while Southwest Airlines, which also takes pride in its highly motivated workforce that outperform its competitors, does not pay any individual bonuses, instead driving commitment through a strong team and customer-oriented culture.

Second, companies in the same industry may differ in both the differentiating organizational capabilities that they pursue and how they strive to strengthen these capabilities through HR and other practices. There is a tendency for firms in the same industry to adopt similar HR practices since the technology of the sector dictates certain enabling capabilities—for example, safety in the airline industry. But the workforce strategy of Ryanair—perhaps the most successful budget airline in Europe—with its emphasis on a contingent workforce and confrontational employee relations, could not be more different from that of Southwest.[50]

Organizational Capabilities in Multinational Firms

In this book, we introduce examples from around the world of successful companies that are able to outperform their competitors in part because of their people management practices: for example, Lincoln Electric in the US, Haier in China, Infosys in India, Merck in Germany, Toyota in Japan, or Schlumberger—with the head office functions distributed around the world. While they deploy very different HR practices, all these companies are clear about which organizational capabilities are needed to support their business model, and they make sure that their HR practices drive the necessary actions and behaviors.

However, as these companies internationalize, the challenge they face is how management practices that successfully support organizational capabilities in one country can be adapted to another. The troubled journey of Lincoln overseas shows how difficult it can be to transfer organizational capabilities abroad—the underlying HR practices do not necessarily travel well to a different environment. Lincoln Electric executives regarded their HR practices as a major source of competitive advantage. Yet these practices generally failed when transferred to the newly acquired units abroad. As an organization expands internationally, culture and institutional context make the issue of how HRM contributes to company performance even more complex.

THE HRM WHEEL

Along with strategy implementation, the concept of organizational capability provides the center point for HRM activities in any business organization. The strategy and intended organizational capabilities should be reflected in the underlying HRM principles and guide the development of distinct HR practices that are supported by different roles played by the HR function, leading in turn to a set of desired organizational outcomes.

We use the metaphor of the "HRM Wheel," presented in Figure 1-3, to capture the dynamic and interdependent relationship between these four elements of HRM in multinational corporations. We will discuss each part of the HRM Wheel in turn, but we will focus in particular on the guiding principles, as these determine to a large degree what kind of HRM architecture will be implemented inside the firm.

FIGURE 1-3
The HRM Wheel

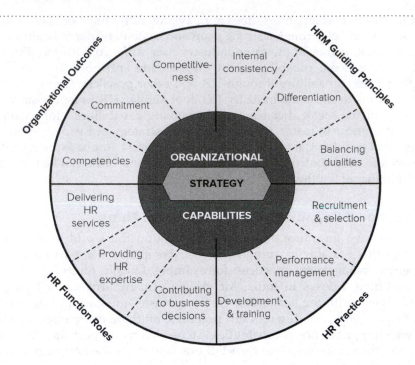

Setting the Guiding Principles

We propose that three guiding principles are at the foundation of HRM in multinational corporations:

- Internal consistency
- Differentiation
- Balancing dualities

The three principles are complementary, although in practice most multinational companies employ them sequentially—starting with consistency, then developing a more differentiated approach, and finally tackling the dualities that become evident in cross-border people management.

Internal Consistency

The principle of internal consistency refers to the way in which the firm's HR practices fit with each other and with the features of the work organization, such as the degree of specialization of work tasks and the extent to which work is organized around teams rather than individuals. For example, if a firm invests a great deal of money in skill development, it should emphasize employee retention through feedback, competitive compensation, and career management; otherwise those valuable employees may be poached by competitors. It should also empower such employees to contribute to the organization and reward them for initiative.[51]

Some form of explicit management philosophy will help ensure this consistency across practices, and such powerful combinations of HR practices lead to a whole that is more than the sum of its parts. Conversely, having a reward system that pays aggressively for individual performance when the work is organized around teams would constitute what some describe as a "deadly combination" of work practices.[52]

Consistency is important for organizational performance. Let us return to Lincoln Electric to illustrate this point. Lincoln has a highly consistent approach to HRM, and its widely publicized piece-rate and bonus systems are only one part of a finely tuned set of practices that evolved over 50 years.[53] The factory workers view themselves as individual entrepreneurs who are rewarded generously if they perform well. The US plant is basically run by the workers, with only one supervisor per 58 workers.[54] The incentive system goes hand in hand with a belief in the equality of management and employees—no-holds-barred consultative mechanisms, open-door practices, and total transparency about company results. Similar compensation principles apply to executives, managers, and factory workers. The appraisal system has evolved step-by-step over the decades and supports the strategy of the firm: high quality at the lowest possible cost and flexibility to meet changing demand.

In practice, there are three different aspects of consistency to consider. The first is *single-employee consistency*—whether employees experience appraisal, promotion, compensation, and other HRM elements as complementary or conflicting. When staff experience these practices as inconsistent, owing to poor design or conflicting management priorities, performance suffers through loss of motivation, commitment, and initiative.[55] The second aspect is *consistency across employees*—whether employees in similar roles and making the same contribution are treated equally despite differences in gender, ethnic origin, or background (e.g., expatriate vs. local).[56] The third aspect is *temporal consistency* or continuity over time. If practices and policies are constantly changing, there will be confusion and dysfunctional frustration among employees.[57] All three aspects of consistency can be found in Lincoln Electric's US operations.

So far, we have focused on consistency in terms of the content of HR practices—the way in which the firm recruits, selects, develops, and manages the performance of its employees. However, these practices should also display consistent themes or messages, and an explicit management philosophy or value system often supplies the necessary coherence.[58] If the messages picked up by employees through work practices are clear and consistent, a positive effect on employee attitudes and behavior can be expected.[59] But sometimes HRM rhetoric conflicts with the reality that employees perceive, and this can undermine HR's credibility. We have seen an example during our work in Brazil, where some well-intentioned executives championed an HRM philosophy they had learnt in the US and Europe, while local staff typically saw the message as so remote from their reality that the HR function was discredited.[60]

All this highlights the importance of consistency between the espoused HRM strategy and policies, and the actual practices in different parts of the organization. For instance, company executives may state that they have a merit-based pay system. But if the firm does not have valid processes for making sure that employees are in fact paid on merit, the staff may feel unfairly treated, leading to a drop in organizational commitment and effectiveness.[61]

The challenges of achieving a good fit between HRM strategies, policies, and practices are particularly difficult in multinational corporations with operations in different cultures and institutional contexts. While the firm may espouse a worldwide HRM philosophy supported by globally standardized policies, actual practices often reflect the local context and therefore differ across countries. Local managers often ignore the global philosophy and policies—"Great idea, but unfortunately it does not apply here"—and the result is inconsistency in the deployment of HRM across the organization.

Differentiation

While there are good reasons for emphasizing internal HRM consistency, there is a risk of taking consistency too far. Companies that only focus on building and optimizing a well-integrated set of consistent HR practices run the risk of creating a inflexible system that may be costly and difficult to adapt to changing demands. Therefore, the principle of consistency must go hand in hand with the principle of differentiation.

While differentiation in HR practices due to geographic location receives most attention in the HRM literature—especially when it relates to multinationals—there are actually at least three complementary notions of differentiation that need to be considered:

- Differentiation across employee groups
- Differentiation across subunits (geographies and/or business lines)
- Differentiation from other firms, both multinational and local[62]

First, not all employee groups are equally important for the success of the organization. Firms that apply the same HR practices across all employee groups run the risk of underinvesting in the talent that is crucial for long-term success while overinvesting in people who are easily replaceable. Practices that are appropriate for one part of the workforce may not be optimal for another.

The arguments in favor of differentiating HR practices among employee groups are compelling and in line with what we see in many corporations. One study of Spanish firms concluded that 70 percent used all four modes of employment;[63] another showed that companies did indeed use different combinations of HR practices to manage employee groups that varied in terms of strategic value and uniqueness.[64]

While the benefits of differentiating HR practices between employee groups apply to most organizations, differentiation across subunits is of particular importance to multinational firms. Failure to make sensible adaptations to different environments may be costly, as the Lincoln case shows. The US executives spearheading the company's internationalization believed strongly in the effectiveness of their work practices, and so these were introduced without much adjustment in the newly established or acquired subsidiaries abroad. However, local managers often disagreed with the appropriateness of (for example) worker consultation or autonomy over working hours, while local employees and unions rejected other practices. In some countries, the proposed practices were simply illegal.

Lincoln's approach may seem naïve, but many firms have walked the same path with great enthusiasm. Successful companies, particularly those that have operated unchallenged for long periods of time on home markets, sometimes adopt a universalist approach to HRM when they expand internationally. They find out the hard way that some degree of local differentiation is necessary—which can in turn compromise the consistency of HR practices and necessitate a careful rethink of the company's management approach.

Does this mean that companies must always adapt their practices to fit with the cultural and institutional environment? Is "When in Rome, do as the

Romans do" always a good guideline? Such a conclusion would be as naïve as believing in "the one-best-way."

In our view, the Lincoln story should not be interpreted as implying that reward and appraisal systems that link compensation closely to individual and/or company performance will never work in, say, Germany. After careful analysis, an appropriate conclusion might be that such an approach to HRM might work in Germany: *if* the firm is able to recruit staff who find such a reward system attractive; *if* the work system can be designed to measure individual performance; *if* the compensation system complies with local labor law; *if* appropriate practices can build employee trust in management; and so on.

Some of these *if*s might rule out the use of such a system or render it excessively expensive, but highly variable reward systems may pop up in the most unlikely places if properly implemented.[65] Lincoln's mistake was not that it tried to take its unique approach to people management abroad. When firms globalize it makes sense to build on what makes the company unique and successful in its home country. However, the Lincoln management may have misjudged how different its management approach was from local norms, and how difficult it is to change the behavior of managers and employees in acquired companies who had no experience of the Lincoln Way.[66]

Some HR professionals consider it inappropriate to be different from local firms in a foreign culture. However, having HR practices that are distinctively different can help to recruit and retain local talent who are attracted by the unique features of the multinational. The hallmark of cross-cultural understanding is being able to go beyond rudimentary stereotypes, knowing where one has to conform to the environment and where one can be different. Understanding where to push and where to give in to cultural and institutional considerations—in short, how to balance the two—is part of the global know-how at the core of people management in the transnational corporation.

This brings us to the third and probably most potent aspect of differentiation, focusing on the distinctiveness of the firm's approach to HRM. Sustainable competitive advantage rarely comes from copying others; it invariably comes from being different from other firms. Differentiation stems from how the firm's unique combination of HR practices makes it stand out from other organizations, often in subtle and invisible ways that are embedded in the culture of the enterprise.

While the necessity for competitive differentiation is widely accepted within the fields of strategic management and marketing, its importance has received less attention in HRM. In particular, recruitment, development, and performance management are three HR processes with great potential for creating differentiation. For example, attracting and retaining the right people involves marketing the firm as an employer. Unless the firm stands out from its competitors in the labor market, it is unlikely to appeal to potential employees with the required skills and attitudes. In the Cleveland, Ohio, area where Lincoln Electric's main factory is located, the company's unique work practices are well-known. This enables the company to recruit self-reliant individuals who are attracted by its highly competitive work system. Lincoln's strong employer brand is an important reason why it has been so successful in the US, but it is also one element of its competitive advantage that is not easy to transfer abroad.

Other firms that follow a distinct path to developing competitive capabilities are also known for paying careful attention to recruitment and selection.

Toyota's meticulous assessment of all job candidates from hourly workers to senior executives is legendary.[67] And P&G with its traditional (some might say archaic) emphasis on long-term careers and promotion from within attracts several hundred thousand applicants worldwide. It rigorously selects the less than 1 percent of the applicants that it deems the very best—no apologies there for not being trendy.[68] But in both the P&G and Toyota cases, differentiation also goes hand in hand with consistency, which takes us to the third guiding principle of multinational HRM—balancing dualities.

Balancing Dualities

The importance of balance—deciding how far to focus on one particular goal, issue, or principle at the expense of another—is one of the central messages of this book. We will elaborate more on this issue later in this chapter. Here we limit our scope to the consistency–differentiation duality.

In case of a multinational firm, there are no simple answers to the questions of how, and how far, to adapt HR practices abroad. While differentiation across locations can help the multinational achieve a better fit with the various environments in which it operates, too close alignment of HR practices to each external location (country or region) is likely to lead to a loss of integration—global inefficiencies, lack of learning across units, and problems of control and coordination.

The tension between differentiation on the one hand and the consistency that facilitates integration on the other has traditionally been resolved through structural choices; indeed, differentiation and integration form the fundamental DNA of organizational design.[69] Corporations build their basic structure—traditionally differentiating either by geography (regional structures) or by business (product line structures)—to maintain consistency and coordination within units but allowing differentiation between them. However, the situation of the transnational organization is more complex. It faces multiple pressures for differentiation—on geographic/regional, business, customer or global account, and global project lines—as well as increasing needs for coordination. We discuss the structural choices that companies can use to respond to these pressures for multidimensional organization in Chapter 4.

Multinational firms also use social mechanisms to address this duality of high needs for both differentiation and integration.[70] Relationships between employees from different parts of the corporation help people to understand and deal constructively with the often conflicting goals of local responsiveness, global efficiency, and inter-unit coordination. Additionally, corporations may invest in developing shared values and a global mindset among their employees—that is, a way of thinking that incorporates the dualities and contradictions that they face in their daily work.

Designing Core HR Practices

With the three guiding principles in mind, the next step is to put them in action. Every firm has to cope with a number of basic and vitally important HRM tasks, such as getting the right people into the right place at the right time—attracting, motivating, and retaining people. These are the core tasks of HRM, the facet that is most familiar, and which is dealt with in myriad books on the topic. Organizational performance will suffer if these tasks are not executed well. To guide our discussion, Table 1-2 provides a simple framework summarizing the key HR practices.

We start with a brief introduction to these practices and highlight some of the key challenges that multinationals have to confront. We should point out that with our focus on managers and knowledge workers in multinational firms, we address the important area of labor and industrial relations only briefly in the context of institutional differences among countries. We will discuss many of the specific HR practices in considerable detail later in Chapters 6–9.

Recruitment and Selection

With worldwide skill shortages, companies across the world face the challenge of attracting new employees with the desired skills and competencies. Without an appealing and differentiated employee value proposition, including a set of people management practices that potential job applicants will find attractive, it is difficult for a firm to fight the "war for talent" that characterizes emerging and growing markets in both good and bad times.[71] How can global firms build a strong employer brand in different parts of the world? The importance of brands has long been recognized in global marketing, and contemporary HR thinking about employer branding has clearly been influenced by insights from the field of marketing.[72]

The most suitable people have to be selected on the basis of their fit with the specific vacancy, their future growth potential, and the organization. A variety of selection and assessment methods are used to review external and internal candidates for jobs but with differences in their applicability across cultures and legal contexts. The importance of diversity is increasingly acknowledged in multinational firms across the world, yet most multinationals still staff their top positions with men from the home country and a remaining challenge for most corporations is how to do more than pay mere lip service to diversity.

Another issue for multinationals is whether to develop their own talent or recruit from outside. But regardless of the balance between build and buy, any investment in the selection and development of talent will not be viable unless the company can retain people to profit from the investment. An attractive compensation package and good development opportunities, a sound relationship with the boss, and the possibility of maintaining a healthy work-life balance are just some ways to reduce the attrition of core talent.

Performance Management

Performance management is a process that links the business objectives and strategies of the firm to unit, team, and individual goals and actions through periodic performance appraisals and rewards. It has three successive phases: setting goals and objectives; evaluating and reviewing performance as well as providing feedback; and linking this to rewards and development outcomes. Implementing this process creates a number of challenges for any multinational firm.

Effective goal setting depends on healthy two-way communication between superior and subordinate.[73] Hierarchic and gender differences can make this

TABLE 1-2

Key HR Practices in Multinationals

Recruitment and Selection
- Workforce planning
- Employer branding
- Recruitment
- Selection
- Induction and socialization
- Termination and outplacement

Performance Management and Rewards
- Job evaluation
- Goal setting
- Performance measurement
- Appraisal and feedback
- Compensation and benefits
- Rewards and recognition

Development and Training
- Training (on-the-job and off-the-job)
- Talent assessment and reviews
- Succession planning
- Career management
- Coaching and mentoring
- Leadership development

International Mobility

Communication[A]

Labor and Industrial Relations[A]

[A] In this book, these practices will be considered only in passing.

difficult, varying from one culture to another, as does corporate status (e.g., expatriate vs. local). Similarly, cultural issues may impact the applicability of various performance management tools, such as 360-degree feedback.

Praise may be generally well accepted around the world, though even here there are cultural features—for example distinguishing one individual in a collectivist culture. But multinational firms find dealing with low performance consistently to be difficult. "Maintaining face" is a sensitive issue in some Eastern cultures, while in others legal constraints circumscribe an employer's discretion on performance issues.

More than any other element of the HRM Wheel, performance management puts into stark relief the perennial tensions of global integration versus local adaptation. This is of particular relevance to multinationals, like Lincoln, where the performance management system is one of the core tools to drive its differentiating capabilities.

Development and Training

Developing future global leaders is a high priority for the multinational firm and is usually one of the major strategic preoccupations of top management. But what is a good leader and how can a multinational with many distant operations identify people with leadership potential outside the home country? There are two main difficulties: first, there are significant perceptual differences about what constitutes good leadership among different cultures; and second, the skills needed at senior leadership levels are different from those at lower levels.

People develop most by taking on and learning from challenges. For international leaders, this implies demanding assignments, working outside their domain of functional and geographic expertise. Most new or promoted employees do not immediately have the skills needed for their jobs, so these must be developed through on-the-job learning, coaching, mentoring, or formal training. However, the bigger the challenges that people take on, the higher the likelihood that they will make significant mistakes that can be costly for the firm. Training, coaching, and mentoring should therefore be part of what we call a people risk-management strategy. Furthermore, an increasingly important task for most multinationals is integrating top-down and bottom-up approaches to talent development.

Defining HR Functional Roles

This book is about how multinational corporations can deal with the challenges of global operations and improve their performance through the way they manage their employees. We argue that this task is a joint responsibility of top executives, line managers, and HR managers and professionals, but in this section we will focus mainly on the tasks and roles of the specialized HR function.

The academic HR literature contains several conceptualizations of the tasks and roles of the HR function.[74] We distinguish between the three following roles:

- Contributing to business decisions
- Providing HR expertise
- Delivering HR services

These three roles correspond to the way in which many multinationals organize their HR function. For instance, Unilever structures its HR functional activities into HR services (with Accenture doing much of this work within the scope of a long-term outsourcing agreement), expertise teams, and business partners. P&G initially organized all basic HR tasks into three regional service centers, and later outsourced them to IBM, retaining responsibility for development of HR practices and business support.

We provide a brief overview of these different roles below. In Chapter 14 we will elaborate on each of these roles in more depth and discuss how multinationals can develop the required competencies among their HR professionals.

Contribution to Business Decision-making

The business decision support role describes the activities of HR professionals who work directly with line and top managers on business, organizational, and HR challenges. Those occupying this role typically report to the person in charge of the business unit, with an indirect (dotted line) relationship to the corporate HR department. In contrast to the specialist knowledge of the HR professionals responsible for process and content development, the business decision support role requires broader generalist competence.

A key part of the role is to contribute to strategy discussions by highlighting the people aspects of strategy implementation and capability development. HR professionals should have a seat at the table when these discussions take place—which not always is the case.[75] Senior HR managers also work with senior management on strategically important issues related to organizational design and cohesion, talent management, succession planning, performance management, knowledge and change management, acquisitions, and alliances—strategic challenges we discuss later in this book.

Individuals playing the business decision support role often become natural link pins between business units and the functional centers of expertise in the corporation, as well as the HR service centers. Yet not all this work is strategic. An indispensable part of the role is dealing with more mundane HR operational tasks and helping line managers to resolve employee issues and concerns.

Provision of HR Expertise

The key outcomes of the HR expertise role are HR practices that help the firm maintain and enhance the organizational capabilities needed to execute its business strategy.

Professional knowledge of state-of-the-art HRM is a necessary point of departure for this role. Learning from others is essential—but blind pursuit of the latest best practice is not. Decisions should be based not on trends but on a thorough analysis of what is needed to support the organizational capabilities of the firm. Central to the HR expertise role are the three guiding principles of HRM presented earlier: consistency between HR practices and with other parts of the work organization; differentiation across employee groups and subunits, as well as from other firms; and balancing critical dualities, such as global integration and local responsiveness.

Given the constant pressure to do more with less, organizing HRM process and content development is a challenging task for any multinational firm. The organization of global expertise depends on the structure of the company, but the traditional solution is to have functional experts at headquarters with a global responsibility for tasks such as talent and performance management. It is essential that these experts have deep international experience, and an awareness of how their home country lens can bias their perceptions. Another solution is to decentralize responsibility for developing policies, processes, and tools to a center of global expertise located in a subsidiary that has particular capabilities in the area in question.

HR Service Delivery

The key task in the HR service delivery role is for core processes to be carried out at low cost and with a desired service level. The interface with HRM process and content development must be managed carefully.

Over the last years, considerable pressure has been put on HR departments to cut costs and reduce the number of personnel involved in administrative tasks. In response, e-HR solutions have been developed that shift much of the transactional work to employees themselves using self-help tools; service centers have been established; and elements of HR have been outsourced.

In firms that have invested in e-HR solutions, employees can obtain online answers to a range of questions about holidays, pensions, regulations, and routine transactions.[76] While investments in standardized HR processes and IT systems can be considerable, they can also enable the introduction of new capabilities, for example facilitating global internal labor markets and cross-border deployment of professional talent.[77]

Shared service centers began to emerge as firms realized that many administrative tasks could be carried out in a more standardized manner, undertaken at a central location in the country, or on a regional basis. A clear trend has been to locate service centers in low-cost settings in Central America, Central and Eastern Europe, and India.

Certain HR processes have been outsourced for many decades; companies rely on headhunters and recruitment firms for recruitment and selection and on business schools for management training programs. The trend toward outsourcing larger parts of HR has continued in recent years, often in combination with a standardization of HR practices across the world. However, firms should obviously keep in-house practices such as leadership development that are strategically important.

Although effective HR service delivery is unlikely to translate into any sustainable competitive advantage, failure to execute these basic services can put the firm at a competitive disadvantage. It is a vital enabling capability, and the importance of efficient, high-quality HR services must not be underestimated in the search for what may seem like more prestigious and high-profile roles for the HR profession.

Focusing on Organizational Outcomes

HR practices, guided by a set of principles and with the HR function playing important roles, ultimately lead to desired organizational outcomes of human resource management—the final element in the HRM Wheel framework outlined in Figure 1-2. We have identified three interwoven critical outcomes:

- Competencies
- Commitment
- Competitiveness

The first outcome focuses on the quality of people in the corporation; the second highlights the attachment of employees to the organization; and the third is focused on long-term business success.

Competencies

The competencies of employees and managers is the first outcome of HRM. Do employees have the knowledge and skills needed for the firm to implement its strategy? The world is full of strategies and business plans that are discounted by analysts and investors who know that the enterprise does not have the human capacity to execute them better and faster than its competitors. To what extent are current and planned HR practices building the employee and leadership competencies needed to develop and retain over time the intended organizational capabilities of the corporation?

The required competencies go beyond the job requirements in ways that are seldom discussed in the traditional HRM literature. Given the importance of coordination in the transnational firm, its HRM activities play important roles in shaping what we call the social architecture of the global organization: its social capital (the structure and strength of social relationships between individuals); the values, behavioral norms, and beliefs of organizational members; and the global mindset that leaders and other members of multinational organizations must display. These three social dimensions are important determinants of the ability of employees to carry out their jobs in a global organization characterized by interdependence. P&G introduced recently a new element to their corporate credo: "Mutual interdependence is a way of life."

Commitment

HR practices, such as performance feedback, coaching and development, and attention to fair process in decision-making,[78] also shape employee attitudes, which may be just as important for firm performance as knowledge and skills. While the literature on organizational behavior deals with many different employee attitudes, which companies often measure using so-called engagement surveys, employee commitment to the organization is particularly relevant.[79] Several studies have confirmed that a high level of affective commitment is associated with better firm performance[80] and individuals who are highly committed are less likely to leave the organization.

The multinational must excel at worldwide implementation or execution of operational strategies and business plans. Execution depends on both good planning and commitment on the part of employees to the decisions that are made. Since most decisions will arouse some degree of resistance, particularly from successful or autonomous units, it is important that the way in which those decisions are reached is seen as fair in order to maintain commitment and loyalty. Indeed, the execution of strategy and business plans is at the heart of strategic human resource management and facilitating the management of change is a vital part of the business decision-making supporting role of HR professionals.

Competitiveness

The ability of the firm to retain its competitiveness over a prolonged period of time is the third organizational outcome of the HRM Wheel. The impact of HRM on firm performance is at the center of a hot debate that has been raging for some years. Much of this debate has focused on the choice of HR practices. Although there may not be a single best way of managing people, the evidence suggests that having a coherent set of HR practices that promote the development of employee knowledge and skills, social capital and commitment to the organization, and its strategy pays off in most circumstances.[81]

However, one limit of prescriptive viewpoints concerning HR practices is that they are static, whereas our world is highly dynamic. All industries periodically go through cycles of growth and decline, created by fluctuations in supply and demand for their products or services. In 2008/9, we witnessed one of the most dramatic changes in the global economic climate since the Great Depression in the 1930s. In some industries, companies went from booking record profits to suffering record losses in the course of three to four months. In a turbulent environment, sustainable performance depends on being able to cope with these cycles, anticipating the downturn in boom times and building for the future in lean periods.

Paradoxically, the most difficult time to invest in people is during times of growth, when managers are typically scrambling to take advantage of opportunities and are too impatient to invest in long-term global processes. The best time to make these changes and investments is during lean periods—as long as the firm has made sure it has sufficient funds in anticipation of a downturn. Indeed, we suggest that the best metaphor for understanding long-term development of multinational organizations is steering—navigating smoothly between good and harsh times, between global integration and local responsiveness, between short term and long term.

Egil Myklebust, who headed Norsk Hydro for ten years, understood this well. Norsk Hydro was a major Norway-based international company focused on cyclical industries like fertilizers, metals, and oil. Myklebust had known many ups and downs, and he told us that his role as CEO was to cut off the tops and bottom of the cycles. "In the boom times, when everyone is scrambling to launch projects and to hire people, my role is to push for caution and make sure there is ultra-sound justification. Otherwise hasty actions will worsen the downturn that surely lies ahead. And when people are taking the axe in the pits of the downturn, I have to push people to be bold and optimistic; otherwise we won't be in a position to take advantage of the good times ahead."[82]

Dualities and HRM in the Transnational

Myklebust's comment points to the difficulty we have in pinning down the concept of organizational effectiveness: first because organizational effectiveness is a multidimensional concept, and second because those dimensions involve opposites such as short term and long term. There are multiple opposing dimensions underlying our thinking about effectiveness—control and flexibility, internal and external focus, focus on both means and ends.[83] To be effective, an organization must possess attributes that are simultaneously contradictory, even mutually exclusive.

We refer to such opposites as dualities, while others call them paradoxes.[84] They are not either/or choices, the appropriateness of which depends on a particular context, but dualities that must be reconciled or dynamically balanced. Some of the many dualities facing organizations and groups are shown in Table 1-3.

One important insight of duality or paradox theory is that any positive quality taken too far becomes negative or pathological.[85] Instead of trying to maximize something, an organization should try to ensure that it maintains at least a minimal level of attention toward a desirable attribute. For example, an organization requires a minimal degree of consensus but not so much that it will stifle the dissension that is the life blood of innovation; and it needs a minimal degree of contentment, sufficient to ensure that key people remain with the firm, but not so much that arrogance or complacency emerges.

The pace of change has recently highlighted many of the paradoxical features of contemporary business organizations. In the past there were long periods of evolution within an existing product life cycle, alternating with short periods of revolutionary crisis when the technology changed.[86] Fueled by the pressures of globalization, pendulum swings have become more frequent as competition compresses time frames. As product life cycles speed up, as swings between undercapacity and overcapacity shorten, ambidexterity in the sense of doing two disparate things at the same time becomes vital.[87]

In such a world of rapid change, firms have to leverage their existing resources to make profits today and at the same time develop new resources that will be the source of their profits tomorrow. Leverage (called *exploitation* by academics) involves concern for efficiency, execution, production, and short-term success, but excessive focus leads to what has been called "the failure of success." Resource development (or *exploration*) involves innovation, learning, risk-taking, experimentation, and focus on long-term success.[88] However, an excessive focus on development is risky, compromising the survival of the firm. While the transnational firm faces the local–global dilemma, it also faces this exploitation–exploration dilemma.

Steering between Dualities

Opposing forces—such as differentiation and integration, external and internal orientation, hierarchy and network, short term and long term, planning and opportunity, rational analysis and emotional involvement, and change and continuity—can never be reconciled once and for all. They create tensions that must be anticipated and managed.[89]

The navigator is a useful metaphor for understanding how to deal with these tensions.[90] The job of the navigator at the helm of a vessel is to manage a constant but varying tension between the need to maintain a particular course and changing winds and currents. Steered by a skilled navigator, the path of a boat toward its destination is a series of controlled zigzags in response to wind and current. The unskilled helmsman fights to maintain headway, overcorrecting when the boat is blown off course, failing to anticipate the storms and calms that lie ahead. The resulting path is a series of wild zigzags as the boat veers from crisis to crisis.

TABLE 1-3

Some of the Dualities Facing International Firms

Managing today's assets—building tomorrow's assets
• Satisfying customer needs—being ahead of the customer
• Short term—long term
• Exploitation—exploration
Loose—tight
• Opportunistic—planned
• Entrepreneurship—control/accountability
• Flexibility—efficiency
Competition—partnership
Low cost—high value-added
Differentiation—integration
• Decentralization—centralization
• Unit performance—corporate integration
• Individual accountability—team responsibility
Change—continuity
• Speed of responsiveness—care in implementation
Professional—generalist
• Technical logic—business logic
Taking risks—avoiding failures
Task orientation—people orientation

Tensions caused by dualities can lead to virtuous or vicious circles of organizational development.[91] Most firms have to steer between opposing forces like functional excellence and inter-functional coordination, low cost and high flexibility, and mass and niche marketing. Some firms focus on a fixed strategy, for example, aligning the firm to the development of functional excellence. This might lead to initial success. But when that success is threatened by opposing pressures (for example, slow decision-making caused by lack of coordination among functions), leaders often respond by reinforcing what led them to be successful in the first place—increasing the pressure for functional excellence. This may lead to a crisis, where new leadership is brought in to build coordination. The pendulum swings from functional excellence to coordinated teamwork.

In contrast, the leaders of other firms appear to anticipate the need for a change in course, gently steering specialized functions toward greater teamwork before the problems of slow decision-making show up. Alternating between one course and the other, as the Norwegian CEO earlier noted, they steer toward their aims of higher profits and better return on investments in a virtuous spiral of increasing capabilities in both functional excellence and integrated teamwork.[92] Mastering this process is of critical importance to transnational firms.

Dualities and Transnational Management

Understanding dualities is a cornerstone for effective transnational management, since the transnational enterprise is one that can overcome the contradictions between local responsiveness, global efficiency, and exploiting knowledge on a worldwide basis, as Ghoshal and Bartlet noted. There are two particular dualities confronting the transnational enterprise that we highlight in this book—the duality of local responsiveness *and* global efficiency and that of resource exploitation *and* resource exploration.

We discussed already how many so-called multidomestic firms internationalized by decentralizing responsibilities to their subsidiaries and local business units. Decentralization has many advantages, including proximity to customers, a heightened sense of accountability, more local innovation and entrepreneurship, and better employee morale of local staff. But local responsiveness has a shadow side. After initial success, it often leads to reinventing the wheel, duplication of back office functions, slow response to technological change, and costs that cannot compete with globally efficient competitors. These "handmaidens of decentralization," as Bartlett and Ghoshal called them, often prompt firms to swing to centralized control, until bureaucracy, loss of responsiveness, and the inability to retain good people turn the pendulum to decentralization once again.

After several swings, organizations begin to realize that decentralization (local responsiveness) and centralization (global integration) are a duality. Even though there may be an immediate advantage to each approach, a future movement in the direction of the organization must be anticipated. One executive expressed this with apt advice to senior management: "Organize one way, manage the other way." If the structure is currently being decentralized to encourage local responsiveness, senior management attention should be focused on building coordination links across units. If the central functions and control are being beefed up, the focus of attention should be on preventing the loss of local entrepreneurship.[93]

Organizing one way but managing the other way requires a change of thinking among local leaders. While acting as local entrepreneurs, they also need to have a clear understanding of global strategy. Strategic management becomes a process that involves all key leaders around the world, and local managers need to have a global perspective. The role of people in central staff positions, including corporate HR, is not to tell local people what to do or to solve their problems for them—that would be incompatible with the need for local responsiveness. Instead, central staff must act as network leaders, getting people together to face up to common problems.[94]

The challenges of managing dualities are of crucial relevance to HRM. All organizations maintain corporate control and coordination through hierarchy, budgets, rules, and centrally managed processes and procedures. But as the needs for coordination grow, more rules, more control, and more bosses at the center simply will not work; this will only kill local entrepreneurship and drive away good people. These classic tools need to be complemented with more subtle mechanisms of horizontal coordination, such as lateral structures, social architecture, leadership development, performance and knowledge management. These coordination tools are to a large degree the application of HRM.

OUTLINE OF THIS BOOK

The stage having been set here, the two next chapters review the globalization strategies of local responsiveness and global integration in depth. In Chapter 2, we explore what local responsiveness means for HRM by looking at the multi-domestic firm, with a particular emphasis on how multinational corporations adapt to the local cultural and institutional context. Chapter 3 focuses on the strategy of global integration through the lens of the meganational enterprise, framing the subsequent discussion of control and coordination mechanisms.

We look at the different methods of coordination. Structural coordination mechanisms examined in Chapter 4 include multidimensional structures, cross-boundary teams, cross-boundary roles and steering groups, as well as virtual teams. Social coordination mechanisms of social capital, shared values, and global mindset are discussed in Chapter 5. The next four chapters (Chapters 6–9) deal with key processes in international HRM: talent acquisition, performance management (including compensation), leadership development, and international mobility.

The next four chapters examine complex people management challenges in global firms: facilitating change through HRM (Chapter 10), knowledge and innovation management (Chapter 11), cross-border merger and acquisition integration (Chapter 12), and managing alliances and joint ventures (Chapter 13).

The final chapter addresses the implications of recent and future developments for HR professionals in multinational firms.

The focus of this book is explicitly on international HRM in large complex multinational firms rather than small or medium-sized enterprises, although a number of issues that we will cover are of direct relevance for a broad spectrum of firms. We will present examples from firms drawn from all regions of the world, including eBay and GE from the US, Toyota from Japan, Haier and Alibaba from China, European multinationals like Zara, Kone, and Shell, and companies without clear nationalities such as ArcelorMittal and Schlumberger. Each chapter starts with a short case, highlighting the challenges that we will discuss.

As the HR contributions to internationalization increase in importance, the boundaries between the HR function and line management become blurred, as do the boundaries with other management functions, such as strategic planning, information technology, marketing, corporate communication, and operations. Throughout this book, we will be taking a broad managerial perspective, addressing "the manager," regardless of whether that manager works as a line or general manager or as a professional in the HR function. However, from time to time, we will also address challenges that are specific to HR in most firms. The convention that we use is to refer to "HR" whenever we mean the functional domain and "HR practices" when referring to corporate practices in managing people for which the HR function is at least partly responsible. When we talk about human resource management, or HRM, we are adopting a generalist perspective.

TAKEAWAYS

1. Control and coordination of dispersed operations have always been a key challenge for multinational firms; people management is central to how companies have addressed this challenge.

2. Multinational firms have muddled through organizational dilemmas and contradictions, often in a pendulum fashion. The contradictions become apparent as firms are pushed to be both responsive to local needs and globally integrated—a hallmark of the "transnational organization."

3. All multinationals face transnational pressures, but not with equal force. HRM can help firms align local responsiveness with a high degree of global integration.

4. In transnational firms, HRM has increasingly been acknowledged as one of the key tools to implement global business models and build long-term competitive advantage.

5. To add long-term value, people management has to support the development of organizational capabilities that differentiate a multinational from its competitors.

6. The important guiding principles of HRM are internal consistency of human resource management and work practices; differentiation among employee groups, between locations, and from other competitors; and balancing dualities.

7. Every international firm has to cope with a number of basic but vital HRM tasks: attracting and recruiting, managing and rewarding performance, and developing and retaining people. The core HR task—getting the right people into the right place at the right time—is an enabling capacity that must not be neglected.

8. The HR function covers three roles: contributing to business decisions; providing HR expertise; and delivering HR services. Each of these distinct but interrelated roles is important and needs to be staffed by competent HR professionals.

9. Competencies, commitment and competitiveness are the key outcomes of HRM—competencies that underlie organizational capabilities; commitment to the organization as well as to its strategies and plans; and long-term competitiveness.

10. Organizational effectiveness is inherently paradoxical, requiring steering between opposing forces. Two key dualities which need attention are local responsiveness *and* global efficiency, and resource leverage *and* resource development.

NOTES

1 Berg and Fast, 1983; Hastings, 1999; Bartlett and O'Connell, 1998.
2 Siegel and Larson, 2009.
3 Björkman and Galunic, 1999; Björkman, Galunic, and Lockard, 2015; Siegel, 2008; see www.lincolnelectric.com.
4 Moore and Lewis, 1999.
5 Ibid., p. 230.
6 Carlos and Nicholas, 1988. On the other side of the world, southern Chinese clans spread their hold across Southeast Asia in the fourteenth and fifteenth centuries.
7 In academic terms, this is known as "agency problems" and concerns the extent to which self-interested agents will represent their principal's interest in situations where the principal lacks information about what the agent is doing. According to agency theory, principals can invest in collecting information about what the agent is doing or seek to design an incentive system such that the agent is rewarded when pursuing the principal's interests.
8 Wren, 1994.
9 Even by the early 1990s, FDI had only rallied to around 8.5 percent of world output (Jones, G. 1996). The latest data show the stock of outward FDI to be 33.7 percent of global GDP in 2014 (World Investment Report 2015, UNCTAD—available at http://unctad.org/en/PublicationsLibrary/wir2015_en.pdf).
10 Chandler, 1990.
11 Schisgall, 1981.
12 Jones, G. 1996, p. 173.
13 Price Waterhouse and Coopers & Lybrand later merged to form PricewaterhouseCoopers (PwC).
14 Vernon, 1977.
15 FDI refers to investments in units abroad over which the corporation has control, thus excluding purely financial (portfolio) investments.
16 Vernon, 1966; Stopford and Wells, 1972; Johanson and Vahlne, 1977.
17 Ashkenas *et al.*, 1995.
18 Such clusters of critical factors helped particular nations to develop a competitive advantage in certain fields—such as German firms in chemicals or luxury cars, Swiss firms in pharmaceuticals, and US firms in personal computers, software, and movies.
19 At the same time, Chinese outward FDI also increased dramatically. In 2014, Chinese outward FDI was second only to that of the US (World Investment Report 2015, available at http://unctad.org/en/PublicationsLibrary/wir2015_en.pdf).
20 See http://fortune.com/global500/.
21 Bartlett and Ghoshal, 1989. The origins of the aphorism apparently go back to urban planning in 1915, and it is today used by governments as well as business corporations. To this we can add Hedlund's (1986) related concept of *heterarchy* and Prahalad and Doz's (1987) studies on the

multi-focal organization, all of which have origins in Perlmutter's (1969) geocentric organization. See Westney (2014) for an overview of research on the organization of multinational corporations.

22 Doz, Bartlett, and Prahalad, 1981; Doz and Prahalad, 1984, 1986.

23 Bartlett and Ghoshal, 1989.

24 The original company name of Panasonic was Matsushita Electric Works.

25 Since the term is generic, we use "international" when referring to Bartlett and Ghoshal's (1989) use of the term.

26 Although NEC clearly had the grand vision, with its notion of combining computers and communication (long before the emergence of Cisco), it was unable to implement that vision. A big part of the problem is that it was never able to globalize and go where the talent was.

27 A good example of this change is in the pioneering research on corporate strategy of Porter (1980). Porter argued that strategy was choice, and his data showed that there was a clear choice between two generic strategies: cost differentiation (low cost) or market differentiation (customer orientation). As he put it, firms that pursued both low cost and high customer orientation were stuck in the middle—lower on indicators of success such as profitability. But Porter's data had been collected in the 1960s and 1970s, before globalization began to have its impact. By the time that his influential work on strategy was published, corporations were struggling to find ways of doing things better *and* cheaper. It was no longer *either-or* but *both-and*.

28 Ghoshal and Bartlett, 1998, p. 65.

29 Rosenzweig and Nohria, 1994; Björkman and Lu, 2001.

30 See Nohria and Ghoshal (1997) for a classification of the business environments of multinational firms.

31 Martinez and Jarillo, 1989.

32 Edström and Galbraith, 1977.

33 "Three times the number of managers were transferred in Europe at [one company rather than the other], despite their being of the same size, in the same industry, and having nearly identical organization charts" (Edström and Galbraith, 1977, p. 255).

34 Perlmutter, 1969.

35 Ibid., p. 13.

36 Michael Porter (1985), who laid much of the foundations for the field of strategic management, noted that "horizontal strategies"—what was to be more widely known as global integration— are the most important contribution for HRM.

37 See, for example, Pucik (1984a, 1992), Taylor, Beechler, and Napier (1996), De Cieri and Dowling (1999).

38 Cited by Bartlett and Ghoshal (1992).

39 Porter, 1980.

40 Barney, 1991.

41 Boxall, 1996.

42 Grant, 1996, p. 377.

43 The term "dynamic capabilities" is used to describe the firm's ability to create new organizational capabilities in response to changes in the environment (Teece, Pisano, and Shuen, 1997; see Zollo and Winter, 2002, for a slightly different definition).

44 Grant, 1996; see also Ulrich and Lake (1990) for an early HRM-based discussion of organizational capabilities. For a contemporary perspective on organizational capabilities, see Teece (2014).

45 A psychological contract is the (often informal) perceptions of the individual and organization of the employment relationship, including the reciprocal promises and obligations implicit in it (Rousseau, 1995; Guest and Conway, 2002).

46 Barney, 1991.

47 Enabling capabilities is sometimes referred to in the literature as *ordinary* capabilities.

48 The concept of functional and coordination capabilities was developed in collaboration with Robert Diab. For an empirical application see R. Diab and V. Pucik, "Competing on Capabilities: Can China's Auto Parts Companies Become Global Tier-One Suppliers?" *China Europe International Business School Working Paper*, 2015.

49 Merck KGaA holds the global rights to the name and the trademark "MERCK." The exception is North America, where it is represented by the EMD brand, which stands for "Emanuel Merck Darmstadt." US-based Merck & Co., which was a subsidiary of Merck KGaA until it

was expropriated in 1917, holds the rights to the name and the trademark "MERCK" in North America. In the rest of the world the US company operates as MSD, Merck Sharp & Dohme, or MSD Sharp & Dohme.

50 Human Resource Management International Digest, 2007.

51 See Boxall and Purcell (2003) for a presentation and discussion of the "ability, motivation, and opportunity" (AMO) model.

52 Becker *et al.*, 1997.

53 For details on the evolution of Lincoln Electric's approach to HRM, see Berg and Fast (1983) and Björkman and Galunic (1999).

54 Siegel, 2008.

55 Bacon, 1999. Another example is a collection of studies by British researchers on employee experiences with HRM (Mabey, Skinner, and Clark, 1998).

56 It is particularly important that comparable employees in the same location are treated similarly (Baron and Kreps, 1999).

57 Ibid., 1999.

58 See Baron and Kreps (1999) for a detailed discussion of the importance of consistency between HR practices, notably in Chapter 3.

59 Bowen and Ostroff (2004) conceptualize HRM as a signaling system. When HR practices send distinct and consistent messages, employees are motivated to understand and adopt attitudes and behaviors consistent with the strategy and goals of the firm.

60 Tanure, Evans, and Pucik, 2007. Legge (1995) critically elaborates on a long-standing clash between the rhetoric and the reality of HRM in Europe.

61 Kepes and Delery, 2007.

62 There may also be some differentiation across business lines. This fourth aspect of differentiation is particularly relevant when business units differ in the organizational capabilities they use to compete.

63 Gonzáles and Tacorante, 2004. However, it must be noted that the classification of employment types is a considerable challenge in empirical research.

64 Lepak and Snell, 2002.

65 See Chapter 7 for a discussion of this point.

66 Lincoln's management might have done a better job in managing a new approach to people management in the acquired units. We discuss management of change and M&As in Chapters 10 and 12.

67 Liker and Hoseus, 2008.

68 "P&G Leadership Machine," *Fortune*, April 13, 2009, p. 16.

69 This refers to the classic principles of differentiation and integration in organizational design. See Lawrence and Lorsch (1967), Mintzberg (1979), Galbraith (1977), and many other works in this domain.

70 These social mechanisms are discussed in Chapter 5.

71 The consulting firm McKinsey coined the "talent war" expression to capture the reality in many industries (Chambers *et al.*, 1998).

72 Sparrow, Brewster, and Harris, 2004.

73 Lawler (2003a) summarizes the research on this issue.

74 Readers may be familiar with David Ulrich's well-known so-called Four Box Framework (Ulrich, 1997), with two operational and two strategic roles. Ulrich suggests that there are two operational HR roles: that of the "administrative expert" and that of the "employee champion." Our HRM service delivery role incorporates Ulrich's administrative expert role, while our HRM development role contains elements of administrative expert and also elements of Ulrich's strategic/long-term roles of the "strategic partner" and "change agent." Finally, our business support role is closest to Ulrich's strategic partner and change agent but also contains aspects of the employee champion. More recently, Ulrich and Brockbank (2005) identified five roles for the HR function: employee advocate, human capital developer, functional expert, strategic partner, and HR leader.

75 We will return to this question in Chapter 14.

76 Ulrich and Brockbank, 2005.

77 This is discussed in Chapter 8. As we note there, these global open job markets are helping IBM achieve its vision of becoming a globally integrated enterprise.

78 Fair process in decision-making is referred to throughout this book but particularly in connection with managing change in Chapter 10.

79 Psychological empowerment is another important attitude. The individual's perception of being able to decide on and/or influence relevant issues related to his or her own work is one integrated part of psychological empowerment; the feeling of having the necessary knowledge and skills is another. Both academic research (e.g., Spreitzer, 1996) and company anecdotes confirm that psychological empowerment has a positive effect on company performance. For research on affective organizational commitment, see Allen and Meyer (1990).

80 For a review of such studies, see Kuvaas (2008).

81 Huselid (1995), Lepak and Snell (2002), and Guthrie (2001), respectively.

82 By 2009, the name of the company had been changed to Hydro and only the metals industry business had been retained.

83 Quinn and Rohrbaugh, 1983.

84 Evans and Doz, 1989; Evans and Doz, 1992; Evans and Génadry, 1998. See also Smith and Lewis (2011) and Smith (2014).

85 Historians have been well aware of these swings. Indeed Arnold Toynbee's monumental *A Study of History* is built on the insight that the decline of civilizations occurs when a society pursues its success formula to excess (Toynbee, 1946). One of the earliest articles on duality theory, on the theme of organizational seesaws, emphasized this point (Hedberg, Nystrom, and Starbuck, 1976).

86 Greiner, 1972; Tushman and O'Reilly, 1996.

87 Organizational ambidexterity is discussed by O'Reilly and Tushman (2013) and by Birkinshaw and Gupta (2013). We explore this and the related concept of strategic agility in Chapter 10.

88 March, 1991.

89 Evans and Génadry (1998) argue that it is tension between opposites that should be the dependent variable in organizational research.

90 Hampden-Turner, 1990a.

91 Hampden-Turner, 1990b.

92 Evans and Doz, 1989. Similar examples of steering are provided by Brown and Eisenhardt (1997, 1998). They show how successful firms in fast-moving industries steer between the need for semi-structures (clarity of roles, deadlines, and priorities) and improvisation (opportunism and open communication).

93 See Klarner and Raisch (2013) for research on "rhythms of change" in the context of the change–stability duality.

94 The implications for leadership are the subject of more and more frequent study; see Evans (2000) and Lewis, Andriopolous, and Smith (2014), as well as Zhang *et al.* (2015) and Nakarni and Chen (2014) for empirical studies on paradoxical leader behaviors.

2

Becoming Locally Responsive

SUMMARY

Challenge

As companies expand abroad, responding to multiple local contexts and differentiated needs becomes increasingly complex—and difficult

Analysis

For effective local responsiveness, companies must be able to learn about three key dimensions of the context:

- Cultural (knowing yourself and others)
- Institutional (knowing the socio-political context of where you are)
- Network (knowing whom you talk to)

Solutions

- Cultural models help identify local needs, but use them with care to avoid unhealthy stereotypes
- Start with the home country as a first step towards understanding how institutional contexts influence HRM practices
- Step outside the "comfort zone" as communication quality depends on diversity of information
- Localization starts at the head office and requires sustained commitment
- To go local—adapt ... but don't always play by the local rules

eBay versus Alibaba in China

In March 1998, Meg Whitman was recruited to become the CEO of eBay—three years after the French entrepreneur, Pierre Omidyar, had founded the e-business firm. At the time, eBay had only 50 employees, US$4.7 million in revenues, and operated only in the US. When she stepped down as CEO of the California-based firm ten years later, eBay was present in close to 40 countries and had more than 15,000 employees, approximately 100 million active users, and about $8 billion in annual revenue.[1] By any standards, eBay is a highly successful multinational corporation. However, in spite of its market dominance in many countries around the world, it has struggled to grow in some key markets in Asia.[2]

eBay's entry point to Asia was Japan in 2000. Its business model for Japan, as for all the other international markets it had previously entered successfully, was essentially the same as for the US—notably the user fee structure and no media advertising. Its local Web site was also similar to the company's US version, with no special features to attract and serve local users. However, eBay was not the first mover in the Japanese market. Its US competitor Yahoo had already formed a joint venture with the Japanese Internet company Softbank and invested heavily in an aggressive advertising campaign to promote its services.[3] By the time eBay went online, following the lengthy process of building its 100 percent-owned company from scratch, Yahoo had already built a loyal customer base that eBay was not able to seduce away. Two years after its entry to Japan, eBay pulled out.

As the company looked at other opportunities in Asia, eBay's management was determined to learn from its failure in Japan. Rather than starting from zero, eBay entered Taiwan, Korea, and India through partnerships and partial acquisitions of local firms. This was also the strategy chosen in potentially the biggest market opportunity of all: China. In March 2002, eBay first bought a 33 percent stake and then full control in EachNet, China's first and largest online consumer-to-consumer (C2C) trading site led by a Shanghai native who had graduated from Harvard and developed EachNet with eBay as his model. Within a short time, eBay/EachNet had become the clear market leader for C2C business in China, with a dominant 85 percent market share. EachNet's staff were Chinese, but since its outset it had been modeled on eBay.

However, local competition began to push back very quickly.[4] The biggest challenge came from a start-up formed by Chinese Internet entrepreneur Jack Ma. Ma already had a highly successful business-to-business auction site called Alibaba (in which Softbank from Japan and later Yahoo were major investors). He was concerned that eBay/EachNet would establish a beachhead from which to attack his very profitable B2B activities. So, in 2003, Ma locked up his team for six months in his house to set up his own e-commerce company Taobao ("hunt for treasure") as a direct competitor to eBay. "[eBay and Yahoo] are the sharks in the ocean, and we are the crocodiles in the Yangtze River," said Ma. "When they fight in the Yangtze River, they will be in trouble. The smell of the water is different."[5] Its portal was crowded with multicolored links that appealed to the Chinese user, contrasted with the clean design of eBay/EachNet.

In China as elsewhere, eBay added fees based on the value of a deal to the listing fees that EachNet charged. Taobao did not charge any such fees and Ma promised that his company

would not do so for at least three years.[6] Faced with the eBay giant, Taobao's employees were encouraged to "do a handstand" to see the world differently, finding solutions to the tough competition. While eBay's Chinese site had a layout and features similar to those in rest of the world, Taobao presented a site full of popular local features (such as horoscopes). Critically, Taobao developed a new payment system linked to physical delivery of the goods, as Chinese customers did not fully trust the credit card-based systems like PayPal that eBay was using. Taobao—unlike eBay—also allowed the seller and buyer to interact directly. In a society that was still uncomfortable with the Internet, this was an effective way of dealing with issues of trust among people who do not know each other personally. Finally, to build customer confidence, Taobao decided to provide customer service support by telephone, again, not something supplied by eBay.[7]

The challenges of integrating EachNet and eBay further aggravated the latter's problems. Many members of the original EachNet team left the company, feeling that they had been sidelined after the acquisition, when eBay managers from places like Germany and Taiwan were brought in to help with the integration. In order to achieve economies of scale, eBay moved EachNet's Internet platform to its US-based global server, as it had done systematically when integrating other foreign units. In the process, several locally developed design features were removed. Once the site was on the global platform, requests to localize the content of the Chinese site had to be approved from the US. Local employees felt that headquarters "did not listen to them."[8]

Despite following Taobao's example with free product listing, eBay's market share was down to 20 percent by the end of 2006. Although Meg Whitman had promised, after the failure in Japan, that eBay would do a better job in adapting its activities to the local market in China, the company was unable to do so. In December 2006, eBay announced a fresh start, forming a joint venture with Tom Online, a wireless Internet company controlled by Hong Kong tycoon Li Ka Shing.[9] All eBay/EachNet business would be merged into a joint venture managed by Tom Online; only eBay China's global trading remained independent. In 2014, eBay had a 2 percent market share.

In 2014 Alibaba, now the world's largest Internet retailer, prepared to enter the US market by recruiting a former US Treasury chief of staff to help tailor its international strategy. Rather than taking Amazon and eBay head-on in their home territory, the more conservative approach was to allow US retailers such as Nieman Marcus to sell to Chinese consumers.[10] Will Alibaba succeed in the US or fall into the same traps as eBay in China?

OVERVIEW

The story of eBay in Asia provides a vivid example of the potential problems facing multinational corporations that fail to adapt to local demands and competitive conditions. In this chapter we examine how firms respond to the diverse environments they face in international markets. Local responsiveness involves responding to differentiated needs in different markets and to the local context. Companies that focus on responding to local conditions take a *multidomestic* approach to management.

In this chapter we examine how companies can deal with three sources of diversity. They must know themselves and others (cultural diversity), know where they are (institutional diversity), and know whom they talk to (network diversity). Then we discuss how they can localize by attracting and retaining local managers, though surprisingly this all starts at the head office. In conclusion we observe that local responsiveness does not necessarily mean playing by the local rules.

THE IMPORTANCE OF LOCAL RESPONSIVENESS

The managers of subsidiaries in multidomestic firms have targets that they must meet, but they can achieve them in a way that is locally responsive. Local responsiveness represents the capacity to sense and answer to the varied needs of customers and other stakeholders. At the core of the multidomestic strategy is the argument that the capability of responding in a locally appropriate way helps to overcome the "liability of foreignness" that firms may suffer from when entering new markets.[11] This liability comes because foreign companies do not understand the local culture, institutions, and networks. As we have seen in the case of eBay, not knowing how to manage in the unfamiliar environment, and/or not having products and services that fit local requirements, puts foreign companies at a disadvantage compared with their local competitors. Internet companies in particular may fall into the trap of thinking that users all over the world are the same.

Local responsiveness was the route followed early in the internationalization process by companies such as Nestlé and Unilever at the beginning of the twentieth century. In an era when communication and transport were restricted, customer preferences around the world were fragmented. Perhaps more importantly in those days before modern logistics, the cost and delay of shipping goods internationally offset the economies of global mass production for all but a limited range of products. However, as trade barriers decreased and technologies increased our ability to overcome geographic barriers, companies began to feel fewer pressures to be responsive and focused more on capitalizing on economies of scale.

More recently, the market leaders have become more evenly matched on access to capital, know-how, and technology. In a world of increased global connectivity,[12] local responsiveness has acquired additional value as a source of competitive advantage. Even Coca-Cola, which for most of its existence constituted the archetype of a firm pursuing a meganational strategy, felt the need to "rediscover" its own multi-local heritage, triggered by the slow responsiveness of the global headquarters in Atlanta to changing local markets and to food safety incidents around the world.[13]

In the process of "rediscovering" local responsiveness, our understanding of it has also changed. The term "local" used to imply "national," whereas today it means "differentiated." Nations remain important drivers of differentiated needs, but they are by no means the only ones. One of the challenges for multinational companies is to respond to differentiated needs more finely, market by market. In fact, "local" refers to any market that is distinct from others.

In addition, cultural distance remains important in our global era. From the multinational firm's point of view, some regions and markets may be more distant than others.[14] For example, research on foreign companies in Brazil revealed that those coming from countries with strong ties to Brazil (in terms of language and institutional similarity, geographical proximity, colonial history, and immigration) were usually more successful than firms from countries with weaker ties to the country.[15] Also, there is some evidence that firms moving step-by-step to culturally distant countries, after establishing a presence in more proximate countries, are more successful than those that expanded by directly entering distant markets.[16] Given such findings one might urge managers to pay careful attention not just to market opportunities but also to ease of entry in terms of social, cultural, and institutional factors, especially with respect to their impact on human resources.

Business Advantages of Local Responsiveness

A locally responsive company is likely to be more receptive to local trends, emerging needs, and product usage patterns—and therefore less likely to miss subtle market opportunities. By presenting a local face and acting like a domestic firm, the foreign firm may reach a wider customer base and compete more effectively in local labor markets. Responsiveness also includes a firm's business practices, such as the way it handles relationships with suppliers, distributors, and local government, and the approach it takes to people management.

The dimensions of local responsiveness come from a mix of market, organizational, and political considerations (see the box "Business Dimensions of Local Responsiveness").

Business Dimensions of Local Responsiveness

Industry characteristics

In certain business sectors, there is little competitive advantage to be gained from standardizing or coordinating across different subsidiaries. For example, non-branded foods and small household appliances face weak forces for global integration because of an absence of scale economies. Cement companies, such as Lafarge and CEMEX, engage heavily in local production in every country they have entered. This is largely because the shipping and tariff costs neutralize any cost advantages of centralized sourcing.

Customer needs

Historically, branded packaged goods companies, such as Danone (foods) or Unilever (nondurable goods), have tended to respond to different customer expectations, preferences, or requirements. But even businesses with global formulae, such as McDonald's or Disney, may be forced to modify their offerings to cater to local traditions or expectations. For example, European dining habits forced both Disney's theme park in Paris and McDonald's European franchises to abandon cherished no-alcohol policies applied in the home market.

Local substitutes

Competition from local products or services with different price/performance characteristics may lead a company to local adaptation. Nestlé varies its infant cereal recipes according to local raw materials—in Europe they are made with wheat, in Latin America with maize and sorghum, and in Asia with soy. Whirlpool, contrary to its worldwide policies, introduced a locally manufactured brand of appliances in Eastern Europe to compete against low-priced competition.

Markets and distribution

National differences in market structure and distribution channels can have repercussions on pricing, product positioning or design, promotion, and advertising. For example, the distribution infrastructure, particularly in emerging markets, may require adjustments to product design or packaging in order to cope with the challenges of dust, heat, or bumpy roads.

Host government regulations

Host government concerns—for national development or national security—may force a business to be locally responsive. Petrochemical firms have to build close relationships with national authorities controlling a resource that is critical for economic development. Local content requirements can force a firm into development partnerships with suppliers. Retail practices that are standard in the US, such as opening 24/7, or refunding the price difference on any item sold for less elsewhere, are illegal in Germany.

Conforming to local business practices and developing ties to local authorities are especially important. If a firm becomes a local insider, it is more likely to have a say in the shaping of new policies and regulations and to be invited to play a significant role in industry or trade associations. In this way it can gain valuable information and have a better chance of participating in local deals. As global oil companies like Shell and Exxon recognize, it is important to interact closely with local authorities in the regulated world of petroleum exploration and marketing. However, there are also potential dangers. Being too close to the authorities can create its own risks, for example, if the local government comes under attack for questionable practices.[17]

Another example is from the Internet search industry. For several years Google had a Chinese-language version of its search engine (google.com) that operated outside of China. However, the Chinese government closely monitored the search engine, continuously using a firewall to block access to sites blacklisted by the government and slowing down the search in general. In 2006, Google decided to open up a new Chinese-speaking version in China (google.cn), and the company agreed to adhere to Chinese self-censorship laws and regulations.[18] However, the decision by Google to follow Yahoo and Microsoft in accepting self-censorship in China was heavily criticized in the US.[19] When Google reversed course in 2010 in response to a hacking attack originating in China, announcing that it would no longer censor searches there, the Chinese authorities retaliated. Access to most Google products has been essentially blocked (including Gmail and Google Scholar); whereas a third of all searches in China were on Google in 2009, it had less than 2 percent market share in 2014.

People Challenges of Local Responsiveness

Alongside the business arguments for local responsiveness, there are equally compelling arguments for taking a local orientation in people management. Of all the management domains, people management is generally seen as the most sensitive to local context.[20] Cultural differences are one reason, but by no means the only one. National regulatory pressures are equally if not more important—on workplace representation, employee participation, fiscal incentives for training, acceptable practice when hiring and firing, working hours, and so on.

Some countries regulate employment practices closely, whereas others leave more discretion to the employer. For example, firms in the US can set their own overtime policies and seldom pay professionals for overtime. In Japan such practices are nominally illegal yet not uncommon, but in Germany they would land the company in court. Moreover, HR practices are typically subject to scrutiny by labor unions, whose strength and attitudes to management vary by nation and industry (more about this later in the chapter).

These characteristics make people management more context-specific than accounting, marketing, or manufacturing, which tend to adhere more closely to parent company norms. Because people management tools are context-specific, one response is simply to delegate HR practices entirely to the local subsidiaries—an approach that might be characterized as "When in Rome, do as the Romans." Yet this is too simplistic.

The adjustment of HR practices to the local context is often framed as a Hamlet choice: *to adjust or not to adjust, that is the question*. In fact, people management is not a monolithic domain. For example, research on foreign companies in China shows significant differences in the degree of local responsiveness of recruitment, training, compensation, performance appraisal, and promotion criteria,[21] and we explore reasons for these differences in this chapter. Also, HR practices for rank-and-file employees may correspond more to local norms than practices affecting executives.[22]

Some HR practices are more contextually bound than others. Some can be regarded as high context, others as low context, to borrow from Hall's terminology.[23] Low-context practices are more explicit, based on clear frameworks and applied in a similar fashion across cultures—such as job design criteria and objectives, and measures of employee performance. High-context practices have a stronger dependence on local norms and values, such as conflict resolution, and how objectives are set and performance appraisals conducted.

UNDERSTANDING DIVERSITY

To capitalize on the advantages of responsiveness companies must respond to diversity across countries. In this section, we focus on the sources of diversity across countries and how international firms respond to this diversity in the way they manage people.

We present and discuss three perspectives for understanding diversity. They relate to the cultural differences between the context in which the parent company and its local subsidiary are embedded (know yourself and others), to the institutional configuration of the environment (know where you are), and to the company's way of networking (know whom you talk to).

Know Yourself and Others: The Cultural Perspective

This perspective maintains that the values (i.e., notions of what is desirable) shared by people or members of a social group are at least to some extent shaped by collective beliefs, behavior, and artifacts.[24] Members of a society internalize certain values, beliefs, and behavioral norms that become more or less taken for granted. Culture is believed to influence and thus differentiate management practices across societies as well as other collective groups such as industries and organizations.

From the cultural perspective, attention typically focuses on how the local culture influences the management practices of foreign firms in the country. But the starting point for sensible local responsiveness is recognizing that the parent organization is embedded in the societal culture of its home country. This cultural embeddedness may have an effect on its international strategy, on how the multinational controls and coordinates its foreign units, and on the views held by parent company executives about effective management practices. Simply put, before you try to understand other people as well as the practices and strategies that may be effective abroad, you had better understand yourself. In this chapter we will focus on societal culture, postponing our discussion of organizational culture to Chapter 5.

Mapping Cultural Differences

The most influential body of literature concerning values in international business relates to cultural differences between countries. Its foundation is Hofstede's landmark book *Culture's Consequences*, which describes research conducted 40 years ago grounded in one of the largest databases about workplace values ever analyzed—attitude surveys of 116,000 IBM employees in 53 countries.[25] The study showed that despite IBM's strong integrative culture, national culture played an important role in differentiating work values.

Hofstede identified five "universal" dimensions along which cultures could be compared: individualism/collectivism, power distance, uncertainty avoidance, masculinity/femininity, and long- versus short-term orientation. Hofstede argued that these five dimensions influence the way in which organizations are structured and managed.[26] His quantitative measures of culture gave birth to the notion of "cultural distance" between home and host country and allowed the cultural perspective to infiltrate other fields of international business research. Others showed that there were bigger differences in managerial beliefs among people working for the same company in different nations than among people working for different companies within one nation.[27]

Following a similar line of inquiry, Trompenaars and Hampden-Turner showed the importance of opposing values, such as achievement versus ascription and universalism versus particularism.[28] They identify seven cultural "tensions" (see Table 2-1) that they believe companies (and managers) should be aware of, since these could influence the transferability of management practices across borders.

A multinational team of researchers (GLOBE) conducted another large-scale study of cultural differences, based on data from over 17,000 managers in 62 societies.[29] Partly overlapping with Hofstede's conceptualization of cultural dimensions, the GLOBE project identified nine cultural dimensions along which societies can be ranked.[30] Table 2-2 shows the scores for a number of countries.

GLOBE dimensions, like differences around assertiveness, allow us to understand the problems of interpersonal relations and teamwork when working across cultures. When there is a conflict or a problem that arouses strong feelings, people from some cultures (Israel and the Netherlands, for example)

TABLE 2-1
Seven Cultural Tensions

1. **Universalism versus particularism:** When no code, rule, or law seems to cover an exceptional case, should the most relevant rule be imposed, or should the case be considered on its merits?

2. **Analyzing versus integrating:** Are managers more effective when they break up a problem or situation into parts or integrate the parts into a whole?

3. **Individualism versus communitarianism:** When people reach decisions or make choices, should they consider their own best interests, or should they base their choices on the considerations of the wider team, organization, collectivity, or community to which they belong?

4. **Inner-directed versus outer-directed:** Should managers be guided by internal standards, or should they be flexible and adjust to external signals, demands, and trends?

5. **Sequential versus synchronic view of time:** Should managers get things done as quickly as possible, regardless of the negative impact that their actions may have on others, or should they synchronize efforts so that completion is coordinated and the negative impact minimized?

6. **Achieved versus ascribed status:** Should individuals be judged primarily or solely by their achievements, or by their status, as reflected in age, length of service, or other ascriptions?

7. **Equality versus hierarchy:** Should subordinates be treated as equals and allowed to exercise discretion in decision-making, or should relationships be delimited by hierarchy?

Source: Adapted from C. Hampden-Turner and A. Trompenaars, *Building Cross-Cultural Competence* (New York: Wiley, 2000).

TABLE 2-2
The GLOBE Study on Cultural Practices
(Scale 1–7)

Dimension	US	Germany[A]	France	Sweden	Russia	China	Japan	Brazil	Egypt
Power distance: Extent to which members of a collective expect power to be distributed equally.	4.9	5.3	5.2	4.9	5.5	5.0	5.1	5.3	4.9
Uncertainty avoidance: Degree to which a society, organization, or group relies on social norms, rules, and procedures to alleviate the unpredictability of future events.	4.2	5.2	4.4	5.3	2.9	4.9	4.1	3.6	4.1
Societal collectivism: Degree to which organizational and societal institutional practices encourage and reward collective distribution of resources and collective action.	4.2	3.8	3.9	5.2	4.5	4.8	5.2	3.8	4.5
In-group collectivism: Degree to which individuals express pride, loyalty, and cohesiveness in their organizations or families.	4.3	4.0	4.4	3.7	5.6	5.8	4.6	5.2	5.6
Performance orientation: Degree to which a collective encourages and rewards group members for performance improvement and excellence.	4.5	4.3	4.1	3.7	3.4	4.5	4.2	4.0	4.3
Assertiveness: Extent to which individuals are assertive, confrontational, and aggressive in their relationships with others.	4.6	4.6	4.1	3.4	3.7	3.8	3.6	4.2	3.9

Future orientation: Extent to which individuals engage in future-oriented behaviors, such as delaying gratification, planning, and investing in the future.	4.2	4.3	3.5	4.4	2.9	3.8	4.3	3.8	3.9
Humane orientation: Degree to which a collective encourages and rewards individuals for being fair, altruistic, generous, caring, and kind to others.	4.2	3.2	3.4	4.1	3.9	4.4	4.3	3.7	4.7
Gender egalitarianism: Degree to which a collective minimizes gender inequality.	3.3	3.1	3.6	3.8	4.1	3.0	3.2	3.3	2.8

ᴬ Refers to West Germany (former Federal Republic of Germany)

Source: R. House, P.J. Hanges, M. Javidan, P.W. Dorfman, and V. Gupta (eds.), *Culture, Leadership and Organizations: The GLOBE Study of 62 Societies* (Thousand Oaks, CA: Sage; 2004).

will tend to be direct and assertive in confronting what they see as the issue; others will find this distressingly aggressive, to the point of loss of face (Japan and China). In low-context cultures such as the US, words like "Yes" have a clear meaning, indicating assent. But in high context cultures like Japan, the meaning of a word depends on the context in which it was expressed. When used as a response to a question from an angry superior, "Yes" may mean that "the circumstances give me no choice except to respond in this way." Indeed, as both GLOBE and Hofstede suggest, there are differences from one culture to another in the extent to which subordinates feel free to challenge their bosses (power distance). Without such understanding, conflict can split the team and undermine performance.[31]

The Cultural Context of Motivational and HRM Theories

The proponents of the cultural perspective on organizations argue that cultural values condition organizational practices. Consider the case of people management. Hofstede argued that the motivation theories dominating management thinking reflect American cultural values, especially individualism.[32] They stress achievement and self-actualization as the ultimate human needs. These assumptions may not hold true in other cultures.

Indeed, one can tease out some of the cultural assumptions underpinning standard HR practices, from selection to socialization.[33] For example, some of the underlying assumptions in the area of performance management have particular resonance in the US—the idea that goals can be set and reached (assuming control over the environment) and that objectives may be given a 6- to 18-month time frame (assuming that time can be managed). Managers and subordinates are expected to engage in a two-way dialogue to agree what has to be done, by when, and how. Again, this assumes that power differences allow this to happen— that employees have the right to input in determining their goals and that they are eager to take responsibility.

Does performance mean the same thing to everyone? Is there an objective best approach to performance management? In the US-influenced rhetoric, performance management is focused on results delivered by the individual. The American advice is: "Begin with an absolute focus on results."[34] Individual appraisal is crucial for linking results to pay. Contrast this with the Japanese concept of performance management. Toyota focuses on *Kaizen,* or continuous improvement, steered by collective action. *Kaizen* is an umbrella for a variety of processes oriented toward continuous improvement—including statistical tools, total quality management (TQM), suggestion schemes, and small group consultation. Japanese management efforts are directed at supporting and stimulating the efforts of subordinates to improve the processes that generate results, and the time horizon for improvement is longer than in the West. Appraisal focuses on employee skills and efforts (discipline, collaboration, and involvement) that lead to continuous improvement, rather than on short-term results.

In summary, culturists suggest that the development of HRM theories is based on a set of assumptions that are deeply embedded in one culture—the US, where many of the most influential HR scholars and consulting firms are based. This limits the applicability of this template to other cultures. The ultimate expression of this cultural perspective is the memorable description of HRM as "a contemporary manifestation of the American Dream."[35]

Should Companies Adjust HRM to the Local Culture?

So far we have focused on the influence of the firm's home cultural context on HRM. However, to what extent should the cultural environment of a subsidiary abroad influence local HR practices? Conventional wisdom suggests that national culture matters a great deal. Although we agree that cultural issues are of significance for international HRM, we also believe that it is important to examine critically the assertion that multinationals must adapt to the local national culture.[36]

First, the within-in country differences in values turn out to be substantially larger than the differences between countries. Studies show that the passport explains less than 5 percent of the global variance between individuals.[37]

Second, these studies also point to the considerable overlap in values by individual members of society that can be found even between countries that are culturally distant (see Figure 2-1 for a graphic illustration of this).[38] This means that companies can try to select people in a particular culture who fit with the values of their organization rather than with the typical values of the host nation. For example, in France, Lincoln Electric can recruit and select individuals whose values fit well with Lincoln's famous performance-based

FIGURE 2-1
Distribution of Individual
Values in Two Countries

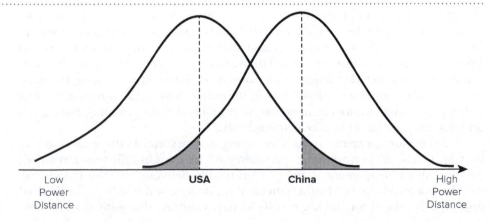

Low
Power
Distance   **USA**   **China**   High
Power
Distance

compensation system. In fact, Lincoln has successfully operated in France since 1955 with an HR system that is more like the one it has in its Cleveland plant in the US than those found in local French organizations. This example points to the importance of selection (we discuss this further in Chapter 6).

Third, another assumption behind the culturist argument is that a misfit between national culture and management practice will reduce effectiveness. For example, providing performance feedback that is public will not work in a Chinese culture where maintaining face is extremely important. Indeed, there are numerous stories that testify to the risk of implementing alien HR practices in overseas units. However, there are also examples of foreign and indeed local firms that have successfully introduced HR practices at odds with local values and practices. In Chapter 7 we discuss the case of consumer appliance manufacturer Haier, whose fully transparent performance management system has become famous in China; while controversial, it has helped attract many young employees to join the company.

While the cultural fit argument would lead us to expect that HR managers of different nationalities would have different views about the effectiveness of HR practices, in fact they largely agree on which practices contribute to enhanced firm performance.[39] For instance, HR managers in Japan, China, the US, and the regions of Europe have rated the effectiveness of pay for performance systems almost identically.

Research shows that multinational firms have considerable leeway when deciding which HR practices to implement overseas. It is perhaps more effective to present the HR practices in a way that is compatible with what people perceive to be important in their local culture, as opposed to aligning practices with that culture's average values (see the box "A Commentary on the Culturist Perspective"). For companies trying to adapt their HRM strategies to local needs, it is not enough to focus on cultural values. The cultural lens needs to be supplemented by consideration of institutional factors.

A Commentary on the Culturist Perspective

Cultural explanations hold intuitive appeal for international managers. They supply multiple plausible interpretations for the many difficulties of working with people from different countries. That is both the strength and the weakness of the cultural perspective.

A compelling case can be made for the importance of the cultural perspective in understanding different attitudes toward authority, teamwork, and conflict resolution.[40] However, as discussed above, the cultural perspective tends to overemphasize value differences and neglect the fact that the cultural traits found in a particular country represent only a central tendency.

Successful people management requires knowledge of differences within a culture as well as across cultures. While cultural distance can be a barrier to effective cross-cultural interaction, another substantial barrier is outsiders' lack of comprehension about diversity *within* a given culture. A potential danger of relying on cultural studies (like those of Hofstede, Trompenaars, and the GLOBE team) is that they create a notion of what all people from a certain country are like. We may have stopped stereotyping gender and race; we need to tackle culture with the same determination.

(Continued)

A further reason for caution is that cultural stereotypes are mostly rooted in historical beliefs about people from other countries, and while national cultures seem to change slowly, cultural values and practices do co-evolve as societies are transformed. Mainland Chinese society is a case in point. While China has traditionally been a high power distance country,[41] characterized by high in-group collectivism, young urban Chinese exhibit a considerably higher degree of individualism and a more modest level of power distance. They are also more assertive than the previous generation. Human resource practices that were aligned with traditional Chinese values 20 years ago may not be suitable in China today.

Local managers often use culture as an alibi for failing to introduce change, protecting local fiefdoms against interference from the head office. Because culture is impenetrable, it is difficult to argue against these explanations. When the local manager in Thailand tells the head office that "confronting poor performers is not possible here for face saving reasons," there is some truth in the excuse—but it is also an exaggeration. Often, the approach, rather than the objective, has to be altered.

Know Where You Are: The Institutional Perspective

Management have some discretion in whether or not to adapt to cultural differences but less so to institutional differences between countries.[42] As noted earlier, working practices that are acceptable in one country (like working a 50-hour week in the US) may be questionable in another country and illegal in a third (as a 50-hour week would be in Germany, for instance). This reflects social, legal, and political differences that are captured by the institutional perspective on diversity of management practices around the world.[43]

The Ease of Doing Business index, developed by the World Bank, expresses this well. From an institutional perspective, Singapore is currently seen as the easiest country to do business; it is straightforward to start a new business there, register property, get credit, pay taxes, have a contract enforced, and hire and fire employees. Near the bottom of the table is Venezuela. See Table 2-3 for details.

Let us look at the contrasting institutional environments for human resources in two European countries: Denmark (ranked 10th for Ease of Employing Workers) and France (ranked 148 on the same scale). In Denmark, there are few restrictions on hiring a new worker, considerable flexibility about working hours, and few constraints on firing someone (for example, there is no obligatory legal settlement). This is combined with a union environment, which, for more than 100 years, has favored working through agreements with top management rather than strikes. Denmark has a favorable institutional environment where the responsibility for HRM lies with line managers, with the HR function in a weaker advisory role. By contrast, in France, newly hired employees have by law to be given a permanent contract after an initial trial period; this makes it expensive and difficult to fire people. The working week was reduced to 35 hours in 2000, and after that date, employees could not be made to work longer if they did not wish to do so.[44] The French union environment has a long adversary heritage, and the HR function has by law and by tradition a more powerful role in who is hired and in determining employment conditions.

According to the institutional perspective, there are alternative ways of organizing economic activity (for one well-known example of institutionalist reasoning, see the box "Six Successful Configurations of Capitalism"). The key to understanding business behavior in different countries lies in the interrelationships between economic, educational, financial, legal, and political systems. Societal factors strongly influence issues at the core of people management, such as compensation, training, job design, industrial relations, and by extension company performance.

TABLE 2-3
Ranking of 17 Countries on Ease of Doing Business and Ease of Employing Workers

Country	Ease of Doing Business Rank[A]	Rigidity of Employment Index[B]	Firing Costs (weeks of salary)	Ease of Employing Workers[C]
Singapore	1	0	4	1
Denmark	4	10	0	10
Korea	5	45	91	152
United States	7	0	0	1
United Kingdom	8	14	22	28
Germany	14	44	69	142
United Arab Emirates	22	13	84	47
Netherlands	27	42	17	98
Japan	29	17	4	17
France	31	56	32	148
Spain	33	56	56	160
Italy	56	38	11	75
China	90	27	91	159
Indonesia	114	40	108	157
Brazil	120	46	37	121
India	142	30	56	89
Venezuela	182	79	Not possible	180

[A] This overall index averages indicators on 11 topics such as starting a business, getting credit, enforcing contracts, and paying taxes, though Ease of Employing Workers is not included.
[B] This averages three sub-indices on a 0–100 scale: difficulty of hiring, rigidity of hours, and difficulty of firing.
[C] Overall ranking, averaging the rigidity of employment and firing costs indices.
Source: *Doing Business 2015 Report*, World Bank Group (www.doingbusiness.org). Data for the Labor Market (the three last columns) is from the Doing Business 2009 Report. Ranking reported from 17 out of 189 countries.

Six Successful Configurations of Capitalism

As viewed by sociologists, capitalism is not a single economic approach. Researchers suggest that there are at least six successful configurations of capitalism, each distinguished not only by distinctive differences in ownership patterns and business objectives but also by different employment practices that shape and constrain the way in which companies conduct business.[45]

1. The main purpose of the *Anglo-Saxon individualist form*, dominant in North America and the UK, is to provide returns to shareholders (shareholder value). The focus on short- to medium-term returns tends to drive HR practices; employment security is relatively limited and firms rely on fluid labor markets to recruit managers and professionals externally as needed.

2. The stakeholder perspective characterizes the more *communitarian European form* in large organizations. Here social contracts and obligations are important: German firms have, for instance, been characterized as having patient capital, with HR practices based on co-determination of employees and management, long-term employment security, and a fairly high reliance on internal promotions.[46]

(Continued)

3. The *European industrial district form* of networked enterprise, based on family ownership (but also involving skilled employees committed to the firm), is found in Italy and Scandinavia. Its aim is to optimize the interests and values of the family owners and senior professional managers associated with the firm.

4. The prime purpose of the *Japanese form* of capitalism, with its institutional cross-shareholding and lack of strong owners, is the stability of the organization. Lifetime employment of core employees and slow promotions are its most visible HR manifestations.

5. The *Korean chaebol* is simultaneously oriented toward retaining the influence of the entrepreneurs and their family successors as well as growth strategies supporting national economic development. While labor relations are often contentious, the emphasis until recently has been on lifetime employment of managers recruited from top Korean universities.[47]

6. The *Chinese capitalist form* is represented by family businesses throughout the Southeast Asian diaspora, and increasingly in mainland China. It exists primarily to serve the ambitions of owners, with trusted long-term employees playing important roles in the firm but with relatively few efforts to build formal HR systems.

This is a reminder that although there has been some convergence toward the Anglo-Saxon model of capitalism in recent decades, we can still identify differences across firms in different institutional environments.

The Institutional "Voids" in Emerging Markets

The institutional perspective is helpful in understanding the problems and opportunities of emerging markets, including the so-called BRIC nations (Brazil, Russia, India, and China). In developed markets, companies rely on an institutional structure that is sometimes taken for granted—highways and roads to distribute goods to consumers; vocational schools and universities that supply skilled technicians, engineers, and managers; and legal systems that protect property and allow for the resolution of disputes. In many emerging countries, this infrastructure is poor, indeed sometimes entirely lacking. There is an "institutional void."[48]

The cost and difficulties of adaptation to these institutional voids—the lack of skills that is pervasive in many emerging countries, the bureaucracy or corruption of the local or national government, and labor market practices that are branded as exploitative and unethical back at home—are such that multinational corporations find these markets difficult and expensive to penetrate.

India is a country with many such voids. The strong information technology industry in India exploits these institutional voids. Tata Consultancy Services, Infosys, and Wipro have become global players in providing software services in part because they know how to select, recruit, and train technicians at low cost from a complex web of schools of varying quality, offering salaries that are lower than multinationals would have to provide.

Multinational companies sometimes have to partner up with local governments and educational institutions to create an ecosystem that fills such a void. An example is Rolls Royce who wanted to build an advanced manufacturing and research facility in Asia to produce aero engines and fan blades. Confronted with the lack of skilled aerospace technicians, they built a partnership with the Singapore Workforce Development Agency, the National Trade Union Employment Agency in Singapore, and local polytechnics to develop the necessary training and qualifications programs. This resulted in a steady stream of recruits with the skills for aerospace manufacturing, providing 500 jobs in 2012, the first year of operations.[49]

Labor Relations Varies with the Context

The role of labor unions is a notable example of how the local institutional context can influence a company's international operations. Wal-Mart is well-known for its strong antiunion stance at home in the US, but its employees in China work under a union contract as required by law and enforced by various administrative practices.[50] Restructuring of Pfizer Japan ran into severe problems, forcing a CEO resignation under pressure from the company union—headed by company managers.[51]

Countries differ radically not only in trade union membership but also in collective bargaining coverage and in union involvement in collective consultation and company communications. In some countries like France, unions have an influence that goes far beyond their formal membership; only 7 percent of employees are union members but 90 percent of enterprises are obliged to adhere to collective agreements where unions have a strong role. In the US, only 11 percent of employees are unionized and 15 percent are covered by collective bargaining agreements, whereas more than three quarters of Scandinavian workers are union members and even more are covered by collective bargaining agreements. In Korea with its confrontational heritage, union membership is less than 10 percent today. In Singapore and Japan 18 percent of employees are covered by collective bargaining, but 80 percent in Australia. Worldwide, trade unions have lost membership during the last 30 years, including in Asia, although they have become stronger in China.

The structure of the unions differs significantly. In many European countries as well as in the US, unions are formed mainly around industry sectors and/or professions. However, in Japan it has been common to have separate unions for each corporation. In some countries, like China, the government only recognizes one union, the All China Federation of Trade Unions (ACFTU). All companies there are expected to have trade unions, and even foreign firms that usually resist unionization—such as Wal-Mart—have unions (and sometimes communist party cells) in their Chinese units. The role of ACFTU has traditionally concentrated on welfare issues, but recently the trade union has become much more involved in negotiations about collective contracts for employees and issues related to layoffs and dispute settlement.

In Europe, works councils are typically required in all but the smallest firms, and the European Works Council Directive covers all companies established in the EU member states. Corporate decisions that influence employees in significant ways must be discussed with the works councils. Although these have limited decision-making power, they often serve as important communication channels and as a sounding body for employees. However, from a management perspective, the obligation to discuss decisions in works councils may lead to delays in the decision-making process.

Some regard the influence of national business systems as declining, pointing to the individualization of HRM practices in Japan, to changes in the Korean *chaebol*, and to what Nobel-Prize economist Joseph Stiglitz called the Anglo-Saxonization of management.[52] Indeed, there has undoubtedly been some convergence of multinationals from different countries on an "Anglo-Saxon" model for people and organizational management.[53] However, this convergence may be more nuanced than it often appears. One investigation into the Anglo-Saxon influence on European multinationals reveals important variations.[54] Though French and German multinationals are adopting Anglo-Saxon practices in the fields of executive compensation, job restructuring, and corporate governance, they do so in a local manner. For example, German preoccupations with long-term orientation and social responsibility have been merged with new concerns for shareholder value and responsiveness, leading to distinctly German ways of responding to the latter. Layoffs through restructuring are more moderate than in Anglo-Saxon countries, accompanied by an emphasis on partnerships and cooperation with the workforce.[55]

Overall, the institutional perspective emphasizes that firms are constrained by their local environments. But again there are dangers in relying excessively on this view (see the box "A Commentary on the Institutional Perspective"). Irrespective of institutional constraints, in an increasingly professional and knowledge-based world, employees and managers are more and more aware of management practices in firms from other countries. Executives everywhere are bombarded daily by press reports on the latest global business and management trends in the US and elsewhere. The idea of cultural or institutional cocoons where firms are prisoners of their own national heritage is less and less true. It all depends on whom you talk to and whom you view as role models—and this leads us to the network perspective on diversity.

A Commentary on the Institutional Perspective

Government regulations, educational systems, and political norms vary from one country to another. We apply the institutional perspective when thinking of foreign countries, but for the multinational firm there is a risk of being blind to the extent to which the home country context puts its mark on people management issues, just as home country cultural values do. As a company internationalizes, it should reflect on the way in which the institutional context of its own home country has shaped its HR strategy and how this influences its approach to people management abroad.

Foreign subsidiaries in fact face dual institutional pressures—from the parent organization and from the local environment—which they need to balance.[56] Executives in these subsidiaries, and particularly HR managers, need strong negotiation skills, particularly if headquarter executives are unaware of these local institutional constraints. Headquarters may take a decision to cut headcount or to introduce new work practices globally, and such actions are strongly constrained by the local environment. Local managers cannot simply refuse to comply; they have to be objective about what is feasible and argue cogently for it.[57]

One of the dangers of the institutional perspective is to exaggerate the strength of local institutional pressures. While labor laws and regulations may indeed restrict the range of possible HR actions, local managers often have taken-for-granted views about what works and what does not with respect to the management of people. There may be strong local professional norms concerning what constitutes appropriate corporate practices. For example, many foreign firms regarded the German market as off limits to takeovers until the British mobile phone operator Vodafone shattered the perception of impenetrability by acquiring Mannesmann. German firms such as Daimler and E.ON have eagerly embraced "shareholder value," reorienting their accounting systems to Anglo-Saxon standards as they entered the US stock exchange. We can also observe an increasing number of Japanese corporations divesting unprofitable units and even laying off employees as they restructure their operations.

In this respect, a number of observers foresee a gradual global shift toward the more market-oriented institutional mechanisms prevailing in the US business system. American commentators, in particular, often feel strongly about the virtues of the free market open economy, resenting the degree of state intervention and regulation that prevails in many parts of Europe and Asia. On the other hand, the 2008/9 global financial crisis, ascribed by many to under-regulation (or poor regulation), has further fueled this debate.

Know Whom You Talk To: The Network Perspective

Beyond similarities in cultural values or institutional context, organizations define themselves by the company they keep. Business is conducted through networks and learning or adaptation is guided by connections. Through their networks, multinational organizations face pressures to conform to so-called best practice, and this is particularly relevant to the HR/personnel domain since professional associations have long played an important role in prescribing what is "best" in people management.

The networks to which a company belongs can make a big difference to what it views as important, as demonstrated in a study on HRM in foreign and local firms in Ecuador. The study showed little transfer of HR techniques between multinationals and local firms. Managers in local Ecuadorian firms compared themselves to other local firms, and the multinationals compared themselves to other multinationals operating in the country. They constituted two separate networks with virtually no overlap—and no transfer of know-how.[58] Indeed, one of the clearest findings in network theory is that people network with others who are similar to them.

It is understandable that multinationals do not learn from local firms in countries where local firms are smaller and perceived as less sophisticated than their own subsidiaries. Why would multinationals cultivate contacts with lower-status players? What could they learn from them? Yet a similar phenomenon is also visible in Japan, where one would expect exchange between Japanese multinationals and locally based foreign subsidiaries. In fact, they are two separate worlds. Foreign companies in Japan pay higher wages than local firms, since their salary surveys compare them only with other foreign firms. Most are not even aware that they are paying this *gaijin* tax (foreigner tax) because they would never think of networking with an indigenous Japanese corporation. Some Japanese managers working for foreign subsidiaries even have their own union, the Foreign Affiliated Managers Association (FAMA). These managers seldom cross over to Japanese multinationals or vice versa.

Learning from Friends When Abroad

Managers working abroad have a particular incentive to build networks with those from other multinationals since they are not sure about how specific HR practices will fit into the local context. Expatriates who are responsible for introducing practices that may be risky, expensive, and hard to reverse are naturally keen to discuss the benefits, or frustrations, that others may have experienced when implementing similar changes. As one network expert puts it: "Adopting innovation entails a risk, an uncertain balance of costs and benefits, and people manage that uncertainty by drawing on others to define a socially acceptable interpretation of the risk."[59] And there is evidence that firms tend to imitate changes previously adopted by network peers.[60]

All this suggests that local adaptation of HR policies and practices may be influenced as much by what other foreign subsidiaries are doing, or what regionally based consultants recommend, as by the experience of local firms or best practices back home. A study of foreign firms operating in Russia highlights this three-way tension. It showed that the HR practices of foreign firms "were more similar to their parent firm's practices *and those of other foreign firms operating in Russia* than to HR practices in local Russian firms" (our italics).[61]

Similarly, in China, while some HR managers we interviewed in multinational firms complained about constantly being contacted by local firms interested in learning more about their approach to HRM, foreign firms seemed to be much less interested in learning about HRM in local Chinese companies.[62]

Sharing the same clubs, sending their children to the same schools, living in the same areas, expatriates from different multinationals quickly develop strong ties, especially in developing countries. Such relationships provide natural channels for sharing useful information about what works and what does not. A firm's choice of HR practices therefore also reflects the information received from networks to which its employees belong.

Global Trends—and Fashions

Of course, firms can also look outside their immediate networks for ideas about what they should do and what may work. Increasingly, organizations have access to a kind of surrogate network in the form of cases gleaned from business professors, consultants, management gurus, and journalists. These fashion setters carry best practices and benchmark information across borders, geographical or industrial.[63] Each proposes new exemplar companies and organizational innovations. Companies are exposed to the routines and practices of key international competitors. What self-respecting international manager has not heard of GE's Workout or Toyota's Production System? In a broad sense these companies and practices become part of an organization's extended network—legitimate sources of comparison.

In the 1980s and early 1990s Japanese management was the rage, only to be replaced by global worship of General Electric and its CEO Jack Welch, and then by Apple and Steve Jobs. Through the business media, new leading edge practices reach a broad audience and converge on a company's executives from several points at once. This can create intense pressure to follow suit in order to maintain the appearance of a "legitimate," "modern," or "progressive" organization, as defined by the reference network. This is plain bandwagon imitation.[64]

Access to what is "in" has been spurred by the rapid rise of social media. Executives in Africa, Asia, or South America may be just as familiar as their European or North American counterparts with the latest innovative practices—or raging controversies. Accenture's decision to abolish annual performance reviews drew instant commentaries from HRM experts around the world. When the *New York Times* published an article critical of Amazon's employment practices in its Seattle headquarters,[65] within hours, hundreds of Chinese bloggers commented on its implications for employment practices in China.

International networks may rapidly spread concepts such as value innovation or 360-degree feedback, but successful adoption means that they have to be worked coherently into the fabric of the firm. Indeed a detailed study on the transfer of Japanese TQM (total quality management) practices to five firms in the US showed that while simplified rhetoric may be necessary to kick-start the process of transfer, successful implementation requires detailed technical attention and adaptation to the specific circumstances of the enterprise.[66] Despite initial skepticism, 360-degree feedback can work well in Asian environments but only if attention is paid to issues like respondent anonymity or the impact of *guanxi*. There may be generic ideas, but there are no generic solutions.

A Commentary on the Network Perspective

As employees around the world have ever-expanding access to a variety of information sources (they are also more mobile and some get part of their education abroad), the network perspective will gain even more importance. Broader networks tend to produce more new ideas. As shown by a survey of 25 innovative entrepreneurs and 3,000 executives who have good track records of managerial innovation, innovators carefully maintain broad networks and take every opportunity to seek out the views of others.[67] We will discuss in Chapter 11 how future innovations are less likely to come from the R&D labs of the home country and more likely to spring from combining knowledge through networks of contacts across the world—and the same could be the case for future HRM practices.

In this context, being connected only to those who think like us may foster blindness to how one can take advantage of new opportunities—especially in emerging markets. There, the trendsetters in organizational practices are often local multinationals—for example, Infosys for talent management, Huawei for operational excellence, Lenovo for M&A execution, or Xiaomi for business model innovation. And there is a whole range of up-and-coming innovative companies in many other markets, still operating below the radar of the global business press but already well-known on the social media.

Most large companies today are still less digitally aware than the average teenager, but this will change, as today's teenagers become tomorrow's new employees. However, with the rapid spread of alternative communication platforms, there is a danger that the fascination with the tool may get ahead of the content. We see an increasing number of HR professionals (prodded by their bosses) investing efforts in chasing the latest apps to connect, monitor, and respond to inputs from the virtual world. While a slow response to a critical social-media message may create long-lasting damage, overreaction can be just as harmful.

In order to remain alert to new opportunities to access information, but at the same time to avoid flash-in-the-pan fashions and preserve consistency and a healthy balance of views, we need to be aware of the ways in which our networks shape our perceptions of reality. Homogenization of perspectives leads to impoverished choices. We need to network widely and not just with those that are similar to us. Interacting with external networks is quickly emerging as an important organizational capability.

Five Influences on Decision-Making in the Multinational Enterprise

Cultural diversity, institutional factors, and the company's informal networks shape the ways in which multinational corporations manage people. Practice depends on the context, and all these factors constitute different sources of contextual influence.

A good way of summarizing the challenges of responding to the diversity of a global world is to point out that there are at least five different influences on international HR practices: the *mother country*; the *mother company* and its distinctive culture and institutionalized practices; the *local cultural and institutional context*; *other foreign firms in the country*; and *other global companies* (see the box "Five Sources of Influence on the Multinational").[68] Earlier in this chapter, we emphasized two in particular: the mother country and the local cultural/institutional context. While internal consistency pushes the multinational toward a particular configuration of policies, work systems, and practices, it is subject to the pushes and pulls of many different forces.

Five Sources of Influence On the Multinational

Country-of-origin effect

HR and other corporate management practices reflect cultural and institutional conditions in the home country, and these practices are then transferred to foreign units. The time perspective of the parent company is a case in point. US firms, where the tenure of top managers depends on annual if not quarterly results reported to shareholders, are likely to have a shorter-term perspective than traditional German firms, where bankers and employee representatives may have a strong influence on the board of directors.[69]

Company-of-origin effect

Companies develop distinctive HR practices that are successful at home and then transfer these to foreign environments. Lincoln Electric's story in the late 1980s illustrates this, though the transfer abroad was less successful. When Cisco recruits a native Brazilian engineer for its operations in that country, it is looking for an engineer who deviates from the hierarchic Brazilian norms, someone who is likely to thrive in its competitive networked culture.

Host country effect

Some firms adopt local isomorphism as a strategy— "Strategy may be global, but everything else is local implementation." Companies that expand internationally through acquisition and alliance are more likely to experience the pressures of local isomorphism than those that grow by setting up greenfield sites.

Foreign firm network effect

In situations of uncertainty about what constitutes best practice, organizations often look at others and then mimic what they do or collectively develop a consensus about what to do. As discussed earlier, we often see that the networks to which foreign firms belong produce common notions about appropriate HR practices.

Global convergence effect

Knowledge today flows easily from one region of the globe to another. International companies compare themselves with others with international experience and model their practices on these. Diffusion of technology and management practices means that national effects become less important than the globalization effect.

The debate about whether management practices around the world, including HR practices, are converging or diverging is not new. Different forces or "effects" exist simultaneously and will continue to do so in the years ahead. While scholars may continue to debate which is more important, companies like Berlin-based Rocket Internet are built on the capability of exploiting all five forces. Rocket International is a tech incubator firm founded in 2007 that launches and grows tech companies at astonishing speed—with 2015 revenues of $5 billion across 110 countries and 35,000 employees. With a culture of sharing knowledge, it spots successful Internet business and replicates them in new markets, often in emerging countries.

IMPLEMENTING LOCALIZATION

As discussed in Chapter 1, companies typically internationalize by sending key people abroad—through expatriates. To be locally responsive, HR practices need to be appropriately adapted to local conditions, but this is not sufficient. Responsiveness typically goes hand in hand with localizing management— how top positions are staffed in overseas units and also the influence of local managers on key decisions.

Our concept of localization goes beyond staffing and retention, equating it with the degree of local responsibility for decision-making. A subsidiary may have only one expatriate, but if that individual takes all decisions of importance, the subsidiary's degree of localization will be low. This will also be the case if a local general manager has to check out every decision with corporate headquarters. On the other hand, a high degree of localization is not synonymous with complete subsidiary autonomy. A high degree of localization simply implies that the local subsidiary managers are responsible for their decisions and live with the consequences of their actions.

Although local responsiveness does not always imply localization—experienced international managers can often be effective representatives of the local voice toward the corporate center; local responsiveness through expatriates is difficult to sustain in the long term. The difficulties facing eBay in China were partly associated with the fact that the company was not able to retain talented Chinese managers. Note that Alibaba recruited a top US executive, a Treasury chief of staff, onto its senior management team to help steer its entry into the US market. Rather than do what observers had expected, taking on Amazon and eBay head-on in their home market, Alibaba's US strategy is to help smaller American businesses to enter and sell in the Chinese market.

Attracting and Developing Local Managers

One key aspect of localization is systematic investment in the recruitment, development, and retention of local employees who can take over the running of local operations. Unilever provides one of the earliest documented examples of this policy in action. Sensitive to the national aspirations of newly independent countries, the company started to replace expatriates with indigenous managers. Known internally as the "ization" policy, it started in the 1930s and 1940s with "Indianization" and "Africanization" of local subsidiaries.[70]

Since then, localization has become part of the corporate mantra for multinational enterprises around the world. Local employees nearly always have a better understanding of the vernacular—the cultural, institutional, and business environment in which the company operates—and they are usually better at managing a local workforce. Localization helps foreign multinationals penetrate the network of personal and business contacts needed to build and consolidate a presence in the country.

Authorities often evaluate foreign firms by their degree of localization, while the media, politicians, and trade union officials also tend to stress the importance of local talent development. Some governments—for example, most of the Gulf states—impose quotas, restrict work permits, or impose fiscal controls on expatriate salaries. Therefore most companies with a long-term commitment to a particular local market will see localization as a necessary step to gain social acceptance and avoid a colonial or ethnocentric image.

Employee commitment and motivation are also influenced by the degree of localization. Unless senior managers can convince local employees that they understand and honestly represent local interests to headquarters so that local employee concerns are given due consideration, they may have difficulty eliciting commitment. Employee commitment is also likely to suffer if decision-making is centralized at corporate headquarters. This was demonstrated in the negative reactions of local managers toward the way eBay integrated the newly acquired EachNet and transferred decision-making authority for many areas to its US headquarters.

Opportunities for growth and advancement are important concerns for local employees—and dissatisfaction with those opportunities is one of the most frequently cited reasons for turnover. Heavy reliance on expatriates is often perceived as blocking promotional avenues for local managers and a sign of the company's lack of trust in them. In contrast, the presence of influential local executives in a subsidiary supplies role models for younger employees and improves recruitment and retention.

Two interrelated problems continue systematically to plague corporate efforts to localize. First, because of high demand and limited supply, competent local managers are often hard to find. Second, once found, they may be hard to retain. These two problems sometimes create a "catch-22" dilemma. If good local managers are going to leave us in any case, why bother to invest time and money in developing them?

Building Local Management

While there are no silver bullets to solve these problems, there are initiatives that many companies can implement, starting with a focus on the attraction and development of local talent (this is discussed further in Chapters 6–8).

1. **Establish a visible presence** In many emerging markets, there may be a genuine scarcity of talent with specific functional or managerial competences, while competition in the labor market is keen. The challenge even for well-known international firms is that they do not enjoy the reputational advantage over their peers that they may have at home.

2. **Adjust selection criteria** Developing a generic set of recruiting criteria is often difficult. For example, we will see in Chapter 8 how KONE, a global elevator company based in Finland, was obliged to modify its global criteria for evaluating potential when facing rapid expansion in China. Selecting on "competencies" may not work in emerging markets. Instead, recruiters may look for candidates with above all the right attitude since functional skills can be developed through on-the-job and off-the-job training.

3. **Sell careers, not just jobs** When talking to prospective recruits, the company should communicate its localization objectives and connect those plans to the career prospects of local managers. When Schlumberger recruits engineers in Russia, they know that they have the same career prospects as those recruited in France or the US and that the performance criteria are the same. A reputation for thorough training and skill development can enhance the outcome of the recruitment efforts.

Because of the difficulties of attracting and retaining experienced managers, some companies choose to "grow their own timber." They take on young recruits, placing more emphasis on their future potential than on their current professional or technical skills. This entails large investments in their training and coaching as well as in international assignments. It may even involve building local training institutions, as many multinational firms have done in China.

Recruiting locals who have graduated abroad is another popular strategy to address the talent gap. However, in some emerging markets such as China, tensions between locals and "pseudo-locals"—returnees with freshly minted foreign MBAs commanding salaries well above market rates—produce the same resentment that used to be provoked by the lavish packages granted to expatriates.

In mature markets, attracting talent is more likely to be a problem of accessing the appropriate labor pool. For example, the number of top-class Japanese managers who can be lured from local corporations to foreign firms is still relatively small (though growing). Many headhunters who service multinationals in Japan find it difficult to spot or access high performers in local firms and therefore limit themselves to searching among executives already in the *gaishi-kei* (foreign-affiliate) world.

Retaining Local Talent

A disproportionate number of local managers trained to take over expatriate positions never actually fill those posts or only do so briefly. The terms and conditions after training may not measure up to what the external market offers to ambitious and well-trained individuals.[71] While the company expects a return on its training investment, competitors poach the most talented individuals.

Given the length of time that is often needed to develop qualified local managers, which may include investing in basic education that the local system has not provided, retention can be a real challenge. Some multinational firms are obliged to hire at least two local trainees for each former expatriate position.[72] Inevitably, this drives up costs and can create a temporary surplus of skilled managers, allowing rival firms to benefit from the company's development efforts. US automobile companies and German carmakers with US manufacturing sites systematically raid Japanese transplants to capture local talent, weakening the latter's ability to localize. On the other hand, that may be a price worth paying if the company is still able to attract and retain the very best.

Inevitably, compensation features prominently among the mechanisms to retain local talent. Paying above market rates is typical, but market rates are less than transparent in emerging countries. This partly explains the curious fact that the vast majority of companies claim to pay in the top market quartile. However, cash is only one part of the compensation package. Today, retention bonuses, stock options, and restricted shares are just as common in Shanghai as in New York, if not more so. Some companies have introduced even more comprehensive packages, including private health programs, interest free loans, or housing assistance.

As a result, salary costs for capable local staff are high around the world. The lament of a general manager of a Japanese bank in London 15 years ago, as he struggled to retain qualified specialists wooed by European and US institutions in the City—"for us localization is no longer a cheap alternative"[73]—can be heard today nearly in any location where multinationals have a significant presence.

An attractive compensation package is necessary but not enough; there are always other companies that can offer more.[74] The decisive factors may have more to do with career development and involvement in decision-making. The multinational firm has to be prepared to develop and promote talented people more rapidly than it traditionally does at home and to support them with the necessary training and coaching. Mapping the career paths of high potential local candidates is an important signal of the company's commitment to them.[75] Social climate may also be important. Company atmosphere, friendship ties, and social activities, combined with the promise of a stable future in a firm with high local growth prospects, have been observed to be decisive factors in local employee retention.[76]

Localization Starts at the Head Office

Localization is unlikely to be successful if it is only a faddish whim of transient expatriate general managers or regional directors. Systematic recruitment and development of local managers requires a long-term organization-wide effort that transcends the good intentions of individual managers, and this means durable corporate commitment from the top. While the positive or negative outcomes of localization efforts are most visible within the subsidiary operations involved, the core of the problem may actually be far away in the corporate center.

The fundamental bottleneck of localization is often the capacity of corporate headquarters to interact effectively with locally hired executives. For example, in last 20 years we have observed several Japanese multinationals that aggressively recruited capable local staff, recognizing correctly that the weakness of local management was an obstacle to faster global growth. However, within a relatively short period the newly appointed local managers left in frustration because they could not get the job done. What was going on?

Historically, the international growth of Japanese multinationals was coordinated through an informal network of Japanese executives, carefully orchestrated from the center that controlled the critical resources. Although nominally in positions of substantial authority, the newly hired local executives were simply not able to secure the resources necessary to drive the local business forward. They did not have the personal connections or even the language ability to communicate with the head office, which was generally staffed by managers without much, if any, international experience. Only when more global-savvy executives replaced these headquarters managers, as for instance happened at Matsushita during the early 2000s, did localization efforts begin to show results.

Companies that fail to take localization seriously right from the start can find themselves caught up in a fruitless process of serial localization. If, for whatever reason, the newly appointed local managers cannot do the job after the expatriates pull out, the subsidiary's performance will inevitably decline. Then expensive troubleshooters from the outside are sent in to fix the problems, followed by a second wave of managers with a new mandate to localize. The efforts have to start again from scratch but by this time in an atmosphere of increased cynicism locally about the company's commitment (or ability) to get it done.

Similarly, when turnover of local managers is high, companies often become reluctant to invest enough in developing local employees, preferring instead expatriates with a proven commitment to the company; this merely confirms suspicions of a glass ceiling for locals. Expatriate-heavy structures restrict career opportunities for local managers, making it even harder to attract or retain local talent. If this continues through several rounds, the morale and motivation of local employees is bound to suffer.

Building a capable local management team does not happen overnight. It needs preparation.[77] Although the corporate or regional HR function is usually in charge of developing plans for the localization of management, most of the day-to-day responsibility for successful localization rests with expatriates in senior management positions *within the subsidiary*. This means paying as much attention to the role of the expatriates as to the locals, as it is expatriates who ultimately carry out the localization strategy. When assigning this responsibility to expatriates, three areas require close attention: (1) the link to expatriate selection, (2) mandate and timing, and (3) measurements and rewards. These challenges are discussed further in Chapter 9 on steering global mobility.

Localization is important, but anything taken to an extreme can create a pathology. Excessive localization can lead to empire-building and ultimately loss of control by the head office. Put simply, if everyone is local, who is global? Indeed, localization should be viewed as a step on the journey toward transnational management development and not as an end in itself. On the contrary, when the corporation is so local around the world that opportunities for horizontal cross-border mobility are limited, it becomes difficult to develop managers with broad global experience.

THE LIMITS OF RESPONSIVENESS

We started this chapter by describing eBay's problems in Asia, attributing them largely to a failure to respond to local circumstances. However, a local responsiveness strategy also has its limits. Indeed, when localization of staff is combined with a decentralized federal structure, it can lead to local fiefdoms and inhibit collaboration. This often results in lost opportunities for the multinational to share best practices and learn across units. It can generate other inefficiencies as well, such as duplication of effort (reinventing the wheel) and resistance to external ideas—the "handmaidens of decentralization," as they have been dubbed.[78]

Just as firms following a meganational strategy (discussed in the next chapter) may fail by blindly applying home strategies and practices to the new environment, so may the multidomestic firm fail by focusing too closely on its local playing field. The ultra-responsive firm may be unable to leverage globally derived knowledge and to lower its costs through global economies of scale. The road to exploiting global economies of scale while trying to maintain local responsiveness—going from a multidomestic to a transnational organization—is a tortuous path involving swings of the pendulum between decentralization and centralization, as perceived by employees.

The Spiral Path to Transnational Organization

Although there is little research on the topic, our experience is that the route from multidomestic to transnational organization, capturing global economies of scale and scope while retaining local responsiveness, is a spiraling and rocky road that typically takes at least ten years.[79] Why does it take so long? Formal structures may change quickly, but changing processes takes more time, and even longer to change the skill sets of key people and mindsets. The route is tortuous, with what managers perceive as swings between global and local.

FIGURE 2-2
Hypothesized Change
Path as a Multidomestic
Organization Moves to
Transnational

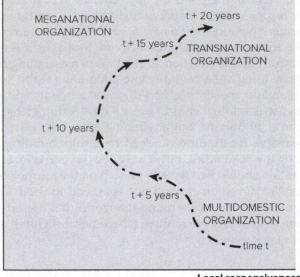

Spiraling paths lead to swings in the pendulum. The route is not a linear path from multidomestic to transnational but a spiral path as shown in Figure 2-2.[80] The multidomestic company needs global integration to ward off low-cost rivals; small-scale manufacturing or engineering facilities around the world need to be consolidated, also to speed up responsiveness to technology change; processes need to be standardized to lower costs and avoid duplication. Easy to spell out on paper, but the process of implementation is difficult.

The managers of the most successful units resist what they see as a loss of autonomy and a dangerous swing to centralized bureaucracy, led by home country executives who have little understanding of the local business. These local managers may at best understand with their heads the need for change, but emotionally they feel less commitment. So they proceed with implementation at a snail's pace.

This creates the swings of the pendulum. Parent company executives get frustrated with the slow progress of integration and global cost reduction, resorting to heavy guns and confirming the fears of local managers. The rumor mill spreads nightmare stories from other companies about the problems of introducing global IT systems and of frustrating customers. These get cited as a reason for putting off collaboration on the new global IT system (which would indeed cut out most local IT departments). When under pressure, people prefer to exploit the processes they know well rather than venture into the uncertainty of developing new ones. Some of the best local entrepreneurs leave. New local executives may be recruited, but it takes them time to understand the business.

Changes in managerial roles   There are also significant changes in managerial roles as the firm moves from multidomestic to transnational. In a multidomestic organization a key role is that of the country manager, who often has full general management responsibility within the bounds of targets and a strategy negotiated with headquarters. However, the country manager's role changes with transnational development.[81] The general management responsibility disappears, and it is replaced by more complex coordination demands that require sophisticated leadership skills rather than simply the ability to exercise authority. This is often experienced as a demotion from general manager to a local functional role, for example as head of sales, or to an ambiguous role as country "host" manager.

In the multidomestic firm, the career structure for local managers is relatively straightforward; people become a bigger king or queen as they move up. But the leadership career structure in transnational firms involves significant transitions, as we will see in Chapter 8; the role of a country or regional manager requires quite different skills from those of a local business unit manager. For example, new competencies are needed in coordinating without authority and in structuring important but ambiguous strategic tasks.

Some corporations believe that you cannot teach old country managers new tricks, and the more successful they are, the more likely they are to resist—so new people must be brought in. The evidence is not clear. We remember a discussion with an Asian country manager in a multinational corporation that was trying to build more global integration. This change meant that his role had shifted from being the P&L boss to becoming in effect a local sales and marketing manager. Our man experienced the change as a demeaning demotion rather than an opportunity to develop new coordination and leadership skills. "Is this change permanent?" he asked. "Or is it just one of those temporary organizational fads that will blow away?" Having been convinced that the change was real and permanent, he became one of a small minority of Asians in the firm who set out to adapt and develop new skills. Five years later, he was promoted to corporate vice president, heading up all front-end marketing operations across Southeast Asia.

The inpatriation of local managers to the regional or global headquarters is another big step toward transnational organization. To ensure international mobility, Unilever has long had a policy of reserving at least one slot on all management teams in both emerging and developed countries for an expatriate—a European in Asia and an Asian or Latin American in Europe. Traditionally, the risk of local empire building is attenuated at 3M by an informal rule that executives cannot become managing directors in their own country. Promising local managers are appointed as heads of subsidiaries in other countries. This reduces the danger of indigenous managers becoming fixtures for several decades and clogging the career pipeline, and it ensures that local stars gain international exposure.

Regionalization On this spiral path, it is often most practical to find economies of scale first at a regional level, grouping small units into larger units (or regions) so as to improve coordination.[82] The regional headquarters usually assume two roles, *strategy development and implementation* and *providing common administrative services*.[83] In the HR arena, the regional staff often assumes responsibility for leadership development.

It has been argued that the world's major corporations are in fact regionally oriented rather than global in their scope.[84] Competition takes place principally within these regions rather than across the globe. Some suggest that the concept of "transnational" only applies to a small percentage of firms, the vast proportion of multinationals being predominately focused on a region or even a country.

Local Responsiveness Does Not Necessarily Mean Playing by Local Rules

One somewhat paradoxical outcome of successful localization is the recognition that local responsiveness does not always mean playing by local rules. Indeed one of the benefits of localization is that indigenous managers have a better sense of which local rules they can break. Local managers have a better sense of *intracultural* variation—tolerance for differences within a nation. They also tend to have a better awareness of the strengths of cultural values and norms, and the likely effects of breaking them. They also know how flexible national and local institutional structures are.

The transnational ideal is local managers who have been exposed to global methods and practices through their networks and time spent in lead countries, perhaps working with expatriates who are in the local subsidiary to gain international experience. Rather than embracing the local way, they can redefine the boundaries of what is considered "local"—showing smart disrespect. Finding ways to operate that neither mimic local firms nor copy the way multinational corporations do things in other parts of the world may be the seed of innovations that can subsequently benefit the corporation as a whole.

TAKEAWAYS

1. Local responsiveness helps the firm overcome the disadvantages of being an outsider in a country or market with distinctive needs. With increased globalization, local responsiveness is valuable as a source of innovation and competitive differentiation.

2. HR practices are more sensitive to local context than finance, marketing, and other organizational routines. Within HRM, some practices are more sensitive to context than others.

3. The fact that cultural values influence HR practices does not necessarily mean that companies have to adapt to local cultures. There are wide variances in values within any nation, and a number of local employees may indeed find practices that deviate from those of local firms to be attractive.

4. The HR practices of multinationals are shaped by their home country institutional context, and these practices may need adjustment when firms operate in different environments.

5. In many emerging markets, multinationals have to deal with institutional voids—the absence of an institutional infrastructure that supplies firms with qualified personnel and provides a structure for dealing with people-related issues.

6. Networking is important for learning how to adjust and solve local problems, as well as to be aware of emerging trends. Managers skilled in building wide networks can use them to guide how to adapt abroad.

7. Localization means local influence on decision-making, with local managers playing key roles while drawing on inputs from expatriates as well as headquarters and other subsidiaries.

8. Localization of management requires a long-term strategy with commitment at all levels, especially among expatriates, to the development of local successors.

9. The route from a multidomestic to a transnational organization is typically a spiral path that involves swings of the pendulum between decentralization and centralization. Regional organization is often set to mediate the tension.

10. Local responsiveness does not necessarily imply playing by local rules though it does require knowing which rules can be broken, and how. Excessive local responsiveness tends to inhibit collaboration across boundaries, and may be as harmful to performance as excessive centralization.

NOTES

1 "eBay Marketplace Facts", June 30, 2008; Corporate Factsheet, *www.ebay.com*.
2 The caselet builds partly on the IMD teaching case series "Alibaba vs. eBay," IMD-3-1842 to IMD-3-1844, 2007.
3 "How Yahoo! Japan beat eBay at its own game," *Business Week*, June 4, 2001.
4 "An upstart takes on mighty eBay," *Fortune*, November 15, 2004.
5 Jack Ma's speech can be found in the 2012 film *Crocodile in the Yangtze*.
6 "The Taobao offensive," *Red Herring*, June 27, 2005.
7 "eBay's Tom Online deal: Timely lessons for global online company managers," *China Knowledge Wharton*, February 14, 2007.
8 Ibid.
9 Ibid.
10 *Reuters*, 2014. "Alibaba in major initiative to court Chinese consumer for U.S. retailers", www.reuters.com
11 Zaheer, 1995.
12 Friedmann, 2007.
13 As Coca-Cola's new CEO noted in 2000, "In every community, we must remember we do not do business in markets, we do business in societies... [This means making] sure that we stay out of the way of our local people and let them do their jobs" (Daft, D., "Back to Classic Coke," *Financial Times*, March 27, 2000, p. 16). But the company swung the pendulum too far from the global to the local, and then back again, and has been struggling in recent years to get the balance right.
14 One framework of note conceptualizes the "local" in terms of distance from the home country of the multinational. In Ghemawat's CAGE framework, there are four dimensions to distance—cultural, administrative (what we call institutional), geographic, and economic. See Ghemawat (2007).
15 Rangan and Drummond, 2004.
16 Barkema, Bell, and Pennings, 1996.
17 This happened to Shell, which had strong links with the regime of the former Nigerian military leader, General Sani Abacha. Consumers around the world perceived Shell as colluding with a corrupt government, compromising its corporate image.
18 Google has for many years removed links to pro-Nazi Web sites in Germany.
19 Google executives were called into Congressional hearings to defend their actions and many commentators on social media were highly critical of Google. See Thompson, C., "Google's China problems (and China's Google problems)," *New York Times*, April 23, 2006.
20 Rosenzweig and Nohria, 1994; Gooderham, Nordhaug, and Ringdal, 1999; Mayrhofer and Brewster, 2012.

21 Lu and Björkman, 1997. A study on multinationals in Greece reported similar findings (Myloni, Harzing, and Mirza, 2004).

22 Rosenzweig and Nohria, 1994; Goodall and Warner, 1997.

23 Hall and Hall, 1990.

24 In his influential model of culture, Schein (1985) proposes that there are three levels of culture: (1) basic assumptions, (2) values, and (3) surface manifestations, such as artifacts and behavior. Most research on national culture has focused on the values held by individuals in the country in question. However, there are a large number of definitions and conceptualizations of culture, a review of which is beyond the scope of this book.

25 Hofstede, 1991 and 2001.

26 See, for example, the debate in *Journal of International Business Studies*, 2006, issue no. 6.

27 Laurent, 1983; Gerhart and Fang, 2005.

28 See Trompenaars, 1993; Hampden-Turner and Trompenaars, 2000. The work of Trompenaars was strongly influenced by the dilemma (duality) concept of Hampden-Turner.

29 For critical reviews of the GLOBE study, see several articles in *Journal of International Business Studies*, 2006, issue no. 6.

30 House *et al.*, 2004.

31 See Meyer (2014) for an interesting and practical culture map, assimilating and building on the work of Hofstede, Trompenaars, and GLOBE. It is built around eight dimensions of culture such as communicating, evaluating, and disagreeing.

32 Hofstede, 1980 and 2001.

33 Schneider, 1988; Schneider and Barsoux, 2003.

34 Ulrich, Zenger, and Smallwood, 1999, p. 171.

35 Guest, 1990.

36 See Holden, Michailova, and Tietze (2015) for articles.

37 Gerhart and Fang, 2005.

38 See Beugelsdijk *et al.* (2015).

39 Stahl, Björkman, *et al.*, 2007.

40 See Meyer (2014).

41 Hofstede, 1991.

42 Brewster and Wood, 2012.

43 Wood *et al.*, 2012; Wood, Brewster, and Brookes, 2014.

44 Institutional environments are subject to change, and the business community in France has long been lobbying for less restrictive employment practices. Some reforms were launched, but the gap with countries on the top of the list remains wide.

45 Redding, 2001; Whitley, 1992 and 1999; Orrù, 1997. These configurations are also known as "business systems," "industrial orders," or "varieties of capitalism." See Morgan (2007); Wood *et al.* (2012); and Wood, Brewster, and Brookes (2014) for reviews.

46 Koen, 2004.

47 Cho and Pucik, 2005.

48 Khanna and Palepu, 2006 and 2010.

49 Kwan and Siow, 2013.

50 "Unions triumphant at Wal-Mart in China," *International Herald Tribune*, October 13, 2006.

51 "Pfizer to slash Japan costs without job cuts," *Boston.com News*, May 29, 2006.

52 Stiglitz, 2006.

53 Pudelko and Harzing (2007) show that the HR practices in the foreign subsidiaries of German and Japanese multinationals have converged toward dominant US practices.

54 Ferner and Quintanilla, 1998.

55 Ibid., 1998.

56 Rosenzweig and Nohria, 1994; Kostova and Roth, 2002.

57 The consequent importance of negotiation and influence skills for international human resource managers is discussed in Chapter 14.

58 Maria Arias, personal communication.

59 Burt, 1987.

60 Hauschild, 1993; Westphal *et al.*, 1997.

61 Fey *et al.*, 1999. See also Child and Yan (1998) and Björkman and Lu (1999) who observed the same in joint ventures in China.

62 Björkman *et al.*, 2008; Sumelius, Björkman, and Smale, 2008. See also Braun and Warner (2002).

63 Micklethwait and Woolridge, 1996; Abrahamson and Fairchild, 1999.

64 Abrahamson and Fairchild, 1999; Abrahamson and Eisenman, 2008.

65 Kantor, J. and D. Streitfield, "Inside Amazon: Wrestling big ideas in a bruising workplace," *New York Times*, August 15, 2015.

66 Zbaracki, 1998.

67 See Dyer, Gregersen, and Christensen (2008). Among the 25 entrepreneurs they interviewed were Lazeridis, the founder of Research in Motion, David Neeleman of JetBlue, and P&G's AG Laffley. These innovative executives networked externally more widely than their peers, and their innovative ideas typically came from such networks. The same was true for 3,000 surveyed executives, and this has been found to be true for lower-level employees (Morris, Zhong, and Mäkhijä, 2015).

68 Ferner and Quintanilla (1998) discuss four of these; we have added the influence of other international firms in the local context.

69 Loveridge, 1990.

70 Kuin, 1972.

71 Cohen, 1992.

72 Wong and Law, 1999.

73 Terazono, E. "Japanese Banks' Local Feel," *Financial Times*, January 29, 1997.

74 Compensation is discussed in Chapter 7.

75 Wong and Law, 1999.

76 Fey, Engström, and Björkman, 1999.

77 Two separate studies of localization of management in foreign multinationals in China found that the effort spent planning the localization process was positively associated with its outcome (Fryxell, Butler, and Choi, 2004; Law, Wong, and Wang, 2004).

78 Bartlett and Ghoshal, 1989.

79 An exception is the small number of firms, typically in high technology sectors, that are multinational from the time of their origins. See also the "metanational" concept developed by Doz, Santos, and Williamson (2001).

80 Ghoshal and Barlett (1998, 2000) described this pattern of change in multinationals. The *spiral model of change* has been also examined by Mintzberg and Westley (1992), Hampden-Turner (1990a), Brown and Eisenhardt (1998), and Lewis (2000). It can be contrasted with two other models of organizational change. The first is an *evolutionary model* seen in the school of organizational or population ecology (Hannan and Freeman, 1989), which builds on Weick's influential Darwinian model of change processes: variation-selection-retention (Weick, 1979). See also Kimberly and Bouchikhi (1995). By contrast, the Organizational Development movement was built on *transformational assumptions about change* elaborated in the punctuated equilibrium view of change (Tushman, Newman, and Romanelli, 1986). See Pettigrew (2000) for a commentary.

81 See Birkinshaw and Hood (1998) and related research by Birkinshaw.

82 Ghemawat (2007) calls this aggregation.

83 Lasserre and Schütte, 2006; Lasserre, 1996.

84 Rugman and Verbeke, 2004 and 2008.

3

Achieving Global Integration

SUMMARY

Challenge

Companies with business models that require tight global integration are often seen as ethnocentric and not adaptive enough to meet market demands

Analysis

Achieving effective global integration rests on:

- The ability to implement appropriate (and flexible) mechanisms of global control
- The ability to simplify and standardize HRM processes and practices

Solutions

- Focus on performance management as a backbone of output control
- Build shared values through socialization to promote integration without hierarchy
- Use expatriates in corporate agency roles to move decision-making closer to the market while preserving integration
- Be aware that standardization of HRM has many advantages, but it can lead to harmful over-centralization
- Deploy horizontal coordination tools to balance integration and responsiveness

The Global Rise of Zara

Over the past decade, Zara and the other affiliates of the fashion retailing group Inditex (the world's largest apparel retailer) have successfully overcome the global economic recession and come out on top. Headquartered in one of the hardest hit countries, Spain, the flagship brand of the Inditex group has over 2,000 stores in close to 90 countries on all five continents, and much of its success is attributed to a business model known as "fast fashion"—rapidly churning out fashionable designs at affordable prices. As a result, Zara is often seen as responsible for the major transformation of the global apparel industry and consumer purchasing patterns.[1]

How they do it is of great interest to other retailers, not only in the clothing business but also in electronics, food, and entertainment. While part of its success rests on reaping benefits from global standardization of fast fashion preferences, Zara's tight operational control stands out, not only on cost and logistics, but in all aspects of its global processes – including HRM.

Zara's headquarters in Spain sets the company's strategy and manages the global HR function. The HR managers are organized by geographical area and each supports around 15 stores on all HR issues. Part of the HR manager's responsibility is to ascertain that store managers present the brand in a similar way to customers anywhere in the world and that all stores are globally integrated through a common culture. Store managers are often rotated from one location to another to strengthen the corporate culture and ensure that best practices move from store to store and country to country.

In each country, the country and HR managers hold weekly "brand meetings" with the store managers to discuss store performance and best practices. One manager explained, "We cover the sales, the budget, the appointments, the sanctions, and all the operational points and make sure that [Zara's] culture and the law is respected."[2] HR and country managers constantly visit stores to explain the culture directly to the staff and to monitor store performance. In addition, each store regularly receives manuals that include information about the chain and its management, human resource practices, information systems, and the environment. But for most store processes there is no exact formal template spelling out how something needs to be done. Rather, each store is given guidelines based on core principles related to the Zara culture.

This approach allows each store to respond to local expectations while maintaining a strong global brand. For example, corporate headquarters require that clothes be replenished from backrooms on a continual basis in every store. How exactly this gets done depends upon the country manager and individual store managers. By focusing on principles instead of following the details of a brand template, Zara maintains an integrated global approach that allows for local adaptations.

By following guiding brand principles, country and HR managers not only make sure that stores and headquarters remain closely connected but also ensure that they take feedback and learn valuable practices from local stores. Learning from the stores, however, needs an openness to new ideas in a company that requires most of its activities to be globally similar and integrated.

OVERVIEW

Zara became a leader in fashion retailing by pursuing a strategy of global integration, leveraging its standardized design and distribution process into global dominance through superior pricing and speed. In this chapter, we build on the Zara story to explore the benefits of global integration strategies and to outline the key mechanisms of global integration and their implications for the organization and how people are managed.

Global integration relies on vertical control to ensure that operations are aligned across functions and countries. We review four principal control mechanisms and related HRM processes: output control supported by performance management, normative control enabled by socialization, personal control exercised through expatriation, and process control embedded in standardization of organizational procedures.

Companies who follow a meganational approach to organization frequently use global integration strategies. But if they only use vertical controls, companies cannot effectively balance the need to be both globally integrated and locally responsive. In the final section we present a framework describing horizontal coordination tools used by transnational firms to balance multiple strategic perspectives.

THE IMPORTANCE OF GLOBAL INTEGRATION

In Chapter 2, we discussed the need for international firms to respond to local requirements. We argued that *local responsiveness* is achieved primarily by delegating decision-making responsibility to local units and by appointing local managers to the top management teams of subsidiaries.

In this chapter we discuss how firms can achieve global efficiency through a high level of integration of their international activities. With increased global competition, efficiencies of scale and cost supported by *global integration* are becoming a competitive necessity in a number of markets where decentralized strategies were dominant in the past. Global integration means that the different parts of the corporation constitute a whole and that decisions are made based on a global perspective. The desired outcome is alignment of resources optimizing global performance.

Among the factors favoring integration are the emergence of global consumers, supported by growing homogeneity of tastes; the diminishing importance of country borders with regional integration in Europe, Latin America, and Southeast Asia; and the increasing importance of fast decisions and operational speed.

The need to respond rapidly to changes in market requirements, but at a lower price point than competitors, meant that Zara had to build many standardized processes for fashion design and distribution. Zara also developed a strong corporate culture that helps the company to deploy these processes globally. The outcome is a global brand—aligned across all countries where Zara is present.

Advantages of Global Integration

There are a number of reasons why companies may choose to follow a route of tight international integration (see the box "Business Advantages of Global Integration").

Business Advantages of Global Integration

- *Economies of scale.* A company can lower its unit costs by centralizing critical value chain activities, such as manufacturing or logistics. This may involve having a small number of large facilities to make products for export or creating a network of specialized and focused operations spread around the world that are tightly controlled by the central hub. This allows Zara to carefully manage its investments and to maximize economies of scale in manufacturing, sourcing, and logistics.

- *Links in the value chain.* Sometimes competitive advantage comes from tight links between value chain activities—making sure efficient hand-offs between R&D, manufacturing, and marketing across different countries allows the firm to stay ahead of macroeconomic, technological, and competitive changes.
- *Serving global customers.* To the extent that customers are integrated and operate on a global basis, their suppliers may be forced to adopt a

(Continued)

similar structure. Subsidiaries do not serve isolated customers; prices, quality standards, and delivery terms are determined globally. For instance, international law firms are expected to deliver the same service to their global clients regardless of where they are served.[3]

- *Global branding.* A consumer product company like Coca-Cola promotes a unified brand image around the world. Coke standardizes both its formula and advertising themes (its two critical success factors) to a high degree, gaining efficiencies in the use of marketing tools like advertising and merchandizing.
- *Leveraging capabilities.* Some companies expand globally by transferring capabilities developed in the home market. The international expansion of both IKEA and Walmart depends on supply-chain management skills that allow these companies to pursue their traditional low-price strategies around the world.
- *World-class quality assurance.* Key processes are standardized and centrally controlled to maintain competitive advantage. The pharmaceutical giant Merck manufactures locally to meet government requirements. Its manufacturing processes are complex, however, and these are standardized in order to maintain high quality.
- *Competitive platforms.* Tight control of local subsidiaries by central headquarters may allow rapid response to competitive conditions and redeployment of resources to facilitate expansion worldwide. For example, in the past, tightly centralized Japanese multinationals penetrated new markets through price subsidization funded by profitable operations elsewhere.

Global integration does not necessarily imply selling identical products in the same way all over the world. What it does mean is that decisions about how to address local customer needs or market differentiation are made by managers who have an integrated global point of view. The strategies of export-driven Japanese, Korean, and Chinese manufacturing companies—relative latecomers to internationalization—typify this. Their tightly integrated product development and manufacturing functions at home provide economies of scale in cost, quality, and product innovation—supplying the world with automobiles, cameras, copiers, consumer electronics, and other products through their sales subsidiaries abroad.

Similarly, global integration does not mean centralization of all aspects of a company's operations. It may be limited to a particular product, function, or value chain segment. For example, to capitalize on its ability to develop new products and rapidly launch them across the world, P&G strives to deliver globally branded products worldwide in a standardized fashion. Advertising and pricing of products, on the other hand, are more adapted to local needs. For Zara, ensuring that global integration does not become too rigid—restricting its ability to adapt quickly to shifting local consumer preferences—is a constant challenge.

A similar strategy can be observed in the digital industry. When Google first started selling its Apps for Work in India, the products were sold online, using the same approach as in developed markets and requiring customers to pay in US dollars. Then, after a series of complaints and the loss of many potential clients, Google customized its sales and advertising strategy to the Indian market, with payment in local currency.[4]

All multinational firms integrate at least some of their operations; even those operating as holding companies, who give broad independence to their foreign subsidiaries, must integrate some corporate functions such as finance in order to exercise the appropriate governance. Global integration, just like local responsiveness, is always a matter of degree.

The Meganational Firm

Many companies choose to expand internationally while maintaining close control over the value chain—the string of primary activities (R&D, manufacturing, logistics, etc.) and support activities such as HR and procurement that are the source of added value.

In companies pursuing global integration, the development of new knowledge takes place mainly at the global hub, usually the corporate headquarters or the worldwide product division. Foreign subsidiaries depend on the center for resources, direction, and information. They act as product delivery pipelines to foreign markets, implementing the strategies of the parent company. Most decisions are made from a global perspective; in the extreme, the firm operates as if the world were a single market.

In Chapter 1, we defined companies that use this "one-country" approach to creating competitive advantage as *meganational* firms.[5] For such companies, mastering global integration, including its support through HR practices, is the essential capability driving business success. IKEA is another global retailing example, as described in the box "IKEA: The Yellow and Blue Meganational," bringing globalization to a mass-market home furnishing industry that previously was considered a local business.

The meganational approach is popular among companies offering products with features that are similar around the world, or where maintaining key activities in the value chain at the center can create a competitive advantage in terms of speed of product development, cost reduction, or quality improvement.[7] However, as with IKEA and Zara, meganational firms can also be found in other industries in which the forces for local responsiveness are supposedly high—such as McDonald's and Pizza Hut in fast food.

Meganationals are not only found in North America and Europe; many international companies in Japan and Korea fit this description. The strategy of global integration served them well for a considerable period; it helped Toyota and Samsung to achieve positions of worldwide market leadership.

IKEA: The Yellow and Blue Meganational

The Swedish furniture retailer operates more than 350 stores in nearly 50 countries. IKEA's strength comes from its ability to optimize work processes worldwide—integrating product design, low-cost manufacturing, logistics, and efficient service.

Although consumer marketing is normally associated with strong influence of different cultural preferences, IKEA global processes are built around a tightly controlled standard marketing concept.

Key strategic decisions at IKEA emerge from a fast-moving process of data gathering and analysis, consultation, and conflict resolution. Different perspectives are actively encouraged but get aligned quickly, enabled by the fact that many senior executives around the world come from the same place—Sweden.[6] They share a common language and cultural background, and they are used to working with each other.

Specially trained "IKEA ambassadors" have been assigned to key positions in all units, charged not only with the transfer of know-how but also with inculcating the "IKEA Way" among its staff around the world. This has allowed IKEA to standardize its entire supply chain from product design to customer delivery more effectively without a push back about the rigidity of the operational procedures.

A meganational firm may be perceived as ethnocentric—by employees in subsidiaries abroad or by host governments—and indeed sometimes this may be the case. Decisions may seem to be made at the expense of the subsidiary's interests, with the corporation's home country having an undue influence. The composition of the top management team at the center, typically dominated by home country nationals (nearly all from one region in Spain in the case of Zara), further strengthens this perception. Additionally, expatriates from the home country often have key roles on local management teams to maintain close links with the head office.

Not surprisingly, Japanese multinationals, with their historical preference for a meganational approach, consistently have a greater presence of expatriates from the parent country in local management than multinationals from other countries.[8] How to overcome this tendency to become ethnocentric is one of the challenges facing many meganational firms.

Some companies, such as Coca-Cola or Toyota, have used a meganational strategy as the first step of internationalization, moving to a different strategic posture as they progress. Some degree of meganational strategy can be detected in most cases of early internationalization when resource constraints require careful central control. Other firms, such as Apple or McDonald's, maintain their meganational orientation for an extended period of time because it fits with their products and/or markets. What all meganationals have in common is a strong reliance on a mix of tools enhancing centralized (vertical) control.

The Tools of Global Integration

Efficient global operations require global control. Historically, the levers of global integration have been primarily those that enabled centralized control over dispersed operations.[9] This observation is consistent with frameworks in organizational theory. The idea underlying these frameworks is that as the degree of complexity and uncertainty of tasks increases, a progressively wider range of control mechanisms will be employed. Simple mechanisms such as rules and procedures can manage simple tasks. But as the complexity of the task increases, direct supervision, planning, and more complex levers of control will come into play.[10]

When talking of integration tools or mechanisms, it should be pointed out here that integration mechanisms are sometimes referred to as tools of control and sometimes as tools of coordination, both in popular usage and in textbooks. Control and coordination are two closely related concepts that are difficult to separate.[11] As we explained in Chapter 1, we use the term "control" when power and authority are overt and the mechanism is hierarchic in nature.[12] We use the term "coordination" when the mechanisms focus on enhancing lateral (horizontal) interactions that lead to adjustments among different organizational units and individuals.

Global *control* mechanisms can be classified broadly into four types:[13]

- Output control
- Normative control
- Personal control
- Process control

Output Control

Output control is focused on the negotiation of objectives or targets, rather than on behaviors or course of action—in other words how these results are achieved. This is analogous to market rather than hierarchic ways of governance. Targets that have been agreed constitute quasi-contractual obligations, typically backed up by explicitly stated rewards and sanctions. Bonuses are linked to the achievement of results, and the ultimate sanction may be replacement or dismissal for nonperformance.

The trend in most global companies toward greater rigor in performance management (objective setting, evaluation, and rewards—to be discussed in Chapter 7) reflects an emphasis on output control. To avoid an excessively short-term orientation, output control is guided by some form of planning system that focuses on working through the trade-offs between long-term strategic objectives and short-term outputs (financial targets and budgets as well as operational goals).[14]

Normative Control

In comparison with personal control, normative control (sometimes called normative integration) is more implicit and subtle. It typically means defining—often top-down—and then inculcating values, beliefs, and behaviors that employees are expected to learn so that these are internalized and followed. (We discuss shared values, beliefs, and norms at more length in Chapter 5.)

People can be recruited on the basis of their potential fit with these values and norms, which can also be taught, both through formal socialization programs and through informal interaction with other organizational members. Those who demonstrate adherence to corporate values and behavioral norms are chosen for positions of responsibility. To the extent that employees share common norms and values, they can be trusted without the necessity for rules, procedures, and supervision.

Personal Control

Personal control is anchored in the managerial hierarchy of roles and responsibilities, where decision-making authority is concentrated at the center of the organization. Since all organizations are organized in a hierarchy, some degree of personal control is universal. This is the most direct and personalized form of control. The center takes key decisions, supported by direct supervision—for example, by visits to foreign operations by senior executives.

Personal control through expatriates can be used to replace and complement headquarters centralization. Trusted expatriates make decisions on behalf of headquarters and they monitor the implementation of central decisions. Personal and hierarchic control mechanisms are one of the foundations of a *meganational* strategy.

Process Control

In its simplest form, process control involves imposing rules—though few rules can cover all situations in a multinational. Rules take the shape of standardized procedures, typically in written form and increasingly supported by IT-based tools. These can come to constitute an internal governance system, for example, mandating the processes for recruitment, for signing external contracts, or concerning safety measures.

Standardization can also take more sophisticated forms, including the development of complex global work processes and systems. Standardization can apply to skills (training people in how to approach customers or handle a performance appraisal) as well as knowledge (codifying new knowledge on customer solutions so that it can be diffused across operations).[15]

Implementing Global Integration

The four different control mechanisms are largely complementary. Almost all organizations have some centrally concentrated hierarchy, some standardized procedures, some degree of results-based negotiation and planning, and some prescribed values and behavioral norms. Firms tend to employ certain levers of control more than others, however, leading to different organizational configurations. Figure 3-1 shows how companies might simultaneously but differentially focus on these four aspects of control.

Research suggests that companies pursuing global integration tend to rely on centrally driven hierarchic mechanisms, notably personal and process controls, while locally responsive firms rely more on output control than other control mechanisms.[16] Normative control mechanisms that rely on strong socialization and buy-in into particular behavioral norms are back in fashion (they first gained popularity in the 1980s when the Japanese "miracle" was widely admired), now being applied by many of the emerging meganational Internet-economy giants, such as Apple, Amazon, and Alibaba.[17]

There are also differences between countries of origin, with respect to the type of control exercised by the headquarters.[18] US firms tend to depend on

FIGURE 3-1
Integration Control
Mechanisms

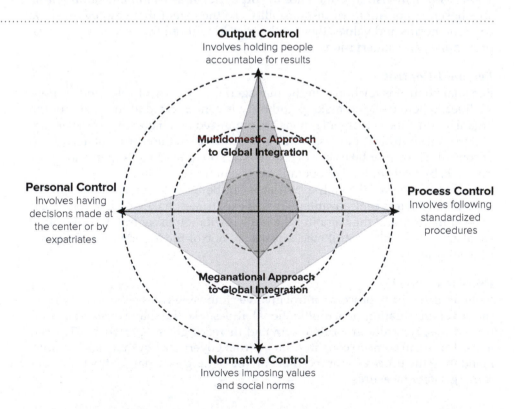

process and output control, Japanese multinationals use a larger number of expatriates (personal control) to integrate their foreign operations, and European companies rely more on normative integration than firms from the other regions,[19] at least with respect to controlling their affiliates.

SUPPORTING GLOBAL INTEGRATION THROUGH HRM PRACTICES

All four control mechanisms represented in Figure 3-1 are closely intertwined with people management practices. We will describe the mechanisms of control associated with global integration strategies, addressing first output control and normative control though leaving most of the discussion on these two topics for later chapters.[20] We will then focus on personal and process control and their links to HRM.

Global Integration Through Performance Management—Output Control

When one thinks of meganational firms, the first image that usually comes to mind is centralized decision-making at the all-powerful headquarters. This is misleading. Senior managers at the center would become overloaded with operational details—as the scope of international operations expands, decision-making would break down. Everything would stop until the headquarters decides. It would also be hard to attract and retain capable local staff, who would feel alienated at slow decision-making by distant bosses with limited understanding of local circumstances.

As we pointed out, alignment of dispersed resources is critical for effective global integration. The objective of output control is therefore to create and monitor the measurements relevant to achieve this alignment, usually through a performance-management system that fosters decisions and behaviors consistent with a global orientation, independent of location, and that rewards global rather than local objectives.

Among all control mechanisms, output control through performance management has the broadest application; all multinational firms, regardless of their business model or strategic posture, want to monitor the business performance of their subsidiaries. When ABB—in its heydays of radical decentralization—was divided into 5,000 profit centers (served by 140 IT systems), it still ran an impressive standardized and transparent financial control system providing senior management with information needed to steer the global business.[21] However, in firms trying to capture the benefits of global integration, what is particular about output control is that it focuses mainly, if not exclusively, on what matters at a global level. Consequently, the performance-management process will mostly reflect common standards and global objectives.

A meganational will provide targets and measurements not only for what to do, but also how to do it—which is seldom the case for multidomestic firms—since control is often tightly linked to process standardization. Since measuring global contribution at the local level may be difficult, the company will typically decide to rely on well-socialized expatriates (personal control). Research has shown that the higher the percentage of expatriates in a subsidiary, the lower the levels of output control deployed.[22]

Achieving Global Alignment

During the early stages of internationalization, a period when most companies adapt a meganational approach, profits are often measured only at a world-wide level, while local subsidiaries operate on the basis of budgets, with cost and sales targets. Business results may be reported locally for fiscal reasons, but these local figures are often arbitrary. In the big picture, they do not matter. But as the business grows, transfer pricing, interest on internal loans, and corporate function allocations (including HR, licensing fees, and recharging the cost of expatriates—we leave tax optimization aside) may all influence the bottom line of the subsidiary and distort the measures of its performance to a great degree.

One paradox facing meganational firms is that even if everything is rigorously measured, no one really knows what products and services are actually profitable since local "results" do not reflect business reality. Asking a plant manager in the Czech Republic, who reports (daily) to the global product group of a US-based meganational, about her plant ROI elicits only an amused smile: "What do you want it to be"? More than 80 percent of "costs" are negotiated with vendors globally or allocated based on a global formula.

It is not uncommon that the corporate view of the subsidiary gleaned from financial reports is quite inconsistent with what the results would be if operated as an autonomous unit. Headquarter cost allocation and purchasing control are only some of the reasons. Business strategy decisions can also impact local profitability. For example, for competitive reasons, firms pursuing global integration may adopt aggressive pricing policies in a particular market, causing the local subsidiary to operate with a loss. Therefore, when local business results are subordinated to global results, it is meaningless to hold local managers responsible for performance in the sense of traditional profit-and-loss accounting.

For these reasons, effective output control and performance management is based on measurements that go beyond traditional financial reports, usually targets focused on specific aspects of the value chain or customer market. For example, globally standardized cycle time or quality data are valuable measures in manufacturing, and many global consumer product firms rely on detailed worldwide customer satisfaction surveys, controlled by headquarters, to obtain comparable non-biased feedback from local customers. An argument can be made that among meganational firms, effective implementation of output control can be a differentiating organizational capability—as demonstrated by Amazon, Maersk (number one in global shipping), or Zara.

Another paradox of output control in a meganational is how to encourage sufficient local initiative (see box "Dualities of Output Control"). For example, many multinationals operating in emerging markets need to figure out how to respond to market penetration from local competitors who offer "good-enough" products—providing acceptable quality at low price, thereby attacking the market share of established premium product suppliers. In theory, a meganational firm should be well positioned to take the necessary decisions to

Dualities of Output Control

The objective of output control in a meganational is to align activities around a standard set of relevant metrics. Strict standardization of measurements can guide how "output" is monitored, evaluated, and shared within the firm. At the same time, global integration through output control may enhance opportunities for local adaptation. Properly designed output measures may enable local subsidiaries to customize their product and service offerings to specific market niches and opportunities—while leveraging the scale and scope advantages of global integration. Just as it is done in Zara, full transparency of measurements is a necessary precondition.

Research shows that output specifications can be effective in getting employees to find the resources they need to adapt products to meet local client needs.[24] For example, managers at McKinsey tell their associates that they do not care how something is accomplished, but they will be evaluated on their ability to help the client reach specific objectives. Associates are under pressure to deliver results for the client regardless of whether or not this is consistent with what has been done by the company beforehand. At the same time, associates are expected to turn to others inside the organization who have worked on similar projects. This ensures a degree of global integration while allowing for local adaptation at the same time.

counter this threat—investing in product redesign to lower the cost and then providing incentives to the local unit to price its products aggressively. In practice this seldom happens, because performance measures at the operating level discourage such actions. If local managers are rewarded for meeting their margins (set globally), they will not be keen to launch a lower-priced product. This is the lesson GE learned when they attempted to sell a low-cost CT scanner in India—getting the whole organization behind it required changing the performance measurements.[23]

Global Integration Through Socialization—Normative Control

The Brazilian construction giant Odebrecht, which earns about half of its revenue abroad, has a strong internal culture that emphasizes training, meritocracy, and decentralized decision-making. To internalize the culture, new employees are expected to study the founder's books and are quizzed about their teachings. In the first five years, corporate acculturation makes up a big part of their annual appraisals. A closed Facebook called Odebrecht United has more than 17,000 members, mostly employees. The result is a sense of loyalty that verges on the religious.[25]

Odebrecht is a good example of a meganational relying on normative control as a tool for global integration. Normative control helps companies like Odebrecht influence the behavior and attitudes of employees without specifying what should be done and how. It is a subtle and powerful tool of global integration, often complementing other mechanisms of global control.

The purpose of normative control is to ensure that key employees worldwide make decisions and behave in accordance with the values, beliefs, and norms of the global corporation, reflecting its corporate culture. Some degree of normative integration is always necessary as it helps to develop an integrative mindset among employees. Without normative integration, communication across borders would be time-consuming since people would have interpreted information in different ways and have different frames of reference. If there were no commonality of norms, attitudes, and values across the organization, other tools to integrate the firm would be inherently more difficult to implement.

The main tool to establish normative control is socialization (see the box "Organizational Socialization"). People who move up the career ladder will be those who have successfully internalized the expected behaviors.

IKEA, introduced earlier in this chapter, has also invested heavily in socialization efforts that ensure people are on board with the "IKEA way." Guided by its core values, IKEA strives to recruit people who will blend well with the IKEA culture of humility, simplicity, and cost-consciousness. It prefers to hire people without much previous work experience, focuses heavily on socializing them early, and then develops them quickly by delegating responsibility and frequent rotations.

In IKEA's case, the foundation of corporate culture goes back to the founder and long-time CEO Ingvar Kamprad. In fact, in many past and present meganationals, the values and norms come explicitly from the top, reflecting the thoughts, beliefs, and personalities of the founders/CEOs (be it Jeff Bezos at Amazon, Steve Jobs at Apple, or Jack Ma at Alibaba—three companies already mentioned as champions of normative control).[29] However, the top-down socialization can also be less overt, bundled in organizational customs, routines, and rituals.

However, IKEA is also a good example to counteract the mistaken belief that socialization necessarily results in conformity. One of its core cultural

Organizational Socialization

Socialization as defined by social scientists refers to the "process by which individuals acquire knowledge, skills, and dispositions that enable them to participate as ... effective members of groups and the society."[26] While psychologists, sociologists, and anthropologists have researched this domain for a long time, the study of organizational socialization is relatively recent, building on the recognition that the culture of the organization is maintained through this process.

Socialization works essentially through an often unconscious process of reward and punishment. When people behave in the right way, they are made to feel good. When they behave in the wrong way, they are ostracized, made to feel bad, or even punished. Through this process, members of the organization learn a common language and conceptual categories that facilitate

communication (for example what "quality" means). They come to understand the criteria for inclusion and exclusion in groups, how decisions are reached, the criteria behind the power structure, and the reward/punishment system. They learn the acceptable ways of handling disagreements and conflict, the rules of the game for peer relationships, and the ideology that gives meaning to the organization, often expressed through symbols and stories.

The approaches to socialization may be individual or collective (e.g., training); they may be formal (guided by explicit values such as at IKEA or Odebrecht) or informal (through interactions with colleagues).[27] Socialization theory suggests that when individuals are new to the job or the organization, the pressures of socialization will be strongest.[28]

tenets is the importance of acknowledging and learning from errors, anchored in the well-known quote from Kamprad's writings: "Only while sleeping one makes no mistakes." Acceptance of errors implies freedom of action, improving the status quo. Kamprad's own reluctance to travel with herds, his going against the grain, became a fundamental aspect of life at the company and led it to attract innovative thinkers.[30]

The Weakness of Strong Normative Control

While normative control contributes to global integration, excessively strong normative control may lead to loss of strategic flexibility. Cultural cohesion or organizational glue, as we have called it,[31] can be taken to the extreme of conformity, indeed unformity and cloning. So normative control has to be administed in moderate doses and with care, without forgetting the importance of maintaining openess and flexibility. An experienced executive expressed this well with an analogy:

> One of my son's hobbies is building model aircaft. The key to building an aircaft that will fly is dosing the glue at the right places. Too little glue at the key spots, and the plane falls apart when you try to fly it. But sometimes he falls into the opposite trap. He and the plane get covered with the glue, and the plane is so heavy with glue that it won't fly. It is the same for organizations—some are so sticky that they can't fly.

Meganational firms are often unable to see the constraints created by the uniformity of normative control—even if the list of core values may list openness and learning. In the early 2000s, corporate HR in Nokia cancelled a series of executive training programs which took high-potential managers to Silicon Valley. The objective of the visits was to observe and learn from an ecosystem which was different from Europe, and especially from Finland (where most of the young talent came from), and then to translate the learning into action plans challenging the existing business strategy. However, as Nokia was riding high, coming from virtually nowhere to become the number one global manufacturer of mobile phones, looking outside for disruptive business models was not encouraged. Just a decade later, Nokia was forced to exit the business—defeated by Apple and Samsung.

The values and norms that were beneficial at one point in time may be inappropriate when markets and technologies change. The potential risks of a strong culture include "inertial, myopic thinking and orientation to the past… The ties that bind may also blind."[32]

Socialization and Expatriation

In meganational firms, socialization often involves extensive mobility through which individuals learn the culture of the firm and its nuances. Transfers, especially geographic moves, typically involve some degree of sacrifice of family and personal life, and the experience of sacrifice has long been shown to be part of commitment building in modern organizations as in primitive tribes.[33]

Since normative control is exercized abroad in part through expatriates, it is important that these expatriates be well socialized into the parent firm before being dispatched abroad. Indeed, it is unlikely that expatriates will be entrusted with major responsibilites unless they have demonstrated their understanding and commitment to the corporate perspective. This is why normative and personal controls are closely interconnected.

Global Integration Through Expatriates—Personal Control

Global integration requires that key managers worldwide are on the same wavelength. One way to ensure this is through expatriate staffing—shifting the locus of decision-making to the affiliates while assuring that a global view prevails.

Expatriation is a form of direct, hierarchic, personal control;[34] headquarter executives usually trust their expatriates more than they trust local employees. As pointed out above, trusted expatriates are also likely to have been thoroughly socialized into the corporate values and norms, and are well-versed in company business processes.

It Is not "Where" but "Who"

We have already noted that a certain degree of decentralization is essential even in meganational firms. However, decentralizing decisions to affiliates does not necessarily increase their autonomy. There is a lot of confusion about this, since autonomy in multinational companies is often perceived as synonymous with the locus of decision-making.[35] If decisions are made at headquarters, subsidiaries are said to have little autonomy; if decisions are made locally, then they have high autonomy. In fact, making decisions locally does not necessarily imply autonomy if the decisions are made by expatriates rather than local managers. Who makes the decision may be as important as where the decision is made.

The typical pattern in meganational firms is that home country expatriates, well socialized in the parent company norms and with strong social ties to headquarters managers, occupy key positions in the subsidiaries. For many firms this may be a key post, like general manager or financial controller. For others, it may be a critical technical position, such as the brew master at Heineken.[36] Indeed, sending expatriates to subsidiaries can have the same results as centralizing decisions at headquarters.[37]

For example, research has shown that many Japanese firms delegate substantial decision-making power to local subsidiaries. However, this may not mean more local responsiveness, as such devolution is highly correlated with a large presence of Japanese expatriates.[38] In other words, while many decisions are made locally, they are made by Japanese expatriates based on what they believe is best from a global perspective. Local executives may not like centralization (critical decisions are made in Tokyo or Nagoya), but they also find it hard to live with this more subtle pseudo-decentralization. No matter how hard some Japanese companies try to open and enlarge their management pool, skeptical observers doubt the impact of such efforts.[39]

The Evolution of Expatriate Management

Expatriation has been a tool of organizational control since the early stages of civilization. The box "Holding the Roman Empire Together" provides an example of early efforts on global integration relying on "expatriates."

Holding the Roman Empire Together

The use of expatriates is as old as international business. Hence, the effective management of expatriation—or more broadly of international transfers—remains one of the foundations for the implementation of international management.

The geographical reach and longevity of the Roman Empire can be regarded as a prodigious feat of international management. Rome expected those in charge of even the most distant part of the Empire to be more than just representatives; they had to make the right decisions on behalf of Rome. One of the binding forces of the Empire was the careful attention paid to the selection, training, and socialization of Rome's expatriates, the generals and governors entrusted with the governance of far-flung provinces.[40]

Such positions required a long apprenticeship in a highly trained and organized army. Governors were selected exclusively from consuls who had held high state office. By the time they were dispatched abroad, the ways of Rome were so ingrained in their minds that they would not need policy guidance—nor had they means of getting such advice. They were "centralized within."

This policy of administrative decentralization coupled with tight socialization of the local decision-makers created strong, self-contained provinces or "subsidiaries." A tribute to their robustness was that the Roman Empire survived even the fall of Rome (a sort of involuntary divestiture) when the center of the Empire moved east to Byzantium.

Early in the history of international business, typical parent country employees stationed abroad operated like viceroys—directing daily operations, supervising the transfer of know-how, communicating corporate policies, and keeping the home office informed about relevant developments in their assigned territories. Assignments were decided on an ad hoc basis, occasionally supported by crash courses in language and foreign culture. Since foreign assignments often meant being at a distance from the politics of career progression in the parent company, financial incentives were used to make foreign postings attractive.

The needs of global integration remain the major factor driving expatriation today, but other objectives are gradually increasing in importance. Let us examine these and their implications in more depth.

The Multiple Drivers of Expatriation

With respect to the logic behind expatriation, one can differentiate between *demand-driven* and *learning-driven* international assignments.[41] Traditional expatriate jobs fit mainly into the former category: employees who are dispatched abroad to maintain control (directly in senior positions or indirectly through functional influence) or to fix a problem or address an operational challenge. On the other hand, cross-border mobility can be used to enhance individual development or organizational learning. Many assignments combine both elements, but in most cases it is clear which of the two dominates.

In addition, expatriates differ in the time they spend in an assignment abroad. Historically, most assignments were relatively long term, often lasting two to four years.[42] Recently, more and more assignments are short term, less than one year, linked to a specific task or need. Figure 3-2 puts assignment purpose and length together into a framework for understanding the nature of expatriate roles.

FIGURE 3-2
The Purpose of
Expatriation: Demand-
driven vs. Learning-driven

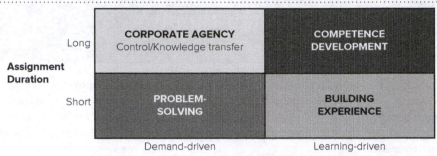

In many cases, expatriates are assigned abroad for a relatively long period of time as agents of the parent firm in order to accomplish a variety of tasks related to managing the operations and/or oversight of the subsidiaries. Representing headquarters and exercising control, or the transfer of knowledge and management practices, drives the demand for their services abroad. The expatriates serve a *corporate agency* role. The majority of expatriate postings in the past were of this type, and even today such assignments, while less dominant, are still the most common.[43]

In other cases, the demand for expatriate contributions is driven by relatively short-term start-up or problem-solving needs, and the length of the assignment is determined by the time it takes to address the task. We call this a *problem-solving* role; the expatriate brings knowledge and competencies that were not available locally. Obviously, when the gap persists, the length of the problem-solving assignment can be extended.

With the development of local managerial and professional capabilities, there is less demand for expatriate assignments to fill a local technical skill gap. At the same time, companies face an increasing need to develop global coordination capabilities. The focus of these *competence development* and *career enhancement* assignments is on organizational capabilities and individual learning (the latter postings tend to be shorter) rather than deploying skills or transferring practices from other parts of the multinational—a purpose fundamentally different from control.

Does this mean that each type of assignment will be administered with a different approach? So far, this is not the case. While academics call for a contingent approach to expatriation,[44] the overall trend in the field is toward increased standardization of mobility policies and practices, managed from the corporate center.[45] To understand this paradox, it is necessary to consider that—like in Zara and many other multinational firms—the legacy purpose of expatriation is to support global integration. Even today, this history (and pressures to reduce cost) to a great extent influences how most companies think about managing international mobility.

Who Are Current Expatriates

In the past, the notion of "expatriate" brought to mind a middle-aged, male executive dispatched from a first-world headquarters to a third-world subsidiary. In fact, this stereotype was never true, and it is even less so today. Most international transfers are within economically advanced countries; the countries with the highest population of resident expatriates are the US, China, and the UK.

A 2015 survey profiled international assignees in 143 multinationals from the Americas (51%), Europe, the Middle East, and Africa (43%), and Asia Pacific (6%):	**TABLE 3-1** **A Portrait of Expatriates**

- 46% of the assignees were younger than 40 years old.
- 19% of the assignees were women.
- 80% were accompanied by a spouse/partner; 4% of the assignees had partners of same gender.
- 55% of the "single status" assignments were expected to be for 3–12 months, 45% more than one year.
- 11% of the spouses were employed both before and during the assignment, 48% of the spouses were employed before, but not during the assignment, 4% during but not before the assignment—the rest (37%) were not employed before or during the assignment.
- 52% had children with them during the assignment, 2% with dependent parent(s).

Other findings

- The most common assignment objective was filling a managerial or technical skills gap, followed by building management expertise.
- 88% of global companies expect their international assignment population to stay the same or increase.
- 86% of global companies don't have a formal repatriation strategy.

Source: Brookfield Global Relocation Services (2015) (www.brookfieldgrs.com).

Table 3-1 provides an overview of some characteristics of today's expatriates around the world, based on a comprehensive survey of mostly North American and European multinationals. The key observation is that the expatriate population is increasingly diverse in its ethnic origins, gender, age, and the roles expatriates are expected to perform.

In a number of multinationals, many international assignees (a term now preferred to the old term "expatriate") are relatively young because of growing use of expatriation as a tool for learning and development, and many come from countries other than the home of the parent company. And as companies throughout the world are removing obstacles to gender diversity in management, an increasing proportion of expatriates are women.

The Expatriation Challenge

Making an expatriate assignment a success for the individual, the family, and the firm is an issue relevant to all multinationals. How much of a challenge is this? Based on our experience, it is quite significant but probably less than often thought. The box "Expatriate Failure: How Real Is the Problem?" examines some commonly held beliefs about this issue.

Expatriate Failure: How Real Is the Problem?

Until recently, a typical study on any topic linked to expatriation was framed by an introduction about the high cost of expatriates and the high frequency of assignment failure, especially in American multinationals.[46] However, while the direct costs of relocating an expatriate are real, there seems to be no studies that have empirically linked failure rates directly with company or subsidiary performance.

There has been no shortage of references to high expatriate failure rates, with claims that more than a third

(Continued)

of expatriations are aborted.[47] But does the empirical evidence support these claims? The answer is a surprising but unambiguous no. It seems that a persistent myth of high failure rates (that is, early returns of the expatriate to the home country) has been created by "massive (mis) quotations" of a handful of articles on US multinationals, some dating back to decades ago.[48] The real failure rates appear to be considerably lower. For instance, the 2015 Brookfield survey reported that 7 percent of expatriates returned early without having completed their assignments,[49] and other studies have reported similar figures.[50]

It is conceivable that the exaggeration of expatriate "failure" may have slowed down the adoption of some useful recommendations. When companies compare their failure rates with the alarming "average" presented in some textbooks, their situation does not look too bad. Why spend resources on what does not seem to be broken?

However, is "premature return" an adequate reflection of expatriate failure? One can argue that expatriate failure should continue to be examined, but using other measures. It may be far more damaging for a company if an expatriate who fails to meet expectations stays until completion of the overseas assignment. If underperformance in the job is included in the analysis—either as the result of poor selection or adaptation—failure rates may indeed be considerably higher.[51] Still, according to available data, expatriate retention rates in multinational firms are comparable, if not lower, to the ratios for overall employee population.[52]

Visible signs of expatriation failure, such as premature returns or resignations, may be less frequent than commonly believed. But given the investment necessary to support international assignments and the benefits that can be derived from effective expatriation, managing the international mobility process is an important (and growing) responsibility of the HR function—and not only for the meganational firms. In fact, the more the purpose of expatriation moves beyond control and other corporate agency tasks, the more important it is to align international mobility with other key HR processes and practices—a topic that we will address in detail in Chapter 9.

Global Integration Through Standardization—Process Control

The last important facet of global integration is the standardization of key operational procedures. Shared global standards support output control, ensuring more consistent performance in terms of cost and quality as well as compliance with environmental and safety standards. How can a company hope to be globally integrated if each unit has its own tailored way of measuring quality, its own IT system, its own distinctive approach to managing accounts receivable, and its own way of recruiting and training people? Process standardization also enables the transfer of the work organization as a complete system to a foreign location, perhaps the ultimate example of meganational strategy. But, just like international mobility, deployment of consistent processes worldwide is relevant to most multinational firms—in particular with respect to standardization of HRM.

Maintaining Global Standards in Operations

Ask anyone anywhere for a list of companies that deliver the same product around the world, and it is likely that McDonald's, the largest global fast-food company operating in some 120 countries, would be on the list. Whether you are in Tokyo, Moscow, Paris, or Cincinnati, the experience of ordering, buying, and eating a meal at McDonald's is virtually the same, although menus may vary with local tastes.[53] What attracts customers to McDonald's is the consistently high service level, from product quality to speed of order execution, from the ambiance of the stores to their hygiene. Every aspect of McDonald's operations is designed to satisfy customer expectations based on standards that are universal around the world. Nothing is left to chance or individual discretion.

A big part of McDonald's success is its ability to transfer expertise developed first at home to other markets worldwide. Global standardization of practices through operation manuals is an important tool. All McDonald's restaurants are required to conduct 72 safety protocols every day.[54] Even more critical is a relentless focus on education and training, led by Hamburger University and its regional "colleges" throughout the world.[55] McDonald's operating system has for many years been a model for scores of other businesses in which personal contact is an essential part of delivering value to customers.[56]

Another example of effective process standardization can be seen in Infosys. Its processes and IT-based solutions are offered to roughly 1,000 clients across 50 countries.[57] Infosys's competitive advantage comes from its ability to optimize its internal work flow worldwide—integrating consulting diagnostics with IT solutions. At the core are tightly controlled routines where consultants in the field work closely with programmers in India and key locations to provide solutions that are both timely and high in quality. This approach requires efficient and tight process control that does not allow for course deviations.

Transplanting the Work System

Probably no other case of large-scale standardization has received more coverage in the media and in academic literature than NUMMI—a joint venture created by GM and Toyota in 1982 to manufacture a small car on the site of a closed General Motors (GM) plant in Fremont, California.[58] The box "Transferring the Toyota Production System to NUMMI" focuses on the transfer of Toyota's manufacturing system to Fremont. Many in the US automobile industry expected that the transfer would fail, assuming that Japanese manufacturing methods were too deeply dependent on Japanese culture. However, the venture was an instant success, and NUMMI became the US leader in quality and productivity within three years.

Transferring the Toyota Production System to NUMMI

In 1963, GM opened an automobile assembly plant in Fremont, California. By the late 1970s, the plant employed over 7,000 workers but ranked lowest in productivity, and was one of the worst in terms of quality, in the entire GM system. Relations between management and the union were marked by distrust, daily absenteeism was almost 20 percent, drug abuse and alcoholism were rampant, and first-line supervisors were known to carry weapons for personal protection. The plant was finally closed in the 1982 recession.

Under an agreement between Toyota, GM, and the United Autoworkers' Union, the plant reopened in 1984 as NUMMI, a joint venture between the two automakers. Toyota recognized and accepted the same union bargaining committee that existed under the old GM system and 85 percent of the initial workforce was hired

(Continued)

from the pool of laid-off GM employees. After two years, the plant was 60 percent more efficient than a comparable plant fully owned by GM. How did this happen? Part of the change came from integrated HR and manufacturing processes, using intensive involvement of the workforce in a way that simultaneously empowers and controls them.[59]

Just as important was the deliberate and extensive socialization of NUMMI employees into the new system. First, when deciding whom to rehire there was a heavy emphasis on the selection of employees who had the ability to function within the NUMMI philosophy. Second, Toyota sent no less than 400 trainers from Japan to explain the Toyota methods to the US workforce. At the same time, 600 of NUMMI's blue-collar employees were sent to Japan for between three weeks' and several months' training at Toyota factories. This included classroom training and working alongside Toyota workers. As part of the training, NUMMI employees were asked to suggest improvement to the famous Toyota manufacturing system. The approach was not "Now you have to learn to work this way" but "Can you help us all to improve?"—cross-cultural action learning at its best.

The whole transplant effort was headed by a bicultural leadership group combining expatriates from Toyota in key plant positions, a small number of GM managers (mainly finance and procurement), and other Americans recruited from outside (including HR).[60] The plant itself was organized around teams, with a three-level hierarchy (in contrast to five or six levels in traditional GM plants). Most of the original team leaders went through the training in Japan, and many of them were subsequently promoted to managerial positions at the Fremont plant.

For over 25 years, and despite considerable improvements in productivity of the US automobile industry, NUMMI remained the benchmark to beat, comparable in quality with Toyota's operations in Japan.[61] Today, the factory is owned by Tesla, the pioneer producer of electric cars.

Part of the appeal of NUMMI to GM was the possibility to learn firsthand the organizing principles of lean manufacturing and to deploy them in its own operations, but GM struggled to make this happen. There were several reasons: a culture of plant autonomy and a distrust between workforce and management, but also an inconsistency of existing people management practices with the new work organization.

There is no doubt that HR practices played an important role in the success of manufacturing practices in Japan.[62] And the effective transfer of a work system may not be possible without at least some degree of transfer and thus standardization of HR practices. HRM factors included team-based production, worker participation in problem-solving, job rotation, few job classifications, single status, and high levels of training.

It should be noted that while Japanese automotive firms transferred these practices to most of their overseas plants, there was often considerable adaptation.[63] For example, while job rotation practices were similar to those in Japan, problem-solving team methods were adjusted, and compensation was comparable to local rather than Japanese norms. The adoption of new measurement tools (output control), rigorous selection and socialization (normative control), and extensive use of expatriate coaches (personal control) certainly reduced the impact of operating in a different cultural and institutional environment.

The importance of HRM alignment for transplanting the work systems cannot be overstated. When Toyota tried to replicate NUMMI's success in India, it transplanted the work processes but neglected to rethink the alignment of HRM processes, struggling for over a decade to get the plant to a desirable level of performance.[64]

Global Standardization of HRM

The desirability and degree of global standardization of HRM policy and practices is an issue that extends beyond the realm of meganational firms (just like all other elements of control). Arguments in favor of global standardization together with arguments for local adaptation, are summarized in Table 3-2.

A number of factors drive and support global standardization. For example, global standardization is associated with *scale advantages* as investments in the development of HR tools, and procedures are divided among multiple units. Standardization of HR practices can also enable further *specialization within the global HR function*, as there may be less need for replication of functional expertise across units. With similar HR tools and processes implemented throughout the corporation, questions related to functional subareas can be referred to the corporate functional specialist, regardless of where the person is located.[65]

With standardized HRM, employees share a vocabulary and beliefs about the business, facilitating communication and collaboration.[66] Also, when all units share the same HR practices, they are more likely to identify with the corporation as a whole. Finally, standardization of practices can contribute to enhancing perceived equity within the corporation, further stimulating inter-unit cooperation.[67] The more the value chain activities are integrated across different units of the corporation, the stronger the argument for alignment of HR practices will be.

While global HR standardization can have significant positive effects, such efforts often encounter difficulties, partly because they go against legitimate pressures for local adaptation of HR (see Table 3-2).[68] As discussed in Chapter 2, it may be quite easy to standardize HR philosophies (or guiding principles) and general policies, but actual practices are likely to differ across foreign units.

Which HR practices benefit from standardization, and which will not? There are differences between HR practices in the perceived benefits to be gained through global standardization. Table 3-3 presents the findings of research on the HR practices for white-collar employees in Western multinationals in China. Practices related to performance management showed the highest degree of global standardization. The *criteria* (principles) behind HR practices tend to be more global than implementation aspects, such as the *level*

Global Standardization	Local Adaptation
• Serves as control mechanism	• Fits with local cultural, institutional, and labor-market considerations
• Allows specialization and scale (cost) advantages in the HR function	• Helps fulfill local legal requirements
• Facilitates the use of IT-based HR tools and processes	• Appropriate HR practices may enhance local goodwill and image
• Can transfer best HR practices and work systems	• Motivates host country managers to have locally developed HR practices
• Global (foreign) HR practices are sometimes preferred by host country nationals	
• Facilitates coordination across units	

TABLE 3-2
Advantages of Global Standardization and Local Adaptation of HR Practices

TABLE 3-3
Degree of Global Standardization and Local Adaptation of HR Practices in Western-owned Firms in China

	Global Standardization[A]	Local Adaptation[A]
Methods used when recruiting new local managers and professionals	4.4	3.9
Criteria used when recruiting new local managers and professionals	5.0	4.1
Amount of management and professional training	4.4	3.4
Content of management and professional training	4.7	3.6
Relative importance of financial bonuses as a percentage of total compensation	4.1	4.2
Criteria employed to determine financial bonuses	5.1	3.8
Methods used to appraise (assess) the performance of professionals and managers	5.4	3.7
Criteria used to appraise (assess) the performance of professionals and managers	5.4	3.7

[A] Global standardization was measured by asking managers how similar (on a scale from (7) "very similar" to (1) "very different") subsidiary HR practices were with those in the multinational's home country operations. Local adaptation was measured with a similar question about the similarity between subsidiary HR practices and practices found in local firms.

Source: I. Björkman, P. Budhwar, A. Smale, and J. Sumelius, "Human Resource Management in Foreign-owned Subsidiaries: China versus India," *The International Journal of Human Resource Management* 19, no. 5 (May 2008).

of employee compensation and the *methods* of recruitment, which are more influenced by local conditions.

The choice of standardization versus adaptation should not be reduced to an either-or dilemma. In our view, the real question is *what to standardize across the globe*, *what to regionalize*, *what to localize*, and *what to reinvent* when adapting work practices, including HRM, to another environment. For example, multinationals may transfer some aspects of how people are recruited and selected from the parent company, they may copy some aspects of how this is done in local organizations, and they may develop some entirely new ways to deal with certain issues. Some HR functions may also be managed at a regional level (Asia Pacific or Europe, for example), leading to some regional standardization. The outcome is, to a greater or lesser extent, *hybrid* HR practices found in most foreign subsidiaries.[69]

In summary, with respect to talent management (attraction, recruitment, and selection), it is easy to agree on global principles, but adaptation is inevitable the more one gets to the nitty-gritty level of practice. This is also true for performance management. There are strong arguments for standardizing performance management practices, though local adaptation is typically needed in what we call the "downstream side" of performance appraisal, evaluation, and rewards. Finally, leadership development, including the management of mobility, will inevitably follow regional and global norms because of its close link to global integration.[70]

Another point to consider is the difference between formal *implementation* of corporate practices abroad and their *internalization* by subsidiary managers and employees.[71] While the depth of standardization matters, it is also crucial that users have internalized the underlying principles. Indeed, the most challenging element is often the thoroughness of internalization, the "state in which the employees at the recipient unit view the practice as valuable for the unit and become committed to the practice."[72]

Although policies and practices can to some extent be imposed by the headquarters through various control systems, there are no simple means available to influence positively the attitudes of subsidiary employees toward an "imposed" system. Lack of attention to "selling" a certain practice may lead to it being adopted only on the surface[73] or even being openly resisted.[74] The enforced adoption of a practice without a belief in its value will, at best, lead to superficial compliance and a low level of internalization.

Indeed, the use of top-down control mechanisms has been found to be unrelated to the internalization of the global HR processes and tools imposed on foreign subsidiaries. Rather, it is the existence of strong interpersonal relationships between key global and local actors that helps explain why some foreign subsidiaries show a higher level of internalization of transferred HR practices[75]—which brings us to the topic of the transnational approach to global integration.

A TRANSATIONAL APPROACH TO GLOBAL INTEGRATION

Despite many successful examples of global expansion through the globally integrated meganational approach, failures are not hard to find. Walmart's botched attempt to enter Germany and Korea provides a cautionary tale to all companies with a strong meganational heritage; having strong norms about how things should be done in a company may be helpful for integration, but these norms can also create blinders for managers who need to make certain adaptations in order to succeed in the local market.[76] Walmart was ill aware of the need to adapt their product offerings and service approach. For example, having greeters stand at the door when customers entered the building made both customers and employees feel uncomfortable in Germany and Korea. Also, Walmart did not believe that they needed to work cooperatively with the unions—while gaining union cooperation was not a key success factor in places like the US, it certainly was in Germany and Korea.

If Walmart managers had been more open to adapting to the expectations and needs of their customers and employees in Germany and Korea, the company might still be there. Better yet, they might have learned something about how to work more collaboratively with foreign employees, a lesson that could have been applied elsewhere. The necessaity of learning from the local environment and integrating that knowledge within the global company is one of the factors that has led many meganational firms to examine the limitations of the hierarchical approach to global integration.

The Limits of Meganational Integration

A number of causes push companies to move away from a reliance on top-down control. Probably the main weakness of global integration strategies built on vertical control is the the firm's restricted ability to respond quickly to rapidly evolving market opportunities, needs, and demands—of customers, host governments, or local employees—its *lack of local responsiveness*.[77] Some other limitations faced by companies taking a meganational approach are listed below:

1. Lack of autonomy—not encouraging local initiatives
For example, the leading global chip manufacturer Intel is run out of its headquarters in California's Silicon Valley. Intel adopts a typical meganational approach with many standardized processes and the use of expatriates to ensure global integration. Until a few years ago, competing on economies of scale and scope in R&D and manufacturing, Intel had a policy called "Copy Exactly," which discouraged experimentation at individual factories. Engineers and technicians would painstakingly clone proven Intel manufacturing techniques from one plant to the next—down to the color of workers' gloves, wall paint, and other features that would seem to have no bearing on efficiency.[78]

Today Intel still follows this same model of replication, but with a twist. They now try to encourage local initiatives by giving more profit and loss responsibility to their subsidiary units.[79] However, in a meganational company steeped in the control mode of governance, if local units are suddenly given the unconstrained right to do things in a local way and for local benefit only, waste can be expected. To avoid a swing in the pendulum, the process of encouraging local initiative involves careful steering to avoid excessive and costly adaptation.

2. Lack of innovation—only top-down, not bottom-up
Meganationals can be outstanding innovators—think Apple—but this innovation nearly always comes from the center. In theory, vertical controls do not preclude local innovation, but in practice the meganational approach to management often does not provide much space for new ideas to be heard, let alone implemented on a global scale. IKEA or Toyota may promote cross-subsidiary or cross-plant coordination, but sharing knowledge on process improvement is not the same as allowing opportunities for new radical ideas to bubble up from the bottom.

The challenge of tapping into the creative potential of employees is very much on the mind of Zara's CEO; not only does his company need to be globally fast and efficient, it also needs to be continuously improving.[80] To do so requires not just tight control over the operations, a capability at the core of Zara's competitive advantage, but also building up a new capability in enabling bottom-up change.

The advantage of an integrated firm is that valuable new ideas can quickly be spread across the world—if they reach an attentive center. For example, Zara stores in Japan have developed a practice of five-minute staff meetings before opening time to discuss the day's objectives. Corporate HR then made sure that this innovative practice, consistent with Zara's norms and values, is now introduced within all Zara stores.

3. Lack of engagement—fewer decisions left to be made locally
Digitalization allows a stronger focus on control. The performance and behavior of people can be monitored more and more easily, and data can be centralized at the center and then used to make decisions which in the past were made locally. Less strategic decisions can even be relegated to computers—freeing up time for managers to make higher-level decisions. Also, as more key business

decisions (e.g., what product to market to different segments) are generated using complex algorithms, managers rely more on processes that are established by predetermined criteria rather than engaging in dialogue with the people involved.

Digitalization impacts HRM as it increases the control and power that a company can exert over its people.[81] For example, companies such as Facebook have piloted a retention process based on algorithms that gathers data from social media Web sites like LinkedIn to make predictions about who is likely to leave a company. Valuable employees are flagged, and direct managers will follow up to see if there is anything the company can do to keep them. While this may be a helpful retention tool, the invasive nature of this and similar tools may create problems in countries with strong data-privacy regulations.

The increasing digitalization and use of predictive analytics to make decisions and provide processes can both strengthen and weaken the meganational. While new digital technologies can increase efficiencies, they may stifle creative thinking by forcing employees to follow data-driven processes and systems. Also, without meaningful involvement in the decision process, employees in distant locations are likely to become disengaged. To avoid such disruptive pressures, more emphasis has to be put on alternative means of integration to foster the necessary cohesiveness of the global firm—bringing us back to the importance of horizontal coordination.

From Control to Coordination

In simple terms, what differentiates the transnational firm from the meganational or a multidomestic company is the way in which a firm exercises authority. There is usually a clear decision-maker—the global or business manager in the meganational or the country manager in the multidomestic firm. The responsibility and accountability of all key managers are closely aligned, clearly defined, and supported by dedicated resources.

This contrasts with transnational firms, where there are few such "general managers." The identity of the "boss" may vary with circumstances and priorities, business, function, customer, etc. There are multiple priorities: on one strategic priority, a person may be the boss, and on another s/he may be a subordinate, and on a third a colleague. Task forces or steering groups create forums outside the formal structures that allow employees to influence the direction and execution of business strategies in a way that is not possible within the simple hierarchical organization.

In the transnational firm, vertical control is less about getting a task done and more about providing a foundation to connect people in different parts of the organization to get the task done. However, one should bear in mind that without standardized processes, the complexity of the transnational may become difficult if not impossible to manage—one of the lessons of early matrix organizations as we will see in the next chapter. In that way, a transnational can achieve strategic objectives better, cheaper, and faster than in a more simple meganational or multidomestic firm—at least that is the theory behind the transnational, though we will see in the chapters ahead the challenges of putting theory into practice.

Taking a transnational approach to integration means that you are concerned with knowing which subunits in the firm need to be connected and what are the best ways to ensure *coordination* among all who need to be involved with a decision and its implementation. If the locus of authority in the meganational or multidomestic firm is vertical, the locus in the transnational is vertical *and* horizontal. As we pointed out, vertical control and horizontal coordination are complementary, but managing the tension between the two is one of the principal challenges—and contributions—of HRM in transnational firms.

Let us try to understand the logic behind this transnational transformation of organizations, where coordination and collaboration have to go hand in hand with hierarchy and control, where local responsiveness cannot be sacrificed on the altar of global integration. There are three different perspectives to illustrate a transformation that is ongoing at the present time. First, we look at the competitive realities facing multinational firms; then we consider the workforce or people perspective; and finally we consider how all of these changes fit with one of the emerging paradigms of organizational theory—the firm as a network.

The Competitive Perspective

Today's multinationals face a different situation from the past. The American, European, and Japanese companies that led the process of internationalization in the post-World War II era either exploited home-based scale economies or transferred home-grown knowledge to their subsidiaries abroad. In both cases, their know-how and critical resources were located at the center. However, there are not many companies left in this position today and there will be even fewer in the future.

Consider some of the realities:

• Subsidiaries abroad may be of paramount importance to the multinational, sometimes representing market opportunities larger than at home. This has long been the case for multinationals from smaller countries such as Switzerland and Sweden. Whole business lines may be run from these other countries, and there will be multiple locations that must be linked together. Also, the technical and managerial sophistication of some lead subsidiaries may outstrip that of the parent country; information therefore has to flow both ways between the subsidiary and the headquarters.

• Many multinational companies are differentiated, in the sense that subsidiaries vary in their strategic importance, capabilities, and resources.[82] Rigid structures, undifferentiated policies, and traditional notions of planning cannot cope with this. For subsidiaries that are "strategic leaders," planning may involve intensive interaction with the headquarters, whereas distant "contributors" may be left alone, as long as they meet their targets. In the former, staff-development and compensation policies may be negotiated to balance corporate and local interests, whereas contributors usually adjust to local practices.

• Companies can no longer afford to be deliberate—which means slow. The pace of competition, the need to make decisions quickly without compromising on cost and quality, has increased. Instead of competing with companies that were weak on financial resources and technical and management expertise, traditional multinationals such as Nestlé and Unilever now compete not only with nimble local players with global ambitions in many different battlefields around the world but also with cost-driven private equity-controlled firms such as Kraft Heinz. With the ongoing waves of global consolidation, the pressure to be aligned globally is likely to increase.

- In many industries, future competitive advantage cannot be secured through further economies of scale, downsizing, and delayering. Even best-of-breed companies, like Toyota, that pushed the limits of operational improvement, now realize that future competitive advantage can only come through leveraging know-how across their global affiliates. Furthermore, the flow of innovation is changing from center-to-local to local-to-center or even local-to-local.

Collectively, all these trends mean that the traditional focus on headquarters–subsidiary relationships is giving way to the question of how to coordinate relationships, how to build and maintain ties, and how to manage a complex web of connections. The focus on center-to-subsidiary relations remains, but to this one adds subsidiary-to-center(s) and subsidiary-to-subsidiary ties.

The People Perspective

The transition to a network-based society based on people's knowledge rather than their manual skills has also led to changes in ways of managing people. First, right across the world the workforce has a much higher level of education and training than two decades ago. Innovation has become more important, and traditional hierarchical firms found that they could neither attract nor retain the new generation of skilled knowledge professionals they need. Highly educated employees require motivation and a raison d'être for working in a company that goes beyond financial rewards. Second, employees no longer need to be in the office to work; with email, the Internet, and wireless phones, people work from home, from other subsidiaries, or from whereever they happen to be. Third, cooperation is increasingly important; today's organizational world is less about individual roles than about teams and groups.[83]

The top-heavy control model of the multinational organization cannot cope with the realities of global markets. The cost of multiple layers of supervision and control started to weigh heavily on the profitability of companies. To meet the growing coordination needs, it is necessary to develop self-control rather than boss-control, and for this American practitioners coined a new term—"empowerment."[84] This in turn requires new skills such as leading without authority. The outcome is that more attention needs to be placed on selection, skill development, objective setting, feedback, and other tools of people management.

The Network Perspective

Organizational theory has shown that as the environment becomes more complex, and as information processing demands increase, the organization has to complement its reliance on hierarchic modes of integration with attention to horizontal coordination (see Figure 3-3).

The best way of coordinating in simple and stable environments is to use rules and standard operating procedures, hierarchic referral (ask the boss), and planning systems that lead to goal setting (explicit performance contracts).[85] But as complexity and turbulence increase, these hierarchic mechanisms can no longer cope. On the one hand, the organization can try to reduce the need for

FIGURE 3-3
Vertical Integration and
Horizontal Coordination

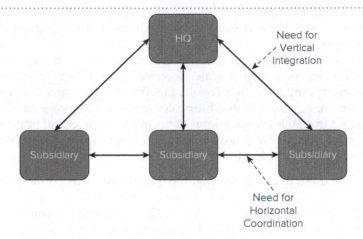

Source: Adapted from teaching notes developed by C. Bartlett.

information processing by outsourcing nonessential activities, or by creating self-contained units, like independent business units.[86] On the other hand, like Zara in our opening case, organizations can increase their coordination capacity by building a strong organizational culture and building lateral relationships, complemented by investments in vertical information systems. Research shows this gradual shift from structure to horizontal coordination.[87]

Consequently, it has become increasingly common to think of organizations as networks of internal (and external) relationships. In bureaucratic or mechanistic structures, there is a low degree of connectivity; relationships are asymmetric (top-down with little upward feedback) and centralized (focused on a few key actors in hierarchical positions). In contrast, organic or adaptive organizations are characterized by dense, strongly interconnected networks. The capacity for coordination is much higher.[88] For organizations to be successful, they must satisfy the principle of requisite complexity—the internal complexity of the firm must mirror the complexity of its external environment; that is, they should have a sufficient number of lateral and reciprocal relationships.[89]

However, this is not to suggest that more complex is always better. The appropriate degree of horizontal coordination will depend on business strategy: a company should not create more coordination mechanisms than required since these mechanisms (coordinating roles, steering groups, and other forms of cross-boundary teamwork) imply additional expense in terms of resources, management time, and energy.

In summary, the three perspectives on the transnational firm introduced here all lead in the same direction and emphasize the importance of horizontal coordination as a capability to help multinationals be both locally responsive and globally integrated.

Horizontal Coordination Mechanisms

Expanding on our brief introduction to coordination in Chapter 1, our framework of the horizontal coordination mechanisms is shown in Figure 3-4. Because coordination is applied for a purpose, the term "organizational glue" can be used to describe the underlying processes and practices (some companies refer to this as "cohesion management"). Glue is something that can be used to stick

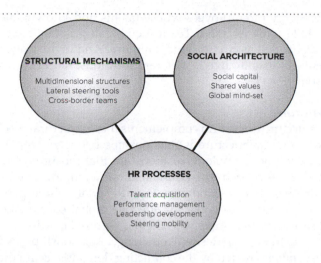

FIGURE 3-4
Horizontal Coordination
Mechanisms

two parts of an organization together for a specific purpose. Glue technology is to a great extent the application of human resource management.[90]

There are three elements of coordination or glue technology—structural mechanisms (dicussed in Chapter 4); social architecture (discussed in Chapter 5); and key global HR processes for acquiring talent (Chapter 6), managing performance (Chapter 7), developing and retaining global leaders (Chapter 8), and steering cross-border mobility (Chapter 9). We start with a brief overview of these three elements.

Structural Mechanisms

Organizational structure spells out who does what and who reports to whom. Structures can be based on different dimensions, and in a simple world one dimension dominates. Small firms have functional structures, larger firms have either business or geographic structures, and sometimes a combination of both. However, making a choice on a single dimension of alignment—product, geography, function, and (increasingly) the customer—is difficult, since transnational firms need the ability to act simultaneously on all these dimensions. Therefore, many multinationals have chosen to implement multidimensional structures.

There are a wide variety of multidimensional structures (we will discuss the major types in the next chapter), each requiring different ways of horizontal collaboration to complement top-down hierarchical decision-making. This includes lateral steering tools centered on an individual or a team that coordinates decisions across the various business units, thereby broadening the perspectives that can be brought to bear on strategic decisions. Individuals charged with these roles may have a high degree of responsibility but not necessarily much formal power or independent resources. Temporary or permanent steering teams are responsible for coordinating various activities and decisions across organizational boundaries, replacing bosses at the center of the traditional organization.

Cross-boundary teams and projects are basic building blocks of coordination in today's corporations. Different types of teams are set up to respond to many different challenges. Teamwork allows the organization to mobilize the collaborative energy of employees whose talents and knowledge are relevant to the immediate issue at hand. Team membership is flexible; teams can be formed and disbanded as circumstances require. And in the transnational firm, the team members usually live in different locations, requiring competence in working virtually.

Social Architecture

The social architecture of the firm complements these structural mechanisms. The foundation of social architecture is relationships between people, increasingly facilitated by electronic technology, relationships that constitute the social capital of the firm. In firms with rich social capital, information flows quickly and freely across intra-organizational boundaries. Social capital, where people trust and understand each other, is essential for effective global coordination, making it easier to mobilize scarce resources when help is required in a distant subsidiary or to secure access to those with desired knowledge. Relationships also help resolve the inevitable conflicts created by the conflicting demands facing the global firm.

Another important part of the social architecture of the firm is shared values (discussed earlier in this chapter as a normative control mechanism). Values, beliefs, and norms that are held in common across all or part of the global firm form the core of the organizational culture. Shared values facilitate the trust that is essential for effective horizontal coordination, conflict resolution, and knowledge transfer. Relationships between people are unlikely to add much value unless there is some degree of cohesion in the way in which people think and behave.

Global managers need to be able to cope with conflict and contradiction. This leads to the third element of social architecture in a multinational firm—the global mindset. We define it as a set of attitudes that predispose individuals to cope constructively with competing priorities (for example, global versus local priorities) rather than advocating one perspective at the expense of others. It includes awareness of diversity across businesses, countries, cultures, and markets; the ability to interpret business issues without being biased by the perspective of a single country, culture, or context; and, most importantly, the willingness to accept the legitimacy of multiple points of view.

Global HR Processes

Multidimensional structures and the social architecture of the firm are enabled by core human resource and organizational processes. Four interconnected global HR processes are particularly important for supporting coordination capabilities in global firms: talent acquisition, performance management, leadership development, and steering employee mobility. We already introduced these HR processes in Chapter 1 and will discuss them in considerable depth in Chapters 6–9.

GLOBAL INTEGRATION 2.0

It should be emphasized that horizontal coordination does not replace vertical control—it transforms it. The corporate executive becomes a strategic coach rather than a controller. General management becomes a responsibility of all middle and senior managers rather than a role occupied by one person. The focus of planning shifts from content to process, with an emphasis on working through conflicts and building commitment to strategies.[91] As for corporate staff, their roles change from functional experts to network facilitators, with new skills in capturing, assimilating, and ensuring the transfer of expertise around the world. Global or regional processes for connecting different activities together replace rigid policies. Measurement and data analytics become instruments for enhanced self-management and learning rather than instruments of control.

Many of the advances in IT technologies aim to enhance the organizational ability to generate new insights and react accordingly, by combining different aspects of social media, big data, and machine learning in a way that allows firms to analyze and capture in real time what is happening in the world around us. All this should help HR managers to act more quickly and with more confidence about the impact of their decisions. For example, one company we have worked with is Insidesales.com, a rising tech start-up with offices in the US and UK. This company uses algorithms to assess the personality traits of new hires. They track and monitor employee performance for all recruits in the companies where they work. As the data increases, the accuracy of their predictions increases. Clients can use these traits to help with their selection decisions.

However, the technology that provides insight for corporate decision-making may also result in unintended consequences. What should in principle be open and flexible modes of global coordination and collaboration, facilitatated by digital technology, may actually move the organization back to a more standardized process that looks and feels more like the old-style "headquarters knows best" approach to global management—but without the happy expat taking the locals out for a beer. And in any case, the expats are all virtual now!

TAKEAWAYS

1. Global integration means that business decisions are made from a global perspective. In the extreme, the meganational firm operates as if the world were a single market.

2. The key control mechanisms supporting global integration can be classified into four types: output control through achieving agreed results; normative control through corporate values, beliefs, and norms; personal control through decision-making; and process control through formalization and standardization.

3. The focus of output control is to create alignment through agreement about targets or objectives. The broad trend in many global firms towards greater rigor in performance management reflects an emphasis on output control.

4. Normative control (socialization) helps companies to influence the behavior and attitudes of employees through internalization of corporate values and norms without relying on overt bureaucratic or hierarchical procedures and routines.

5. Personal control reflects the hierarchy of roles and responsibilities in which authority is concentrated in the center of the organization. Personal control through expatriates can be used to complement or replace headquarter centralization.

6. Process control and global standardization of HR practices is associated with a number of advantages, including subsidiary control, transfer of best practices, and scale advantages in the global HR function.

7. Vertical control mechanisms cannot cope with the complexity of demands facing the transnational firm. Taking a transnational approach to integration involves connecting subunits across the global organization.

8. Horizontal coordination in the transnational firm does not replace vertical control or organizational hierarchy—it transforms it.

9. There are three elements to the "organizational glue" of global coordination: (1) structural mechanisms; (2) social architecture; and (3) global HR processes: talent acquisition, performance management, leadership development, and international mobility.

10. Increased information flow facilitated by new technologies enables deeper integration of organizational processes (including HR operations), but it also opens the door for companies to revert back to meganational approaches to HRM.

NOTES

1 Caro and Albeniz, 2014.

2 Zeynep, Corsi, and Dessain, 2010.

3 Segal-Horn and Dean, 2008. The automotive industry is another example of a business in which suppliers must be able to serve their customers globally.

4 Based on personal conversations with the director of business development at Google, September 2015.

5 We prefer the term "meganational firm" to Bartlett and Ghoshal's "global firm" (1989). "Global" may be confusing because of the generic nature of the word; as suggested in Chapter 1, it is a word that has many meanings.

6 Stahl *et al.*, 2012.

7 Within the same industry, companies may pursue different internationalization strategies, often following the path that led them to success in their home markets. Nohria and Ghoshal (1997) find empirical support for the match between industry and structural fit. Scientific measurement instruments, cement products, industrial chemicals, aircraft engines, and mining machinery are among the industries that are traditionally globally integrated.

8 Pucik, Hanada, and Fifield, 1989; Kopp, 1994; Yoshihara, 1999; Oki, 2013.

9 Prahalad and Doz, 1987, p. 160.

10 See Galbraith (1977); Lawrence and Lorsch (1967); Mintzberg (1989); Martinez and Jarillo (1989); and Harzing (1999).

11 Organizational theorists typically see control and coordination as the same in principle, and there is often some confusion around terminology. Both are means to achieve organizational goals. Harzing summarizes the literature by saying that "control is a means to achieve an end called coordination, which in turn leads toward the achievement of common organization goals" (Harzing, 1999, p. 9).

12 The terms "control" and "coordination" were explained in Chapter 1.

13 The classification we use is largely drawn from Harzing (1999), who reviews the literature on control mechanisms.

14 One study of diversified corporations identified three different approaches to output control (Goold and Campbell, 1987). In "financial control" companies, objectives are set in terms of financial performance. In "strategic control" firms, objectives cover longer-term strategic objectives and annual financial targets. In "strategic planning" firms, there is far more emphasis on the planning process, driven by the intention to develop bold strategies. Objectives blend both short-term financial targets and long-term strategic aims.

15 Standardization is a prerequisite for process control, as it is nearly impossible to formalize work processes that are not standardized.

16 Harzing, 1999.

17 Leydesdorff, 2012; Kunda, 2009.

18 Harzing, 1999.

19 Studying 287 headquarters of MNCs in nine countries, Harzing (1999) found that personal control (centralization) was used more by British and German corporations than their Swiss and Swedish counterparts. The latter made much more use of normative control through socialization and building networks for mutual adjustment (controls used infrequently by French and Japanese firms with respect to their subsidiaries). Formalized control through standardization and output control was most strongly employed by UK and German firms, and least by Japanese corporations. Other studies have also found that US firms use extensive output control and Japanese firms use personal control through expatriates (e.g., Chang and Taylor, 1999).

20 Issues related to normative control will be addressed in Chapter 5 (social architecture) and output control in Chapter 7 (performance management).

21 Barham and Heimer, 1998.

22 Harzing, 1999.

23 Singh, J., "GE Healthcare: Innovation for Emerging Markets," INSEAD Case Study, 2011.

24 Morris, Zhong, and Makhija, 2015.

25 "Odebrecht: Principles and values," *The Economist*, August 22, 2015.

26 Brim, 1966.

27 For dimensions of socialization processes see Van Maanen and Schein (1979).

28 See Ashforth *et al.* (2012).

29 Top-down dissemination of values and norms is not limited to meganational firms. For example, Johnson & Johnson's long and successful history of decentralization is firmly anchored in its Credo values—written first in 1943 by the member of the founding family and chairman general R.W. Johnson.

30 Denison and Lief, 2008; Jonsson and Foss, 2011.

31 Evans, 1993.

32 Staber, 2003, p. 416.

33 Corporate rhetoric encouraging employees to transform the world or "with the best" 24/7 is another example of commitment-building rituals common, for example, in companies such as Amazon.

34 As Brewster (1991, p. 33) comments: "For the key managerial postings, at least, it is clear that management in these organizations trust their 'own' people to operate as they are required to do, more than they trust the locals they employ."

35 Hennart, 1991.

36 Japanese subsidiaries abroad often have locals heading functions such as marketing and sales but Japanese nationals in roles demanding close liaison with Tokyo (usually product planning and finance).

37 Egelhoff, 1988; Hennart, 1991.

38 Pucik, 1994.

39 Rudlin (2000), a former manager of a large Japanese trading company, argues that advances in information technology allow Japanese managers to increase the exclusivity of informal communication. In the past, phone conversations in Japanese were at least audible to local staff. While they may not understand, they get an idea that something is going on and follow up with questions. With one-on-one e-mail, the locals are totally excluded.

40 Jay, 1967.

41 Pucik, 1992. Empirical support has been found for differentiating demand-driven and learning-driven assignments—a study of 1,779 assignees found that turnover intentions varied with the nature of the assignment (Stahl *et al.*, 2009).

42 When followed up with yet another international transfer, expatriation can become a career, a pattern not uncommon in many international firms.

43 Brookfield's 2015 Global Mobility Trends Survey.

44 The need for a contingency approach to expatriation was first raised by Mendenhall and Oddou (1985). See also the empirical research of Stahl (2000).

45 Brookfield's 2015 Global Mobility Trends Survey.

46 Black, Gregersen, and Mendenhall, 1992.

47 Some researchers suggest that expatriate failure rates in European multinationals may be lower than in the US because of more effective European expatriate policies (Brewster and Scullion, 1997), better selection (Scullion, 1995), and more emphasis on the value of international experience (Björkman and Gertsen, 1993). An alternative explanation may be that European multinationals accept lower standards of performance to avoid the loss of face involved in a premature return (Scullion, 1995).

48 Harzing, 1995.

49 Brookfield's 2015 Global Mobility Trends Survey.

50 Björkman and Gertsen, 1993; Forster, 1997.

51 Forster, 1997.

52 Brookfield's 2015 Global Mobility Trends Survey.

53 In this respect, diffusion of strikingly similar Apple stores around the world follows a similar logic.

54 www.mcdonalds.com/corp/about/factsheets.

55 The company's legendary founder, Ray Kroc, recognized the power of training. "Hamburger University" (HU) was started in 1961 in Oak Brook, Illinois, only six years after Kroc acquired the business from the McDonald brothers. By 2015, the school had trained more than 330,000 students around the world. Equipped with state-of-the-art technology, it is part business school, part technical workshop, but is mostly a teacher training college. Its students are mainly operating managers with at least 2,000 hours of prior local training, and their mission is to go forth and teach others at home (Wohl, J., "Hamburger University grills students on McDonald's operations," *Chicago Tribune*, April 18, 2015).

56 "McDonald's Franchisee Adds a Personal Touch to Its Services," *Foodservice*, June 2015.

57 *Investor Sheet*, Infosys.com. Retrieved July 27, 2015.

58 For the early history of this joint venture see O'Reilly and Pfeffer (2000).

59 Adler, 1999; Pil and MacDuffie, 1999; and O'Reilly and Pfeffer, 2000.

60 The small number of GM managers assigned to the joint venture seriously impeded transfer of learning back to GM.

61 Wyman, O., "The Harbour Report North America 2008"—available at http://www .reliableplant.com/article.asp?articleid=12134. In 2009, when GM was forced to restructure under a prepackaged bankruptcy process, the company decided to withdraw from the joint venture.

62 James and Jones, 2014.

63 Womack, Jones, and Roos, 1990; MacDuffie, 1995.

64 James and Jones, 2014; Morris and Snell, 2011.

65 Comparative studies of multinationals from different parts of the world have found US corporations to have the highest degree of global standardization of their HR practices (Harzing, 1999; Björkman and Lu, 2001; Ferner *et al.*, 2004).

66 Farndale and Paauwe, 2007.

67 Almond, Edwards, and Clark, 2003.

68 See, for example, Kostova and Roth (2002), Paauwe (2004), Rosenzweig (2006), and Farndale and Paauwe (2007) for discussions of the pressures on multinationals to pursue both global standardization and local responsiveness of HR practices.

69 Ferner, Almond, and Colling, 2005.

70 The reader will find this issue, namely what in the domain of HRM to globalize and what to localize, discussed throughout this book, notably in the chapters on HR practices.

71 Kostova, 1999; Kostova and Roth, 2002. A third element, beyond the implementation and internalization of practices, is their integration with other relevant and related subsidiary practices (see Björkman and Lervik, 2007). The integration of practices refers to the links and connections that develop between the focal practice and the culturally and institutionally established processes and practices in the subsidiary (Lervik, 2005), and is therefore another important sign of successful transfer.

72 Kostova and Roth, 2002, p. 217.

73 Meyer and Rowan, 1977; Kostova and Roth, 2002.

74 Blazejewski, 2006.

75 Ahlvik and Björkman, 2015.

76 "Wal-Mart Finds That Its Formula Doesn't Fit Every Culture," *New York Times*, August 2, 2006.

77 Kobrin, 2015.

78 "When Intel says 'copy exactly,' it means it," *China Daily*, May 30, 2006.

79 Morris and Vanderson, 2015.

80 Zeynep, Corsi, and Dessain, 2010.

81 Kantor and Streitfeld, "Inside Amazon: Wrestling Big Ideas in a Bruising Workplace," *International New York Times*, August 15, 2015.

82 Bartlett and Ghoshal, 1998, p. 122. They distinguish between different types of national subsidiary according to their strategic importance and their level of resources and capabilities—strategic leaders, contributors, implementers, and black holes.

83 Broeckx and Hooijberg, 2007.

84 The concept of "empowerment," with its emotive connotations, has created a great deal of misunderstanding. The best formulation of what this implies is to be found in Mills (1994), who provides the following formula: Empowerment = Goals x Delegated "Respons-ability" x Measurement and Feedback. The term "respons-ability" (our word) means having the necessary skills to respond. This formula emphasizes both the hard and soft elements of empowerment.

85 Galbraith, 1977.

86 This can extend to corporate spin-offs such as the separation of KONE's elevator and cranes businesses (the spin-off of Konecranes from KONE in Finland) and the split between Hewlett-Packard (computers) and Agilent (the original HP instruments business).

87 To cite but three examples of this shift in research focus, in his value-chain analysis Porter argued for the importance of "horizontal strategies," viewing these as the most important contribution HRM makes to the way in which a firm adds value (Porter, 1986). Martinez and Jarillo (1989) reviewed the stream of research on coordination in multinational firms, clearly noting this shift in focus from hierarchic and structural mechanisms to informal and lateral means of coordination. St. John *et al.* (1999) studied how 48 international firms managed links between marketing and manufacturing. They found that firms with relatively simple multidomestic strategies used traditional planning and scheduling methods, while firms with more complex global strategies used a wider variety of coordination tools, including lateral teams and relationships. Firms with the most complex transnational strategies used the widest range of coordination mechanisms.

88 Baker, 1994; Ibarra, 1992.

89 Nohria and Ghoshal, 1997, p. 189. Requisite complexity is a concept borrowed by management theorists from the field of cybernetics (Ashby, 1956).

90 Evans, 1993.

91 Planning becomes learning, to use the image of a former Shell corporate planner (De Geus, 1988). See also Mintzberg (1994).

chapter

4

Structuring Coordination

SUMMARY

Challenge

Traditional tools of top-down control cannot cope with the complexity of organizational demands facing transnational firms

Analysis

Well-managed multinational firms have developed a variety of structural coordination tools:

- Multidimensional structures aligned with the business strategy
- Lateral steering processes that promote accountability at the lowest level possible
- Cross-boundary teams used as basic building blocks of coordination

Solutions

- Ensure that managers *share* responsibility for coordination across business units
- Establish lateral steering roles or mechanisms - such as business coordinators, global account managers, or functional councils
- Develop leaders with ability to steer the business without formal authority
- Train global team members to collaborate effectively across borders
- Provide managers with opportunities to learn to work in "split egg" ways

Integrating Nestlé

In April 2000, Nestlé—the world's largest food and beverage company with 250,000 employees and close to 500 factories in over 80 countries—launched a US$3 billion IT initiative. The Global Business Excellence program (GLOBE) was to transform the Nestlé organization from a loose "federation of independent markets" into a company showing a common face to customers and suppliers around the world.[1]

While the program could nominally be seen as a massive SAP rollout (in itself a complex undertaking), the purpose went far beyond building a new IT platform. Peter Brabeck, the then CEO of Nestlé, was explicit about the final goal:

"I want this to be very clear. With GLOBE we will create common business processes, standardized data, and a common IT infrastructure—but do not think this is an IT initiative. We are going to fundamentally change the way we run this company."

In Brabeck's view, Nestlé's decentralized structure, which had brought the company much success in the past, no longer fitted the new realities of global competition.

Traditionally Nestlé had been structured as a cascading pyramid of major zones and markets—usually countries. Each business was essentially local, neatly aggregated to larger geographical units, all finally coming together in the corporate center. Running alongside this organization in a coordinating role were half a dozen strategic business units, such as beverages, dairy products, and infant nutrition.[2] The role of the business unit managers was to increase integration across geographies with a particular focus on new product development but without profit and loss responsibility.[3]

The company's strong focus on product customization to local tastes was the foundation of Nestlé's success; but this also created duplication and inefficiencies, with sales overhead costs well above its competitors.[4] A fragmented supply chain did not provide the desired economies of scale. Bargaining power with cross-border suppliers and retailers was weak; some large customers had better pricing information about Nestlé products in different markets around the world than the Nestlé central office.

Internal coordination was also difficult, as each country's organization and systems had been operating independently. Identical products had different product codes in different countries, and in HR there was no common grading and compensation system. With different titles for similar positions across countries, it was almost impossible to agree on who was at the same hierarchical level or performed the same job. Even for senior managers, salaries and bonuses were difficult to compare.[5]

The aim of GLOBE was to build a common platform for Nestlé's global operations but the formal structure of the company would remain for the most part configured as a matrix of geographies and businesses. As Nestlé was determined to maintain its focus on local markets, the company did not want to move too far away from its culture of decentralization. However, in order to cope better with the competitive challenges it faced, it had to become more globally connected and aligned.[6]

Nestlé needed to find an alternative route that would balance the benefits of local initiative with global leverage but remain in line with Nestlé's long-standing business principle of "putting people ahead of the systems." Senior management believed that maintaining local decision-making autonomy while simplifying and standardizing core processes would achieve this. By flattening the organization, and assigning more coordinating responsibility to cross-border and cross-functional teams, the company hoped to move away from the vertical hierarchy to a more flexible network structure, which it believed is more suitable to the new generation of company employees.[7]

One of Nestlé's key leverage points for enhancing lateral coordination has been global implementation of common HR processes—from a single worldwide performance management system to comprehensive talent reviews, as well as succession planning based on a common grading system and structured leadership development (for a global talent pool of about 2,200 people). However, this does not mean that Nestlé's corporate HR function rules over local companies by issuing detailed global policy directives. Instead it uses a lot of virtual teamwork to reach a consensus on HR process objectives and tools, thereby working toward consistency and coherence across the world.[8]

OVERVIEW

The Nestlé case illustrates how changes in the global competitive environment have exposed the limits of traditional hierarchic structures to cope with the complexity of international business. The purpose of this chapter is to review how global firms can complement vertical integration with structural elements of horizontal coordination, and the vital role of HRM tools in facilitating this.

Making effective decisions in multidimensional structures requires lateral steering mechanisms that can supplement, if not replace, traditional top-down hierarchical decision-making. Perhaps the best way to address the complex business challenges facing global organizations is through cross-boundary collaboration. Indeed, one might argue that teamwork is a core characteristic of most organizations in the global economy.

MULTIDIMENSIONAL STRUCTURES

In the previous chapter we explained why multidimensional structures are a vital element of coordination in transnational firms. Multidimensional structures have their origins in matrix organization (see the box "The Matrix Heritage"). As multinational organizations expanded globally they were organized by business or product *and* by geography or market.

The Matrix Heritage

Many of the corporations that expanded abroad 50 years ago had multiple product lines and were moving into markets in different regions around the world. Should they organize by worldwide product division or by geographic region?[9] Several US and British companies were inspired by the success of the first matrix organization, NASA, in sending man to the moon.[10] Citibank, Corning, Dow, Exxon, and Shell among others adopted the idea of matrix as a guiding principle for their worldwide organization.

Right from the start, some management scholars urged caution. One study demonstrated that implementation was hindered by traditional management styles,[11] and it was also pointed out that matrix was much more complex than reporting lines. For a matrix to work, it should be built into control and performance appraisal systems, teamwork, conflict resolution mechanisms, relationships, and leadership development, leading to a proposition that matrix has more to do with HRM than it has to do with structure.[12] However, few of the companies that opted early on for the matrix solution had such supporting elements in place.

In these circumstances, most companies found matrix structures difficult. Managers were uneasy about the separation of authority and responsibility. The new arrangements generated power struggles, ambiguity over resource allocation, buck-passing, and dilution of accountability. Worse still, the traditional matrix of product and geography did not account for other important dimensions—corporate functions, market segments, or key customer accounts. In theory, a manager reported to two bosses and conflicts between them would be

reconciled at the apex one level higher up. However, it was not unusual to find companies where managers were reporting to three or four bosses, so that reconciliation or arbitration could only happen at a very senior level. The matrix initiative, originally introduced to help cope with complexity, seemed to be contributing to it.

The difficulties with implementing an effective matrix solution together with the growing importance of speed in global competition led many firms to abandon matrix.[13] While matrix might ensure the consultation necessary for sound decision-making, it was often painfully slow.

Weary of the matrix, other firms attempted to keep control of international activities with central staff. This was particularly true for German and Japanese multinationals that were largely export-oriented with sales subsidiaries abroad. It took a long time to work through decisions in German *Zentralebereiche* (central staff departments), and particularly in Japanese *nemawashi*[14] (negotiation) processes of middle-up consultative decision-making. But the disadvantages were initially outweighed by the quality of decision-making and commitment to implementation that accompanied the consensus-oriented decision-making. The complex consultative processes worked reasonably well as long as everyone involved was German or Japanese.[15]

As with matrix, this approach was initially successful but eventually led to inefficiencies and paralysis, as the staff functions at corporate and divisional levels overexpanded in an attempt to cope with growing coordination needs. Again, speed of decision-making was the Achilles heel.

With some employees reporting to two bosses,[16] such matrix structures were intended to allow a balance of influence between the product (business unit) and market/geography (country) perspectives inside the company. However, global matrix is a difficult structure to maintain because of the inevitable conflict of priorities between the different units of the organization.

Companies using a matrix structure usually attempt to regulate the balance with carefully written rules of engagement, specifying the responsibilities of each role. However, no matter how well defined the responsibilities are, overlaps and tensions are inevitable as the complexity of the business increases. And the distribution of power is mostly vertical—power to one dimension means less power for the other, which contributes to further escalations of conflicts.

The evolution of ABB—a Swiss-based global engineering firm created through a merger of two European competitors—under the leadership of Percy Barnevik is perhaps the best-known illustration of challenges facing a global company attempting to implement a complex matrix organization.[17] Barnevik's vision was to create a global company that would be able to deal effectively with three internal contradictions: being global and local, big and small, and radically decentralized with centralized reporting and control. The key principle was local entrepreneurship, so most decisions were to be done at the lowest possible level in the 5,000 profit centers that become the foundation of the ABB organization.

The company abandoned this matrix ten years later. What went wrong? There were few unifying processes in place, aside from the financial reporting system. Even at a country level there was no common IT, HR, or purchasing. While Barnevik and his team traveled extensively to propagate his vision and ensure knowledge sharing across units, most people operated in business unit silos. Entrepreneurship flourished, but synergies were limited. With time, the complex structure became unwieldy, and costs spiraled out of control.

Barnevik's successor attempted to reestablish discipline by shifting power fully to global businesses. But the businesses had no tools to exercise meaningful influence, and the reorganization resulted in fragmentation and chaos at the operating level. When the next CEO, in the middle of yet another reorganization, finally proceeded to build from the top the core group-wide processes the company needed, their disconnect from operational reality only further deepened organizational paralysis.[18]

Several CEOs—and another major crisis—later, ABB is back to a multidimensional structure—still attempting to match the benefits of "One ABB" with the power of local entrepreneurship. ABB's current multidimensional organization is not a balanced matrix (in fact use of the word "matrix" was banned for a while); product divisions take the lead in business development, and functions are integrated globally, while the role of countries and regions is to create appropriate synergies.

Two Insights Leading to the "Return of Matrix"

Because of highly visible failures, matrix structures were gradually going out of fashion, but the matrix problem was more alive than ever. To be effective, multinationals had to manage two dimensions—or more. Both practitioners and researchers turned their attention to how coordination and collaboration—lateral interactions, mutual adjustments, and teamwork—could provide the flexibility of matrix without its proven disadvantages. Research reviews had shown that there were two dimensions of matrix management:[19]

- *Structure*: The dual or multiple authority relationships (formal vertical reporting lines)
- *Collaboration*: The horizontal communication linkages and teamwork (for example, between product and country managers) that matrix organization fosters

Most of the disadvantages appeared to stem from the former, while most of the advantages originated in the latter.

Two insights followed these observations: the first insight (building on the previous criticism of the matrix approach) was that matrix is difficult to manage unless the organization has well-defined common processes—notably an effective IT infrastructure and HRM system. The second insight was that it is necessary to build collaboration *before* you introduce matrix. These conclusions found support in new ideas in organizational theory about coping with growing demands of information processing and decision-making in complex firms.[20] Organizations require strong capabilities in two areas: first in information processing and second in coordination and teamwork.

Gradually it became clear that the matrix challenges of control and coordination in multinational firms were essentially issues of people and information technology rather than a question of strategy and structure. Matrix, as two leading strategy scholars were later to say, is not a structure, it is a "frame of mind" nurtured more than anything else by careful human resource management.[21] During the last 15 years, matrix has returned in the shape of different multidimensional structures, as described in this chapter, with an added emphasis on horizontal coordination and collaboration within the framework of common processes.[22]

It should be pointed out that managers typically refer to any multidimensional structure as a "matrix." But the emerging multidimensional organizations have often more than two dimensions; product, geography, function, and customer are the dimensions most frequently used and may be also supplier and technology. IBM, one of the most complex multidimensional organizations, is organized around over 40 product groups, geographic regions, technology sectors, as well as strategic business units focused on customer segments, distributors, and suppliers. Also, matrix implies balance between the two dimensions, but this is not necessarily the case in multidimensional organizations.

Today, leading global firms and management scholars alike recognize that vertical structural solutions (balancing power) alone are not an appropriate response to business complexity; they have to be supplemented by complementary horizontal coordination mechanisms.[23] Conversely, the portfolio of coordinating mechanisms should match the specific strategy and governing structure of the organization.

Emerging Forms of Global Multidimensional Structures

Before addressing the specific tools of horizontal coordination, we will first review some of the most distinctive examples of multidimensional structures in global organizations today (see Table 4-1: Configuring the Multidimensional Organization). While all of them reflect the multidimensionality of transnational

TABLE 4-1
Configuring the Multidimensional Organization

Strategic Focus	Organizational Solution
• Leveraging subsidiary competence	• Differentiated network
• Fostering global optimization	• Globally integrated enterprise
• Building customer intimacy and operational efficiency	• Front-back organization

firms, they also respond to different organizational priorities of respective business strategies. In particular, three sets of internal and external factors are instrumental in shaping these new structures:

1. The evolution of capabilities and knowledge within the firm
2. The global drivers of competitive advantage
3. The importance of aligning closely with customers.

It is important to bear in mind that the choice of how to structure the global organization is also heavily influenced by its administrative heritage, that is, its historical development as a multinational firm.[24]

The focus of a global company organized as a **differentiated network** is on leveraging competencies and capabilities initially developed in its local subsidiaries for worldwide advantage. Put simply, it can be described as a *bottom-up* process of business unit globalization. Multidomestic firms with strong local subsidiaries, such as ABB or Nestlé, are typically in the forefront of the move toward a differentiated network. Differences in competitive priorities among key markets may also foster the need for differentiation.

The objective of a company organized as a **globally integrated enterprise** is to achieve competitive advantage by locating specific activities in the best place worldwide and finding ways to link or integrate these activities across the world.[25] In this case, the process of globalization of business activities is *top-down*. Firms such as IBM, CEMEX, or Bharti Airtel are examples of companies that follow such an organizational approach.[26]

The **front-back organization**[27] is another emerging form of a multinational organization. The customer-oriented parts of the company are aligned locally to respond to market needs (the front end) while those parts of the company that may benefit from global synergies are organized along global lines (the back end). This avoids the disadvantages of a full-blown matrix, limiting matrix connections to front- and back-end coordination. Many "international" firms[28] (for example, HP and P&G, and most recently J&J) have been realigning their global organization in this direction.[29]

These three emerging forms are organizational archetypes. A single corporation may contain different archetypes since the choice of an appropriate structure is often made at the business rather than corporate level. In some businesses, the emphasis may be on countries and geographies in order to respond to local opportunities (or political pressures); in others, the aim is to optimize global efficiency and to support new product development. The focus may vary from one business to another and also over time.

From a human resource management perspective, these different organizational forms pose different people challenges, so it is important to understand why these forms emerged and what is necessary to enhance their effectiveness.

Recognizing the Importance of Subsidiaries: The Differentiated Network

Multidomestic companies such as Nestlé grew mainly by investing in the development of local capabilities. The idea behind the differentiated network organization is that these valuable capabilities should no longer be managed solely from a local perspective; subsidiary capabilities should be leveraged regionally and globally, using horizontal coordination.[30]

Rather than simply executing a headquarter-designed strategy in a local context, which is what happens in multidomestic firms, the subsidiaries are now expected to become active contributors to global strategy—even strategic leaders—benefiting from location-specific advantages that can be leveraged across the broader organization. This idea is particularly powerful when a subsidiary has developed an area of excellence geared to the local country's opportunities.[31]

The "center of excellence" concept is integral to the differentiated network organization (although found in other forms of global enterprise as well). A center of excellence is an organizational unit that has been explicitly recognized as a source of value creation. For example, the lead role for Nestlé's core confectionery business is entrusted to the UK subsidiary.[32] Some centers of excellence have developed from long-term experience in dealing with a demanding customer; others derive their unique position from external sources. Among global financial firms, for example, private banking is often run from Switzerland, options and derivatives products from New York, and foreign exchange products from London.[33] In principle, a global firm operating as a differentiated network draws on multiple centers of excellence with supporting capabilities widely dispersed around the world.

One size does not fit all, and so the design may vary from one part of the organization to another. In Nestlé, despite GLOBE's worldwide rollout, some business units are not tied to this platform. For example, the firm's leading market position in China rests on its ability to steer a complex "one country-two systems" organization[34] where some businesses report to global divisions while others are managed locally but all within the GLOBE framework. These are managed side-by-side with global JVs (with a separate operating structure) and several rapidly growing local partnerships. These partnerships, while majority-owned by Nestlé, have retained local top management; and even the corporate language is different—Chinese rather than English.[35] The resulting organization chart is complex (see Figure 4-1 for an overview of the Nestlé China organization) and difficult to steer without strong horizontal linkages.

In terms of the challenges for HRM, trust and collaboration are very important and must be nurtured – in Nestlé China, one senior HR leader is fully dedicated to this role. In ABB, one of the guiding principles was that disagreements between parallel units within the network (for example on internal transfer pricing or product specifications) should be resolved by the managers themselves and not delegated upward to top management. As the company folklore had it, one could ask twice for help, but the third time top management would put someone else in the job who could handle conflict resolution without involving superiors. When senior management intervenes on details and plays the role of arbiter (a problem not unique to ABB or Nestlé), organizational politics kicks in with a vengeance and trust disappears. There is no end to the upward escalation of conflict, and in the end this can paralyze the organization.

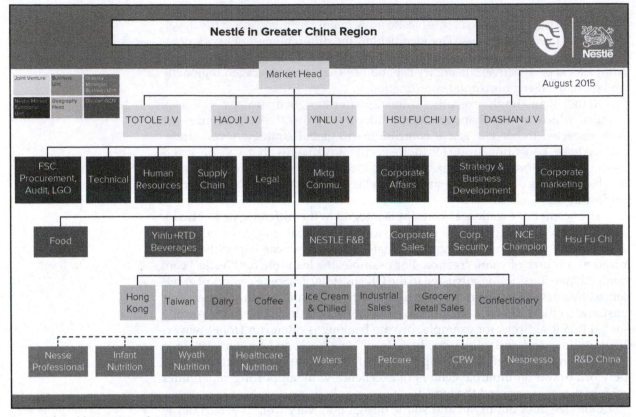

Source: Adapted from company documents

FIGURE 4-1
Nestlé Greater China
Organization Chart

Leveraging Distributed Capabilities: The Globally Integrated Enterprise
According to Sam Palmisano, the former CEO of IBM, the essence of the globally integrated enterprise is a shift in the focus of strategic decision-making "from what products to make to how to make them, from what services to offer to how to deliver them."[36] On the assumption that national boundaries are less and less relevant to corporate practice, organizational capabilities and cost advantages are purposely nurtured for global optimization and leverage. However, in contrast to a traditional meganational firm, these capabilities can be located anywhere, not only in the mother country.

IBM is perhaps the most visible example of a global company pursuing this approach (see Figure 4-2)—self-described as a tightly knit network without a central hub.

For example, IBM spends roughly $40 billion annually on goods and services to run its business. The procurement function is consolidated into three operations centers for America, Asia, and Europe. There is no need for local procurement departments in the 100 and more countries where IBM operates.[37]

Procurement is not the only example. In pursuit of global optimization, all IBM support functions are integrated on a global scale and specialized tasks are outsourced to internal and external experts, who can be located anywhere in the world.[38] As an illustration, the IBM's growth market operations are supported by HR specialists in Manila, accounts receivable are processed in Shanghai, accounting is done in Kuala Lumpur, procurement in Shenzhen, and the customer service help desk is based in Brisbane.[39]

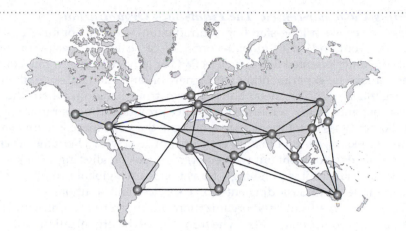

FIGURE 4-2
IBM's Globally Integrated
Enterprise Model

Source: Adapted from IBM, 2009 Annual Report, http//www.ibm.com/annualreport/2009/2009_ibm_annual
.pdf, accessed March 12, 2011.

One factor enabling the development of a globally integrated enterprise is the lowering of trade barriers, which enables a better flow of goods and services across national or regional borders. The second factor is the IT revolution, which allows standardization of business processes across subsidiaries, driving costs down, and measuring profitability where it counts—at the level of every customer.[40] The third—and decisive—factor is the emergence of a global talent pool; expertise and knowledge have no boundaries.

As a result of the interplay of these three factors, companies can treat different functions and operations as discrete parts of the value chain and pull them apart and back together again in most efficient combinations. The decision on how to do this is based on strategic judgments about where the company wants to excel, and where it thinks it is better to leave it to its partners. The responsibility for making this work resides with the specialists in global functions.[41]

In globally integrated firms, operating systems based on global standards link the entire company (including the outsourced elements). When everything is connected, work flows to places where it will be done best; that is, most efficiently and with the highest value added. And the workforce may move as well: the IBM global delivery center in Brno (Czech Republic) numbers 70 different nationalities among the more than 3,000 employees.[42]

Implementing the globally integrated enterprise poses a number of people management challenges, notably the need for a globalized approach to talent and workforce management. Also, for operating managers, skills in working laterally without authority are essential as most of the resources they need to deliver results lie outside their formal responsibility. A collaborative leadership style and strong partnering skills are vital. For employees, global opportunities are available, but they are also exposed to worldwide competition for their work. They must have tools at their disposal for rapid upgrading and development of skills, as well as the ability to work anywhere, regardless of location. For this reason, training and development are fundamental pillars of the IBM's HR strategy.[43] All this requires a lot of cross-border coordination and within-border flexibility.[44]

Becoming Customer-centric: The Front-Back Organization

In order to resolve a long-standing contradiction—how to combine customer focus (the front end) with global economies of scale (the back end)—some global consumer-oriented firms, such as P&G or J&J, are trying to gain competitive advantage by experimenting with a new organizational design: the front-back organization.[45] The metaphor is drawn from banking, where the front office is customer facing, while the back office provides administrative support. Several other types of companies are moving in the same direction, for example Belgium's Bekaert, a leader in the steel wire industry, with a heritage of centralized product development but with emerging focus on aligning with key local customers; or HP, as it is pursuing a transition from a global product-centered business model to value adding enterprise services and solutions.

The core of the front-back organization is a dual structure in which both halves are multifunctional units.[46] The front half of the organization (outside)—marketing, sales, and customer service—is focused on customer needs and market opportunities (usually organized around specific customer segments or markets). The back half (inside)—R&D, manufacturing, and supply chain functions—is focused on global efficiency and product excellence (usually organized along business and functional lines). P&G believes that such organization structure helps to combine global scale benefits with local focus (see Figure 4-3 for a schematic illustration of P&G organization).

Front-back organization is not aiming to achieve a balance. It is fundamentally a customer-centric, not product-centric, design. Even for the back-end, the primary objective is maximizing end-user benefits. Nor is it a matrix structure. There is a clear separation between global product divisions, market-facing units, and supporting global functions, each with their own P&L and limited multiple reporting. The different parts of the organization usually come together on the organization chart only at the very top of the senior executive team, but this is complemented with extensive lateral linkages between businesses, countries, and functions.

In the telecommunication equipment business, Nokia[47] moved from being product-centric to customer-centric when telecommunications around the world

FIGURE 4-3
P&G's Model of Global
Organization

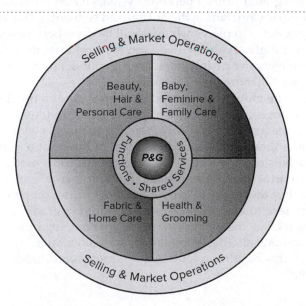

Source: Adapted from company documents

became deregulated, and operators such as China Mobile or Vodafone looked for support in designing, building, and maintaining their networks. Nokia responded by creating a customer operation division in which teams—reporting to account managers—were charged with providing total solutions (products and services) for specific customers, while the rest of the firm was organized along product or functional lines. Each unit functioned like a small consulting firm that could react quickly to customer demand. The key measurement was customer satisfaction and the share of customer business obtained by Nokia. This encouraged employees to do what the customer wanted, including installing equipment from competitors if the customer's specification demanded it.[48]

A key challenge facing front-back organizations is that they demand a high degree of coordination as well as skill in contention management. When HP, with its long history of decentralization, launched its attempt to implement a front-back organization in the early 2000s, many observers were doubtful about its chances of success. *BusinessWeek* commented that the company was "betting on an approach so radical that experts say it has never been done before at a company of HP's size and complexity."[49] It took HP five years and a new CEO to get the new organization firmly in place. Similar challenges were encountered by other firms moving toward this kind of model, and even widely admired multinational companies such as P&G aborted their original radical front-back design for a more modest organizational overhaul.

For the HR professionals, implementing a front-back organization brings a range of challenges, from the development of senior executives capable of working comfortably with the tensions embedded in this design, to the design of a performance management system that focuses either on the customer or on the product (depending on the unit in the firm), while at the same time supporting collaborative behavior. Ideally, this kind of organization is ambidextrous[50]—local *and* global, excelling at short-term execution while pursuing the long-term vision of creating new markets—not an easy task without a full line of other coordinating mechanisms.

Leadership Implications

All of these new organizational forms are flatter than the traditional hierarchic organization, not only because there are fewer hierarchical levels but also because—for reasons of speed—decision-making is less centralized than in more vertically oriented firms.

Because of this emphasis on bringing decision-making closer to where decisions need to be made in the organization, there is a popular belief that networks and hierarchy are opposites and that the former are replacing the latter. This is not at all the case. Networks need some form of hierarchic leadership authority. Without strong leadership to establish clear goals to which people are committed, networks can become debating clubs, with the risk that the "extreme of chaos" could replace the other "extreme of excessive order."[51]

However, networks, along with leadership style and the underlying skills needed, do transform the nature of leadership. As we pointed out earlier, enabling or coaching management replaces the traditional command-and-control approach, and skills in influence and collaboration become vital. Similarly, while strong headquarters leadership is needed, this is no longer based on the authority to tell people what to do, since headquarters has less and less of a monopoly on expertise and experience.

Headquarters managers have to provide what we call network leadership (sometimes referred to as parenting[52]), for example, bringing value to the network by building cross-border links between affiliates in order to reap the benefits of coordination and knowledge sharing. Network leadership at the center also involves leveraging functional capability, providing specialist expertise that is well adapted to the different parts of the enterprise.[53] For managers with operating responsibilities within the network the key issue is aligning responsibility and accountability. The implications are discussed further in connection with the management of leadership transitions in Chapter 8.

Aligning Responsibility and Accountability

In multidimensional organizations, managers not only are responsible for achieving results for their own units but also have shared accountability for successful strategy implementation across units. Viewed with the lens of hierarchic control, the overlapping accountability could be seen as a problem, although from the perspective of horizontal coordination, it is quite natural. While accountability can be shared, it cannot be delegated (or avoided), and it often includes an obligation to monitor and challenge others. Nestlé's conceptualization of the responsibility and accountability interface for senior managers is presented in Figure 4-4.

The accountability of managers at Nestlé goes beyond their own area of responsibility and may include areas that they should influence but cannot directly impact through their authority. In global firms with multidimensional structures, this means that managers have to take into account the perspectives of other relevant actors before taking decisions in their areas of responsibility. All of this requires transparency in goals and results, rigorous but practical decision-making tools to align who is responsible for what (see the box "Clarifying Roles and Responsibilities"), and not the least a close alignment with people strategies—from talent development to performance management.

FIGURE 4-4
Responsibility and Accountability at Nestlé

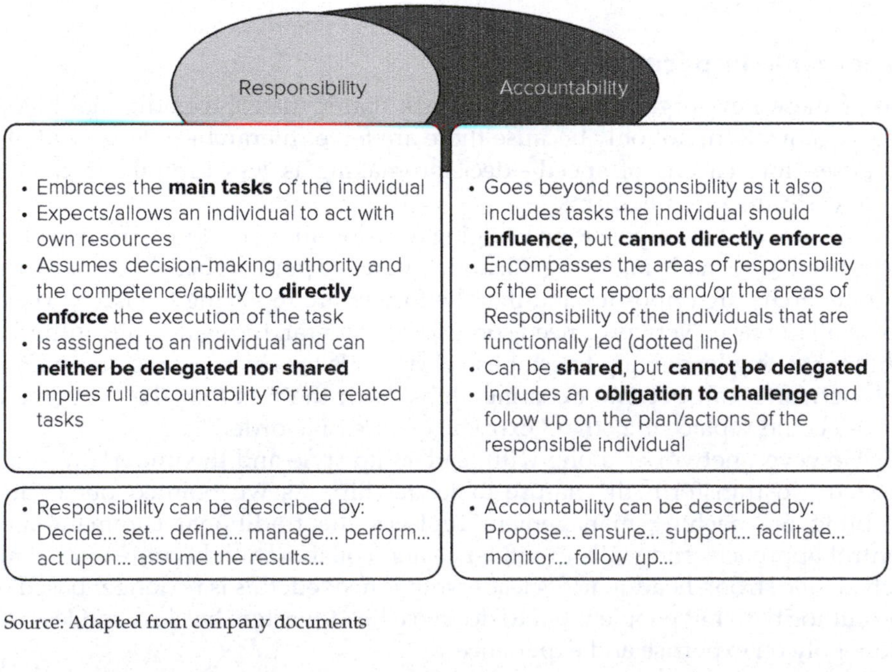

Responsibility	Accountability
• Embraces the **main tasks** of the individual • Expects/allows an individual to act with own resources • Assumes decision-making authority and the competence/ability to **directly enforce** the execution of the task • Is assigned to an individual and can **neither be delegated nor shared** • Implies full accountability for the related tasks	• Goes beyond responsibility as it also includes tasks the individual should **influence**, but **cannot directly enforce** • Encompasses the areas of responsibility of the direct reports and/or the areas of Responsibility of the individuals that are functionally led (dotted line) • Can be **shared**, but **cannot be delegated** • Includes an **obligation to challenge** and follow up on the plan/actions of the responsible individual
• Responsibility can be described by: Decide... set... define... manage... perform... act upon... assume the results...	• Accountability can be described by: Propose... ensure... support... facilitate... monitor... follow up...

Source: Adapted from company documents

Clarifying Roles and Responsibilities

Roles and responsibilities in a multidimensional organization are often unclear; at one extreme, nobody feels responsible for decision-making, at the other extreme everyone wants to be involved. Drawing on project management techniques, a frequently used tool for clarification is the responsibility chart (known as a RACI chart), showing who is responsible (R), who should approve (A), who should be consulted (C), and who should be informed (I).

For example, a global product launch requires decisions and consultations on product design, packaging, sales forecasts, and pricing—involving different regions, sales and marketing functions, and other corporate functions including senior management. The process starts with a facilitator listing the decision areas and the respective roles on a chart that is completed by the different actors; then they all meet for a half day (typically starting with completely divergent views) to reach agreement on roles and responsibilities.

Sources: J. Galbraith, *Designing Matrix Organizations That Actually Work* (San Francisco: Jossey-Bass, 2009) and P. Rogers and M.W. Blenko, "Who has the D?: How clear decision roles enhance organizational performance," *Harvard Business Review* (January 2006).

LATERAL STEERING TOOLS

As pointed out above, past research has shown that effective multidimensional organizations require and depend on horizontal linkages to coordinate activities and decisions across organizational boundaries. Given the complexity of decision-making in multidimensional organizations, it would often be inappropriate if go or no-go, resourcing, and other key decisions were taken without consulting different perspectives. Lateral steering can facilitate cross-boundary collaboration to coordinate regionally, to manage the introduction of a new technology, or to tackle other complex problems—all without introducing the complexities of a vertical structure. And most importantly, lateral steering can increase commitment to action, to the extent that key actors can be involved as members of the group (see the Box "The Global Ocean Trade Management Team at WWL").

Other benefits of lateral steering are flexibility and avoidance of formal bureaucracy. While it is difficult—and slow—to change the structure of an organization, lateral roles or steering groups can be set up and disbanded from one day to the next as priorities emerge and change. The composition of the steering groups can also shift, along with the priorities. For example, a Scandinavian firm that is organized on worldwide product lines decided that its operations in Asia were of strategic importance and needed greater coordination across businesses, as well as careful resourcing. Within a few weeks it set up an Asian board, consisting of the COO, the heads of two divisions active in Asia, and three key individuals from its Asian operations. Projects that were floundering now came under the supervision of this board, and new projects were set up. When the projects moved to the implementation stage, the internal board disbanded and passed the responsibility on to operational executives.

Lateral steering can take many different shapes and forms—as internal boards, formal or informal steering groups, functional councils, product

The Global Ocean Trade Management Team at WWL

WWL, a logistics company based in Oslo, is the world's leading car carrier. Its ocean transportation business is divided into six major trades, each controlling shipments from one continent to another, with each trade manager having full P&L responsibility for the specific trade. Trade managers report to respective heads of regions. At the same time, all trades are linked to each other. A ship bringing cars from Japan to the US should continue taking US cargo to Europe and finally European cars to Asia. The key to WWL's business success is optimization of capacity utilization across the whole fleet, taking into account differences in profit margins on different trades and customers.

In theory, the optimal solution could be calculated and imposed from the center, and until recently this was the way the business was run. However, as the business grew and became more complex, this centralized approach was destroying local accountability and initiative toward customers, who are primarily local. Today, it is the collective role of the global ocean team (composed of all trade managers) to coordinate among the different trades, so that both global and regional priorities can be optimized. The team meets face to face several times a year, but it is continuously in touch by e-mail and teleconferencing.

development committees, strategic development councils, and regional boards. Alternatively, the steering group may be a single person, for example someone who has vertical functional responsibility for a business unit but also horizontal responsibility across businesses in a region. The purposes of both forms of lateral steering are complementary and most multinational firms use a combination of the two. We will start our discussion with individual coordinating roles, moving on to team-based steering in the second part of this section.

Lateral Leadership Roles

Cross-border brokering and integrating roles are often assumed by individuals. In global firms, these managers will hold titles like project manager, program manager, global account manager, or process owner. But, regardless of title, they all have two common features. First, they are responsible for decisions in a specific domain, which they implement through coordination across different units. Second, they execute their role with little formal authority, since authority remains with the line organization.[54] As shown in Table 4-2, in most

TABLE 4-2
Examples of Lateral Leadership Roles

Leadership Role	Objectives
Business/area coordinators	Coordinate among units that report to different leaders, facilitate efficient resource utilization, and fill the alignment gaps that the formal structure does not cover.
Global competence leaders	Coordinate development of competencies required by current and future business strategy and ensure that accumulated knowledge is harnessed effectively.
Global account managers	Managing the interfaces between important customers and the different units of the global firm across various geographies and the value chain.
Alliance managers	Appointed on a corporate level, responsible for planning, negotiating, and implementing alliances (discussed in Chapter 13).

global firms there are at least four critical operational domains that may require lateral leadership.

Business/Area Coordinators

The role of business, product, or area coordinators is to coordinate and optimize regional or global activities, from sourcing and product development to marketing and supply chain management.[55] Some are focused externally, aligning the organization toward vendors or customers; others are focused on creating synergies inside the firm.

The nature of the role depends on the configuration of company activities. In Nestlé, business unit managers (Nestlé's term for business coordinators) do not manage a business in a specific geography but concentrate on the global business as a whole. Most Nestlé profit centers still focus on markets (countries), and the coordinators exert influence through participation in the planning process, as well as through control over product development and new product launches. Product specialists in W.L. Gore perform a similar horizontal alignment function.[56]

At Toyota, the role of coordinators is to link overseas operations to the parent firm, bridging the language and cultural barriers for local unit managers. Coordinators are responsible for facilitating access to global resources, ensuring the horizontal flow of information with other parts of the company, and alignment of local operations with the company culture (we will return to this issue in the next chapter).

As with any coordinating role, the power and legitimacy associated with the position matters a great deal. But power does not need to be overt; Nestlé's business coordinators are traditionally recruited from among the most accomplished country leaders. With proper staffing, coordinators can exert influence even when they have no formal authority because they are effective at influencing the behavior of others. Good coordinators know the business and use their networking skills to obtain the information they need and their personal credibility to get things done.

Global Competence Managers

Functional managers have long been recognized as important for the coordination of activities in global firms, especially with respect to facilitating communication among dispersed functional specialists, assuring timely diffusion of best practices and promoting innovation within a particular discipline.[57] However, there is one important dimension of functional responsibility, closely connected to human resource management, which often requires a dedicated role, namely developing new capabilities. Consider the following example.

A Japanese manufacturing company expanded rapidly over the last decade, building satellite plants in emerging regions of the world such as China and Eastern Europe. However, new plants were invariably completed at a cost higher than the budget, and they were slow in reaching the expected level of performance. Analyzing the cause, the company discovered that each project was handled as a one-off, essentially a learning assignment for some of their high potential managers. Today, as the company continues to expand, it considers new plant construction and start-ups as a fundamental capability, with a dedicated manager (seated in the global manufacturing function) responsible for ensuring that each project is staffed with an appropriate mix of experience.

A global competence manager is responsible for aligning the company business strategy with competence development within the function. It is one thing to declare that the company is going to expand in Asia; however, it is far from simple to ensure that company has the talent and capability on the ground to make this happen. Competence managers look ahead at the nature of the business challenge, and together with the HR function they design appropriate steps to fill any possible gaps. This might include attracting employees with new skills to the organization, as well as making sure that existing competencies are retained as the company evolves.

A complementary area of responsibility is to look after the long-term health of the function. This happens at Shell, for example, a company with global competence managers embedded in most professional functions, including HR. These managers are members of senior leadership teams and assume responsibility for a number of operational tasks in global talent management—making sure that the function attracts and develops a sufficient number of young high potential graduates, facilitating opportunities for cross-border experience, and, in general, ensuring that the function has the competencies to deliver on business expectations. Career managers at Michelin perform a similar role, although they also take care of specific talent pools.[58]

Global Account Managers

The scope of operations of customers in many industries, such as automobiles, IT service, and telecommunications, is increasingly global. Customers demand common and consistent quality and delivery standards across all these operations worldwide, global (lowest possible) pricing, and support in all locations. To respond to these demands, many companies have implemented global account management, with the objective of presenting one face to the customer. These managers coordinate across businesses and geographies and provide a voice for the customer inside the organization.[59] Some companies establish global account structures to differentiate themselves from the competition by developing long-term relationships with their key customers.

There are three generic approaches to the design of global account management, depending on how the firm manages the balance between global and local responsibility for the customer interface.[60] In the first, ownership of the customer and P&L stay with the country; the global account manager plays the role of cross-country coordinator, information provider, and influencer. The second and probably most common approach is a matrix, where an account manager reports both to the local sales organization and to a corporate global account management function. For both these approaches, managers in global account roles have responsibility and accountability for the client but no formal power or independent resources. Only in the third approach—still rare but increasing in frequency—does the balance of power lie with the global account manager. This structure may be appropriate if global customers are seen as more important than local sales.

Implementing global account management can be long and painful because it adds a whole layer of complexity to the organization. Even more importantly, it usually involves shifting the balance of power within the global organization, and therefore meeting resistance (see the box "Implementing Global Account Management").

Implementing Global Account Management

Implementing a global account structure is a complex process. As far as time and deliverables are concerned, targets should be realistic.

- Historically, the best customers are often close to their local suppliers and value this relationship. Gaining the necessary cooperation from local subsidiaries is therefore an important early step in the implementation process. It is advisable to involve local managers in setting up global accounts.
- The shift in power between countries and global accounts will have an impact on firm culture. Companies must put in place appropriate policies and systems to support this transition, not least in human resources. Senior executives must be seen to support the change.

- The global account manager is not a salesperson. The role is essentially internal—communicating, facilitating, and coordinating—not external. Selecting individuals with the skills and competencies that fit this role is the foundation for effective global account management.
- Training global account managers requires appropriate resource. IBM invests in training of account managers at the same level as developing senior executives.

Sources: J. Birkinshaw and J. DiStefano, "Global account management: New structures, new tasks," In *The Blackwell Handbook of Global Management: A Guide to Managing Complexity*, ed. H.W. Lane et al. (Oxford: Blackwell Publishing, 2004); G.S. Yip and A.J.M. Bink, "Managing global accounts," *Harvard Business Review* (September 2007).

From an HR perspective, the key issues relating to global account management are selection, performance management, and training/development. Deep knowledge of the business, interpersonal skills, cross-cultural communication skills, and comfort in leading without authority are some of the key criteria for selecting managers for this role. In terms of performance management, while maximizing the revenue flow is as important as it is in any other sales and marketing role, other soft factors such as the quality of the relationship with the customer should also be taken into consideration.

Lateral Steering Groups

The second important instrument of lateral coordination—cross-border steering groups—includes cross-regional business teams, strategic development councils, product development committees, and regional management boards, as well as various other formal and informal steering groups. While the structure of the firm may be quite simple, cross-boundary steering groups help to align the organization by providing platforms to bring a variety of perspectives to bear on issues in the steering group's area of responsibility.

Using cross-boundary groups to steer strategic or operational projects or problems provides flexibility in the governance of the transnational firm.[61] Cross-border steering groups can help the firm to coordinate globally or regionally to launch a business initiative, manage the introduction of a new technology, align and standardize processes across various boundaries, and tackle other complex problems—all without introducing the complexities of a matrix structure. Such groups can also manage emerging areas of business or nurture new strategic activities until they are large enough to become a part of the mainstream organization.

Cisco is a global company that has embraced the steering group concept. Under the banner of "speed, skill, flexibility" the company coordinates its global operations with three business councils at the VP level to focus on product decisions, 15 boards to facilitate coordination among functions, and many working groups below to execute and implement the decisions taken.[62] The steering group idea took off when the senior executives realized that the company's functional structure precluded the company from moving quickly into new markets. Putting managers in cross-functional and cross-regional teams helped to break down traditional silos and led to faster decision-making. Lifelike videoconferencing and social media are widely used to share information, avoid duplication, and coordinate activities. However, not all managers made the transition to the new style of work; as many as 20 percent of Cisco senior executives could not handle the new requirements or did not accept the revamped compensation system tied to teamwork.[63]

While one purpose of a steering group is to engage multiple perspectives in decision-making, groups need to stay small to be effective. Steering groups are not representational committees; those who have tried to run complex companies by committee have usually failed. Also, the roles and responsibilities of steering boards and councils have to be clearly defined and well communicated throughout the company.

Some cross-border steering groups, such as business coordination teams and functional councils discussed below, are set up to complement the formal organization. Other global teams are temporary, created to address specific operational problems by mobilizing the collaborative energy of employees whose talents and knowledge are most relevant to the issue at hand.

Business Coordination Teams

Business and cross-functional coordination teams are typically set up to supplement a traditional matrix, for example, to integrate product strategies across regions by linking marketing and supply chain units, to launch a new product in multiple countries, or to service global accounts when an account manager's role is not sufficient. A coordination team may have access to its own resources, as well as responsibility for achieving specific objectives. The team members are appointed by senior management, which gives them authority and legitimacy.

In order to maximize the benefits of the Renault and Nissan alliance, cross-company teams (CCTs) and cross-functional teams (CFTs) were introduced by Carlos Ghosn after his appointment as Nissan's CEO. [64] The role of the CCTs (with the chair of each team coming from Renault and vice-chair from Nissan, or vice versa) was to coordinate operations and to search for synergies between the two firms. The mission of the CFTs was to streamline processes in specific functional areas, such as purchasing, and sales and marketing. The CFTs were limited to ten members to facilitate fast action, but they were supported by sub-teams set up to explore specific issues and to work out action plans. Both CCTs and CFTs are now a part of the permanent governance structure of the Renault–Nissan alliance, complemented by a small group of alliance functional directors responsible for accelerating synergies and best-practice sharing.

Regional management is one area where business coordination teams are used with increased frequency as part of a transition from a multidomestic to a regional structure. GE grew in this way to become one of the largest companies in Europe with over $40 billion in local revenues, although it has only recently established a European head office. All necessary coordination was implemented through horizontal councils and task forces with limited budgets and no formal resources. Not surprisingly, nomination to any of these coordinating bodies was a badge of honor for any up-and-coming GE executive.

Functional Councils

In many global firms, functional councils perform a number of essential coordinating and governance roles.[65] The role of such councils is first and foremost to align functional and business strategy, a critical task when business units are operating globally while functions are organized locally. The councils set global priorities for the function and monitor implementation. They can also drive standardization of practices and processes, which increases efficiency by reducing unnecessary duplication. If established at an operating level, these councils can be a good vehicle for communication and sharing best practices to develop and leverage functional capabilities worldwide.

Functional councils are increasingly used to steer the global HR function in large complex companies like ABB, P&G, and Shell. Keeping them small to maintain focus, these councils might consist of managers heading key expertise areas in the head office, HR leaders from regions or lead countries, and HR managers from the business divisions. Similar councils may be cascaded down to regions or even countries. One of the important roles of such councils at intermediate levels is to monitor the performance of high potential employees and provide them with opportunities for career development.

Although one advantage of steering groups is flexibility, their roles and responsibilities need to be clearly defined and well communicated to ensure that decisions can be taken quickly. Accountability, with clear deliverables, is essential; otherwise there is a risk that steering groups will become a drain on people's time and energy or bureaucratic representational committees with no credibility and little influence. As Cisco has learned, alignment with human resource practices is essential.

Senior management must actively encourage, recognize, and reward horizontal collaboration. Performance management becomes an essential tool, since objectives need to be aligned and decisions executed across borders. The selection and development of leaders and steering group members should reflect the requirements facing organizations relying on strong horizontal coordination.

Lateral Leadership Competencies

Probably the most important distinction between staffing vertical and horizontal structures is that in vertical structures, the authority vested in a position defines what the occupant of the role can do, while in a lateral structure it is *who* is in the job that will determine what gets done. Essentially, authority comes from the person in the job. What do we know about leadership competencies essential for effective lateral coordination? Table 4-3 provides a summary of some of the key skills.

Managers in lateral leadership positions usually have a mix of functional and interpersonal competencies, ranging from technical expertise and analytical skills to communication and cross-cultural skills. As they don't have large budgets, staff, or direct authority over resource allocation, they have to rely on persuading and influencing networks of people inside and outside the firm; so credibility and integrity are essential for this role. The ability to assume responsibility without full authority and effectiveness in mobilizing resources across organizational boundaries are another important competencies for lateral leaders.

TABLE 4–3
Lateral Leadership Competencies

- Assuming responsibility without authority
- Effectiveness in mobilizing resources across the organization
- Skill in managing conflicts and steering through tensions
- Working proactively under ambiguity
- High degree of cultural flexibility and adaptability
- Experience and ability to work virtually
- Ability to build trust through professional credibility and personal integrity

Developing the Necessary Social Understanding and Networks

To be effective, lateral leaders require an in-depth understanding of the organization. Because of the tacit nature of knowledge required to be an effective lateral leader, most companies try to grow their own.[66]

One of the best ways of developing the coordination skills of lateral leaders is through various forms of international assignment, especially if they are properly structured around the learning dimensions of the expatriate role.[67] The value of mobility can be further enhanced through global and regional meetings, participation in international projects, social gatherings, and training events that deepen personal ties. And since experience gained in international assignments develops horizontal coordination, an organization should have incentive and reward systems to make these assignments attractive.

The success of lateral design depends a great deal on the depth and quality of the company's social capital—in essence, the network of links between people in the organization. In Chapter 5, we will elaborate on the contribution of social capital to horizontal coordination.

BUILDING CROSS-BORDER TEAMS

Cross-border teams (often called global teams) are a fundamental coordination mechanism in transnational companies as they provide a way of tapping into the diversity of perspectives and experiences residing in different parts of a multinational. Like any other team, a cross-border team can be defined as a small number of people with complementary skills who are committed to a common purpose, with a set of performance goals for which they hold themselves accountable.[68] However, cross-border teams also face the challenge of managing cultural diversity and coping with virtuality, as members are located in different parts of the organization.[69]

Cross-border teams can bring together the best people in an organization to work on a specific task without having to consider where those members are located. They can also draw on wider networks of information and expertise.[70] Instead of an army of headquarter staffers, a few network leaders are needed to form a cross-border team for a specific purpose, with appropriate members drawn from units with relevant expertise. Such teams can drive change fast by cutting across layers and boundaries. Speed is a critical advantage of these teams; they can be put together quickly, and their composition can be changed equally rapidly if needed, providing firms with invaluable flexibility.

Because the team members typically share neither a common socialization nor a common location, creating effective cross-border teams has turned out to be more difficult than expected.[71] Geographic and cultural distance interact to create obstacles to team performance,[72] and much of our discussion below will focus on the particular challenges in teams that work virtually to a greater or lesser extent.

There is some evidence that the effectiveness of the transnational team is likely to be bipolar—either disastrous or superb—whereas national teams are more likely to be simply satisfactory.[73] On the one hand, there is a higher probability of relational conflict in the multinational team, associated with hostility, distrust, cynicism, and apathy. If the differences are left unmanaged, the team may blow up, compromise, or fizzle out. On the other hand, multicultural teams can be very effective because of the higher levels of cognitive conflict—complementary differences in knowledge, perspectives, and assumptions.[74] There is evidence that cross-national teams take significantly longer to reach decisions but that they consider a wider range of options than homogeneous teams.[75]

Foundations for Global Teamwork

Teamwork within a unit is difficult enough, and the obstacles multiply with international and virtual teams.[76] Below are several enabling factors and obstacles to the establishment of effective cross-boundary teamwork that are particularly relevant for international HRM.

Clarity on Goals and Deliverables

One of the most ubiquitous findings about cross-border teamwork is that success depends on the clarity of the task and goals.[77] Clear goals and deliverables distinguish a team or a project group from a committee. If the mandate remains fuzzy, as is often the case initially, the project group risks developing into a time-wasting talk shop, no matter how important its mission. Since most team members will typically have their own operational roles to undertake, lack of clarity undermines commitment to the project and creates a self-fulfilling prophecy. Shell, a company with substantial experience with global teams, encourages clarifying goals by insisting that all such groups should prepare their brief and obtain buy-in for it from appropriate sponsors.

Over-ambition is a related trap, setting up too many cross-border groups that overstretch the organization. The difficulties facing the specialty chemicals division of a European firm illustrate this problem. The division grew organically, complemented by a number of acquisitions. In the words of its HR director:

> There was a clear need for consolidation, which initially took the shape of a series of conferences, internal seminars and workshops. These started to break down some of the barriers, and then we set up a series of project groups to work through challenges that had been identified by senior management. With hindsight, we were too ambitious—there were about 20 project groups and this overloaded the organization. Five or six were successful, but many developed into time-consuming discussions that led nowhere. A certain cynicism started to prevail because the many failures drowned out the successes. This problem remains today because no one really believes in collaboration.

There is some evidence that larger, critical projects (in relation to the size of the business) are more likely to succeed than smaller projects because they receive more attention and sponsorship from senior management.[78] The latter are forgotten in the allocation of necessary resources. It is also important to ensure that successful cross-border projects gain sufficient internal visibility.

Importance of Staffing

Cross-boundary teams are often put together to provide diversity of perspectives, so selecting people to work in the team involves balancing multiple criteria, such as technical or functional skills, representation of different parts of the firm, and the dual interests of global integration and local responsiveness. However, it is difficult to incorporate all this diversity because team size is limited. There are also arguments for taking personal characteristics into account, like cross-cultural sensitivity, emotional self-control, and the ability to work autonomously.[79]

The internal difficulties of team management, as well as cost and scheduling problems, appear to grow exponentially with the size of the team. Psychologists suggest that the optimal number of people in a team is typically five to nine and never more than 10 to 15.[80] Where technical constraints argue for larger teams, the task has to be structured so that it can be broken down into work for subgroups.

Understaffing to the point where the team does not have members with necessary perspective and experience is dangerous, but overstaffing also has serious drawbacks. One of the paradoxes of staffing project teams is that some of the most energized and committed groups are those where the members complain about being overworked and understaffed. This has been called "optimal under-manning" or "n-minus one staffing," keeping the team lean and mean rather than representational and consequently bureaucratic.[81] Another paradox is that the available people are rarely the right people; indeed, this is probably precisely why they are available. In this sense, the formation of a project team is a political process, as the box outlining "Staffing Nestlé's GLOBE" illustrates.

Staffing Nestlé's GLOBE

Nestlé's GLOBE team was formed in April 2000. The whole team was expected to grow to about 300 professionals at its peak, supported by scores of outside consultants. At the core, however, the project would be led by a small leadership group of fewer than a dozen managers.

Thirty-nine-year-old Chris Johnson, previously responsible for Nestlé's business in Taiwan and without any direct IT experience, was nominated to head up the GLOBE team. He would also become the youngest member of Nestlé's group management, the team of nine top executives heading the company, for the duration of his appointment as the head of GLOBE. He reported to the CFO of the company.

Chris's boss provided him with a short list of people he recommended for the GLOBE core leadership group. Some of them reported to the CFO, and some worked in the IT department at headquarters and had been involved in previous integration projects that had failed. Some were very experienced but close to retirement, and others, according to Chris's peers, were not well respected in the markets.

As Chris was considering whom to select, he learned that several of these candidates had already been promised a position on the GLOBE team. Chris now had to decide what to do next. Accept the CFO's recommendations in spite of his doubts? Find a compromise? Reject all candidates in whom he had no confidence?

Chris Johnson decided to confront his boss: "Either I pick the people or I quit!" It was the only time during the GLOBE project that he laid it on the line; as he saw it, it was a way of telling everyone that he would take full responsibility for the success or failure of the GLOBE project.

Sources: J.P. Killing, "Nestlé's Globe Program (A): The Early Months," Case study no. IMD-3-1336; and Video, IMD, Lausanne, 2003.

When individuals see a successful project forming, they are eager to join it—and conversely they are quick to jump ship if it looks as though it will flounder.

The members of cross-border teams are responsible for testing and probing with their own parts of the organization to ensure effective buy-in.[82] This means that their personal credibility with their own units in the firm must be high. Team members have to be able to command the time and attention of people outside of the team over whom they may have no direct authority, but whose support is essential.

Global Teamwork Builds on Relationships

Teams are chosen to confront complex problems and conflicting pressures, and there is widespread agreement from both research and experience that personal relationships facilitate the working of international teams. There will always be cultural differences of one type or another, even between people of the same nationality. Without personal ties, these will invariably handicap the task. Therefore, in the start-up phase it is important to commit time to building linkages face to face.

High-quality relationships characterized by trust and respect, cooperation, and commitment are important in all teams but even more so in virtual teams.[83] And cross-border teams must pay additional attention to relationship-building, since identity, cooperation and trust are not easy to build and maintain virtually.

Research shows that team members tend to begin their work together with a basic willingness to trust each other in order to get the work done, though such "swift trust" is also relatively fragile.[84]

Working in Cross-Border Teams

Many lessons on working in face-to-face teams also apply to virtual teams. However, the absence of face-to-face, co-located contact, and the fact that team members come from different contexts, puts additional emphasis on appropriate communication, managing conflict, team leadership, appraising and rewarding team performance, and quality of team learning processes—all part of the HRM domain.[85]

Communication

Some studies suggest that electronic mail increases the quantity of communication but lowers its quality. There is substantial evidence that electronic communication is less effective with ambiguous or complex tasks where there is no neat technical answer, and when negotiating interpersonal or complex technical conflicts.[86] The more complex the team project, the more important it becomes to pay attention to building trust and face-to-face relationships, as discussed above. In a study of global R&D management in 14 multinational enterprises, the senior product development manager of the company with the most sophisticated electronic communications commented:

> Videoconferencing, integrated CAD/CAM databases, electronic mail, and intensive jet travel all contribute to lowering the communication barriers. All things considered, however, the most effective communication, especially in the beginning of a project, is a handshake across a table to build mutual trust and confidence. Then and only then can electronic tools be really effective.[87]

The communication challenges faced by virtual team members come from two main sources.[88] First, because any technology is lower in richness and social presence than face-to-face interaction, team members lose much of the contextual information that they usually rely on to understand each other well. Second, most electronic communications are asynchronous—there is a lag time between the exchange of messages, reducing the immediacy and efficacy of feedback. This is exacerbated further by communications across time zones.

In some ways, intercultural communication can be more effective when it is written rather than oral. E-mail can help those who prefer the written word; it gives them time to digest and think through a reply. In many cultures, people prefer working through the written word, and even within the same culture, some people prefer writing to speaking.[89]

The complementarity of electronic and face-to-face communications is well summarized in this quote from one of the pioneering books on network organization:

> What the electronic network can do is to accelerate as well as amplify the communication flow, but its viability and effectiveness will depend critically on the robustness of the underlying social structure. This implies that one has to be careful in substituting face-to-face ties with electronic ones. It is vital to maintain a critical ratio of face-to-face to electronic interactions. It may be even more critical to maintain face-to-face relationships with those individuals who can serve as bridging ties, gatekeepers, champions and so on.[90]

The failure of global teams is often attributed to communication difficulties and conflict arising from cultural differences. But this is a difference in degree, not kind. Even a local project team faces complexity and conflict because of the diversity of its members, with a consequent risk of misunderstanding and personality clashes. In transnational teams, that diversity is greater, with correspondingly greater risks of failure.

When people come from different cultures to work virtually, many norms need to be clarified. Is it reasonable to call someone at home during the weekend? What is a reasonable delay in responding to an e-mail? When someone goes on vacation, can one expect them to check their e-mail? What does "urgent" mean? Some organizations use explicit communication protocols or charters to steer formalization of issues that need to be addressed.[91]

Managing Conflict

As we argued earlier, given the diversity of cross-boundary teams, contention and conflict are inherent in such teams. However, conflict is not necessarily a problem. Task or cognitive conflict, due to different information or assumptions, can be productive, hence the importance of diversity in teams; but relationship or emotional conflict (about behaviors, the way things are said, or conflicts of personal interest) can be highly disruptive for teams, especially if there is low trust between team members.[92] Relationship conflicts easily become personal. They typically erupt when teams run into obstacles, notably when they experience their first performance problems and receive negative feedback from outside.[93]

Often it is not conflict itself but avoidance of conflict that disrupts the team. The most important skills needed by leaders of global teams are those that enable them to bring cognitive and emotional conflicts to the surface and work through them. Because virtual teams cannot pick up visual cues, they may find it difficult to detect a conflict before it mushrooms. Failure to respond to an e-mail expressing a position can easily lead to misattribution and undermine trust. Does the nonresponse signify disagreement, anger, lack of interest—or simply that the other parties are busy with other important work?

In some cultures, silence or lack of explicit endorsement indicates disagreement; in others, silence could mean a tacit approval. In one action-learning global leadership development program, the team met face to face the day before the final presentation to the CEO after working virtually for six months. A British member of the team had prepared the presentation material, based on the key recommendations she believed the team had agreed on during numerous teleconferences. Her Japanese colleagues appeared stunned by what they saw on the screen. Finally one of them pointed out, "But—we have never agreed to this." Apparently, during the teleconferences, as American and European team members vigorously debated the recommendations, the Japanese were silent, and no one bothered to check their understanding and agreement. Needless to say, the next 24 hours were very intense.

One lesson these team members learned was the importance of safeguarding an open dialogue: setting up ground rules so that everyone can be heard, making sure that potential conflicts and disagreements surface early in the process. Beyond this, there is little conclusive research on conflict management strategies in virtual teams.[94] We know, however, that conflict resolution is highly dependent on team culture and trust among team members. We will come back to this issue in the next chapter, when we discuss the importance of social capital and relationships in maintaining cohesion in the global firm.

Importance of Leadership

Leadership is clearly a critical contributor to the effectiveness of global teams. The leader has to be highly skilled in coaching behind the scenes, conflict resolution, and team building (see box "Leadership Roles in Cross-border Teams"). Ability to leverage team diversity, people-oriented leadership, and skills of team leaders to act as boundary-spanners are another three important leadership factors influencing global team effectiveness.[95]

Leadership Roles in Cross-border Teams[96]

Developing and communicating a compelling vision of the team's collective goals and potential outcome is one of the most important aspects of leadership.[97] When team members understand and are committed to a vision, they trust the leader and are more motivated to work toward its realization. A strong vision also allows more autonomy and empowerment among team members: if everyone understands the team's goals and direction, team members trust each other to act on their own on behalf of the team.

Every team needs a *clear task strategy and defined roles*, an organized workspace (which, in a virtual team, means access to appropriate information and communications technology), and explicit interaction norms that include coming to meetings well-prepared with a clear

(Continued)

understanding of the objectives. Virtual teams that do not manage these processes carefully often simply fail to get off the ground. It is the leader's role to *ensure that these basic processes are well structured* and that related resources are available and supported.

Another role of the leader in a global team is *facilitating relationships and building trust*. It is important for team members to engage in healthy dialogue and conversations, both social- and work-related, to build social and intellectual capital. With the absence of visual cues, the leader of the virtual teams has to check regularly for understanding and potential conflict; the leader should have cross-cultural experience and be sensitive to contextual differences in behavior.

The leader must also ensure that the team does not become too inwardly focused. An *external focus on scouting* (identifying expectations and tapping into outside knowledge), *ambassadorship* (building buy-in and sponsorship as well as keeping track of allies and adversaries), and *coordinating with other groups* in the firm are also vital for high-performing teams.[98]

Finally, the leaders should be particularly attentive when the team runs into its first major obstacles, such as negative feedback from key sponsors. This is the time when conflicts erupt, and the leader needs to *make sure that the group learns how to deal with obstacles constructively.* This may require time-out meetings, especially for a virtual team, as well as revisiting norms. High-performing teams are characterized by how they deal with the rough times rather than by the honeymoon period.[99]

The leadership skills required may vary at different stages of the team project. In the early stages, advocacy skills are needed to build legitimacy, obtain resources and break through bureaucratic barriers. At the intermediate stage, catalytic skills in building commitment and negotiating with external stakeholders are required. And integrative skills in coordinating and measuring progress are necessary as the project nears fruition.[100]

While co-located teams often benefit most from a leader who acts as a facilitator, virtual teams need a leader who provides clearly defined direction and removes ambiguity from the process. Researchers find formalized coordination usually works best in globally distributed teams. When a team works together in the same office, you can have loose job descriptions, possibly even with two people sharing elements of the same role. That does not work with virtual teams. Team leaders have to formalize roles and responsibilities—starting with their own.[101]

An experimental study of virtual teams where the members came from different countries showed that effective leaders demonstrated the capacity to perform contrasting leadership roles simultaneously. For example, they were able to act as empathetic mentors while asserting authority in influencing the responsibilities of members.[102] The dualistic demands of cross-boundary project work are one of the reasons why such assignments are an important element in the process of developing leadership competencies and global mindset.

Appraising and Rewarding Teamwork

Unless the project assignment is full-time, a major problem in cross-boundary teamwork is the tension between responsibility for the regular job and the demands of lateral teamwork, leading to appraisal and reward difficulties. Individuals are asked to work on cross-border teams and then reprimanded because of poor performance in their own job. Cross-border teamwork can overstretch the organization unless people have settled into and mastered their operational jobs before they are assigned to cross-boundary teams.

The appraisal and reward system can sometimes discourage teamwork. Appraisal and reward systems that take cross-boundary performance into account are not simple, but they are becoming commonplace in project-oriented organizations like professional service firms. At Accenture, senior partners spend up to a quarter of their time on appraisal of partners and managers, collecting the views of clients, research and back office departments, managers, and subordinates. "You are not going to be receiving a top bonus this year because although the client is happy, the research department did not get the collaboration it needed."[103] Using 360-degree appraisals and similar multi-rater input to capture the opinions of team clients and members is also increasingly common.

As described in the box in the next section "Learning How to Work in 'Split Egg' Ways," people are often paid for their performance in the job but promoted for the initiative that they show, notably through cross-boundary teamwork.

Promoting Feedback and Learning

Most global firms would be well advised to follow the route of IBM and leading professional service firms that are in the forefront of developing processes for cross-border teamwork—ensuring that every project ends with a learning review that contributes to individual and organizational know-how. We often find that managers do not spontaneously seek out learning as an outcome, although they quickly realize its importance when it is signaled to them.

The HR function has an important obligation and opportunity here. We recall advising the human resource executives in a major information technology firm to become involved in four key global projects that the firm was setting up. Project expertise and management of cross-boundary teams was clearly a critical future capability in this industry, and there was no internal know-how about the implementation of such complex global projects (such as how to staff and motivate the teams, or how to speed up the process of successive adoption by countries). To our regret, the HR function turned down the opportunity: "Sorry, but that is not part of our job." No one undertook the process-leadership role, mistakes were made, but more importantly, there was no feedback and learning.

IMPLEMENTING STRUCTURAL COORDINATION

Multidimensional structures, lateral steering, and cross-border teams cannot operate in isolation; as we pointed out repeatedly, they can be effective only if other mechanisms of lateral coordination are properly designed—notably the shared norms and values that facilitate trust as well as appropriate talent and performance management processes.[104] Indeed, enabling lateral coordination is a big challenge—and a big opportunity—for international HRM.

Combining coordinating and operational responsibilities requires managers to work in matrixed or "split egg" ways that are becoming typical for leaders and professionals in transnational firms (see box on "Learning How to Work in 'Split Egg' Ways"). In this sense, for many managers in multinational firms, the matrix gets built into their roles in the sense of having to do one's job AND take responsibility for lateral coordination.

Learning How to Work in "Split Egg" Ways

Instead of resolving the conflicting priorities that face transnational organizations—local versus global and short-term performance versus long-term strategic innovation—through formal reporting lines, these dilemmas can be built into the roles of individual managers. As a consequence of the shift to lateral coordination, all leaders, and an increasing number of managers and professionals, have to learn how to work in matrix roles or what we call split egg ways (see the diagram below, which looks like an egg divided into two).

In the past, the traditional line–staff organization responded to conflicting priorities by segmenting them structurally. Line managers and employees in the business units and subsidiaries had an operational focus. Their attention was centered on local targets and budgetary constraints with a short-term time horizon. The responsibility for long-term global strategic development lay with senior leaders and the staff at headquarters. However, these neat line–staff and headquarter–subsidiary distinctions created a bureaucracy where much fell into the cracks between the two. Line managers had no commitment to the plans developed by headquarters, which often failed to reflect the realities in the field. At a time when speed was becoming a

vital competitive edge, this way of organizing was simply too slow.

One response to this challenge is to deal with these conflicting needs through the redefinition of managerial roles rather than through the structure. The responsibility for strategic initiatives and lateral coordination is added to the operational responsibilities of the manager, in what we call the manager's project role. The manager in the business unit now has two roles, *operational* and *project*, as shown in the split egg diagram. During the first year in a new job, the operational role will often take 100 percent of the available time. But after settling into the job, the manager (especially those with high potential) is now expected to spend, say, 30 percent of his or her time or work on change or improvement projects with a longer-term and cross-boundary perspective, typically involving formal or informal teamwork.

The need to free up time to get involved in cross-border initiatives, project teams, and coordination work obliges the manager to delegate many of the operational tasks for which he or she is responsible—"empowering" direct subordinates. Managers must now take the nuts and bolts of HRM seriously—paying attention to selection, performance management, and the development of their staff.

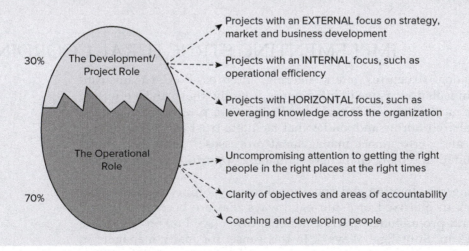

30%   The Development/ Project Role

Projects with an EXTERNAL focus on strategy, market and business development

Projects with an INTERNAL focus, such as operational efficiency

Projects with HORIZONTAL focus, such as leveraging knowledge across the organization

The Operational Role

Uncompromising attention to getting the right people in the right places at the right times

Clarity of objectives and areas of accountability

Coaching and developing people

70%

This is the managerial role of the person—in the sense of "doing things right." But people are not promoted just for their performance in doing things right; they are promoted to higher levels because of the leadership initiative that they show in the project role—"doing the right things."

In the old days, managers were people in the middle whereas leaders were people at the top. In today's transnational firms, capable individuals at different levels have to exercise skills in both *management*—getting agreed results through people in their areas of responsibility—and *leadership*—taking cross-boundary initiatives, and adding value through coordinated strategic projects.

The split egg role is not a radically new role concept (McKinsey introduced the metaphor of the T-shaped manager back in the 1970s).[105] In most firms, it has always applied to high-potential managers who are expected to deliver on their operational targets and to earn visibility by working on broader development projects. In Chapter 8, we discuss further the role of the split egg in global leadership development as well as some of the pitfalls of this way of working.

One critical implication of using split egg roles is the increased importance of HRM for the global firm. Managers learn to pay careful attention to talent selection, getting the right people into the right places. Performance management is essential. In short, when they experience split egg pressures, managers learn that one of *their* most important tasks is human resource management.

Matrix Everything—Except the Structure

One way of summarizing the challenges of organizing the global firm is to stand conventional thinking on its head.

Let's go back to the law of requisite complexity. Global firms face the highest degree of environmental complexity, and the law of requisite complexity says that the internal complexity of a firm must mirror external flexibility. This is still best captured by the matrix concept. The environment is highly matrixed—product markets, geographies, customer segments, management functions, core technologies…. Organizations cannot avoid matrix. But matrix does not have to mean only structure. In order for a multidimensional organization to operate smoothly, the organizational culture must also think and breathe matrix. Matrix has to be built into control and coordination systems, performance management, leadership development, teamwork, conflict resolution mechanisms, relationships, and attitudes.

So matrix everything—except the formal structure! This could be a good guideline for a global organization. Like every guideline, do not take it to the extreme. There is a role for matrix structures of dual reporting relationships in most organizations. However, to manage complexity, matrix through project groups, steering committees, internal boards, management processes, business planning, and measurement. A project team can be set up quickly; an internal board can be formed, reconstituted, or disbanded in a few days; roles and responsibilities can be rapidly revised— in contrast, it takes time and energy to align or change structure. Matrix roles and responsibilities, so that people have vertical and horizontal accountabilities. And matrix minds and mindsets; we will be discussing how to do that in the next chapter.

TAKEAWAYS

1. Global firms complement vertical control mechanisms with structural elements of horizontal coordination. HRM tools play a crucial role in facilitating this.

2. Multidimensional structures have their origin in the matrix organization. The global matrix is inherently difficult to maintain because of the inevitable conflict of priorities between the units. Effective matrix management requires clearly defined common processes and building strong horizontal linkages.

3. The focus of global companies organized as differentiated networks is on leveraging competencies and capabilities initially developed in their local subsidiaries for worldwide advantage.

4. The objective of companies organized as globally integrated enterprises is to achieve competitive advantage by locating specific activities in the best place worldwide, and finding ways to link or integrate these activities around the world.

5. In front-back organizations, the customer-oriented parts are aligned locally to respond to customers, while those parts which may benefit from global efficiencies and scale are organized along global lines.

6. Lateral steering tools provide a flexible and potent means of global coordination while promoting accountability at the lowest level possible. These include lateral steering roles and lateral steering groups.

7. Business or area coordinators, global account managers, as well as alliance managers, are examples of lateral steering roles. Effectiveness in such roles requires the ability to exercise leadership with little formal authority.

8. Cross-boundary teams are the basic building blocks of horizontal coordination. Global virtual teams with members who are not co-located and who do not share the same context need to invest in building and maintaining trust through face-to-face interactions.

9. The generic lessons of team management apply to cross-boundary teams, but the risks of failure are greater unless principles such as goal clarity, attention to staffing, managing conflict, team leadership, and feedback/learning are applied rigorously.

10. In many global firms, managers are not only responsible for achieving results for their own units but also have shared accountability for successful strategy implementation across units. They must learn to work in "split egg" ways.

NOTES

1 The information about Nestlé was obtained from several case studies, company documents, and personal interviews with company executives.

2 Killing, 2003b.

3 Galbraith, 2000.

4 Killing, 2003b.

5 Interview with Paul Broeckx, former senior vice president, Corporate Human Resources Division, Nestlé, December 2005.

6 GLOBE was rolled out on time and on budget in key pilot countries, but its worldwide implementation took longer than anticipated.

7 Nestlé internal company document, "Nestlé on the Move," Human Resource Department, Nestec Ltd., Vevey, Switzerland.

8 Interview with Paul Broeckx, former senior vice president, Corporate Human Resources Division, Nestlé, December, 2005.

9 This question was raised by the Harvard Multinational Enterprise project, initiated in 1965. See Stopford and Wells (1972).

10 By sending man to the moon President Kennedy was determined to win back over the Russians who had taken a lead in the space race. NASA was responsible for this mission. It was a mission that could not fail, and it had to be achieved within a decade. However, Congress would not put up the enormous funds that this would require. Faced with Kennedy's insistence, NASA invented matrix organization, violating the sacrosanct organizational principle of one-person-one-boss. Engineers would report to a functional boss and to a project or program boss.

11 Argyris, 1967.

12 Davis and Lawrence, 1977.

13 A widely publicized article by a well-known management guru questioning the use of matrix structure accelerated the decline (Peters, 1979).

14 The *nemawashi* process in Japanese firms is an informal process of consultation, typically undertaken by a high potential individual, involving talking with people and gathering support for an important decision or project.

15 Many German international firms had an unusual structure abroad, where the sales subsidiary was run jointly by a local general manager with a German commercial manager on a *primus inter pares* basis, facilitating this consensual approach.

16 This was a radical departure from the "one boss" model enshrined in the classic principle of unity of command (one-person-one-boss). For this reason, the matrix has been regarded by some as the only totally new twentieth-century form of organization.

17 Barham and Heimer, 1998.

18 Zalan and Pucik, 2007.

19 Ford and Randolph, 1992; Martinez and Jarillo, 1989.

20 Galbraith, 1977.

21 Bartlett and Ghoshal, 1990.

22 For an overview of matrix organization, see Galbraith (2009).

23 Nadler and Tushman (1997) analyze organizations in terms of the vertical architecture of groupings and the horizontal architecture of linking and aligning. A similar approach is taken by Ghoshal and Bartlett (1997).

24 Bartlett and Ghoshal, 1989.

25 Palmisano, 2006.

26 "Business is Going Native Again," *Financial Times*, April 9, 2014.

27 Galbraith, 2000.

28 As explained in Chapter 1, "international" firms excel through their ability to transfer expertise in particular from the center to less-advanced overseas environments, allowing local firms more discretion in adapting products and services (Bartlett and Ghoshal, 1989).

29 This is also the case for many pharmaceutical companies (for example, GSK) that need a front end oriented to national regulatory authorities as well as customers, while R&D and manufacturing are global.

30 Ghoshal and Nohria, 1987; Nohria and Ghoshal, 1997.

31 Galbraith, 2000.

32 Frost, Birkinshaw, and Ensign, 2002.

33 Galbraith, 2000, p. 42.

34 Nestlé's expression of "one country—two systems" follows the common phrase used in the media to describe the relationship between China and Hong Kong—now part of China, but retaining distinct governance.

35 Five semi-independent joint ventures account for more than one-third of Nestlé's sales in China. A detailed description of how Nestlé nurtured one of them—Totole—into a leading global chicken bouillon maker is contained in Chong (2013).

36 Palmisano, 2006.

37 Sanchez, 2007.

38 Even IBM, which pioneered the concept of a globally integrated enterprise, has some "global" activities in multiple locations, as localization of capabilities is an increasing concern of host governments.

39 Gibbs, Heywood, and Weiss, 2012.

40 Strikwerda and Stoelhorst, 2009.

41 The evolution of IBM as a globally integrated enterprise is mapped out in Kanter (2009).

42 Sanchez, 2007. The overall headcount as of 2014.

43 IBM's approach to talent management is described in Chapter 8 on page 255.

44 Morris and Calamai, 2009.

45 Galbraith, 2011.

46 Galbraith, 2002.

47 Nokia has gone through a number of radical transformations since its establishment in 1865. Its origins were in rubber, pulp, and paper. It shifted to wireless telecommunications in the 1980s and just 20 years later became the world's largest producer of mobile phones—and the Nokia Networks division is one of the leading suppliers of equipment for mobile operators. However, with the emergence of smartphones, Nokia was not able to compete with Apple and Samsung and the mobile phone business was sold to Microsoft in 2014. At the time of writing, telecommunication equipment is Nokia's main business area.

48 Galbraith, 2011.

49 "The radical: Carly Fiorina's bold management experiment at HP," *BusinessWeek*, February 19, 2001.

50 Birkinshaw and Gibson, 2004.

51 Gittell (2000) illustrates the importance of hierarchy for coordination. This study contrasts the flat organization of American Airlines, which has broad spans of control and rigorous performance management, with the smaller spans of control at the phenomenally successful Southwest Airlines. The price that American Airlines pays is poor coordination. In contrast, supervisors at Southwest play cross-functional coordination roles—diffusing blame and providing coaching and feedback.

52 Goold and Campbell, 1998.

53 We discuss network leadership and the implications of exercising leadership without authority in Chapter 8.

54 Galbraith, 2000.

55 Galbraith, 2014.

56 Manz, Shipper, and Stewart, 2009.

57 Bartlett and Ghoshal, 1992.

58 Francis *et al.*, 2004.

59 Galbraith, 2000.

60 Birkinshaw and DiStefano, 2004; Yip and Bink, 2007.

61 Ghoshal and Bartlett, 1997.

62 For the evolution of Cisco's lateral steering, see Gulati, Wagonfeld, and Silvestri, (2014).

63 "Cisco Systems layers it on," *Fortune*, December 8, 2008.

64 Donnelly, Morris, and Donnelly, 2005. In total, about 1,500 managers and professionals from both companies were involved in lateral steering activities.

65 In some firms, the composition of functional councils is similar to functional management teams; the designation "council" puts an emphasis on horizontal communication and collective deliberation.

66 Galbraith, 2000. See the discussion on building or buying talent in Chapter 6.

67 Pucik, 2006.

68 As defined by Katzenbach and Smith (1993).

69 For a comprehensive review of research on global virtual teams, see Gibson, Huang, Kirkman, and Shapiro (2014).

70 Jonsen, Maznevski, and Davison, 2012.

71 Ibid.

72 MacDuffie, 2007. See also Kiesler and Cummings (2002) for research on the effects of proximity and distance on groups.

73 Adler, 1991.

74 Amason and colleagues argue that handling these two faces of conflict is critical for team performance (Amason *et al.*, 1995). Affective conflict is associated with team failure, while cognitive conflict is associated with team success. Their empirical research (Amason, 1996) supports this argument, leading them to suggest that knowing how to steer a group toward constructive conflict is the key to successful team management.

75 Punnett and Clemens, 1999.

76 Katzenbach and Smith, 1993; Johansen *et al.*, 1991; Mannix and Sondak, 2002; Gluesing and Gibson, 2004; Ancona and Bresman, 2007; Brett, Behfar, and Kern, 2012; Jonsen, Maznevski, and Davison, 2012.

77 Davidson Frame, 1987; Ferrazi, 2014.

78 Hedlund and Ridderstraale, 1995.

79 Blackburn, Furst, and Rosen, 2003.

80 For a classic discussion of team size effectiveness see Belbin (1993).

81 Snow, Miles, and Coleman, 1992.

82 Although it was not international in focus, Ancona and Caldwell's (1992) study of new-product team managers showed that effective teams follow cycles of external activity (aimed at molding the views of senior management, getting feedback, and general scanning) and internal processes. See the work on X-teams undertaken by Ancona and Bresman (2007).

83 Ferrazzi, 2014.

84 Jarvenpaa, Knoll, and Leidner, 1998; Jarvenpaa and Leidner, 1999. For more on the importance of trust in cross-border virtual teams, as well as the practical implications, see Duarte and Snyder (2006). For more on "swift trust" see Meyerson, Weick, and Kramer (1996).

85 For a review of research on HRM role in managing global teams see Gibbs and Boyraz (2014).

86 Duarte and Synder, 2006.

87 It is estimated that the "half-life" of a personal meeting in R&D networks—the time it takes before trust falls below a dangerous threshold—is less than three months. See De Meyer (1991, p. 56).

88 Jonsen, Maznevski, and Davison, 2012.

89 Jin, Mason, and Yim, 1998; Canney Davison, and Ward, 1999.

90 Nohria, 1992, pp. 304–5.

91 See Duarte and Snyder (2006); Lepsinger and DeRosa (2010); and Watkins, M., "Making virtual teams work: Ten basic principles," *Harvard Business Review*, 2013, https://hbr.org/2013/06/making-virtual-teams-work-ten-/.

92 Simons, Peterson, and Task, 2000. See Hinds and Bailey (2003) for a comprehensive model of conflict in virtual teams.

93 Peterson, Behfar, and Jackson, 2003.

94 Jonsen, Maznevski, and Davison, 2012. See Duarte and Snyder (2006) for an outline of strategies, tools, and techniques for work in virtual teams. And see Behfar *et al.* (2008) for a framework and empirical research on conflict resolution strategy in non-virtual teams.

95 Zander, Mockaitis, and Butler, 2012.

96 Our basic sources are Jonsen, Maznevski, and Davison (2012) and Zander, Zetting, and Mäkelä (2013).

97 Bass and Stogdill, 1990; House *et al.*, 1999.

98 Ancona and Bresman, 2007.

99 Peterson, Behfar, and Jackson, 2003.

100 See Snow *et al.* (1996). Behavioral complexity theories of leadership seem appropriate to understand these demands. These theories argue that leadership effectiveness depends on the ability of managers to display multiple, dualistic leadership styles, supported by a high degree of cognitive complexity (Denison, 1996; Hart and Quinn 1993). Situational leadership ideas, widely used on training programs, embody the same notion.

101 We are grateful to José Santos for his insight on the need for formalization in virtual teams. While mutual adjustment is possible in face-to-face teams, this is not possible in virtual work. Consequently the leader needs to formalize and structure the context of the task.

102 For a managerial review of research on leadership in virtual teams, see Zander, Mockaitis, and Butler (2012).

103 Ghoshal, 1991; Lorsch and Tierney, 2002.

104 We will return to these issues in Chapters 5 and 8.

105 See Hansen and von Oetinger (2001) for an update on the T-shaped concept, applied to knowledge managers.

5

Constructing Social Architecture

SUMMARY

Challenge

Multinational organizations are social entities, but often lack the social architecture to connect people across borders – the essential condition for global coordination

Analysis

Building the social architecture of the company requires:

- Social capital: The relationships among the employees in the corporation
- Organizational culture: Values, beliefs and norms shared by people in the multinational
- Global mindset: Openness towards others and ability to balance competing priorities

Solutions

- Cross-border councils, committees, and projects are the foundation for building social capital
- Enhance global social capital and common culture through HRM practises such as selection, socialization, training and international mobility
- Use shared values to build trust which is essential for effective lateral coordination and conflict resolution
- Safeguard the foundation of global mindset – equal opportunity for all regardless of passport

The Social Architecture of Toyota

What later became Toyota Motor Corporation began as an automotive department established within the textile machinery maker Toyoda Automatic Loom Works in 1933. Exports to the US started in 1957, and in 1962 the company began its first manufacturing operation abroad, in Brazil. Toyota added overseas plants in Thailand in 1964, a first US factory (a joint venture with General Motors) in 1984, and the first European car plant began production in Britain in 1992. By 2014, Toyota occupied the number one position in the global automotive market, with

12 domestic and 52 vehicle plants in 26 countries outside Japan, employing altogether 340,000 people. Most of the foreign plants had been set up during the previous 20 years, with teams of technicians and managers from Japan playing a crucial role in the process. The close relationships between team members, and between them and the parent plants in Japan, were important for the transfer of knowledge necessary to start new operations.

The business principles guiding Toyota's operations today were originally developed by the founder of Toyota, Sakichi Toyoda, in the 1930s, but unlike many other Japanese firms, these principles were never codified in a way that would make them easy to communicate. As the international expansion of the company made it increasingly difficult to centralize decision-making at headquarters in Japan, clarification and strengthening of the Toyota global operating philosophy was seen as an essential precondition for diffusion of authority to locations abroad.

After discussing and refining how to express company values over a period of several years, the first internal draft of the Toyota Way was presented in 2001. There are five core elements of the Toyota Way: challenge (focus on analyzing and solving problems to improve performance); *kaizen* (continuous improvement); *genchi genbutsu* ("go see for yourself," or "go to the source," a principle for analyzing and solving problems); respect for people (with different opinions and perspectives); and teamwork.

Along with the Toyota Way, the company formulated the Toyota Business Practices, an articulation and explication of the Toyota Way with a focus on how to analyze and solve operational problems. All Toyota employees throughout the world are expected to master and use these practices. The Toyota Business Practices provide a common language for all Toyota employees and units. Both the Toyota Business Practices and the Toyota Way are covered extensively in training programs for domestic and foreign employees.

The Toyota Way is one of the key tools for integrating and coordinating the company's global operations, especially in the manufacturing area, and participants in internal meetings and development programs spend extensive time discussing how to use it. Toyota puts considerable emphasis on selection and socialization processes. Job candidates at all levels are rigorously screened to make sure that they fit into the Toyota culture, and new members of the organization go through a comprehensive orientation program before they are turned over to their work departments, where the socialization process continues.[1]

The start-up phase is crucial to the establishment of new overseas manufacturing units. When Toyota began to expand internationally, it made a rule that a specific plant in Japan would be responsible for training people in each overseas operation. However, with the increasing number of new production facilities abroad, this system reached its limits. Instead, Japanese coordinators are sent to the foreign units to instill Toyota's philosophy, concepts, and manufacturing methods. Each coordinator spends between three and five years abroad, with the first generation serving as teachers, the second as coaches, and the third as advisers. The first non-Japanese trainers/coordinators from plants in Kentucky and Canada were dispatched abroad in 2007.[2]

In spite of its immense commercial success, Toyota is facing several challenges in managing its international operations. Even with heavy investment in education, the company still does not have a sufficient number of international trainers and coordinators. Employee turnover in some overseas operations makes it more difficult to develop a workforce that has internalized the values, behavioral norms, and management processes that have emerged and been refined in the Japanese operations. Toyota does a good job in socializing new recruits into the corporation, but nonetheless attrition is a significant problem. And learning a culture does not happen overnight. Toyota former President Katsuaki Watanabe went so far as to say: "I don't think I have a complete understanding even today, and I have worked for the company for 43 years."[3]

OVERVIEW

Both Toyota's top management and external observers agree that the Toyota Way is a key ingredient in Toyota's global success. However, while Toyota may be special in the degree of attention it pays to disseminating its culture worldwide, every organization is a social entity in which values, social relationships, and employee mindsets make a difference. In this chapter we focus on how to build what we call the *social architecture* of the multinational firm.[4] We will explore three aspects of social architecture, focusing on how "corporate social architects" use different people management tools and processes to construct the architecture and the ensuing outcomes: (1) relationships among the employees (social capital); (2) shared values, beliefs, and norms (organizational culture); and (3) global mindsets.

We begin this chapter with a discussion about social capital—the ways in which personal relationships and networks can serve productive purposes. Social capital among employees greatly contributes to enhanced interunit collaboration and coordination. Shared values facilitate corporate coordination, and we continue by exploring multinational firms through the lens of organizational culture. We discuss positive and negative aspects of strong organizational cultures, identifying ways in which corporations can try to manage their culture. The mindset of executives, managers, and employees is important for the functioning of multinational firms. In the third section, we concentrate on two perspectives of global mindsets. The first is cultural, and it refers to individuals' openness and interest in other nations and cultures; the second is strategic in the sense that it denotes an individual's ability to hold competing strategic priorities (such as local responsiveness and global efficiency).

LEVERAGING SOCIAL CAPITAL

As we saw in the Toyota case, social networks are essential during the early phases of internationalization. Historically, with limited means to communicate and share information, companies had to put their trust in key managers expatriated to distant subsidiaries. Today's multinational firm relies heavily on advances in information technology; without mobile phones, e-mail, and the Internet, the coordination of geographically dispersed activities would be a lot more difficult. But whenever there is a need to collaborate across borders, to transfer and assimilate know-how, or to resolve conflicts or differences in perspectives, employees act in the same way as their less e-enabled predecessors; they rely on those they know, trust, and understand. One of the paradoxes of globalization is that the power of technology to connect people can be harnessed effectively only if there are close relationships between those involved in the exchange of information. It is captured by the cliché that we live in a world of high tech and high touch.

In any organization, deep social relationships improve communication between people and facilitate the development of trust and collaboration, allowing the firm to pursue common objectives with minimal friction. Relationships between employees are especially important for companies that operate across borders. Many of the elements of coordination discussed in this book would not be effective without person-to-person relationships.

Sociologists have analyzed social relationships and networks for many decades, but in the past, informal networks in business organizations were often viewed with suspicion—bringing harmful personal politics into the workplace through the influence of old boy networks and office mafias. The view that the social networks of organizational members are critical for effective coordination has only recently gained acceptance. In this section we examine the multinational from a social capital perspective, focusing on interpersonal relationships between people within and across units and organizations.

What Is Social Capital and Why Do We Care About It?

The term *social capital* refers to the benefits that derive from the connections and interpersonal relationships of people within an organization and with people outside.[5] This constitutes an intangible resource—a form of capital in the same way that human skills constitute human capital. Let us start with the justification for describing these benefits as social capital.

First, personal relationships can be used to access other resources, such as information, or support for the implementation of decisions that have been made. The relationships that were formed between local employees and expatriates sent out from Japan to the newly established Toyota factories abroad continued to facilitate exchange of information and problem-solving long after the expatriates had returned to Japan.

Second, investments in relationships are like a stock that may yield future returns. For example, doing someone a favor, treating them well, or spending time together builds social capital that can be used to call in a favor later. But third, like human capital, social capital needs to be maintained; otherwise it will depreciate over time as the personal relationship fades.

In a multinational firm social capital has three distinct but interlinked dimensions—structural, relational, and cognitive.[6] The *structural* dimension is mainly concerned with links between people or units, such as the network of ties between actors.[7] The *relational* dimension focuses on personal relationships and the trust, obligations, and shared identities that individuals have developed through a history of interaction. While the structural dimension is concerned with the existence (or otherwise) of links between individuals and units, the relational dimension deals with the strength of those relationships. Finally, the *cognitive* dimension encompasses organizational phenomena such as shared languages and systems of meaning among parties. Here we discuss the structural and relational dimensions of social capital, and will explore its cognitive dimension, in the form of global mindsets, later in the chapter.

One interesting aspect of the structural dimension is the position of an individual as a *bridge* between different networks. Building on classic insights into the strength of weak ties for landing a new job,[8] the structural perspective stresses the advantages in terms of access to information and new ideas of being able to bridge otherwise unconnected networks.[9] Subsidiary managers in a multinational corporation who have personal relationships with key people at corporate headquarters act as bridges—or "boundary spanners"[10]—between the local environment and the corporate parent organization. When boundary spanners share their thoughts and feelings about headquarters with local employees, they mold staff attitudes toward the parent organization.[11] Inpatriates who return to the subsidiary after assignments at corporate headquarters or elsewhere in the multinational play similar boundary-spanning roles.

The focus of the relational perspective on social capital is often on the group or network as a whole. The emphasis here is on internal *bonding*. There is commonly a sense of mutual obligation and trust among individuals who share a common history and/or background.[12] Without personal relationships, there is limited trust. People who have close relationships with each other are more likely to share information and offer assistance, facilitating collaboration in the social network.[13]

Over time, close relationships among individuals can become a feature of an entire group or organizational unit. For instance, in a global R&D team of people who have a long history of working together, all members of the unit or organization can tap into the common social network.

The individual and collective benefits of social capital are summarized in the box "Advantages of Social Capital."

Resolving Conflict through Social Capital

Conflict is an inevitable part of work and life in any social organization, particularly in the multinational given the contradictions and tensions that it faces. An important aspect of the relational dimension of social capital is conflict resolution, and at the heart of contention management is the fact that most conflicts are best worked out through social relationships.

Managers sometimes ask us how conflicts in transnational management can be minimized. It is the wrong question. While too much conflict is destructive, a total lack of conflict may lead to equally destructive apathy and complacency. In fact, successful companies in fast-changing environments encourage fact finding and divergent arguments, so that they are as fully prepared as possible when the moment for decision-making comes.[23] Different perspectives, and fresh assumptions that may challenge received ideas, can be both positive and

Advantages of Social Capital

Individuals who bridge different social networks have been found to gain superior *access to information* about opportunities, new research findings, or business ideas that are likely to be useful to the unit where they are working. For instance, the personal contacts of a manager often determine how the firm will enter a new market,[14] while social relationships within and outside multinationals allow employees to search effectively for solutions to problems. Attempts to create corporate "Facebooks" build on this. Close relationships are particularly useful when information is sensitive and when sharing it requires a high level of trust. Strong bonds are also beneficial for *sharing complex and tacit knowledge*.[15] In a tightly integrated social network, new information flows extensively between the members, producing teams where people share a common knowledge base.[16]

Both internal and external social capital can contribute to improved *innovativeness* for the firm.[17] Individuals with extensive external networks can bring in experts to work on projects and use these contacts to access, acquire, and combine information and knowledge with resources in their own organization.

Further benefits of social capital are *solidarity* and *collaboration*. Shared values, beliefs, and behavioral norms often develop in tightly integrated social networks and

the members may develop a common language for discussing work-related issues. There is also greater willingness to subordinate individual goals to collective goals and actions.[18] Moreover, individuals with strong bonds may be more willing to take initiatives that serve the goals of the unit, venturing outside the scope of their formal job descriptions. In the multinational corporation, the more units depend on each other, the more they can benefit from social capital to help coordinate their activities.[19]

Through the private social relationships of employees with friends and acquaintances, a firm can tap into a pool of potential job applicants. Studies have shown that people hired through referrals tend to stay longer and perform better than those employed through other recruitment methods.[20] Furthermore, employees are less likely to leave a firm if they have good relationships with others working there.[21] Thus social capital facilitates *employee acquisition* and *retention*.

Finally, social capital can also be viewed from a *power and influence* perspective. When a person has built up a set of obligations from others, they can be used to influence their actions. Individuals spanning social networks—especially if they are the only bridges—can exploit this situation to negotiate favorable terms for their business units.[22]

productive. High quality relationships increase the likelihood that people will present different viewpoints and the probability that conflicts can be turned into constructive and novel solutions.[24]

Clearly, organizations and societies differ in how conflicts are framed and solved. At GE, Jack Welch was a master at constructive debate. He spent up to 25 percent of his time at GE's management training center, where he presented his views on the challenges and goals to GE managers and then expected them to argue back. "His theory is that if an idea can't survive a spirited argument, the marketplace surely will kill it."[25] However, not many Asian executives are comfortable with this kind of confrontational problem-solving approach, so despite its commitment to boundaryless behavior and business expansion in Asia, GE's leadership under Welch was viewed by some as US-centric.

The GE dilemma is far from unique. L'Oréal, the successful cosmetics firm, is over 100 years old. Its cultural values were built around contention management, embodied in a dualistic value system (to be a "creative poet" and a "financially conservative peasant" at the same time), and in practices such as using confrontation rooms for making key decisions. This worked well and contributed to L'Oréal's success—as long as all key managers were French and deeply socialized into such practices. But as the firm expanded internationally, L'Oréal's distinctive approach to managing contention gradually weakened, as the firm localized its management. Therefore, one of the challenges of firms such as GE and L'Oréal is to develop norms for contention management as well as close social relationships that allow people of very different backgrounds to collaborate effectively.

To guide constructive debate, some of the general guidelines that stem from research and practice are shown in Table 5-1.

How to Build and Manage Social Capital

Informal social networks emerge in all social settings. In the past, organizations were driven by relationships that were often formed early in life—the old boy network, the clan formed at university, and the team of people who built up the company. And it has for a long time been known that individuals who

TABLE 5-1
Resolving Conflict

- **Ensure that there is agreement on goals.** Absence of agreement about goals (or vision or strategic criteria) will lead to political infighting and unconstructive debate.

- **Actively listen before you disagree.** Showing the other person that you have understood their views increases the probability that they will listen constructively to yours.

- **Data, data, data ... Measurement, measurement.** A focus on facts keeps dialog constructive. Companies with cultures of constructive debate tend to believe in measuring everything.

- **Ensure balanced input.** If certain functions or units are left out of the debate, it is likely that they will not be committed to implement decisions made.

- **Explore multiple alternatives to enrich the debate.** Focusing only on your preferred option to simplify the process of debate will increase the probability of conflict when the time comes to make a decision.

- **Inject humor into the decision-making process.** Trust the psychologists—research shows that humor can keep tension constructive.

- **Focus on the issues, not personalities or individuals.** Much conflict could be avoided by making sure that it is the idea that is challenged, not the individual who voiced it.

are located closer together are more likely to form ties.[26] However, rather than allowing yesterday's networks to steer business development, relationships in the proactive transnational firms need to be built with today's and tomorrow's needs for coordination in mind.

Building and maintaining social capital poses particular challenges for firms spanning vast geographical distances, time zones, and cultures.[27] Multinational firms can shape informal social relationships and networks through complementary structural solutions. For example, the existence of international councils, committees, and formal project teams influences the pattern of interactions and relationships that evolve within the firm and with other organizations. Even if the interaction is initially mostly task oriented, gradually, more social aspects and bonds are likely to develop.

One of the challenges facing firms is how much to "manage" the informal professionals networks that emerge spontaneously within and across organizations, now frequently described as communities of practice. These communities are characterized by largely informal interaction and collaboration around a common set of interests, such as functional expertise in an area of technology. The participation in such networks can be encouraged by recognizing contributions as a legitimate part of a person's work, accounting for this in performance evaluations and promotion decisions. The firm may also provide budgets for travel and workshops as well as technological support. However, too much micromanagement can kill the intrinsic motivation of those participating in these communities of common professional interest.[28]

While creation of social capital has traditionally been viewed merely as a by-product of HR practices, the formation of social relationships should be viewed as a key outcome of proactive people management.[29] Take recruitment and selection practices. Companies may try to increase the likelihood of social capital formation in a particular unit by selecting people on the basis of their organizational cultural and social fit. And on-boarding activities are also used to build relationships between new recruits and senior leaders.[30]

Indeed, multinational firms have long viewed interpersonal communication skills as a basic competency for people in professional as well as leadership roles. For example, companies recruiting from international business schools say that an essential attribute they look for in potential recruits is interpersonal skills in dealing with people who are different from themselves. An additional benefit is the extensive global social networks that graduates have built up during their studies.

Other HR practices also impact the creation of social capital. The way some firms encourage and support mentoring relationships between junior and senior employees can contribute to the formation of social ties. The motivation of boundary spanners to share their social capital with others depends in part on whether such behavior is acknowledged within the employee performance appraisal system.[31]

Leadership training programs are used to mix employees from different parts of the global organization who usually do not meet otherwise. Learning teams are constructed to ensure a good mix of people from different backgrounds; team building exercises are undertaken; and action learning assignments provide excellent opportunities for participants to get to know each other better while working on important projects. As stated by the head of executive development for a major telecommunications firm: "The personal

Ten Days in the Desert

Some years ago there was a merger between a large French company and its British competitor to form the largest packaging group in Europe. On paper, the merger made a great deal of sense, but business analysts discounted the potential advantages because they felt that two such arch-competitors would continue to fight with each other. The president of the newly formed group decided to invest seriously in building relationships.

The top 25 executives, half French and half British, were told to clear their desks for ten days. They were flown to Saudi Arabia and then on by helicopter into the middle of the desert. Landing on a sand dune, they got out and found two caterpillar trucks with camping equipment, food, and water, and, as the helicopter took off, a letter from the president saying that he looked forward to seeing them in four days' time for their first management meeting at a hotel in Riyadh. This unexpected outward-bound experience was a dramatic but successful way of breaking the ice and building new relationships. Making it to the hotel without undue incident, it was a real "team" that spent the next four days hammering out ways to develop the strategy for the new group. The team building paid off in open and constructive debate, leading to several creative conflict resolutions. The strategy was highly successful, and the firm's share price soared.

relationships that the participants build are an extremely important part of the outcome of our programs."[32]

Well-planned getaways and meetings may also play important roles in building social capital (see the box "Ten Days in the Desert"). In this example, the relationship building had a clear objective, namely developing a strategy for the merged organization.

However, unless there is a well-thought-out purpose for why people are brought together, the cost may exceed the benefits. Consider the case of a Belgian corporation formed by the merger of a dozen companies in different but complementary industries ten years earlier. Each year, the senior executives met for a three-day conference. But after seven years, people began to complain about the time-wasting "annual Mass" (as they called it) when all they did was discuss business results and exchange views about what had happened in the past. Although the exercise had been useful for the first few years, and some superficial social relationships had been formed, these had never been deepened through subsequent collaboration between the companies.

Management training and development programs can also be used to build social relationships with managers from key business partners. The Swedish telecommunication equipment corporation, Ericsson, offered for many years their main Chinese customer organizations the opportunity to send participants to its internal MBA program. In addition to the impact on Ericsson's internal human and social capital, the program strengthened the external relationships of Ericsson employees with managers in telecom service providers from all parts of China.

Finally, conferences and forums, sabbaticals, leaves of absence, and short-term exchange assignments either within or between firms encourage the development of social networks. Employee transfers and visits across borders are particularly relevant within global firms. As the Toyota case illustrates, expatriates (and inpatriates) play especially important roles, as they bring their social capital with them and create new social relationships in their host organizations.

Social Capital across Cultures

While social capital is important in all cultural and institutional contexts, there are differences in how one goes about building it and how social relationships influence management and business.

One study explored the functioning of social capital in a comparison of French and US enterprises. Successful French managers, like their American counterparts, had extensive personal networks, though social capital was found to develop in a different way. French managers tended to have long employment relationships with their firms, and the managers' networks—which were mostly within the organization—reflected this. Their limited social capital outside the firm was built on contacts formed during executive education programs, demonstrating the role that management training plays in building social networks. In contrast, the networks of the more mobile American managers reflected work relationships with people from a wider variety of firms, brokering a wider range of potential innovations, though perhaps at the expense of the capacity to leverage networks within their organization.[33]

China exemplifies a society where social capital (*guanxi*) plays a crucial role. Strong personal relationships are typically formed through family ties, shared provenance (coming from the same villages), and studying together. There is also a well-established tradition of using trustworthy individuals to broker introductions to unknown others, the "third person" acting as a guarantee for the trustworthiness of all parties. Experienced managers, consultants, and academics stress the importance of creating *guanxi* with employees, business partners, suppliers, customers, and government officials. Foreign firms can adopt one of two basic strategies. They can either buy external *guanxi* by recruiting individuals who already have relationships with important stakeholders or develop their own *guanxi* over time.

However, China's high regard for social capital is by no means unique. Countries in Central and Eastern Europe—and even Switzerland, where mandatory military service for males traditionally builds networks across social groups—are other examples of countries or regions where what often matters is "who you know."

Managing the Darker Side of Social Capital

Most discussions about social capital in organizations focus on its positive contributions to firm performance. However, social capital also has a potential dark side.

A high level of bonding within a social group may mean that the group is closed to outsiders. An example of this is language-based social networks in multinational firms. Although most large multinationals use English as their official corporate language, in reality individuals and units tend to form social network clusters based on their languages. Japanese corporations have been criticized for having strong networks of Japanese-speaking executives that are difficult for nonspeakers to break into. Employees of a large Finnish multinational who did not speak Finnish complained about the "Finnish mafia."[34]

The former CEO of IKEA, Anders Moberg created a public stir when he addressed an MBA class and advised all foreign employees who really wanted to advance in the company to learn Swedish.[35] Although his comments were intended to urge future employees to understand the culture of the parent organization, they nonetheless point to the disadvantage shared by the large majority of staff who did not master the language. It has also been shown that fluency in the corporate language is positively associated with the level of trust and shared understanding within global organizations.[36]

Social categorizations produce in-groups and out-groups. Gender researchers have criticized the persistence of male-dominated networks of executives, arguing that old boy networks lead to discrimination against women. Although many corporations put considerable efforts into diversity management, the top layers of most global firms are still dominated by men, often from the corporation's home country.[37] Strong local bonding may also make it difficult for expatriates and short-term visitors to become integrated in a unit.

Close social relationships and a high level of solidarity may make an organization too inward-looking. Little new information will reach the members of the group, who are too loyal toward each other to engage in an external search for new ideas and opportunities. For instance, a set of strong personal relationships with the people working for a local supplier may prevent the firm from noticing and seeking out better alternatives. The not-invented-here syndrome may be particularly prevalent in units with strong internal bonding.[38]

One crucial question for the corporation is who will appropriate the potential advantages that accrue to individual employees who bridge different social networks. As a private good,[39] social capital is an asset that individuals can use to improve their own situation; indeed, social relationships are the basis for many nefarious forms of corruption. But leaving corruption aside, take the example of a corporate scientist who gains access to important information that would benefit other members of the product development team. There is no guarantee that the individual will share the information because sharing would weaken his or her own position.[40]

Finally, it is important to recognize that there are costs (money and time) associated with developing and maintaining social networks, for both the company and the individual. Investments in social relationships are means rather than the ends; however, the extent to which employees will use their social capital to the benefit of the corporation is to a large extent a question of how aligned their values and goals are with those of the corporation.

SHARING VALUES GLOBALLY

The Toyota Way reflects a system of values and accompanying behavioral norms that evolved informally over the years. New members of the organization learn the Toyota Way gradually, partly through an oral tradition of stories and anecdotes, and partly by observing and learning from events and behavior around them. The writing and publishing of the Toyota Way, and continual reference to it by executives, further strengthen the company's culture and sharpen the Toyota identity.

Scholars and managers have shared an interest in organizational culture for several decades. Today, the term is widely used in the business community not only to describe and explain corporate practice but also to explain performance. Managers are advised to investigate the cultural fit between the partners in international alliances,[41] problems encountered in mergers and acquisitions are often explained by clashes in culture,[42] and some companies recruit above all for cultural fit, reasoning that skills can be learnt.

Shared Values, Beliefs, and Norms

We focus here on one common way to view culture—as a system of shared *values*, defining what is important; shared *beliefs* about one's own corporation and its context; and associated *norms* that define appropriate behavior and action in the organization.[43] Largely tacit mental assumptions (values and beliefs), shared by members of the organization, are at the core of the concept of organizational culture, manifesting themselves in organizational symbols, rituals, the language used by employees, and the stories told by people in the organization.[44] Members of an organization may be unconscious of the beliefs and values they share.

When top managers say, "we have to change our culture," they are usually expressing their view that values, norms, and behavior need to be better aligned with corporate strategy. As we have seen, organizational culture can be a tool of normative control;[45] a primary purpose of shared values in this case would be to ensure that corporate goals and objectives are followed. But in the context of social coordination in multinationals, shared values have much broader purpose; they facilitate bottom-up initiatives and horizontal collaboration and initiatives, not only top-down compliance.[46]

As companies move to the transnational stage, shared values become even more important. While consistency in strategy execution is still critical, shared values facilitate trust, which is essential for effective lateral governance, horizontal problem-solving, and knowledge creation. IBM, for example, believes today that in a knowledge-based world where talented individuals always have other options, the only way of integrating people into the firm is through values and norms that are broadly shared and internalized, steering necessarily autonomous action at every level of the organization.

The Benefits of a Strong Culture

Most observers would unhesitatingly describe Toyota's organizational culture as "strong." An organizational culture can be considered *strong* if its values, beliefs, and norms are widely shared and intensely held by members of the organization.[47] A strong culture increases consistency of behavior among employees. In a multinational firm, the advantage of a strong culture is that it engenders coordination and facilitates interaction among employees and units who know what to expect from others. Common behavioral norms provide guidelines for ways to behave in different situations; and widespread agreement about values provides a basis for deciding how to act without formal rules.

Strong organizational cultures enhance goal alignment. When there is clarity about corporate goals as well as appropriate behavior and practices, employees face less uncertainty and can react quickly when confronted with unexpected situations. In Toyota, the focus on challenge and *genchi genbutsu* has been internalized by employees as a natural way to approach problem-solving. Goal alignment also facilitates coordination, as there is less room for debate about the firm's best interests.[48]

There is some evidence for the hypothesis that strong organizational cultures are associated with better and more reliable performance.[49] However, other studies have failed to find any significant relationship between cultural strength and company success. One reason for these somewhat inconclusive research findings are the potential costs associated with a strong culture. Firms with a strong culture often lack internal diversity and may have difficulty adapting to changes in the business environment that require radical shifts in strategy and operational modes.[50]

Corporate Versus Local Unit Identification

But are corporations that span dozens of countries and have a number of different businesses characterized by only *one* organizational culture? In reality, there may be significant differences in values, beliefs, and norms across units. Not only do we often find that foreign subsidiaries constitute *subcultures* within the multinational; we also find that employees are torn between their allegiances to the local unit and the global parent organization. This tension between the local and the global allegiance has been analyzed in research on *organizational identification.*

Organizational identification refers to the strength of an employee's identification with the organization in which the person works.[51] Identification tends to be stronger if there is a good match between the employee's and the organization's values, a relationship that often becomes deeper the longer the person has been employed.[52]

Organizational identification has many positive effects for a corporation. If employees throughout a multinational firm identify with the parent corporation and feel positively toward its leadership, their self-esteem and self-motivation will be enhanced. Organizational identification also facilitates cooperation across units since employees share values and loyalties. But this does not imply that allegiance to the local unit in which they are working will be detrimental to the performance of the company.

Indeed, in multinational enterprises and other large organizations, employees often identify with several organizational entities. For instance, an expatriate manager may have a strong identification with the corporation as a whole and at the same time be psychologically attached to the subsidiary where she is working. Such *dual organizational identification* is beneficial since it fosters sensitivity to both corporate and local interests and concerns, and it may help the manager to be a "bi-cultural interpreter" between the local unit and the rest of the corporation.[53] In fact, employees who have dual loyalties—to the corporation as a whole and to their own local unit—may be more effective than those who identify only with the global organization.[54] For instance, a subsidiary manager in a consumer goods company may play an important role in balancing between the pressure from headquarters to adopt a globally standardized brand strategy and the necessity to adapt that strategy to local conditions.[55]

There is some evidence that subsidiary managers identify more with their own unit than with the parent corporation, especially host country managers[56], but even expatriates experience dual identification.[57] Rather than trying to weaken subsidiary identity, corporations should try to strengthen corporate identity.[58] There are several ways of doing this. First, make sure that employees in subsidiaries spend time at corporate headquarters; second, communicate positive characteristics of the corporate identity actively and persuasively; and third, signal international career opportunities for employees from all geographical units.

Building Shared Values

Shared values across the units of a transnational firm cannot be imposed through a top-down process. They are diffused through continuous and consistent reinforcement, based on interactions between like-minded individuals from different parts of the multinational. What really counts is what people do—particularly their leaders—not what is said on the corporate website. Therefore every aspect of people strategies, from communication to performance management, has to be aligned with the desired values and behaviors. The diffusion of shared values requires what is called values-based leadership.

The firm's HR practices play a central role in shaping and strengthening the values that underlie organizational culture. Selection is one of the most important instruments. When they recruit and select employees either for entry positions or promotions, many successful firms strive for a fit with existing (or desired) values. Trying to reengineer the fit for existing employees is much more difficult.

In any multinational firm, the extent to which culture is shared is influenced by a range of factors. The most critical of these are:

- The broader culture and institutional environment in which the corporation was founded.
- The beliefs and actions of founders and other important past and current leaders, as well as explicit efforts at defining and communicating the corporate values.
- Processes of employee socialization.
- International employee transfers.
- Monitoring how well employees adhere to corporate values and norms.

Each of these factors will influence the choice of HR tools and practices used to develop and reinforce the organizational culture of a global firm.

The Interface of National and Organizational Cultures

As we discussed in Chapter 2, organizations reflect to some extent the societal environment in which they have been established. For example, the collaborative values often found in Japanese firms reflect traditional Japanese societal values.[59] Companies can use such features to enhance their image among customers and prospective employees. The values of LVMH, a company selling luxury goods, champagne, and spirits reflect the refinement and elegance associated with its French origins. The cultures of BMW and Audi are rooted in the importance of engineering in German society.[60]

However, although there is a relationship between societal and organizational values, many successful firms are cultural outliers, with unique cultures that do not fit a national pattern. A close-up analysis of the culture of companies from the same country and in the same industry can reveal striking differences. Take for instance the values of Toyota and Honda. Although the values and philosophies of these two Japanese competitors may appear similar at a distance, Honda's culture stresses the importance of individual ambitions and performance, and being aggressive in the marketplace. Honda's founder, Honda Soichiro, once told a reporter: "Each individual should work for himself. People will not sacrifice themselves for the company. They come to work at the company to enjoy themselves."[61] Honda also focuses more on R&D and innovation than Toyota. We need to look beyond national heritage to understand differences in organizational cultures.

Organizational cultures are anchored on a *distinct* set of shared values. Within their home country, few managers would question the benefit of such cultural differentiation. Leading-edge companies are seldom scolded by the business press for having a different management style than their competitors. Indeed, culture is viewed as an important source of competitive advantage. Idiosyncratic cultures and values are celebrated and often emulated. However, for many multinational firms, it can be a challenge to maintain social cohesion around unique values while expanding globally and responding to local cultures.

While it is fine to be unique or different at home, being different in a foreign culture is frequently considered rude and arrogant. For example, when Michelin's management in China decided to promote the company global values among its Chinese staff, many observers were critical of their decision, arguing that the company should follow the "Chinese Way" rather than the "Michelin Way."[62] Nevertheless, many successful international firms have chosen to implement the same business values globally. For example, Johnson & Johnson had a "no bribes" policy that makes no allowance for locally "accepted" business practices long before other firms subscribed to the same principle.

Organizational Values: Historical Legacy or Engineered Outcome?

There is wide agreement that founders and significant leaders often exert considerable influence on organizational culture. We have already mentioned several in our discussion of normative control, we can add numerous others such as Honda Soichiro, Zhang Ruimin (Haier), Ratan Tata (Tata Group), Sam Walton (Wal-Mart) and Jack Welch (GE) as examples of founders and long-term CEOs whose values and beliefs shaped their corporations. Some of their values and beliefs helped their organizations deal with critical situations in their history. Learning from such events can become important elements of the culture of the company, even as it expands around the world.[63]

Some of these corporate leaders have written up their values, beliefs, and personal stories in books.[64] Many firms consciously use *stories*, or sagas, from the history of the organization to describe significant accomplishments of their founders or other key leaders to highlight important aspects of their culture. The stories anchor the present in the past and provide legitimacy for how things are done in the organization today. It has become customary to present these war stories on the corporate website for the benefit of internal and external visitors.

Shared language is one precondition for strong cultures, helping employees to communicate effectively, even across considerable geographic and cultural distance. Firms with strong cultures often develop their own vocabularies that new organizational members have to learn. And this learning lasts; former employees of GE or Toyota can be spotted even years after they left their original employers based on the language they use.

Material symbols can also be used to reinforce the values of the organization. The layout of corporate headquarters, the types of cars that executives are given and how they travel, and the dress code and behavior of managers are all symbolic expressions of organizational values. Take, for instance, the corporate culture of IKEA, with frugality (and relentless focus on cost reduction) being one of its core values. This is well understood throughout the whole organization from stories that are told about the behavior of the company founder, Ingmar Kamprad: how he drives an old Volvo; that he travels in economy class and stays in budget hotels.

Many global firms try actively to create a set of corporate values. The so-called *values jamborees* at IBM have received widespread attention. In July 2003, IBM chairman Sam Palmisano invited all employees at IBM worldwide to participate in a 72-hour Web-based discussion of what "we represent to our-selves and to the rest of the world." More than 22,000 members of the organization participated in the experiment, which was followed by a large number of analyses and discussions leading to the formulation of IBM's three values: (1) dedication to every client's success; (2) innovation that matters—for our company and for the world; and (3) trust and personal responsibility in all relationships. HR programs and policies were redesigned in line with these values. Other large multinational corporations have engaged in similar jamborees when redefining their corporate values.

Managing Employee Socialization

Along with selection, employee socialization is probably the most important tool for building global corporate culture, as pointed out earlier in Chapter 3. Every organization is unique, and so new members need to learn its ropes and how they can function effectively within it. For newcomers to become committed to the organization and be able to contribute effectively, they need to feel socially accepted—that they have become insiders.[65] Although socialization occurs whenever an individual changes roles and moves across boundaries within the firm, the process is most intense when first entering the organization.[66]

New employees go through the first part of the socialization process before they officially join. The signals sent by firms to the labor market influence the kind of applicants that they receive.[67] The more distinct and consistent the messages that the corporation sends to the labor market via its Web site and advertisements, the more likely applicants are to fit the cultural values, leading to better commitment to the firm. Multinationals like Toyota, Cisco, and Unilever have developed elaborate presentations of their company on their Web pages in which they describe what it is like to work in the company.

Many firms have formal induction programs for new employees, and there is ample evidence that such programs improve the outcomes of the socialization process.[68] At Toyota, new members of the US organization go through a comprehensive five-week orientation program. Every hour of the induction program is specified. Subsequently, the new hires are transferred to their own unit where the focus shifts to on-the-job training.[69] For newly recruited managers induction training is weighted more toward individualized mentoring.

Socialization is not an issue for entry-level employees only; it is equally important for externally recruited managers and senior executives if they are to perform well in their new company. One US executive, recruited to a high-level position in Toyota, went through a period of 12 weeks in a US engine plant, followed by 10 days visiting plants (including suppliers) in Japan. A senior Toyota manager served as his mentor, giving him assignments and feedback and discussing his experiences on a continuous basis.[70] The socialization process was aimed at helping the US manager to understand Toyota's values as well as its management and production principles through an intensive firsthand experience. He also began to develop personal relationships with people in different parts of the corporation.

One of the challenges in managing the socialization of new managers is the delicate balance that has to be achieved between socialization and desired change.[71] Socialization should be seen as a two-way process, where the organization is striving to influence new members who, conversely, may have been recruited to bring new competencies. If the corporation is inert and hostile toward changes associated with recent hires, the potential value of the new ideas brought into the firm is lost and the incomers are likely to leave.

Rolls-Royce, the aircraft engine firm competing with GE, has been successfully expanding into new geographies. It recruited senior executives from across the world, with the aim of globalizing its traditional British culture. Rolls-Royce's top management recognized that this recruitment drive would not only involve socializing new executives into the firm, but also entail the resocialization of managers who had spent their entire careers in Rolls-Royce into new ways of thinking. Recognizing that close social network building was vital, the vehicle for the reciprocal socialization was a six-month management program offered periodically to a mix of roughly half new recruits and half old timers. The program was sponsored by the CEO, who ran the first day of the initial five-day training, briefing participants on strategically important projects on which teams then worked intensively together, reporting their recommendations back to him and top management.

International training programs, with sessions taught in different parts of the world, combined with cross-national teams working on action learning projects may also be used to influence the participants' values, beliefs, and behaviors. AGC Group, one of the leading global glass manufactures, has its headquarters in Japan and significant operations in Europe and Asia. It has made the dissemination of the "Asahi Way," a global coordination tool, the focal point of its senior leadership program.

Finally, international mobility is another key tool for diffusion of shared values. Toyota is a good example of a multinational firm that consciously uses international assignments, and increasingly also involving non-Japanese employees, to transfer the parent company culture to new production facilities around the world. Toyota is not alone in using expatriates as a way to diffuse shared values to different parts of the corporation.[72] Expatriates have been labeled "bumble-bees," because they fly across units and pollinate local employees with corporate values, beliefs, and behavioral patterns.[73]

However, as we will discuss in Chapter 9, multinationals also transfer employees *from* foreign subsidiaries to headquarters or other corporate units. This is done not only to learn the business or inform headquarters about the local perspective, but also with the objective of helping the inpatriates absorb parent company values and beliefs. In a number of multinational firms, it is well understood that a prerequisite for locally hired high potential employees to reach senior positions is a successful pilgrimage to head office.

Monitoring Adherence to Values and Norms

Virtually all multinationals administer some kind of employee surveys at regular intervals. For instance Toyota carries out an Employee Morale and Opinion Survey in its US units every 18–25 months. Many corporations use these surveys not only to obtain feedback from their employees on a range of issues, but also to measure how well corporate values and corresponding behaviors are followed. The results are then typically fed back to the unit and discussed. If necessary, corrective measures are agreed and implemented.

As with so many other aspects of organizational life, organizational culture will not take hold if senior management does not walk the talk. One of the most difficult decisions is how to deal with high-performing managers who compromise company values. Companies with strong cultures practice zero-tolerance: compliance first, performance second. In one US pharmaceutical firm, a highly successful general manager of a Chinese subsidiary was asked to resign because he tolerated sales practices that were incongruent with corporate values. Although the official announcement was very discreet, within days, everyone in the company worldwide understood that values are nonnegotiable.

Challenges in Managing Organizational Culture

Firms with strong cultures typically have explicit values, indeed often a clearly understood management philosophy like the Hewlett-Packard Way, the Lincoln Electric Value System, or the Toyota Way. Explicit values are the backdrop against which the practices can be calibrated. This is desirable because it is not specific work practices that create a competitive culture but the coherence and consistency between those practices.

The potential upside of having a strong organizational culture is significant, but heavy-handed management efforts to manipulate the culture easily backfire. Indeed culture management may be viewed as social engineering, which in the extreme can lead to an Orwellian "1984," when socialization and training are manipulation in disguise, and empowerment means making someone else take risks and responsibility.[74] In multinationals, attempts by headquarters to influence employee values and norm may be perceived as colonialism, as expatriates and parent company managers imposing their values and norms on the local workforce. In a similar way, top management's claims about corporate identity may be challenged by employees in subsidiaries, who strive to preserve the elements of the subsidiaries' identity and organizational culture that they value.[75]

In addition, successful cultures may breed complacency, some core principles may be put aside for a convenience sake, or proven values can actually become a hindrance in addressing new challenges. This became evident in Toyota's slow response to the quality problems experienced in the United States in 2009–2011. In view of some experienced observers, Toyota was "overwhelmed by demon of complexity"—too many products in too many markets.[76] However, problems with deploying "Toyota Way" also played a critical role (see box "Why Toyota Lost Its Way?").

Why Toyota Lost Its Way?

- Toyota's traditional credo has been "quality first, then quantity follows", but this faded away when the company goal changed to become number one in the world. Toyota did not have a sufficient number of quality control experts to support the rapid expansion of its product portfolio and overseas growth.[77]
- Because of the fast growth, the quality of relationship with suppliers suffered; Toyota employees with insufficient experience applying "Toyota Way" were assigned to global technical centers to work with and monitor new suppliers—who also lacked experience in Toyota practices and standards.[78]

- Toyota's culture is to focus on facts—and internal studies did not show that Toyota design or production causing defects reported by customers. The government investigation eventually concurred. But blaming the customers for causing the quality problem turned out to be a major marketing fiasco.
- Internally focused senior executives in the headquarters did not pay sufficient attention to expectations of regulators, media and public opinion in overseas markets, and consequently, they were slow to respond to what was perceived as a local problem.[79]

As Toyota's difficulties in the US illustrate, even for the "best-of-breed" companies, sustaining culture in day-to-day operations is riddled with challenges. The existing literature, examples of multinationals that have been successful in managing their cultures over a long period of time, and our own experience suggest that culture management requires:

- A profound understanding of factors influencing human behavior across cultures
- Consciousness of the key elements of the existing culture that the firm wants to retain and those that it would like to change (and why)
- The involvement of employees from different parts of the corporation in the process
- Attention to how decisions and actions are interpreted by organizational members across units and borders
- Attention to the realignment of the whole range of HR practices in all parts of the firm
- Parent company executives as well as local managers who "walk the talk"
- A long-term perspective, recognizing that change in culture requires continuity in change

The careful management of organizational values at the Indian IT giant Infosys provides a good example of many of the points we have mentioned here; see the box "Walking the Talk at Infosys."

Walking the Talk at Infosys

The top management of India's Infosys deeply believe that shared values and principles give the corporation its character and provide the sustained integration they feel its 165,000 employees need.[80] The values were those of Narayan Murthy and his seven colleagues, who established the firm in 1981 and built a leading global IT-services corporation. The values are formalized as client value, leadership by example, integrity and transparency, fairness, and excellence.

These may sound like trite phrases, but they are imbued with meaning for Infosys staff precisely because of the example of their leaders. Indeed, being a role model is embedded in the second of the five values. Narayan Murthy, former CEO and chairman, set the example by living in the same two-room apartment he and his wife moved into in 1984. He says, "I truly believe in leadership by example. I have realized that it is the most powerful way of creating trust in your ideas. Before doing something, you must do it yourself." For example, he used to travel frequently on company buses. When complaints were made about bus travel, Murthy's comments were taken seriously. He also believed in rapid communication and his management team responded to all internal e-mails and inquiries within 24 hours.[81]

Recruits in this fast-moving company are hired and promoted not for their IT skills but for their ability to learn quickly and for their fit with company values. The concern today is how to maintain these values as the company expands its operations around the globe.

LEVERAGING GLOBAL MINDSET

Several years ago, one of the Nokia's divisions providing telecommunications infrastructure participated in a study of how managers perceive a company's global strategy. The survey showed that some parts of the organization, such as product lines, had a highly global orientation. Other parts were strongly local, for example, sales companies in emerging markets. The initial reaction of most executives was positive: "This is exactly the type of differentiation we need—strongly integrated product lines worrying about global economies of scale and locally oriented sales units worrying about local opportunities."

Their view changed as they realized that, as a result of this differentiation, conflicts were being pushed up to senior management for arbitration, overloading their agendas and causing delays in decision-making. While the product managers did indeed need to be global, they also needed to work conflicts through with local sales units—and vice versa. Consequently, Nokia launched a number of initiatives, ranging from management education to changes in profit and loss accountability in order to develop more balanced perspectives and the necessary global mindset.

Leadership is essential for addressing the contradictions of transnational enterprise, but it is insufficient. The key lies in the minds of people inside the enterprise—requiring a particular intellectual orientation to business problems and an open and positive attitude toward other cultures and people. We call the attitudes and the required cognitive structure that underlie such thinking a *global mindset*.[82] What is a global mindset, and how does one develop it?

What Is Global Mindset?

The organizational challenges of globalization require new skills for managing diversity as well as changes in how managers frame business problems. Perlmutter's now-classic typology of ethnocentric, polycentric, and geocentric orientations or mindsets of managers in multinationals formed a framework for subsequent thinking about this issue. Perlmutter identified a need for more "geocentric" managers, "the best [wo]men, regardless of nationality, to solve the company's problems anywhere in the world."[83]

What is the difference between geocentric managers and expatriates? Expatriates are defined by location; they are managers working in a different country from their own. In contrast, geocentric[84] / global[85] / glocal[86] / transnational[87] managers—the terms have been used in similar ways by different authors—are defined by their *state of mind*. They are people who can work effectively across organizational, functional, and cross-cultural boundaries. Not all expatriates are global managers; in fact, many expatriates have an ethnocentric orientation.[88] At the same time, managers in key subsidiaries may not be expatriates, but they need to have a global mindset.

There are two different and complementary perspectives on global mindset, one rooted in a psychological focus on the development of managers in multinational firms, and the other coming from scholars and practitioners with a strategic viewpoint on the transnational enterprise. Let us briefly review these two perspectives.

The Cultural Perspective

The first perspective views global mindset as *the ability to accept and work with cultural diversity*. Cultural self-awareness, openness to and understanding of other cultures are the core elements of the cultural perspective (some scholars prefer the term "psychological perspective") on global mindsets.[89] In contrast to an ethnocentric mindset, a person with a global mindset "accepts diversity and heterogeneity as a source of opportunity."[90]

In line with this perspective, the term "transnational manager" has been coined to describe cultural "citizens of the world," individuals defined by their knowledge and appreciation of different cultures, able to tread smoothly and expertly between cultures and countries throughout their career.[91] It has been suggested that people with a global mindset tend to have broader perspectives than people with a traditional domestic mindset; they try to understand the context for decision-making and are suspicious of "one-best-way" solutions. They accept life as a balance of contradictory forces, facilitating their ability to handle tensions and conflict. They value diversity, channeling it through teamwork, and show more creativity in problem-solving. They view change as an opportunity rather than a threat, are open to new initiatives, and focus on process rather than structure to deal with the ambiguities and needs for adaptation in multinational firms.[92]

Few individuals possess all these qualities, but those who do are likely to be better equipped to deal with the challenges of working in transnational firms.

The Strategic Perspective

The second complementary perspective on global mindset, and the one that we will address in more detail, focuses on a way of thinking (or cognition) that reflects conflicting strategic orientations and can therefore be labeled a *strategic* perspective.

Since most multinational firms face strategic contradictions, scholars have emphasized the need for "balanced perspectives," arguing that a critical determinant of success in multinationals lies in the cognitive orientations of senior managers—their cognitive ability to cope with complexity embedded in the business.[93]

Diverse roles and dispersed operations must be held together by a management mindset that understands the need for multiple strategic capabilities and views problems and opportunities from both local and global perspectives. The task is not to build a sophisticated structure but to create a matrix in managers' minds.[94] The "matrix in the mind" concept captures the notion of global mindset and the idea that contradictions need to be built into the way of thinking of managers and leaders in the transnational firm.

As we discussed earlier in this book, the main strategic drivers in the transnational enterprise are global efficiency, local responsiveness, and worldwide coordination. So the strategic perspective on global mindset expects individuals to *hold competing priorities* rather than to advocate one dimension at the expense of the others.[95]

Obviously, not all companies need to develop a transnational mindset in order to do business across borders, although we believe that an increasing number of firms will need to develop in this direction. A multidomestic or meganational mindset may sometimes be just as appropriate, depending on the strategic posture of the corporation.

Measuring Global Mindset

Measurement is a powerful tool for development. Using repeat surveys to evaluate global mindset provides management with an indicator of the effectiveness of development activities. Global mindsets have been measured in different ways, some focusing on the psychological/cultural dimension, some on the strategic.[96]

It is possible to measure the strategic global mindset orientation of different parts of the multinational (see Table 5-2),[97] assessing the capacity of individuals to understand a complex global strategy and thereby steering its implementation.

Some years ago we undertook a study of Nokia Networks, mentioned at the beginning of this section. The data showed that global efficiency/integration was valued more than local responsiveness, highlighting a polarity between the global orientation of worldwide product lines and the local orientation of downstream units responsible for regional sales and customer services. Corporate staff held more balanced views, but with a relatively low orientation toward both global integration and local responsiveness, reflecting difficulties in reaching consensus. Previously the company had handled the tensions of conflicting polarities through informal dialogue among the close-knit network of leaders who shared common experiences and values. However, as the business expanded, the ability of a small network of leaders to address all the issues was increasingly strained. This global mindset needed to be shared by a much larger managerial population.

What did the company do? They actively communicated the need to increase local responsiveness and rotated the leadership team to give more responsibility to executives with local experience. Profit and loss accountability was decentralized. 250 managers were involved in action learning programs to find ways of increasing lateral coordination, replacing vertical integration. The next round of the survey 18 months later showed a significant shift in the desired direction.

How to Develop Global Mindset

While it may seem obvious that multinational firms will need more managers with global mindset both at headquarters and in overseas units, translating this attractive vision into an operational reality is not simple. Research indicates that the experience of occupying complex roles over time will lead to an increase in the level of global mindset.[98] How does one go about developing global mindset among managers and employees before they are promoted to global executive roles? How can HRM tools help? It all starts with recognizing diversity.

• **Global efficiency/integration:** the centralized management of dispersed assets and activities to achieve scale economies.
• **Local responsiveness:** resource commitment decisions taken autonomously by a subsidiary in response to primarily local competitive or customer demands.
• **Worldwide coordination:** the level of lateral interaction within and between the network of affiliates with respect to business, function, and value chain activities.

TABLE 5-2
Measuring Global Mindset

Source: T.P. Murtha, S.A. Lenway, and R.P. Bagozzi, "Global Mindsets and Cognitive Shift in a Complex Multinational Corporation," *Strategic Management Journal* 19: 2 (February 1998).

Equal Opportunity for All—Regardless of Passport

Perhaps the biggest barrier to the development of global mindset is the impression of local staff around the world that one's passport counts more than one's talent. If developmental opportunities are restricted to people from the parent country, or those from a few lead countries, local employees will tend to retain local perspectives—the only direction relevant for their own futures.

From a long-term perspective, a truly global enterprise must satisfy a simple but demanding test: does it matter where employees enter the organization? Today, there are probably only a few companies that can meet this benchmark, especially if global actually means outside of the northern hemisphere. It takes decades of effort to ensure that selection criteria are not biased toward one cultural group and that early identification of talent works just as well in Karachi or Johannesburg as it does in New York.

Why do these barriers persist? Historically, most operational HR activities in multinational firms were decentralized to individual country organizations. In principle, this is logical; after all, the vast majority of employees will always be "local," embedded in the local culture and impacted by the local institutional environment. However, when HR localization is taken too literally, and everyone is treated as local, who is "global?" A natural outcome of this approach is that nationals of the country where the corporate center is located are considered implicitly "global," but all others are "local" and have only a limited chance of advancing on the corporate ladder.

The emphasis on global mindset requires a major shift in HR orientation, with regional HR managers having a particular responsibility for building global mindset as well as for leadership development.

Building on International Mobility and Project Work

International assignments develop many different aspects of global mindset, as outlined in Table 5-3.[99]

TABLE 5-3
How Mobility Enhances Global Mindset

- Transfers develop the portfolio of skills associated with global mindset, such as championing global strategy, facing up to cross-border conflicts, and handling complexity. Individuals with deep international experience show more creativity in problem-solving.[100]

- Transfers develop skills in handling cultural diversity. An individual learns that there is more than one way "to skin a cat" and that different ways have merits. This also counteracts the cognitive tendency to think in terms of cultural stereotypes.

- As managers move from a local subsidiary role to a regional or global coordination role and back, they know that they may inherit any problems of excessive localism (or globalism) in their next job—which may moderate the natural tendency to swing the pendulum too far.

- The need to balance different pressures is built into many jobs. The career prospects of the international assignee depend on being able to satisfy the performance requirements of the subsidiary, *and* the demands of headquarters staff, *and* perhaps those of the assignee's mother country.

- Someone with experience of working abroad is more likely to be put on international project groups and councils, to be appointed to cross-border steering groups, and to be a link in best practice transfer, all of which reinforce the development of global mindset.

- Individuals who speak several languages tend to have a more global mindset. Language training combined with international experience can contribute to increasing the level of global mindset in the multinational.

However, given the cost of international mobility, multinationals need also to use other ways to increase the global mindset of their employees. Cross-border projects are an excellent alternative tool to develop global mindset. The purpose of the project group (or cross-border steering group or internal board) is to bring different perspectives to bear. The skills learnt through project work include the ability to work with peers who may have different perspectives on how to approach the problem, setting goals on important but ambiguous tasks and working through conflicts.

Enhancing Global Mindset through Management Training

Another important tool to develop global mindset is training. This underlines the appeal of recruiting from business schools with internationally heterogeneous student populations. The educational process, with its emphasis on classroom discussion, team approaches to case studies, and international consulting projects, is designed to maximize the give-and-take of multiple opinions and orientations, giving the students a better understanding of the richness of perspectives and the value of tapping into other people's knowledge.

Many companies, including Johnson & Johnson, Unilever, and GE, use in-house training to speed up the development of global mindsets. Staff in GE's management development center designed short, intensive, and experiential action learning programs to foster GE's internationalization. As part of these programs, multicultural action learning teams of GE managers were sent to China, Russia, and India to work on specific company problems in these regions, as well as to collect information on GE's best and worst practices around the world. The teams immersed themselves in the issues relevant to each region and reported on their findings, outlining business opportunities to top management. Even today, many years later, former participants reflect on their "global leadership" training as one of the most influential events of their career.

Most of the company-specific programs that we undertake with multinational firms have the development of global mindset as an objective. A typical scenario is a two-week seminar for 36 select executives. The concept behind such programs is simple: lock up a group of executives off-site; get them to understand each other's problems and their interdependencies through project work and discussion of appropriate cases, guided by the conceptual understanding and encouragement of outside faculty; and facilitate the face-to-face relationships that will allow them to work through the challenges. In short, build global mindset and appropriate behavior.

Adjusting Performance Metrics

Our research at Nokia Networks showed that expatriates had far more "balanced" perspectives than their domestic counterparts, showing high understanding of the interplay between global and local forces and the need for coordination. However, to the company's surprise, there were no significant differences in mindset between expatriates returning to Finland after six months' absence and those who had never left home. At headquarters, roles, responsibilities, and corresponding performance criteria were heavily skewed to the global at the expense of the local. Repolarization of the mindset followed quickly.

One of the key steps top management took was to adjust performance management metrics to push for more balanced perspectives. Shared performance indicators, tied to a common global strategy, also facilitate the resolution of conflicts across boundaries.[101]

The Role of Senior Executives

Global mindset starts at the top. The first step is its articulation and reinforcement by top management, in clear and consistent language, across all levels and units. During his tenure as CEO of ABB, Percy Barnevik spent more than 200 days each year visiting ABB's units around the world, personally presenting his vision of a global enterprise to thousands of managers and employees. For many years, "Barnevik's slides" served as a common source of reference down through the organization. Barnevik did not believe that communicating ABB's business vision and strategy could be delegated. Many other top executives agree: corporate leaders like Carlos Ghosn of Renault-Nissan and former Shell CEO Jeroen Van der Veer are famed for the amount of time they have spent roaming the world to spread the word.

Global mindset is not just part of a vision statement; it is manifested in the way a company makes strategic decisions and goes about their implementation. While top management provides the context for the way to think about global strategy, it is up to the senior managers in business units, functions, and regional or country organizations to make global mindset a reality throughout the organization. Their respective roles may be different, but they ultimately share the responsibility for the synergy between responsiveness and integration.

Rethinking the Global Mindset Paradigm

At this point, it may be useful to remind ourselves that global mindset—and its strategic dimension in particular—is about holding and using multiple perspectives that at first glance may appear contradictory. In their passion to promote global mindset, academics and practitioners have a tendency to see global or cosmopolitan as superior to local, calling for a "universal way that transcends the particulars of places."[102] "Local" is taken to mean parochial and narrow-minded.

However, in our view, global mindset requires the opposite approach to such one-dimensional universalism; it calls for a dualistic perspective, immersion in local "particulars" while retaining a wider cross-border orientation. It is important to consider that a genuine emphasis on global mindset implies recognizing that diversity includes tolerance of people who are not "global," either through lack of opportunity, personal choice, or circumstances. Anything taken to extremes risks becoming pathological—and global mindset is no exception. This is true for companies as well as for individuals.

During the last decade, a catchy paradigm—"Think globally, act locally"—has often been used to capture the concept of a progressive global corporation that considers the whole world its market but at the same time carefully nurtures local priorities and requirements. However, implementing this vision has turned out to be a longer and more difficult process than most companies envisioned.

What is the problem here? In a multinational firm that used this popular slogan on the first page of its annual report, one local subsidiary manager commented: "Our firm is organized on a simple premise. When operating under stress—and that is most of the time—*they* do the thinking, and *we* do the acting." In other words, thinking and acting are two separate roles, performed by two separate groups. The headquarters takes the strategic initiatives, which the locals are left to implement.

In contrast, global mindset is about the ability to keep and use contradictory perspectives. It is also as much about learning as about doing. To be truly global implies openness to learn from the experience of others and to understand and appreciate how others (local customers, employees, or competitors) think. However, the ability to satisfy those needs with a superior value proposition is dependent on the *global* mobilization of corporate resources, whether these are leading-edge technology, economies of scale, or global standards of performance and quality.

Perhaps the way out of the global/local dilemma is to return to the logic of the globalization process. Today, it is not enough to act locally in a fragmented country-by-country fashion. Leveraging R&D investments, manufacturing assets, logistics, IT infrastructure, service platforms, and operational know-how for competitive advantage requires a world-scale approach. At the same time, customer needs are increasingly individualized, and customers throughout the world exhibit a strong preference to be treated as individuals—the secret of the business model implemented by Ritz-Carlton (providing extraordinary personal service to its hotel clients) or the mass customization perfected by Toyota. Similar tendencies are increasing among corporate customers: they want it their way, unique to their particular situation, but at best possible global price and quality—and speedily. This can only be achieved if the whole organization can act as one.

What, then, is the competitive advantage of a global firm? In simple terms, it is the ability to tap into and mobilize the company's *capabilities*, wherever in multinationals they may exist, to satisfy local *customer needs* in different parts of the word. It may be useful, therefore, to rephrase the original paradigm. Building a company with a global mindset is really about developing an organization that can *learn locally and act globally*—in a way that competitors cannot match.[103] Perhaps this is a contradiction, but such is the nature of globalization.

In summary, the idea behind global mindset is that managers must have the capacity to accept the legitimacy of multiple perspectives. Inevitably, multiple perspectives lead to tensions between different subunits of the multinational; yet most tensions can be worked out through relationships supported by norms of collaborative teamwork. This brings us back to the concepts of social capital and shared values discussed earlier in this chapter; these three aspects of social architecture are closely intertwined.

TAKEAWAYS

1. Every organization is a social entity. One of the key HRM issues in multinational firms is building the company's social architecture.

2. Three elements of social architecture are of particular relevance to global organizations: relationships among the employees (social capital); shared values, beliefs, and norms (organizational culture); and global mindsets.

3. There are three aspects of social capital: structural (emphasizing position within a network); relational (focusing on trust and mutual obligations); and cognitive (encompassing shared meanings).

4. In firms rich in social capital, information flows quickly and freely across intra-organizational boundaries. Social relationships also help resolve the inevitable tensions and disagreements created by the conflicting demands facing global firms.

5. Organizational culture can be understood in terms of values, beliefs, and norms that are held in common across all or part of multinational firms. Shared values facilitate the trust that is essential for effective lateral coordination, conflict resolution, and knowledge transfer.

6. The extent to which values, beliefs, and norms are shared throughout the firm is influenced by a range of HR practices. The selection of future employees, their socialization, and international mobility are commonly used to maintain and strengthen organizational cultures.

7. In multinationals, employees often identify with both their local unit and the corporation as a whole. Dual organizational identification can be beneficial if well balanced, since it fosters sensitivity to both corporate and local interests.

8. There are two different and complementary perspectives on global mindset. The first is a *cultural* perspective and refers to the openness toward other nations and cultures; the second is a *strategic* perspective that denotes a person's ability to balance the firm's competing strategic priorities.

9. The foundation for developing a global mindset is equal opportunity for all, regardless of where they enter the firm. The major HRM tools to build such a mindset are international mobility, cross-border projects, and training.

10. Building companies where employees have global mindsets means developing organizations that can *learn locally and act globally*.

NOTES

1 Liker and Hoseus, 2008; see also Osono, Shimizu, and Takeuchi (2008).

2 Stewart and Raman, 2007.

3 Ibid., p. 80.

4 Our concept of "social architecture" focuses on the social dimensions of how multinationals work. In this chapter we focus on the people management tools that corporate "social architects"—both in HR and in line and top management positions—can use to influence social capital, shared values, and global mindset of the employees of the organization.

5 Kostova and Roth, 2003. There is no shortage of definitions attempting to express the value of social ties and relationships in the organization. Lengnick-Hall and Lengnick-Hall (2006, p. 477) define social capital as "the intangible resource of structural connections, interpersonal interactions and cognitive understanding that enables a firm to (a) capitalize on diversity (b) reconcile differences."

6 Nahapiet and Ghoshal, 1998.

7 The structural ties between actors have been the key focus of social network research. See, for example, Kilduff and Tsai (2003); Kwon and Adler (2014).

8 In his influential work, Granovetter (1973) found that people who were trying to change jobs were more likely to find interesting opportunities through their "weak ties" (acquaintances and friends of friends) than through their "strong ties" (close friends). Close friends would typically provide few leads that they had not thought of, whereas acquaintances often had leads into totally new networks and opportunities.

9 The bridging/structural perspective on social capital was pioneered by Ronald Burt (1992). Much of his work emphasizes the returns for an individual who brokers "structural holes," that is, the bridging of two networks that are spanned by one person only.

10 Kostova and Roth, 2003; Barner-Rasmussen *et al.*, 2014.

11 Kostova and Roth, 2003, p. 309.

12 Ibid.

13 Neves and Caetano, 2006.

14 Ellis, 2000.

15 We discuss how social capital can contribute to knowledge sharing in Chapter 11.

16 Adler and Kwon, 2002.

17 For instance, Tsai and Ghoshal (1998) found a positive relationship between interunit social capital and innovativeness.

18 Leana and Van Buren, 1999.

19 Kostova and Roth, 2003.

20 Lengnick-Hall and Lengnick-Hall, 2003.

21 Dess and Shaw, 2001.

22 Adler and Kwon, 2002.

23 Brown and Eisenhardt, 1998.

24 Maznevski, Davison, and Jonsen, 2006.

25 Tichy and Sherman, 1993, p. 60.

26 Kwon and Adler, 2014.

27 Taylor, 2007.

28 Lengnick-Hall and Lengnick-Hall, 2003.

29 Ibid.

30 Erickson and Gratton, 2007.

31 Kostova and Roth, 2003.

32 Sonja Weckström-Nousianen, Nokia Corporation, personal communication, 2008.

33 Burt, Hogarth, and Michaud, 2000.

34 Marschan-Piekkari, Welch, and Welch, 1999.

35 Björk, 1998.

36 Barner-Rasmussen and Björkman, 2006.

37 As pointed out by Hearn, Metcalfe, and Piekkari (2006), international HRM is seldom examined from a gender perspective.

38 Adler and Kwon, 2002; Hansen, Mors, and Løvås, 2005.

39 Leana and Van Buren, 1999.

40 Adler and Kwon, 2002.

41 See, for example, Child, Faulkner, and Tallman (2005).

42 See, for example, the collection of papers in Stahl and Mendenhall (2005).

43 O'Reilly and Chatman, 1996; Ravasi and Schultz, 2006.

44 See, for example, Hatch (1993).

45 See Chapter 3.

46 Nohria and Ghoshal, 1997; Taylor, 2015.

47 O'Reilly and Chatman, 1996; Levy, Taylor, and Boyacigiller, 2010.

48 Sorensen, 2002.

49 Ibid.

50 Ibid; Welch and Welch, 2006.

51 Mael and Ashforth (1992, p. 104) offer the following formal definition of organizational identification: "The perception of oneness with or belongingness to an organization, where the individual defines him or herself in terms of the organization(s) in which he or she is a member." See Ashforth, Harrison, and Corley (2008) for a comprehensive review of the literature on identification in organizations.

52 Reade, 2001.

53 Gregersen and Black, 1992; Vora, Kostova, and Roth, 2007; Smale *et al.*, 2015.

54 Doz and Prahalad, 1986. See the discussion on expatriate allegiance in Chapter 9.

55 Stroh *et al.*, 2005. For a review of research on multilevel identification in organizations, see Ashforth, Harrison, and Corley (2008).

56 Vora, Kostova, and Roth, 2007.

57 Stroh *et al.*, 2005. See also Chapter 3.

58 Ashforth, Harrison, and Corley, 2008.

59 Dore, 1973.

60 Ralston *et al.*, 2008.

61 "Soichiro Honda: Uniquely driven," *Business Week*, August 17, 2004.

62 Francis *et al.*, 2004.

63 Schein, 1985.

64 See Kamprad and Torekull (1999).
65 See Bauer *et al.* (2007) for a comprehensive analysis of newcomer adjustment during organizational socialization.
66 Bauer, Morrison, and Callister, 1998.
67 Hence the importance of managing the employer brand, as discussed in Chapter 6.
68 Bauer, Morrison, and Callister, 1998.
69 Liker and Hoseus, 2008.
70 Spear, 2004.
71 Van Maanen and Schein, 1979. See Klein (2004) for an interesting assessment on how to assist outsiders to achieve this balance.
72 The pioneering work of Edström and Galbraith (1977) recognized the role of international transfers as a mechanism of organizational socialization.
73 Harzing, 2001.
74 Sisson, 1994.
75 Ravasi and Schultz, 2006; Welch and Welch, 2006.
76 For example, see http://knowledge.wharton.upenn.edu/article/under-the-hood-of-toyotas-recall-a-tremendous-expansion-of-complexity/.
77 Ibid.
78 Cole, 2011.
79 Ibid.
80 www.infosys.com, February 17, 2015.
81 Agrawal and Kets de Vries, 2006.
82 Levy *et al.* (2007) discuss different definitions of global mindset.
83 Perlmutter, 1969, p. 13. Perlmutter's seminal work was introduced already in Chapter 1.
84 Ibid.
85 Pucik and Saba, 1998.
86 Begley and Boyd, 2003.
87 Adler and Bartholomew, 1992.
88 See for instance Black *et al.* (1999a) and the discussion about expatriates in Chapter 9.
89 Levy *et al.*, 2007. "Cosmopolitanism" has been proposed as an underlying dimension of the psychological/cultural perspective.
90 Govindarajan, V. and A. Gupta, "Success is all in the mindset," *Financial Times*, February 27, 1998, pp. 2–3. Similarly, Kanter (1995) sees this as a difference between new "cosmopolitans" and "locals," to employ terms that had been developed earlier by the sociologist Gouldner to describe the difference between people who identified with the wider profession as opposed to those who identified with the "local" interests of the firm.
91 Adler and Bartholomew, 1992.
92 Rhinesmith, 1993.
93 Levy *et al.*, 2007.
94 Bartlett and Ghoshal, 1989.
95 See Murtha, Lenway, and Bagozzi (1998) and Levy *et al.* (2007) for further elaboration, also for the distinction between the strategic perspective and alternative frameworks.
96 Levy *et al.*, 2007. Javidan's Global Mindset Inventory has a broader psychological orientation, measuring intellectual, psychological, and social capital from a global mindset perspective (Javidan and Walker, 2012; www.globalmindset.thunderbird).
97 Murtha, Lenway, and Bagozzi, 1998. These measures can be used to evaluate the way in which individuals working in different areas, functions, and business units understand corporate global objectives. For example, do managers in global product divisions conceptualize the importance of global efficiency/integration and responsiveness in the same way as managers in country units? What about managers with international experience, as opposed to those who pursued local careers?
98 Story *et al.*, 2014.
99 Arora *et al.*, 2004; Nummela, Saarenketo, and Puumalainen, 2004.
100 See Maddux and Galinsky (2009) and related research on mobility, discussed in Chapter 8.
101 Performance management is discussed in Chapter 7.
102 Kanter, 1995, p. 60.
103 Pucik, 2003.

chapter

6

Acquiring Global Talent

SUMMARY

Challenge

Demographic changes and gaps between the supply and demand for skilled employees constrain the ability of multinational firms to optimize their global resources.

Analysis

Meeting the talent needs within a changing global environment requires careful attention to:

- Managing attraction as well as selection from external and internal talent pools
- Balancing dilemmas such as make vs buy, home country vs local focus, short term vs long term

Solutions

- To guide selection decisions, define desired competencies around specific skills and values
- Build differentiated employee value proposition and consistent employee brand
- Develop relationships with schools in key markets to enhance the quality of the talent pipeline
- Provide talented individuals worldwide with access to career opportunities
- Make sure that long-term talent strategy is not compromised by short-term thinking

The Next Big Talent at Infosys

One of the world's largest software firms, Infosys started in Bangalore, India, in 1981 on a shoestring budget of $250. From its inception, Infosys bet on technology helping to shrink cultural, geographic, and administrative distances. Its biggest innovation was a new way to provide information technology, software engineering, and business process consulting services by an efficient workforce organized by time zones to accomplish tasks in different geographic locations at a fraction of the cost. In this regard, Infosys was born global and had to compete in a worldwide playing field from day one. To succeed in this global game, Infosys had to invest heavily in its talent pools, regardless of where they were located. Today, Infosys revenues are close to US$ 9 billion and it has over 176,000 employees. Its success has been one of the factors behind India's emergence as the global destination for software services. Its employee stock options created some of India's first salaried millionaires.[1]

In 2015, the Infosys top management decided that the primary focus for the head of HR would be on recruiting and selecting "the next big talent."[2] The next big talent represents people with rare skills of strategic value to the company in a global market. In the early years, India was a valuable source of well-trained talent; but as the business services industry in India shifted from a focus on low cost to providing high value, Infosys recognized that global talent is the key to sustaining competitive advantage. Since the company employs people from nearly 90 different nationalities, a big challenge was to globalize the employment brand and to recruit top graduates in its key markets in the Americas, China, and Europe. In all of these regions, they needed to find people with the right competency mix—people with exceptional skills and a strong appreciation for cross-border collaboration.

Having built a strong global reputation, Infosys has freedom to choose; it typically selects less than 1 percent of college-level applicants—with an emphasis on selecting for "learnability." This creates a recruitment and selection challenge: how do you ensure you are attracting and selecting the "right" 1 percent? One solution is to expand and improve the quality of the talent pool, so Infosys provides training for faculty to help align university curricula with industry (and their own) needs. In addition, they invite students to visit the Infosys campus. While improving the education and selection of students in places like India and China, such actions have also created a foundation for enhancing college recruiting in countries like the UK and US. All of these activities increase the likelihood that Infosys will attract and select the talent it wants.

Another recruitment and selection practice of Infosys is known as InStep. InStep provides internship opportunities for students from top universities throughout the world. Interns are sent to India to work on a specific project for a few months. This allows them to get to know the culture of Infosys, learn about India, and gain a greater understanding of the Infosys client.

But selection does not stop with the hiring decision. Infosys provides many opportunities for new employees to find their best fit. For example, an employee working in HR may want to move to consulting, so one way to test the market is to seek an internship for a month or two within the consulting division. After the internship, the employee can go back to HR or apply for a full-time position within the consulting division. As one manager put it, "instead of that person potentially leaving for a different career opportunity, they can explore other opportunities within the same company." With over 176,000 employees, managing these career opportunities across multiple countries requires an effective internal talent market. Infosys has spared no expense on developing a state-of-the-art intranet system that allows people to see what other types of opportunities might exist inside. In fact, Infosys' intranet has been voted among the "Top 10 intranets" worldwide.[3] While its primary purpose is to facilitate employee collaboration, it also provides a platform for posting jobs, assessing performance, and improving Infosys' ability to find talent within the company worldwide.

OVERVIEW

A global IT services company like Infosys has few fixed assets and no legacy positions; it lives off its know-how, embedded in the talent of its workforce. In that sense, Infosys is a typical multinational in today's knowledge economy. What is notable about Infosys is that it took some bold strategic decisions concerning global talent attraction. It began with a strong talent pool in India and has quickly moved to a transnational model of harnessing talent from all over the world.

In this chapter we build on this story to examine the value of talent management. We first discuss the need for talent management and then demonstrate cutting-edge ways by which companies are managing their talent portfolios in a shifting global environment.[5] Next, we discuss ways by which companies can effectively recruit and select employees using a transnational approach that helps them balance the need to be both locally responsive and globally integrated.

WHAT IS TALENT MANAGEMENT AND WHY IS IT SO IMPORTANT?

Talent management is the process through which organizations anticipate and meet their need for key human capital.[6] Basically, it involves getting the right people into the right places at the right time.

Multinationals excelling at talent management do a good job in implementing key people management practices: recruiting and selecting talented people, managing their performance, and developing and retaining them. The different people management activities should not be viewed as silos but as interdependent elements in the overall talent management system of the corporation. For example, in Infosys, the focus on top talent in selection and recruitment is also reflected in the performance management system. Based on their appraised performance and potential, future leaders are identified relatively early and then selected for special attention and investment in terms of training and other development activities.

In this chapter we will focus on the recruitment and selection of talent, leaving performance management to Chapter 7 while leadership development is examined in Chapter 8 and global mobility of people in Chapter 9.

The rising interest in global operations, driven by growing markets in Asia and other parts of the world, has called managers' attention to the need to more effectively manage talent. To create competitive advantage, companies have to take a global perspective in attracting, recruiting and selecting, and developing talent, just as Infosys is doing.

What Do We Mean by Talent?

Talent represents individuals who are in a position or role that has a direct impact on company competitiveness.[7] Such individuals are considered "A-players," usually comprising high-level managers, high-potential and high-performing individuals, and those with rare knowledge and skills that are of strategic value to the firm. Hence, employees may be considered as talent regardless of their formal position or place; the crucial question is whether or not they are key to the enabling and differentiating capabilities of the corporation.

This approach addresses a key tension in talent management: should companies focus on A-players who are important for building capabilities to implement the strategy of the firm, or on a wider group—even a majority of all employees—who may also play an important, but nonstrategic, role in the organization? Different companies have different definitions of the talent management scope, but in our view, talent management should focus on identifying which types of individuals matter most for the firm. Valuable individuals typically have tacit knowledge and deep experience for a particular role that cannot be found easily in the external labor market.[8] It would not make economic sense to invest equally in a clerical employee who can be easily replaced and in a functional expert with high leadership potential.

An alternative (or complementary) perspective on how to manage talent is focused on positions, not individuals.[9] It distinguishes between strategically important A positions, supporting B positions, and replaceable C positions that do not differentiate the firm,[10] as shown in Table 6-1. Positions are defined primarily by their strategic impact, the required range in performance levels, and need for firm-specific know-how. Other characteristics that distinguish A, B, and C positions are differences in the scope of authority and the consequences if someone in that role makes mistakes.

These three types of positions do not necessarily correspond to hierarchy, pay scales, or the difficulty of recruiting for the position. Take the airline industry as an example. The people who negotiate landing rights, with higher variability in their performance, are more critical to the success of the firm than the pilots who come immediately to mind when thinking of talent—pilots are more

TABLE 6-1
Which Jobs Make the Most Difference?

	A Positions STRATEGIC	B Positions SUPPORT	C Positions STANDARD
DEFINING CHARACTERISTICS	Has direct strategic impact *and* high performance variability *and* requires firm-specific know-how	Has indirect strategic impact OR has strategic impact with little performance variability	Required for the firm to function but has little strategic impact
Scope of authority	Autonomous decision-making	Specific processes need to be followed	Little discretion in work
Primary determinant of compensation	Performance	Job level	Market price
Effect on value creation	Creates value by enhancing revenue	Supports value-creating positions	Has little positive economic impact
Consequences of mistakes	Missed revenue opportunities	May be very costly and can destroy value	Not necessarily costly
Consequences of hiring wrong person	Lost training investment and revenue opportunities	Sometimes remedied through hiring of replacement	Easily remedied through hiring of replacement

Source: Adapted from M.A. Huselid, R.W. Beatty, and B.E. Becker, "A Players or A Positions?" *Harvard Business Review* (December 2005), pp. 110–17.

replaceable. So it would make sense for an airline to carefully select and groom such negotiators. Regulations ensure that all pilots have to be well trained and qualified, and so their roles might be considered as supporting B positions. Ground staff might be considered C players, managed according to the market.

With emphasis on A-players and A-positions, we would define talent management as deliberate actions to recruit, select, manage the performance of, develop, and retain those individuals who, individually or collectively, have the capability to make a significant impact on the long-term competitiveness of the firm.[11] This approach to talent management may however lead to a tension between a focus on "A players in A positions," who are essential for strategy execution, and the need to engage the majority of employees, who may also play an important, but nonstrategic, role in the organization's operations.

Why Is Talent Management So Important?

The growing importance of talent management reflects four fundamental shifts in the nature of the supply and demand for skilled employees reflecting changing demographics, globalization, mobility, and the learning economy.

Shifting Demographics

Due to inescapable demographic trends in most developed countries, there has been a decline in the size of the talent pool that will continue for the next 20–30 years (partially compensated for by immigration). There is a bulge in the number of older people approaching retirement and fewer young people, especially those at the productive career stage of their thirties. Figure 6-1 shows the demographic profile of Germany for 2014, shaped like a diamond. The German figures are not atypical; Japan and Italy have an even more serious demographic problem, while the situation is similar but less severe in Scandinavia, Singapore, and the US.

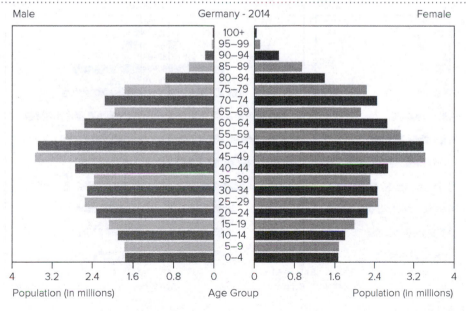

FIGURE 6-1
German Demographic Profile in 2014

Source: www.census.gov/ipc/www/idb

However, the population of less-developed countries has been quickly growing and will continue to grow for the foreseeable future, except in China where the population is aging due to the one-child policy that lasted until 2015.[12] China's working-age population is expected to be much smaller by 2050 (see Figure 6-2).

Despite the rapid growth of working-age people in other emerging markets such as India, economic growth also creates a talent shortage due to the lack of needed skills. In fact, the top concerns of CEOs today are not related to finances, marketing, operations, or strategy. Rather, their top concern is the shortage of qualified staff.[13]

The demand-supply imbalance is particularly pronounced in the market for young professionals. While there has been a boom in university enrollments in India, China, and Brazil, the quality of graduates is uneven. Language skills are not always emphasized, and local educational systems often do not foster skills valued by multinationals, like taking initiative and teamwork. One survey estimated that only 10 percent of Chinese engineering graduates were suitable to be hired by multinationals, in comparison with 50 percent of such graduates from Central European countries. But companies like Infosys and Cisco, which invested earlier in partnerships with elite local technical institutions in places like China and India, are now reaping the benefits as they are able to recruit top professionals.

Shifting Globalization Trends

While saving on labor costs still remains an important reason for deciding to move operations abroad, access to qualified personnel influences 70 percent of offshoring decisions.[14] Shifts in the supply of talent are increasingly leading firms to look to emerging countries, not only for lower-cost outsourcing in non-core areas but also to staff strategically important functions such as R&D, product development, and engineering services. Cisco created a second headquarters

FIGURE 6-2
China Demographic Trend for 2050

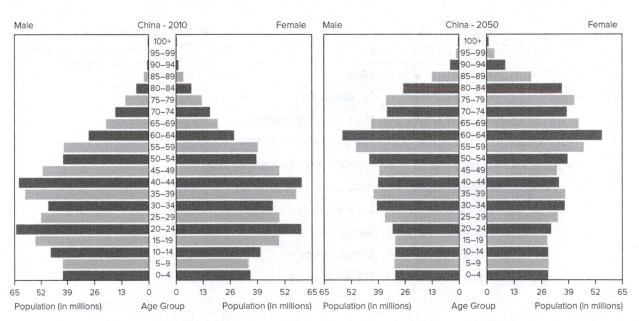

Source: www.census.gov/ipc/www/idb

for global innovation in Bangalore.[15] São Paolo is now one of the global hubs for Internet banking expertise and financial information forecasting.

Talented local people are often interested in obtaining skills and experience by working with a multinational and then leaving to join a local firm or start their own business. The story of the rise of Alibaba and Taobao at the expense of eBay in China, told in Chapter 2, is an example.

Shifting Individual Mobility

The Internet has created a major shift in the information symmetries around employment. Today, exploring what the external job market offers is as easy as the click of a mouse. Internet job sites such as Eurojobs.com and Monster.com provide targeted information on available jobs in all major countries of the world, while other sites such as Glassdoor.com provide inside information on prospective employers. Software provided by service companies allows employees in a different country to go through the entire interview process virtually. This facilitates mobility, which has steadily increased as firms also use Internet recruitment to poach skilled individuals from competitors.

The influence of mobility and the changing power balance is profound. Retention has become a vital element of talent management, inseparable from attraction and development. Unless firms can manage retention, any investment in talent development may be wasted. Organizations may become more reserved about employee training and development since there is a risk that the employee may exploit the benefits by moving elsewhere; it is safer to try to poach experienced talent from others.

Shifting to a Learning Economy

As we move step-by-step into a learning economy, company performance becomes increasingly dependent on the skills of its employees. This trend is also known as upskilling and refers to increased problem-solving and knowledge work.[16] In organizations that live entirely off their ability to learn—consulting and legal firms, investment banks, and academic institutions—the CEOs of top firms often spend 25–40 percent or more of their time on talent management.

This means that upskilled employees need to be managed in a more integrated fashion, where the employees themselves make most of the decisions on how work is conducted, rather than in a traditional hierarchic way where managers make major decisions. In the same way the deskilling of workers was sometimes seen to be a conscious management strategy to increase control over workers and make the management process easier, the upskilling of workers is spurred by the external forces of globalization and technological innovation as well as the saturation of domestic markets and greater international competition.[17] These factors "have forced employers to find smaller market niches that demand quicker reactions to changing markets and, in turn, a more flexible workplace where jobs are defined more broadly and workers have greater control over them."[18]

The Challenge of Emerging Skills Gaps

The evolving dynamics in the demand and supply of talent brought about a recognition that the problem facing companies around the world is not a shortage of talent as such but an imbalance between skills needed and skills available in specific countries and industry sectors. For example, in 2014 there were estimated to be 8 million vacant positions in Europe and the US. At the same time, there were almost 25 million unemployed in Europe.[19] In Asia and other emerging markets, talent management is one of the top concerns of CEOs because of the difficulty in finding skilled people. To take a specific occupation, Internet networking, the estimated gap in the number of employees needed in Asia Pacific was 700,000, while the gap in the Middle East was proportionately even greater.

There are many data illustrating the worldwide skills gap.[20] What are the causes of such an imbalance? There are many. The educational infrastructure in some countries does not facilitate the development of the needed talent. Surveys suggested that 60 percent of US college graduates could not find a job in their field; 30 percent of South Korean graduates were not employable, while many jobs requiring technical skills went vacant there. There are impediments to the migration of talent from abroad that might compensate for demographic and skill shortages; sectors of the population such as women are sometimes outside the talent pool; labor laws in some countries make it so difficult to fire people that employers are cautious about taking a risk in hiring people; and with increased demand, firms are reluctant to invest in training for fear that people will take those skills elsewhere to increase their pay. All of these together have a major impact on the competitiveness of countries, industries, and even individual firms (see the box "Talent Competitiveness across the World").

Talent Competitiveness across the World

The Global Talent Competitiveness Index (GTCI) allows one to understand the strengths and weaknesses of 93 countries at different levels of economic development.[21] This composite index measures the ability of countries to attract, grow, retain, and facilitate two types of human capital—technical-vocational skills and global knowledge skills—that contribute to productivity (typically measured as GDP per capita).

Switzerland, Singapore, and Luxembourg are the world leaders on talent competitiveness—land or sea-locked

GTCI Ranking The "Top 20" out of 93 countries	
1. Switzerland	11. Norway
2. Singapore	12. Netherlands
3. Luxembourg	13. Finland
4. United States	14. Germany
5. Canada	15. Austria
6. Sweden	16. New Zealand
7. United Kingdom	17. Iceland
8. Denmark	18. Belgium
9. Australia	19. Estonia
10. Ireland	20. Japan

countries with few other resources than their people—that have a long heritage of socioeconomic policies favoring talent growth and attraction (see Table 6-2). For example, Switzerland is a successful country and the most innovative nation in the world as measured by the Global Innovation Index, with one of the highest levels of income per capita.[22] At age 12, all Swiss school children have to start thinking about their vocation, and at 15 they have to choose whether to pursue a generalist education or a vocational track that combines practical work as an apprentice with formal education.[23] 70 percent chose the vocational track, and some observers believe that the dual educational system largely explains the country's track record on innovation and national competitiveness, as well as its high rate of employment (youth unemployment is 3.6 percent while it averages over 25 percent across southern Europe).[24]

Some other insights from the GTCI analysis are as follows:

- China, ranked #41 and Malaysia (#35) have strong profiles in terms of the formal education needed to grow talent. Brazil is positioned at #49, while India (#78) has particular weaknesses in retaining its talent. The oil-rich Emirates have successfully invested in attracting talent and building a strong educational system, ranking 22 out of 93 countries.
- Tertiary education in most countries exploded as it became clear that we were moving into a knowledge-based world—a six-fold increase in China over 20 years until 2010, a 16-fold increase in India. But in many countries, this has been at the expense of vocational education, which became the inferior option. Today the skills gap is biggest among technicians and professionals who come from such a vocational background.
- Despite the political sensitivity of immigration, most of the high income countries of the world are open economies that try to attract talent, though Japan and South Korea remain exceptions. The economics of talent attraction clearly support this.[25]
- Social mobility, the ability to get ahead regardless of one's family background, is strongest in the Nordic countries, with the US being in a lower position.

Economic growth and innovation depend on talent, and governmental action is needed to ensure an appropriate supply of skills. But this takes time. Skills gaps are often best dealt with when business partners up with educational institutions and government or local authorities; Infosys is an example of such ecosystems in India. And skills gaps also put in sharp relief the proposition that talent management capability can be a source of competitive advantage.

BALANCING ACTS IN TALENT MANAGEMENT

Developing talent management capability involves balancing many opposing tensions. We have already touched on one such tension—the need to focus on A players who are important for strategy, at the risk of elitism, as opposed to the pressure to focus on the wider majority, at the risk of diluting resources. We explore two additional tensions here, and we will discuss the balancing of short and long term at the end of the chapter.

Should We Build or Should We Buy?

A key decision is whether to staff future expansion through internal resourcing or through external recruitment—whether to build or buy talent. In the past, this sort of "supply chain" question would rarely be asked. Companies tended to have undifferentiated talent strategies. Some firms grew primarily through external recruitment at all levels; to get promoted you had to change companies. Other firms grew through developing their own talent in internal labor

TABLE 6-2
Internal Labor Markets—Advantages and Disadvantages

Advantages	Disadvantages
• Developing firm-specific skills	• Higher talent management costs
• Building loyalty and commitment	• Training risks absorbed by company
• Better screening of job candidates	• Lack of flexibility; higher salary costs
• Potentially lower supervisory costs	• Slower to adjust in times of change
• More control over salary levels	• Insular; fewer insights into competitors
• Encourages sharing of information	• Risk of various "glass ceilings"
• Better maintenance of the culture	• Risk of overstaffing or understaffing

markets (ILMs). What are the pros and cons of building your own timber—development through ILMs?[26]

ILMs are characterized by long-term mutual attachment between the organization and its workforce. Promotion is from within and there is an emphasis on experience, which is equated with seniority. ILMs are well studied,[27] and their advantages and disadvantages are summarized in Table 6-2. One of the major strengths of the ILM is its capacity to nurture firm-specific strategic skills and complex capabilities in the shape of experienced experts or leaders who also have broad functional and market know-how and who are committed to the firm. But well-functioning ILMs require effective talent management practices. A poorly managed ILM can become an expensive training ground benefiting competitors who will poach the most talented individuals.

The institutional environment influences the balance between build and buy. Japan, Germany, France, Italy, and Switzerland are among the countries where internal resourcing dominates, either by custom or forced on firms by labor legislation. For example, in France and (until recently) Italy, employees in all but the smallest firms receive a permanent contract after an initial probationary period, which makes it difficult and expensive to terminate employment. Successive governments have tried to open the labor markets to bring more market flexibility, though resistance from unions and employee groups is strong. On the other hand, in Denmark, the Netherlands, Britain, and Hong Kong, strong ILMs are less frequent, even among large firms. The emphasis on internal development has steadily declined in the US, and as we discuss later, the US is probably the region with the strongest preference for buying talent. In Russia, much of Central and Eastern Europe, and China, the external labor market orientation dominates today, despite the history of state-owned enterprises with ILMs controlled by the Communist Party.

The nature of the knowledge and skill in a particular industry is another important factor determining the balance between build and buy. Build strategies prevail in capital-intensive industries that depend on complex knowledge and skills, such as the oil industry. Graduates are recruited for long-term careers, and sophisticated talent management processes steer internal resourcing. Functional oriented structures also facilitate talent management in pharmaceuticals.[28] But in the fast-moving worlds of software development and IT, the pattern has been to rely on buy strategies, especially in the US.

Cappelli argues that there should be a mix of build and buy, guided by the answers to four key questions:[29]

1. For how long will the talent be needed? The longer the time horizon, the easier it will be to recoup investments on internal development.

2. Is there a career hierarchy of skills and jobs that facilitates internal development? This is most obviously the case if there are clear functional development paths.

3. Is the culture of the firm part of its competitive advantage? If so, this favors ILM development rather than recruiting those who have no understanding of the culture.

4. How accurately can one forecast demand? The less accurate the forecasts, the greater the risks with internal development.

Companies with broad domains are asking themselves whether they should consider having different talent strategies in different businesses. For example, in oil companies, project management is critical for strategic development, so a build strategy may be appropriate here, while a buy strategy may be favored in downstream marketing operations. But people strategies affect organizational governance, and this raises new dilemmas. Is it possible to maintain two increasingly different businesses under one roof?

And yet another tension is emerging. Both "build" and "buy" strategies aim for a similar outcome—an employee capable of doing the job. But who is the employer? Thirty percent of the staff at Google are contract staff, and the problems of having insiders and outsiders on the same team have attracted criticism.[30] In Japan and in Europe, a sizeable proportion of the younger workforce is employed through temporary work service providers. Perhaps the initial question will soon need to be modified: "build, buy, or rent?"

Should We Adapt (Locally) or Be Consistent (Globally)?

Talent management, in the widest sense of the management of staff, has traditionally been a local matter. As we discussed in Chapter 2, national cultures differ, and laws and labor markets vary greatly. But even in multidomestic firms, there is usually a corporate-led global focus on leadership succession for senior management, including attention to managing the localization of executives.[31]

Some transnational firms have been broadening the globalization of talent management to all strategic positions that are important to firm strategy and its execution. Our Infosys case is an example, where global talent management covers engineers in emerging countries. Infosys did not succeed in recruiting the best engineers in China and Russia by doing this the local way. It succeeded by applying in China the methods that it had honed at home in India, helping local educational establishments to become world class and then training a Chinese recruit in the same way as it would train someone in India.

When considering people who will occupy strategic positions, companies see numerous advantages to global consistency in talent management, driven by the central HR function with the support of top management, and assisted by IT platforms:[32]

- They can build competitive advantage throughout the world by finding and developing the best people in local markets, as in the case of Infosys.
- Global consistency facilitates the ability to deploy talent across geographic locations to where it is needed. It is difficult to identify and move talented people unless the standards for talent are the same, so it is important to have the same competence- and performance-based standards for the evaluation of individuals.

- Using a global database of qualified talent, candidates can be quickly identified. Combined with computer-based platforms in open-job markets, skilled professionals can be more quickly deployed to new opportunities and projects, particularly on a regional basis.
- The use of common processes and measures makes global workforce forecasting and planning possible, using new analytic techniques and simulations.
- Many firms suffer from the herd effect—for example, moving all IT services to Bangalore, with resulting wage inflation. Companies skilled in global talent management can take advantage of second tier locations, where there is greater variability in the quality of talent.[33]

Local managers are often ambivalent about such global processes, arguing that *they* are different. How does one know whether this simply reflects resistance to change or a substantive competitive reality? Because of local conditions, a global practice might indeed have to be adapted or it may be too expensive to implement.

The advice from companies that have introduced global staffing processes is to push back, asking people to prove that they really are different. However, local buy-in is increased if the local leaders can shape execution in ways that reflect sensitive local issues. P&G allows differentiation where there is a legitimate business need or where the longer-term benefits outweigh the short-term concessions, shooting for 85:15 or 90:10 ratio of standardization to customization.[34] The test of a good global staffing process is that it allows the firm to fill local positions with better candidates than it could using a local platform, and possibly cheaper and faster as well.[35]

This balance is an issue that we will pick up in our discussions on recruitment and selection. While a multinational firm may achieve consistency in concepts, principles, and the use of some techniques, there are inevitably local differences when one gets down to practices and behaviors rooted in a specific context.

MANAGING RECRUITMENT

Recruitment is the practices and activities carried out by the organization with the primary purpose of identifying and attracting potential employees.[36] Without attention to global recruitment, multinationals risk being trapped in the ethnocentricity of the mother company. Take the case of a leading European firm that has a strong reputation as a leader in international HRM. Despite decades of attempting to internationalize the talent pipeline by promoting the development of local managers, the senior leaders remained by and large graduates of the top engineering schools in the mother country. The turning point was when they realized that the problem was under their noses—the home country received more attention and resources from HR and the senior line than other countries. They were able to recruit the best people at home, who then received the best induction and career mentoring. The people who moved later into leadership positions tended to be those who had experienced the best start to their careers. If they were to internationalize the talent pool, they would have to do an equally professional job of attraction and recruitment in other countries—exactly what Infosys is trying to do in many of the countries in which it operates.

Forecasting the Need for Recruitment

If a company is to have a strategic and proactive approach to talent management, this begins with the ability to forecast the supply and the demand for talent. This is particularly true if a company engages in building its own internal supply of talent—recruiting people young, and then training and developing them to create a pipeline of talent. Workforce planning, as it is called, can help you to correctly forecast talent needs. Recruitment and staffing plans resulting from competency-gap analysis are included in the resource plans of leading multinationals. Senior management assesses these gaps as part of the strategic planning process.

Our discussions with Infosys have pointed to a renewed interest in anticipating talent shortages by working with universities to ensure that a sufficient number of students are prepared to work in the IT sector.[37] One program known as "Campus Connect" gets representatives into universities to work with students and professors to help with curriculum development. Another program, "Catch-Them-Young," gets Infosys HR managers into primary schools, helping promote interest in math and sciences.

Because the quality of data within Infosys is high, Infosys can run simulations to undertake scenario planning that helps them decide how much they need to be involved in upstream recruiting efforts, such as going into secondary schools. They are able to track employee movements in the organization, understand when employees are likely to leave, and understand what factors make a future employee most effective once they are hired. By doing this kind of forecast analysis, Infosys has been able to globally standardize their recruiting efforts to ensure that talent gaps are filled.

Reaching Out to Attract Talent

A key question in recruitment is how to reach out effectively to potential candidates. There are a variety of different vehicles for attracting and recruiting talent.

Relationships with local universities, technical schools, and business schools. For large and leading corporations this is the most common route for entry-level recruitment of technical professionals and high potentials.[38] For example, Emerson has joint training programs with technical universities in China and the Philippines, while Volkswagen has established strategic alliances with Chinese universities and technical institutes, forming part of their internal corporate universities. The German automotive supplier Continental has Continental universities in Mexico City and Romania. Concerned that Vietnamese universities were not providing students with up-to-date technical knowledge required to work in Intel, the company sponsored students to get an engineering degree at a US school. After successful completion of the program, students are provided employment at Intel in Vietnam.[39]

Internships. Firms can identify prospective recruits among students who are offered short-term internships—a recruitment strategy popular among many

Western multinationals. Cross-border internships are growing, especially for MBA students. Infosys offers internships in India for talent it wants to recruit from foreign markets. At the same time, such internships allow students to evaluate potential employers, leading to a better fit.

Contests, competitions, and fellowships. This means organizing contests with prizes and offering employment to the winners or using fellowships to attract outstanding candidates. Google organizes periodic worldwide programming competitions to test contestants' Internet programming skills. In the meat industry in the US, firms select their future managers on the basis of national carcass-judging championships. These contests allow companies to hire nontraditional students who would normally not pass their employability requirements.

Employee referrals. Companies with strong ILMs, such as Lincoln Electric, as well as many smaller and high technology companies, widely use employee referrals to attract new employees. This approach, if applied with appropriate checks and balances, can not only save on recruiting costs but also has been shown to lead to faster socialization, higher retention, and better performance among those recruited.[40] As long as the risks of nepotism are minimized, referrals work particularly well in networked cultures like China.[41] In fact, some companies, such as Dell, have eased their global policy of not hiring family members. They have found that having multiple family members work for the same company increases their commitment.

Internet. Recruitment through Internet is rapidly becoming common practice throughout the world. Global platforms for job search are growing rapidly, as are portals focusing on specific occupational specialties. Social networking sites such as LinkedIn.com are increasingly being used for recruitment purposes. The problem with web recruitment is the high cost of screening and selecting from a large number of candidates, though the use of automatic selection tools and web competence testing can help. Companies are also using sophisticated tools to identify passive job seekers who might have browsed their website. Such individuals may be contacted with an e-mail or even a phone call from someone asking if they would be interested in talking about career possibilities at their company.

Advertising. Attention-grabbing advertising can be effective, especially when a firm is largely unknown. Early on, when Infosys was still struggling in India, it ran an ad featuring the headline: "Only 64 brilliant young engineers are destined to conquer the world of software. Find out if you are one of them this Saturday." This advertisement inspired more than a thousand applicants and created a stampede. Companies still take out traditional advertising in newspapers and specialized magazines, but those media are being replaced by nontraditional and web-based methods; for example, Google advertises for talent in cinemas and on billboards.

Professional recruiting firms and agencies. Executive search firms started to internationalize their operations decades ago because those that could offer services in different world regions were at an advantage with multinational clients. Such internationalization has spread to recruitment agencies that specialize in particular types of talent, such as medical technicians or IT specialists. A number of firms have outsourced the whole recruitment process to a service provider, in some cases worldwide. This approach has its pros and cons, but it provides little advantage for a firm that has competent recruiting processes in place and is an employer of choice.[42]

The effectiveness of different recruitment channels varies with national culture, though not as widely as the selection methods we discuss in the next section. It is important to analyze the effectiveness of alternative recruitment sources and methods in any particular market. GE questioned the effectiveness of recruiting MBAs from top business schools, deciding instead to build relations with well-regarded tier-two engineering schools and sourcing managers from the military.[43] In fact, most of GE's current senior executives, aside from CEO Jeff Immelt, are graduates of lesser-known colleges and universities.

Valero, the oil refining corporation that grew from 3,000 to 22,000 employees in the space of ten years, uses dashboards to monitor different methods in the recruitment chain, such as ads on job boards. Valero is one of a growing number of firms applying supply chain thinking to speed up hiring and reduce the expenses associated with it. When a new refinery opens, skills are sought from around the world—project managers from the US, outsourced engineers from Canada, and programmers from India.[44]

Global Employer Branding

Attracting talent basically means marketing the firm to recruits. Companies that enjoy a strong reputation and a powerful brand can profit from this, as Infosys does in India, allowing the company to grow from about 66,000 to over 170,000 employees over five years without compromising the quality of its services.[45]

Companies target particular candidate profiles, leading them to apply branding techniques that are derived from marketing and customer analysis. If firms can create a distinctive image in the recruitment market then they will attract only the right people. This means thinking of recruits as customers, segmenting the talent market, and using analytic techniques to identify whether the brand image is effective in attracting the right talent.[46] Branding signals a distinctive corporate identity—but to capture value, firms need to associate this with a program of internal branding, as does BMW, to ensure that employees are attitudinally and behaviorally ready to deliver on the brand.[47]

Building a Differentiated Employee Value Proposition

Attracting or keeping a desired employee is based on the same principles as attracting and keeping a desired customer. This is the idea behind the *employee value proposition* (EVP), a balance of "get" and "give up."

The "get" side, the value that the company offers, is more than just pay, benefits, and morale. Just as some customers will pay more for a product that provides reliability or prestige, people will often choose to work for lower pay than elsewhere in one company because that company offers something distinctive that they value. That distinctive offering might be challenging work, a high degree of autonomy, strong friendship and social bonds, learning opportunities, a reputation in the community, or an image of social responsibility.

The "give up" side of an EVP is often ignored, though it varies widely from one firm to another. Employees give up something in order to work, and the price they pay varies from one firm to another. Some firms, for example a global investment bank, ask to be prioritized 24/7 in the lives of their talented people, who must be willing to work evenings, to travel extensively, and to tolerate high stress loads. Talented people will only be willing to work for this kind of firm if there is an equal "get," or value they receive, in return. Other organizations may demand less of a commitment, with more flexibility to balance work and family life. As a result, they need to offer less to make an attractive employment proposition.

How can one figure out the best value proposition to attract and retain desired employees? In contrast to the employer brand, which should be consistent across the firm, an effective EVP is differentiated, varying with the employee group and the geographic market. This requires being aware of the different elements that can form an EVP and carefully assessing the relevant market in order to figure out which elements to highlight.

For example, for Federal Express (FedEx) in China, the drivers of the vans are a key employee group. FedEx suffered from excessively high turnover as their experienced drivers were lured away by more highly paid opportunities with local courier operations. Assessing potential levers aside from pay, they found that emphasizing the FedEx values of safety and security, building a sense of pride in accident-free driving in immaculately clean vans, succeeded in bringing turnover rates down decisively.[48]

For Infosys, the most important elements of the EVP across all countries consist of (1) rewards that provide partial ownership to the employees, (2) learning opportunities that help people develop their technical and leadership skills, and (3) emotional attachments that help people feel listened to and validated by the organization. Emotional attachments come from a culture that is interested in applying ideas and suggestions from employees. It also allows them to fulfill their need to be socially responsible and make a difference in the world. Whether it be in providing an environmental clean-up program for employees to become involved with or a big-brother/big-sister program, Infosys has found that the emotional component of their EVP has been key to people wanting to be a part of the Infosys company.

The potential elements in an employee value proposition are shown in Figure 6-3.

- The *rewards* are an obvious part of the package. But rewards go beyond pay and benefits, including intangibles such as a sense of belonging, affiliation, and progressive career development. Traditional Japanese enterprises offer low entry salaries to their core talent but provide relatively secure long-term careers.
- Attributes of the *job* may attract talent to the firm, notably the challenge of the work, its autonomy, or the learning opportunities associated with it.
- Features of the *company*, its culture, value system, and reputation may be assets, allowing the firm to highlight them in targeted campaigns. The reputation and values of the firm may enhance an individual's social reputation, even in his or her private life. For young employees worldwide, a firm's reputation for social responsibility plays an increasingly important role.
- The firm's *leadership* or *capability* development image may be part of the value proposition for attracting high potential recruits. P&G's reputation for brand management and thoroughness of its competence development

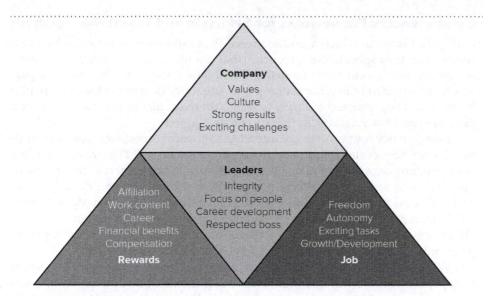

FIGURE 6-3
The Employee Value Proposition

process attracts recruits who know that even if they do not find the ideal career match inside P&G, they will leave with a plus on the CV because of the company's reputation for rigorous grooming of marketing professionals.

Through interviews and surveys, the EVP of a targeted group can be assessed, focusing messages on the most attractive elements. Focused recruitment efforts may be more cost-effective than broad reputational campaigns.

When the talent war is severe, companies are often forced to segment talent markets. "Life cycle differentiation" is an example. Life cycle differentiation means tailoring EVPs to highlight desirable elements for a target age group, whether this is housing, educational opportunities, autonomy, or flexible work practices. The old concept of cafeteria benefits was based on this idea, now extended by modifying the EVP according to life cycle needs—offering learning and challenge to younger staff while emphasizing flexibility and meaningful work for the older generation.

MANAGING SELECTION

Selection involves identifying the most suitable person from a pool of candidates—internal and/or external.[49] It focuses on assessing the fit between the candidates and the job or career opportunity. The way in which this is done may bias recruitment or promotions, so selection is closely linked to the management of cultural, gender, and other forms of diversity.

In this section, we discuss four issues: the framework for selection (competencies); selection methods, focusing on the external candidate pool; the management of diversity, with a particular focus on gender and ethnicity; and the challenges of internal selection. The latter is particularly important for multinational corporations since it deals with the identification of global talent among local employees.

Competencies: Frameworks for Selection and Talent Management

One of the ways in which a multinational firm influences selection is by identifying the firm-specific competencies that should guide selection decisions. A competence is a cluster of related skills, abilities, and traits that enable a person to act effectively in a particular job or situation. One important distinction is between deeply rooted *qualities*, or traits/motives, that might guide selection decisions and behavioral *skills* that can be developed.

Competency frameworks are intended to ensure consistency across recruitment, selection, socialization, and development actions.[50] They also provide a common language for line managers and HR professionals across the matrix of operations to steer talent selection, performance management, development, and decisions that will help build desired capabilities. As Reuben Mark, former CEO of Colgate-Palmolive says, "Competencies are the glue that joins all of our HR processes; they factor into our various employee training and development programs as well as our promotion and compensation decisions."[51]

While the idea of providing such a global platform for talent management is appealing, the journey is fraught with frustration and disillusionment. Competence frameworks are often too generic to be useful, means become ends, and company task forces spend large amounts of time and money generating sterile wish lists of desirable qualities. Why is this competence journey so difficult?

A study of 31 North American firms found that a major reason for this confusion in linking organizational needs to individual competencies is that there is not one guiding logic but at least three. Twelve of the firms took what we call a *performance-based approach*, nine adopted a *strategy-based approach*, four used a *values-based approach,* while others adopted hybrid approaches.[52] Each logic has its merits and disadvantages, so that there are trade-offs rather than a single correct approach. Our experience is that the source of confusion stems from people using the concept of competence in different ways, without realizing that they are applying different logics that involve trade-offs. These three approaches are summarized in Table 6-3.

The Performance-based Approach

The performance-based approach says that we should focus on the characteristics of high performers so we can reproduce more of them.[53] A firm that wants to recruit and train sales staff for an emerging market might employ the methodology to develop criteria for selection and training, and to guide regular assessments, perhaps adopting skills-based compensation linked to those competencies. Depending on how it is applied, the performance-based approach is potentially rigorous. The study of real managers gives legitimacy to the "soft" domain of talent management and facilitates its acceptability and implementation. Above all, the performance-based approach is pragmatic, and with appropriate cultural adjustment the results can easily be incorporated in performance appraisal guides, selection criteria, and training schemes around the world.

However, there are some disadvantages when the performance-based approach is applied to strategic talent. It is fundamentally a rear-window methodology, oriented toward the past and the status quo rather than to the future. While there may be merit in using such logic in a slow-moving industry, the

	Description	Advantages	Disadvantages
Performance-based approach	Competencies based on behavioral research on high-performing individuals	□ Grounded in actual behavior □ Air of legitimacy □ Involves people, which fosters acceptance	□ Based on the past, not the future □ May omit intangible and unmeasurable competencies □ Requires extensive resources
Strategy-based approach	Competencies forecast to be important in the future for the successful implementation of company strategy	□ Competencies based on the future, not the past □ Focuses on learning new skills □ Can support organizational transformation	□ The scenario for the future may be incorrect or distant □ Difficult to implement unless top management "walks the talk"
Values-based approach	Competencies based on a holistic view of norms and values	□ Can have strong motivating power □ Can provide strategic stability for long periods of time, especially in fast-growing environments □ Provides "glue" or integration	□ Depends on the ability of top leaders to communicate a holistic philosophy of management □ Competence development process may lack rigor □ Can be difficult to translate into actual behavior

TABLE 6-3
Three Competence Logics Guiding Talent Management

Source: Adapted from J.P. Briscoe and D.T. Hall, "Grooming and Picking Leaders Using Competency Frameworks," *Organizational Dynamics* (Autumn 1999), pp. 37–51.

approach is poorly suited to the discontinuities of a fast-moving competitive environment or to the complexities of a multidimensional professional service firm. Since it is based on historic data, the performance-based approach may perpetuate an outdated structure of career paths.

The Strategy-based Approach

The strategy-based approach is forward-looking, built around where we want to go. The original theory behind "strategic human resource management" emphasized translating strategy for the future into current implications for talent selection and development, thereby implementing strategy faster.[54] This is the approach that some strategy scholars advocate as an integral element of their balanced scorecard approach to strategic management and execution.[55] What skills or competencies does our talent need in order to execute our strategy? How well are we providing those competencies? And how do we fill the gaps through training, development, performance management, and rewards?

While the strategy-based logic lacks the rigor and legitimacy of the performance-related approach, especially for people lower down in the firm, its big advantage is that it is oriented to the future. It is often appealing to the senior management of firms undergoing substantial transformational change and to those in fast-moving competitive environments.[56]

Consistency of behavior at senior levels—walking the talk—is important. As ABB's founder and former CEO Percy Barnevik once commented, "If we talk about the need for fast decision-making and then top management procrastinates on important decisions, then it just isn't credible."[57] Fast decision-making needs to be matched by fast and thorough communication throughout the organization. While the need for new behaviors aligned around a change in strategy may be obvious to top management, it may be far from clear to middle-level managers in distant subsidiaries, where the decisions on recruitment and promotions are taken. The competencies may be seen as the whim of the current CEO or as headquarters politics.

The quickest way to implement the strategic approach is to bring in new strategic skills from outside, as happens at the top in times of crisis. Extraordinary promotions are also effective in communicating strategic signals in complex multinationals—for example, a particular individual, widely regarded as a maverick, is promoted to a position of major responsibility.

The Values-based Approach

While the values-based logic behind talent development may be linked to a competency framework, it is part of a broader philosophy of management linked to strong normative integration. For example, Infosys not only recruits for "learnability," it applies this value to all internal selections right up into senior management.[58] Why is this seen as a "value" and not as a "competence"? It is a value because it does not represent how much someone knows or how proficient they are at a skill. Rather, it reflects attitudes and beliefs—Infosys wants professionals who are constantly interested in learning new things and pushing the boundaries of their own knowledge.

Indeed, selection on the basis of specified attitudes and values is arguably one of the most powerful ways of building and maintaining a strong culture. The values-based approach provides potentially powerful glue or integration, particularly in a knowledge-based organization that cannot rely excessively on hierarchic mechanisms of control.[59] In the box "GE's Values-Based Approach to Selection," we discuss how GE has approached selecting talent in a global market.

GE'S Values-Based Approach to Selection

McKinsey Consulting initiated the idea that talent is scarce and that there is a war for talent. However, this is not necessarily the whole story. Despite the fact that more and more people go to university, there is still a scarcity of talent. This stems in part from how talent is recruited and selected by the firm.

For example, GE had been working for some time to reduce the weight of a jet engine in order to increase fuel efficiency. They figured out how to reduce the weight of the engine but could not figure out how to reduce by 33 percent the weight of the bracket that holds the engine onto the airplane wing. They had engineers with PhDs from top schools like Stanford and MIT, but still had no luck. Finally they decided to open up the problem to people outside of the company. They had 700 applications from 56 companies. The winning design came from a 22-year-old engineer who ran a motorcycle mechanic shop with his brother in Indonesia. No one at GE would ever have hired this Indonesian mechanic. He did not have the right pedigree or credentials. However, he was not only able to meet the GE requirements of reducing the bracket weight by 33 percent, he actually reduced the weight by 84 percent.

Talent is out there. It is the approach to acquiring the talent that makes it seem scarce. Companies have begun to realize this and have put much more effort into their hiring practices, so from now on there is no basic formal requirement to be hired by GE. You don't even have to have finished school. All you need to do is demonstrate the five key value-based traits that GE now looks for when hiring talent:

1. Hunger to win: how motivated are you to follow your purpose
2. Integrity and transparency: others need to be able to vouch for your ability to keep your word
3. Accountability: how do you own the space others give you?
4. Resiliency and grit: the ability to withstand trials in life
5. Learner: do you hunger for growing and discovering?

Source: This box is largely based on the work of R. Krishnamoorthy, "Competing for talent in every geography," *Harvard Business Review* (June 2014).

Adapting Competencies in the Transnational Firm

Global competencies need to be translated into behavioral indicators in order to steer selection decisions, both those involving external recruitment and those focused on internal promotion or transfer. Cross-cultural validation studies undertaken by companies show that there will inevitably be differences in behavioral indicators from one culture to another, as well as from one business to another. For example, a specific skill within the competence of "managing people" at supervisory levels might be providing feedback. In an individualistic culture, such as the US, the appropriate behavioral indicator might be "confronts people constructively on their failings," whereas in a collective culture, such as Thailand, this might read as "ensures that subordinates know how they stand while maintaining team effectiveness." In defining "external relations" in a petrochemical company, the downstream exploration business might emphasize community relations, while customer relations would be highlighted in the upstream marketing business.[60] The "teamwork" competence may apply across cultures but with very different indicators in different settings.

There is a real tension between the need for differentiation and the need for consistency. Unless the competence framework is developed in close partnership with top management and the line, there is a risk that line managers will pay no attention to what they see as an "HR exercise" that ignores the pragmatic needs for differentiation, trying to impose one size on all. The need for differentiation across countries will often be invoked by local subsidiaries arguing for their own local way in choosing the competencies that guide selection.[61]

Selection Methods: The Importance of Context

The role of selection at entry recruitment is to minimize the risks that accompany long-term employment as well as to ensure fit with the future job. Selection is the area of human resource management where cultural and institutional differences play the biggest role.[62] For example, in the UK there is a long-standing belief in the empirical prediction of performance. The role of selection is to gather relevant information through interviews, testing, and assessment vehicles. In France, selection systems are based more on clinical assessment, to size up fit for long-term employment, not to predict outcomes.

In countries like France where employees have legal rights to long-term employment after a probationary period, the HR staff has the role of vetting people. Contrast this with Denmark, where there are few legal restrictions on hiring and firing; recruitment decisions are largely devolved to line managers.

The use and interpretation of different selection methods vary from one country to another:

- **Interviewing.** Interviews are widely used everywhere. However, structured interviewing, where each applicant is asked the same questions, is the norm in the US and has been shown to have much higher predictive validity than the unstructured interviews commonly practiced in many other countries.[63] So companies such as IBM, Accenture, and Shell that want to globalize talent management practices focus on developing structured templates for interviewing.[64]

- **Testing.** Attitudes toward psychometric testing vary with culture, with the strongest belief in its predictive ability in the UK. Today there is widespread awareness of the cultural biases in testing instruments when used across different cultures, though some tests, like General Mental Ability, have been shown to have high predictive validity across different contexts.[65] Faced with cultural differences in selection, companies are advised to respond by searching for cross-culturally validated testing instruments, and there is a lively service industry in this domain. Consulting firms and some companies make more use of simulation instruments than psychological tests, particularly when guiding the selection of technical and managerial talent.

- **Assessment Centers.** Well-designed (albeit expensive) assessment centers using interviews, role plays, presentations, tests, and simulations are considered to be a rigorous and valid way of screening talent, either at recruitment or for the internal assessment of potential. Yet assessment centers do not translate well without adaptation to the new cultural context. Simulation cases may have to be rewritten for a different setting, and different norms will have to be worked out for tests.[66]

Bear in mind that selection should be seen as a *two-way process*, especially where highly talented individuals are concerned. The candidate's impressions of the enterprise are influenced by assessment content and the way in which selection is undertaken—they can be seen as a first step in the socialization process. A well-intentioned HR department can put off talented individuals by creating an impression of cumbersome and bureaucratic procedures. A test or simulation that has not been adapted well to the local culture, or that goes against practice in that region, can create the impression of an ethnocentric corporation where locals have few possibilities for progression.[67]

Selection and Diversity Management

Diversity and selection are closely interwoven. Selection bias—favoring people of a particular gender, color, or cultural origin in recruitment and promotion—is a significant factor in discrimination. There are many facets to diversity, which in the US focuses on minorities in organizations—women, older people, blacks, Asians, Hispanics, native Americans, gays and lesbians, and the disabled. However, the salient aspects of diversity management vary from one culture to another. In Canada, a key issue is Francophone versus Anglophone, both of whom are predominately Caucasian. In many European countries it is the sizeable immigrant population—Turks in Germany and Muslims of diverse nationalities in France. In much of Asia, it is ethnic background—balancing Chinese, Indians, Malays, Bumiputras or ethnic locals in Singapore, Malaysia, and Indonesia. For multinational companies, the obvious dimension of diversity is national background, as well as gender.

The characteristics of the selection system clearly influence bias. Selection systems like open-job resourcing, where candidates can apply for positions and where the selection criteria are formally spelled out, favor unbiased decision-making.[68] But systems that are closed, in the sense that candidates must be nominated by headquarters and where the selection criteria are more informal (simply the judgments of the assessors), are more likely to be biased, as a study on whether international careers are open to women has shown.[69]

In terms of gender discrimination in the developed world, Japan has the fewest women in the workforce; around 65 percent of adult Japanese women are employed but only 1 percent of the most senior-level executive managers are women. The equivalent figure for China is 9 percent and 15 percent for Singapore.[70] Despite beefed-up legislation and some change, there are many subtle obstacles rooted in the Japanese employment system. These include an attachment to traditional performance assessment, where objectives are vague, and the willingness to sacrifice oneself for the company.[71] Scandinavia also has a low percentage of women in management positions in the private sector; many women are finding better career opportunities in government and public service. In some Arab countries, such as Saudi Arabia, gender discrimination is anchored in religious beliefs.

In the traditionally male-dominated oil exploration business, the French-American firm Schlumberger has implemented a range of diversity initiatives to raise the percentage of professional women in the workforce:

- There is a special program to identify high potential women at an early career stage and to provide them with high profile positions.
- There are recruitment targets: for example 40 percent of R&D hires should be female.
- Nearly half of Schlumberger's recruiters are female, acting as role models; such recruitment jobs are two-year stepping stone assignments before moving into management.
- Schlumberger has undertaken many actions to be an employer of choice for dual career people, including helping partners of international assignees to find local employment, flexible work schedules, and leaves of absence.
- Female employees are encouraged to join and develop networking groups that are managed locally but that coordinate activities globally with other groups.

Employee surveys at Schlumberger and Shell assess how individual and workforce diversity is respected by measuring *inclusiveness*. The results of annual attitude surveys are analyzed to see if the scores given by women in a particular country, business group, or function are lower on relevant questions, like support from the boss or opportunities for development. Low inclusiveness scores lead to feedback and appropriate action.

The American view on diversity typically emphasizes the business case. IBM argued that its heavy investment in diversity, initially in the US, would pay off in a billion dollars of revenues in the next five to ten years through a better understanding of its female, gay, and ethnic minority customers.[72] Other business reasons for diversity include improved ability to attract and retain talent, as well as enhanced innovation and problem-solving ability. Schlumberger's expansion into emerging markets was based on a long-standing principle that recruitment should broadly parallel the geographic distribution of revenues. Surveys show that virtually all Fortune 500 companies view global diversity as an important or very important issue. But with respect to gender, research in other parts of the world, including Europe, suggests that the business case for gender diversity is less widely accepted there than in the US.[73]

One of the open questions for multinational corporations is whether a global strategy is best for diversity management. IBM's approach, which originated in the US, is global.[74] The company created global task forces, reporting to a high executive level and with strong representation from the targeted minorities. A global structure of regional or business councils at lower levels is responsible for specific initiatives, complemented by the creation of employee network groups. A similar approach was implemented in Shell. Other multinational corporations prefer to take a decentralized local approach, since equal opportunity laws and norms vary from one culture to another.

However, nationality and cultural background remain the most challenging issues for multinational firms, as they struggle to escape their home country roots. As an executive working for a large, fast-moving consumer goods firm told us, "My handicap is not that I am a woman but that I am Chinese." From the earliest days of globalization, the forecast has been that multinational companies will gradually move from an *ethnocentric* to a *geocentric* orientation, where the key indicator will be national diversity at the top.[75] In most global firms, irrespective of the national origin, this has yet to happen.

The Challenges of Internal Selection (Assessment of Potential)

How does a multinational corporation spot and select talent from within its ranks? This question is important: usually only those selected will be offered development opportunities and training with the intention of moving them into leadership roles. If selection into this pipeline, as it is called, is focused on males from the home country, those are the people who will come out of the pipeline into executive roles. So how do global companies identify leadership potential?

Regional Differences in Internal Selection (Assessment of Potential)

There are many ways of assessing talent or leadership potential within the multinational firm. The traditional ways of doing this vary from company to company and from nation to nation.

The Elite Cohort Approach. Many Japanese corporations in the latter half of the twentieth century adopted what we call the elite cohort approach.[76] Cohorts of graduates are recruited from target universities for long-term careers and then moved around the organization during a seven-to-eight-year trial period. Once the trial period has ended, the rules change and career progression becomes a tournament, with "winners" and "losers."[77] The merits of this approach are that selection has been rigorously undertaken, assuring the development of a highly socialized leadership elite whose loyalty is unquestioned, whose skills have been meticulously honed, and who have a strong grasp on the subtle problems of coordination.

However, this approach is incompatible with localization. Since potential is identified at the time of recruitment, all the people entering the cohort pipeline are Japanese. Consequently, the output of the pipeline is Japanese. Even when Japanese firms attempt to include foreign employees in the cohort, the practice of appraising potential cautiously over a number of years discourages the best, who want quick signals that they have a future. As a consequence, while Japanese work practices at the factory level are widely admired, Japanese firms have a poor reputation for manager development, particularly in service industries such as banking and entertainment. However, since the elite cohort approach has been successful, it is not easily modified.[78]

The Elite Political Approach. What we call the elite political approach, which characterizes some US firms, is the typical pattern in establishment companies in Latin Europe. We can take France as an example. As in the cohort approach, potential is identified at entry: recruits come from schools that specialize in grooming an elite for positions of future leadership responsibility.[79] The graduates of the best *Grandes Ecoles* are virtually guaranteed a position as a top leader (the only question is the size and stature of the firm), and they will immediately enter into a position of managerial responsibility, without any trial period.[80]

The equivalent of this in the US would be firms that recruit graduates with top MBA degrees from Ivy League universities. One could argue that some elite consulting firms and investment banks, such as McKinsey and Goldman Sachs, play the same role in the US and elsewhere as selection grounds for senior-level appointments.

The Functional Approach. Historically, German firms exemplified the functional approach, a third model for internal assessment and talent management, though variants can again be found throughout the world. It is less elitist in nature, and the distinctive feature is that leadership is associated with functional expertise rather than managerial leadership.

Once recruited into the company, employees follow the apprenticeship tradition, which is deeply rooted in German heritage. The objective is twofold: first, to provide the recruits with a broad exposure to the business and organization; and second, to assess where their talents really lie. At the end of this trial period they are assigned to the function that appears to suit them best.[81] The advantage of the functional approach is the in-depth expertise that it develops, shown by the meticulous attention to detail that is associated with the renowned quality of German engineering. The disadvantage is the slowness of decision-making in organizations with strong silos, especially when it comes to strategy in a fast-moving world of global competition.

The Do-It-Yourself Approach. For US companies, the growing consulting and tech industries have been pushing companies to find talent internally by providing existing employees with self-guided tools to help themselves move onto bigger and better positions in the organization.[82] Traditionally known as the country with perhaps the weakest belief in internal talent management, a US model is beginning to emerge from what companies like Google and Apple are doing.

Companies like PwC and Juniper Networks have abandoned the traditional US talent management approach of simply hiring someone from outside the company if they need a new technical skill-set. Instead, they are investing more in ongoing communications with employees to improve skills of the workforce they already have. The role of HR is not necessarily to train but to facilitate a developmental dialogue between the manager and her subordinates to help them get the skills they need to excel in the company.

Microsoft, Adobe, and Deloitte have moved in a similar direction. They broke up the traditional promotion ladder and are providing a more open and flexible framework to accommodate employee needs and to adapt to rapid shifts in skill requirements. For example, Deloitte found that they increased employee engagement and their ability to adapt to shifts in project goals by ensuring that managers were having short, weekly coaching sessions with employees rather than simply sending them to formalized training programs.[83] While this model allows flexibility for workers, it also pushes the company toward a stronger meganational approach of developing leaders mostly within the parent country context.[84]

Transnational Approach to Assessment of Potential

Each of these four approaches has distinctive strengths, but they share the danger of an excessive reliance on the parent-country labor market. They come under pressure from progressive globalization. One of their limitations is that talent and potential, particularly in the elitist models, is identified so early. While there are clear advantages to this (talented people can be exposed to developmental challenges over a longer period of time), it easily leads to a parent country bias, as well as an excessive number of people in the pipeline who leave for other firms.

Consequently, a different approach has emerged that is more in tune with the needs of the multinational enterprise, particularly those facing transnational challenges. The distinctive features of this model are that it is not elitist, in terms of identifying potential at entry, and that it decentralizes the responsibility for functional development to its local subsidiaries, while managing selection into the leadership and global talent ranks tightly at corporate level.

The pattern that has developed in multinational corporations, such as Exxon and IBM in the US and Nestlé and Novartis in Europe, is to decentralize the responsibility for recruitment to local units.[85] The parent country itself becomes just another local unit, and the corporate recruitment or staffing unit is separated from the mother country.[86] The role of the reconfigured corporate function is not to recruit in the parent country, it is to beef up the rigor with which local companies undertake recruitment and staffing (typically aided by a guiding competence-based logic). Local subsidiaries recruit not just for jobs but also for potential.[87] Local recruits pursue their career within the local company, typically moving upward within functions for the first five to eight years. One could call this a *locally managed functional trial*. The corporate task is then to distinguish those with wider potential from the ranks of local talent.

Since potential is not identified at the time of entry, a wide variety of techniques are used to identify internal people with potential.[88]

- Local general managers may be asked annually to submit the names of their high potential individuals, who will then be scrutinized or even sent through an assessment center. The task of developing high-potential local talent may be one of the key performance indicators (KPIs) for the local unit.

- Expatriates working in local firms are required to identify local high potentials, including their possible successors.

- If there is a regional structure, identifying potential is a particular responsibility of the regional HR manager working with local subsidiaries.

- In some firms, potential is identified in a more subtle way, through local nominations for a landmark corporate "young managers" educational program, in which the training staff observe the behavior of participants closely.

- Local personnel who are given exceptional salary raises may come under particular scrutiny, as will those individuals who are assigned by local subsidiaries to work on cross-boundary projects.

- Exxon used to use a peer ranking methodology,[89] and multiple appraisal remains a reliable method of making such judgments—getting a group of managers who are familiar with the local people around a table for a frank discussion of their qualities. While the choice of a competence-based logic in no way resolves the problem of identifying potential, it provides a common language and concept of potential to guide these methods.

One of the implications is that global performance management will become particularly important, since internal selection should be based on common standards for performance evaluation. We will explore further some of the dilemmas around this issue in Chapter 7.

INTEGRATING SHORT AND LONG TERM IN TALENT MANAGEMENT

Rigorous talent management fundamentally boils down to attention and resources. The most difficult aspect is that it requires a high degree of attention from three internal stakeholders: top management, notably the CEO; the global HR function; and line managers in general. The HR function cannot do this alone, as talent management cannot be separated from business strategy; the development of organizational capabilities comes largely through ensuring that the necessary talent for the future is closely aligned with other elements of operational and business management. In fact, learning to organize and manage talent globally is becoming an important differentiating capability for a growing number of firms such as Infosys.[90]

Developing a Talent Management Mindset

The alignment of talent management with corporate strategy requires the active involvement of senior leaders. Nevertheless, a global survey of CEOs, business unit leaders, and HR professionals indicated that the most significant perceived obstacles preventing talent management from delivering value are first, that senior managers do not spend enough quality time on it, and second, that line managers are not adequately committed to people development.[91]

At a minimum, senior and line management should be involved in the following activities:

- Ensuring that global talent considerations are taken into account early in the strategy formulation process, translating business strategy into talent strategy.
- Forecasting talent skill supply and demand, diagnosing gaps in organizational capabilities, and taking proactive measures to fill them.
- Supporting appropriate talent attraction and selection processes at all levels of the organization.
- Reinforcing a talent mindset by making sure that talent management discussions are business priorities throughout the global firm.

Commitment to a talent mindset is perhaps the most challenging of these activities. All too often, line managers give only token acceptance to talent management, treating it reactively—for example, by recruiting sales people only when new products take off. They hoard their own high performers to achieve short-term goals and are unwilling to share talent across businesses or geographies. Out in the field, far away from the headquarters, talent management can sometimes seem like a vague long-term concern that has little bearing on the day-to-day actions for which they are rewarded.

Therefore, the key to developing a consistent and comprehensive talent mindset is the ability to reconcile the tension between short- and long-term perspectives. In its early stages of growth, many outside observers said that Infosys should spend more time on building operational efficiencies and less time on building a long-term talent pipeline. Infosys responded by pointing out the need to take a long-term talent approach to be able to achieve both long- and short-term objectives. As one HR director pointed out to one of the authors, "developing talent for the long-term is our number one goal. But this doesn't mean we can lose sight of the immediate issues we're facing. If an employee is not happy with his job today, it's going to affect your bottom-line tomorrow."

Companies can become trapped in a vicious cycle of HR boom and bust if leaders are excessively reactive and pay attention only to the short term. In a downturn, the first budget to be cut is recruitment, followed by training. When the business cycle is at its lowest point, there is a temptation to cut costs to the bone by laying people off, sometimes in ways that compromise the motivation and loyalty of survivors. When the upturn comes, there are not enough skills left in the company to take advantage of the growth opportunities. Managers scramble to fight short-term fires, hiring people with excessive bonuses and frustrating others. If before there were no budgets for training and development, now there is no time to do training and development well. Problems with underperforming people are pushed aside—until the next downturn, when they are laid off. And so the cycle repeats itself.

Even firms known for long-term thinking, such as those in the oil and gas industry, have fallen into this trap. Oil prices are by nature cyclical and unpredictable, and when the price of oil hit an all-time low of $10 a barrel, Shell,

Exxon, and the other major players stopped all recruitment, faced with an obvious need to cut operating costs. For several years there were no new jobs in the oil industry, hundreds of engineers and geologists were laid off, and many departments of petroleum engineering at Western universities literally had to close their doors. Then later, when the oil price jumped to over $100 a barrel, the skilled workforce needed to resume aggressive oil exploration was nowhere to be found, as technical graduates from emerging oil-producing countries would typically prefer to join their national oil company—or Schlumberger, the now booming oil services provider that had demonstrated a longer-term strategic staffing perspective. At great expense, the oil majors rebuilt their recruiting machine—but with the oil prices on the way back down, the pendulum swing in attracting talent is bound to happen again—unless companies learn from their past mistakes.

L'Oréal had an exemplary way of dealing with this cycle. Top management openly acknowledged that one of the most important tensions to manage is the conflict between the short-term bottom line and long-term development, and that in decision-making there is a natural tendency to privilege the short term, since it is so immediate and concrete. The role of the human resource function at L'Oréal was to act as the guardian of the strategic and long-term perspective, especially concerning decisions about recruitment, promotion, and the development of people. This did not give HR a right to veto; however, it did give them the right to stop the music and say, "Time out! Let's look at the long-term arguments before we decide." Sometimes the decision would favor the short term, sometimes the long term, and sometimes a creative solution favoring both would be found.

TAKEAWAYS

1. Talent consists of individuals with the right competencies who are in positions or roles that have a significant impact on company competitiveness.

2. The talent management process anticipates and meets companies' needs for individuals with the required competencies. Demographic changes, individual mobility, and global competition add to the importance of talent management.

3. The problem facing companies around the world is not so much a generic shortage of human capital but one of skills gaps—imbalance between skills needed and skills available in specific functions, industries and countries.

4. Multinational firms can build competitive advantage through talent management by providing opportunities for the most qualified individuals, regardless of their passport or gender.

5. To attract talent in local markets, multinationals need to build strong employer brands, elaborate differentiated employee value propositions, and balance global consistency with local adaptation.

6. To build a strong talent pipeline, many multinationals have found value in developing relationships with local universities, influencing how students are trained, and getting them interested in working for their companies upon graduation.

7. Selection involves identifying the most suitable person from a pool of candidates—internal or external. Selection should be closely linked to the management of gender, nationality, ethnicity, religion, and other forms of diversity.

8. Multinational corporations often guide talent management processes by specifying desired competencies. However, there is often confusion in how to define competencies, which comes from mixing three different competence definitions—based on logics of performance, strategy, or values.

9. Approaches to internal selection include: (1) the elite cohort approach, (2) the elite political approach, (3) the functional approach, and (4) the do-it-yourself approach. The transnational approach can be described as a locally managed trial, encouraging local units to develop their functional talent and then selecting the best.

10. When making selection decisions, companies need to make sure that local short-term staffing needs do not drive out long-term skill building and global talent development.

NOTES

1 Gupta and Shapiro, 2014.

2 Rao, H. and D. Hoyt, "Infosys splits HR head role to focus on top talent management," *The Economic Times*, March 4, 2015.

3 Patil, 2007.

4 "Infosys: Building a talent engine to sustain growth," *Stanford Case HR-30*, October 4, 2007.

5 Morris, Snell, and Björkman, 2016.

6 Cappelli and Keller, 2014.

7 Huselid, Beatty, and Becker, 2005. See Cappelli and Keller (2014) for a discussion of what talent means, as well as the conceptual approach and practical challenges in talent management.

8 The dimensions of value and uniqueness, used by Lepak and Snell (2007), are similar, though their perspectives are slightly different. The former focuses on positions or roles, while the latter focuses on the nature of the knowledge required.

9 Huselid, Beatty, and Becker, 2005.

10 The employment orientation is likely to be market-oriented, and C-positions may be outsourced.

11 Morris, Snell, and Björkman, 2016; Ingham, 2007; and Stahl, Björkman, *et al.*, 2007.

12 US Census Bureau, International Database statistics, 2015. See www.census.gov/ipc/www/idb/ for worldwide demographic statistics by region and country.

13 Kim, S., "The challenge of filling the skills gap in emerging economies," *The Guardian*, October 7, 2014; Kalman, D., K. Narayan, K. Oehler, R. Schuler, and M. Walker, "The global talent index report: The outlook to 2015," *Economist Intelligence Unit*, 2015.

14 Manning, Massini, and Lewin, 2008.

15 "Cisco's Wim Elfrink: 'Today, we are seeing what I call the globalization of the corporate brain,'" *Knowledge@Wharton*, July 16, 2009. http://knowledge.wharton.upenn.edu/article/ciscos-wim-elfrink-today-we-are-seeing-what-i-call-the-globalization-of-the-corporate-brain/

16 Snell and Dean, 1992.

17 Cappelli and Keller, 2014.

18 Cappelli, 1996, p. 141.

19 http://ec.europa.eu/eurostat/statistics-explained/index.php/Unemployment_statistics.

20 McKinsey, 2012; Oxford Economics, "Global talent 2021: How the new geography of talent will transform human resource strategies," 2012, Retrieved 2015, from https://www.oxfordeconomics.com/Media/Default/Thought%20Leadership/global-talent-2021.pdf; Lanvin and Evans, 2014; OECD, 2013; WEF, 2014; Yoo, Pepper, and Garrity, 2014.
21 Lanvin and Evans, 2014.
22 For INSEAD's Global Innovation Index web site, see global-indices.insead.edu/gii/.
23 70 percent select the vocational track producing butchers and bakers as well as technicians in robotics and bank managers. There are many crossover paths into universities and higher technical institutions, and half of the ministers in the Swiss government are products of early vocational education.
24 Lanvin, Evans, and Rasheed, 2014.
25 Boeri *et al.*, 2012; Freeman, 2010; Rowthorne, 2008.
26 Bidwell (2011) argues that external hires will perform worse than internal promotees, get higher pay, and show lower loyalty. He provides data from a financial services firm in the US to substantiate this.
27 Lee, Bachrach, and Rousseau, 2015; Baron and Kreps, 1999.
28 Cappelli, 2008, p. 121.
29 Ibid.
30 Harkinson, J., "Google's Low-Wage Contract Workers are Poised to Unionize," *Mother Jones*, July 27, 2015.
31 Scullion and Starkey, 2000.
32 Wiechmann, Ryan, and Hemingway, 2003.
33 Farrell, Laboissière, and Rosenfeld, 2006; Manning, Massini, and Lewin, 2008.
34 Ryan, Wiechmann, and Hemingway, 2003.
35 The issue of "cheaper and faster" often creates another tension. While the global platform is likely to reduce HR cost in high-cost countries, it may increase HR expenses in low-cost locations. When subsidiaries are directed to absorb this increase under the "one-firm" banner without seeing much tangible benefit, a push-back is inevitable.
36 Orlitzky, 2007.
37 See also Yoo, Pepper, and Garrity (2014) for an example from Cisco.
38 Stahl, Björkman, *et al.* (2007) found this to be true in their survey of 37 MNCs from North America, Europe, and Asia. See also Manning, Massini, and Lewin (2008).
39 "Intel's Vietnam Engineering Talent Pipeline," *Bloomberg Businessweek*, June 26, 2014.
40 Castilla, 2005.
41 Breaugh, 1992; Morehart, 2001; Cheung and Yong, 2006; Lengnick-Hall and Lengnick-Hall, 2003.
42 Sparrow, 2007; Lawler *et al.*, 2004.
43 For a fuller description of GE talent management process see the introductory case on GE in Chapter 8.
44 "The 10 most forward-thinking leaders in workforce management," *Workforce Management*, March 13, 2006.
45 Stahl, Chua, *et al.*, 2007.
46 Hieronimus, Schaefer, and Schroder, 2005.
47 Sparrow and Otaye, 2015. In China, new BMW engineers start their internal training with driving lessons—to better appreciate the feeling of driving a BMW-branded car.
48 Personal discussion with Prof. Stewart Black, INSEAD Singapore.
49 The literature on selection tends to focus on the former, neglecting the challenge of selecting high potentials from among the existing employees.
50 Winterton (2007) notes that a major reason for the adoption of competence frameworks in the 1990s was the need to replace formerly supply-driven training and development systems with demand-driven models, linked to desired capabilities. But the meaning of competence varies according to cultural context, with different meanings in the US, UK, France, and Germany.
51 Morrison, 2007.
52 Briscoe and Hall, 1999. In Chapter 8, we discuss brand-specific competencies linked to the development of firm-specific leadership skills.
53 Chatman and Cha, 2003.
54 Fombrun, Tichy, and Devanna, 1984.
55 Kaplan and Norton, 2008.
56 Bartlett and McLean, 2003.
57 The quote is from Kets de Vries (1994).
58 Kets de Vries, Agrawal, and Florent-Treacy, 2006.

59 See the discussion of Toyota and the section on culture as shared values in Chapter 5.

60 These observations are based on the experience of both Shell and BP. See also Sparrow and Hiltrop (1994).

61 See the case study and commentaries in Morrison (2007).

62 There is a vast research literature on selection methods and tests according to culture and context. See, for example, *The International Journal of Selection and Assessment*. See Brewster, Sparrow, and Vernon (2007) for a more detailed overview from the perspective of the international corporation.

63 Cook, 1999.

64 Ryan, Wiechmann, and Hemingway, 2003

65 Schmidt and Hunter, 1998.

66 Sparrow, 1999.

67 Wiechmann, Ryan, and Hemingway, 2003.

68 Open-job resourcing is discussed at length in Chapter 8.

69 Harris, 1999.

70 "Japanese Women and Work: Holding Back Half the Nation," *The Economist*, March 29, 2014.

71 Benson, Yuasa, and Debroux, 2007.

72 Thomas, 2004.

73 Nishii and Özbilgin, 2007.

74 Thomas, 2004. See Ciceri (2007). Also, there is a danger that "global" can mean applying US criteria worldwide.

75 Perlmutter, 1969. We discuss the issue of diversity in leadership development and top management teams in Chapter 8.

76 The elite cohort approach is not confined to Japan. For example, the Danish group Maersk, a Fortune 100 shipping and oil conglomerate, used such an approach to management development until recently, though with some different features from the Japanese.

77 Pucik, 1984.

78 Given accelerating globalization, this has long been described as the Achilles heel of Japanese management practices (Bartlett and Yoshihara, 1988).

79 At junior high and high school in France, students are progressively screened out into discipline streams. The top graduates then spend two years preparing for a competition to get into the *Grandes Ecoles* (graduate schools). The choice of college depends strictly on one's national ranking in this competition. At the top colleges, education focuses on preparing people for future leadership responsibility.

80 The virtue of the French system is that leaders in the business corporations of the establishment have close relationships with senior government ministers and officials—often they were classmates at a *Grande Ecole*. Consequently, French enterprises have been successful in sectors where government-business cooperation is important—defense, atomic energy, utilities such as energy and water, and telecommunications.

81 Responsibility for coordination was assumed at a senior level by management committees guided by the strongly consensual norms that are characteristic of large German enterprises.

82 Chapter 8 provides further detail on both a top-down and bottom-up approach to developing talent within the organization.

83 Buckingham and Goodall, 2015.

84 Cappelli, 2015.

85 For a comprehensive example of global talent management see Chapter 8.

86 This often happens in tandem with a corporate reorganization, where the global headquarters is separated from the mother country.

87 See our earlier discussion on localization in Chapter 2.

88 For more on potential identification and development see the discussion on global talent management in Chapter 8.

89 Exxon, an early pioneer in international management development, for many years used an annual procedure whereby each manager across the world was given a list of names of people in their immediate working environment. The manager had to rank these names in order of perceived potential. The rankings were summarized, and the final ranking was the basis for a more intensive qualitative review. However, the procedure was eventually abandoned because the judgments reflected performance rather than potential.

90 Lewin, Massini, and Peeters, 2009.

91 Lanvin and Evans, 2014.

chapter

7

Global Performance Management

SUMMARY

Challenge

In multinational firms, performance management is essential for effective coordination, but reconciling global and local perspectives is difficult.

Analysis

Building effective performance management systems requires:

- Recognition that performance management is a critical tool for global coordination
- Differentiation based on deep understanding of local cultural and institutional context

Solutions

- Ensure consistency across all elements of the performance management process
- Maintain a global approach "upstream", mix global and local approaches "downstream"
- Align scorecards and rewards to reinforce global mindset and encourage cross-unit collaboration
- Hold managers at all levels accountable for execution of performance management

Managing Performance Daily at Haier

One spring day in early 1985, anyone visiting the facilities of Qingdao Refrigerator General Factory, a home appliance manufacturer in the northeastern Chinese city of Qingdao, would have been forgiven for thinking that company CEO Zhang Ruimin had taken leave of his senses. Just a few months after taking the helm of this virtually bankrupt company, at the age of 35, this former city official gathered all factory personnel in the factory courtyard. There, they watched a group of co-workers take sledgehammers to implement an order from their young CEO: "Destroy all refrigerators that have been found to be defective in even a minor way." Zhang had a clear message: the factory would no longer produce substandard products. Instead, a high quality of products and services would become the foundation of its global brand.[1]

Thirty years later, Zhang had turned the small loss-making refrigerator factory into a group of more than 240 subsidiaries and 30 design centers, plants, and companies, employing over 50,000 workers. Haier (as the company is known today) was one of the world's top makers of large home appliances with more than US$30 billion in revenues, US$2.4 billion profits, and over 10 percent global share with a particularly strong position in washing machines and refrigerators.[2]

A guiding principle of Haier's management system is OEC (Overall, Every, Control and Clear). "Overall" means that all performance dimensions have to be considered. "Every" refers to everyone, every day, and everything. "Control and clear" refers to Haier's end-of-work procedure each day, which states that employees must finish all tasks planned for that day before leaving work—they are responsible for managing their own workload and reporting to their supervisor.

To support OEC, Haier uses a variety of performance management and motivational tools. For example, a key aspect of Haier's performance management is the system used for performance evaluations and promotions—and demotions—based on the concept of a racetrack. All employees can compete in work-related "races" such as job openings and promotions, but winners have to keep racing—and winning—to defend a title. There is no such thing as a permanent promotion. In keeping with this philosophy, every employee in the Haier Group undergoes frequent and transparent performance appraisals—going against the traditional Chinese culture in which "face" is extremely important.

However, accountability is not shared equally. According to Haier's 80:20 principle, superiors are respon-

sible for 80 percent of results (good or bad), and subordinates for 20 percent. Each manager's performance is reviewed weekly. The criteria for the evaluation involve both achieving quantifiable goals and the degree of innovation and process improvement. At the end of the month, managers receive a performance grade of A, B, or C. The results of this evaluation are announced at a meeting for middle- and upper-level managers on the eighth day of each month. Those judged as being ready to move to a higher position are transferred into the Haier talent pool.[3]

Haier has a formal policy for managing employees who do not meet set expectations. The consequence of continued performance in the bottom 10 percent after three negative reviews (either quarterly or annually), despite remedial training, is dismissal. The flip side of this approach is the emphasis on recognizing and rewarding successes and creativity. If an employee develops or improves a product, or suggests an efficient new procedure, the innovation carries the employee's name, and a notice to this effect is prominently displayed.[4]

Another important feature of Haier's HR system is a close connection between performance measurements and compensation. The company provides each employee with a "P&L book," which is updated daily and breaks down and quantifies the financial outcome of the employee's efforts. The bottom line is directly linked to the salary received by the employee. In Haier's language, employees do not receive salaries but their share of profits.

Haier is one of the first Chinese manufacturers to have established manufacturing bases overseas. An interesting question is whether the management practices that seem to have earned the company such success in China are transferable to other cultures as it continues its international expansion. For example, how would American or European employees respond to Haier's approach to managing performance? And if Haier chooses not to apply its performance management approach abroad, will this constrain its ability to coordinate global activities?

OVERVIEW

Haier is a good example of a company with well-defined performance management. Building on the Haier case, we will clarify what global performance management is and why it is important. We will then examine both the "upstream" side of this process, which focuses on determining the strategic and operational goals that should be the fundamental drivers of business performance, and its "downstream" side, which includes individual and team performance appraisal, feedback, performance evaluation linked to talent management processes, and rewards. This discussion leads to the conclusion that commitment to rigorous performance management is more important than the sophistication of the methodology.

Performance management can play an important role in supporting global coordination. Therefore, we will discuss how performance management may impact various types of lateral steering, notably global account management. Second, more broadly, we will examine factors influencing performance management in global teams. We conclude this chapter by discussing two questions critical to the implementation of global performance management: why the "ownership" of performance management is with line management, not with HR; and how performance management systems can contribute to building distinctive capabilities.

WHAT IS GLOBAL PERFORMANCE MANAGEMENT?

We define global performance management as a process that links the strategies and development organizational capabilities of a global firm to unit, team, and individual goals and actions. It involves periodic appraisal and evaluation, with reward and development activities that are in turn linked to the outcome of the appraisals. Global performance management includes three successive elements:

1. Specifying desired performance—setting objectives and goals at all levels
2. Reviewing and evaluating performance—providing feedback and plans for corrective action
3. Linking results to financial rewards—differentiating high performers

An essential characteristic of the performance management process is the consistency and tight link across the three elements—simple in principle, but potentially complex in practice, since the three phases of performance management are all too often disconnected—especially in companies operating across multiple cultural and institutional boundaries.

In much of the human resource management literature this concept of performance management is associated with the practices of some well-known Anglo-Saxon firms. But in a competitive world performance management is a process that has no boundaries, as the Haier example illustrates, and many innovative ideas influencing contemporary performance management have been pioneered by firms outside the US and Western Europe.[5]

Why Is Global Performance Management Important?

In a multinational firm, the performance management process should provide alignment between corporate, business, geographic, and functional objectives.

It guides a company's global people strategy, providing input to all functional HR processes, from recruiting and staffing to development and compensation. It links these clearly to the enhancement of corporate and business capabilities. And there is also increasing empirical evidence that across countries performance management is one of the management practices positively associated with firm performance.[6]

Except for executives at the highest levels, strategic goals are typically rather abstract for employees. Increasing shareholder value, decreasing time-to-market, enhancing customer orientation—what do such strategies mean for the behavior of people around the world? Effective performance management makes what is abstract concrete. It helps employees to focus on what they have to do, recognizes and rewards them for doing so, and makes clear the consequences of poor performance and behavior.

Good performance management processes should:

- Provide clarity about people's roles, objectives, and contribution to the business, thereby allowing greater autonomy
- Generate regular feedback on performance so that there is effective learning complemented with ongoing coaching and career development
- Make visible what performance is expected and what rewards (monetary and non-monetary) this will bring to the employee

This is particularly important in a transnational firm that relies on horizontal coordination, since clear goals, metrics, and the other elements of performance management are essential for building the necessary teamwork.[7]

Some leading-edge firms view their performance management process as a genuine source of competitive advantage and are secretive about their approach. As one global HR vice president commented, "We would no more show our performance appraisal form to a bunch of outsiders than Cola-Cola would let you come in and look over the secret formula for Coke."[8]

The Global Performance Management Cycle

For a multinational company, perhaps the most important question to ask is whether it should adopt a single global performance management process, differentiate the process by business or region, or allow each local company to develop its own particular process. Historically, multi-domestic firms were more local in their approach to performance management, while meganational corporations preferred a strong global orientation. While arguments have been made that performance management is or should be country- or culture-specific,[9] the overall trend has for many years been toward more globally integrated, or at least aligned, performance management systems. Among all HR practices, performance management (with the exception of the reward element) tends to be the most globally standardized.[10]

However, the extent to which one can generalize about benefits of a global or local approach may depend on the phase of the performance management process. Let us therefore break the process of performance management down into some of its elements, starting "upstream" with the planning and objective-setting cycle and then moving "downstream" toward appraisal, evaluation, and rewards.[11] The whole performance management process is presented in Figure 7-1.

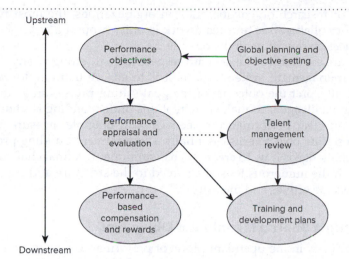

FIGURE 7-1
Global performance
management process

THE "UPSTREAM" SIDE OF PERFORMANCE MANAGEMENT

The focus of the upstream side of performance management is on setting global objectives. The first step in the performance management process is determining the strategic and operational goals that should be the fundamental drivers of business performance.

Goal setting is one of the most influential paradigms in the business management field. Hundreds of experiments and studies involving thousands of individuals on all continents have demonstrated that clear and challenging goals boost performance. As noted in a review of four decades of goal-setting research, "So long as a person is committed to the goal, has the requisite ability to attain it, and does not have conflicting goals, there is a positive linear relationship between goal difficulty and task performance."[12] A good example of the power of goal setting in practice is the rapid growth of $25 billion Brazilian private equity firm 3G—the owner of AB InBev (the world's largest beer company introduced in Chapter 1) and several other well-known consumer good companies such as Burger King, Heinz, and Kraft—built on a simple premise: getting excellent people, giving them challenging goals, and sustaining a meritocratic culture.[13]

Multinational firms can use many different approaches to set objectives (long-term strategic focus versus short-term financial focus, detailed planning versus entrepreneurial decision-making, etc.), each with their own embedded paradoxes and limitations.[14] The details of these different processes are beyond the scope of this book, but the specific approach chosen by the multinational in the upstream stage of performance management should be aligned with its global strategy and its organizational structure.

However, with the increase of cross-border activities, the issue for most companies engaged in international business is not if they should set global objectives. The issue is their scope and how to go about setting these objectives in a way that mobilizes the organizational energy in the desired direction and contributes to the coordination and cohesion of the firm. As it was noted in a summary of research on collaboration in organizations, the most fundamental lever for collaboration and teamwork is unity around a concrete goal that clearly places competition on the outside.[15]

There are several challenges with respect to goal setting in any global performance management system. The first is to ensure that employees around the world interpret the outcome of the goal-setting process in a similar way. The second challenge is to make sure that this understanding is translated into relevant and clear performance objectives with tangible measurements. The process of setting objectives is essentially a commitment-building process, and the third challenge is how to create such commitment. A final challenge is how to deal with the numerous tensions related to the structure and content of the performance objectives and measures.

Developing a Shared Meaning of Objectives

The first priority in the upstream phase of performance management is therefore making sure that employees worldwide share an understanding of what the goals actually mean. Different interpretations of a goal, and equally important, different readings of the consequences of not achieving the objective, can cause a great deal of confusion. In some firms a goal is a promise that must be respected, and so great care will be devoted to planning that goal. In others, a goal is a stretch aspiration that most people will fail to achieve. In yet other firms, the norm is "no surprises" so that goals become up-and-down moving targets. This is aggravated by differences in cultural heritage, both organizational and national. The box "When is a Goal a Goal?" presents two contrasting examples.

When is a Goal a Goal?

At A.P. Møller-Maersk, a Danish Fortune Global 500 firm in the container transport and shipping industry, the meaning of a goal or target is very clear throughout the company's worldwide operations. A goal, once agreed and accepted, is a promise to deliver. This means exercising what the now deceased owner of the company called "constant care"—debating and reviewing thoroughly with all parties any commitment that one will make since it is precisely that—a commitment. As the owner used to say, "Your word is your bond"—and everyone knows that he meant it. Not meeting a commitment will have serious consequences, maybe dismissal.

In contrast, at GE—another company known for its approach to performance management—the concept of a goal is different but equally clearly defined: It is a stretch target that the majority of people will fail to meet. As GE's annual report notes: "GE business leaders do not walk around all year regretting the albatross of an impossible number they hung around their necks. At the end of the year, the business is measured not on whether it hit the stretch target, but on how well it did against the prior year, given the circumstances. Performance is measured against the world as it turned out to be: how well a business anticipated change and dealt with it, rather than against some "plan" or internal number negotiated a year earlier."[16]

GE views most goals as stretch targets, it rewards well those who make significant progress on reaching them, but failure to hit these targets is not penalized. At the same time, as at Maersk, certain essential targets must not be missed, and these are specified since it is important to avoid setting stretch goals in areas where meeting a particular performance level is critical.[17]

Maersk and GE (both corporations that have been successful over a long period of time) have different approaches to performance management, to planning goals, and to their review and consequences. It is not that one conception of a goal is right and the other is wrong—in both cases, there are trade-offs. It is more a question of whether the business units and countries across the world are playing the same game with the same rules. Playing by different rules creates intense frustration that spills over negatively into many other areas of cross-border collaboration.

There are also cultural differences in underlying assumptions about the meaning of goals that affect performance management. For example, school systems in different countries socialize people to think about goals in different ways. Americans are brought up in the belief that the top A-grade is achievable. In contrast, French school children are evaluated on a 20-point scale, where a 15 represents an unusual distinction and an 18 is virtually unprecedented. Time horizon plays a role. The Japanese and Koreans are more likely to accept an ambitious goal ten years in the future that represents an aspiration, whereas most Westerners prefer a more tangible and achievable time scope.

More convergence is to be expected since technology is changing the process of performance management, including appraisal and development, bringing about an increase in timeliness and transparency of the goal-setting process. Some companies, like global hospitality giant Starwood, have long had goals posted on their intranet for consultation by peers and subordinates. Accenture has developed a Facebook-style program where employees post two to three weekly goals that can be viewed by fellow staff members, along with a couple of objectives for each quarter.[18] A hot area for venture capital investment is creating software through which employees and their bosses set long- and short-term goals, logging their progress on digital dashboard that everyone in their company can see and comment on.[19]

Deciding on Measurement Scorecards

What gets measured gets attention. This old idea is no less valid when it comes to implementing processes of global coordination. In our research and work with managers operating in global businesses, we have consistently seen gaps between the desired and actual level of collaboration and coordination. Why is the level of coordination low? This is partly because mechanisms such as teamwork and knowledge sharing are missing, but even more fundamentally because the performance management measures and outcomes do not encourage managers to do what they personally believe should be done. When measurements change, so do behaviors. In the HR arena in particular, attention needs to be given to what cannot be easily measured; see the box "Getting Clarity on Unmeasurables."

There are at least two strong arguments for using a common and consistent system of measurement scorecards throughout the multinational firm, including at least some cross-border performance measures:

- Global scorecards reinforce a global mindset among employees by making the nature of the global business visible and tangible for managers and employees in the company.
- Joint performance objectives encourage dispersed units to collaborate, thereby reducing the conflicts that often exist across organizational boundaries, such as between sales/service units and global product groups.

Getting Clarity on Unmeasurables

Some goals are difficult to measure, notably in the people development area. Take for example talent development. Goals such as "ensure that the top 5 percent of the professional workforce have clear development plans" may be too general and too undifferentiated to be useful. How can one get clarity around objectives that are not easy to measure?

Asking people to develop action plans and then reviewing those plans is one way of doing this. "Develop an action plan within one month for the development of the top 5 percent of the professional workforce, and review this with your boss and the regional head of HR." That plan is much more concrete, and specific goals can be set on the basis of the review.

Also, well-designed cross-border measurement scorecards help to decentralize responsibility. Without such metrics, clear accountability is impossible and relationships between the corporate and unit levels are likely to oscillate between unhealthy extremes of laissez-faire management-by-exception and detailed bureaucratic control over decision-making that dampens local initiative.

The existence of transparent and clear metrics allows decentralized initiatives and facilitates constructive debate between corporate and subsidiary levels. The aim is both to help local managers identify and diagnose problems and to allow top management monitor that performance. The purpose is to help rather than interfere: "What's the problem? What are you doing to fix it? And how can we help?" And one of the ways of helping is to suggest to local managers that they go and talk with higher performing units.

One European oil exploration firm uses peer groups of business unit managers to add punch to the goal-setting process. The managers of each business unit enter into an annual performance contract with top management and are then free to deliver the results in whatever way they wish. But the "peer assist" process requires managers to get their plans, including investment plans, approved by their peers before finalizing the performance contract with top management. "The peers must be satisfied that you are carrying your fair share of the heavy water buckets," said the company's deputy CEO. "The old issue of sandbagging management is gone. The challenge now comes from peers, not from management."[20] Half of the unit manager's bonus depends on the performance of the unit, and the other half depends on the performance of the peer group. The three top-performing business units in a peer group have also been made responsible for improving the performance of the bottom three.

Focused measurements linked to core business strategies can be powerful in ensuring coordination. Early on in its international expansion, one US high-tech firm faced the challenge of cracking the Japanese market with its semiconductor and telecommunication products. Several previous initiatives had failed. But this time it not only changed its product offering and marketing strategy but also modified the performance appraisal criteria for scores of managers worldwide. The change was very simple. One open-ended sentence was added to the list of annual appraisal criteria for 300 senior managers worldwide: "What have you done to support the company's Japan strategy?" Within weeks, phones started ringing in the company's Tokyo office, with colleagues inquiring how they could help—with information, knowledge, technical resources, and even people on short-term assignments.

Thus, a common approach to performance metrics needs to be shared across the globe. Many multinationals have established clear guidelines for setting individual goals throughout the corporation, often deployed under an acronym of "SMART": Specific, Measurable, Achievable, Relevant, and Timely.[21] To ensure focus, Starwood limits goals to five—the so-called Big Five, consisting of three financial targets and two qualitative objectives, as does AB InBev. And to stimulate cross-border learning within companies, the emphasis has to be not only on "what" has been accomplished but also on "how" it was achieved.

Advances in information technology and social media allow real-time measurement worldwide. State-of-the-art IT infrastructure enables global firms like Cisco to close the books on a daily basis. In some companies this may create a fear of "big brother," but if properly used, it can enable self-monitoring and autonomous corrective action at the front line. Using social media, the real-time reviews by peers provide more accurate measures of how individuals are performing within teams and across departments. With social recognition, individual and team achievements are captured at the moment they happen.

Building Commitment

Strategic planning processes used by many firms in the past typically involved a small group of senior executives and planners working on the numbers, leading to strategic objectives that were understood by only a handful of people—without any communication of the logic behind the numbers to the rest of the organization.[22] Consequently, there was little commitment, so implementation of these objectives was often ineffective. Therefore many companies today put a great deal of effort into making sure that not only the goals but also the strategic logic behind the goals are thoroughly communicated and well understood by the whole organization.[23]

For example, a Nordic multinational firm decided to confront the problem of traditionally slow implementation of a worldwide reorganization. The HR group prepared advice on how subsidiaries should communicate this to employees. However, the executive committee also announced that a special bonus would be paid to business unit managers in six months, based on the results of random interviews with subsidiary staff about their understanding of the purpose behind the reorganization. Indeed, the level of understanding of what needed to be done, and why, increased dramatically.

Money talks even in Scandinavia, but probably the best way of translating information into understanding and then action is having a dialogue. A critical task in the planning cycle is therefore creating opportunities for such dialogue to occur. Examples are interlocking "conferences" that bring together hundreds of key executives, with intensive preparation to ensure two-way discussion; training programs to introduce a common language for reviewing, say, strategic marketing; workshops that bring together heads of businesses for a week of intensive confrontation on issues that have been suppressed; "workout"-type processes; the "peer assist" process mentioned above; and fishbowl meetings where local management teams present their plans to top management while other teams sit in on the review.[24]

As global companies introduce multidimensional organizations, the planning and goal-setting process has to be adjusted accordingly in order to avoid confusion about who is responsible for what, making sure that goals of different units are reconciled and aligned.[25] The "responsibility chart" introduced in Chapter 4 as a tool for coordination can also be used for alignment of goals in the performance management process. Whatever tools are used, gaining clarity on responsibility and accountability is critical.

Building commitment to goals is as important at the individual level as at the unit level. As noted earlier, there is a wealth of research showing that goal setting improves employee performance since individuals are more committed to meeting the goals that they themselves have decided upon.[26] But does this hold true across cultures? There are certainly cultural differences in the roles that subordinates tend to play in the goal-setting process. In cultures characterized by large power distance, the superior commonly decides on the objectives. For instance, one study of performance management in Western multinationals in China concluded that the objectives were set by superiors more often than in their home countries.[27] Nonetheless, even in China, two-way communication about employee objectives helps produce stronger goal commitment, and involvement in goal setting has indeed been found to have positive performance implications across settings and cultures.[28] See the box "Game-style Performance Management at Shanda Games" on building goal commitment among millennials.[29]

The perception of fairness is critical for acceptance of performance management. Recent research on performance management in multinational firms have shown that in terms of procedural justice, it is important to make sure

Game-style Performance Management at Shanda Games

Shanda Games (SNDA) is the third largest online game developer in China, with over US$600 million in revenues and more than 2,500 employees in 2015. Not surprisingly, its performance management systems mimics a video game, with an objective of providing real-time performance feedback, compensation perceived as fair and equitable, transparency in promotions, and effective employee motivation.

Under the game-style management system, there are 100 Shanda "SD" positional levels with different salary levels corresponding to different experience value points (EVPs). EVPs can be obtained by completing daily tasks related to their positions or projects (initiating projects, or implementing projects initiated by other colleagues or assigned by the department).

Each SD position has a range of 20 sublevels. The employees can be automatically advanced to a higher level within his or her position category with a corresponding salary raise and bonus as long as accumulated EVPs meet the standards for advancement. Every day, they can check their position-based EVPs, project-based EVPs, the EVP gap between the present position level and the next higher level, and corresponding salary levels, using the "Blood-level Bar" on the user interface.

A senior HR executive at SNDA commented about the benefits of the game-style performance management: "The transparent system enables employees to see clearly their respective targets and the gap... Convinced that they are master of their own fate, employees will get motivated to create value for themselves—and for the company."

Source: Personal interviews at Shanda.

that employees are involved in setting targets that they can actually influence, while the employee perceptions of distributive justice are largely driven by the perceived link between performance appraisal and outcomes.[30]

Tensions in "Upstream" Performance Management

In the process of deciding on the structure and content of their global scorecards, companies must strive to balance several tensions embedded in this process:

- The mix of financial versus non-financial targets
- Short-term versus long-term goals
- Unit-level versus corporate-level objectives
- Incremental versus breakthrough initiatives
- Standardized measures versus localization of objectives

There are no "once-and-for-all" or "best practice" answers for resolving these tensions; they simply require continuous attention from senior management as well as HR as the global organization and its environment evolves.

Financial versus non-financial targets   The limitations of using only financial objectives as measures of performance are well understood and the trade-offs between various financial measures and their impact on corporate performance are also reasonably well mapped.[31] More difficult, and more critical, is deciding what non-financial targets need to be included in the global scorecards, how they should be measured, and what their weight in the overall evaluation should be.

Against this background, the balanced scorecard approach (see the box "Balanced Scorecards" below) has a particular appeal—provided that it is simple and focused—since it forces recognition of and debate on the dualities that underlie performance.[32]

Balanced Scorecards

The concept of the balanced scorecard was developed by Kaplan and Norton.[33] They observe that financial measures report on the outcomes but do not reflect how the organization manages the drivers of future performance. Therefore, instead of a narrow focus on financial results, they propose looking at the strategy to create value from four different perspectives:

1. **Financial** The strategy for growth, profitability, and risk viewed from the perspective of the shareholder
2. **Customer** The strategy for creating value and differentiation from the perspective of the customer

3. **Internal business processes** Strategic priorities for various business processes that create customer and shareholder satisfaction
4. **Learning and growth** Priorities for creating a climate that supports organizational change, innovation, and growth

Kaplan and Norton do not specifically address human resources, except as internal business processes. Perhaps this omission is due to difficulties in measuring human resources.[34] Whatever the reason, the omission of a critical component of performance management is considered

(Continued)

by some as a major problem and limitation of the balance scorecard approach.[35] Some firms have dealt with this by including human resources issues in the learning and growth dimension of their scorecards.

Becker and Huselid attempt to bridge this gap by introducing the concept of the *HR scorecard* focused on measuring the contribution of the HR function to multiple objectives, such as financial, (internal) customers, operations, and HR strategy.[36] The workforce scorecard measures workforce mindset and culture, workforce competences, leadership, and workforce behavior, all leading to workforce success in achieving the strategic objectives of the business.[37]

While financial indicators may have the virtue of simplicity, the balanced approach is more aligned to a world of paradoxes and dilemmas. However, the dilemmas of performance management do not disappear with the balanced scorecard—they just become more explicit for managers.

Short-term versus long-term goals   While short-term goals rightly emphasize business deliverables, the measurement scorecard should counterbalance this by adding longer-term objectives. Cutting costs for short-term survival by laying off employees in the time of crisis, for example, may be painful, but the real challenge is cutting costs without jeopardizing the long-term future. Many of the long-term issues may focus explicitly on people-related dimensions and it is the responsibility of HR managers to ensure that such considerations are taken into account even in difficult times. Unfortunately, the HR function in many corporations is excessively reactive, carried away by growth aims in good times and slashing headcount in difficult periods.

This tension does not surface only in times of crisis. In most firms, long-term and short-term planning are tackled sequentially. Strategic planning is an initial step that leads to operational planning and budget decisions. From then onward, the strategic goals exist only in the distant background. When operational goals in a subsidiary far from headquarters are translated into individual objectives, the connection with corporate strategic objectives is typically vague at best. Targets that are inherently long term, such as talent development, tend to get pushed out in the process.

Unit-level versus corporate-level objectives   There are good reasons to establish challenging but achievable goals for which the unit in question can really be held responsible, motivating managers to work hard to reach them. However, as we have already pointed out, a narrow focus on the individual units may lead to behavior that is suboptimal for the global organization as a whole.[38] Most multinationals therefore establish both local and global (sometimes also regional) objectives for their foreign units. The mix and weight of objectives can change from year to year, as warranted by corporate priorities.

Incremental versus breakthrough initiatives   The performance management process tends to focus on incremental rather than breakthrough change. There has been valid criticism that most global measurement systems have a built-in bias toward optimization, replication, and predictability.[39] They tend to drive out disruptive learning; responding to new and unfamiliar knowledge may have long-run benefits, but it typically involves short-term adjustment costs and losses due to experimentation. Therefore, there may be a need for a long-term "breakthrough" process to complement the traditional short-term focus of operational goals.

Some firms have moved to parallel goal-setting processes where operational objectives are separated from the long-term goals—with active top management involvement and focus on the latter. At GE, long-term company-wide stretch targets are included in the global scorecard, such as a step increase in operating margins, Six Sigma quality targets, and not least leadership development objectives. These are reported to the shareholders in the annual report. Other companies, such as Intel, have similarly broadened the conception of performance management to complement the cycle of operational planning with strategic actions oriented toward long-term breakthroughs.[40]

Standardized measures versus localization of objectives   Multinational firms are rarely, if ever, faced with the same competitive position, the same economic situation, and similar institutional contexts in every corner of the world. Marriott and Citibank use worldwide customer satisfaction measures, but individual units can hardly be expected to achieve precisely the same scores.[41] Therefore, even the most globally standardized performance measures should reflect the differences as they are cascaded down to local level. However, the logic behind differences often gets "lost in translation." For example, it is natural in a time of economic recession to mobilize the whole organization worldwide to cut costs by setting specific cost-reduction targets. Yet it is counterproductive if this is expressed as a ban on adding headcount in business units that have an opportunity to increase profitability though growth.

It is also important to recognize that even in the context of a common strategy, specific goals vary from one business to another and from one subsidiary to the next; thus different performance indicators within the scorecard should be given different weights. Local goals must reflect local competitive realities; otherwise the next stage of the process—appraisal and evaluation—is doomed to run into problems.

Yet at the same time, if goals are mainly local, the opportunities for cross-unit synergies may be neglected. The box "Obstacles to Global Collaboration" illustrates the consequences of using performance measures that encourage local sub-optimization.

Obstacles to Global Collaboration

In order to increase focus and eliminate wasteful internal competition, a European engineering company—in which each business unit was evaluated strictly on the basis of its own P&L—allocated responsibility for the US market for power transmission to its US subsidiary. At the same time, responsibility for development and production of a specialized component gear was consolidated in Switzerland in order to gain sufficient economies of scale in a relatively small global market.

In the process of collaborating on a project in the US, the Swiss engineers developed a close relationship with a US customer—who then wanted to use the Swiss-made equipment on another project in the UK. However, since the final contract for delivery in the UK involved a US customer, both the US and UK subsidiaries had to be brought in on the deal. With each claiming their share of the potential profits, project terms became unattractive to the Swiss, and the opportunity was lost.

Source: Adapted from Y. Doz, J. Santos, and P. Williamson, *From Global to Metanational: How Companies Win in the Knowledge Economy* (Boston, MA: Harvard Business School Press, 2001).

THE "DOWNSTREAM" SIDE OF PERFORMANCE MANAGEMENT

The "downstream" of the performance management process consists of individual and team performance appraisal, feedback and rewards, as well as performance evaluations linked to talent management processes.

Performance appraisal serves multiple functions—communication on organizational objectives, working out tensions in boss–subordinate relationships, providing information for self-improvement, guiding training and career development, preparing evaluations for talent assessments, providing the basis for pay decisions, and leaving paper trails to justify dismissals—many of which are in conflict with each other. Timing is also important. Unlike Haier, most US and European firms have had a policy of yearly performance appraisals for all employees,[42] but the appraisal cycle at Cisco, Intel, and some other high-tech firms takes place every six months. More frequent performance-related communication feedback is becoming increasingly popular. Deloitte has replaced annual reviews with quarterly or project "performance snapshots" and relies on employee weekly check-ins with managers to keep performance on course.[43]

Performance Appraisal Challenges

There is an ever-expanding range of appraisal practices—some reflecting the latest managerial fad, while a few leaving a lasting impact on the way companies throughout the world approach this complex process; "forced rankings" popularized by GE are perhaps the most visible example. But any appraisal is rife with challenges, as experienced practitioners know and as HRM textbooks show.[44]

There is no shortage of evidence that performance appraisal may have unintended negative consequences and calls for abolishing performance reviews altogether are not infrequent.[45] The father of the total quality management movement, Edward Deming, argued forcefully that appraisal is so dysfunctional that performance improvement efforts should be focused on system improvement—getting at the root problems—rather than on symptoms that appraisal often raises.[46] Other critics of the process may not go so far, but it is obvious that what is appropriate for one situation is often inappropriate for another. This is true in a domestic company and, even more so, in the case of a multinational.

A big part of the challenge of getting it right is again that of global/local differentiation. The trend has been toward more globally integrated performance management practices—also downstream. We would argue that although multinational firms need a global template for the appraisal process, local business units may need some leeway to adapt that template to their circumstances. What is crucial is buy-in among senior management in the subsidiaries on how it should be executed in practice.

It is common to hear local objections and doubts, "Our culture is different, our labor laws are special, performance differentiation is not feasible, our operations are not mature enough." Some of these obstacles may be real, but in our experience many objections reflect the unwillingness to take on probably the most difficult part of any manager's role—to provide timely, fair, and constructive performance feedback. The fact is that most managers, irrespective of culture, find managing performance—especially formal appraisal—to be difficult, time-consuming, and uncomfortable.

Fitting Performance Appraisal with the Local Environment

The concept of performance appraisal practiced today in many multinationals was developed in a Western context (mainly by US-based firms) and an argument can be made that it might not always suit the context of other cultures. There are myriad cultural obstacles to Anglo-Saxon-style performance appraisal, many of them well described in the management literature,[47] ranging from the relationship between the employee and the organization and the nature of the manager–subordinate relationship to feedback and preferences about outcomes.[48]

For example, the manager–subordinate relationship is conceived differently in different cultures. In many cultures, the idea of a two-way dialogue in which the subordinate should be free to challenge the perception of the boss goes strongly against the heritage of what Hofstede calls "power distance."[49] In collectively oriented cultures, behaviors that demonstrate loyalty and cooperative spirit are likely to be just as important as the ability to achieve sales targets, unlike the situation in most Western firms.

Also, it is often argued that one legacy of the Maoist years, reinforced by the strong authority of the boss in the traditional Chinese culture, is that Chinese employees often avoid initiative for fear of being punished.[50] Some Asian cultures do not share the sense of internal control of the Anglo-Saxons—how should a Western executive react when an Indian colleague inexplicably puts off a decision, perhaps having read a horoscope indicating that this would be an unfortunate time to make a choice? However, there is no need to travel to the Orient to see global performance management constrained by the cultural and institutional context.[51] As late as the mid-1990s, German academic reviews of HR practices made no mention of appraisal practices or performance management.[52]

Still, as we have learned from the example of Haier, making assumptions about a company's performance management based on the cultural or institutional context in which it operates may be misleading. If a company considers performance management to be one of the key factors behind its competitive advantage, these constraints may be seen as secondary. As one of Haier's HR executives commented to us: "We don't want Haier to be an average Chinese company, so why should we follow what an average Chinese employee may like to believe in?" Haier's full transparency in sharing appraisal outcomes is perhaps the most dramatic example.

Frequently, the influence of culture on corporate practice is exaggerated. Thirty-five years ago, it was predicted that management-by-objectives (MBO) would never take root in France because of the prevailing concept of authority, the avoidance of face-to-face conflict, and the negative connotations of control in that culture.[53] Yet only a decade later a survey of large French companies reported that over 85 percent had a policy of fixing objectives for managers and conducting annual performance appraisal reviews.[54] Similarly, leading firms in Italy and Germany have been rushing to introduce performance management approaches built around objectives and appraisal as an element connected with greater decentralization of accountability. In Japan, where performance evaluations were traditional practice but conducted without formal feedback to the employee,[55] face-to-face performance interviews are now a standard part of managerial routine.

As discussed in Chapter 2, generalizing about cultural differences may be misleading. In a study of how American and Japanese MNCs transferred their performance management practices to Vietnam, the former—although more distant in terms of cultural values—were more successful in gaining acceptance.[56] There are signs of considerable convergence among multinational companies toward perceived best practices in performance management.[57] At least in the private sector, even domestic firms in Western and other countries are moving closer together in their approaches.[58]

Still, to customize the global performance management process to suit the local environment requires the multinational firm to consider the following issues carefully:

- To what extent can the global firm implement practices that are at odds with the local institutional and cultural context? Being different may be difficult but acceptable, yet complying with local laws is essential. In Germany, for example, all information pertaining to appraisals is open to employees.
- What can be learned from other firms—not just other worldwide firms but also successful locally owned companies whose performance management diverges from common local practices? If they can do it, why not others?
- How far is it possible to go in adapting locally without breaking consistency within a global firm? Without global performance management in place, many other global people strategies will be difficult to implement.

There is no simple answer to any of these questions, and one size definitely does not fit all. At the same time, commitment to implementing a rigorous appraisal and feedback process is more important than the sophistication of the methodology.

Providing Feedback

One element of performance management that often creates controversy with respect to cultural context is feedback, given different ways of addressing a potential conflict in different cultures. While the discomfort that surrounds critical feedback is more or less universal, leading to many of the problems with appraisal, it may be particularly acute in certain cultures. A study of performance appraisal practices in the three Chinese cultures of Hong Kong, Singapore, and Taiwan showed a common preference for group-oriented appraisal rather than individual assessment (though otherwise there were significant differences on most other dimensions of appraisal).[59]

Asian cultures tend to deal with sensitive issues, such as negative performance feedback, in subtle and indirect ways; the idea of constructive confrontation is an alien concept for many Chinese and Japanese, though one should not generalize. While it is probably true that most Chinese employees resent direct negative feedback, there are others who view the Haier-like "racehorse" environment as superior to the traditional emphasis on educational credentials and personal connections.[60]

However, despite the many cultural and institutional differences, there is evidence that "Anglo-Saxon style" appraisal feedback is spreading across the world, even in Japan—at least in multinational firms.[61] In China, where foreign companies were often told that direct feedback is nearly impossible to implement because of potential loss of "face," some firms are learning from Haier and breaking the mold. Similarly, as we discussed above, firms in Continental Europe have gradually introduced performance management approaches built around objectives and appraisal as an element connected with greater decentralization of accountability. Multiple rater appraisals are gaining popularity,[62] particularly for developmental purposes, as outlined in the box "360-Degree Feedback in Multinational Firms."

There is one practice concerning performance management that definitely applies across cultures: it is vital to train supervisors and managers in how to conduct appraisals. Virtually all multinationals with successful performance management processes have realized this, and performance appraisal training is today mandatory in many leading firms.[63] Such training stresses the importance of well-prepared periodic appraisal discussions as well as ongoing coaching as ways to improve a person's performance.

360-Degree Feedback in Multinational Firms

Many firms around the world have developed feedback systems to provide managers with direct input on their strengths and weaknesses as leaders. A number of different approaches have developed, but they all share one thing in common—individuals' own assessments of their behavioral skills are contrasted with the assessments of their bosses, peers, and direct reports. These assessments help managers to see the differences between the perceptions they have of themselves and those that others have of them.

360-degree leadership assessments can be used for both development and evaluation. While there may be some overlap in these two aims, there are some important differences. Organizations that use 360-degree feedback for evaluation and appraisal often encounter problems in getting honest feedback. Participants will tend to select respondents whom they think will provide positive feedback if they think that it will be used to evaluate them. For this reason, many firms use the results for development purposes, trying to keep 360-degree feedback separate from the performance appraisal process. As organizations acquire experience with 360-degree feedback systems, with greater acceptance of the process, they are better able to juggle the competing goals of evaluation and appraisal.

Attitudes to the process of giving and receiving feedback vary across nations. In general, countries with high-power distance and a dislike of conflict will be the most resistant to 360-degree feedback. However, there is now empirical evidence that some 360-degree assessment tools can be used with a reasonable confidence in different parts of the world and many differences occur at the firm level rather than the national level. Individual firms differ in terms of power distance and the management of conflict and may resist attempts at feedback. When a leadership 360-degree system is introduced into any organization for the first time, it is normal to have skepticism until the system becomes accepted and individuals become more comfortable with giving and receiving feedback.

Sources: M.A. Peiperl, "Getting 360-degree feedback right," *Harvard Business Review* (January 2001), pp. 142–7; J. Ghorparde, "Managing five paradoxes of 360-degree feedback," *Academy of Management Executive* 14, no. 1 (2000), pp. 140–50; A.S. DeNisi and A.N. Kluger, "Feedback effectiveness: Can 360-degree appraisals be improved?" *Academy of Management Executive* 14, no. 1 (2000), pp. 129–39; D.R. Denison, L.M. Kotrba, and N. Castano, "A cross-cultural perspective on leadership assessment: comparing 360-degree feedback results from around the world," *Advances in Global Leadership* 7 (2012), pp. 205–28.

Performance Evaluation: Linking Appraisal to Outcomes

The next component of the performance management cycle is the link between appraisal and rewards (compensation and promotion) as well as development outcomes such as learning opportunities and individual development plans, or the inclusion (or exclusion) of the person from corporate talent pools. Again, context matters. For example, a study of Chinese employee reactions to Western objective setting and appraisal systems showed that while the processes of negotiating expectations and of performance feedback were often key for Western staff, it was the link between performance and career development that was most appreciated by the Chinese.[64]

One output of the appraisal is the formal performance evaluation of the employee that typically feeds into talent management and leadership development processes. Although some well-known firms such as Accenture or Medtronic have moved at least partly away from ranking employees,[65] performance evaluation usually involves differentiation. Typically, employee performance is rated on a three- or five-point scale relative to others in the organization within the same or similar grade.

A critical issue that arises from such evaluations is how to deal with high and low performers. Leading firms around the world are redefining the standards in performance evaluation, getting tough in the process and opening up new controversy. Their aim is to motivate and reward the best, but some also systematically weed out those who are underperforming relative to their peers.

A well-known champion of explicit ranking and tough performance standards has been GE's former CEO Jack Welch. GE's globally used review of performance and potential is based on the so-called vitality curve and focuses primarily on rewarding, retaining, and developing the top 20 percent of "A-players" and quickly removing the "C-players" in the bottom 10 percent.[66] While post-Welch GE and Microsoft are seen as backing away at least partly from a strict enforcement of the vitality curve,[67] for others such as AB InBev, rewarding the best it is the core of their company culture (See the box "Brewing High Performance at Anheuser-Bush InBev").

Brewing High Performance at Anheuser-Busch InBev

Working for the world's largest brewer may not to everybody's taste but that is fine with Carlos Brito, the company's chief executive.[68] "People that are brighter, more committed, deliver more, produce more, create more value, build better teams, are better leaders, inspire people to achieve higher things—those guys need to be treated in a very different way than the other guys that are good, but not amazing."

AB InBev, with key operations in the US and Brazil, and a global head office in Belgium, sees itself as a meritocratic company, with a strong culture of informality and transparency. Staff are encouraged to quiz their leaders, who sit at central desks in open-plan offices. Many liken it to the way start-up employees have access to their company's founder-entrepreneur. However, transparency does not mean equality. "In our company we say that fairness is to treat different people differently," explains Brito. Considerable rewards, in cash and equity, are available to those who hit tough targets at company, unit, and individual level. When targets are missed, bonuses vanish.

The company encourages a sense of discomfort. Brito says: "Every year we look at the top talents and we say, OK, are they stretched, are they getting too comfortable?...

[If they are] it's time for us to start taking people more often out of their comfort zones... We believe that people only grow when [they're] from time to time sat outside of [their] comfort zone."

Performance is constantly monitored, and reviewed formally once a year, using 360-degree feedback. Underperforming staff are given six to nine months to improve. Brito denies AB InBev operates a forced ranking system. Yet, he says, at some point you must say to laggards: "Look, you're a very smart guy, there are other companies out there but for us it's not working. You live only once, don't waste your time here, go somewhere else while you are young."

Not surprisingly, the company has its share of critics, objecting to work environment of high pressure, internal competition, and relentless drive to reduce cost.

One of the justifications for firing low performers is that it may be better to force people out so that they have the opportunity to restart their careers without the handicapping disadvantage of a bad reputation. A reputation as a low performer is often a self-fulfilling prophecy (see the box "The Set-Up-to-Fail Syndrome"). People acquire poor reputations, they are passed from one department in the firm to another, and their performance—and self-confidence—continues to suffer. In these situations, as argued by Welch, early action may be better not only for the company but also for the individual.[69] A growing number of multinational firms identifies low performers but then allows time to turn the individual either around or out.

The Set-Up-To-Fail Syndrome[70]

The set-up-to-fail syndrome can develop whenever managers start to view certain subordinates as lower performers. Often, these implicit judgments occur early on in the boss–subordinate relationship—within a matter of weeks rather than months and based on initial impressions of attitude or potential. They can have a lasting impact on the performance and development of the subordinates concerned.

What the boss thinks of as a "supporting" style may come across to the perceived lower performer (PLP) as overly controlling. Often, they do not receive the same resources, information, and opportunities as their colleagues who are viewed as more capable, making it difficult to prove the boss wrong. Their motivation is hit by the boss's close monitoring. Feeling micromanaged and underappreciated, PLPs may lose confidence in themselves and in their boss, and they disconnect from their jobs.

Within a short time, the PLPs may therefore start demonstrating the very attitudes and underperformance that the boss had anticipated, which means the boss has no reason to question his or her own role in the process. In fact, the self-fulfilling process becomes self-reinforcing as the boss adopts a more intense "remedial" approach.

Managers need to be mindful of the set-up-to-fail syndrome when working with subordinates from other cultures since there may be differences in views on what constitutes effective subordinate behavior. What the subordinate in a certain culture views as deference to the superior may be seen by the expatriate boss as a lack of initiative, triggering a negative cycle of interactions.

Circumstances today favor the spread of the syndrome—increasing bottom-line pressures for results creating hard, driving bosses; wider spans of control so that bosses have less time for each individual subordinate; and the prevalence of A-B-C quota systems of performance evaluation.

Closing the Loop: Challenges in Global Compensation

From an employee perspective, together with opportunities for training and development, financial rewards are the most immediate outcome of the performance management process. In this respect, historically, reward and compensation policy was typically the most local area of performance management, although often within a broad global structure, such as some version of the Hay system of job classification. The one problematic and highly complex area was compensation for international staff (mostly home country expatriates) who moved from country to country. Today, this is changing and companies are considering how to harmonize the compensation of their employees across their worldwide operations. Without such harmonization, implementing a global approach to performance management would be very difficult.

The basis for a global approach to compensation is a common compensation and reward *philosophy*. Such a common philosophy and at least some communality in compensation, benefits, and rewards across units are needed to create a common employee value proposition. This can mean, for instance, that the firm has a global policy concerning the average compensation level compared to the local market (that is, the company aims to compensate its employees at a certain percentile) and that common criteria are used to determine rewards. Base pay, benefits, and actual levels of total compensation for most employees may still differ across countries.[71]

However, it is increasingly difficult to uphold differences in compensation among employees from different geographical units. The examples described in the box "How Should the Bonus Be Paid?" show that what is global and what is local is far from easy to determine.

How Should the Bonus Be Paid?

An American software company operates development centers in California and Bangalore India where the programmers are paid in line with local market rates. A critical project that involved extensive coordination between the two locations required a radical redesign, with a deadline that could only be met through extraordinary effort. The company decided to offer a significant bonus to all the programmers involved as long as the redesign was undertaken in time. But how should be this bonus be distributed? In proportion to base pay, taking into account the income gap between the US and India? Equally among the two groups? Or in proportion to the individual contribution to the success of the project, irrespective of work location?

Consider also the dilemma facing GIC in Singapore, the government fund management firm charged with investing the country's financial reserves on world markets. In the past, it recruited local professionals to fill fund management and analyst jobs, paying them according to local civil service standards. As GIC expanded overseas, it hired talented non-Singaporean staff—again paid locally, but often more than their counterparts at head office. Today the top foreign staff members are being transferred to Singapore on a permanent basis—and how should they be paid? The salaries of their peers in foreign-owned financial institutions in Singapore reflect international market conditions; paying less would violate external market equity, making it impossible to retain the best. But if foreign hires are paid at global rates, this will create internal inequity with their Singaporean colleagues. So why not treat all professionals as "globals"? That is possible, but it would then create external inequity with respect to other government employees.

Similarly, top managers at one of Norway's largest international corporations did not worry if a few Americans earned more than them because the Norwegian state would take most of any increment in taxes. But when a large number of middle-level professionals around the world were earning significantly more than the head of a global business at home, it created a disturbing sense of inequity, leading them to advocate a worldwide review of compensation practices. While the members of management teams of subsidiaries are today typically part of a common corporate system of performance-based reward management, many companies wonder if variable compensation, skill-based reward practices, and risk-based compensation such as stock options should not be generalized across local operations.

The design and implementation of reward systems—from pay-for-performance to team-based pay, from stock options to executive compensation—is highly dependent on context.[72] There are national legal constraints (for example, it is difficult to pay on a piece-rate basis in Germany or not to pay for overtime in Japan) and differences in taxation systems often argue for local differentiation. Several studies drawing on an international HR practice survey show cross-national differences in compensation practices, for example, in using financial incentives, although the trend is towards increasing similarity.[73] However, national culture is only one element of context. Variations in norms and values within cultures are just as important as variations across cultures.[74] Consequently, there is considerable variance in compensation practices across firms, industries, and sectors within most nations.

In some country or industry environments it is accepted that employees may share some of the unit- or firm-level risk, whereas elsewhere such choices may be constrained by custom or regulation. For example, the approach to reward management at Lincoln Electric (combining pure piece-rate compensation and generous bonuses with norms of transparency to create a strong culture of self-reliance) is fundamental to the success of that firm. Such an enterprise might be obliged to consider extremely carefully the location of its operations. It might avoid countries where institutional barriers render its reward system nonviable, and it should pay meticulous attention to the selection of people (as Japanese firms have done when establishing operations in the US). In other firms, compensation practices may be less strategic and consequently more of an issue for local management.

In either case, global reward decisions are full of difficult questions. One such question is how rewards should be tied to the balance of global versus local results. There are convincing arguments that compensation should only be linked to outcomes that the employee can influence.[75] However, this would mean that linking pay to global results would only benefit a select few in the organization. Others assert the opposite, pointing to the evidence that firm performance improves when the individual rewards at all levels are at least partially tied to broader objectives,[76] and there is some evidence that multinationals have a preference to export incentive practices from the headquarter to subsidiaries.[77] For example, Novartis uses merit-based bonuses worldwide irrespective of locations, as the company believes that this practice is instrumental in promoting a performance-oriented organizational culture.[78]

SUPPORTING GLOBAL COORDINATION

Unless both upstream and downstream elements of performance management are aligned to reward broader dimensions of performance beyond one's job or immediate business unit, it is unlikely that we will see strong collaborative behavior or support for wider global corporate initiatives. From this perspective, the performance management process is an indispensable part of global coordination.

We will consider two aspects of global coordination where performance management may have a particularly strong influence. First, we will discuss how performance management may impact various mechanisms for lateral steering, among others global account management. Second, more broadly, we will examine factors influencing performance management in global teams.

Enabling Lateral Steering

There are several imperatives worth repeating that are essential for performance management to support horizontal coordination:

- The underlying approach to measuring performance has to be global in order to make the various mechanisms of horizontal coordination work in a synchronized manner. It is the internal *consistency* and *coherence* of practices and norms that create an environment for lateral coordination.
- Having a global scorecard does not mean that everyone must have the same goals. However, it is important to address the inevitable tensions regarding conflicting priorities through *clear guidelines* concerning the process and the principles on how these should be handled.[79]
- The conflict between individual job responsibility and the demands for lateral coordination and cross-boundary teamwork (the operational and project roles) must be acknowledged. Top management needs to recognize explicitly the benefits and contributions of global collaborative behavior.

The difficulties in balancing global and local requirements are likely to be most acute when individuals who are not performing well in their own jobs, or whose units are underperforming, are asked to work on cross-border projects, coming under unreasonable pressure to improve their own individual performance *and* to work on lateral coordination teams. Only people with credibility can successfully manage the inevitable tension between conflicting but legitimate priorities that naturally emerge in any global business.

Lateral coordination roles typically demand superior leadership skills and they complement job mobility as a platform for developing global leadership competencies.[80] A good performance management strategy is *to pay* for local job results but *to promote* for demonstrated global leadership in "split egg" coordination roles. This ensures that future leaders are drawn from a talent pool with a proven global mindset and an excellent track record in working across borders. Without recognition and incentives, it may be difficult to attract high potentials into positions requiring challenging lateral responsibilities.

Project-oriented global professional service firms like McKinsey and Accenture are in the forefront when it comes to applying performance management that facilitates cross-boundary coordination activities. There, senior partners spend up to a quarter of their time on evaluating contributions of managers and partners, collecting 360-degree views from clients, other managers, subordinates and support groups.[81]

Enhancing Collaboration

In Chapter 5 we discussed the vital role of three elements of social architecture in supporting horizontal coordination. However, global social networks, shared values, and global mindset are unlikely to be effective without continuous reinforcement through both subtle and explicit recognition and rewards. This imperative is recognized by many leading multinationals, irrespective of national origin. The now popular expression "boundaryless behavior" was coined by Jack Welch, who during his years at the helm of GE was determined to break down the silos and foster cross-border collaboration.[82] IBM based in the US, Toyota based in Japan, Nokia based in Finland, CEMEX based in Mexico, Infosys based in India, and Haier based in China have all included in their performance management system explicit measures intended to support global collaboration. See Table 7-1 for an example drawn from a leading multinational consulting firm.

However, cross-border collaboration does not and should not eliminate constructive competition inside the organization. Competition as such is not destructive, though it can quickly become so when measures and rewards are solely focused on individual outcomes.

Many years ago, one of us had the privilege to discuss this issue with Honda Soichiro, the founder of the automotive company bearing his name. Honda himself was famous for his love of racing and fierce competitiveness. He was asked: "Excuse me, Honda-san, but isn't there a contradiction between your emphasis on competition and the core Japanese value of *wa* [harmony]?" Honda pondered the question for a few seconds and then answered: "No, there is no contradiction. Collaboration inside a company is a must. And if I help you more than you help me, then I win."

Performance Management for Global Accounts

Global account management (GAM) is one area where lateral coordination needs to be built into performance management, and this is far from simple. Typically, the GAM unit is embedded in the global sales organization, where tight links between individual performance (for example reaching sales targets) and short-term financial rewards are the accepted norm, even in companies that do not believe in pay as a source of motivation for most employees. However, if ABB in Germany sells a piece of equipment to a Volkswagen factory in China, who should get the credit for the sale? The sales manager in China, the sales manager in Germany, or the global account manager for Volkswagen sitting in Switzerland?

Most companies resolve this problem by double/triple counting, giving the credit to all involved based on some pre-agreed formula (ideally not too complex!). Extra time spent on perfecting the internal allocation of profits does not create much value for the customer—as global account result comes almost by definition from team efforts.[83] More difficult than finding the "correct" bonus formula is figuring out how to motivate global account managers to

TABLE 7-1

Appraising Global Collaboration at Bain

- Client contributions: What have you done to build our relationship with customers or clients?

- People development: What have you done to recruit and develop the talent for future partners?

- Knowledge contribution: What have you done to increase the intellectual capital of the firm?

- Reputation building: What have you done to enhance the reputation of the firm?

- One firm behavior: What have you done to build relationships within the firm?

Source: J.R. Galbraith, *Designing Matrix Organizations that Actually Work* (San Francisco: Jossey-Bass, 2009).

look beyond the short-term sale cycle and consider the long-term relation-ship with the customer—in effect acting as customer representatives inside the organization.[84] This supports the argument that performance management for global accounts must be anchored in outcomes other than money—individual competence development, career advancement, opportunities to work in an international environment, or building relationships with other good people.[85]

A related challenge is how to motivate people outside the global account team to offer the necessary support. Collecting and disseminating customer feedback on a regular basis, with quick follow-up action, is the starting point for orienting the performance management process in this direction.

Appraising and Rewarding Global Teams

The insight of Honda's founder on aligning collaboration and competition is also relevant for global teamwork. Effective team appraisal should recognize and reward good team players and discourage behaviors that are not condu-cive to global team effectiveness.[86]

Performance Appraisal Criteria for Global Teams

There seems to be broad agreement that the appraisal of team members should go beyond task-specific criteria to include team process items such as collabora-tive problem-solving, support of other team members, and effective conflict res-olution. Since preferred styles of conflict resolution may differ across cultures, what should be rated is resolving conflicts (with implied sensitivity to cultural differences) rather than adherence to a particular approach.

The use of objective criteria to evaluate individual contribution enhances the fairness of the process. Indeed, a major challenge for many managers of global virtual teams is their inability to observe physically the contributions of individuals. Therefore, it is important to evaluate team members on what they actually accomplish, using measures such as customer satisfaction or peer rat-ing, rather than what they appear from a distance to be doing. When managers have objective data at their disposal, contamination of evaluations by percep-tual or cultural biases is also less likely.[87]

But how objective are data such as peer ratings collected across different cultures? Research data suggest that team members from collectivist cultures may give more generous evaluations of their fellow team members than those from more individualistic cultures.[88] Also, members from highly assertive cul-tures might be more likely to provide negative feedback than those in less asser-tive cultures.[89]

How to Improve Global Team Appraisals

How can companies enhance the effectiveness of the appraisal of global teams? The typical recommendations from both researchers and practitioners are simi-lar to those one would give for any generic appraisal:

- Include criteria on the quality of the process and a multidimensional mix of objective and subjective ratings.
- Enhance the fairness of global peer evaluations by training all raters and using job-relevant rating scales.
- Get managers (and team members) to provide ratings that differentiate between low and high performance.

Increased emphasis on process-related criteria may also help tackle the difficult choice between rewarding team members for their individual contributions or the accomplishments of the team. It may seem obvious to reward team members for the output of the team, but research evidence is contradictory; in virtual settings, team-based pay seems to contribute to social loafing as often as it leads to high performance.[90] And even with the best of intentions, the priorities of the daily job usually prevail over more distant team targets.

Given the difficulty in aligning individual and team-based rewards, it is not surprising that some observers see inadequate reward and recognition practices as the single most important factor behind failures of global teams.[91] In this respect, linking positive team behaviors with individual financial rewards may be one way of incentivizing individual team members to support team performance.

While research on performance appraisal in global teams is still in its infancy, some conclusions seem to be holding reasonably well, as indicated in Table 7-2.

In most circumstances, full-time global teams where the cross-border linkages are important and regular, such as global key account teams, should be rewarded on the basis of team performance, not on the performance of the individual members. If the extent of cross-border linkage is only moderate, financial incentives are less important, as global teams provide many intrinsic rewards: learning challenges, increased visibility, and opportunities to build personal social capital. However, the best way of appraising and rewarding individuals is through the talent review process; indeed cross-boundary projects are an integral tool of leadership development.[92]

TABLE 7-2

Rewarding Global Teams: Some Research Observations

- Team-based reward strategies require stability of group membership.
- Some cultures (e.g., US) may prefer rewards based on individual performance, although there is no conclusive evidence on what this implies in the work setting.
- It is not only about money; independently of cultural differences, recognition and career opportunities are often as motivating as financial rewards.
- Involvement of team members in designing the reward structure may help foster its future effectiveness.
- High task interdependence increases the valence of team rewards relative to individual-based rewards.
- In project-based global teams, objective setting, the focus of appraisals, and the rewards should be tailored to the stage of the project.

IMPLEMENTING GLOBAL PERFORMANCE MANAGEMENT

Performance management is an indispensable part of global coordination and there is an ever-expanding range of practices—some reflecting the latest management fads, others leaving a lasting impact on how companies around the world approach this complex process. What is appropriate for one situation may be inappropriate for another, and probably no other element of people strategy generates as many debates and controversies as performance management.[93]

We have summarized the ideas discussed in the chapter in Table 7-3, showing best practices in global performance management.

With respect to the global/local tension during the implementation, we have stated at the outset that this should be considered in the context of the full performance management cycle. In our view, there is little doubt that the upstream setting of strategic objectives should be globalized; there is a worldwide trend, even at lower levels of management and among

TABLE 7-3
Best Practices in Global Performance Management

Design Principles
- Coherent—aligned to global strategy, capabilities, and values
- Simple and easy to use in multiple languages
- Flexible to reflect changes in the nature of the business
- For everyone, not only for high performers

Processes
- Line accountability/ownership
- Globally consistent but reflecting local differences
- Focus on dialogue, not the process or the form
- Senior management commitment

Measures
- Explicit link to global and local business goals
- Not only what but also how
- Customer feedback incorporated
- Support for collaborative behavior

Outcomes
- Understanding what needs to be delivered
- Key inputs to guide global mobility and development
- Link to tangible rewards
- Commitment to action

Fundamentals
- Fair and transparent
- Motivational—creates energy
- Remains constant; it is not changed all the time
- Should not be another bland system—differentiate!

professionals, toward objective-based management as opposed to an activity-based approach built around job descriptions. Performance appraisal is the area in which there are the strongest arguments for a mix of global and local approaches, while many multinational firms are coming to the conclusion that performance evaluation should be rigorously global. The higher the position of the employee, the greater the likelihood that a global approach will be applied. Still, the path to successful implementation is far from straightforward. Even companies that pioneered the global approach to managing performance, such as GE, have found that cultural and institutional environment matters.[94]

Aside from the issue of whether to adapt to the local context or implement a global approach, there are two other overarching issues that frame the implementation process:

- Clarifying who is responsible for implementation of the global performance management system
- Shared understanding on how performance management systems can contribute to differentiation and building distinctive capabilities

Who "Owns" Performance Management?

Although the general idea of performance management is now widely accepted by multinational firms across the world, its implementation invariably runs into problems unless there is top-down commitment starting with senior management—including local management teams.[95]

Why is the commitment from the top so critical? Although HR usually provides the administrative and coaching support, the responsibility for making the process work lies with the line management. If senior managers are seen as visibly taking the time to engage in managing performance, including its developmental aspects, others will follow. For example, the attention that senior bankers pay to appraisal at Goldman Sachs is legendary in the finance industry, collecting 360-degree views, data, and opinions from around the world, feeding them back and working them through, carefully balancing judgments on individual achievement and teamwork. Tremendous care is also given to the design and administration of the bank's compensation system, which must balance rewards for individual achievement and support for the team.

In other words, performance management is a time-consuming and difficult task—in any culture—especially when it involves giving some employees honest feedback on less than stellar performance, justified by solid facts. This requires regular performance monitoring to collect that data—and then a lot of coaching to help the employee to improve. So how can global companies motivate their managers across the world to devote their most limited resource—their own time—to this difficult process? The answer is: through performance management!

What happens to managers who are doing a good job of performance management? And to those doing a bad job? If the answer is that there is no difference and no consequences for how those managers themselves are evaluated, then any performance management system is likely to fail. [96]

Creating Differentiation

Traditionally, debates around performance management systems in multinationals were about "fitting" it into the local context, usually the environment of the local affiliate. We will conclude this chapter by pointing to the *opposite* challenge. The deeper issue is not how to fit, but how to build distinctive capabilities—how to differentiate (the last point in Table 7-3).

In Chapter 1 we identified differentiation as one of the guiding principles for HRM in multinational firms, and performance management is one area of HRM where differentiation can indeed have a large impact. Lincoln Electric is an example of a successful corporation that is strongly differentiated from its competitors by its approach to performance management, reaping the benefits. However, when such companies go abroad, they typically have a dilemma, as Lincoln did; their approach to performance management may not fit with the local context. Does this mean that there is no benefit for a multinational firm from differentiation in its performance management practices—either from local firms or from other multinationals?

Not so long ago, a review of global performance management commented on the need to align it with the local context as follows: "The notion of 'sharing' rewards or credits for an accomplishment is as foreign a notion in individualistic countries, as say, an 'employee of the month' award would be in collectivistic countries like Japan, China, or Malaysia."[97] This makes intuitive sense—or does it?

Let us return to Haier. Today, one of the most coveted performance-related awards in the company is the "employee of the month" for young employees with less than five years' tenure in the firm. However, this award is not only a plaque on the wall. When employees are selected for the award, their parents are invited to Qingdao for a dinner with the CEO Zhang, today one of the most widely recognized corporate executives in China. At the dinner, Zhang presents the parents with a personal letter thanking them for bringing up such an outstanding child—now a great contributor to Haier's future. The next day, the company PR machinery ensures that the letter and the picture of the parents with the CEO are reprinted in the hometown newspapers.

Is it motivational? It is! Does this mean that the researchers cited above were incorrect? Probably not. On average, employees in collectivist societies may indeed not care much about generic "employee of the month" awards. However, the award as deployed by Haier is not generic. Haier has found a way of making this individualistic reward into something distinctively Chinese, in a manner that differentiates Haier from any other company in China—and probably the world. The way Haier rewards its employees of the month reflects the context of contemporary China as well as leveraging the reputation of the firm as a leading Chinese multinational. It is effective because in essence it is very Chinese, but at the same time because it is not in any sense typical. It differentiates.

The lesson from Haier is that differentiation through performance management is neither a question of ignoring culture nor one of "fitting with culture." Rather it means understanding, respecting, and reflecting culture at a much deeper level than broad generalizations about individualism and collectivism. Global companies need to be deeply sensitive to local cultural contexts not because they should emulate local practices but because this knowledge can show them how to differentiate. As discussed earlier, this may mean paying close attention to selection or socialization. Or, as with the Haier "employee of the month" scheme, it may involve tailoring a practice so that it is meaningful and powerful in the local context.

When a firm is creative in the way it locally adapts its management practices, rather than simply following what is done in the home country or emulating what local firms do, that may inspire other subsidiaries to be similarly innovative. Haier's subsidiary in the US, for example, has to think through its employee award schemes. Should it copy the practice carried out in China? Probably not, because there is no Zhang in the US. Should there be instead a traditional US-style plaque and acknowledgment on the company Web site? Or, are there other firms in the US that have distinctive and successful ways of rewarding outstanding employees? Is there a creative way in which the US subsidiary can differentiate itself and reinforce its competitive advantage while remaining true to the spirit of the Haier way?

Performance management is often viewed in mechanical terms as following either global or local practices, rather than as innovating to build distinctive sources of competitive advantage. Despite the weight of a process that in many multinationals is the most centralized of HRM processes, we see in the tension between the global and the local many opportunities for differentiation—as long as one tunes into what "local" means with creative sensitivity. In the future, we expect to see more multinational firms that foster continuous horizontal and bottom-up knowledge sharing and learning (not copying) around performance management practices within the enterprise.

1. Performance management includes three successive phases: the specification of what is desired performance, involving setting goals and objectives (upstream); the review and evaluation of performance, including feedback; and linking the evaluation results to financial rewards and development (downstream).

2. Internal consistency and coherence of performance management practices is essential for lateral coordination in global firms. Tight linkage across the three phases is critical—simple in principle but complex in practice.

3. There is little doubt that the upstream setting of strategic objectives should be globalized. Performance appraisal is the area in which there are the strongest arguments for a mix of global and local approaches.

4. There are at least two strong arguments for using a common and consistent system of measurement scorecards throughout the multinational firm. Global scorecards reinforce a global mindset among employees, and joint performance objectives encourage dispersed units to collaborate.

5. In global firms, performance measures should include the benefits and contributions of collaborative behavior.

6. Problems in managing performance are most acute when individuals who are not performing well are asked to work on cross-border projects, coming under pressure to improve performance, and at the same time work on global teams.

7. Good performance management strategy to promote lateral steering is to pay for local job results but to promote for demonstrated global leadership in the "split egg" coordination roles.

8. Performance appraisal of global team members should include team process items such as joint problem-solving, support of other team members, and team conflict resolution.

9. Differentiation through performance management is neither a question of ignoring culture nor one of "fitting with culture." Global companies need to be deeply sensitive to local cultural contexts not because they should emulate local practices but because this knowledge can show them how to differentiate.

10. Commitment to rigorous performance management is more important than the sophistication of the methodology.

NOTES

1 Pucik, Xin, and Everatt, 2003 (revised March 31, 2010); "Haier and higher," *The Economist*, October 12, 2013.
2 "Haier group," *Euromonitor*, September 2014.
3 "Haier and higher," *The Economist*, October 12, 2013. Zhang, 2015.
4 Some observers noted that Haier's focus on creativity and freedom given to engineers to design and build their own product led to a bewildering array of product categories and specification—diluting the company's cost advantage. See "Haier's purpose," *The Economist*, March 18, 2014.

5   One should avoid associating performance management with a particular culture, as in some popular characterizations. We know of many well-established Anglo-Saxon firms for whom the performance management ideas discussed here are as alien as for the Chinese state-owned enterprises in the era before the period of economic reforms.

6   Bloom *et al.*, 2012.

7   Ibid.

8   As reported by Grote (2000), a survey of best practice in performance management ran into problems when many clearly model companies declined to take part.

9   Festing *et al.*, 2012; Peretz and Fried, 2012; Varma, Budhwar, and McCusker, 2015.

10 Björkman *et al.*, 2008.

11 It may be noted that Vance (2006) in his discussion of global performance management uses the terms "upstream" and "downstream" with a different meaning than we do.

12 Locke and Latham, 2006. See also Locke and Latham (1990). Goal-setting theory is not without its critics, however. Ordonez *et al.* (2009) argue that one should be aware of the side effects of goal setting in the shape of neglect of non-goal domains, inhibited learning, reduced intrinsic motivation, and a rise in unethical behavior.

13 Correa, 2013.

14 Goold and Campbell, 1987.

15 Hansen, 2009.

16 Quoted from the GE 1994 Annual Report.

17 Stretch goals have a dual purpose—they promote organizational effectiveness and personal growth. Although these purposes are not mutually exclusive, organizations usually employ stretch goals for one reason or the other. See Kerr and Landauer (2004). A critical review of stretch goals pursuit is presented in Sitkin *et al.* (2011), with a response by Kerr and LePelley (2013).

18 "Job review in 140 keystrokes," *Business Week,* March 23 and 30, 2009.

19 "Raising efficiency the Silicon valley way," *International New York Times*, March 16, 2015.

20 This process is described by Ghoshal and Gratton (2002), and the quotation from the company deputy CEO is taken from this article.

21 Kerr and LePelley (2013) traced the origin of SMART goals to GE's New Manager's Manual published in 1984.

22 Mintzberg, 1994.

23 Biron, Farndale, and Paauw, 2011; Sumelius *et al.*, 2014.

24 Building on his experience as head of planning for Royal Dutch/Shell, De Geus (1988) argues that planning should be considered as company-wide learning rather than an analytic process—one of mobilizing people and building commitment to action in the lower reaches of the organization.

25 Galbraith, 2014.

26 Locke and Latham, 1990, 2006, and 2013.

27 Lindholm, 1998.

28 Latham, 2004.

29 For discussion of "gamification" of performance management in the US, see http://blog.rise .global/2015/02/16/gamification-for-performance-management/.

30 Sumelius *et al.*, 2014.

31 Becker, Huselid, and Ulrich, 2001; Huselid, Becker, and Beatty, 2005.

32 There is empirical evidence that business analysts assess long-term performance in terms of top management's balanced attention to financial, employee, and customer stakeholders (Kotter and Heskett, 1992).

33 Kaplan and Norton, 1996 and 2001.

34 Ibid., pp. 144–5.

35 Flamholtz, 2005.

36 Becker, Huselid, and Ulrich, 2001.

37 Huselid, Becker, and Beatty, 2005, p. 70.

38 One of the frequent criticisms of MBO-type processes is that they place too much emphasis on individual objectives (often to facilitate the determination of individual rewards) at the expense of collective commitment to a broader business strategy.

39 Doz, Santos, and Williamson, 2001, pp. 98–9; Goss, Pascale, and Athos, 1993.

40 Burgelman and Grove, 2007.

41 Vance, 2006.

42 In Japan, until recently, performance appraisal for younger employees in many established firms may have taken place several times during the year—but without direct feedback. See Pucik (1989).

43 Buckingham and Goodall, 2015.

44 Varma, Budhwar, and DeNisi, 2008; Cascio, 2012.

45 For example, Culbert, 2010.

46 Deming, 2000.

47 Schneider and Barsoux, 2003.

48 See Schneider and Barsoux (2003); Cascio (2012). See also Hofstede (1999). On the other hand, Festing, Knappert, and Kornau (2015) have argued that gender-specific preferences regarding performance management have a more consistent impact than national culture.

49 Hofstede, 2001.

50 See Shen (2004) for an analysis of performance management in Chinese corporations.

51 See Claus and Briscoe (2008) and Cascio (2012) for a review of research on performance management in multinationals.

52 Sparrow and Hiltrop, 1994, p. 557.

53 A frequently cited study is that of Trepo (1973), which Hofstede, Trompenaars and other culturalists frequently use as an example.

54 Reported by Sparrow and Hiltrop (1994).

55 Pucik, 1984b.

56 Vo and Stanton, 2011.

57 Faulkner, Pitkethly, and Child, 2002; Shadur, Rodwell, and Bamber, 1995; Harzing and Pudelko, 2007.

58 Shadur, Rodwell, and Bamber, 1995.

59 Paik and Stage, 1996. For example, Hong Kong managers disliked participative appraisal practices, whereas the Taiwanese accepted close supervision more than those in Singapore or Hong Kong.

60 Recently Haier began to experiment with replacing internal 360-degree feedback with direct market-driven ratings from users. See Zhang (2015).

61 Claus and Briscoe, 2008.

62 One of the main objectives of the 360-degree feedback is to eliminate idiosyncratic rater effect, removing individual rater's peculiarities of perceptions—a problem illustrated well in Scullen, Mount, and Goff (2000).

63 Biron, Farndale, and Paawe, 2011; Cascio, 2012. Sumelius *et al.*, 2014.

64 Lindholm, 1998.

65 For example, "Accenture CEO explains why he's overhauling performance reviews," *Washington Post*, July 23, 2015.

66 "Jack Welch: 'Rank-and-Yank'? That's Not How It's Done," *Wall Street Journal*, November 14, 2013.

67 Microsoft which for a long time screened out about 5 percent of its workforce abolished this policy in 2013.

68 "AB InBev hard-nosed kings of beer," *Financial Times*, June 15, 2015.

69 Welch, 2005, p. 45.

70 Manzoni and Barsoux, 2007.

71 According to research by Yanadori (2011), a subsidiary location accounted for a significant proportion of variance in managers' base pay in ten subsidiaries of one US MNC in the Asia-Pacific region.

72 Bloom and Milkovich, 1999. See also Bloom, Milkovich, and Mitra (2003); and Festing, Eidems, and Royer (2007).

73 Mayerhofer *et al.*, 2011.

74 Pucik, 1997.

75 Expectancy theory argues that there should be a tight linkage between (1) the efforts made by the employee (or team/unit), (2) how the performance of the person is measured, and (3) rewards associated with measures of performance.

76 Milkovich and Newman, 2005.

77 Rosenzweig and Nohria, 1994; Ferner and Almond, 2013.

78 Siegel, 2008.

79 In the multidimensional organization of ABB, the customer must come first, the corporation second (including the business area and/or country), and the profit center third.

80 See the discussion on mobility and action learning in Chapter 9.

81 Ghoshal, 1991.

82 Ashkenas *et al.*, 1995.

83 Galbraith, 2000, p. 219.

84 To give this long-term perspective, many firms want global account managers to be willing to stay in their jobs for a long period of time, seven to eight years or more. IBM, for example, also makes a big investment in training global account managers who need strong general management skills to manage the network of relationships with the firm and that of the client firm. These positions often suit the requirements of high potential managers who want some stability in their private lives for family reasons.

85 Birkinshaw and DiStefano, 2004.

86 Gibson and Kirkman, 1999.

87 Kirkman *et al.*, 2002.

88 Kirkman and Den Hartog, 2004.

89 House *et al.*, 2004.

90 Social loafing effects have been found in a variety of countries. See Kirkman and Den Hartog (2004, p. 252), and Thompson (2000).

91 Kirkman and Den Hartog, 2004.

92 The talent review process and the role of such teams in leadership development are discussed in Chapter 8.

93 In an earlier review of relevant research, Cascio (2006, p. 193) concluded that the field of global performance management is "largely unchartered." Six years later, the conclusion remained the same (Cascio, 2012, p. 201).

94 Bartlett and McLean, 2006.

95 Biron, Farndale, and Paauw, 2011; Sumelius *et al.*, 2014.

96 Lawler, 2003b; Cascio, 2012.

97 Kirkman and Den Hartog, 2004, p. 253.

chapter

8

Developing Global Leaders

SUMMARY

Challenge

The shortage of global leaders is one of the main obstacles to successful execution of global business strategies

Analysis

Multinationals need solid HRM processes for developing and retaining leaders with skills to manage a global business. These include:

- Identifying and developing global leadership potential across cultures
- People risk management to help employees learn from challenging assignments

Solutions

- Use functional and geographic mobility to develop global leaders
- Constantly emphasize coaching, training, and feedback
- Watch out for tradeoffs and dilemmas when identifying and developing leadership potential—there are few universal solutions
- Strike the right balance between top-down and bottom-up approaches to leadership development

Evolution at GE, a Model for Leadership Development

One hundred years ago, Charles Coffin succeeded Thomas Edison as chief executive officer (CEO) of General Electric (GE) and, with his belief in meritocracy through measured performance, laid the foundations for what was to become renowned as GE's "leadership engine." Refined by successive CEOs and brought to fame during Jack Welch's tenure (1981–2001), Coffin's enduring achievement earned him *Fortune*'s award of "the greatest CEO of all time" in 2003.[1]

The idea behind the leadership engine is that a leader is a steward of human capital, whose primary job is to leave a legacy of talent that can carry the company forward. This is what GE's top executives believe—and the corporation has become a model for talent development that is emulated globally. This reinforces, indeed underlies, the strength of GE's brand—and executive search agencies around the world target GE as a talent-rich firm. When we meet former GE managers in China, Germany, or the US, they invariably speak highly of their GE training. Former GE executives have moved on to head up a wide range of international firms, from ABB in Switzerland to Boeing and Honeywell in the US and Lixil in Japan.

Coffin laid the foundations with a premonitory emphasis on merit, while Welch brought a focus on candor and honesty when he took Session C, GE's core process for talent review, development planning, and succession management, out into the businesses. Every spring, the CEO and senior vice president of human resources (HR) visit each of GE's operating units and hold a daylong audit, assessing the performance of the management team and the potential of rising talent. A follow-up takes place six months later.

"We have made leadership development the most important element in our work," said Welch. "We focus on some aspect of it every day. It is in our blood. We put people in the right job and let them develop a strategy, in that order. You can't start with strategy and then appoint someone to execute it. So my most important job is to choose and develop business leaders who are bright enough to grasp the elements of their game, creative enough to develop a simple vision, and self-confident enough to liberate and inspire people."[2]

GE introduced metrics to drive this in the shape of a "vitality curve," ranking individuals into As (top 20 percent), Bs (middle 70 percent), and Cs (bottom 10 percent) on performance, potential, and fit with company values. Linking this to rewards—and punishments, since the bottom 10 percent would not be there next time round—created shock waves around the world. Today's CEO, Jeff Immelt, remains committed to the vitality curve reviews, though the 20–70–10 percentages became more flexible.

Appointed in 2001, the day before 9/11, Immelt is himself a product of the GE leadership development process. A Harvard MBA, he chose to ignore warnings that it would take ten years before he met Welch and got any visibility (he met Welch within a month). Soon considered as one of the top 150 high potentials (HiPos), he succeeded in a series of tough challenges, including saving a business.

Immelt's strategic focus is on innovation, technology, and continuous internationalization. During the last decade, the company has moved from heavy US exposure to businesses generating more than half of their revenues from outside America. Talent management means achieving these strategic aims. "Every initiative I'm thinking about gets translated into recruiting, Crotonville [training], and Session C [development reviews and succession planning]. When you step on the gas here, it really goes."[3] For example, to translate innovation into action, each business was asked to identify five high-level "pillar jobs" that involve the challenge of building customer-facing innovation. Top management reserves the right to fill these positions with the candidates of their choice. In this way, GE makes sure that its best people will be given the challenge of leading a breakthrough opportunity that, if successful, could be grown into a new business. Its learning development center at Crotonville, the first American corporate university, today offers courses in Munich, Shanghai, Bangalore, and elsewhere.

In 2015, GE started to modify the performance review system that had become a model for many firms. The forced ranking fitted poorly with the needs of the millennial generation, and the annual performance review process was too burdensome. It was to be replaced with an app built around near term goals that helped a manager to getting real-time coaching to improve performance. The annual review discussion with the boss would remain, leading to pay and bonus decisions.[4]

Globalization of leadership development also remains a challenge. Immelt never held a position outside the US, and in 2015 only three of the top 18 corporate executives were not Americans.[5] Still, GE tries hard to develop a global executive team. Immelt and his colleagues go out of their way to meet with high potential employees when they are on trips abroad, and GE continues to win nominations as one of the best three companies in the world for developing leaders.[6] When Immelt nominates his successor, we will know the outcome of this effort.

OVERVIEW

More than almost any other firm in the world, GE has built a reputation for the quality of its leadership development, to the point where the many former GE executives who occupy CEO positions in other *Fortune* 500 companies outperform their peers.[7] But even at GE, leadership development is evolving to meet the needs of a technology-driven global age, where annual development reviews give way to real-time performance coaching.

In this chapter, we start by reviewing competencies for global leadership, as well as guiding principles on how to develop them. We then highlight challenges in identifying and developing potential leaders, as well as retaining the best, exploring some of the dilemmas around leadership development practices. We conclude the chapter by outlining how global leadership development can facilitate global coordination in transnational firms.

GLOBAL LEADERSHIP

The task of developing future global leaders is a priority for multinational firms. Even in international firms that normally pay scant corporate attention to HRM, leadership development is invariably an area of top management concern.[8] With accelerating globalization, surveys of Fortune 500 enterprises have shown that 85 percent were concerned about the insufficient supply of global leaders—people with the ability to manage uncertainty, and with the organizational and business savvy and the cross-cultural skills needed to run such a business.[9]

It is above all the growth in emerging markets that fuels the gap,[10] where there is a shortage of local functional and professional managers with the breadth of skill needed to operate in today's complex multinational. Indeed, rapid growth combined with a small pool of experienced leaders means that the lack of global leadership skills has been the primary workforce challenge for enterprises doing business in Asia Pacific, as well as Latin America.[11] This is a problem confronting not just the traditional multinationals but also the new players emerging locally with global ambitions.

The challenge of global leadership development is also reflected in the composition of top management teams. When it comes to the background of those at the senior levels—and despite decades of attention to diversity in talent management—top leadership positions in most multinational companies still remain dominated by parent-country nationals (see box "Global Gap at the Top").

Global Leadership Competencies

The belief that global leadership requires different skills than "domestic" leadership is widely shared. When David Whitlam, then CEO of Whirlpool, was steering the company's transition from a domestic US player to a global firm, following the acquisition of Philips' appliance division, he commented: "I've often said that there's only one thing that wakes me up in the middle of the

Global Gap at the Top?

Many of the best known global firms have a majority of their workforce located outside of the home country. With their long history of recruiting talent and leadership development all around the world, it could be expected that the composition of the top management teams would reflect the global diversity of their workforce. This does not seem to be the case. In 2013, only 13 percent of global Fortune 500 firms have a CEO born outside of the headquarter country. The figure for the executive teams was only slightly higher at 15 percent. Among the Fortune 100 nonfinancial firms, both figures increase to about 30 percent, but they sink to single digits among the smaller global firms.

European companies are the most cosmopolitan with 23 percent of foreign bosses, but this includes a large number of CEOs born within the European region. The figure for the US is 13 percent, including immigrants who entered the workforce in the US after graduating from US universities. Companies from English-speaking countries and those that are highly developed can draw on a wider talent pool, but the number of CEOs and executive team members who were promoted to their current positions after being recruited outside the home country are still woefully small. Across countries, the presence of a nonnative CEO increases substantially the share of foreign-born executives on the top executive team.

Source: P. Ghemawat and H. Vantrappen, "How global is your C-suite," *Sloan Management Review* 56:4 (2015), pp. 72–82.

night. It's not our financial performance or economic issues in general. It's worrying about whether or not we have the right skills and capabilities to pull the strategy off … It is a simple and inescapable fact that the skills and capabilities required to manage a global company are different from those required for a domestic company."[12]

While there seems to be agreement that leading a global company requires a particular skill set, there is no accepted definition of global leadership or established body of tested theory.[13] Still, a substantial literature has addressed the question of what competencies global leaders need to be effective and how these can be developed.[14]

Many global leadership competencies have been singled out and these can be viewed as a pyramid, as shown in Figure 8-1. At the base is the global knowledge and understanding that comes above all through contact with people of different backgrounds while working and living abroad, as well as through education and experience. Then certain threshold leadership traits are required—we discuss openness to challenge and learning agility later in this chapter. The next three layers form the core global competencies, including attitudes and interpersonal and systemic skills.

Many of these competencies have been discussed in other chapters, but we see four as particularly important for global leadership. Global leaders need a *high tolerance for ambiguity*, along with *the ability to work with contradiction* that is at the heart of global mindset. It is also clear that leaders need *strong interpersonal skills* in building multinational relationships, including emotional self-control and the ability to handle conflict. Finally, *the ability to exercise influence without authority* is essential for effective lateral coordination.

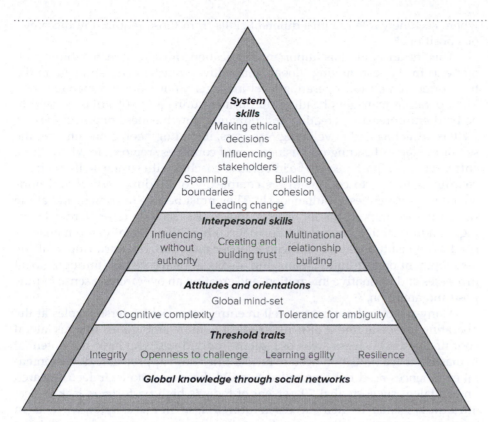

FIGURE 8-1
The Pyramid Model of
Global Leadership

Source: Adapted from A. Bird and J. Osland, "Global Competencies: An Introduction," In The Blackwell Handbook of Global Management, eds. H. Lane, M. Maznevski, M. Mendenhall, and J. McNett (Oxford: Blackwell, 2004).

Some people would like to believe that such global skills can be learned at home by working with a diverse workforce. However, the prevailing view is that the experience of living and working overseas is indispensable for the development of over half of all significant global competencies.[15] While many important business lessons can be learned at home, most deep attitudinal or cultural lessons about leadership that go beyond simple intellectual understanding are learned best through international mobility. We believe that the experience of living and working abroad—not merely traveling—is necessary to develop emotional depth of understanding of global business.

Leadership Transitions

One of the limits to the idea of mapping out global leadership competencies is that the leadership skills needed at one level in the multinational firm are different from those needed at the next level. A long tradition of research, gaining momentum in the last decade, has explored this notion of leadership "intransitivity," the recognition of which goes back more than 40 years to the humorous "Peter Principle."[16] Leadership involves a set of behaviors that differ from managerial behaviors. The challenges of making a transition to a new role as a leader, requiring a new identity, have been explored by many researchers.[17] The concept of leadership as a "pipeline" captures this, a series of transitions where each new role requires different skills from those required in the previous position.[18]

This intransitivity has important implications for global leadership development. In the fast-moving global competitive environment, strategic initiatives often come from operating-level managers, not from top management. The operating managers heading up business units and subsidiaries need to be bold entrepreneurs, creating and pursuing new business opportunities, as well as attracting and developing resources, including people. In contrast, the senior managers heading up businesses and countries/regions, to whom these entrepreneurs report, need to be integrative coaches with strong skills in lateral coordination, able to cope with the complexity of holding vertical and horizontal responsibilities simultaneously. They must be able to stretch, and at the same time to support, the local units; they must facilitate cross-border learning, building strategy out of entrepreneurial initiatives. Finally, top managers need to be institutional leaders with a longer time horizon, nurturing strategic development opportunities, managing organizational cohesion through global processes and normative integration, and creating an overarching sense of purpose and ambition.[19]

Many people who perform well in entrepreneurial leadership roles at the operating level will find it difficult to adjust to more ambiguous roles as lateral coordinators in business areas or regions. Individuals who have the potential to master such a transition need to be identified, and appropriate developmental experiences need to be provided to build these new skills. Indeed research on top talent suggests that 70 percent of today's high performers lack critical attributes essential to their success in future roles.[20] In this chapter, we focus in particular on the transition from operational roles to business area or regional leadership positions.

While the ability to make a particular known transition is important, the ability to cope with transitions in general will become an important overarching competence for leaders—hence, the importance of learning agility, to which we return later.

THE PRINCIPLES GUIDING GLOBAL LEADERSHIP DEVELOPMENT

We start our assessment of the principles and tools for steering global leadership development with an overview of the experiences that successful global executives identify as contributing most to their own development. Researchers interviewed 101 senior executives from 36 countries, covering all major regions of the world, who worked for 15 different multinational corporations, including ABB, Shell, Unilever, and Johnson & Johnson.[21] Table 8-1 shows the key events that these executives saw as contributing most to their development, classified into four categories of experience.

Major line assignments, particularly those involving managing change, figure prominently, as do special projects and consulting roles. Also high on the list are mobility and transition experiences that led to a deep change in perspective, such as culture shock and career shifts. Above all, people develop through challenging assignments and experiences.

% of people describing the event as a key developmental experience	
Foundation Assignments	
• Early work experiences	12
• First managerial responsibility	7
Major Line Assignments	
• Business turnarounds	30
• Building or evolving a business	16
• Joint ventures, alliances, mergers, or acquisitions	11
• Business start-ups	10
Shorter-Term Experiences	
• Significant other people	32
• Special projects, consulting roles, staff advisory roles	24
• Development and educational experiences	23
• Negotiations	8
• Stint at headquarters	7
Perspective-Changing Experiences	
• Culture shock	27
• Career shifts	21
• Confrontations with reality	18
• Changes in scope or scale	17
• Mistakes and errors in judgment	10
• Family and personal challenges	8
• Crises	7

TABLE 8-1

The Developmental Experiences of 101 Successful Global Executives

Source: M. McCall and G. Hollenbeck, *Developing Global Executives* (Boston: Harvard Business School Press, 2002).

Challenge Is the Starting Point

We often take managers back to basics by asking them, "How do you develop people?" They quickly come with a number of responses: through feedback, coaching, mentoring; setting goals, assigning responsibility; encouraging learning from mistakes, training, and so forth. Some people emphasize that development happens on the job. But they often miss the most central point—at the heart of development is the simple principle that people learn most by doing things they have not done before.[22]

People develop above all through challenge, by venturing outside their comfort zone. Test this yourself. Ask others to tell you about the experiences that were most valuable for their development. Surprisingly enough, people hardly ever mention training and education. Some may talk about a relationship with a significant mentor or role model. But the vast majority will describe some stretching challenge that they worked through, often succeeding but sometimes failing, often in professional life but sometimes in private life, sometimes planned but equally often by chance. Indeed, a common denominator we found in our research on leaders who make a difference, in technical or managerial positions, is that they respond more positively than other people to challenge, seeing opportunities where others perceive threats.[23]

There are good reasons for regarding challenging jobs that are well aligned with the strategic priorities of the firm as being owned by the corporation rather than the business, as GE does with "pillar jobs"—opportunities to lead customer-facing innovation that are stepping-stone challenges to higher positions. The most important question in talent development is probably, "Who gets the important experiences?" Challenging jobs should not go to people with low potential to grow.

Cross-Boundary Mobility as a Key Tool

Although the concept of leadership varies with culture and context, as discussed in Chapter 2, there is more agreement on how to develop leadership skills. Mobility—the movement from one function or geographic location to another—is the critical lever. Through the transition to new challenges outside their expertise, people learn how to lead, and they develop the authority of leadership as opposed to the authority of expertise.

People who pursue careers in organizations typically start by developing their talents within a particular function or discipline. A capable person will move up through supervisory and managerial responsibilities, developing knowledge and skills in people management, goal setting, planning, and budgeting. There are various transitions to be mastered during this upward path, notably the transition from being an individual contributor to being a people manager.[24] If the company feels that someone has leadership potential, it should put that person in a position where s/he has to learn to lead. Moving to another function or across borders to another culture removes prior experience and expertise, placing people in challenging positions where they have to learn integrative leadership skills of setting direction and aligning people, while focusing on strategic development. The box "The Route to the Top" provides a powerful example.

The Route to the Top

The most important tools for leadership development are not assessment techniques or MBA programs, or any other form of training. It is challenge through mobility—experience in a job outside one's expertise or home culture, where one has to learn how to deliver results through the expertise of others who are different from oneself.

The story of a senior executive in a major multinational corporation illustrates this point. When we interviewed him a number of years ago, he was president of an important subsidiary in Asia, had an excellent record of leadership success, and had deep skills in the management of people. He told us:

> What led me to this position? It is quite simple. I was trained as a geologist and spent the first seven years of my career trying to discover oil. One day when I was

heading an exploration assignment, they called me to the headquarters and told me that they wanted me to take over the responsibility for a troubled department of 40 maintenance engineers on the other side of the world. Geology is the noble elite, and maintenance engineering is somewhere between here-and-hell in the value system. I didn't want the job—in fact my first thought was that they were punishing me for some mistake I had made—and I told them that I knew nothing about maintenance engineering. "We're not sending you there to learn about engineering," they said. "We are sending you there to learn about leadership."

> With a lot of doubts, I took the job, and I was there for just over four years. And I learned practically everything I know about management and leadership in that job—all I've done since is refine what I

picked up there. Mind you, it was the most stressful job I've ever had—it nearly cost me my marriage! Fortunately, they sent me on a management training program during the first three months, and that helped me to understand what was happening and how to adjust—otherwise I might not have survived.

Afterwards I returned into a more senior position in oil exploration, but I'd completely changed as a result of that experience with the maintenance engineers. Later, this executive became CEO of one of the largest multinational corporations in the world.

Functional mobility entails moving outside one's area of expertise. Another type of mobility is geographic. Both types foster situational skills—the ability to handle context. Early studies provided suggestive evidence that mobility fosters the "helicopter" ability to see the context and big picture and yet to zoom in on the details,[25] and most companies including GE acknowledge that international experience is desirable if not essential for leadership of a multinational corporation.

Today there is research evidence that in-depth multicultural experience builds genuinely new perspectives and enhances creativity—an effect that is not achieved through international business tourism. Research subjects were given a well-known creativity test, to stick various objects on a wall so that they do not fall. People who have in-depth international experience are, statistically, more likely to solve the problem compared to people who have never lived abroad or even people who travel widely. This is a robust finding that has been replicated with different tests and in different cultures and regions.[26] Multicultural experience is positively related to creative performance (learning from insights, idea generation, and remote association) as well the ability to exploit unconventional knowledge and creative ideas.[27]

International experience is thus indispensable for success. Take the "haute couture" fashion sector. Research shows that the longer creative directors of global fashion houses had worked abroad (the depth of their international experience) and the more foreign countries they had worked in (the breadth of their exposure), the more creative they were.[28] Karl Lagerfeld, one of the most influential persons in fashion, is an example, a German who is today based in Paris after working in Tokyo and New York.

Learning How to Work Vertically and Horizontally at the Same Time

As we have shown throughout this book, many tasks in today's multidimensional firms require the capacity to take horizontal leadership initiatives while assuming responsibility for results in one's own job. Therefore, an important tool of leadership development is cross-boundary project assignments—what we call working in split egg ways (see the box on this and Figure 4-1 on page 132). According to a survey of 12,000 business leaders around the world, special projects within the job that allow cross-functional exposure, the honing of project management skills, and fostering business acumen were at the top of the list of tools for effective leadership development.[29]

When working in split egg roles, conceptual differences between management and leadership start breaking down. The individual is expected to be both an effective manager (doing things right in the operational role) and an effective leader (doing the right things in the project role). The former involves operational performance management; the latter requires leadership initiative, guided by the long-term strategic priorities of the firm. The pyramid of skills for global leadership that were mentioned earlier in this chapter is developed through split egg assignments:

- **Exercising leadership without authority** Much of the work as a leader in the multidimensional firm requires influencing people in others part of the firm, without having any formal authority over them. These skills become more and more important as managers move up the organization; involvement in top-of-the-egg initiatives fosters such skills.

- **People management skills** How do you free up 20 or 30 percent of your time for project initiatives when you are also accountable for delivering on tough operational targets? Having good people to whom you can delegate becomes a matter of personal success. Managers in split egg roles learn to pay rigorous attention to staffing—getting the right people into the right places—as well as to negotiating performance objectives and coaching subordinates. In short, managers learn that one of their most important tasks is the management of human resources.

- **Team skills** Various team skills are vital in the multidimensional organization—building trust and respect, managing conflict and contention, negotiating clear goals on complex and ambiguous tasks, learning to take time out to build relationships, balancing the internal focus on team cohesion with the external focus on managing stakeholders.[30] Working on cross-boundary projects fosters the learning of these and related teamwork skills.

- **Distance working and virtual team skills** Since much of the work on cross-boundary projects will by necessity be done virtually, this know-how is also honed in this way. This includes knowing how to blend face-to-face and virtual communication effectively, building a rhythm in distributed work, and preventing obstacles from becoming self-fulfilling problems.[31]

- **Dualistic thinking and global mindset** Working in split egg or matrix ways builds a dualistic sense of responsibility for both short- *and* long-term results, for performance *and* innovation, and for local *and* regional or global results. This kind of experience is one of the key ways of developing a strategic global mindset in the most talented managers in a firm.

One can safely argue that no one in a transnational organization should move into a position of leadership responsibility without proven ability in cross-boundary teamwork—which also means accountability for getting results.

People Risk Management

The flipside to the argument that people develop most through challenge is that the bigger the challenge, the greater the risk of making mistakes. When people go through career transitions, like the first move abroad or outside their area of expertise, they will naturally rely on skills and know-how they acquired in the past. They make mistakes, become overstressed, and make more mistakes. Close supervision could minimize this risk—but that would take away the challenge. So what is needed is people risk management—the second element of development—referring to support in the shape of coaching, mentoring, feedback, assessment, and training.

Companies sometimes express this as the 70–20–10 principle: 70 percent of development happens on the job, 20 percent through feedback, coaching, and relationships with others, while 10 percent occurs through training. However, the last 30 percent can make a big difference.

Training as Risk Management

From the firm's perspective, an important aim of transition training is to minimize the risk of costly mistakes. This means that training has to be *synchronous*, closely linked to the challenge of the new assignment or project. All too often, training takes place when people are available, even though this may be the worst time from the value-added perspective. Training that is not linked to current experience largely goes in one ear and out the other. Bosch, GE, IBM, Shell, Toyota, and many other multinationals try to supply the necessary training just-in-time.

Such "promote-and-then-develop" practices are changing the training scene—courses are shorter, and enrollments are decided at shorter notice. Often, they are designed and delivered by outside contractors as modular programs that fit around the new job, and e-learning may replace or support classroom training. Synchronous training may also give people the courage to take measured risk. When a person moves into a new job, she often has a sense of what should be done, but there are usually obstacles—a boss who will not back the change, peers who are hostile. Timely training can boost an individual's confidence to tackle these obstacles.

A positive challenge for one person can be a difficult experience for another. Consequently, coaching, feedback tools, and assessments are widely used in connection with management training programs to ensure that individuals have a good sense of their own strengths and weaknesses and can actively map their development journey.

Leadership training is big business. US companies alone spend almost $14 billion on leadership programs.[32] But even well-designed training has its own risk. Many firms fear that with increased visibility, trained and educated employees can easily be poached. Indeed, some economists even warn against investing in generalized skills training and executive development programs because these increase an individual's market value and ability to negotiate a higher salary. The consequence of this logic may be declining investments in internal development, with detrimental long-range consequences.[33] By way of contrast, research shows that investment in general-purpose skills may have a beneficial firm-specific effect by reinforcing employee commitment to the firm.[34] There is clearly a balancing act to be managed here.

Action Learning

Action learning is an explicit attempt to couple work on an important strategic challenge, typically a team project, with tailored support, training, and coaching for the team.[35] There is usually a double aim—to tackle some important cross-boundary challenge and to develop the global leadership skills of high potential individuals. Action learning differs from split egg team projects in that learning, rather than the quality of task delivery, is the prime aim, though there is a real task challenge. Action learning projects will usually report to high-level sponsors in senior management.

Currently, a majority of company-specific training programs, whether run in-company or outsourced to a business school, involve some degree of action learning. This requires training providers to have sophisticated skills in program design blending classroom and action learning methods, including coaching and 360° assessment and group coaching. It also requires proper buy-in from top managers involved in identifying suitable strategic challenges for action learning.

Coaching and Mentoring

One of the most important sources of development is relationships with other people—the positive and negative role models of good and bad bosses, internal or external coaches, and mentors.[36] Coaching often refers to the activities of an external professional who assists an individual or team in professional and personal development in a nondirective way, sometimes in connection with a formal training program. With the right coach, this is potentially a good way of providing just-in-time risk management.

Coaching originated in the US, though as an indication of its scope, a survey reported that six out of ten British organizations use coaching as part of leadership development with either outsider or insider coaches.[37] The experience of leading business schools is that the competence of good professional coaches comes from a combination of management experience, training in psychological processes, personal insight, and other-centeredness.

The term coaching also describes a particular supervisory style that facilitates risk management.[38] Take GE as an example of a company known for its emphasis on supervisory coaching. GE managers confront challenging stretch goals. It makes sense for the boss to adopt a coaching stance: "How can I help you to achieve those impossible stretch targets? What can I do to support you, are there any obstacles that I can help remove from your path? Because if you achieve those impossible stretch targets, I the boss will achieve my impossible stretch targets too." With its new performance development app, GE wants to shift the focus of development from being evaluation driven to coaching for performance improvement, allowing managers to get supportive assistance from the boss and all quarters.

Mentoring is sometimes grouped with coaching, although it is conceptually distinct. In mentoring, an experienced leader or professional is paired with a high potential person in a longer-term reciprocal relationship, as at the Finnish multinational KONE (see the box later in this chapter). It is practiced widely and informally in professional service firms in the transition to the role of partner. However, it can be difficult to organize formal mentoring relationships, partly because of the personal and emotional nature of such relationships and partly because the mentor's contribution may not be visible. Professional organizations can encourage and reward mentoring by asking middle-level associates to identify mentors. This information is then publicized to highlight the contribution of those who are playing this important developmental role.

Mentoring and "buddying" systems can take myriad shapes and forms.[39] Companies in highly competitive sectors, where close links between technological and commercial skills are important, sometime buddy up a HiPo duo for mutual development.[40]

For their mutual benefit, Cisco hooks up company veterans with managers from Jordan, Saudi Arabia, South Africa, and elsewhere who are on a talent acceleration program in Bangalore.[41] Another multinational we know pairs up key sales managers in local countries with R&D managers at the headquarters, each acting as a host to the other. The relationship provides local sales managers with insights into the technical pipeline and allows R&D managers to scope and test out opportunities for these technologies in the field. IBM has long used shadowing (watching experienced managers at work and sharing their day-by-day tasks) as a way of grooming talented individuals. A survey of how 25 multinationals go about developing local leadership also shows widespread use of mentoring, with nearly two-thirds assigned a mentor (ideally a more senior local person rather than an expatriate).[42] Having a local mentor contributes significantly to expatriate success and knowledge sharing.[43]

Feedback

Providing timely, constructive, all-round feedback is one of the most useful facets of people risk management. 360° feedback systems have long been standard practice in many firms, typically linked to development but sometimes incorporated into performance management practices. In the past it was argued that such feedback systems were culturally bound and would not function in, for example, an Asian setting. But our experience and research findings suggest that 360° approaches do work well there, as long as they are undertaken in a professional way and with strict adherence to the principles of anonymity.[44]

Nevertheless, cultural issues concerning feedback are important, as discussed in Chapter 7 in the context of performance appraisal. One of Welch's most important contributions to GE was to normalize direct, candid, and rapid feedback, legitimizing the open discussion of development needs. But these norms are not easy to apply in cultures where feedback is usually more indirect.

MANAGING GLOBAL LEADERSHIP DEVELOPMENT

Developing global leaders starts off with the question of *who* to develop. Who should scarce and expensive resources be focused on? Who should get the challenging jobs that are vital to strategic success? Who can be considered as corporate rather than local talent? In other words, who has global leadership potential?

In this section we discuss how multinational organizations go about identifying leadership potential in people in their operations around the world, and then how they develop their capabilities in line with the principles outlined earlier. We explore the dilemmas that are associated with this process of talent management. The box on "Global Talent Management at KONE" provides an overview of how an $8 billion multinational, one of Finland's leading corporations, tackles global leadership development, and how it is adapting an approach that has served it well for decades to China. KONE's approach to talent management builds on recruitment and selection issues discussed in Chapter 6, as well as the performance management issues in Chapter 7.

Global Talent Management at KONE[A]

While Nokia's phenomenal rise and fall has drawn attention to Finland, it is another multinational that is recognized locally as "Best Employer" and having "Best HR" practices, namely KONE. With US $8 billion in sales and close to 50,000 employees, KONE is one of the four leading players in the global elevator industry. The biggest growth opportunities are in China, and despite being a latecomer, KONE is the market leader there. Talent management has played an important role in KONE's international expansion.

The foundations of talent management were laid in the 1970s when the firm's international expansion through acquisitions began. Globalization of HRM processes including talent started in the early 2000s, spurred by the commitment of a new CEO, Matti Alahuhta, to deliver the best "People Flow" experience. At the heart of global talent management is an annual Leadership and Talent Review (LTR), which focuses on the occupants of 500 leadership roles worldwide.

During this review of key people and positions, all businesses and geographic areas must

- identify high potentials;
- nominate successors to key positions; and
- decide on development actions for people in key positions.

Areas and businesses are expected to nominate 1–5 percent of their staff for review, and there are about 300 employees designated as HiPos worldwide who do not currently occupy key positions. Identifying high potential at an early career stage is seen as desirable so that individuals can benefit from special development (KONE leadership educational programs, cross-functional moves, and mentoring as well as coaching), but individuals must have been with KONE for six months before they can be nominated for review.

To steer this review process, top management sets annual targets including on diversity (gender and culture), development (proportion undergoing job rotation), and recruitment (external versus internal sourcing). "High Potential" means the ability, commitment, and motivation to succeed in more senior leadership positions, defined by four criteria that are shown in Figure 8–2.

KONE follows the 70:20:10 principle, believing that 70 percent of development happens through job, project, and rotational challenges; 20 percent by learning through

FIGURE 8-2
High-Potential Criteria at KONE

High Potential Criteria

Performance
- Consistently strong ratings (3 or 4) in performance appraisal (what and how) Especially the How (values and leadership behavior for those in managerial positions)
  - Decision-making
  - Executing
  - Winning through people
  - Collaborating
  - Strategic and business acumen

KONE HiPo competencies
- Proactive communication
- Drive and persistence
- Conceptual thinking
- Flexibility
- Interpersonal sensitivity
- Self-confidence

Basic requirements
- Strong educational background (at least BSc- level degree or equivalent)
- Fluent English
- Typically from Grade 4–5 (IPE 50–57)
- Enough time in KONE (>6 months) to demonstrate performance and behaviors

Motivation to become a leader
- Interest and ability to accept cross-functional or cross-border assignments
- Self-awareness and learning agility, i.e., motivation and capability to learn and develop
- Stretching beyond responsibility of current role (geographically or functionally)
- Mobile
- Growth capacity: current +1 or +2 levels

others (all HiPos have a mentor and many receive special coaching); and 10 percent through formal education and training. It is clearly the commitment of senior management, and notably the CEO, to this and to the LTR process that makes it work. The CEO attends almost all senior leadership programs.

A "walk and write" approach is used at LTR meetings to stimulate fair input and discussion. The management team wanders around the room, writing comments on the posters of candidates, leading to presentations on these and discussion. Reviewing the succession plan for the top positions is also part of the meeting, giving a measure of the "bench strength" of areas and businesses, as well as indication of the need for external recruitment, and the urgency of renewal in management teams. As is practice in the Nordic region, succession candidates are not usually informed of their status.

China posed particular challenges for this globalized talent management process. Capitalizing on its technological leadership in elevators, KONE set out in 2005 to catch up in China, successfully riding the crest of the construction boom to secure a leading position by 2013. Recruiting 1,000 new staff each year, a recruitment slogan was "Come to work for the fastest growing company," which helped overcome KONE's lack of visibility. KONE's staff teaching at 50 technical schools also assisted in recruitment. But there was a shortage of HiPos: few of the Chinese managers satisfied the basic requirements, notably fluent English. The size and growth of China, virtually a continent unto itself, led KONE to relax the global criteria, designating "local" HiPos who did not have to speak English. The relaxation of language requirements also motivated local managers to speak up and become more proactive. Finally, the HiPo identification process in China was pushed down to the branch level.

Source: A. Smale, I. Björkman, and J. Saarinen, "Pushing the Right Buttons: Global Talent Management at KONE Corporation," University of Vaasa and Aalto University; available through the Case Centre.

Identifying and Assessing Potential

We suggested earlier that perhaps the most important question in talent development is who gets the challenging jobs—in other words who gets selected. As discussed in Chapter 6, selection involves identifying the most suitable person from a pool of candidates—internal and/or external. It focuses on assessing the fit between the candidates and the job or career opportunity— here the future global leadership role. Selection is the area of HRM where cultural and institutional differences play the biggest role.[45] The traditional ways of selecting people for leadership roles—of identifying potential—vary from company to company and nation to nation. But the prevailing pattern today in international corporations is what we call the *transnational model of internal selection* (see Chapter 6). According to this model—exemplified by both GE and KONE—local companies recruit and develop professionals for functional jobs, and individuals from within these ranks are subsequently identified as HiPo using assessments of performance and potential. One survey found that 60 percent of large corporations used this approach, asking local affiliates to identify talent that can be moved into corporate development programs.[46]

This assessment typically is part of an annual or periodic review, as with GE's Session C[47] or KONE's LTR. At GE this starts with performance reviews that are first bottom-up in the businesses and then top-down with the CEO. At the heart of such a review there is usually an assessment of people on two or more dimensions, often in the shape of what is known as a nine-box assessment. Figure 8-3 shows the framework used by the pharmaceutical giant Novartis.[48]

FIGURE 8-3
"Nine-Box" Assessment of Performance and Potential: An Example from Novartis

Performance objectives				᙮ NOVARTIS
Exceeded expectations	Superior results/ unsatisfactory behavior	Superior results/ good behavior	Exceptional performer and recognized as role model	
Fully met expectations	Good results/ unsatisfactory behavior	Strong performer (fully acceptable level of performance)	Superior behavior/ good results	
Partially met expectations	Unsatisfactory performer	Good behavior/ unsatisfactory results	Superior behavior/ unsatisfactory results	
	Partially met expectations	Fully met expectations	Exceeded expectations	**Values/ behaviors**

Evaluations of performance are collected, representing one dimension of the framework. The performance of individuals is sorted into three (sometimes four or five) classifications, according to a rough bell curve that is similar to GE's "vitality curve". The definition of the second dimension, which we summarize as "potential," varies from firm to firm. At GE potential is a combination of suitability for promotion and values, as expressed in *behaviors*. At Novartis, potential is gauged by whether someone demonstrates the key values and behaviors that the company looks for in its future leaders. At KONE, it is six competencies that are deemed desirable together with the assessed motivation to become a leader.

The review process should not only focus on identifying and then developing individuals in the top right-hand box of Figure 8-3, who are strong on both dimensions—those in all four corner boxes require attention. Obviously, those who are high performing and high potential should be moved into the most challenging assignments with appropriate training and support. Retention and development plans need to be worked out for high performers who are not currently seen as having leadership potential, for they may be critical to the performance of the firm. It is worth emphasizing that GE, Shell, and other companies that depend on the quality of their engineering and functional talent focus a great deal of attention on the development of people who are likely to pursue careers only within their functions. And deep questions need to be asked about those who are high potential but underperforming. Are they misfits? Are they being constrained by difficult bosses? Finally, most companies want to identify the underperforming people with low potential—to turn them around or to turn them out.

Assessing Learning Capacity
Individuals vary in their ability to handle big challenges and to learn from their experiences. Some people seek out feedback proactively, consult with others, and in effect organize their own coaching; others do not, preferring to do what has worked well for them before. As the box "How fast do you learn?" outlines, learning agility is an important element of leadership potential, and for many companies it is *the* most important factor.

How Fast Do You Learn?

People's learning speeds vary.[49] One study of 838 managers in six multinational corporations explored the individual characteristics that distinguished successful global leaders from solid performers who lacked leadership potential.[A] Eleven characteristics differentiated the two groups, and factor analysis showed that there were two different underlying dimensions, as shown in the table below. The first dimension, encompassing characteristics like the courage to take risks, captures the willingness to assume challenge. The second dimension, with characteristics like seeking out feedback and learning from mistakes as well as criticism, expresses learning agility.

Eleven Characteristics Distinguishing High-Potential Leaders from Solid Performers in Six International Corporations[A]

Factor 1: (Willingness to take on challenge)
- Seeks opportunities to learn
- Is committed to make a difference
- Has the courage to take risks

Factor 2: (Learning agility)
- Adapts to cultural differences
- Is insightful: sees things from new angles
- Seeks and uses feedback
- Learns from mistakes
- Is open to criticism

Other Characteristics
- Acts with integrity
- Seeks broad business knowledge
- Brings out the best in people

[A]Three companies were European multinationals, one American, and one Australian. The ratings were undertaken by the bosses of the 838 subjects.

Source: Adapted from G. Spreitzer, M.W. McCall, and J. Mahoney, "Early Identification of International Leadership Potential: Dimensions, Measurement, and Validation," *Journal of Applied Psychology* 82, no. 1 (February 1997), pp. 6–29.

The importance of learning agility for leadership development has long been recognized, both by corporations and in more academic studies. For example, a study of 90 prominent leaders in fields from the arts to business singled out personal learning ability as the quality most required for leadership;[50] and it has been described as a meta-competence for managers.[51]

As indicated in Chapter 6, Infosys recruits professionals at entry level for "learnability." When Infosys was smaller, it could be choosy in selecting on the basis of technical skills, but not once it became a leading player recruiting thousands of professionals each year, in a software process arena where the rate of change is rapid. Learnability is defined as consistent ability in deriving generic knowledge from specific instances. Potential leaders are tested for how quickly they can learn new concepts and then apply them to unfamiliar situations.[52]

Dilemmas in the Global Leadership Development Process

There are several dilemmas in the process of identifying global leadership talent and deciding who should get the most rewarding developmental opportunities. We focus on those that are particularly salient to the multinational setting.

When to Identify Potential?

A lot of career politics is associated with getting visibility early on in the eyes of top management in order to secure the challenging jobs that count. However, there are dilemmas associated with the age at which potential should be identified—early or late?

Japanese companies have historically identified potential at the time of graduate recruitment, leading to an extended developmental trial period.[53] This makes sense in a culture where individuals pursue lifelong careers in the same firm and because it is still not common for firms in Japan to recruit from outside. In Anglo-Saxon countries, however, other firms are likely to poach HiPos, especially if the enterprise has a reputation for selection and development. This happened to Procter & Gamble (P&G) back in the past when it developed a reputation as a top-notch incubator, feeding the management ranks of competitors in the fast-moving consumer products industry.

Alternatively, one could argue for the late identification of talent, by which time experience and track record enable one to make good judgments on potential. However, this strategy is similarly flawed since top talent may get frustrated and leave, and there is insufficient time for high payoff developmental actions.[54] If talented international employees are identified much later than those in the home country, their leadership prospects will be compromised. Indeed, this may be a factor explaining why GE was less successful in developing leaders from their Asian operations. Talented individuals in the US were spotted much earlier than their counterparts in Asia—Immelt came to the attention of Jack Welch when he was 27—but until recently GE had few regional corporate offices outside the US that could take on the task of identifying and developing regional talent. This is one reason why GE has created additional corporate offices in Dubai, Panama, and elsewhere.

How Much Transparency?

A key challenge in talent identification is procedural justice,[55] and multinationals should try to ensure that the evaluation of performance and potential is undertaken on a globally consistent basis. However, once a judgment has been made about who has potential, there are often dilemmas concerning the appropriate degree of transparency about the decision.

As in KONE, multinational firms from egalitarian cultures wrestle with the issue of whether or not to inform HiPos about their status after talent reviews. The differential treatment of such employees in terms of developmental support or compensation can be a sensitive matter. If the HiPo status is not visible, this can lead to frustration and turnover among high performers who do not feel adequately recognized. Being formally recognized as one the talent pool is found to increase willingness to accept challenging assignments in the future.[56]

However, if HiPo status is communicated, there are two corresponding fears: first, good performers who were not identified as having HiPo are likely to lose motivation and leave; and second, unrealistic expectations about advancement might be raised among those identified as having potential. The former is unavoidable, endemic to any "quota" process, and one can argue that keeping people in the dark about their career progress in the hope that they will stay in the firm is shortsighted, if not unethical. As for the second fear, if one accepts that people develop through challenge, then one consequence of being identified as HiPo is an expectation of a career stretch. It is both difficult and ill advised to hide this designation, though most companies choose to communicate it with a certain amount of discretion.

Some companies have responded to these dilemmas by encouraging self-nomination instead of top-down identification. Commonwealth Edison in the US allows people to nominate themselves as HiPos, submitting a list of peers and superiors who will be asked to provide references, similar to the process of tenure review in the academic world. At Tatweer, a Dubai group, employees must apply for a place on a HiPo program, going through a challenging process of assessment and reviews with outside consultants. They are then expected to continue to perform at a high level in their current job while they participate in the program. Those who are not truly motivated and capable will simply shy away.[57]

Ensuring that judgments on potential are reviewed regularly can mitigate some of the risks associated with transparency. Those who are not yet identified as HiPos have then an incentive to work themselves into the designated talent pool; while those that are labeled as HiPo realize that they need to continue to prove themselves to progress in their career. The quality of these periodic reviews is arguably one of the most important aspects of talent management.

Who Should Be Accountable?

A major challenge for multinational corporations coming from a heritage of local responsiveness is how to get the local company to pay attention to leadership development at early career stages. In a tightly run, cost-conscious local operation, there may not be much room for high potential people with advanced degrees and high expectations but no hands-on experience. Furthermore, operationally oriented local HR managers may be ill equipped to cope with the challenges of recruiting, developing, and retaining such individuals. In some cultures, senior management may also be reluctant to recruit young people who want to go beyond the job by exercising initiative.

Given that the skill requirements at one level of responsibility are different from those at the next level of leadership, the process of identification and development of high potential individuals should be managed by the corporation or region, not by the business or country, so as to ensure the mobility and people risk management that is vital for development.[58] GE and other firms are explicit about this: those individuals become what many multinationals call, formally or informally, "corporate property."

A widespread obstacle for leadership identification in multinationals is the natural tendency of subsidiary managers to act in their own interests and hide their best people.[59] The more one praises an indispensable individual, the more likely it is that the person will be moved elsewhere under the banner of leadership development. A survey of HR executives from multinational firms singled out this problem as one of the major challenges in talent management.[60] Consequently, chief executives such as A.G. Laffley who used to head up P&G are adamant about the importance of releasing talent, since talent development is a corporate value on a par with financial performance.[61] For them, hiding talent is an act of corporate disloyalty. KONE and Haier are among the many multinationals who include the leadership development of others as a performance criterion.

In the past one might have expected loyal expatriates, representing the corporate perspective, to combat such silo tendencies; but in many markets the senior ranks are increasingly local. This is why nurturing talent becomes a key responsibility of regional management or of an experienced HR manager who works with subsidiaries across the region. Schlumberger, the world's leading oilfield services provider, navigates this issue by reengineering the whole process. In countries where local management is operationally focused and strongly technical in orientation, the corporate or regional HR function recruits individuals with perceived high potential, who are then placed in entry-level functional jobs in a third country with a reputation as a talent incubator. When these recruits have successfully mastered the core operational roles, they are repatriated to their home country for the next step as engineering or service managers—ready to move again as they progress through the organization.

How to Avoid Bias in Global Talent Reviews?

The purpose of differentiation between people, for example, on two dimensions as in nine-box reviews, is not just to place people's names in boxes, but to ensure that an open dialogue takes place about their performance and potential, as well as the development implications. However, it is not uncommon for talent reviews to be nothing more than formal rituals performed by a quasi-representative committee of stakeholders defending their favorite candidates. Local bosses are often reluctant to discriminate among their managers. At a KONE talent review in Asia, a country head rated all his managers as "exceeding expectations." At the meeting the regional executive told him that, "if you rate them all as excellent you prevent them from growing"—and it was a light bulb moment for that country manager.[62]

One pitfall is that these reviews are often biased against managers who are far away from the home country and who do not have personal relationships with key decision-makers sitting at headquarters.[63] The head office people with power may give an individual who locals see as talented only token consideration. Consciously or unconsciously, they do not trust local inputs and ratings, and they give at best a formal stamp of approval to the person. Moreover, there is an inevitable halo effect—candidates who share certain similarities with the evaluators are judged as having higher potential.[64] Local units learn that their views are not taken into account, so they start taking the process lightly—the makings of a self-fulfilling prophecy. The consequence will often be that the best local employees will look for opportunities outside the firm; at which point, head office says, "why bother to invest in them, as they will leave in any case?" To minimize such risks, companies may follow the example of GE and make sure that their senior executives get to know local talent or follow the practice of KONE in setting targets for particular regions or key countries.

That someone who may be less qualified gets a promotion or developmental opportunity is not the most important consequence of biased decisions—people's qualifications can often be debated. The important consequence is the loss of procedural justice and the diminished credibility of both the review and the appointment-making process in the eyes of managers (and potential leaders) around the world. Exemplified by GE's Session C review, the quality of information, candid dialogue among line executives, and professional preparation by both line and HR should lie at the heart of the talent review.

How to Move Beyond Identification?

The purpose of formally identifying and reviewing people with leadership potential is to ensure what we term "unnatural acts"—value-added actions that would not happen unless attention has been paid to fair assessment of potential. An example of an unnatural act would be ensuring that local nationals who do not have an impressive education but who demonstrate high potential come to the attention of senior management; and that they are provided with special coaching to accompany a challenging assignment that would otherwise have been given to an expatriate.

In this respect, many multinational firms fall into the trap of engaging in excessive identification and assessment of potential, at the expense of development action. This is partly because the identification side of leadership development involves work that can be facilitated by the HR function, increasingly using globally standardized tools and processes. On the other hand, HR can undertake little on the development side without the commitment of the local business managers—apart from sending someone on a corporate training program or assigning them a mentor.

This has important implications. First, companies are advised to be selective, even conservative, in their judgments about who is of high potential, because it is preferable to under-forecast than over-forecast future needs. Undertaking rigorous reviews is time-consuming, and not worth doing unless it is done well. And if the catch net is too wide, it will dilute the attention given to it by line managers. At KONE no more than 5 percent of the workforce can be considered as HiPo, in line with the practice of other multinationals with proven track records in leadership development.[65]

Second, senior line managers in the business or functional units must adopt a talent development mindset and take ownership of leadership identification and reviews. The HR function has to undertake important groundwork, but it is the attention of line managers and those at the top of the organization that counts. The former CEO of P&G, cited above, commented: "I spend a third to half of my time on leadership development [...] Nothing I do will have a more enduring impact on P&G's long-term success than helping to develop other leaders."[66]

Developing Potential

A simple logic linked to mobility guided the development of leadership potential in many leading multinational organizations in the past. Candidates for top positions should have experience in the home country, an established market abroad, and an emerging market. They should have a turnaround management project providing change management experience, as well as experience in a headquarter staff role. They should have experience in multiple business areas within the firm. But consider the implications. If potential was identified when someone was in his or her late 20s, and if that person were to move successfully into senior management no later than his or her mid-40s, this implied less than two years in each position. The consequence, as we discuss later in this section, was that people developed skills in starting things off but not in deep execution and the management of change.

Today, firms are more selective in the way they frame the necessary development experiences. In its leadership principles, InBev explicitly says that the type of challenges people experience is more significant than the function in which they experience them. InBev sees the best development experiences as coming from the following categories of roles:

- Challenging people roles, where leaders acquire experience in supervising and developing large numbers of people
- Challenging assignments outside an individual's expertise
- Challenging commercial roles: customer-facing experience is regarded as vital for developing brand-related competencies deemed essential in its beer business
- Challenging expertise roles: each individual should have a functional area of expertise to fall back on in case of need.

Since mobility is so important for global leadership development, the difficulty of optimizing both short-term performance and long-term development underlies most of the dilemmas faced by multinationals in developing potential. This is seen clearly in challenges around decision-making on promotions and assignments.

Balancing Demand-Driven and Learning-Driven Assignments

When planning appointments, there are often real trade-offs between immediate performance, which argues for appointing a manager with the skills and experience required, and learning and development, which will mean nominating a HiPo individual who will learn from the experience. This is similar to the distinction between demand- and learning-driven international mobility discussed in Chapter 9. It should be the role of the HR to voice these trade-offs so they can be managed objectively.

When a key position opens up in a unit, there will typically be a local functional candidate with many years of experience, a loyal and low-risk person who is sure to perform solidly. And there may be another candidate from the regional talent pool, an outsider to local operations with less experience but who might bring new ideas and extraordinary results that would rock the boat, developing into a higher-level executive. Who should get the position? There are no standard answers, though the preference of local management is usually clear. Unless there is a countervailing force in the shape of a strong regional HR manager who has the backing of senior line management, the conclusion is foregone. Paradoxically, the longer-term outcome is that local managers will continue to complain that senior leadership remains dominated by expatriates. In this sense, multinational leadership development can be described as guerilla warfare.[67]

Companies often find it particularly difficult to find positions abroad for learning-driven development. Headquarters may have the clout and legitimacy to find such assignments for home country employees with high potential—building on the traditions of expatriation. However, finding developmental jobs in the US or Europe for talented staff from emerging countries is often difficult. ABB deals with this through norms of swapping—if you want to send someone abroad, you have to be prepared to take in someone from outside. 3M has a general principle that the country managing director should not be a local person, thereby ensuring opportunities for geographic mobility at senior levels.

Focusing on A-Positions as well as A-Players

Sustainable competitive advantage comes from building strong organizational capabilities that are hard for others to imitate. Leadership development should therefore ensure that future leaders acquire experience in domains regarded as key capabilities, such as brand management for a beer company like InBev. This means that talent reviews should not just focus on the individuals—the so-called A-players—but also on the A-positions, the "strategic" jobs that are critical to a firm's competitive advantage, as discussed in Chapter 6.[68] Given its strategy of market innovation, GE identifies market-facing roles in building a new business as A-positions (along with acquisition roles). Indeed, one can argue that the systematic identification of positions that differentially contribute to an organization's long-term competitive advantage should be the starting point for any strategic talent management system.[69]

In tightly networked multinationals such as Nestle, Shell, and Unilever, the career of a HiPo employee will consist of a series of such A-positions, accentuating the development of firm-specific skills as well as generalist leadership—mastering networks, understanding the complex value chain, and confronting specific business and organizational challenges.[70] The flipside of this firm-specificity is that these individuals have fewer options at the same level of responsibility outside the firm should it become clear that their future inside is limited. Functional expertise travels well from firm to firm, but firm-specific, generalist experience has limited market value.

Achieving the Right Amount of Mobility

Most managers will pursue careers within functions, never moving outside them or their home countries; as noted earlier, companies like GE take functional development seriously. While mobility is a key lever for intransitive leadership development, there is a danger of taking mobility and learning to extremes. Too much mobility will compromise the ability to *implement* new initiatives—there is little that can be executed thoroughly in 18–24 months, especially at middle and senior management levels. After all, it is not strategy and plans that count, but the quality of their execution. This is the reason why one should talk of mobility rather than "job rotation."

Especially in emerging markets with many career opportunities, rapidity of movement in some companies becomes a quasi-indicator of potential. This creates a zigzag management pattern where newly appointed leaders of local units seek out initiatives that respond to the strategic intentions of senior management. Just as their local actions are taking hold, the individual is promoted and moved. If the successor is cut from the same cloth, he or she will take the unit off on a different initiative, since there are few rewards for implementing changes started by someone else. The consequence is that local organizations go through periodic campaigns—cost cutting, customer orientation, time to market, and so forth—but never develop deep capabilities in any of these domains.

Instead, the key to achieving the right amount of mobility should be to ensure that there is a clear link between accountability and tenure when planning assignments. If the assignment is learning driven, aimed at building experience, it is unlikely that the individual will be responsible for performance and capability building; the assignment can be of short duration. But if the assignment is demand driven and the individual is responsible for performance, then those assignments should be of longer duration, depending on the time it takes to ensure effective implementation.

Succession Planning or Talent Pools?

Succession planning consists of developing a plan to fill key positions as they become vacant. Succession planning is widely practiced in Europe, but less so in the US except at the most senior levels; in Asia succession planning has mostly been used at operational levels because of the severe talent shortages that companies experienced during the boom years.[71]

Succession planning has come under attack for being excessively mechanical. In reality, the decision about who gets the job is often made through informal discussion without consulting the succession plan, which is sometimes viewed by line managers as little more than a ritual of the HR function. Indeed, in flat organizational hierarchies, the decision to indicate person X as a likely successor for position Y may be somewhat arbitrary. Also, the requirements for a role may change after the original plan was agreed, or a new CEO may have different criteria for leadership appointments. When only 60 percent of the moves occur as planned, this may spill over into skepticism about the whole process of leadership development. In fact, in the US a majority of companies have abandoned all pretensions at succession planning.[72]

Succession planning may in many firms be complemented by talent pools, reservoirs of people with skills linked to critical organizational capabilities who can in principle be deployed across functions, businesses, and geographies.

The typical scenario in many multinational firms today is that the local business unit is expected to engage in succession planning in its own interest, while the region or corporate level control a talent pool of HiPo managers. When a position becomes vacant, the local unit will propose its own successor, while corporate HR will consult the talent pool to see if there is a suitable individual who would benefit from the role and contribute to it. This leads to a review of who is the most appropriate candidate.

Balancing Top-Down and Bottom-Up

The approach to managing leadership development in multinationals, as we have outlined it, is naturally top-down, directed from the center, because of the intransitive "unnatural acts" that leadership development involves. The expense involved is justified by the fact that leadership development is a critical item on the strategic HRM agenda of most international enterprises, as mentioned at the outset of this chapter, typically driven by the CEO and even the board. But an open-market, individual-driven, bottom-up approach to talent management is spreading, often known as "open-job resourcing." As discussed in our opening case, GE is shifting the focus from ranking-centric annual performance reviews to apps that help employees to assess their learning needs, facilitating access to development opportunities. Multinational firms will have to pay increasing attention to striking the right balance between the two approaches, which we would argue are not mutually exclusive.

Some major corporations, like Carrefour and Honda, did not have a corporate HR function until a relatively late stage in their history, when it was created to manage global leadership development. Honda's founder, Honda Soichiro, believed that people management and marketing were so important that he did not wish to compromise line management's responsibility by functionalizing them. However, Honda found it had to make an exception for leadership development. Without a dedicated role, functions and countries took local perspectives with too short a time horizon; leadership development took place within silos and without the necessary mobility.

Until recently, leadership development in most multinationals has largely been managed in the top-down way, which means that the organization took the prime responsibility for managing the careers of its strategic talent. For non-strategic staff, external recruitment has come to prevail in the US and increasingly throughout the world, complemented more and more by intranet-based, open-job resourcing (internal labor markets). In some multinational firms, bottom-up staffing through open-job markets is now spreading up the hierarchy to professionals and management.[73]

Accelerated by the global standardization of HR processes and the development of e-HR technology, the spread of bottom-up approaches is driven by the prospect of being able to deploy talented people and ideas across borders far more effectively, rapidly, and cheaply than with conventional top-down methods. However, there are major obstacles to realizing these benefits. One of the far-reaching implications of open-job resourcing is that the responsibility for career development shifts from the company to the individual. An increasing number of multinationals are now capitalizing on major investments they have made in self-help, e-based HR technology using GE-style apps, as well as standardized global HRM processes to develop platforms aimed at helping people to help themselves—in line with the best interests of the firm.

Among large companies, IBM pioneered this way by creating an e-platform that provides self-help in learning, networking, mentoring, career track management, and other elements of traditional top-down career management. The firm has also completely changed its formerly secretive attitude about its work strategy to one of internal transparency. Cisco's internal job market is built around a "jobs can find you" principle, according to which people are expected continuously to look for job openings that correspond to their aspirations. On the company side, Cisco carefully plans the competencies and roles needed to implement its short- and medium-term strategies. These openings and the underlying strategy are made transparent through the intranet, and people worldwide can apply for openings that most closely match their aspirations.

At Starwood Hotels, all positions up to the level of regional manager are posted on the global intranet, leading to increased mobility, though positions at and above regional manager are managed top-down. Open-job resourcing continues to spread upward into the managerial ranks of multinational firms, though rarely if ever to the most senior levels. All positions at Hewlett-Packard, except for the top 100, are available on the internal open market, as they are at

Microsoft. At Shell, positions up to the top 250 have been posted internally for more than a decade.

Striking the right balance between a top-down and a bottom-up approach to leadership development has become a question of how far down in the multinational firm to cascade centrally managed talent pools and globally standardized practices of leadership development—and how far up in the firm to allow individually driven practices such as posting jobs on internal job markets and facilitating self-help via apps or e-platforms. We expect the interplay between top-down and bottom-up approaches in leadership, management, and professional development to be one of the interesting frontiers for practice in the future.

We witnessed one major multinational that abandoned its well-honed top-down management development processes that were correctly seen as somewhat ethnocentric, replacing them with global open-job resourcing. The outcome was predictable—few young talents volunteered for "unnatural" challenging assignments, leading a decade later to appointments of untested leaders to positions with significant responsibility. Some passed, but others failed—with major cost to the business. Recently, the company corrected the course—learning how to mix effectively the top-down and bottom-up approaches to global talent management.

Managing Retention

The major reason why many companies, particularly in the Anglo-Saxon world, are reluctant to invest in the training and development of their people is that this increases their value—and the likelihood that they may leave.[74] Therefore, retention must be an integral part of talent management, and this includes the management of technical talent (see the box "The Development and Retention of Technical Talent"). Firms that do a good job of recruitment and development

The Development and Retention of Technical Talent

Talent development processes often focus exclusively on managerial leadership talent, to the exclusion of technical talent that may be critical for the future of the firm. We noted earlier that nine-box reviews should pay attention to the development and retention of those with high performance but lower managerial leadership potential, and this is particularly true for emerging markets where the "talent war" centers on technical or functional talent. The definition of "potential" may include technical leadership potential, as at IBM.

Where technical talent is strategically important, companies set up separate talent governance processes led by executives with a technical background, as at IBM, Schlumberger, Air Liquide, and Lockheed.[75] They focus on STEM[76] recruitment, on defining competence levels linked to career/salary progression, as well as on mapping out associated career paths.

In some companies, dual-career ladders fell out of favor when a study pointed out the gap between the theory and the reality that technical ladders were becoming a parking lot for failed leaders.[77] Others, like Schlumberger, have implemented technical ladders successfully, with a progression at senior levels from senior to principal to adviser and on to fellow.

but who manage retention poorly will have borne all the costs of talent development, while other firms capture the benefits. Unfortunately, it is typically the most talented people, whom firms can least afford to lose, who leave for higher pay and bigger opportunities elsewhere.

Why Do People Leave and What Can Be Done About It?

The scholarly research on turnover and retention suggests that there are multiple reasons for attrition,[78] and there is a large practitioner literature on the reasons why people leave a firm.[79] With this in mind, let us review some of the implications for managing retention.

1. Compensation When asked in an exit interview about the reasons for leaving the organization, most people will say that they are getting a higher wage packet in their new job. But this does not necessarily mean that higher compensation is the solution to retention. Experienced HR professionals will point out that typically it is not money that leads someone to look outside in the first place but some other cause for disgruntlement—lack of clear development opportunities, a difficult boss, or problems in work–life balance. And if a talented individual is prepared to change job and organization, they will invariably gain an increase in compensation. Raising salaries across the board to solve retention would only price the company out of business. It is important to consider all aspects of the employee value proposition (as discussed in Chapter 6), of which compensation is only one element.

Nonetheless, compensation still matters. To retain strategic talent using compensation as a carrot it is vital to know how employees view the local job market opportunities in comparison with the global salaries of HiPos (see Chapter 7). In countries where it is possible to use stock options and retention bonuses, these may be effective in boosting retention. People may leave after their options are exercised, but this is at least predictable.

Financial penalties can sometimes be used to discourage unilateral resignations. For example, employment contracts that include retention bonds (often with family guarantees) are widely used by the public sector in Singapore to retain employees who have benefited from education or training support from the government or the employer. The aim is to ensure that they remain with the sponsoring organization for a prescribed period of time to secure a return on the development investment. In the private sector, such contracts, while not uncommon, are difficult to enforce.

2. The quality of the relationship with the boss Line managers are responsible for many areas of potential dissatisfaction contributing to turnover: coaching, providing feedback, giving recognition, and offering growth opportunities. They are also central to other dimensions of retention management, such as work–life balance, where the superior typically has considerable discretion, regardless of corporate policy and practice. HR professionals often argue that much of the problem of turnover lies in the hands of the direct supervisor. A popular way of expressing this is the aphorism that "people don't leave companies, they quit bosses." This is one reason why multinationals invest in supervisory training—the benefits of improved retention as well as employee engagement typically more than outweigh the cost.

One of the contentious issues in retention management is that line managers tend to see it as the responsibility of the HR function, often linked to compensation and benefits, while HR professionals want line managers to take the prime responsibility for retention. However, creating a talent mindset where line managers accept that they must pay attention to subordinates can be difficult. This is true even in North America, where it is now common for at least senior managers to have retention objectives among their key performance indicators.

If the firm has an internal job market that allows employees to apply freely for other internal positions, the boss is obliged to pay attention to actions such as listening to staff that will increase the engagement and loyalty of key subordinates. Half of companies in the US allow employees to apply for another internal position without permission from the boss.[80] But creating this talent mindset can be more challenging in the environment of emerging countries, like Russia and China, where bosses often have an eye on the door themselves and are not used to considering people management as part of their role. Indeed they may take their best performers with them when they leave!

3. Work–life balance The biggest source of work dissatisfaction in the opinion surveys of many leading multinationals is poor balance between professional and private life, often voiced by the millennial generation of young professionals. One reserve to note here is highlighted in the research of one of the authors, based on 14,000 managers across the globe, which showed that perceived work–life imbalance may hide other problems, notably different types of mismatch between the job or company and the individual.[81] In contrast, individuals who thrive on their jobs and work environments will often live with their work–life dissatisfaction for protracted periods of time.

In order to retain talent, companies respond with a range of work–life programs to juggle work and family commitments, as well as child-friendly working practices. Infosys successfully tackles retention with a group of workplace initiatives—including family involvement—that mimic the best aspects of university life and aim at avoiding impersonal bureaucracy amid rapid growth.[82] Flexible working hours are spreading, practiced by two-thirds of European companies and by large firms in other regions, from Singapore to San Francisco. While telecommuting appears to be particularly effective with respect to retention among dual-career couples with children, only 24 percent of a sample of 300 corporations across the globe offers this, and we rarely see it in Asia.[83] Thoughtless practices—such as Friday conference calls, New York time, that compromise the weekend for those in Asia—should be eliminated.

4. Personal growth opportunities In rapidly growing markets, such as China or India, outside career opportunities that offer not only better compensation but also a significant increase in responsibility are a major cause of turnover.[84] Often, talented employees can move quickly from local or regional jobs to positions with global responsibilities—for example, with aspiring local multinationals. Here, an opportunity for a "split egg" assignment, such as participation in a significant global project, or adding coordinating responsibilities that provide visibility with senior management, may be at least a temporary remedy. Coaching and mentoring are other tools to counter this inevitable trend.

5. Talent development In the long term, people will only stay if they feel the organization has no "glass or bamboo" ceilings and that they get a fair chance to prove (and enhance) their skills. Therefore, a transparent structure for talent development that is clearly based on performance and potential is the critical tool for combating attrition. In multinational firms, this means establishing positive role models for local staff. The perceived lack of development and career opportunities contributes greatly to attrition, especially among talented local individuals. If local employees are unsure of their future in the firm, particularly when they see senior jobs going first and foremost to expatriates, they will naturally keep a close eye on outside opportunities. But this is also true of firms in the US, where senior positions are often filled by outsiders.

6. Location It may be easier to recruit people in talent cluster locations like the San Francisco area for the IT industry, the north of Italy for the fashion industry, or in urban conurbations such as Shanghai and Sao Paulo. But it is also easier for other firms to poach talent in such places, and attrition will certainly be higher. The HR strategy of software firm SAS focuses on providing generous employee benefits and a highly congenial flexible work environment—but it is located in North Carolina, far from the technology hub on the Pacific coast. Their attrition rate is low in an otherwise volatile industry and this stability gives SAS a competitive advantage over its competitors, where many members of software development teams are either learning the ropes or looking for opportunities elsewhere. Companies may be able to choose secondary locations where it is easier to socialize and retain talented individuals (like Vietnam rather than China).

Overall, there is no simple recipe for talent retention in all contexts, which is why this matter must be high on the agenda of talent reviews focused on technical as well as managerial leadership in all regions of the multinational enterprise.

LEADERSHIP DEVELOPMENT AS A FACILITATOR OF GLOBAL COORDINATION

One of the reasons why leadership development will continue in some degree to be top-down in multinational firms is that it is a powerful vehicle for global coordination. In the past, decisions followed reporting lines up to top management. However, that process was too slow and bureaucratic. As we have discussed extensively, global firms have therefore started to build lateral coordination mechanisms such as cross-border councils and steering groups. How can they go further? Explicit career pathing for high potential leaders is one effective way.

Let us take an inter-functional example. The firm specifies publically that no-one will get onto the management team in the commercial division unless they have proven themselves in at least one middle-level position for a reasonable period of time in the operations division—and vice versa. What are the consequences? First, the consequent mobility will develop a better quality of leadership since managers are obliged to hone their leadership skills via cross-functional moves. Second, it ensures that the leaders at the top have broad perspectives, the "matrix in the mind" that comes from assuming the responsibility for results in another discipline. Third, it builds social capital between key people in the two disciplines, with the trust that will allow them to work through inevitable differences in functional interest. And fourth, this changes the culture of the enterprise. Ambitious young professionals who want to move into leadership positions quickly learn that it is vital to be professionally competent in one's base discipline, but also important to build networks and collaborate with other functions.

Building coordination capabilities in a multinational firm requires "unnatural acts" that will only occur if there is senior management intervention with the HR function playing an important supporting role. If a company is to get out of its dependence on home country expatriates in key positions, talented locals need experience in challenging line positions at the headquarters that will provide them with the matrix perspectives, the global mindset, and the social networks that will equip them for senior leadership positions in their regions. Yet these positions are precisely those that high potential home country nationals are jockeying to obtain. Without strong top-down leadership, the path to transnational "global-*and*-local" organizational development will be inevitably slow.

TAKEAWAYS

1. Global leadership development is a top priority in most multinationals. Among the reasons are the increasing rate of change in the environment, growth in emerging markets, and the importance of leadership development for ensuring global coordination.

2. Tolerance for ambiguity, the ability to work with contradiction, strong interpersonal skills, and the ability to exercise leadership without authority are key competencies for global leaders. But there is no universal list of global leadership competencies because leadership is intransitive—the best performer at one level is not necessarily the best performer at the next.

3. Leaders develop above all through challenging opportunities and assignments. Mobility across countries and functions is important, complemented by split egg type cross-boundary projects.

4. Challenges have to go hand in hand with people risk management—coaching, feedback, training, and mentoring in different shapes and forms.

5. Learning agility—the ability to learn fast and well from challenging experiences—is an important element of leadership potential.

6. At the heart of the traditional top-down approach to leadership development are rigorous reviews of talent in different parts of the firm, typically based on the assessment of performance, potential, and/or respect for key values.

7. The purpose of potential identification is to ensure "unnatural acts" of development that would not happen without top-down intervention. Companies should be selective in their judgments about who has high potential.

8. Firms should focus on individuals in the A-positions as well as on the A-players. Having A-positions distributed globally is the starting point.

9. There are several central questions in leadership assessment and development. How can multinationals assure that talent will be identified regardless of location? Should potential be identified early or late; and how transparent should firms be about the judgments made?

10. Bottom-up "help yourself" career development, using e-technology tools and supported by internal job markets, is in some leading firms complementing top-down leadership identification and development, except at the highest levels.

NOTES

1 Bartlett and McLean, 2006; Pucik and Lief, 2007.
2 "Follow the Leader," *Industry Week*, November 18, 1996, p. 16.
3 Bartlett and McLean, 2006.
4 "Why GE had to kill its annual performance review after more than three decades," *Quartz*, August 13, 2015, qz.com/428813/ge-performance-review-strategy-shift/.
5 This is still the case for a large number of US-based multinationals, including global giants such as IBM and J&J.
6 An annual award conducted by the Hay Group with *Chief Executive Review*, based on polling peers, academics, and experts. GE was second placed in 2013 and third placed in 2014 (with P&G and IBM), winning the award many times during the previous decade. Only 31 percent of the 790 firms reviewed in 2007 were US based. See www.chiefexecutive.net/.
7 Lehmberg, Rowe, and Philips, 2009.
8 Scullion and Starkey, 2000. See also a recent survey of corporations in over 40 countries, where only 25 percent of HR executives cited their organization's leaders as high quality (DDI, "Global leadership forecast 2014/2015: Meeting Tomorrow's Business Challenges," www.ddiworld.com/leadershipforecast).
9 Gregersen, Morrison, and Black, 1998; Black, Gregersen, and Morrison, 1999; Ready and Conger, 2007.
10 In the BRIC countries of Brazil, Russia, India, and China, the shortage of management talent is most acute at senior country levels (Ready, Hill, and Conger, 2008).
11 IBM, "Unlocking the DNA of the adaptable workforce: The Global Human Capital Study," 2008, www.ibm.com/cy/pdfs/HR_Study_2008.pdf.
12 Maruca, 1994, p. 142.
13 Mendenhall *et al.*, 2012.
14 For reviews of this literature on global leadership competencies, see McCall and Hollenbeck (2002); Mendenhall (2006); Mendenhall *et al.* (2008); Caligiuri and Tarique (2012).
15 Hollenbeck and McCall, 2001.
16 The Peter Principle suggested that employees will rise in a hierarchy until they reach their level of incompetence (Peter and Hull, 1969). It is a notion today captured popularly in Dilbert cartoons.

17 See Kotter (1990); Hill (1992); McCall (2004); Guillen and Ibarra (2009); Ibarra (2015). Considerable research suggests important skill changes as individuals transition from novice to middle and on to senior leadership levels (Lord and Hall, 2005).

18 Charan, Drotter, and Noel, 2001.

19 See Bartlett and Ghoshal (1997) for a description of the model of management roles and competencies in the transnational organization.

20 Martin and Schmidt, 2010.

21 See McCall and Hollenbeck (2002). The 101 executives (46 European and the rest from other parts of the world) in the study held positions such as CEO, executive vice president, managing director, country manager, business unit manager, and controller. The interviews focused on key events in their own development.

22 McCall, Lombardo, and Morrison, 1988.

23 Evans, 1974 and 1992. See also McCall, Lombardo, and Morrison (1988). Top leaders of notable multinational firms have the importance of providing challenge firmly in mind. For example, the consistent aim of Mads Ovlisen, architect and former CEO of the leading pharmaceutical multinational Novo Nordisk, was "to be the best and a challenging workplace." According to Ovlisen, these are two sides of the same coin.

24 Charan, Drotter, and Noel, 2001. See Hill (1992) for an analysis of the transition from individual contributor to manager.

25 Muller, 1970. See other studies in the journal *Advances in Global Leadership*.

26 See Maddux and Galinsky (2009), and many other publications by them and other co-authors.

27 Leung *et al.*, 2008.

28 Godart *et al.*, 2015.

29 DDI, "Global leadership forecast 2008/2009: Overcoming the shortfalls in developing leaders," by A. Howard and R. Wellins, 2008, www.ddiworld.com/leadershipforecast/.

30 These team skills, necessary for lateral coordination, were discussed in Chapter 5.

31 See the discussion in Chapter 4 in the section "Building Cross-Border Teams."

32 McKinsey Quarterly, "Why leadership-development programs fail," January 2014.

33 Cappelli, 2008.

34 Galunic and Andersen, 2000. In any case, almost all training is general, in that it would be useful to at least some alternative employers.

35 Action learning was reportedly disseminated first by Revens (1980). See also Conger and Benjamin (1999). See Raelin (1999) for a review of action learning. It should be noted that in a high-context society such as Japan, learning processes are mostly project oriented or experiential—there is little emphasis beyond school and university on Western-style didactic learning (Nonaka and Takeuchi, 1995).

36 McCall and Hollenbeck, 2002.

37 "Learning and development: Annual Survey Report 2008," CIPD, United Kingdom, www.cipd.co.uk/NR/rdonlyres/3A3AD4D6-F818-4231-863B-4848CE383B46/0/ learningdevelopmentsurvey.pdf.

38 Goleman, 2000.

39 See Higgins and Kram (2001) for a review of mentoring from a wider network perspective.

40 Competitive advantage in many industries depends on coupling technical capabilities with market-facing customer knowledge. While some coordination can be provided by structural mechanisms such as cross-boundary steering groups, tight coupling in leadership roles can come from what Intel calls "two-in-the-box" assignments. These are development assignments where shared responsibility for managing a significant project is given to two people, one with a strong technical background who may be on a career ladder to a senior technology management position and the other with a strong commercial or business background who is on a high-potential managerial ladder. For further analysis, see Alvarez and Svejenova (2005). The research of Belbin (1981) on eight complementary team roles provides an underlying rationale.

41 "Gamechanger," *BusinessWeek*, March 12, 2009.

42 Eddy, Hall, and Robinson, 2006.

43 Carraher, Sullivan, and Crocitto, 2008.

44 Lepsinger and Lucia, 1997.

45 There is a vast research literature on selection methods and tests according to culture and context. See, for example, *The International Journal of Selection and Assessment*. See Brewster,

Sparrow, and Vernon (2007) for a more detailed overview from the perspective of the international corporation.

46 "Leadership 2012," Research Report, Corporate University Xchange, Harrisburg PA, 2007; cited by Cappelli (2008, p. 145).

47 The origins of this process title, Session C, apparently go far back into the history of GE's strategic and business planning processes. Originally this included sessions A and B, but these have long since been abandoned.

48 Chua, Engeli, and Stahl, 2005.

49 Spreitzer, McCall, and Mahoney, 1997; McCall, 1998; McCall and Hollenbeck, 2002; Hollenbeck and McCall 2001. See also Lombardo and Eichinger (2000).

50 Bennis and Nanus, 1985.

51 Briscoe and Hall, 1999.

52 Agrawal and Kets de Vries, 2006.

53 Pucik, 1984.

54 This was shown by a natural experiment that occurred at Exxon some years ago. Many Exxon executives started their careers at one of the two refineries in the US. However, senior management consistently came from one of them, Baton Rouge. Why? There was only one explanatory difference—at Baton Rouge, leadership potential was identified at age 27–28, at the other refinery the target age was in the early 30s.

55 Gelens *et al.*, 2014.

56 Björkman and Mäkalä, 2013.

57 The Commonwealth Edison and Tatweer examples are taken from Cappelli (2008, pp. 197–9).

58 Martin and Schmidt, 2010.

59 Mellahi and Collings, 2010.

60 Guthridge, Komm, and Lawson, 2008.

61 "Best companies for leaders," November 2005, www.chiefexecutive.net.

62 Smale, A., I. Björkman, and J. Saarinen, "Pushing the right button: Global talent management at KONE Corporation," Aalto University and University of Vaasa, Finland, available via Case Centre, 2014.

63 Mellahi and Collings, 2010.

64 Mäkelä, Björkman, and Ehrnrooth, 2010.

65 Eddy, Hall, and Robinson, 2006.

66 "Best companies for leaders," November 2005, www.chiefexecutive.net.

67 McCall 1998. Cappelli (2008) points out that great value in talent management comes from exactly that process of spotting "hidden" local talent and nurturing its development, rather than developing more obvious talent that is already clearly labeled by degrees and qualifications and thereby more likely to leave the firm for opportunities elsewhere.

68 Huselid, Beatty, and Becker, 2005; Boudreau and Ramstad, 2007.

69 Collings and Mellahi, 2009; Lepak and Snell, 2002.

70 The idea of firm-specific leadership skills has been developed further by Ulrich and Smallwood (2007) using the concept of building a leadership brand. They regard about 60–70 percent of leadership skills as generic (vision, the ability to deliver results, interpersonal skills, etc.) and 30–40 percent as specific to the industry and the capabilities of the firm.

71 DDI, 2008.

72 Cappelli, 2008.

73 See Cappelli (2008) for a more comprehensive overview of these issues.

74 Cappelli, 2008. The cost of replacing an unskilled person is usually one or two times the monthly salary, while for a senior executive it may be 10 or 15 times that monthly salary (Cascio, 2000; also Lawler, 2008).

75 There is a relative vacuum in research on technical talent management. However, see Kim *et al.* (2014).

76 STEM stands for Science, Technology, Engineering, and Mathematics, in other words the technical or professional disciplines.

77 Allen and Katz, 1986.

78 See, for example, a review by Shaw *et al.* (1998) of more than 1,500 studies on the topic; and the meta-analysis by Griffeth, Hom, and Gaertner (2000).

79 See, for example, Branham (2005).

80 Talent Research in 2005 reported by Cappelli (2008).

81 Evans and Bartolomé, 1979; Bartolomé and Evans, 1980. We found that the stress of work, for example in a mismatch between employee and function, spills over into private life, compromising psychological availability. The misfit would feel a sense of work–life imbalance, whereas another individual working the same hours would perceive no imbalance.

82 "The 10 most forward-thinking leaders in workforce management," *Workforce Management*, March 13, 2006.

83 IBM, 2005, "The Capability Within: The Global Human Capital Study," www.ibm.com/services/us/bcs/html/2005_human_cap_mgt_gen.html. This report is the source of other data in this paragraph.

84 Tian, Harvey, and Slocum, 2014.

chapter

9

Steering Global Mobility

SUMMARY

Challenge

International mobility is one of the key tools for enhancing horizontal coordination, but many companies find it difficult to manage cross-border assignments

Analysis

Effective mobility management requires:

- Creating an environment where mobility is seen as positive for employee careers
- Maintaining HR policies that provide a diverse employee population with opportunities for international experience

Solutions

- Provide cross-border career opportunities regardless of the passport
- Link international assignments with leadership development needs
- Pay attention to the family and the implications of dual careers
- Increase the use of short-term learning assignments and other alternatives to traditional expatriate assignments
- Plan for repatriation early in the mobility cycle

Promoting Global Mobility at Schlumberger

Founded by two brothers, Conrad and Marcel Schlumberger, in France in 1927, Schlumberger is now a US$ 48 billion giant in the oil services industry, with no central headquarters, four "principal offices" (Paris, Houston, London, and The Hague), and a Norwegian oilman with extensive global experience as CEO. The Schlumberger brothers invented a way of detecting oil located deep in the ground by lowering electrical wires down a drilling hole. Today Schlumberger offers most of the services that an oil company needs to explore and produce oil, from seismic mapping to integrated project management, on a fixed-fee basis. Even during the slump

265

in the global oil industry, Schlumberger has been able to maintain healthy profit margins—earning more than US$ 5 billion in 2014.

Global oil majors like ExxonMobil and Shell depend on Schlumberger's services, as do the national oil-producing companies that control the bulk of oil reserves around the world, such as Saudi Arabia's Aramco, Brazil's Petrobras, and Kazakhstan's KazMunaiGaz. Countries with oil reserves want to control the revenues from their oil, but they do not have the necessary technical skills. Rather than sharing the revenues with a Western oil major to access those skills, as they did in the past, they have turned to Schlumberger. With over 100,000 mostly professional employees recruited from 140 nationalities, the company is present in 85 countries—including 10 percent working in Russia. Andrew Gould, former CEO who guided the company through a major global expansion, commented that "Russia could one day be as big for us as the US," where Schlumberger gets nearly 30 percent of its revenues.[1]

A good part of the competitive advantage that Schlumberger enjoys over competitors such as Halliburton and Baker Hughes dates back to a bold initiative the firm took in the early 1990s, when it decided that people and technology would be the two strategic drivers of business growth. Its spending on R&D is larger than for all competitors combined. To support its technology focus, Schlumberger recruits in its regions of operations, and it invests actively in developing local talent in petroleum geology and geophysics in emerging markets like Russia, Kazakhstan, and China, building close relationships with the top local engineering schools.

Young employees are attracted to the firm because they know that they will receive the best learning opportunities in the industry through classroom training and project work. One of the pulls for bright engineers in China, Nigeria, and Mexico is that Schlumberger is renowned for treating everyone in the same way, regardless of passport, when it comes to training, careers, and compensation. In a culture where "talent" equates with "engineers," performance is appraised by technical experts rather than managers.

Through lean and fat years, Schlumberger has consistently focused on cultivating great people. They are expected to be highly mobile; a senior Nigerian manager now working back home, for example, may have worked on every continent. Industry insiders envy Schlumberger's ability to attract, develop, and retain the best and brightest and to deploy them where needed, from the freezing tundra of Siberia to the charred deserts of Algeria. Mobility and diversity are integrated into the business model—close to 5,000 employees change country each year.

The status of "international mobile" is at the heart of the concept. It allows the company to do away with the notion of expatriation. Such employees, whether they are working in their own country or abroad, are considered "residents"; others may be "commuters," dispatched on operational assignments as necessary. When "residents" are posted outside of their home countries, they receive a comprehensive package—same for everyone, depending on local living conditions. For residents working in their home countries, these packages fall midway between those for local employees and expatriates—making it easy to return while retaining incentives to move again. However, while abroad, these residents have no commitment from the company that guarantees return home.

Schlumberger does have retention problems. Top drilling experts are lured away by 300-percent salary raises in an industry where talent is a key to success. Each such departure warrants a full investigation. Unlike many other firms, high performers from other disciplines often do a stint in human resources (including the current CEO), and 40 percent of the HR staff are so-called visitors. "The capacity to develop talent from anywhere in the world is one of our key strengths," said Gould, and even its closest competitors would agree, envying the company's profitable growth.[2]

OVERVIEW

International mobility is crucial for multinational firms. It supports the initial expansion and growth abroad; provides a foundation for cross-border control and coordination, contributes to transfer of know-how among various subunits, and helps employees to acquire critical skills and competencies required to manage and steer a global organization. In this chapter we will focus on the challenges of managing international mobility effectively.

We discuss first the drivers and growth of international mobility and the changing demographics of international employees. The core of the chapter explores the key stages of the international assignment cycle—from selection and preparation to compensation and repatriation—and reviews core practices supporting effective cross-border mobility. We conclude with a discussion of current trends, ongoing challenges, and possible future scenarios.

WHY MOBILITY MATTERS

In a number of previous chapters, we have identified international mobility as a critical HRM process supporting globalization. For example, moving employees across national boundaries is instrumental to:

- Reinforcing global integration through the personal control that expatriates exercise since they identify with the corporation rather than the local unit
- Advancing localization to the extent that expatriates share their knowledge and develop local successers
- Enhancing the quality of horizontal coordination
- Building global social architecture by promoting shared values, creating social capital across borders, and developing global mindsets
- Getting the right people in the right place—accessing the best talent and placing those people where they can generate the most value
- Developing the competencies of global leaders as well as providing challenging growth jobs.

In subsequent chapters, we will also illustrate how international mobility supports knowledge management and plays a role in implementing international M&As and strategic alliances. While many operational issues regarding mobility can (and should) be outsourced to specialist providers, setting up a mobility framework aligned with business strategies should be a priority for all multinationals and a key responsibility of the HR function.

Changing Composition of International Staff

In Chapter 3 we presented a framework that identified different roles of the international staff based on the purpose of the assignment (demand driven or learning driven) and its expected duration (long term or short term). We also cited evidence that a large majority of international assignments are still made for agency reasons (management control, problem-solving, or knowledge transfer) and are relatively long term.

It was not surprising, therefore, that mobility policies and practices regarding international staff have been geared to employees on agency-driven assignments—based on a number of assumptions about a typical expatriate's characteristics:

- International assignees are selected from the employees in the parent country
- The expatriate population is homogeneous in ethnicity, gender, and experience—male, experienced, possibly married but with an adaptable spouse, and originating from the parent country

- Expatriate assignments are relatively long term but temporary (three to four years' duration)
- The objective of the assignment is to maintain control over the affiliate and to transfer know-how from the sophisticated parent to the dependent subsidiary
- After completion of the assignment, an expatriate is expected to return home, to be replaced by another expatriate.

These assumptions are less and less valid. The expatriate population is increasingly heterogeneous, and a contingent approach to expatriation is needed.[3] Surveys report that more than 40 percent of international assignees are relocated to/from a country other than the one where the headquarters is located.[4] In a number of multinationals, the prototypical experienced male executive from the parent country is already in the minority.

PCNs, TCNs, HCNs, and Other Species

Many expatriates come from neither the parent nor the host country and are commonly referred to as third-country nationals (TCNs)—in contrast to parent-country nationals (PCNs) or host-country nationals (HCNs). Historically, two factors drove TCN employment: the scarcity in the home country of suitable candidates for international assignments and attempts to hold down the cost of expatriation. For example, a US multinational sought to employ expatriates from the UK, Canada, and Australia, countries with a common language and comparable compensation and living standards. Today, TCNs are sometimes the most talented candidates for a position, although differences in how frequently MNCs from different countries use TCN assignees can be observed.[5]

The buildup of regional coordinating structures fosters an increase in the number of TCNs. Even in US-based multinationals, most expatriates in Central and Eastern Europe come from other EU countries; for multinationals in China, Taiwan is a major source of expertise; and Indian managers and executives are well-represented among international staff in Southeast Asia. Some European companies are experimenting with a single employment status within the EU, possibly rendering the PCN/TCN dichotomy obsolete in that region.

The traditional definition of expatriation also assumed that nationality (passport), ethnicity, and cultural background are correlated. Many recent immigrants and their children (such as American-born Chinese working in China) do not fit this stereotype. Children of past expatriates who grew up abroad, or others who experienced a multicultural environment through education, also bring additional cultural diversity to the expatriate pool. With accelerating globalization, companies are increasingly looking for the most suitable candidate, irrespective of country of origin. For example, the cohort of senior international managers at HSBC—people expected to move globally—includes nearly 400 managers from more than 30 countries. Half of the latest intake were women.[6]

Women in International Assignments

Until the late 1980s, only 3–5 percent of all American expatriates were women. According to recent surveys, this proportion has increased to 20–25 percent in multinationals around the world,[7] still leaving a considerable gap (see the box "Research on Women in International Assignments").

Research on Women in International Assignments

Scholars have identified "three common myths" about female expatriates:[9]

- Women do not want to become international managers
- Companies refuse to send women overseas
- Even when women are interested in international assignments, the prejudices of foreigners against women may render them ineffective.

Exploration of these "myths" stimulated a number of studies of female expatriates, particularly in the United States and Europe.[10] One stream of research focuses on *the desire of women to become expatriates*. Examining responses from more than 1,000 students from multiple universities, Adler concluded that male and female students displayed no differences regarding their interest in pursuing international careers.[11] Similar results were observed in a more recent study.[12] However, there is also some evidence of differences in the willingness of males and females to accept foreign assignments to culturally distant and less-developed locations.[13]

With respect to *willingness to select female expatriates*, Adler concluded that 70 percent of HR professionals in 60 multinational companies were hesitant to choose women.[14] Among the reasons presented were difficulties in accommodating dual careers and gender prejudice in the countries to which women would be sent. It has also been argued that qualified female employees may be overlooked because men make most of the decisions about whom to send, and many hold traditional stereotypes about women in international jobs.[15]

Several studies have focused on *the adjustment and performance of female expatriates*. Female American expatriates were found to be just as successful as their counterparts overseas—even in so-called male-dominated cultures such as Japan and Korea.[16] Other results suggest that male and female expatriates can perform equally well in international assignments regardless of the host country's predisposition to women in management but that female expatriates self-rate their adjustment lower in countries with few women in the workforce.[17] Female expatriates were perceived as effective regardless of the cultural toughness of the host country.[18]

In a string of studies, a number of explanations for the small number of female expatriates have been proposed: cultural prejudices, including low acceptance of working women in certain countries; lack of support and access to male-dominated expatriate networks; inflexibility and resentment by male peers; particular difficulties linked to family and dual-career issues; and the unwillingness of women to accept foreign assignments.[8]

In the past, companies with a high number of women in international assignments were more likely to report problems resulting from the inability of spouses to continue their careers.[19] Even today, and despite progress, it still seems more difficult for women to reconcile international assignments with the careers of their spouses. Not surprisingly, therefore, a higher percentage of women on international assignments are single—approximately 33 percent, compared to about 27 percent of men.[20]

Some studies have pointed out that in international assignments women may actually have an advantage over men. For example, until more women take over expatriate roles, their relative visibility and novelty may enhance their access to local business networks.[21] It has been argued that women tend to possess attributes that make them more suitable for overseas work than men, such as indirectness in communication, good listening skills, and emphasis on cooperation over competition.[22] Also, because female executives have long experience of being "outsiders," they may be better equipped to manage the stress that often accompanies isolation in foreign settings.

MANAGING MOBILITY

Making an international assignment a success for the individual, the family, and the firm requires paying attention to many factors, from the time of initial selection until repatriation. A starting point is the recognition that mobility is a process, not an event, which can be broken down into a sequence of distinct HRM activities (see Figure 9-1).

We will discuss each of these activities in the "assignment cycle" separately, although naturally they are closely linked.[23] The issues relevant to the later parts of the cycle have to be anticipated earlier—for example, repatriation has to be taken into account at the selection phase.

Selecting Expatriates

Surveys show that it is essential for firms to pay attention to technical expertise and domestic track record, and there are some indications that European multinationals give additional weight to language skills and international adaptability.[24] The selection process is often informal and ad hoc, characterized by what Harris and Brewster label the "coffee machine" system.[25] Candidates are likely to be known personally to the senior managers in the parent company, and the real selection decisions tend to be made in informal discussions "by the coffee machine." Discussions on the selection criteria are rare—the position is seldom announced openly (or when it is, it is already clear who the preferred person is), and there is little formal assessment of the person chosen.[26] This is clearly inadequate, and there is broad academic agreement that organizations should make stronger efforts to develop their selection routines. What does research say about the characteristics of successful expatriates?

Characteristics of Successful Expatriates

Researchers have found a large number of factors to be important for successful expatriation. One cross-cultural textbook identified 68 dimensions, 21 of which

FIGURE 9-1
Mobility Management Cycle

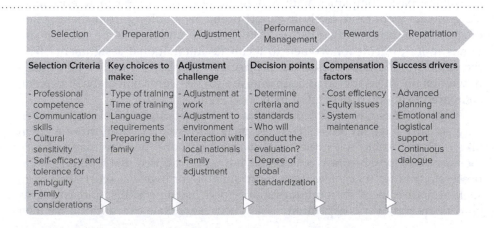

were deemed highly desirable,[27] while another review identified 73 skills necessary for cross-cultural learning.[28] If one adds up all these characteristics, the ideal expatriate is close to superhuman! Most of the key factors, however, can be grouped into the following categories:

- Professional and technical competence
- Relationship and communication abilities
- Cultural sensitivity and flexibility
- Self-efficacy and tolerance for ambiguity
- Family support.[29]

Appropriate professional and technical competence is a prerequisite for most international assignments. Even if the expatriate is not expected to be operationally effective immediately, the person must have the relevant training and experience to learn on the job. However, research indicates that many non-work psychological factors, including the personal situation of the expatriate, are important in predicting the success of international assignees.[30]

A meta-analysis of 66 studies on expatriate adjustment and performance concluded that *relational and communication skills* were the strongest predictor of international adjustment.[31] These help the expatriate build necessary collaboration, giving the person access to local knowledge and the feedback that speeds up learning.[32]

Cultural sensitivity and flexibility refers to the expatriate's ability to understand and respond to differences between countries and situations. Expatriates who are not judgmental about the behavior of foreigners are more likely to learn, adjust, and perform well, and these qualities are found to be positively associated with expatriate performance.[33]

There is evidence from several studies that *self-efficacy*[34] and *tolerance for ambiguity*[35] can help expatriates adjust and perform well on their assignments. The former refers to an expatriate's belief in his or her own ability to act and perform. Individuals with a healthy measure of self-confidence are more likely to act and learn from the outcome of their actions. International assignments often put expatriates in situations where they need to have a high tolerance for ambiguity and the ability to cope with stress.

The adjustment and *support of the family* emerges as one of the strongest predictors of expatriate adjustment.[36] It also features consistently as the main factor influencing expatriates' decisions to return prematurely from their assignments.

The relevance of such traits and skills depends on the expatriate role. For agency-type assignments, clear managerial qualifications and proven leadership skills are the foundation. Such expatriates should also be able to improvise in response to unexpected changes, impart confidence to their supervisors in their ability to deal with difficult situations, and motivate local people to cooperate. For learning-oriented assignments, relationship abilities and cultural awareness may be more important, as these are the keys to accessing new knowledge.

How do international companies respond to these recommendations? The emphasis is clearly on enlarging the pool of potential candidates for international assignments beyond persons from the home country of the multinational and on making sure that the international track attracts those with the best potential to succeed in the firm. Assessments for international assignment are becoming closely linked to the overall evaluation of an employee's potential and are also increasingly rigorous.

Assessment process.   Few multinationals rely on standardized tests for evaluating expatriates, including psychological profiling, cultural proficiency tests, or family-readiness evaluations.[37] There is no shortage of tools, though not all are well validated. Some companies use formal assessments only to evaluate candidates after they have been identified for an international assignment; others screen all college graduates for future success as "global managers."

By far the most common selection method is simply to interview the potential candidate. Appropriately structured interview techniques can increase effectiveness.[38] When formal assessment is used, it is argued that it should not be implemented to screen out unsuitable candidates.[39] Instead, the results should provide the employee with objective feedback. This allows the potential expatriate (and family) to consider carefully all the factors that may influence the success of the assignment, to get advice on how to deal with problematic areas, or to decline the assignment.

Many experienced international firms send potential expatriates on a pre-assignment orientation visit. This helps the local host to evaluate the candidate's fit with the environment and allows the candidate to review the job and location before agreeing. These visits can preempt costly surprises later and may be valuable even after both sides agree to the assignment since the family can anticipate adjustment problems. This minimizes the stress of divided attention between family and work during the demanding period of settling into a new job abroad.

What about the family?   Family considerations have a critical impact on an individual's willingness to relocate and the outcome of the assignment. The decisions of American managers to relocate were found to be influenced by their spouse's feelings about international relocation, by their own attitude toward moving in general, by the number of children at home, and by the employer's transfer policies. One of the major reasons why people are reluctant to relocate is their children's schooling.[40] Opportunities for a spouse or a partner to continue his or her career while abroad is also an important factor in influencing the acceptance decision.

Dual-Career Considerations

Often there are no available jobs for spouses at the new location, a situation aggravated by obstacles like visa regulations, professional licensing rules, and language barriers. And even if a job is available locally, it may not contribute to a meaningful career, reducing the likelihood that the couple will be willing to move.

How can companies respond to this challenge? Multinational firms can use a number of measures to mediate the pressure of dual careers:

- Plan the assignment in terms of location, timing, and duration based on professional preferences and personal circumstances of the couple

- Approach the partner's employer and jointly prepare expatriation plans
- Provide career counseling and assistance in locating employment opportunities for spouses abroad
- Subsidize educational programs for spouses while abroad
- Support entrepreneurial initiatives by spouses
- Cooperate with other multinational organizations in finding jobs for spouses

- Provide reemployment advice to partners after repatriation.

None of these are silver bullets that will solve the problem for everyone, but in most cases, even modest progress in reducing barriers to mobility will have a positive impact on the pool of future global managers.

Virtually all research studies highlight the importance of family well-being, including spouse and children. The lack of consideration of this, in Western cultures at least, emerges as one of the most significant explanations of expatriate failure.[41] The challenges associated with a new job in a new culture, combined with stress on the family, put people under intense pressure, greatly reducing the likelihood of effective adjustment.

The solution? Whenever possible, select a family, not a person. Not surprisingly, a number of international firms involve the candidate's spouse, if not the whole family, in the process of assessment and counseling, particularly in pre-departure training.[42]

Research shows that spouses are more likely to adjust to living in a new culture when firms actively seek their opinion of the assignment.[43] "Buying off" the family to gain acceptance can be shortsighted, as a temporary increase in standard of living can make successful repatriation more difficult.

The issue of dual careers, discussed in the previous paragraphs, is often easier to manage among younger expatriates. Their partners (if there are any) may be more flexible about job opportunities in the local market, as they risk less by taking an international career detour. Placing younger employees who are single or who have small families in international jobs can substantially reduce the total compensation cost; the expenses involved in family expatriation (housing, education, and home leave) can easily surpass the salary cost at lower professional levels.

Is it OK to say no?   We have pointed out that a properly executed assessment can provide a candidate with feedback before making the final decision on whether to accept the assignment.[44] But what happens if the potential expatriate declines the offer?

The answer varies across firms. In some, where management considers international mobility to be an integral part of the employment relationship, a refusal could mean the end of a promising career. For junior staff in some international British firms, or in Japan in the not-so-distant past, expatriate assignments were an inherent component of executive development—the issue was not if, but when.[45] Part of the folklore were tales of hardship endured when the boss called on the second day of the honeymoon. However, it is important to note that these expectations were clearly communicated to staff before they joined the company.

There is a strong case to be made for the principle that an individual should not be penalized for declining a job,[46] especially if acceptance would involve perceived hardship for the family. Lack of commitment or desire to work internationally only increases the likelihood of failure. However, since companies try to ensure that senior executives have international experience, some degree of international mobility is fast becoming a necessary prerequisite for career success.

Preparing for the Assignment

There is strong agreement about the need to invest in thorough training and pre-departure orientation in both the academic and practitioner literature.[47] Early planning and training are important for the growing number of companies where international experience is a key component in management development.[48] Offering pre-departure and arrival support is also a good way to show that the company cares about expatriates and their families.

Insufficient commitment to expatriate training and development is one of the most common criticisms leveled at HR practice in multinational companies. Surveys indicate that most companies offer some kind of cross-cultural training to at least some expatriates and their spouses. According to recent surveys, 39 percent of the companies offered cross-cultural training for all assignments, 45 percent for some, and 59 percent for certain countries only.[49] Training programs are more often organized for expatriates from the parent company than for people from other countries.[50] The programs are seldom mandatory; in reality, many expatriates receive no training before leaving for the assignment.

Let us focus on certain important questions about expatriate training and development. What kind of expatriate training is desirable? When should training take place? Is language competence essential? And again, what about the expatriate's family?

What kind of training?   The greater the cultural distance from the host country and the more social interaction the job involves, the greater the need is for cross-cultural training.[51] Today there is an abundance of training tools in this domain, including cultural briefings, books, videos, case studies, cross-cultural simulations, and Web sites. But not all preparation takes place in a classroom—there are pre-assignment visits, "shadowing" visits while the soon-to-be expatriate is still in his or her previous job, coaching by an experienced manager, and open dialogue on key issues that emerge during the selection process.[52]

The right kind of cross-cultural training is important since a poor program that reinforces cultural stereotypes can have a negative impact on expatriate adjustment and performance. No one training methodology will be universally appropriate—the preparation for a European plant manager who is to be dispatched to China is bound to be different from that of a Japanese bank trainee on the way to New York. The training should be customized to match the needs of the expatriates and their families.

When should training take place?   Some companies start this process a long time before departure to ensure thorough preparation.[53] Others argue persuasively that training about the host culture is best linked to the expatriate's experience and conducted after the assignment begins: the pre-departure orientation is kept brief and practical, and more complex cultural issues are left for later.[54] Early training may build stereotypes, whereas real assimilation involves understanding the subtle differences within a culture, something that comes only with experience. However, from a practical viewpoint, many expatriates, especially those in executive positions, are too busy to attend a formal training program after the start of their assignments. Real-time coaching is usually the ideal solution, albeit an expensive one.[55] Without company commitment and a specific training plan built into the workload, it will be difficult to find time for any formal learning during the assignment.

Some multinationals involve the receiving subsidiary in supporting newly arrived expatriates. Intel has a "buddy system," where local peers are appointed as ad hoc trainers and cross-cultural interpreters for their foreign colleagues. The company also offers training to managers who are about to receive an expatriate.[56] Expatriates who have access to host-country mentors demonstrate superior adjustment to their work and greater interaction with host country nationals.[57]

Is language competency essential?   Everyone would agree that knowledge of the local language is beneficial—but is it a "must" or simply desirable? The answer depends on the nature of the job. Many expatriate jobs are focused on control and coordination, for which English is rapidly becoming the company language. Local language proficiency may not be critical for such assignments. However, when the assignment requires extensive interaction with local customers or local employees who may not speak English or any other global "office language," the ability to speak the local language may be essential.

Accumulated research evidence suggests that language fluency helps expatriates develop interpersonal relationships and adjust to living overseas. However, no clear relationship has been found between language ability and work adjustment, with the notable exception of non-native English-speaking expatriates on assignments in English-speaking countries.[58]

Our own experience suggests an additional dimension to the language issue. Often the effort and commitment shown by expatriates in trying to learn and use the local language counts for far more than their proficiency in it. An effort to learn shows respect for the local culture, and that is appreciated anywhere in the world.

Preparing the family   The expatriate's family, or at least the spouse, deserves the same attention and preparation as the expatriate. The spouse is typically more exposed to the local culture than the expatriate, and learning the local language may be even more important for him or her. Again, learning opportunities after the start of the assignment may be more valuable than pre-departure training, especially as the spouse is unlikely to have the same immediate job constraints.

Adjusting to the Expatriate Role

When people move to an unfamiliar environment, they have to learn to adjust to new behaviors, norms, values, and assumptions. Most people are familiar with the notion of culture shock. Although individual experiences vary, this is fairly often a U-shaped process of adjustment in which an initial honeymoon stage of excitement, stress, and adventure leads to a depressive downswing, a phase of shock, frustration, and uncertainty about how to behave. Ideally, this heralds an upswing of learning and adaptation. Digging further into culture shock, researchers have spelled out three dimensions of cross-cultural adjustment (defined as the degree of psychological comfort associated with living and working in the host country): adjustment to work, general adjustment, and interaction adjustment.[59]

The first dimension is *adjustment to work* in the new environment. If the job is unclear, if there is inherent conflict in the role, and if there is little discretion in the work, adjustment is likely to be difficult. Some companies schedule an overlap with the outgoing jobholder to ease some of these strains. In the globally integrated firm, adjustment to work may be the easiest aspect of adjustment because of similarities in procedures, policies, and tasks across the firm.

The second dimension is *adjustment to the general environment*—reactions to housing, safety, food, education, transportation, and health conditions. These difficulties increase with cultural distance. Companies try to minimize the problems through housing and educational allowances. Previous international experience, effective preparation for both expatriate and family, and spending time with other expatriates before the assignment may facilitate this aspect of adjustment.

The challenge of *adjustment to interaction with local nationals* is generally the most difficult for the expatriate and the family. Behavioral norms, patterns of communication, and ways of dealing with conflict may be different in the new culture, creating frustration or even anger, which may in turn be counterproductive. Each individual's adjustment is linked to the quality of the support network inside the host country, as well as to the time spent with other expatriates before the assignment and to connections with the home office.

Family adjustment matters. To facilitate this, Honda has "family centers" in Ohio and Tokyo to help with the cultural adaptation process. In addition, families of American employees transferred to Japan are "adopted" by Japanese families with similar characteristics (for example, children of the same age). Mentors, who keep the expatriate informed of changes in the home organization, are assigned to each expatriate before departure.

These adaptation challenges are greatly helped by investment in training and feedback. Nevertheless, there are limits to what an organization can do. Much depends on the expatriate's personality, motivation to be transferred abroad, and willingness to learn from the new environment—especially during early stages of the assignment.[60] The ultimate indication of cross-cultural adjustment is the ability to feel at home in a foreign culture without rejecting one's own roots.[61]

Balancing Multiple Allegiances

One element of the adjustment process is finding the right balance between potentially conflicting allegiances to the parent firm and to the foreign operation. Researchers have outlined four generic patterns of expatriate commitment, contrasting those who leave their hearts at home with those who go native (see Figure 9-2).[62]

Free agents are marked by low allegiance to both the parent and the local firm. They are committed to their career. They do not expect to return home, either because they understand that their career in the parent firm has already reached a plateau or because they see their international experience as increasing their value on the external market. Some free agents may do fine in an isolated affiliate, and companies undergoing rapid internationalization may need such hired guns. As a rule, however, their lack of commitment quickly becomes transparent to local staff, diminishing their credibility.

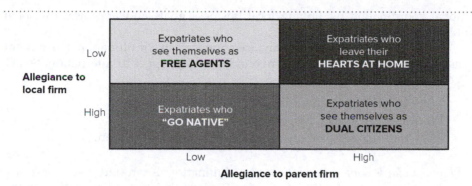

FIGURE 9-2
The Dual Allegiance of
Expatriates

Source: Adapted from S. Black, H. Gregersen, and M. Mendenhall (1992), *Global Assignments: Successfully Expatriating and Repatriating International Managers* (San Francisco: Jossey-Bass).

Another group of expatriates—usually those with long tenure in the parent firm and little previous international experience—*leave their heart at home*, remaining emotionally attached to the parent firm with little allegiance to local operations. This attitude is reinforced by discomfort with the local culture and strong networks with senior executives back home. Their behavior is often ethnocentric, which may antagonize employees or customers, although their ability to work easily with headquarters may make them valuable in situations where close global coordination is required. This group can benefit most from cross-cultural training and other tools facilitating adjustment.

Some expatriates exhibit the opposite pattern and *go native*, building a strong identification with the local firm and culture. They are difficult to repatriate, often preferring to leave the firm and remain in their new home. The parent office finds it difficult to get their cooperation for the implementation of corporate policies and programs. They do not fit well into a meganational firm, though they may thrive in a multidomestic organization that can capitalize on their ability to build trust and support with local employees and stakeholders.

Obviously, the ideal outcome would be to develop expatriates who have *dual allegiance*, although research shows that this is the exception rather than the rule.[63] Expatriates who see themselves as "dual citizens" feel a responsibility to serve the interest of both parties. They deal effectively with the local environment, but they are also responsive to the needs of the parent firm, facilitating the coordination of global initiatives. The work environment—role clarity, job discretion, and a manageable degree of role conflict—is critical to the development of dual citizens. Role clarity and job discretion can be addressed through appropriate job design; manageable role conflict is closely linked to the implementation of an effective expatriate performance-management system.

Appraising Performance and International Staff

In Chapter 7 we discussed the importance of performance management for lateral coordination across the global firm. Probably no other group of employees in a multinational firm has a bigger impact on global coordination than home or third country nationals on international assignments. Performance management of international staff—from senior managers to trainees in development positions—is therefore a critical HRM process that can facilitate (or hinder) global coordination by linking local business goals and appraisal to global objectives and standards.

However, conducting performance appraisals in a multinational firm is not easy, and the difficulties are compounded with respect to international staff. We will focus on three key issues:[64]

- What criteria and standards should be used
- Who should conduct the performance evaluation
- Degree of standardization across the expatriate population.

What standards and criteria to use? Multinationals around the world use similar criteria in evaluating the performance of their subsidiaries, though the specific targets and standards will obviously be different.[65] However, when it comes to the performance-evaluation process of expatriates, there are greater differences between firms. Some companies keep expatriates in the parent-country pool for appraisal purposes, and some treat expatriates as they would a local employee in the same job.

Many environmental factors, such as exchange rate fluctuations, local borrowing costs, and differences in the tax regime, have an impact on the performance of the subsidiary, which in turn will affect the performance evaluation of expatriates occupying senior management positions in these subsidiaries. Defining performance in multinational firms is a complex issue that goes well beyond matters of accounting, and the way in which performance is measured can have a major impact on how expatriates act. In most situations, objective (measurable) performance criteria (global or local) will have to be supplemented with subjective and contextual ones.[66]

Another critical tension that impacts performance criteria for international staff is the difference in the time horizon of expatriates and locals—short-term success in the job versus accountability for the long-term performance of the business unit. Indeed, short-term focus is one of the most frequent criticisms leveled at expatriate managers by their local subordinates.[67] Rightly or wrongly, expatriates are often perceived as caring about results only within the time frame of their expected assignments.

Who should conduct the evaluation? A frequent complaint about international staff appraisal is that many expatriates are evaluated mainly by superiors or HR managers in the home office who may not have much international experience.[68] One global expatriate survey suggested that about 50 percent of the expatriates were monitored and evaluated at least in part by executives in their home countries.[69] Can such raters make a correct evaluation? It seems fair to suggest that only those who can observe them in action can have a solid opinion about their developmental needs. And this may also lead expatriates to spend more effort in managing the center rather than the business. On the other hand, if the performance of the international employees is only evaluated in the host country, there is a risk that the global perspective will be neglected. The use of multiple raters, located both in the host country and in the parent organization, or some form of 360-degree appraisal, is likely to produce the most valid evaluations.[70]

The extent to which local managers have an input into the performance appraisal of expatriates is a good indication of the degree to which the company is following a meaningful localization strategy. Yet such inputs do not eliminate the risk of negative results. In one major multinational, local members of staff were politely praiseworthy of even overtly incompetent expatriates. They knew that if they said anything negative, they would be saddled with the individual for a longer period of time!

Does one system fit all? Most companies use globally standardized procedures and forms for appraising the performance of expatriates.[71] However, the criteria used to evaluate the performance of the expatriate should reflect the purpose of the assignment—be it corporate agency, problem-solving, building experience, or competence development.[72]

One of the lessons from the global expansion of an international telecommunications firm is that performance objectives for international staff should be differentiated in the sense that expatriates who occupy different roles should be measured on different criteria.[73] For example, expatriates in senior manager positions were usually appraised by executives from the home office, and their appraisals were likely to have a longer-term focus. Expatriates in the middle manager group were typically appraised by locally based executives, with the appraisals and incentives linked more to local, short-term goals.

In our view, there is much to recommend in the practice of this corporation. It classified expatriates into five broad groups based on the nature of their job assignment: (1) senior managers, (2) middle managers, (3) business development, (4) project engineers and specialists, and (5) R&D professionals. A tight alignment between the purpose of the assignment and the objectives to be evaluated is a necessary foundation for linking the appraisal to rewards—if the upstream of the performance-management process does not fit, the downstream will fail as well. However, few multinationals at this time have adopted such a differentiated approach, which indeed involves tackling additional complexity.

International Compensation

Decisions on how expatriates should be rewarded can make a big impact on the effectiveness of global coordination—not to mention the cost. Surveys often show that the cost of expatriation is a major concern of international firms.[74] This is not surprising as the total cost burden for the company is estimated at two to four times an expatriate's salary, depending on the location of the assignment and the person's family situation.

Specialized external providers handle many administrative issues concerning expatriate compensation. Over the years, elaborate methodologies have been developed to account for cost-of-living differences between countries, to respond to variations in tax regimes, and to provide incentives for employees to work in so-called hardship areas. However, developing an effective international compensation system is a task that goes far beyond technical analysis. It is linked closely to the company's internationalization strategy, requiring careful attention from the HR policymakers at the top of the HR organization.[75]

The Evolution of International Compensation Strategies

Historically, an expatriate pay package was usually the result of individual negotiations. In the past, foreign assignments were not considered desirable from the point of view of career progression; financial incentives such as relocation premiums were common. The result was generally high expatriate compensation costs that continually escalated, accompanied by corresponding difficulties in repatriation after the completion of the assignment.

With the increasing number of expatriates, the ad hoc negotiation-driven approach outlived its usefulness. The next generation of compensation plans attempted to provide at least a common base—usually the home or host-country salary, whichever was highest—reducing the size of the negotiated component.[76] However, as the number of international employees continued to grow, there was a move away from location-specific approaches to more generic across-the-board compensation.

Today, a number of generic methodologies have emerged (see Table 9-1).[77] The selection of an international compensation plan is influenced primarily by three sets of considerations:

TABLE 9-1
A Summary of International Compensation Systems

	For whom most appropriate	Advantages	Disadvantages
Negotiation	• Special situations • Few expatriates	• Conceptually simple	• Breaks down as numbers of expatriates increase
Localization	• Permanent transfers and long-term assignments • Entry-level expatriates	• Simple to administer • Equity with local nationals	• Difficult with PCNs and TCNs from different economies • Requires negotiated supplements
Headquarters-based balance sheet	• Many nationalities work together for extended periods	• No nationality discrimination • Simple administration	• High compensation costs • TCNs difficult to repatriate
Home-country-based balance sheet	• Several nationalities of expatriates on out-and-back assignments	• Lower cost • Simple to repatriate TCNs	• Discrimination by nationality • Highly complex administration
Modified home-country-based balance sheet	• Many nationalities on project assignments	• Moderate cost • Moderately simple administration	• Lack of conceptual clarity
Lump-sum approaches	• Consistently short assignments (fewer than three years), followed by repatriation	• Resembles domestic compensation practices • Does not intrude on expatriate finances	• Exchange-rate variation makes it unworkable except for short assignments
International pay structures	• Senior executives of all nationalities	• Tax- and cost-effective • Expatriates and local nationals may be on the same compensation plan	• Inhibits mobility for lower levels of expatriates • Lack of consistency among locations
Cafeteria approaches	• Senior executives	• Tax- and cost-effective	• Options needed for each country • Difficult to use with lower-tier expatriates
Regional plans	• Large numbers of expatriates who are mobile within region(s)	• Less costly than global uniformity • Can be tailored to regional requirements	• Multiple plans to administer • Discrimination between regionalists and globalists
Multiple programs	• Many expatriates on different types of assignments	• Can tailor compensation programs to different types of expatriates • Possible lower compensation costs	• Difficulty of setting and maintaining categories • Discrimination by category • Very complex administration

Source: C. Reynolds, *Guide to Global Compensation and Benefits* (San Diego: Harcourt, 2001).

- Cost efficiency—making sure that the plan delivers the intended benefits in the most cost-effective manner (including tax consequences)[78]
- Equity issues—making sure that the plan is equitable irrespective of the assignment location or nationality of the expatriate
- Ease of system maintenance—making sure that the plan is relatively transparent and easy to administer.

The Balance Sheet Approach

We will examine in more detail the costs and benefits of one method that is commonly used by North American and European firms—the balance sheet approach—and we will also review some of the emerging trends in international compensation.[79]

The term "balance sheet" refers to any compensation system that is designed to enable expatriates to maintain a standard of living roughly equivalent to the standard of living in their own country, irrespective of the location of their assignment. As shown in Figure 9-3, home-country salary is divided proportionately into several components. A typical breakdown is goods and services, housing, taxes, and a reserve. Home and host-country expenses for each component are compared, and the expatriate is compensated for the increased cost.

The balance sheet approach is popular, as it is seen as maintaining in a reasonably cost-effective manner the purchasing power of the expatriate, thus eliminating most of the financial obstacles to mobility. In reality, given that many expatriates complain about reduced compensation upon repatriation,[80] this methodology tends to lead to overcompensation—but probably less so than most alternatives.

While the concept of balance sheet methodology is simple, it is complex to implement. For example, what is the home country for the purpose of the balance sheet calculations? When expatriates all come from the same country, work abroad for two to four years, and then are expected to return to their home country, there is no ambiguity. But if expatriates in the same foreign location come from different countries with substantially different costs of living,

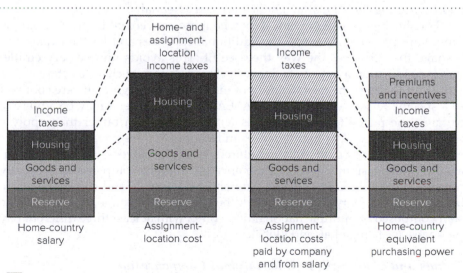

FIGURE 9-3
Balance Sheet Approach to International Compensation

Home-country salary:
- Income taxes
- Housing
- Goods and services
- Reserve

Assignment-location cost:
- Home- and assignment-location income taxes
- Housing
- Goods and services
- Reserve

Assignment-location costs paid by company and from salary:
- Income taxes
- Housing
- Goods and services
- Reserve

Home-country equivalent purchasing power:
- Premiums and incentives
- Income taxes
- Housing
- Goods and services
- Reserve

▨ Additional costs paid by the organization

Source: Adapted from C. Reynolds, Guide to Global Compensation and Benefits (San Diego: Harcourt, 2001).

the result may be unacceptably wide discrepancies in compensation. If the company uses the headquarters location as "home," then expatriates from countries with lower compensation standards will be difficult to repatriate. Some companies use a modified approach (see Table 9-1), where the real home is the base for goods and services, while headquarters standards are applied to housing (the most visible component of total compensation).

While the balance sheet approach is a well-accepted methodology, it has further limits. It encourages people to import their lifestyles, thereby creating barriers between expatriates and locals, especially in countries with lower purchasing power. It also eliminates any incentives for expatriates to moderate their spending patterns as they learn to navigate in the new environment. Further, since a sizeable part of compensation and lifestyle is guaranteed, it is difficult to establish a clear connection between results and rewards.

Alternatives to the Balance Sheet Approach

Increased heterogeneity of international staff may require a "global" compensation package in which national/home origin has no impact, at least for senior executives. Consider the case of the vice president of a US-based firm, leading a global business unit located in Tokyo. If this person comes from the United States or Europe, it is taken for granted that housing arrangements will reflect the lifestyle back home. If the successor happens to be Japanese (for example, just returning from an assignment at headquarters), does this mean that no housing allowance should be paid?

Some versions of a cafeteria approach are becoming increasingly appealing. A weakness of the balance sheet approach is its reliance on norms tailored to the "average" expatriate. Again, the increased heterogeneity of the international staff is creating havoc with this assumption. For example, the balance sheet approach does not work well for those expatriates whose spouses suspend their own careers. For some expatriates, support for their children's education may top the list of essential benefits, while for others it may be long-term care for parents left behind. The cafeteria approach to benefits—pricing such benefits and permitting choice within a limit—is often essential.

For short-term assignments, it may be more convenient to provide simple lump-sum payments to cover the additional expenses and let the expatriates manage their finances the way they see fit. This avoids unnecessary entitlements or intrusion into private financial circumstances, such as tax status.

In some firms, the vast majority of international assignments are confined to a specific region (e.g., the EU or ASEAN). In that case, it may be advisable to tailor the policy to the conditions within that region rather than apply a worldwide policy. Again, differences in treatment of "regional" and "global" expatriates have to be carefully monitored. When employees with similar management responsibility receive dramatically different compensation (usually housing allowance is the biggest differentiator), morale and commitment are bound to suffer. A typical case would be pay inequity among regional office staff composed of multiple nationalities—often with at least three different pay packages: local, regional, and global.

Trends and Challenges in International Compensation

The fact that so many are unhappy with the state of international staff compensation is certainly not caused by a lack of available methodologies. The problem is that most pay methodologies make universal assumptions about where expatriates come from, their roles, and where they are going. However, the population of international employees is increasingly diverse, and no single system can provide satisfactory solutions to the multiple demands of international assignments.

As we argued previously, the motives for cross-border transfers vary from one category to another. If a firm's international staff consists of several categories, then compensation packages should arguably be tailored to the specific needs of each group. For example, the financial services group HSBC has four different categories of expatriates:

- International managers—globally mobile senior executives who are moved from one location to another
- Secondees—managers and professionals who are posted to international locations and expected to return home
- Contract executives—specialists who are hired externally for positions abroad on limited-term contracts
- Short-term assignees—mostly technical staff, each with different compensation and benefits packages[81]

In some firms, this may lead to a unified global compensation plan for the senior executives irrespective of their location, a balance sheet approach for managers and professionals transferred across borders, and essentially local pay packages for entry-level and junior assignees. Alternatively, the company may have one system for career expatriates and another for those on short assignments.

Consequently, when it comes to the choice of compensation strategy for international staff, the starting point is to answer two key questions:

- What categories of international staff should the company have?
- Should all categories of expatriates be paid using the same method?

The answers to these questions will depend on the evolution of the internationalization strategy, the HRM philosophy, and the composition of the international staff population. It is also important to bear in mind that compensation is only one of the factors that determine an employee's desire to accept an international assignment. Nonfinancial rewards, such as learning opportunities and expectations of future career gains, are also important motivators.

One of the growing challenges in the area of international compensation is how to pay TCNs—the fastest-growing segment of the expatriate population. While it may seem logical that pay should be based on home-country levels, with appropriate adjustments and allowances for cost of living, TCNs do not necessarily identify with their home country. And when the differences in living standards between the home country and country of assignment are large, problems are bound to arise.

High-potential TCNs have many alternative opportunities. Again, there is no single best formula for TCN expatriate compensation. The purpose of the assignment, its duration, and the expected work location after its completion (many TCNs do not return home, continuing to the next international assignment) all impact the choice of compensation scheme. Any compensation formula that relegates TCNs to the status of second-class "cheap labor" will cause serious damage to morale inside the organization.

The issue of pay equity between international staff and local employees (and across various national groups within international staff) is also important. While the principle that employees should not be paid less when moving to a different location is well accepted, there are limits. When the cost charged to the local unit for the "package" of an expatriate middle manager equals the cost of 20 production workers, it may be hard to convince local employees of the importance of keeping operating costs down.[82]

A related challenge is the compensation of some "returnees"—employees returning from an assignment to their country of origin, often as expatriates with a newly acquired foreign passport. When a Chinese-born manager returns to China (or a Polish-born manager returns to Poland)—for instance after acquiring a Western MBA—with a compensation package that is superior to his or her former local peers, he or she will face considerable resentment from colleagues with comparable skills but without the "right" passport, who feel they have lost out twice—first, because they could not live or study abroad themselves and second, because they are being bossed by someone who is getting much better pay and who they believe may not be any better than themselves.

The home-country bias of international compensation plans may also be a handicap for international staff from low-cost countries. As pointed out by a Malaysian marketing director, "When expatriates come to us, they end up living in bigger houses than at home. When I was offered a job in New York, I moved from a large bungalow with three helpers to a small flat in Manhattan—and my wife had to interrupt her career to take care of the family." There are no simple and easy solutions to this and other problems of pay inequity—other than a radical shift in total compensation philosophy away from country of origin to job content.

Given the complexity of expatriate pay, it is not surprising that in many multinationals it has become increasingly common even for international assignees to sign local contracts.[83] In the future, the traditional, generous expatriate contracts will be confined to only a select part of the international staff.

Repatriation and Reentry

Most international assignees eventually return home. However, coming home is not necessarily easy. It can be a complex process of renegotiating one's identity, rebuilding professional networks and re-anchoring one's career in the organization.[84] Many expatriates find it particularly difficult to give up the autonomy and freedom they have enjoyed on their international assignment. Even more frustrating are "make-work" assignments, doled out to returnees who are stuck in a holding pattern while waiting for a real job opportunity to open up.

Empirical research with German and Japanese expatriates suggests that the most troublesome expatriation problems result from poor career-management systems and impaired relations with headquarters rather than from maladjustment to the foreign culture.[85] There is also evidence that the "out-of-sight out-of-mind" phenomenon impacts assignees' careers; career advancement has been found to be negatively correlated with the number of international assignments.[86] Further, a growing number of corporations do not guarantee a job in the home organization at the end of a foreign assignment.[87]

When this is combined with the loss of social status and financial benefits associated with expatriation,[88] it is no surprise that many observers argue that the shock of coming home may be greater than the challenges associated with the initial expatriation.[89] Available (but inconsistent) data point to a relatively high turnover of employees after their return from international assignments. Among those who leave, 35 percent do so during the first year after their return.[90] Such turnover would mean not only the loss of the investment the company made in developing its employees but also limits on the transfer of competence. Most importantly, it can create a vicious circle of increasing resistance to international assignments.

As with data on expatriate "failure," however, there are reasons to be conservative about the scope of the problem. Any job transition is stressful, even within the home country.[91] Further, research indicates that a growing number of international assignees view their international work experience as an investment in their own competence and value in the external labor market,[92] so retaining them at the end of their assignment may be a tall order. Nevertheless, multinationals can do more, at relatively low cost, to improve the probability of success.

The best repatriation practices emphasize advance planning to provide real opportunities on return, emotional and logistical support during the transition, and continuous dialogue through formal or informal networking or mentoring programs.[93] In these firms, career managers or advisors monitor the expatriates' development throughout their assignments, keep them informed, and serve as advocates for the expatriates during the home-country-succession planning process.

Some companies fix an end date to foreign assignments to facilitate succession and repatriation planning. Another policy that is frequently applied is to require the dispatching unit to take formal responsibility for finding a position for the expatriate comparable to the one he or she left. However, returning after an absence of three to four years, the repatriate may actually face demotion, the fate of a surprisingly large number of returnees.[94]

Repatriation of TCNs often creates additional challenges. Even with the best career planning, there may simply be no comparable position back at their foreign-country home. Finishing an assignment sometimes forces an agonizing choice—to return home and leave the company or to accept a posting in yet another country, which in turn makes the prospect of a later return even more problematic. For many TCNs this creates an uncomfortable dilemma, raising difficult trade-offs between career prospects and the well-being of the family.

Our experiences with a number of multinational firms suggest two observations on how to increase the odds of successful repatriation. First, seeing is believing. If most senior executives have international experience, this demonstrates the value of expatriation and eases worry about repatriation. Second, the best predictor of successful repatriation is the performance of expatriates before their international assignments. Employees with an outstanding track record before their assignment will usually be easier to place in good jobs upon their return.[95]

Finally, regardless of the quality of the corporation's expatriate-management system, we advise expatriates to be proactive in maintaining good contacts with managers at headquarters and other parts of the organization. Changes take place swiftly and unpredictably in today's corporations, and it is impossible for the HR function to plan for all contingencies. Personal social capital is often crucial for identifying satisfactory job opportunities at the end of an international assignment.

TABLE 9-2
Human Resource Practices That Support Effective Mobility

Staffing and Selection

- Communicate the value of mobility for the company's global mission
- Ensure that those with the highest potential move internationally
- Provide short-term assignments to increase the pool of employees with international experience
- Recruit employees who have lived or who were educated abroad

Training and Career Development

- Make international assignments part of the career-development process
- Encourage early international experience
- Create learning opportunities during the assignment
- Use international assignments as a leadership development tool

Performance Appraisal and Compensation

- Differentiate performance management based on expatriate roles
- Align incentives with expatriation objectives
- Tailor benefits to the expatriate's needs
- Emphasize rewarding careers rather than short-term outcomes

Expatriation and Repatriation Activities

- Involve the family in the orientation program at the beginning and the end of the assignment
- Establish mentor relationships between expatriates and executives from the home location
- Provide support for dual careers
- Secure opportunities for the returning manager to use knowledge and skills learned abroad

A Summary of Global Mobility Best Practices

Table 9-2 summarizes a number of key themes[96] relating to practices that support effective expatriation. Although the suggestions are presented separately for each element of the expatriation cycle, it is also important to bear in mind the links between the different parts.

RETHINKING INTERNATIONAL MOBILITY

Few firms launch their international expansion without at least a small core of managers on international assignments. However, as companies pursue internationalization, various tensions become apparent. These tensions, together with the changing demographics of the expatriate population described earlier, are transforming how companies approach international mobility.

The Tensions in the Mobility Cycle

Five types of tension are common in most international assignment programs:

Cost/investment tensions. The considerable expense associated with international mobility is often viewed as the cost of market entry, to be reduced, if not eliminated, in the long run. Indeed, the need to reduce the personnel cost is often one of the drivers of localization. Yet while most companies can benefit from smarter management of mobility costs, these expenses can also be seen as an essential investment in building the links necessary for managing a transnational firm and learning across organizational boundaries. A cost-driven mobility strategy can lead to "boom-bust" swings. The number of international staff increases in good times, only to be cut when growth slows and recession looms, creating havoc and imbalance in the local organization.

Home/host tensions.   The presence of expatriates, especially in senior management positions, who are insensitive to local cultural norms, who enjoy a superior standard of living, and whose superior value may not be obvious to local employees and stakeholders may generate tensions with the local environment.[97] Host-government officials and regulators may also prefer to interface with locals, who they view as more loyal to host-country interests.

Global/local tensions.   Capable local managers may become discouraged by rotating expatriates in top positions. Either they leave or their willingness to make an effort on behalf of the firm slackens. Over time, this may offset the benefits of an expatriate presence, benefits that include the simple control structure, ease of communication with headquarters, and improved coordination with other corporate units. In addition, as foreign operations increase in size, intimate knowledge of local operations may become as important as communication and coordination with the headquarters.

Short-term/long-term tensions.   Expatriate executives are often criticized for making short-term decisions since their perspective may be limited by the duration of their assignment. They may shrink from taking the risk "on their watch" of taking difficult but necessary actions to secure long-term benefits. Conversely, newly appointed expatriates sometimes experience a heady sense of freedom, or an urge to make decisions that will attract the attention of the head office and promote their careers—in effect, change for the sake of change. On a European Web site frequented by employees of a US subsidiary, one fast-track expatriate was defined as someone who "can outrun his mistakes."

Demand/supply tensions.   The accelerating pace of internationalization has increased the demand for capable and globally savvy managers. However, constraints on international mobility are also increasing, many stemming from family considerations and changing career expectations.[98] Employees are increasingly reluctant to move abroad if it will handicap their children's educational opportunities or mean that spouses have to put their careers on hold. The care of elderly parents is also a growing concern. In a competitive environment, talented people everywhere have alternative employment options.

Alternatives to Traditional International Mobility

Different companies are facing these tensions with different intensity, with the cost issue receiving the most attention. At the same time, the drivers of mobility are changing, with a rise in learning-driven assignments aimed at the development of organizational capabilities and furthering the career development of the employee.[99] Three kinds of responses emerge as alternatives to traditional international mobility based on long-term posting of expatriates:

* Increase in inpatriation—posting of local executives to the company headquarters to support global coordination
* Increase in short-term assignments to reduce cost and increase opportunities for individual and organizational learning
* Replacing expatriation with new approaches to staffing the global organization

Inpatriation: The Next Step in Fostering Global Coordination

Nestlé, Procter & Gamble, Zara, and many other international companies discussed in this book invest substantial resources in the socialization of their local managers. An important tool is a temporary assignment to the head office or parent-country operations. Such foreign nationals on nonpermanent assignments in the parent country of the multinational are frequently called "inpatriates."

The number of inpatriates is increasing worldwide. For instance, European or American multinationals with large operations in Central and Eastern Europe have a considerable number of inpatriates from this region at corporate or regional headquarters. Among global firms, only in Japanese and Korean companies is the number of inpatriates small—despite years of efforts. The language barrier seems to be the greatest (but not only) obstacle.

What kinds of HR policies are best suited to support inpatriation? Are there differences between inpatriates and expatriates that would argue for different HR approaches? The situations facing both groups of employees may be similar, but they are not the same. Most inpatriates are assigned for learning reasons; very few are "corporate agents." Many are young employees or middle managers who come to the parent organization on developmental assignments—to absorb the corporate culture or to participate in project teams. Some come with the explicit aim of preparing themselves to replace expatriates; others stay and join the home organization. One-size-fits-all policies are fraught with difficulties since they are more heterogeneous than expatriates in terms of national origin.

Whereas employees in foreign locations are generally used to interacting with expatriates, with mutual adaptation to the problems of communication, this is often not the case in the home office. Communication problems with inpatriates are often unexpected, and sensitivity to communication difficulties on both sides is required. Indeed, HR may have to support inpatriation through cross-cultural training—for the locals.

A British manager who relocated to the head office in the American Midwest experienced an initial warm welcome, but then social interactions with coworkers cooled off. He felt frozen out. Sharing his concerns with the HR manager, he learned that the locals were upset with his perceived "selfish" values—putting his career ahead of his family, as demonstrated by his leaving two young children behind at boarding school in England. Of course, this was before Harry Potter!

Some companies simply treat their inpatriates as local staff, integrating them into the home-office compensation and benefits programs. They do not provide them with foreign-service premiums, housing support, or related benefits. If the inpatriates are expected to remain permanently in the parent country, this may be the most sensible approach. But for temporary transfers, it may be better to treat inpatriates as they would home-country expatriates on learning assignments, with a degree of support appropriate to the expected length of stay.

Another challenge is a reluctance of some local organizations to expose their "best and brightest" to the home office since they may not return as planned. While such talented employees are posted in the head office, new opportunities there may open up—so why rush back? This may actually be a net gain from the global point of view but can be perceived as a "brain drain" locally. At the same time, dispatching the "second best" defeats the purpose of the inpatriate assignments, so appropriate guidance and monitoring of candidate selection is required.

Short-Term Assignments

Most of the inpatriates' assignments are focused on learning and are relatively short term; moreover, most problem-solving and project assignments also have short spans. So it is not surprising that short-term transfers (less than one year in duration) are the fastest-growing type of international assignment. Some companies limit such assignments to less than six months, while longer transfers are treated as regular international assignments.[100]

Short-term assignments are popular because they offer flexibility and are simpler to plan and execute. Even more important, they cost less; expensive housing and cost-of-living allowances are not necessary. Short-term assignments also facilitate repatriation to the home organization; employees do not need not to uproot the working spouse and family.[101]

Coaching and mentoring will help make such short-term developmental assignments work, but why should the receiving unit invest time and effort in this? While some managers may find working with a mentee from another culture intrinsically rewarding, this makes sense only if there is reciprocity, so the receiving unit also benefits from having its members trained in other locations. One practice that facilitates reciprocity is the "talent swap" (see the box "Talent Swaps Help Develop Skills and Careers"), where for a short period of time employees simply swap their respective jobs.

Talent Swaps Help Develop Skills and Careers

The new sharing economy includes things like house and apartment swaps, car transportation, and co-working spaces. Now the same kind of philosophy is gaining traction in the corporate world, at least for some overseas employees. Talent swaps, foreign assignments in which employees in the same company from different countries temporarily switch jobs, are gaining popularity.

Typically, the two swapped employees share a similar wage-pay structure and skill-experience level, allowing for what is basically a "plug-out-and-plug-in" exchange. These assignments, which typically last less than a year, involve less paperwork and expense than traditional expatriate assignments, where companies have the added cost of moving a family and dealing with schools and costly housing.

A survey by PwC reported that 71 percent of younger workers wanted to work internationally and considered it essential to career growth. In this respect, the swaps are seen as effective for career development to promote early cross-border mobility and to attract and retain employees who are seen as having high potential.

According to the survey, many companies are engaged in this practice on an ad hoc basis but now look to formalize and expand their programs, with more than one in five global businesses planning to introduce the concept. However, there are also downsides: possible loss of productivity, disruption to clients and companies, and unrewarded lateral moves for employees who learn new skills but are not being promoted—and not everybody is in love with that.

One company actively promoting cross-border swaps is Dow Chemical. In the first three years since Dow's talent swap program began, 126 employees in 18 countries across all geographic areas and functions have participated. The goals include gaining cultural fluency, expanding professional networks, and taking people out of their comfort zones. According to the company, of the 76 people in the first two groups of swaps, all returned or will return to new positions or promotions within six months.

Source: "Across Borders, Talent Swaps Help Develop Skills and Careers." *New York Times*, May 15, 2015.

The concept of short-term assignments appeals to common sense, but applying it is often difficult—especially when employee development is the key objective. Visa regimes or language competence may not be symmetrical, so one-for-one exchanges may not be possible. Expectations may not match—sometimes passive "corporate tourism" without meaningful learning is seen as the simplest way to fulfill host obligations, thereby creating frustration among the transferees who hoped to develop new skills. To avoid this, involvement from the corporate center, including budget support, may be necessary.

Global Coordination Without Traditional Expatriates

Aside from short-term assignments, Table 9-3 presents a number of other alternatives to the traditional expatriate model of long-term transfers.[102]

There are an increasing number of foreigners who work overseas without having been sent out by an organization. These employees are not expatriates in the traditional sense of the term, as their expatriation is *self-initiated*, and since they are no longer a small minority, this group is receiving increasing attention.[103] They typically have local employment contracts and no guarantee of remaining employed by the corporation on their return to their home country, even if that happens to be the corporation's home country.[104] The key motivation for seeking such positions may be compensation that is higher than at home, the possibility to work in a desirable location, or prospects for faster promotion and broader career opportunities in the future.

These employees may provide skills and competencies not readily available in the local market that otherwise would have to be covered by a PCN or TCN on a traditional expatriate assignment. Another benefit could be their willingness to stay long term or their language and intercultural competence. However, in terms of supporting cross-border coordination, they may lack the broader global knowledge of experienced expatriates.

Another recent related trend is the increase in *permanent* transfers resulting from localization of expatriates who find the option of returning home unattractive and desire to remain abroad under local (or modified local) terms of employment.[105] This may be encouraged by the corporation because presumably "local terms" means lower cost. However, there may be invisible costs, such as attrition of local talent concerned about a "glass ceiling" of expatriates who never leave or limited transfer of knowledge across organizational boundaries.[106]

A variation on post-expatriate mobility is the *international commuter*. Just as many US executives routinely commute across the continent to their jobs after every weekend, so a new generation of European managers prefers a weekly commute to work, for example, taking the high-speed train between Brussels and Paris. Their priority is securing a stable environment for the family, but companies benefit as well because of cost savings and because they can expand the pool of candidates for international jobs when relocation is not required. A particular category is *rotational* assignments, where the expatriate commutes to another country for successive short, set periods of time followed by a break in the home country.[107]

The ongoing revolution in communications is dramatically expanding the possibilities of *virtual expatriation*—where employees have responsibilities abroad but manage them from the home country. Some managers with heavy international coordination responsibilities spend so much time on the road that it does not matter where these frequent flyers live. Unilever used to allow its regional managers to decide whether they would live in the parent country or the region—either way, they would be traveling a lot in the other direction.

However, virtuality has its limits. No amount of electronic communication can replace human contact. The cost of fewer international postings may be more short-term trips. During business downturns, companies are usually quick to issue edicts against unnecessary travel. In addition, how many times can an individual jet between continents before fatigue sets in? The wear and tear of international travel is a hidden health threat, the cost of which has yet to be calculated.[108]

Global Mobility: Becoming Mainstream—and Less Secure

As international assignments in their various forms become more common, they are also becoming less secure.[109] Expatriate postings in the past provided at least a temporary haven from the turmoil of home-office reorganizations, since the terms for international assignments in most Western companies and virtually all Japanese or Korean companies included the guarantee of a return position.

Now, however, the pattern—in some countries at least—is changing, with fewer companies offering expatriates a guarantee of a job upon their return home. International experience may not be a career booster for all expatriates: management-development assignments may indeed lead to upward mobility, but problem-solving transfers may not. In part, this reflects general changes in the employment relationship—"If we cannot guarantee jobs for people at home, how can we promise them to people abroad?" But it is also a sign that international mobility is no longer exceptional, so companies do not see the need for special treatment.

There are mixed signals here. One clear message from global companies is that international experience is an asset—and sometimes a necessity for future promotions. But, however unintentional, another is that it may carry risks for the assignee's career. There is no question that employees located abroad may have substantially more difficulties in lining up alternative job opportunities at home, or at least that they perceive this to be the case. Not everyone is ready to sign up for a "boundaryless" career.[110] And a *perception* of insecurity naturally leads to skepticism and resistance to international mobility—a paradox in an increasingly connected world.

TAKEAWAYS

1. In global firms, international mobility is essential for horizontal coordination—for building social architecture, including global mindset; and for spotting and developing the best talent.

2. The growing number of women, third-country nationals, younger expatriates, inpatriates, and dual-career families is changing the way companies approach international assignments.

3. Making an international assignment successful for the individual, the family, and the firm demands attention to many factors, from initial selection until repatriation. A starting point is recognizing that international mobility is a process, not an event.

4. The personal traits and skills needed for international assignments depend on the role expectations. Professional and leadership skills are the foundation for agency-type assignments. Relationship abilities and cultural awareness may be more important for learning-oriented assignments.

5. It is important to understand the factors influencing intercultural adjustment and expatriate work performance—adjustment to work, to the general environment abroad, and (most difficult of all) to interaction with the local environment.

6. Family well-being is a critical element for effective long-term mobility. The inability of the family to adjust is often the reason for assignment failure. For dual-career couples, support for the partner's career is becoming increasingly important.

7. Tight alignment between the purpose of the assignment and the objectives to be measured is a necessary foundation of effective performance management of international staff.

8. Selection of an international compensation plan is driven by three considerations: cost efficiency, equity issues, and ease of system maintenance. The balance sheet approach is the most common practice.

9. Short-term transfers are the fastest-growing type of international assignment, especially for the purpose of learning, as they mitigate some of the most common obstacles to mobility: cost, family constraints, and ease of repatriation.

10. In global firms, international assignments are increasingly important for personal growth and development, but at the same time, the career risks connected with working abroad are not insignificant.

NOTES

1 "The stealth oil giant: Why Schlumberger, long a hired gun in oil-field services, is becoming a major force and scaring Big Oil," *Business Week*, January 14, 2008.

2 "Star search: How to retain, train, and hold on to great people," *BusinessWeek*, October 10, 2005. See also Beyer (2006).

3 The need for a contingency approach to expatriation was first raised by Mendenhall and Oddou (1985). See also the empirical research of Stahl (2000).

4 Brookfield Global Relocation Services, *2014 Global Mobility Trends Survey*, 2014, www.brookfieldgrs.com.

5 In a four-country comparison, Tungli and Peiperl (2009) reported that the TCNs were used most often in the UK (38 percent of all international assignees), followed by the United States (23 percent) and Germany (12 percent). Virtually no TCNs were used by Japanese firms.

6 Pollitt, 2014.

7 Cartus, 2014. "Global Mobility Policy & Practices." *2014 Global Mobility Trends Survey*. Brookfield Global Relocation Services (www.brookfieldgrs.com).

8 Moran, Stahl, and Boyer, 1988; Shortland, 2014.

9 Adler, 1984.

10 For a recent review of research on women and international assignments, see Shortland (2014).

11 Adler, 1986.

12 Tung, 1997.

13 Lowe, Downes, and Kroeck, 1999.

14 Adler, 1984.

15 Chusmir and Frontczak, 1990.

16 Adler, 1987; Taylor and Napier, 1996; Tung, 2004.

17 Caligiuri and Tung, 1999.

18 Stroh, Varma, and Valy-Durbin, 2000.

19 Harzing, 1999.

20 Brookfield Global Relocation Services, *2014 Global Mobility Trends Survey*, 2014, www.brookfieldgrs.com.

21 Many of the women in a classic study of Western expatriates in the Pacific Rim reported advantages to being highly visible, and they benefitted from the curiosity of local business people who were eager to meet them (Adler, 1993).

22 Tung, 1995 and 2004.

23 As pointed out by Brewster *et al.* (2014), this interdependence and complexity also impacts research on critical dimensions of international mobility, such as how to measure and determine the outcome of international assignments.

24 Suutari and Brewster, 1999.

25 Harris and Brewster, 1999.

26 Many large multinationals have introduced open job postings on the corporate intranet. For instance, 12 of 14 US, European, and Asian firms studied by Farndale and Paauwe (2007) had such systems. Open job–posting systems may create more openness in the expatriate staffing process.

27 Sparrow, 1999.

28 Yamazaki and Kayes, 2004.

29 Pucik and Saba, 1998; Stroh *et al.*, 2005.

30 Caligiuri, Tarique, and Jacobs, 2009.

31 Bhaskar-Shrinivas *et al.*, 2005.

32 Liu and Shaffer, 2005. Wang and Nayir (2006) discuss differences in the effects of social interaction on expatriate adjustment in China and Turkey. For an informative discussion of how to improve the interaction and collaboration between expatriates and host-country employees, see Toh and DeNisi (2005).

33 Mol *et al.*, 2005.

34 Bhaskar-Shrinivas *et al.*, 2005.

35 Mol *et al.*, 2005.

36 Bhaskar-Shrinivas *et al.*, 2005.

37 Sixteen percent of multinationals surveyed by Aon International in 1997 used family-readiness evaluations, 11 percent used psychological profile instruments, and 11 percent applied cultural proficiency tests ("No common thread in expat selection," Global Workforce, 1998, p. 9).

38 Black *et al.*, 1999.

39 Black, Gregersen, and Morrison, 1999.

40 Brett and Stroh, 1995. According to Brookfield Global Relocation Services (2014 Global Mobility Trends Survey), family concerns and spouses' careers are consistently the most cited reasons for assignment refusals (www.brookfieldgrs.com).

41 Torbiörn, 1982; Black and Stephens, 1989; and Brewster, 1991. However, our own work with international companies suggests that self-reported expatriate failure rates attributed to family issues may be somewhat exaggerated. We have observed several cases where the cause of the failure was poor performance or adjustment, but the explanation given was "family"—perhaps to allow the returnee to save face or perhaps to shift the blame for an expensive selection error outside the HR department.

42 Brookfield Global Relocation Services, *2014 Global Mobility Trends Survey*, 2014, www.brookfieldgrs.com.

43 Black and Gregersen, 1991b.

44 See Dickmann *et al.* (2008) for an analysis of factors influencing the decision to accept an international assignment.

45 For example, Marks and Spencer had for a long time an explicit policy that all managers and high potentials had to be prepared to move home and family once a year, if needed—"If you don't like that policy, don't join us!"

46 Cerdin and Le Pargneux, 2009.

47 A meta-analysis of available studies on cross-cultural training showed a positive relationship with expatriate performance ($r = 0.26$) and indications of a positive association with expatriate adjustment ($r = 0.13$) (Morris and Robie, 2001).

48 For example, Toyota provides one to three years of ongoing training for employees who may be targeted for overseas assignments in a program called "training for overseas duties." Two types of training are offered: preparation for a US assignment and preparation for a non-English-speaking-country assignment.

49 Brookfield Global Relocation Services, *2014 Global Mobility Trends Survey*, 2014, www.brookfieldgrs.com.

50 Harvey, 1997.

51 Tung, 1981; Mendenhall and Oddou, 1986.

52 Harris and Brewster, 1999. See Littrell and Salas (2005) for a comprehensive review of cross-cultural training practices.

53 Preparatory training is at best only a foundation for future learning—unless it is properly designed, it can have unintended consequences. One of the early studies on expatriation to Japan (Black, 1988) showed that pre-departure knowledge was negatively correlated with expatriate work adjustment—probably because the cultural stereotype of Japanese organizations presented in the standard training package did not correspond to the multifaceted reality.

54 Wurtz, 2014.

55 Mendenhall and Stahl, 2000.

56 Toh and DeNisi, 2005.

57 Feldman and Bolino, 1999.

58 Bhaskar-Shrinivas *et al.*, 2005.

59 For conceptual background, see Black, Mendenhall, and Oddou (1991). Several studies have shown that these three dimensions are independent of each other (Shaffer, Harrison, and Gilley, 1999; Cerdin and Peretti, 2000); but see Thomas and Lazarova (2006) for a critical review of the theoretical and empirical support for the conceptualization. Bhaskar-Shrinivas *et al.* (2005) provide a comprehensive review of past research on expatriate adjustment.

60 Firth *et al.*, 2014.

61 Black, Gregersen, and Morrison, 1999. See also the empirical research of Stahl (2000) on the coping problems of German and Japanese expatriates.

62 Summaries of research on expatriate dual allegiances can be found in Black *et al.* (1999) and Stroh *et al.* (2005).

63 Gregersen and Black, 1992, p. 143.

64 While the topic may be highly relevant, data and empirical evidence concerning these issues is still scarce. In contrast to the extensive literature on expatriate selection and development, the research domain of international performance management (e.g., criteria, processes, and outcomes) is quite unexplored. A review article identified only 11 empirical studies on this topic over a 20-year period (Claus and Briscoe, 2008).

65 Borkowski, 1999.

66 Dowling and Welch, 2005.

67 The perception of expatriates as "short-termers" is so common that it may block any effort to drive long-term change. Advice that is often given to expatriates who are assigned to manage a change project is "Never reveal when you are going home!"

68 According to Gregersen, Black, and Hite (1995), only 11 percent of US HR managers involved in planning international assignments have international experience themselves.

69 Brookfield Global Relocation Services, *Global Relocation Trends 2009 Survey Report*, 2009, www.brookfieldgrs.com. Also, one study of 99 Finnish companies operating internationally reported that in 79 percent of the firms, the performance appraisal of expatriates was conducted by the superior located in Finland (Tahvanainen, 2000), while another study of 301 Finnish expatriates found that a supervisor in the host country was the most typical evaluator (Suutari and Tahvanainen, 2002).

70 Gregersen, Hite, and Black, 1996. Cascio, 2012.

71 Gregersen, Hite, and Black, 1996; Shi, Chiang, and Kim, 2005.

72 See Chapter 3.

73 Tahvanainen, 2000.

74 Reynolds, 1995.

75 It should be noted that the field of international compensation is more the domain of compensation specialists and consultants than of academic research. Suutari and Tornikoski's (2001) study of Finnish expatriates is one of the very few exceptions. There is also a stream of research on the compensation disparity between expatriates and host-country employees from a justice perspective (see, for example, Chen, Choi, and Chi, 2002).

76 The idea is that expatriates never receive less than they would be paid at home.

77 For a comprehensive review of international compensation methodologies, see Reynolds (1995, 2001, Chapters 4 and 5) and Tornikoski, Suutari, and Festing (2014).

78 For a summary of tax strategies for international compensation, see Orchant (2001).

79 A survey conducted in 2006 found that 80 percent of the firms applied a balance sheet approach ("2006 Worldwide survey of international assignment policies and practices," *ORC*, New York, 2007).

80 Black *et al.*, 1999, p.180.

81 "Traveling more lightly," *The Economist*, June 24, 2006, pp. 99–101.

82 As we will discuss in Chapter 13, this matter is of particular relevance in the case of joint ventures and alliances.

83 McNulty, 2014.

84 For a comprehensive review of research on repatriation, see Lazarova (2014).

85 Stahl, 2000.

86 Kraimer, Shafer, and Bolino, 2009.

87 "Traveling more lightly," *The Economist*, June 24, 2006, pp. 99–101.

88 Studies referenced in Black *et al.* (1999, p. 219) have shown that about three-quarters of expatriates, regardless of nationality, have experienced significant decreases in their standard of living after returning home.

89 Adler, 1981; Black and Gregersen, 1991a.

90 Brookfield Global Relocation Services, *2014 Global Mobility Trends Survey*, 2014, www.brookfieldgrs.com. Earlier, Black and Gregersen (1999) reported first-year separation rates of 25 percent "of those who completed an assignment [and] left their company . . . within one year after repatriation." In contrast, Brookfield surveys show historical separation rates for returning assignees as comparable to the total employee population.

91 Some turnover can always be expected; see Nicholson (1984) for research on work transitions. When expatriates gain new competencies during their assignments, their market value on the external market may be higher than inside the old organization, so naturally they leave. The return of the spouse to work may result in family relocation that is not compatible with the job offered to the returnee. While many firms undergoing restructuring are loath to terminate employees during an international assignment (partly for legal reasons in some countries), the employees are laid off as soon as they return.

92 Stahl and Cedrin, 2004; Dickmann and Harris, 2005.

93 Black, Gregersen, and Mendenhall, 1992. Allen and Alvarez, 1998; Reiche, Kraimer and Harzing, 2011.

94 Research studies quoted in Black *et al.* (1999, p. 219).

95 Allen and Alvarez, 1998.

96 Pucik and Saba, 1998.

97 In 2013 a typical annual salary for an expatriate manager ranged from 350,000 to 500,000 US dollars. In contrast, a typical annual salary for a local Chinese manager ranged for 40,000 to 80,000 US dollars, as cited in Tian, Harvey, and Slocum (2014).

98 Collings, Scullion, and Morley, 2007.

99 Merck and Exxon send engineers on short-term assignments for technology transfer and personal development. Some European multinationals have long done this.

100 See Tahvanainen, Welch, and Worm (2005) for a discussion of HR implications of the use of short-term international assignments.

101 A complementary trend is that there are opportunities for international transfers later in employees' careers, when they may be looking for lateral challenges and are free of child-rearing constraints. Young local professionals may benefit from such senior executives sharing their experiences.

102 For an extensive discussion of changing forms of global mobility, see Collings, McDonnell, and McCarter (2014).

103 For a review of research on self-initiated expatriates, see Cerdin and Selmer (2014).

104 Suutari and Brewster, 2003.

105 According to KPMG (2013) *Global Assignment Policies and Practices Survey*, 47 percent of surveyed MNCs are using permanent transfer as a form of international assignments.
106 Tait, De Cieri, and McNulty, 2014.
107 Welch, Worm, and Fenwick, 2003.
108 See Welch and Worm (2006) for an extensive discussion about international travelers.
109 Dickmann *et al.*, 2008.
110 This concept was introduced by Stahl, Miller, and Tung (2002).

10

Facilitating Change in Multinational Organizations

SUMMARY

Challenge

Environmental uncertainty requires that global companies respond rapidly to strategic threats and opportunities

Analysis

Companies with superior change capabilities have operationalized two core principles of managing strategic change:

- Effectiveness of change execution depends on the quality of the action plan and its acceptance by people
- In multinationals, paying attention to fair process is important.

Solutions

- Strategies for building acceptance should be tailored to the sense of urgency
- In evolutionary change, invest time in creating opportunities for engagement of all stakeholders
- For radical change, replace key people who do not support change quickly
- To play the role of HR change partner, start with the business strategy and its people implications
- Focus HR activities on building capabilities supporting strategic agility

MedPharm: The Challenge of Implementing Strategic Change

MedPharm is a German subsidiary of a leading US pharmaceutical company that develops and manufactures active pharmaceutical ingredients.[1] Under the leadership of a charismatic founder, MedPharm pioneered the development of new complex drug compounds. Then, to finance expansion, the founder sold the firm to its current American owner. Today MedPharm has five production sites around the world, two in the US, and three in Europe. Plants were initially largely autonomous, but under some pressure from the headquarters, coordination among plants gradually increased mainly with a focus on sharing knowledge about manufacturing methods and quality. This paid off in the shape of effective low-cost operations worldwide, as well as greatly enhanced customer focus.

With fewer blockbuster drugs in the pipeline, the parent firm decided to respond with an aggressive growth strategy involving new products, technologies, and R&D and distribution partnerships, along with targets to increase overall capital efficiency by 20 percent. The newly promoted general manager (GM) of MedPharm explored its future options, working in collaboration with his boss, the head of the global pharma division, and the corporate head of strategy at the parent firm.

The outcome was a new MedPharm vision—to become the main supplier of advanced chemicals to the parent company. This would involve outsourcing the manufacturing of simple compounds to other partners, including low-cost but technically competent Chinese firms, so that MedPharm could focus on complex, high-value products. It would also mean taking the responsibility for managing the relationships with other external suppliers, and strengthening R&D collaboration with the US parent firm. Managing all this would require the development of robust global supply chain.

A team of 50 managers, almost all from the German headquarters and US parent, was set up to detail this strategy, in four working groups, including one focused on the supply chain. These groups presented their recommendations to top management and all managers, including those from the plants and countries, at a three-day working conference in Milan. There was polite resistance from many in the room, including some "heavyweight" plant managers who saw the new vision as an attack on

their autonomy. Still, top management decided to create a new global supply chain function and told the critics to get behind the new direction. Each production plant appointed a key manager to this function with the mandate of aligning the existing supply chain process with the yet-to-be-developed global supply chain platform and the underlying information technology (IT) system.

Eighteen months later, planning began for a follow-up conference to take stock of progress. MedPharm results continued to be good and costs continued to decline. However, in the eyes of the GM, progress on building the global supply chain had been frustratingly slow. "People simply aren't working as a global leadership team," he said. "The results these last few years have been good, but that is irrelevant. Our managers are not yet used to taking a global perspective in addition to their local responsibilities."

Some of the managers commented that, with conflicting priorities, one had to be realistic about time horizons for the supply chain project—attention had to be paid to shortening cycle times in the factories, to staying ahead of the changing regulatory environment, and above all to guaranteeing security of supplies to customers. Many felt skeptical about the projected growth that was a major justification for building the global supply chain function, pointing to only one major new product introduction over the last five years. They saw the whole initiative as part of a growing movement toward centralization and bureaucracy that would undermine the entrepreneurial spirit that had always been a key to MedPharm's success.

Plant managers who were used to fighting battles with the corporate center felt that this initiative too would eventually blow away. With the incessant pressure to cut costs, there were no spare resources and people to invest in the supply chain project—the returns on which, in any case, seemed uncertain and unclear. Meanwhile, the frustration was growing at the parent headquarters, particularly in the IT and finance functions. From their perspective, MedPharm continued to optimize each site at the expense of the whole. The corporate executives were putting pressure on the MedPharm GM. "I thought we had agreement on the vision, but there's no sense of urgency," commented the corporate vice president (VP) for IT. "MedPharm keeps pushing back and putting off the development of the global platform." Others at the US headquarters hinted jokingly that it might be tempting simply to sell MedPharm to the Chinese—things might be more straightforward if they were dealing with an external supplier.

With the follow-up conference scheduled to convene in ten weeks, the MedPharm GM gave his head of strategy and business development and the human resource director the task of developing a plan to resolve the stalemate.

OVERVIEW

Agreeing on the need for the kind of strategic change attempted by Med-Pharm is one thing, but implementing such a decision is another. We start with a review of what the management of strategic change involves. Execution depends on both analysis and acceptance of the decision. We concentrate on the latter, though in two different contexts. The first is the MedPharm situation where there are no immediate pressures for drastic measures—there is a need for *evolutionary change*. The second is where there is a need for *radical change* since the future of the organization is at stake.

The next two sections focus on these two change processes. First, examining evolutionary change, we build on a framework of procedural justice or fair process. We spell out some of the lessons with the help of a five E framework—*engagement*, *exploration* of options, *explanation* of decisions, setting clear *expectations*, and *evaluation* of outcomes. Second, we look at radical change that involves transformation of the culture under survival pressures, involving replacement of key people and rapid introduction of new metrics for performance management.

With these two change frameworks in mind, we review what this means for the important "change partner" role of HR—supporting line managers in the implementation of strategic change. Line managers often tend to focus on the analysis ("what to do") rather than on building acceptance ("how to do it"). Since the pace of external change is increasing, the concluding section of this chapter explores how multinationals can build strategic agility. This requires many of the qualities that we have discussed in this book—global people factors are a key to the development of the capabilities that enable rapid and effective responsiveness to change.

IMPLEMENTING STRATEGY THROUGH PEOPLE

MedPharm had a clear plan for change but it went awry because of people factors. There was no buy-in by local managers who felt that the need for change was distant from the day-by-day operational realities. Indeed, strategy implementation has always been at the heart of strategic HR management. As a contributor to the business, one of the most important roles of HR is managing change.

In managing change, the most important thing ultimately is thoroughness and speed of *execution*. The business world is full of strategies and plans, but financial markets look foremost at the company's history in implementing those plans when they judge the value of an enterprise. Indeed, some studies show that the company's ability to execute corporate strategy is at the top of the list of the intangibles that analysts consider when making their recommendations.[2]

A simple formula captures well the organizational challenges of change management:

$$Q \times A = E$$

Q stands for the quality of the business, economic, and analytic reasoning leading to a proposed action plan or solution. A signifies acceptance of the change and represents the people side of the process. E stands for the effectiveness of change or execution, which will not be high without a high value of A. The box "Change Acceleration at GE" describes a practical application of this framework.[3]

Managers tend to be well equipped to analyze the business environment and develop a plan for change. However, the training and professional experience of most managers does little to develop skills in building acceptance. Consequently, many people who move up into leadership positions have strong skills and experience in Q, but they are often naïve when it comes to A. However, this simple formula recognizes that even a superb Q-solution will fail without attention to the A-side—anything multiplied by zero nets out to zero.

Change Acceleration at GE

In the early 1990s, as General Electric (GE) had not anticipated the Gulf War, it lost considerable money in businesses like aircraft engines because of overcapacity during the recession that followed. While some managers argued for better planning, top management drew a different conclusion—GE had to be capable of responding faster to whatever strategic changes it confronted. The HR function took responsibility to develop what became GE's change acceleration process (CAP), one of the eight organizational corporate capabilities cutting across all businesses, with the guiding formula of $Q \times A = E$.

The basic principle here is that no change happens without leadership. Leaders must analyze the situation carefully, the plan must be sound, and above all, they must be committed to making the change happen. However, before they receive the final go ahead, they must also hold a CAP workshop to work out a strategy for building acceptance. This workshop convenes the key stakeholders for two–four days—perhaps 30–40 people in a project to build a global supply chain, a global cost reduction effort, or a post-acquisition integration—together with a couple of trained facilitators who are familiar with the issues but outsiders to the business in question.

Using a toolkit of exercises, they work through key change management issues:

- How to create a shared need, a common understanding of why the change should take place
- How to communicate the vision to employees in their terms rather than management's jargon
- Where the resistance is likely to be greatest and what to do about it
- How to alter the structure in order to empower champions and sideline those who are likely to resist
- How to ensure that they do not just start off change but make it last

Much of this methodology rests on well-known principles of change management. Over the years, the GE has trained more than 20,000 CAP facilitators, most of them line managers, and every year has applied CAP methodology thousands of times. Recently, GE integrated CAP into one of the other core processes known as Six Sigma for managing process improvement.

A well-thought-out plan—scoring say 7 on a 10-point scale—combined with poor acceptance—say 2 out of 10—leads to very low effectiveness in execution.

Experienced global managers typically view experience in managing major change as the most significant learning experience that equips them for leadership.[4] Managing change in one's own local culture is a first step in learning how to build acceptance, but the challenges in the multinational environment have added complexity. The leader steering the MedPharm global supply chain project (or Chris Johnson leading the Nestlé GLOBE project described in Chapter 4) has to handle quite different contexts facing business units across the world, as well as cross-cultural differences and the barriers of distance. The best way of building acceptance with key stakeholders is through dialogue, and yet when some stakeholders live far away, when there are no existing social relationships, and when they speak the company language less than fluently, there is a temptation to ignore them in planning the change.

Building Acceptance: Is There a "Burning Platform"?

Since resistance to change is inevitable, building and managing acceptance is not easy, especially in large companies with their traditions and culture steeped in past success. Perhaps the best-known framework on managing planned change is the eight-step model developed by Kotter[5]:

- Create a sense of urgency
- Form a powerful coalition
- Create a vision for change
- Communicate the vision
- Remove obstacles
- Create short-term wins
- Consolidate the gains
- Anchor the changes in the organizational culture

These are proven and useful guidelines to help in building acceptance, and GE's CAP methodology converts them into a practical toolkit. However, the experience of most managers is that change is rarely linear, neatly following such steps. Sometimes it is coercive, often a spiral process, and more often than not it is emergent rather than planned.[6] Change is path dependent, contingent on the context.

Kotter's framework and GE's CAP process highlight two aspects of context that lead us to distinguish between two different change models. The first is the *sense of urgency*—a shared and pressing need for change, a sense of impending crisis, often called a "burning platform." At MedPharm, while local managers acknowledged with their heads the need for change, there was no sense of urgency to spur actions that might undermine the comfort of the status quo. Managing change under these circumstances involves building that sense of urgency step-by-step. We call this the *evolutionary change* model. We contrast this with the *radical change* model where there is a clear crisis requiring rapid action—and one of the laws of fast change is that the only way to change quickly is to replace the key people.

This leads us to highlight the second contextual aspect of change: *the availability of committed and determined change leaders*, or what Kotter calls a powerful guiding coalition. Change does not happen unless there is leadership that is driving it. A multinational company can only implement strategic change around the world if it has a pool of capable leaders, experienced in the business and in leading change. When change leaders are not available internally, the company must recruit new leaders from the outside, as often happens.

The first framework that we discuss, *evolutionary change*, focuses on a common situation where change is desirable, in anticipation of future challenges, but there is no burning platform or crisis. Meeting the current business goals is the priority, as the organization changes gradually. The change leadership is there—for example, MedPharm's GM who is determined to build the global supply chain capability—but there is no dominant coalition of executives who feel a sense of urgency. In contrast, the context for *radical change*, our second framework, is a situation where there is a crisis and immediate urgency since the survival of the enterprise is at stake. There is typically a pool of committed leaders inside the firm, with others brought in from the outside, to drive the necessary changes in structure, processes, operations, as well as the cultural fabric that underlies the firm.

These two approaches are not two black-and-white opposites. As we will see in our discussion, there are ways of accelerating evolutionary change (indeed that is one of the objectives of GE's CAP), especially if there is a pipeline of suitable managers who can create a sense of urgency. And after the initial turnaround stage, radical change will always require the skills of building acceptance to anchor a new culture.

EVOLUTIONARY CHANGE: BUILDING ACCEPTANCE THROUGH FAIR PROCESS

In the situation of evolutionary change where there is no shared sense of urgency, the theory of fair process or procedural justice provides a good way of understanding what acceptance means and how to build it. Indeed, research has validated this theory across cultures.[7]

Managers and organizations usually pay close attention to *distributive justice*, the fairness of outcomes—for example, equity and fairness in resource allocation or compensation systems. Distributive justice focuses on resources and outcomes, but the problem with organizational change is that the outcomes will never be fair to everyone. There will always be winners and losers, people or subsidiaries that gain more power and resources while others may even lose their jobs. *Procedural justice* means paying attention to the perceived fairness of the process by which the company takes decisions, so it is also known as fair process. People may be disappointed with the outcome, but if they respect the way in which the organization reached the decision, research shows that they are more likely to retain trust and commitment. Conversely, people may be satisfied with an outcome that favors their interests, but if the process of decision-making was not fair, they still distrust the organization.

Research shows that the concept of procedural justice applies also to the multinational firm and that people indeed are most likely to cooperate in the process of change—regardless of whether they themselves win or lose—if they believe that the change follows the principles of fair process.[8] An empirical study of strategic decision-making in international corporations found that subsidiary managers who believed their company's decision-making processes to be fair showed a higher level of trust and commitment to their organization. This in turn fostered active cooperation in implementing decisions, typically improving performance. Conversely, when managers viewed decision-making processes as unfair, they hoarded ideas and dragged their heels when it came to execution.

If we apply this to the MedPharm change, there are going to be winners and losers with the implementation of the new strategy. Local plant managers will have to change their roles. They will no longer be kings or queens; they will have to develop new skills to perform roles that are more complex. Many local IT staff may lose their job. Yet if the change is to be effective, their acceptance is vital—they must understand this decision, view it as fair, and be supportive of the necessary actions.

Fairness is one of the more critical values in a global organization. One of the reasons why many corporations emphasize fairness is the increasing importance of commitment, as opposed to compliance, as we move to a knowledge economy. As firms become more dependent on talent, the A-factor becomes highly relevant.

Change will always be easier to manage in times of crisis or recession, which legitimizes acceptance of top-down decisions requiring compliance. However, organizational change under conditions of crisis is so constrained that it rarely establishes a solid base for sustainable competitive advantage. For example, we took part in the successful crisis turnaround of a Scandinavian bank some years ago, led by a new chief executive officer (CEO) recruited from outside to save it. Yet, two years later, the CEO had to face new strategic challenges, requiring a more evolutionary process. His change challenge was now how to build a strong, empowered, and committed middle management.[9]

The *Five E* Framework

How does one go about ensuring that employees see a decision as fair, ensuring the necessary commitment to implementation? How can one steer a change process, from plan to full execution, according to fairness criteria? What are the core elements of procedural justice? We summarize them here with a mnemonic: *The Five E's*.[10]

1. People affected by future decisions must be *engaged*—and asked for input. This shows respect and increases the chances that they will see the outcome as fair.

2. The change team should *explore* all options without bias, rejecting only those proven not feasible.

3. Once the leaders take the decision, they should *explain* it thoroughly, so people understand and trust the intentions of the decision-makers, even if they do not agree with the decision.

4. It is important to be clear about *expectations* after the decision is made, translating these into concrete action plans through the performance management system. Appropriate coaching, training, and support ensure that people have the chance to adjust to the new reality.

5. A key part of the fair change process is *evaluation*, reviewing what worked and what did not, to improve the effectiveness in managing change processes in the future.

TABLE 10-1
What Does Fair Process Involve?

Engagement

- People want their views to be heard
- There is a right to refute
- Communication is sincere and genuine

Exploration

- Different options are explored ... and eliminated

Explanation

- People are informed of the decision
- Decisions are based on sound facts and reasoning

Expectations

- Decisions are translated into clear goals, action plans, and behaviors
- The meaning of a commitment is clear
- There is appropriate coaching and support
- Desired behaviors and results are rewarded

Evaluation

- Decisions are applied with consistency
- We learn from our successes and our failures

Our discussion below (summarized in Table 10-1) reviews the application of this framework in the context of the multinational corporation. We also highlight some of the dilemmas it involves.

Engagement

Engagement means involving people in the decisions that affect them by asking for their inputs and allowing them to refute the merits of one another's ideas and assumptions.[11] This means dialogue during the change planning process. Dialogue communicates management's respect for people and their ideas and leads to better analysis and decisions, as well as stronger commitment to implementation.

People will resist change if they see the problem differently, or if they feel they have no voice in setting the direction. An experienced executive put this well when he said, "People don't resist change; they resist being changed." Therefore, a central part of engagement is selling the problem to key stakeholders, thereby creating dissatisfaction with the status quo. To a greater or lesser extent, this will redefine and clarify the nature of the underlying challenge. There is a tendency to define problems in terms of the solutions that one has readily to hand, and engagement minimizes this risk.[12]

The multinational corporation has to cope with cultural differences in how to engage people. Frank dialogue, in the form of open confrontation and contention, is acceptable in the US and quite usual in Israel or Russia. However, "town hall meetings" that GE favors to put bureaucratic problems on the table may be unacceptable in Japan, where communication is usually more indirect. Nevertheless, engagement of key staff is more the norm in Japan than it is in the West—the *nemawashi* process already mentioned in Chapter 4 involves engaging employees through informal discussions. It does take considerable time—decision-making is slow, but leads to thoroughness of execution.

Not everyone needs to be engaged on all aspects of the strategy, business plan, and implications for execution. It is the *key stakeholders*, whose commitment and engagement are necessary. Some of these key actors may be outside the firm (suppliers, unions, and government authorities). Many managers assume that the key stakeholders are the people high up in the hierarchy—if they can get the top managers on board, then it is in the bag. Yet, smart top managers may not back a change plan unless they are sure that key people *below them* are also on board.

For HR, developing skills in stakeholder assessment is important. Who are the opinion leaders and experts, the social network stars and gatekeepers, and the constituencies who could block execution if they were not engaged? What are their interests? In most organizations, there is a sizeable group of people called the "silent majority," who appear passive at the beginning of the change process. They will not align themselves with the change or even pay much attention to it until they see others they respect taking the change seriously. Indeed, effective engagement often follows a progressive strategy— Figure 10-1 summarizes "a step-by-step strategy for engagement." Popularized by the idea of "the tipping point," this way of steering change calls for progressively building awareness, passive then active interest, and ultimately commitment.[13]

Some individuals, called innovators or early adopters, will respond quickly to the change opportunities, although their influence is not necessarily high. After some initial progress and quick wins, the change team should find and target influential champions. When a critical mass of champions gets the attention of the otherwise passive silent majority, the change moves forward, dealing firmly, if necessary, with resistance from remaining holdouts.

There are many tools and techniques for engagement, ranging from mass communication via newsletters or intranet to workshops and training.[14] A "good nose" is necessary for sensing the right tool to use at the right time. Without doubt, the most useful means of engagement is dialogue during face-to-face meetings. This requires a special effort in the multinational firm, where distance and cultural barriers often mean that the change team fails to get out of the office to meet distant stakeholders until too late in the change process. Often headquarter managers misguidedly save on engagement costs and maximize convenience by excluding local leaders until the final stages in the planning.[15] Skills of persuasion, influence, and negotiating are also vital.[16] Regional and country HR managers can give good advice about managing principal stakeholders— because they must usually achieve results without much authority, they may have good mastery of stakeholder analysis and the tactics of engagement.

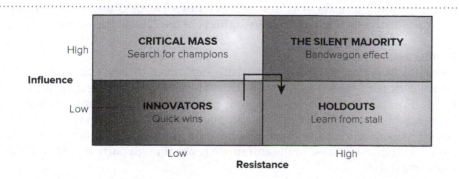

FIGURE 10-1
A Step-by-Step Strategy for Engagement

The traditional levers of engagement are informational or cognitive, oriented toward rational persuasion. However, leaders need to be alert to emotional levers that appeal to the heart. Cognitive levers may be enough to change the strategic direction in a successful organization, but emotional levers help to overcome organizational stagnation or politicized resistance to change.[17] Emotions (positive as well as negative) are contagious and can either handicap or facilitate the change process.[18]

Past research has focused on the negative emotions associated with change—the feelings of anxiety about the unknown that underlies resistance, as well as excessive emotional attachment to the past.[19] In the early stages of change, expressing sympathy and allowing the opportunity for people to vent their doubts and fears may facilitate the inevitable stage of "ending," or giving up on the past.[20] Eliciting hope can help with collective mobilization, for example, emphasizing the new career opportunities after an acquisition. And authenticity in leadership behaviors, such as walk-the-talk transparency, increases the sense of fairness, building trust essential to drive the change forward.

Exploration

In the analysis and planning of change, it is important to explore the different options as well as the implications of possible actions. This process needs to be inclusive, well structured, and most importantly, transparent, if it is to be seen as fair.

Powerful stakeholders, such as local executives or unions, may reject management's option, favoring others. Local managers often favor different options from the headquarter leaders, especially if there is not a strong global mindset in the firm; but they may not be willing to listen to the analysis of the corporate change team unless it is also willing to acknowledge local points of view. Without proper exploration of legitimate alternatives, a stakeholder group may oppose the final decision or implement it only half-heartedly.

The discussion of options can sometimes lead to confusion. Local managers propose a different perspective—and then never hear anything in response from the corporate team until the announcement of the final plan. They are unlikely to consider this fair, accusing headquarter managers of hypocrisy. At the same time, discussion should not linger, options that are not feasible need to be eliminated quickly.

An effective way of exploring options is through focused teams that involve key actors. MedPharm took this route, but local managers were neither adequately engaged, nor involved in exploring options. In contrast, the story of how Canon faced up to the challenges of building an integrated organization in Europe is a successful example (see box "How Canon Consolidated Its European Organization"), as is the way in which Renault's Carlos Ghosn used a structure of cross-functional teams to explore options in the Nissan turnaround.[21]

Explanation

Once the decision is taken, it must be explained to everyone who will be affected, notably those whose commitment is necessary for effective implementation. For the process to be fair, people need to understand that a decision has been reached (the time for debate and questioning is over), that it is based on sound reasoning, that their opinions have been considered, and that the decision is in the best interest of the enterprise (even though particular stakeholders may lose out).[22]

How Canon Consolidated Its European Organization

The leading camera and printer leader Canon had built its presence in Europe through a decentralized network of entrepreneurial local affiliates that were semi-autonomous. This approach initially enabled rapid growth, but later on made it difficult to gain economies of scale and coordinate future expansion. In order to reduce costs, increase profits, and strengthen the brand, Canon decided to consolidate and streamline the organization under a pan-European umbrella.

The main challenge was to obtain buy-in and support for the new operating model from managers and employees in national sales organizations that enjoyed substantial autonomy and stood to lose authority if power shifted to the head office. Canon's European CEO set up four task forces to come up with recommendations for a pan-European organization in specific areas of the business. Careful selection of team members assured that no country or function felt excluded from the planning and decision-making process. Simultaneously, in collaboration with a leading European business school, Canon established an executive development program with action-learning projects complementing the task force agenda.

After a year of intensive discussions and detailed planning, senior managers collectively decided to transform the fragmented federation of countries into a network of subsidiaries with common platforms and strong lateral coordination along major product lines. Processes in key functions such as IT, logistics, finance, and HR became standardized to gain the required efficiencies, and the sales organization was streamlined and unified to strengthen the brand and market position.

Equally important was coordination between previously unconnected units—now accomplished through a variety of functional and customer-oriented cross-border steering groups, pan-European task forces and problem-solving teams, and extensive cross-border transfer of high-potential employees. Nearly all managers appointed to key coordinating roles came from subsidiaries, so from the very beginning the new organization became a source of opportunities for career advancement and personal development.

Five years after the initial decision, with fully restored profitability, Canon Europe became the largest business region in Canon's global family.

Source: V. Pucik and N. Govinder, "Canon Europe: Pan-European Transformation (A), (B) and (C)," Case studies IMD-3-1074 to 3-1076, IMD, Lausanne, 2007.

Senior leaders are likely to be over-familiar with the proposed change and the options: it is no longer news to them. Because the rationale behind the decision is "blindingly obvious," they are often impatient to move to action. Typically, managers at the next level receive instructions in a meeting to inform their respective units. A few e-mails with PowerPoints are sent along with an up-beat corporate video. The result is that supervisors—located a continent away and three levels below, where behavioral change is needed or where costs will be cut—know that the change is coming but have never heard the rationale fully explained. Even if employees have access to the information, without a dialogue needed to convert information into understanding, few fully comprehend what it all means. One of the change management tasks of the HR function is to work with line managers to design communication processes that will effectively build frontline understanding of the decision and its rationale.

The well-known European multinational in the tool equipment business, Hilti, organized an effective explanation process a few years ago following its decision to implement a major change in global strategy and organization. First, information about the change was posted worldwide on the company's intranet. Then HR organized cascading meetings lasting two to six hours for all personnel, right down to the lowest level, meeting with the boss's boss and a consultant. The aim of each meeting was to help individuals understand the rationale behind the change, what it meant for their part of the organization and for their job in particular. A second meeting quickly followed, now with the immediate superior, to work out the implications of the change in terms of targets and action plans. Setting clear expectations is the fourth step in fair process management.

Expectations

Setting expectations means translating decisions into clear roles and responsibilities, SMART targets,[23] and action plans, all with clear rewards and sanctions. Desirable (and undesirable) behaviors should be spelled out. Appropriately structured global performance management process plays an important role here.

Fair process does not imply consensus management. At this stage of change, clarity and credibility of performance and behavioral expectations count for most. If expectations and personal consequences (rewards) are clear, and if employees believe that the change will indeed happen, they will follow. Even those managers who have dissenting views are likely to accommodate—especially if they have had the opportunity to voice their views in the planning stage and see that senior leaders are genuinely engaged in keeping them involved.

Organizational change will always require new skills and behaviors from at least some individuals. Most people are understandably anxious about whether they will be able to master new roles. Consequently, there will be a need for appropriate people risk management, training, and coaching. We have seen many change processes where the implementation was rocky and sometimes even aborted because the HR function was unprepared to provide this support—because it had not been engaged in the planning process early enough. Advance preparation is essential.

New performance metrics have to be set, and it is likely that some individuals will not adjust effectively to their new roles. This will necessitate identifying and preparing a pool of potential successors who can take over from managers who fail to meet expectations after a reasonable period of time.[24] This sort of proactive steering of the implementation process builds the credibility of the organization and its future change capability.

Powerful people in key positions who pay only lip service to the new direction can be some of the biggest obstacles to change. If others sense that change is unlikely to happen because of their opposition, it may create a self-fulfilling situation of collective wait and see. One of the problems with the MedPharm change process was that there was a dominant collective view that the transition to the global supply chain would happen only gradually, sapping the organization's energy and ability to move forward.

Evaluation

The final, often neglected, step in the change process is evaluation or review. As change initiatives occur with increased frequency, a proper evaluation ensures that the organization learns how to improve the change process, and that mistakes made will not be repeated. This is another important role fulfilled by HR.

One of the few multinational firms that takes evaluation seriously is IBM, where there is a long-standing discipline of reviews after every project or change cycle. GE also pays close attention to evaluation, organizing periodic workshops at their Crotonville learning center to diagnose the lessons for the organization from change plans that failed to live up to expectations. Still, we find that most firms at best leave change evaluation to the individuals who were involved, while neglecting organizational learning.

The process of managing major change is an organizational capability that may require dedicated support for continuous learning. At GE, CAP itself is a way of capturing that learning. ABB anchors the responsibility for the management of large global projects, including evaluation and learning, in a corporate-level department. Shell established a corporate project academy to build expertise in this domain. Many other firms have not had the same degree of foresight.

The Tensions Behind Fair Process and the Five E Framework

Any idea of the multinational enterprise as a smooth harmonious entity, a utopian United Nations, is misguided. Tension lies at the heart of the concept of the transnational firm. This means that attention to fair play is important, though the outcomes will never be fair to everyone.

There will always be decisions and outcomes that go against the interests of specific parties—managers, subsidiaries, and businesses. Change or realignment will always create tensions. How can one be sure that such tensions do not damage human and social capital, leading people to become less satisfied, less committed, less loyal—or even to quit the firm? How can one be sure that these tensions do not undermine the delicate webs of collaborative relationships? Paying due attention to fair process and the *Five Es* is vital, and the reason why a growing number of multinational corporations have fairness as one of their corporate values.

Managers in some regions of the world will point to culture differences and say, for example, that "fairness does not mean the same in Korea." It is true that compliance based on respect for traditional authority has been sufficient to drive major changes in the past at companies such as Samsung or Hutchison (based in Hong Kong). However, the scarcity of talent and the growing importance of commitment require a different approach—also in Asia. In some Asian firms, like Siam Cement or Infosys that see talent as a source of competitive advantage, fairness is indeed an explicit corporate value.

How did MedPharm decide to tackle the tensions? Top management recognized (with hindsight) that they focused on the Q in the planning of the supply chain project, without sufficient engagement of the local plant managers and key country staff. Efforts to persuade them that there was no other viable option had been inadequate. MedPharm's GM had therefore asked the head of operations, a leader with high credibility in the organization, together with the HR director to prepare a plan of action, leading to a two-day conference.

The preparation process leading up to a workshop for the top 100 people was a vehicle for intensive face-to-face discussions with all key stakeholders, especially the senior local managers. This was to create a sense of urgency, making sure that everyone understood why it was important to move fast on building the global supply chain. The small organizing team, together with the GM, also concluded that the biggest challenge was a shortage of experienced global leaders who were at ease managing in "split-egg" ways, and therefore a part of the workshop was devoted to the skill requirements for leaders in a world where functional and territorial silos had become dysfunctional. After the workshop, HR established a new program for global leadership development, in partnership with the US parent.

RADICAL CHANGE: USING HRM TOOLS TO BUILD A NEW CULTURE

Radical change may be called for when there is a clear sense of urgency and leaders with commitment to the change. This may be the situation of a formerly successful company, whose strategy no longer meets market needs, now requiring realignment of structure, processes, as well as competencies and culture, with the new strategy. Radical change will draw heavily on human resource management since it usually involves replacement of some of the key people and the development of new performance requirements. It is a process first of taking charge and then of letting go as the new culture takes hold.

Allianz Ayudhya Thailand (AAT) is a case in point. Some years after the German insurer expanded into Thailand, it faced a crisis when its strategy of sacrificing profits for growth led to unsustainable losses for the company. The old business model generated good income for the agents who aggressively opposed attempts by the top management to introduce a new compensation system that would reduce their earnings. As described in the box "Leading Transformation at Allianz Ayudhya Thailand", a new expatriate CEO, Wilf Blackburn, succeeded in turning around the company, despite an environment resistant to radical change.

Leading Transformation at Allianz Ayudhya Thailand

On May 28, 2004, hundreds of sales agents, angry about proposed changes in their compensation system, occupied the Bangkok headquarters of AAT—then the second largest life-insurance company in Thailand. Wearing black (the color of death), singing patriotic songs, and with full coverage from the local media, the protest leaders demanded the resignation of the expatriate president and proclaimed that they would not return to work until their grievances were met.

The expatriate GM had to flee the country under police protection. With the company's reputation in tatters and facing large losses, observers speculated that it would be closed, or sold. To nearly universal surprise, this did not happen. In less than four years, new management transformed AAT from an unprofitable, hierarchical, and demoralized organization to a profitable, modern, and exciting company to work for. How did this change come about?

The strategy chosen by the new leadership team had two elements: change the business and change the culture. On the business side, this required streamlining the product portfolio and shifting to more profitable variable rate policies. The new CEO himself took charge of the agency sales force, communicating directly the urgency of a new market approach focused on customer needs rather than products. To complement this, Blackburn put an equal emphasis on driving radical cultural change to enhance performance, entrepreneurship, and innovation.

The change started at the top. In a bold move, eight senior executives were hired from outside, from industries strong on the new strategic orientations of customer focus and innovation—some from Coca-Cola and P&G, others from Federal Express and IBM. Within three years, 75 out of the 100 executives at the top four ranks of the company left, including most of the expatriates brought in by the previous management.

Lower in the organization, effort was put into rebuilding recruitment—the target employee was young (below 30), well educated, assertive, ambitious, and career driven. To attract and keep employees, HR staff first had to figure out what would be attractive to new employees beyond compensation. At the top of the list were opportunities for growth—in terms of promotions as well as horizontal development via internal job change and international assignments. Very soon, a first group of employees left for assignments of six months to two years at either Allianz's Munich head office or Asian subsidiaries (with their picture in the company's lobby). The company also radically overhauled its performance management system, linking performance to pay against targets and infusing the entire system with transparency from the highest to the lowest level.

To break the bureaucracy and induce innovation, flexible office hours and an open office concept were next. When the renovation of the floor space started, the CEO relocated from the lavish CEO quarters on the upper floor to join other employees on the first floor. "When this happened," Blackburn remembered with a laugh, "they thought that I would be there only until my office got renovated, they couldn't believe I wasn't going to move back!" The new environment looked much more attractive and friendly, and it significantly reduced rental and electricity costs.

These changes did not sit well with many senior managers who had grown up in a culture where face, hierarchy, and status—the size of the office, a personal secretary, and a private driver—were important. The CEO knew that dismantling the office walls was a high-risk decision. He did not "sell" the idea of the open-floor environment to senior managers, he simply said: "There are 24 other insurance companies in Thailand. If you want it so much, you can have an office with one of them."

Following an initial period of doubt, skepticism, and outright resistance, most of the staff came to embrace the new culture that rewarded talent, performance, and the ability to adapt to change.

Six Lessons in Managing Radical Change

Using AAT as an example (among others), let us map out six lessons for managing radical change with a particular focus on the HRM aspects.

1. Provide a clear strategic aspiration

There is a temptation to think of turnaround, bringing a company back into the black, as the focus. In the case of AAT, a major change in the product mix—eliminating unprofitable products that were easy to sell and focusing on new variable rate insurance products—was a big part of the successful turnaround. However, the strategic aspiration was wider. This was only part of a desire to create a more innovative insurance company, requiring a new culture to replace the old authoritarian and bureaucratic organization.

The driver behind radical change is a strategic aspiration that is ambitious, well grounded, and clear, usually driven from the top.[25] In the case of AAT, regional and top management, who were well aware that the insurance market was changing worldwide, took the lead. Blackburn had been part of that process as an executive in the regional Singapore office; his challenge was now how to adapt it to the Thai realities on the ground.

Such an aspiration should appeal to the *head*, the *heart*, and the *hands*, otherwise it will fail to be credible and to provide the necessary continuity in change:

- Appealing to the head means that it should be clear, concrete, and coherent—people should be able to understand it.
- Appealing to the heart means that it should be compelling, challenging, and inspirational, but this dimension of aspiration is usually most problematic. At best, many existing managers nod their heads—or openly protest as at AAT.

- Appealing to the hands means that it should be actionable, inspiring key initiatives such as customer focus and innovation at AAT.

2. Communicating the aspiration

We discussed the vital importance of communication and engagement in the previous section on evolutionary change. This is equally true with radical change. The "new guard" must foster understanding and conviction by communicating the aspiration as a "change story" across the organization, highlighting the wins, making sure that employees know why the changes need to happen and what they will involve.

Doing this fast and effectively is important in radical change, and one of the best ways is role modeling—"walk the talk." Blackburn wanted to break down the old bureaucracy where managers hid behind closed doors, putting in place an organization with the interaction across boundaries that would be indispensible for innovation. The open office concept was an important start, and the new CEO's, move from the executive suite to the first floor with other employees sends a clear message—initially disturbing in the hierarchic Thai culture, but gradually becoming understood and accepted.

3. Replacement of key people who do not support change

The evolutionary model focuses on the engagement of key stakeholders, building momentum through early adopters and then a critical mass of champions. In contrast, there is no time to do this in radical change. At AAT, Blackburn faced critics and opponents at all levels of the organization. There is only one alternative—to replace the key people who are in denial or who resist the need for change. But you cannot replace key people unless you have qualified replacements.

If a company enjoys a strong reputation in the labor market this may be feasible, but the reputation of the firm is rarely positive in the case of a company facing radical change. In some organizations, there may be "young Turks" in middle management who have been arguing covertly for a new strategic aspiration—and they can be elevated into new responsibilities as champions of change. In the case of AAT, the majority of senior and general agency managers were hostile to the strategic vision—and indeed to any foreign-induced change. There was no alternative except to hire people from outside the insurance sector motivated by the opportunity to shake up a traditional industry.

Targeting people with impact on the organization is a key part of replacement. At AAT, the person with the greatest impact was the Chief Agency Officer, a person with "superhuman status" who was deeply opposed to any change. Credibility in this position with responsibility for agencies requires deep actuarial and industry knowledge. It was impossible to find a replacement, so Blackburn had to "step into the boxing ring with the agents" and assume this role himself during the most critical period.

One of the realities of change is that one has to manage the short term—the internal and external expectations—as one moves toward the longer-term strategic vision. Finding qualified replacements who can both deliver operationally *and* pursue the transformational agenda is usually the major constraint. The box "Anchoring Culture Change at IBM" tells how this played out in one of the biggest successful corporate realignments in recent history.

Anchoring Culture Change at IBM[26]

Perhaps the best example of cultural transformation in a multinational organization is that of IBM 20 years ago. Facing a crisis that cost it a third of the profits made over its long history, Lou Gerstner came from the outside to turn the company around, transforming its strategy, structure, processes, and culture. In an organization of 350,000 people across the world, Gerstner's change philosophy was simple: focus on the top 200 people. For eight years, until he passed on a radically changed organization to his successor Sam Palmisano—transforming a computer hardware firm into the world's largest provider of digital services—he stuck with that principle.

A turning point in the transformation occurred after four years. Each year he would convene the top 200 executives to review progress and plans. We paraphrase what he told them:

> One third of you in this room have been working hard to bring about this new IBM. It hasn't been easy, and there have been sacrifices and frustrations. I want to thank those people from the bottom of my heart. Another third – the biggest third – have been sitting on the fence. You say the right words, you sometimes do the right things, but you are not sure that this is going to happen.
>
> And then there is a small third who don't believe in the new IBM, even though you don't voice it openly. We know who you are. It has taken us four years to develop ways of measuring your contribution and behavior. It has taken us four years to find and develop successors who are as capable as you are and who do believe in the new IBM. That last third will not be here in this room next year.

Many of them were not. The middle third came off the fence. The transformational change at IBM was anchored.

However, the belief that strategic change can only happen by replacing key people, because insiders are always too contaminated by the status quo, can be taken too far. The desire to change fast by relying on outsiders may lead to the pendulum swings we described earlier[27]—the local entrepreneurs get frustrated and leave, customers get alienated, results suffer—and the pendulum swings back. Avoiding this mistake is important.

We know of a once beleaguered Italian fashion house where a majority of the key leaders opposed a major strategic reorientation, involving offshoring key processes to low-cost countries, which in their view would compromise their rich heritage. Influential outside stakeholders argued for their replacement, though there was no substitute for their deep professional expertise. Instead, consultants carried out an intensive (and expensive) program of personal coaching to build a sense of urgency, acceptance, and alignment around necessary actions—with remarkable success. Most readers would recognize the name of this fashion house today when they shop for smartly designed but reasonably priced clothes.

4. Restructuring the organization

A big step in radical change is restructuring, putting in place a new structure that reflects the strategic aspiration—moving from a business unit structure to a pan-European organization at Canon Europe, or from a country-focused matrix to a front–back matrix at a global consumer and pharmaceutical firms like P&G or J&J.

When restructuring, it is important to think ahead. One aim of the change process at Canon was to assure that country silos would not be replaced by centralized bureaucracy. For this reason, assignments to most coordination functions at the corporate level were only temporary—an essential training ground for the next generation of frontline executives.

A mistake that happens frequently is to believe that with the new structure, the change is over. Putting new leaders in place and empowering them to drive change is only one step in the transformational journey. Changes in systems and processes, roles and responsibilities, behaviors and culture must follow. Among the most important changes are those in the performance management system.

5. Changing the performance metrics

In terms of anchoring the new culture, changing performance management and its metrics goes hand in hand with developing the new pipeline. Typically, it takes time to do this—performance management is not something that one can tinker with on an iterative basis.

In AAT Thailand, developing a performance culture was a critical aspect of the strategic aspiration. Therefore, the average variable pay component was aggressively set close to 40 percent, allowing some mid-level employees to receive bonuses that amounted to over 80 percent of their annual income. The new system had two components: two-thirds of an individual's performance evaluation depended on achieving the business objectives, while the rest—called "personal responsibility"—was linked to values that AAT wanted their employees to uphold. Employees who did not have individual targets could still earn a bonus based on the overall performance of the company. According to a senior local executive, the new system was "very invasive and not natural for the Thai culture, but it was a system necessary to drive change and performance."

6. Develop a new pipeline of leaders with the competencies that match the aspirations

One cannot continue to rely on outside recruitment for key positions. Training and coaching people in the new desired behaviors are a vital part of change, as discussed earlier. An internal pipeline of talent is essential, as we saw in the case of Canon Europe. This requires careful attention to HRM issues discussed in Chapters 6 and 8:

- Selection of recruits who fit with the new strategic aspirations, followed by careful on-boarding and socialization so that they will not be contaminated by "the old guard" who will inevitably still occupy key positions at lower levels
- Mentoring and buddying programs to ensure that the new talent receives appropriate support from the champions of change and do not get discouraged so that they leave
- Development programs for high potentials, perhaps including action-learning projects that focus on problematic areas needing change[28]
- Career pathing to ensuring that the best get challenging assignments in line with the strategic aspirations of the organization

The Russian nuclear industry, with more than a hundred companies grouped into Rosatom, is one of many examples. When Germany pulled out of nuclear power a few years ago, Rosatom saw an opportunity to accelerate its globalization. However, this required radical cultural change in an industry still Soviet in nature and marked by the aftermath of the Chernobyl disaster 30 years earlier. Working with top and senior management, HR decided that the accelerated development of high potentials was a critical step to move forward. The tool was an action-learning program, with cohorts of high potentials working on projects under the supervision of top management, supported by formal training. It was not a glitch-free process, but change was underway. All this requires active initiative and support from a credible HR function, who should consider themselves as architects of the change process.[29]

THE ROLE OF HR IN SUPPORTING STRATEGIC CHANGE

At MedPharm, the head of HR played a key role throughout the change process. However, despite the close relationship between HRM and strategy implementation, there are still relatively few firms where the HR function lives up to the ideal of being a "change partner" with senior leadership.

HR as Change Partner

A profound understanding of the firm's business strategy and its people implications is the necessary starting point for HR's role as a change partner. Unfortunately, this may not always be the case.

Companies organizing an international HR workshop sometimes contact us. They want input on how they can develop more "strategic HRM" as a part of their company's change efforts. They tell us about all the ambitious change projects that they have under way, in terms of competency management, succession planning, 360-degree feedback, appraisal system development, and the new seminars they have launched on managing change. "That's fine," we say, "But tell us about the strategy for your business and what organizational capabilities you need to build." All too often, there is a long pause… and then: "Well, we'll have to get back to you about that."

HR professionals—at the very least those in senior positions within the function—must know the business well enough to be able to articulate clearly the implications of the new strategy for the organization. Meeting the challenges also requires close interaction between the people in functionally oriented HRM process and content development roles, and those in business support. It is difficult for HR professionals to do a good job in supporting change unless strategic and people planning processes are closely linked.

With their expertise in people and organizational dynamics, HR professionals can play critical roles as sparring partners to line management in discussions about initiating and managing the process of change:

- How to engage key stakeholders, assess inevitable resistance, and empower change champions
- How to communicate the new strategy so that people lower down in the organization and across the world understand the implications
- How to adapt to cultural differences, but maintain the integrity of the core message

- How to "walk the talk" and model the desired change in their own behavior

One of the least recognized challenges in managing change in multinational firms is accepting that change and reconfiguration often takes considerable time to achieve: there is a temporal dimension to HRM—the capacity to anticipate and take the right measures at the right time.[30] It took the pharmaceutical giant GSK ten years to meet its goal of developing a capability in rapid product development. This required creating new work processes in the shape of cross-functional teams; changes in performance management, as well as selection and development; realigning technology and workflows; redesigning career paths; and implanting related shared norms and values. Similarly, it took IBM and Nestlé more than a decade to build a top-class local management cadre for their operations in China.

An important part of the change partner role of HR is helping senior managers to focus BOTH on today's operational requirements *and* realign the organization toward the future. Managers will often put off change since one of the basic laws is that change always comes at a cost—upheaval, disruption, internal focus, as well as large investments of time and energy. One is nearly always better off in the short term by not changing, simply doing better what one did yesterday. On the other hand, HR managers should be concerned if leaders become perhaps too fixated on change—resulting in damage to efficiency and employee morale (we will address in the next section). Communicating these concerns to top management without being labeled a change-blocker requires an HR function that has both credibility and confidence.

The HRM Contribution to the Change Process

The potential contribution of HRM to the change process has so many facets that we can provide only a few examples.

Creating dissatisfaction with the status quo: Change is difficult to manage unless there is an acknowledged need for it. Amplifying dissatisfaction with the status quo through training, two-way meetings, and project groups is an important role for HR, as is ensuring that attention focuses on high-priority problems. In many organizations people are extraordinarily busy, even worried, but they are not focused on the most urgent and important issues.[31]

One of the classic laws of change, which has its roots in the psychology of adaptation, is the inverted U-shaped relationship between change and tension (see Figure 10-2). If tension is low (in other words, if people are happy, contented, apathetic, or complacent because they feel successful), change is unlikely to occur. On the other hand, if the degree of tension is too high, people will react in unpredictable ways to protect their own interests, or they become paralyzed because they see no possible solutions. Change is managed best with a constructive degree of tension.

How can one "heat things up," increasing tension while keeping it constructive? There are four interrelated ways where HR can play the role of a catalyst:

1. Through constant scanning—externally (benchmarking, customer contacts, and competitive analysis) and internally (attitude surveys, management by wandering around, and 360-degree feedback)

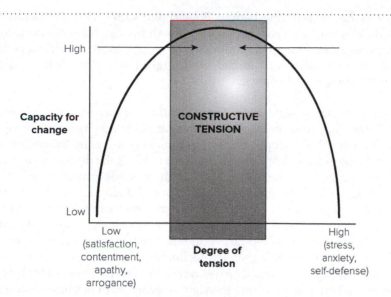

FIGURE 10-2
The Relationship
between Change and
Tension

2. Through sharing information about substandard performance, threats, and opportunities, balanced with the risk of worrying people unnecessarily and distracting them from their work

3. Through internal mobility (enhancing new perspectives by moving people across business and functional and geographical boundaries) or by bringing in new people who see problems with fresh eyes

4. Through the setting of stretch goals, accompanied by performance management (appraisal, incentives, and rewards) and a focus on identifying obstacles that prevent units and employees from achieving their ambitious goals

Identifying key stakeholders: An important exercise in a CAP workshop at GE involves listing all the key stakeholders by name or unit, including external parties, and identifying where they are positioned on a scale from "actively supportive" to "strongly against." The next step is to identify the position where they need to be if the change is to be successful, focusing then on the biggest gaps. What are the interests of these problematic stakeholders? What are the reasons for the gaps? What are the actions to take to bridge the gap?

Promoting champions of change: Change rarely happens as intended without committed leadership. Therefore, it is important to identify leaders who can act as champions of change, to nurture them and develop their change management skills, and to put them in appropriate positions. Radical organizational change sometimes happens simply because a strong leader takes over a unit.[32]

Helping top management to communicate directly with employees: Direct dialogue is the best tool to create an understanding of the need for change and its implications. Yet it can take courage for senior managers, the sponsors of change, to communicate directly with the workforce, and to engage them in dialogue rather than hiding behind PowerPoint slides. One of the most influential HR VPs that we have met viewed one of his key roles as coaching these senior sponsors, building their confidence to engage local stakeholders directly, particularly local managers abroad who might have quite different perspectives on the direction of change.

Designing processes to build commitment fast through face-to-face confrontation of views: How does one accelerate the understanding of the need for change in an organization of 100,000 people, or among employees in a plant located on another continent? One of the important contributions of HR is the design of such engagement and explanation processes—such as the cascade process used by many organizations, or the intensive communication and dialogue in our Hilti example.

It is also important to recognize that what motivates top management is rarely the same as what will motivate middle- and lower-level staff. Information should be relevant to the target audience, and senior management is frequently blind to this, needing skilled facilitation.[33] Messages pointing out that, "we have to change dramatically to become a top-quartile performer by exploiting our assets better and earning the right to grow" will not have much impact on many middle managers and most ordinary employees.

Vision building/agenda setting: Change can progress quickly if the vision or change agenda is clear in the minds of change leaders and staff. All too frequently, top management presents a change solution (e.g., what competitors are doing already) without any clear vision to support it. In these circumstances, it will be difficult to monitor progress. Skilled HR or consultants can facilitate building a vision for the future. Often simple tools, such as backward visioning or "Future Perfect" (write the story as if seen from the future) can kick-start the process.[34]

Helping employees to cope with emotional needs at different stages of the change process: It is important to help individuals cope with the personal transition of major change. There are different needs at the three phases of the transition that individuals go through: "endings," where coping with the emotional pain of giving up what is known and appreciated may be important; "neutral zones," where people need dialogue to explore the future state; and "new beginnings," where they need coaching and training to learn new skills and attitudes.[35]

Dealing with different types of people during implementation: The ability of people to change depends on their willingness and their ability. Some people are both willing and able to change, and they may be candidates for key positions as champions. Those who are willing but lack the knowledge, skills, and attitudes will benefit from training and coaching. Those who are neither able nor willing should be replaced, or at least sidelined. But what about those who are highly capable, essential for delivering today's operating results, but who just do not believe in the need to change? Here there are no easy solutions—the role of HR here is to assist in working through strategies tailored to specific situations—but at the end, no one is indispensable.

Attention to succession management: One of the problems in organizational change is making it last.[36] Paradoxically, there may often be too much change and not enough continuity because all the efforts focused on finding and recruiting change champions, and not on thinking ahead to develop successors. Attention to succession management is important—firms often need successors who will continue the process of implementation rather than having an outsider taking the unit off in new directions—and HR has a clear role here.

Ensuring consistency between words and action: One of the biggest factors hindering change is failure to walk the talk. This is rarely deliberate, and one role of HR is to point out the gap. At an international bank that had invested millions in building a new culture emphasizing empowerment, employees knew that there would be dire consequences if a VP did not have an immediate answer to any question that an executive committee member might ask in the corridor. Until HR pointed this out, the bank's staff was mobilized to keep their VPs informed of anything and everything just in case they were asked a question—totally inconsistent with empowerment.

It is the classic trap, the folly of hoping for X while rewarding Y.[37] The approach of the former long-term CEO of Amgen, Kevin Sharer, has much to commend it. He asked each of his top 75 "What should I do differently?" sharing his own development needs publicly with them while discussing their implications for behavioral change.[38]

Ensuring the balance between short- and long-term pressures: One of the important HRM issues is to ensure that short-term crisis measures do not compromise long-term loyalty when, for example, downsizing. At L'Oréal in the past, the role of the HR function was to argue for the long-term view, to counter the risk that the future would be compromised by short-term imperatives—for example, pointing out that the price of cost reduction through firing employees might be reduced willingness to accept more important process changes down the road.[39]

Overall, we conclude this necessarily incomplete list by noting that Ulrich outlined four roles for HR in the change arena. These roles are the *champion* who promotes the need for change; the *designer* who assists in mapping out an effective change process; the *facilitator* who acts as a coach and catalyst; and the *demonstrator* who is a role model through consistent behavior.[40]

The Dangers of Fixation on Change

Some companies are fixated on superficial change, and this is often the result of poor change management that is excessively focused on delivering solutions without a clear strategic aspiration. Each new management team scrambles around to find new solutions to ongoing challenges. Since employees do not understand the problems, and since there is no clear strategic aspiration, these solutions fail to yield the expected results. Another management team comes in, under even greater pressure to come up with new solutions, and the cycle repeats itself. Gradually, a cynicism about change initiatives builds up. Employees learn to ignore the rhetoric of change, quietly carrying on with their work and their own lives—until real change erupts through crisis. The lesson is that real change requires the continuity provided by long-term vision and goals, but leaving the detailed solutions to those who will implement them.

Excessive mobility under the guise of international management development can exacerbate change fixation. Each new expatriate leader will start a new change initiative—for instance, driving the local unit toward cost reduction. Just as the change is beginning to take hold, the expatriate moves on and a new successor is appointed. Since there are few rewards for implementing what someone else has started, the new expatriate will take the unit off in a different direction. Therefore, successful change requires not only reward for initiating actions but also accountability for full execution, staying in the post as long as necessary to ensure this.

In some firms, top management focuses exclusively on change, improvement, and constant realignment. Each year, the targets are stretched further and further. This creates a treadmill atmosphere where more and more is squeezed out of the organization. Ignoring longer-term strategic and organizational development leads to instability and a deeper crisis in the future.

Having said this, the reality is that continuous change has become a reality in many sectors—with accelerating competition, there are no signs that the pressures for change will go away. In industries such as the high tech, software, professional service, and e-based sectors, the process of change is accelerating. Technological and product life cycles grow shorter, and competitive changes succeed one another in waves. As the process of change speeds up, it is necessary to anticipate future changes and to build the future into the present. This leads us to organizational agility as the next challenge of multinational HRM.

ENHANCING ORGANIZATIONAL AGILITY

In some global industries, major strategic change takes place relatively infrequently—a pattern described as punctuated equilibrium[41]—periods of evolutionary change alternating with spikes of radical change. This has been true for food and most fast-moving consumer goods, as well as basic chemicals or power equipment. An engineer who entered the firm 30 years ago will still deal with the same basic technology as an engineer who starts today.

However, in other globalized industries, such as information and communications technology, the speed of change is rapid, with frequent inflection points when there are major shifts in technologies and markets.[42] If firms adapt slowly, new competitors—either existing competitors who moved faster or nimble entrepreneurial start-ups—can quickly turn yesterday's winners into tomorrow's losers. The disappearance of Compaq, Motorola, and Lucent and the decline of HP and Nokia are examples. In such industries, the capacity for change needs to be built into the fabric of the organization. Strategic agility becomes a survival factor. As multinationals learn to be more agile, speed of responsiveness and change capability are likely to become important competitive success factors in other industries.

Doz and Kosonen have studied multinational corporations in industries where success means thriving on continuous waves of change—Accenture, Cisco, IBM, as well as Nokia and SAP.[43] What are the features associated with their strategic agility? They single out three:

- A high degree of strategic sensitivity
- A strong collective commitment
- Resource flexibility

Let us discuss each of these briefly, with a focus on the HRM implications.

Developing Strategic Sensitivity

Strategic sensitivity means connectedness—a high degree of connectedness with the external environment, and a high degree of internal connectedness through the social architecture. This implies maximizing connections with the outside world of customers as well as with technology hotbeds and universities—constantly scanning for opportunities, threats, market and technological shifts, and innovations. It helps to be present in regions of the world where there are leading developments—as noted earlier, Cisco has split its corporate headquarters into two, the western-facing headquarters in Silicon Valley, and the eastern-facing headquarters in Bangalore, India. Strategic alliances are important tools for scanning and exploring new environments, as are think tanks established with external partners.

IBM has refined the intranet jam process that it pioneered to create shared values, broadening this to innovation jams. An online exchange, connecting 150,000 people for a 72-hour period, including external customers and partners, was first organized in 2006 with the aim of finding ways of moving its latest technologies to market—and this has been repeated since.[44]

All the methods for transferring knowledge internally within the firm, from social networks to people mobility, are part of building strategic agility. Organizational culture is another element, where one might single out the combination of strong ambition (driven by appropriate rewards) along with willingness to experiment and take risks (which implies learning from mistakes rather than punishing them).

There is one critical element from the people management point of view: *the quality of internal communication.* Tapping into external trends, resources and insights is essential, as are successful internal experiments—but if the poor quality of internal communication handicaps the process of working through the implications, this will be of little use. Quality conversations that arouse attention and add value have two characteristics—they are high on either analytic reasoning or emotional authenticity, or both.[45] If internal communication is ritualistic and dehydrated, information is unlikely to spread and processed effectively. Equally dangerous is the situation where communication is handicapped by emotional barriers between top and middle management.

A recent study on the dramatic downfall of Nokia in the mobile phone business highlights the barriers to transparency and engagement.[46] Nokia leaders were broadly aware of competitive threats, but they did not communicate the severity of these threats to the organization because they were concerned about the reaction from the shareholders. Meanwhile, middle managers who were in competition with each other, failed to share negative information with top management since they were afraid of upsetting their superiors. Consequently, senior executives were blind to shortcomings in Nokia's technological and innovation capabilities until it was too late to react.

Indeed, a number of multinationals have invested in enhancing internal dialogue, through training and feedback processes, and a review of global strategic change highlights the importance of facing up to the cultural barriers.[47]

Often managers hoard information as the key to personal power, justified by norms of proprietary secrecy. However, in a fast-moving environment, there are few competitive secrets, and those apply mostly to technological specifications. In such industries, competitive value comes far more from agility, speed of responsiveness, and thoroughness in execution than it does from information per se. Twenty years ago, IBM used to be a secretive firm that was reluctant to share information even internally; today there is a high degree of internal transparency, while reasonable discretion is assured through shared values.

Building Leadership Unity and Collective Commitment

The second key challenge for strategic agility concerns the capability to build alignment around key decisions. Studies of high-performing companies in the hypercompetitive environment of Silicon Valley illustrate this well. While there is constant scanning and hot, high-quality internal dialogue, the top leadership knows how to stop the discussion at an appropriate stage, taking the necessary strategic decisions, and explaining the rationale clearly.[48] The top team has to be totally united and capable of building "act-with-one-voice" commitment to these decisions, aligning the organization around the intended plan of action.

Achieving this is not easy in an organization where senior leaders inevitably have different perspectives as well as big egos. Still, without this capacity for clear, united decision-making with collective commitment, corporations are unable to switch from a mode of behavior focused on exploring options to an action mode of execution. In acquisitions, for example, lack of unity among top management is one of the most important obstacles to merger integration, resulting in a slow integration process from which competitors will benefit.[49]

This is why the collective sense of accountability, together with individual responsibility for one's own unit or function, is so important in the global corporation, as we discussed in Chapter 4. Mobility, especially for high-potential individuals, will nurture this sense of collective commitment, as will fair process management—the ability to engage key stakeholders and explore options, and then to explain decisions and set clear expectations.

There is no doubt that it is easier to build collective commitment to an action plan if all key managers are located in the home country headquarters, as they are in a meganational. Leaders (and the HR function) in a transnational firm must give careful attention to the *Five Es*, engaging key stakeholders of different cultures in distant operations and taking pains to explain decisions when they are taken. Despite the advances in telecommunications, the travel budgets are necessarily high, and it would be dangerous to cut back crudely on such expenses in times of difficulty—when the need for face-to-face communication is at its highest point.

Encouraging Resource Flexibility

Cost is not the only reason for the globalization of business processes and for reorganizing common transactions into regional or global shared service centers—providing resource flexibility may be more important. Information processing, expatriate mobility, supply chain management, payroll, and many other services should no longer be fragmented, or under the thumb of local business or geographic managers. Consequently, the organization can respond much more easily and quickly to market or technological changes, or to the need to reorganize.[50] In one well-known computer firm, studies showed that the average life cycle of a business unit, measured by the length of time before its basic charter was changed, was less than 30 months.[51]

The frontier of resource flexibility is people. Finance and information have long been going through a process of global standardization, but talented people are geographically rooted and resistant to being "standardized." Still, the combination of air travel, virtual communication, and cross-boundary project work has greatly increased the fluidity of HR deployment.

McKinsey prides itself on allowing any of its managers in any location of the world to tap into the expertise of a leading authority on any issue concerning strategy, structure, or leadership—with two or three phone calls or e-mails. Physical mobility among leaders and technical experts, facilitated by global talent pool management, has clearly increased and is most important, as we have stressed throughout this book.[52] In the future, the expansion of open internal job markets, facilitated by globalized self-help technology, may allow companies to deploy knowledge and skills across borders in low-cost ways that have not previously been possible.[53]

However, this means that talented individuals whom the organization wants to retain are no longer under the control of a specific hierarchic unit within the firm. Agile emerging global firms like Infosys and Lenovo have concluded that the only way of integrating such people into the organization, and providing them with a sense of belonging as well as guiding their behavior, is through values-based management, with horizontal coordination replacing hierarchic control.[54]

Established companies such as IBM have put a lot of effort into re-instilling common values, pioneering new web-enabled ways of engaging people. This emotional integration through shared identity and meaning is important to steer collective action and build vital trust. However, a sense of shared identity might be difficult to create in multidomestic companies that have grown through acquisitions and local entrepreneurship; but even here there are opportunities, as illustrated by the Canon Europe case.

Riding the Cycle of Change: Toward an Ambidextrous Organization

Since the global financial bubble collapsed in the fall of 2008, the world economy faced challenges unparalleled for half a century, with consequences that will reach far into the future. Shared values ... people mobility ... high-quality dialogue ... organizations with an in-built sense of fair process—at times of global slump these may seem out of sync with reality. Still, one of the characteristics of agile and high-performing organizations is that they pay as much attention to continuity as to driving change. As the global crisis was starting to bite, the CEO of one exposed global bank commented: "We paid a steep price after former downturns for cutting back on talent. That's not a trap that we will fall into again. The biggest constraint on our future prosperity is not capital or markets but leadership." In the middle of the recession, the bank was preparing to launch an internal campaign to reinforce global corporate values of trustworthiness and responsiveness.

Attention to continuity as well as change, to trust as well as costs, to collaboration as well as individual performance—once again we find that duality or paradox permeates the challenges of strategic agility. When Lego's CEO led extensive restructuring to respond to dramatic changes in the global toy market, his strategic teams wrestled with the need for empowerment and control as well as individuality and teamwork. Such tensions characterized change implementation work throughout the firm.[55]

Another way of expressing strategic agility is to say that global organizations and their leaders need to be ambidextrous—the capability of exploiting and exploring at the same time.[56] As noted by researchers who explored this concept, ambidexterity is ultimately about survival.[57] It is about how IBM moved from hardware to software to services, and how Fujifilm changed from photography to fine chemicals. It is about how HP moved from electronic instruments to minicomputers to printers and is at the time of writing trying to make a transition to services. It is also about the disappearance and decline of once admired global companies like Kodak and Motorola who did not have the ambidexterity to master the upheaval of strategic change.

TAKEAWAYS

1. One of the biggest HRM challenges in multinational firms is ensuring effective execution of strategy. Implementation is largely a question of managing change.

2. There are different conceptual models of change—evolutionary change in situations where there are no immediate pressures for drastic measures, and radical change when the future of the organization is at stake.

3. In situations calling for evolution change, the formula $Q \times A = E$ is a useful rule of thumb. The effectiveness (E) of change is a function of the quality (Q) of the analysis multiplied by employee acceptance (A) of the proposed change.

4. The outcomes of decisions made in any change process will never be fair to everybody. In order to build commitment to change it is important to make sure that the decision-making process is seen as fair.

5. In operational terms, fair process means paying attention to the *Five E*s: engagement of people, exploration of options, explanation of decisions made, setting expectations, and evaluation of the outcomes of the change process.

6. In processes of radical change, the development of a new strategy and organizational capabilities usually requires to realign structures, processes, as well as competencies and organizational culture.

7. Processes of radical change draw heavily on HRM since they typically involve replacement of key people and the development of new performance requirements. It is a process first of taking charge and then of letting go as the new culture takes hold.

8. With their expertise in people and organizational dynamics, HR professionals can play critical roles as sparring partners to line management in discussions about initiating and managing processes of change.

9. Companies need to balance short-term pressures and long-term development. One of the responsibilities of HR is to ensure that short-term crisis measures do not compromise long-term competence needs and employee commitment.

10. To build strategic agility, multinational firms need to pay attention to strategic sensitivity (including transparency of information and quality dialogue), leadership unity, and resource flexibility.

NOTES

1 MedPharm is a fictitious name. The description of the situation is accurate, but we changed various details to protect the company's identity.

2 UAMS and Cap Gemini Ernst and Young, "Measures that matter," part of presentation "How intangibles are driving business performance" (www.uams.be).

3 We do not know the origins of the Q × A = E formula, which GE adopted. In academic literature, one finds this way of thinking about change in Beer and Nohria (2000). They use different terminology, calling the Q-side "Theory E" (standing for economic reasoning), and the A-side "Theory O," meaning organizational reasoning.

4 As discussed in Chapter 8.

5 Kotter, 1996.

6 Mintzberg and Waters, 1985; Mintzberg and Westley, 1992.

7 The concept of procedural justice originated with Thibaut and Walker (1975) in their comparative studies of legal dispute–resolution procedures. For reviews of research on procedural justice across cultures, see Pillai, Scandura, and Williams (1999) and Broekner *et al.* (2000). The interactive relationship between procedural fairness and outcome favorability (or acceptance) is found to be robust and consistent across cultures, though the relationship is stronger in cultures that emphasize people's connectedness to others as opposed to independence from one another (Broekner *et al.*, 2000).

8 For research on the effect of procedural fairness on the acceptance of strategies in the units of multinational corporations, see Kim and Mauborgne (1991 and 1998).

9 The title of a book, "Taking Charge and Letting Go" captures this idea well (Spector, 1995).

10 Kim and Mauborgne (1997) view three elements as important for a process to be fair—engagement, explanation, and expectation clarity. Van der Heyden has elaborated on this framework, developing appropriate instrumentation, and adding two other elements, namely exploration and evaluation (Van der Heyden and Limberg, 2007; Van der Heyden, Blondel, and Carlock, 2005).

11 Note that the term "engagement" has another meaning among HR practitioners, namely involvement and motivation, as in the use of engagement surveys.

12 Evans, 1994.

13 Gladwell, 2000; Kim and Mauborgne, 2003.

14 Beyond face-to-face meetings, the tools of engagement include mass communications (e-mail, newsletters, and intranet sites), workshops, training sessions, benchmarking visits, customer or other surveys, rewards and punishments, third-party leverage (arranging for peers to meet key people), upward lobbying, and decrees.

15 Even at times of headcount freezes, it is good practice not to freeze travel budgets on international change projects.

16 Cialdini, 2001; Conger, 1998; Gelfand and Brett, 2004.

17 Doz and Kosonen (2008) elaborate on this hypothesis.

18 Huy (2002 and 2005) discusses the role of positive emotional management as well as negative feelings in the change process, with a focus on action to express sympathy, hope, fun, attachment, and authenticity.

19 Argyris, 1990; Schein, 1996.

20 Bridges, 1980.

21 For the Nissan turnaround story led by Carlos Ghosn, see Huy (2004).

22 An important example of explanation (discussed in Chapter 12) is the communication about the rationale behind an acquisition, which should take place during the "100 days" following the merger announcement.

23 See discussion in Chapter 7. The acronym SMART applies to objective setting, where targets should be specific, measurable, achievable or agreed, realistic, and with clear time specifications.

24 These stages in implementation are well mapped out by Beer, Eisenstat, and Spector (1990) as a critical path.

25 A study of radical change in a British multinational in the chemical industry showed that the change process did not start with the appointment of a new insider CEO who initiated the turnaround. It began years earlier with the mobilization of small coalitions who were dissatisfied with the status quo. Mid-level managers engaged in a great deal of experimentation at local levels, building experience and confidence in a new strategic aspiration. When the crisis triggered a change at the top, those individuals moved into key positions in a restructured organization. See Pettigrew (1985).

26 Our formal sources for this IBM story are Gerstner (2002), and J. Weeks, "Culture and leadership at IBM," INSEAD case, Fontainebleau France, 2004. But our most important source was an executive who was one of Gerstner's close lieutenants during his tenure at IBM.

27 See the section on "the spiral path to transnational organization" in Chapter 2.

28 This may also include short- or medium-term assignments to other "progressive" affiliates within the corporation.

29 Another example of supporting radical change with leadership development is Tata Steel. Starting from the strategic aspiration of a visionary top executive, it has been transformed within a decade from a distinguished but local Indian steel company into a major player in the global steel industry. The senior executives attended a course in a European business school to help elaborate that aspiration, as well as equipping themselves with the necessary competencies and management know-how.

30 This dimension of HRM is well articulated by Gratton (2000).

31 This is the theme of Bruch and Ghoshal (2002) in a study of four multinational organizations. See Kotter (2008) on ways of creating a sense of urgency.

32 Doz and Prahalad, 1988.

33 See Aiken and Keller (2009). Zohar (1997) argues that people are motivated by five different forms of impact: on society, on the customer, on the company and its shareholders, on the working team, and on "me" personally. Compelling stories should be designed to create as many of these impacts as possible.

34 See Gratton (2000) for ideas and analysis on how HR can facilitate the development of a vision.

35 Bridges, 1980 and 1986.

36 Black and Gregersen (2008) describe the dangers of lack of follow-through in change management at some length. The importance of managing continuity in change is made well in Collins' study *Good to Great*, where he calls this the flywheel effect (see Collins, 2001). See also the discussion in Chapter 8 on the dangers of excessive mobility.

37 Kerr, 1995.

38 Amgen CEO's approach to managing change is described by Aiken and Keller (2009).

39 See the discussion of L'Oréal's management philosophy on p. 195.

40 Ulrich, 1997. See also Caldwell (2008).

41 See Tushman, Newman, and Romanelli (1986) for the punctuated equilibrium model of change.

42 An inflection point is a strategic turning point in the industry, such as a radical change in technology or market. Slow-moving industry leaders often become tomorrow's laggards.

43 Doz and Kosonen, 2008. See Weber and Tarba (2014) for a wider review of research on strategic agility.

44 The example of the IBM innovation jam is presented in Bjelland and Wood (2008). In Chapter 5, we described IBM's intranet jam to create shared values.

45 See Gratton and Ghoshal (2002). For cultural barriers to global strategic change, see Lane *et al.* (2014).

46 Vuori and Huy, 2015.

47 Cultural differences may influence what constitutes effective dialogue. For example, one dimension of quality dialogue that varies from one culture to another (as well as situationally) is direct versus indirect communication. While organizational culture matters, communication in collectivistic cultures is often more indirect, since the desire to be polite and avoid embarrassment may override the importance of rational truth as defined by individualistic cultures (Smith and Bond, 1999).

48 Eisenhardt, Kahwajy, and Bourgeois, 1997; Brown and Eisenhardt, 1997.

49 See the discussion on this issue in Chapter 12.

50 Doz and Kosonen, 2008.

51 Galunic and Eisenhardt, 2001.

52 See Chapter 8.

53 See the discussion on open-job markets in Chapter 8 and on social networks in Chapters 5 and 11.

54 In Chapter 4, we discussed the need for a change in concepts of control. See Chapter 5 for a discussion of shared values and the socialization of talent.

55 See Lewis, Andriopoulos, and Smith (2014).

56 Among the first CEOs to endorse the idea of ambidexterity was GE's Jeff Immelt, describing his goals as "ambidextrous leadership: growth and cost control—and sustained excellence at both." See "Q&A: On the Hot Seat," *Fortune*, 11 December 2005: 75.

57 O'Reilly and Tushman (2013) review the growing literature on ambidexterity.

11

Managing Knowledge and Innovation across Borders

SUMMARY

Challenge

Maintaining competitive advantage in an environment with short product life cycles and competitors who learn fast requires the ability to mobilize knowledge across borders rather than waiting for innovation from the center

Analysis

Enhancing innovation requires managing knowledge across borders in a way that allows the company to

- Tap into valuable tacit knowledge from different parts of the organization
- Acquire information and know-how from sources outside of company boundaries

Solutions

- Align HRM priorities with retention and enhancement of tacit knowledge
- Implement knowledge sharing tools that focus on talent, performance management, and incentives systems
- Design external scanning systems that maximize the benefits of global presence
- Foster innovation by helping employees set goals out of their comfort zones
- Balance people investments between exploiting existing knowledge and exploring new frontiers

Reaching Out for Knowledge at the International Finance Corporation

As the private arm of the World Bank Group, the International Finance Corporation (IFC) provides financial products and consulting services to private businesses in poor countries. The consulting services are closely tied to the financial products as IFC consultants help companies to improve their operations so they can qualify for financing from the IFC. By design, the consulting services division is IFC's vanguard when entering new or challenging markets.

Most of the work carried out by consulting services is done by project teams located in the countries in which the services are offered. Local teams are assembled with talent and skills to address the client needs. They are encouraged to understand the local political, economic, cultural, and technological conditions in which they operate. In order to provide the best solutions to clients, project teams are expected to access both internal and external knowledge resources wherever they may be found, but the IFC has no required process or protocol for how to access this knowledge.

The IFC engages in hundreds of projects a year, and the expert knowledge of even the most seasoned team pales in comparison to the cumulative knowledge of the organization. Some of this cumulative knowledge is only relevant to specific locations, while other knowledge can be applicable and valuable across multiple countries. This presents a major challenge and opportunity for the IFC. Searching for relevant knowledge from other project teams is costly, but if ideas developed elsewhere can be leveraged, savings to the clients may be significant—with possibility of additional benefits of faster delivery and higher-quality solutions due to a broader perspective.

The IFC has found that by getting its local consultants to reach to other project teams operating in different countries, much inefficiency that comes with reinventing the wheel is avoided and new ideas can be developed by building on previous insights in other parts of the organization. Teams can reach out by tapping into personal networks or accessing databases and archives of past projects to see what others have done. By gaining timely access to information about other projects, the team can devise innovative solutions for the client. Indeed, independent research has shown that the farther IFC teams reach outside of their host country, the more impactful and effective their solutions are for the local clients.[1]

However, applying knowledge from one project to another is inherently difficult because of the differences in context—in particular the cultural and institutional settings. Even understanding what another project team did often requires detailed, face-to-face interaction and unique understanding of the companies and government agencies involved. As a result, what one team can gain from another depends on the degree to which the original project was customized, the level of local adaptation required, the extent to which the client became involved in the project, and the uniqueness of the market.

While numerous databases and systems are in place to capture IFC experience, the teams do not know where to go for help, and searching for relevant knowledge is often constrained by project deadlines. These knowledge repositories may range from highly detailed project completion reports required by management, and internal blogs for sharing ideas by people involved in projects, to books, pamphlets, and reports from the communications department. Though valuable, employees often don't have time to explore the wealth of technical information that has been compiled.

Project teams often end up relying only on their local informal networks without seeking out valuable but distant pools of knowledge. And even those teams who do identify new sources of potentially useful knowledge struggle to apply the information if the ideas developed outside their local country are not obviously relevant to their issue. Because of these constraints, many great ideas within the IFC do not get shared and, despite the IFC's best effort, many projects end up reinventing the wheel.[2] Improving knowledge management is therefore high on the management agenda—a task where HR practices and tools can be of considerable help.

OVERVIEW

In a global business environment with shorter product life cycles and competitors that quickly imitate successful innovations, maintaining a competitive advantage requires effective sharing of knowledge.[3] In this chapter, we describe how to manage knowledge and enhance innovation in the multinational firm.

We first discuss how to facilitate knowledge sharing across geographically dispersed units, which depends on cross-unit social networks, organizational values of collaboration and support, and global mindsets among employees. We also review coordination mechanisms, a range of people management practices that enhance knowledge sharing, and how human resource management can support acquiring knowledge from customers, partners, and other external groups.

Sharing knowledge across units, knowledge acquisition from outside the firm, and the recombination of new and existing knowledge are all parts of an integrated process leading to corporate innovations. In the final part of this chapter we examine how international firms can build innovation capability.

SHARING KNOWLEDGE IN THE MULTINATIONAL

Scholars argue that a primary rationale for the existence of multinational firms is their ability to share and exploit knowledge more effectively and efficiently within their organizations than via the market.[4] Multinationals help overcome institutional voids, cultural barriers, and geographic distance by providing processes, common language, and trust among different country subsidiaries.

Knowledge management used to be centered in the home country of the multinational. Today, since capabilities are broadly diffused across regions, new knowledge is expected to come from local units and then shared globally.[5]

While foreign units naturally learn from their local context, solving local problems often requires that subsidiary employees turn to knowledge from technologies, designs, and systems outside of their local contexts. Drawing on knowledge from other units allows employees to leverage tested principles behind a product, service, or system and offer solutions to customer needs not available locally. When units share knowledge with others far away, they increase their chances of finding relevant and new information.[6] Indeed, turning to others outside of the initial geographic domain has been found to account for roughly one-quarter of successful innovations within international firms.[7]

In fact, the importance of interunit knowledge sharing is now so widely accepted that CEOs often identify it as a top concern for the company.[8] One of General Electric's (GE's) five "timeless principles" is the belief that "the ultimate sustainable competitive advantage lies in the ability to learn, to transfer that learning across components, and to act on it quickly."[9] This drove GE to create a boundary-less company by delayering, destroying silos, purging the not-invented-here syndrome, and attempting to create an organization that sees change as an opportunity rather than a threat. Doing so allowed GE to share more knowledge and to share more valuable types of knowledge as well.

Types of Knowledge

When it comes to knowledge sharing, two kinds of knowledge are important to multinationals. *Explicit knowledge* is knowledge that individuals and organizations know that they have—objective, formal, systematic, incorporated in texts and manuals, and relatively easy to pass on to others.[10] Virtually all knowledge stored in IT-based databases and systems is explicit. In contrast, *tacit knowledge* is personal, context specific, and hard to formalize and communicate. Individuals may not even be conscious of the tacit knowledge they possess. Tacit knowledge often underlies complex skills, built on the intuitive feel acquired through years of experience that is hard to put into words.

Explicit knowledge helps companies to improve routine and technical activities—helping the company improve standardized work capabilities. Tacit knowledge helps companies improve their creation capabilities and develop ways to more effectively learn and innovate—helping the company to develop customized work capabilities (see Figure 11-1). However, tacit knowledge is "sticky,"[11] and its stickiness is reflected in the costs associated with sharing tacit knowledge. Because of the relative ease in sharing explicit knowledge over tacit knowledge, employees sharing knowledge across units are more likely to draw upon explicit forms of knowledge than they are tacit forms.[12]

Knowledge-Sharing Challenges

Consider the following example from a firm with which one of the authors has been working. This multinational corporation had six factories around the world, manufacturing almost identical products using the same equipment, the same tools, and roughly the same work processes. The subsidiaries' production yields varied greatly but they neither knew the productivity of the other units nor shared information about the production process. The obvious question to ask in this situation is how to make sure that the units share knowledge with each other, improving the productivity of the laggards and perhaps also that of the top performers.

The degree to which such knowledge sharing takes place depends on (1) the ability and willingness of the provider unit or source to share knowledge and (2) the ability and willingness of the seeker unit to exploit it.[13] When units lack ability or willingness in any of these areas it presents a unique challenge for knowledge sharing. See Figure 11-2 on knowledge-sharing challenges.

Provider Ability—"Foreigner" Challenge

The measure of a unit's ability to share knowledge with others can be labeled its "pedagogical ability."[14] With respect to explicit knowledge, pedagogical ability is shown in the provider unit's proficiency in codifying knowledge in manuals,

---

FIGURE 11-1
Types of Knowledge and
Work Implications

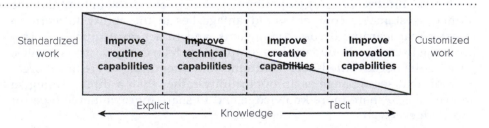

	Seeker of knowledge	Provider of knowledge
Motivation	Not-invented-here challenge	Hoarding-of-expertise challenge
Ability	Absorptive Capacity challenge	"Foreigner" challenge

FIGURE 11-2
Knowledge sharing challenges

Source: Adapted from M. Hansen and N. Nohria, "How to Build Collaborative Advantage", *MIT Sloan Management Review*, Fall 2004.

reports, and physical systems that are available to other parts of the corporation. However, sharing tacit knowledge is more difficult, and the ability to do so is therefore more crucial for successful sharing to take place. It almost always requires interpersonal, often face-to-face, interaction. Good language and communication skills and a good understanding of cross-cultural factors are some of the ingredients of the pedagogical ability needed to share knowledge across borders.

Lack of such skills and understanding creates what is known as the *"foreigner" challenge*. In this case, it requires that units exchanging knowledge already understand one another's culture and have an established interpersonal relationship, particularly in the case of tacit know-how. Without such relationships and understanding, it can be cumbersome and costly to share more than the most explicit knowledge.

Provider Willingness—Hoarding-of-Expertise Challenge

For knowledge sharing to take place, the provider of knowledge must be willing to share it. In the example at the beginning of this section, the manufacturing units were unwilling to share information about their productivity with others, and even less interested in teaching others how to improve their operations, owing to strong competition between plants. Since the headquarter executives were critically reviewing the structure of the company's international network of manufacturing units, the plants were competing for resources, even survival. Why help others learn something that was a key advantage for their own unit? The subsidiary managers were mostly evaluated on their own unit's performance, strengthening their internal focus and reinforcing the multinational's political atmosphere. Thus, the example shows how interunit knowledge sharing is influenced by the performance management system of the firm and the compensation and rewards that go with it.[15] When incentives are misaligned, it often leads to a *hoarding-of-expertise challenge*.

However, when incentives and social norms are in place for sharing, units may be more willing to share. Social status and reputation play important roles in shaping the context for knowledge sharing. People and units should be able to gain status when they are perceived as knowledgeable, and sharing knowledge with other units is a good way to enhance their reputation. Units who are given credit for having shared knowledge are more likely to do so again in the future.[16]

Norms of reciprocity are also important. Units and individuals are more willing to invest in sharing their knowledge with others if they trust them to reciprocate these favors in the future. Teaching others requires considerable effort, and in the absence of strong social relationships between parties, the decision to engage in knowledge sharing is usually based on some calculation of whether or not it is worth the time and money.[17] A higher level of trust is therefore associated with more knowledge sharing, as is the existence of a strong organizational culture where knowledge sharing is an important shared value and norm.

Seeker Ability—Absorptive Capacity Challenge

Not surprisingly, research has shown that the ability of the seeker to absorb new knowledge is a strong predictor of the extent to which the unit shares knowledge.[18] Absorptive capacity is largely an outcome of the existing stock of knowledge—people who know a lot can learn more than people who only know a little. Not having absorptive capacity makes it difficult for affiliate subsidiaries to know where to look for valuable knowledge, creating an *absorptive capacity challenge.*

There are four different levels in the absorptive capacity of a foreign subsidiary, ranging from the capacity to (1) operate assembly or turnkey equipment, (2) locally adapt components, (3) redesign products, and (4) design products independently.[19] The higher the subsidiary's capacity, the more likely the unit will be able to put distant new knowledge into productive use by combining it with the subsidiary's existing knowledge. Developing a high level of capacity to absorb knowledge takes time. For example, even with full corporate support it took HP's Singapore unit 20 years to be able to build up its capability from component assembly to design of new products.[20]

There are paradoxes around absorptive capacity. When two units are similar, it is much easier to understand and learn from the other; knowledge sharing is facilitated. Conversely, similar units have less to learn from each other. The more their knowledge overlaps, the less there is to be gained from investment in knowledge sharing.

Seeker Willingness—Not-Invented-Here Challenge

Absorptive capacity is more than just the ability of a unit to recognize the value of new information, assimilate it, and apply it to commercial ends.[21] It also includes the capacity to unlearn, to challenge existing ways of doing things. Generally speaking, the more satisfied people are with current practices and results, the less willing they are to seek out and absorb what is new. And even if units realize that they are facing a problem that needs to be tackled, inward-looking units with strong internal social networks may not actively search for relevant knowledge held by other parts of the multinational.

Lack of motivation on the part of many units to learn from others is well documented. There is a natural psychological tendency to inflate the perceived quality of one's own knowledge while deflating that of others. The *not-invented-here challenge* has been described in a number of case studies and is particularly strong if a unit is financially successful and has a long proud history.

How to Stimulate Knowledge Sharing

Multinationals can use numerous levers to overcome challenges of knowledge-sharing:

- Improving information about superior performance and knowledge
- Designing structural mechanisms to share knowledge
- Implementing a comprehensive approach to mobility and talent management
- Reinforcing sharing through performance management and incentive systems
- Framing knowledge around the story and not the data

Improving Information about Superior Performance and Knowledge

One way to improve the seeker's willingness and ability to access distant knowledge is to make information on unit performance more widely available. Units perceived by others to be highly capable are more likely to be sought out as sources of knowledge.[22] However, evaluation of a subsidiary's capabilities has a significant subjective element. Studies have revealed that there are only modest correlations between how managers from headquarters and foreign subsidiaries view the capabilities of overseas units.[23] Therefore, it is important to identify superior practices by measuring appropriate dimensions of unit performance.

By making performance data widely available—turning the multinational into a fishbowl where strong performances is showcased—the units can themselves uncover examples of unique and valuable knowledge. For instance, the food machinery company DeLaval (a part of Tetra Laval Group from Sweden) held quarterly meetings for all its subsidiary managers where they were required to present performance data along multiple dimensions. This approach triggered knowledge sharing among the units.[24] Their willingness increased because they realized that others were performing better and might actually have something valuable to share. Their ability increased because they were able to more easily identify sources of valuable information.

Designing Structural Mechanisms to Share Knowledge

Various structural coordination mechanisms, as discussed in Chapter 4, can be used to stimulate knowledge sharing. For instance, product development committees with members from different geographical units and from different functional areas (notably R&D, manufacturing, and marketing) are put together with the aim of tapping into the different perspectives and pools of experience that the members bring to the committee.[25] Temporary international task forces can serve the same purpose. Multinationals may also appoint individuals to liaise between units, for example, as competence managers for a specific functional area or as part of a community of practice.

The Knowledge Management Program (KMP) at the world's largest steel manufacturer ArcelorMittal (formed through Mittal Steel's acquisition of Arcelor) illustrates how multinationals may create horizontal groups or committees to enhance interunit knowledge sharing (see the box "Mittal Steel's Knowledge Management Program"). The KMP process facilitated the integration process in the new ArcelorMittal group and helps build peer networks.

Mittal Steel's Knowledge Management Program

Mittal Steel chose 25 activities, including manufacturing, finance, maintenance, purchasing, legal work, and information technology, as a base for its KMP. For each of these, groups of approximately 20 members from different plants would meet regularly to benchmark the activities and to discuss common problems. For specific problems, the groups would use conference calls and smaller specialized ad hoc meetings. The diversity of the groups was viewed as a particular strength—according to Mittal Steel's chief operating officer: "These countries have some very good technology. The Poles, for instance, have always been good in coke-making, and we have recently had a Romanian manager who was very helpful in sorting out a blast furnace problem in Chicago."

Source: R. Muthu Kumar and S.K. Chaudhuri, "Mittal Steel's Knowledge Management Strategy," Case study no. 305-543-1. ICFAI, India, 2005.

Working in split-egg or T-shaped roles,[26] where managers and professionals have both vertical and horizontal responsibilities, is at the heart of British Petroleum's (BP) focus on global knowledge management in its oil exploration and production business.[27] With the aim of maximizing the benefits of horizontal coordination, peer groups of business unit heads meet regularly. They are given joint responsibility for capital allocation and for setting performance goals, complemented by a host of cross-unit networks on common operational issues. These "top of the egg" knowledge-sharing activities take up to 20 percent of the manager's time. "The model here is an open market of ideas," says one business unit head. "People develop a sense of where the real expertise lies. Rather than having to deal with the bureaucracy of going through the center, you can just cut across to somebody in Stavanger or Aberdeen or Houston and say, 'I need some help. Can you give me a couple of hours?' And that is expected and encouraged."[28]

The knowledge management groups at ArcelorMittal and BP have many of the features associated with open communities of practice. These communities are characterized by some form of collaboration around a common set of interests. They differ from project teams and committees in that the participants' roles are not defined by the firm. Although the focus of these communities is on internal company issues, they may also foster relationships with outside experts. Communities of practice cannot and should not be fully controlled by the firm, building instead on voluntary participation, although corporate support and guidance is essential.[29] The box "Communities of Practice at Schlumberger" provides another corporate example.

Research on communities of practice offers some guidelines on how to make them successful. First, it is most important to have clearly understood objectives and a leader tasked with making sure that knowledge and best practices are shared and developed further. Second, the quality of interactions should be reinforced with workshops, training, exchange of staff, and an appropriate reward structure, with part-time coordination provided on the corporate budget. Unsuccessful communities lack a core group of members, there is little one-to-one interaction and members do not identify with the community, participants have a strong belief in their own competence, and the issues discussed are not illustrated concretely enough for others to understand and visualize them.[31]

Communities of Practice at Schlumberger

At Schlumberger, a Web-based knowledge management system called Eureka links technical experts in its Oilfield Services business into communities of practice, with members having self-created CVs posted on the site. Such communities, formal or informal, exist in all units to exchange tips and conceptual understanding. Schlumberger had tried several times to organize its technical expertise scattered around the world top-down, but without success. Finally, the company leadership recognized that if the firm could not organize the professional lives of its engineers, it should "let them manage themselves." Now Schlumberger has dozens of self-organized communities ranging from chemistry and rock characterization to well engineering.

At Schlumberger, these communities are led by elected leaders, and elections are frequently contested. One of the few constraints is that community leaders need the backing of their bosses; they might spend 15–20 percent of their time organizing an annual conference and an occasional workshop, overseeing the website, and coordinating subgroups. Each technical expert within Schlumberger has two organizational "homes": the formal, hierarchically sanctioned home that corresponds to a position on the organizational chart; and the Eureka technical community, the informal, horizontally linked network of peers who share common interests, goals, and passions about their work in the corporation. According to the former chief executive, Andrew Gould, the self-governing feature was crucial to the success of the Eureka communities since technical professionals are motivated by peer review and esteem.[30]

Mittal refrained from appointing a "best plant" for others to emulate, believing that all units had something to teach others. In other cases, multinationals have appointed geographically dispersed centers of excellence that, among other matters, are in charge of knowledge sharing. Such centers can be formed in various locations around a small group of individuals who are recognized for their leading edge knowledge that is strategically valuable. As a center of excellence, they are mandated to make that knowledge available throughout the global firm, enhancing it so that it remains on the cutting edge.[32] In contrast to parent-driven knowledge development, these centers tend to rely more on informal networks, often acting as a hub for knowledge-sharing activities.[33]

Implementing a Comprehensive Approach to Mobility and Talent Management

The background of people is important because an adequate knowledge base is a prerequisite for absorbing new knowledge from others. Furthermore, those involved must speak a common language well enough to share tacit knowledge. While multinationals from many different countries have adopted English as their corporate language, this has not eliminated the language-related problems in knowledge sharing among geographically dispersed units. A Swedish multinational provides an illustration. Headquarter managers noticed that there was a lack of knowledge sharing between the German subsidiary and its Scandinavian sister units. On investigation, it turned out that the general manager of the German subsidiary was not a confident English speaker and therefore did not participate in the informal discussions with his Scandinavian peers that were intended to lead to exchange of know-how. The appointment of an English-speaking deputy to the German subsidiary solved this problem.[34]

The transfer of personnel is one of the most important levers of knowledge sharing that multinationals have at their disposal. Typically, the transfer and assimilation of complex tacit knowledge into a new context requires the physical relocation of someone with experience—often an expatriate from headquarters or another subsidiary. Inpatriates may be expected to play the same role during assignments at headquarters and on their subsequent return to foreign units.

Many companies have started corporate universities as another way to foster knowledge sharing. For example, Steve Jobs established Apple University as a way to inculcate globally dispersed employees into Apple's business culture and to get them to develop and share knowledge around a common vision and language. Employees are brought in to the university from all over to participate in classes tailored to their positions and backgrounds. The classes are taught on Apple's corporate campus and often focus on clear communication for sharing ideas with peers.[35]

By bringing employees from all over the world to understand the "Apple way" they develop skills and networks that allow them to reach out to peers in distant locations. Doing so decreases the need for expatriates to disseminate knowledge, but inculcates employees with increased willingness and ability to seek and provide knowledge to others within the company.

Reinforcing Sharing through Performance Management and Incentive Systems

The performance management and compensation systems of the firm play significant roles in creating a context for knowledge sharing. Compensation strategies are a frequent obstacle. If individuals perceive that they are rewarded for their "proprietary" expertise and contribution to the firm, sharing knowledge with others will naturally be seen as contrary to their interest.

At Schlumberger, GE, and many other firms, knowledge sharing is part of managers' and engineers' formal performance reviews. Most Schlumberger field engineers have objectives relating to best practices, lessons learned, and other aspects of knowledge sharing.[36] Not surprisingly, an incentive system that encourages collaboration and knowledge sharing is more likely to produce such behaviors than an evaluation system where the hoarding of knowledge and destructive internal competition are tolerated, if not encouraged.[37] For example, a logic of performance management systems which is gaining acceptance in many multinationals is that managers and executives should be encouraged to contribute to company performance at least one level above the unit for which they are responsible. A foreign subsidiary manager may receive a bonus based on the regional or even global performance of the division or the corporation as a whole. This encourages knowledge sharing and wider collaboration between organizational units.

Conversely, tying incentives to the performance of a subsidiary relative to its sister units will create a strong disincentive to share information and knowledge. A retail company where the heads of neighboring areas were married to each other constitutes an amusing example of the perverse effects that such reward systems may have. The general managers (who were husband and wife) failed to share knowledge with each other because their bonuses were tied to the relative performance of the two units![38]

In addition to financial rewards, the career implications of knowledge sharing send strong signals about the kind of behavior that is valued and rewarded in the corporation.

Framing Knowledge Around the Story and Not the Data

In our view, too much emphasis has been placed on the "push" of knowledge sharing and too little on the "pull" from the seeking unit.[39] As the old saying goes, you can lead a horse to water but you cannot make it drink—unless it wants to. Multinationals would do wisely to focus more on stimulating units to adopt knowledge and practices from other parts of the corporation. One way the IFC has done this is by making the water more desirable for the seeker.

The IFC found that encouraging storytelling through a program called "SmartLessons" dramatically increased IFC employees' willingness to search for knowledge.[40] The SmartLessons program provided guidelines and an online platform to share stories about what was going on in the company. Part of the increased interest came from the fact that the stories were fun to read. The program teaches employees how to deliver information through human stories that people can connect with. It offers a simple guide for writing narratives to post online, as well as the services of an editor, who ensures that the articles and multimedia presentations posted on the SmartLessons site really are in story form. Box "SmartLessons at IFC" outlines the organization's recipe for success.

In summary, a multinational can use a number of levers to encourage knowledge sharing. The key, however, is to ensure that levers are consistent with one another and that the intended outcomes are aligned with the corporation's strategy and intended organizational capabilities.

SmartLessons at IFC

Encourage honesty.

IFC considers it a plus if the submissions include descriptions of setbacks and of the emotional impact of the knowledge gained from them. A contributor told us that under the program, "I have felt empowered to write a no-holds-barred account of lessons I learned." For example, a report says finding a management consultant in a particular locale was like "panning for gold—time consuming, generally disappointing, [but] with the odd, exceptional shining star."

Highlight contributors.

IFC provides biographies, including outside interests, to help readers connect with contributors and their ideas. IFC sends out daily "Newsflashes," summarizing stories. The publicity signals that the organization values the knowledge system and creating buzz helps boost readership and increase the pull for information.

Let users determine the value.

Readers can rate each posting by how interesting it is (not its technical perfection). Additionally, the stories are rated by a panel of judges, who award $1,500 twice a year to the top-ranked post; the next-ranked gets $500.

Early survey results show that more than 80 percent of IFC employees who read SmartLessons find them impactful. "SmartLessons are now an integral part of how I think through project design," a user told us. In an organization of some 3,225 employees, SmartLessons are being viewed an average of 1,800 times per month. And, excluding portal pages, the SmartLessons website is one of the most frequently visited of the 159 intranet sites that the IFC tracks.

KNOWLEDGE ACQUISITION

Historically, firms paid little attention to ways in which they might get access to new external knowledge through their international operations. Successful multinational corporations are increasingly those that can tap into new knowledge and ideas from their worldwide networks, combining this with knowledge residing in the parent company with the aim of innovation. In this section, we discuss different strategies for gaining access to external knowledge as well as how to ensure that knowledge is retained. The next section will focus on the innovation process.

Gaining Access to External Knowledge

The tools that multinationals use to enhance knowledge sharing, such as building social networks and mobility, are also relevant for external knowledge acquisition.[41] Besides these, multinational firms have at their disposal additional ways to access knowledge from the outside. The mechanisms for external knowledge acquisition include the following:

- Scanning the local knowledge base for global solutions
- Partnering or merging with other firms
- Playing the virtual market

Scanning for Global Solutions

Scanning encompasses the efforts made by the multinational to gain access to external knowledge through what people read, hear, or experience first-hand. Important observations and innovative ideas can emerge from anywhere outside the multinational. An example is IFC's insights gained by interacting with local consumers, governments, and companies. Although such insights often come as a by-product of ongoing operations, investment in scanning infrastructure may enhance the external acquisition of new knowledge—especially if lateral thinking is encouraged and rewarded.

The establishment of a "listening post" is a fairly inexpensive way to begin, stemming from the practice of sending small groups of soldiers close to the front line to gather information about enemy plans and positions. The Taiwanese PC-manufacturer Acer established a small design shop in the US, through which it acquired knowledge and skills in ergonomic design that were fed back to the parent organization.[42] Ericsson created "cyberlabs" in New York and Palo Alto (next to Stanford University in Silicon Valley) whose task was to monitor developments in these markets and build relationships with local companies.[43]

While listening posts can be a useful way to obtain codified knowledge and help the firm identify potential partners, they are less effective when the firm's target is tacit knowledge as this requires in-depth interaction with other organizations. Moreover, individual scanners and small units typically lack the clout that is necessary for new ideas to be picked up at corporate headquarters. Many multinationals therefore establish comprehensive units in business centers at the forefront of the developments in their respective industries, such as Silicon Valley (high technology), North Italy (fashion), and the City of London (financial services).[44] These districts contain networks of producers, advanced users, supporting industries, universities, research labs, and a fluid labor market with highly competent individuals. Scanning in centers like these takes place through collaboration among firms, but also through trade associations and professional organizations, as well as more informal social networks.

From an HRM perspective, there are pros and cons associated with establishing a unit in hotspot locations. On the one hand, there is an ample supply of people with relevant experience, and the social contacts they provide can be invaluable. However, at the same time there is often fierce competition for talent, escalating salaries, and a risk of losing people to competitors. These tight social networks can serve as a conduit for the company's own proprietary knowledge. And research has shown that firms are likely to lose if they try to constrain their employees in terms of what they are allowed to talk about with others. They tend to get a bad reputation, impairing their ability to hire the best people.[45] The firms coming out on top are those that are better than others at acquiring and exploiting external knowledge.

In the past, it may have been obvious where the Hollywood or Silicon Valley of a particular industry was located. However, the situation today has become more complex. In many high-tech industries valuable knowledge can be found in several pockets around the world, among them Salt Lake City, Utah; Bangalore, India; Cambridge, England; Sophia Antipolis, France; and Tel Aviv, Israel.[46] For example, Bangalore boasts more than 500 tech companies such as Intuit, NetApp, and Infosys.[47] Israel shares similar strength, having more engineers per capita than anywhere else in the world.[48]

Accessing and assimilating complex tacit knowledge requires considerable investment of time and resources. Shiseido from Japan learned this when establishing itself in France to acquire knowledge about designing, manufacturing, and selling fragrances. After an unsuccessful joint venture with a French company, it formed a wholly-owned subsidiary, Beauté Prestige International, to develop and produce fragrances. It also established a high-end beauty parlor in Paris and bought two functioning beauty salons. The company relied initially on expatriates to acquire local knowledge, but this did not work. Eventually, it learned to hire local experts with long-term industry experience, putting them in charge of the French operations. Then, through close observation and the interaction between Japanese expatriates and French employees, Shiseido succeeded in acquiring and transferring desired capabilities.[49]

An important HRM issue when establishing a unit abroad is the company's ability to attract competent personnel at competitive costs. Experienced multinationals always carry out in-depth HR analyses before they set up new units. Questions they typically ask include: Do the local universities produce engineering graduates with the required competence level for an R&D center? Will the influx of other corporations to hotspots like Bangalore or Shanghai lead to salary escalation that undermines current cost advantages?

Partnering or Merging

A significant proportion of knowledge acquisition comes about through partnering. Partners include suppliers, distributors, competitors, and research organizations. Some alliances and joint ventures are established with the explicit objective of co-creating new knowledge, but much knowledge acquisition takes place in partnerships where the focus is on ongoing manufacturing or distribution. Google partners with external developers, advertisers, and users to increase its knowledge base. These partners provide fresh knowledge of the client-base and help Google make better decisions about their products.

Outsourcing has become widely used in virtually all industries. However, while most attention has been given to the outsourcing of support activities, like accounting and customer service to India, companies also use contractors for more advanced activities. For instance, over the last few years, original equipment manufacturers (OEMs) in the mobile phone industry have invested in building their own product development capabilities. The development of a new mobile phone can be a complex process, involving an OEM, a specialized R&D company, and several units from the mobile phone company. In fact, the real breakthrough for Apple's iPhone was not in recognizing the need for a simple and stylish smart phone; it was in working with Xerox, Samsung, Toshiba, and other foreign and domestic suppliers to develop parts and integrated solutions required to turn the phone from concept to creation.[50]

There are many technical and management challenges in acquiring knowledge from partners, but the first step should be developing the social capital needed for the collaboration to run smoothly. Another major task is how to capture the individual learning of the key people involved in such partnerships and translate it into organizational know-how that can be conveyed to others.

Mergers and acquisitions (M&As) are the ultimate form of partnering. The acquisition and retention of local knowledge is a frequent objective in cross-border M&As and therefore we will look at this in the context of managing post-merger integration, discussed later in the book.

Playing the Virtual Market

The new technologies of the digital revolution allow us to link individuals and organizations in all parts of the world in ways that were unimaginable before. Take crowdsourcing as an example: firms can post a specification of what they are looking for on the Internet, together with information about the reward for anyone who comes up with a solution. A much-cited example is that of the CEO of a troubled Canadian goldmine (an intensely secretive industry) who decided to post all the geological data about the mine on the web, offering half a million dollars' prize money to virtual inspectors able to identify ways to successfully exploit the mine. The resulting ideas and gold discoveries catapulted Goldcorp from a $100 million underperformer into a $9 billion juggernaut that is one of the most innovative and profitable mining firms in the industry today.[51]

Companies can also issue more general calls for research projects. The genomics company 23andMe has taken a revolutionary approach to using the crowd in the health-care space. 23andMe allows for patients to perform self-directed research through its platform and amass huge amounts of genetic data.[52]

Virtual markets can have negative consequences if not managed properly. Consider the Digital Designer offering from Lego. The Digital Designer was an online Lego designing tool that allowed users to create and order custom designs from Lego. It was an attempt by Lego to gain insights about user preferences while providing an additional revenue stream. However, the openness of the offering got Lego into legal difficulties over patents and ownership. The venture ended poorly.

Enhancing Knowledge Retention

While codified knowledge can be physically stored in databases and reports, tacit knowledge resides in people. When individuals with unique and valuable knowledge walk out of the door, the company could be losing part of its competitive advantage. What can the firm do to discourage core tacit knowledge from taking that walk?

There are three basic knowledge retention strategies. The first, which we have already discussed, is to *stimulate knowledge sharing among individuals and units*, so that the company is less dependent on a small number of people. While an obvious illustration of this is when people with unique knowledge are approaching retirement,[53] with increasing turnover of professionals across the world, knowledge sharing has to be encouraged on a continuous basis.

A second strategy is to *try to reduce employee turnover* to avoid leaking proprietary knowledge to competitors. We have discussed various mechanisms for retaining employees earlier in the book. However, knowledge retention should also be kept in mind when assessing involuntary turnover, during periods of recession, or when companies are considering relocating operations.

When the price of oil reached its nadir in the late 1990s, many energy firms responded by curtailing exploration activities and laying off experienced staff. Less than five years later, when prices moved in the opposite direction, they had to buy back the same skills from outside at a much higher cost. In some cases they even had to forgo major opportunities, as they simply did not have a sufficiently experienced workforce to manage the projects. We are seeing this same trend today as oil prices have reached record lows in 2015. Many companies have pursued a similar strategy to that of 1999 and will likely experience the same ramifications when oil prices start moving back up.

The third strategy is to *invest in making tacit knowledge explicit*. The Japanese knowledge management scholar Nonaka Ikujiro calls this "externalization." He suggests that metaphors can help individuals to explain tacit concepts that are otherwise difficult to articulate by conveying intuitive images that people can understand.[54] The explicit knowledge can then be codified and saved in databases and the like, where they can be accessed after the people with the embedded knowledge have left the firm. As expressed earlier, the IFC of the World Bank Group has done much to retain the essence of tacit knowledge through stories.

The issue of repatriates illustrates all three strategies. Multinationals typically pay too little attention to how the organization can benefit from the knowledge that repatriates have gained abroad. Many returnees are dissatisfied with the career opportunities they are offered and begin looking for jobs elsewhere—numerous studies show that a large percentage of international assignees resign shortly after returning home.[55] Retention management is therefore part of a successful approach to repatriate knowledge sharing. The receiving organization must make sure that repatriates have opportunities to share knowledge by appointing them to positions where they can work with others on issues related to their experience, and by assigning them to relevant projects and committees.[56] In some situations, reports and presentations can be appropriate tools for capturing and sharing insights gained during overseas assignments.[57]

FROM IDEAS TO INNOVATIONS

In the two preceding sections, we discussed internal and external knowledge sharing. Both activities are crucial for nurturing innovation in the multinational. In this final section, we take a holistic perspective on the innovation process. We begin by pointing to the paradoxical nature of encouraging new ideas in multinationals (see Figure 11-3). We discuss ways to *encourage promising ideas* within the multinational. Next, we explore how companies can move from promising ideas to innovation. Innovation represents the translation of an idea into a good or service that creates value for which the customer is willing to pay. We do this by exploring how companies are *building transnational innovation capabilities* within their subunits. Next, we point out how transnationals are *organizing R&D centers* to help build these capabilities. Finally, we point out how transnationals are *transferring R&D capabilities* to different countries.

Paradoxes in How to Encourage Promising Ideas

While there is little debate about how important it is to identify promising ideas for subsequent development, doing so successfully on a global scale is far from easy. Companies must be able to deal with several paradoxical challenges, each of which has people management implications:

- Promoting unit diversity *and* standardization
- Encouraging chance encounters *and* providing focus
- Focusing on the hot spots of the industry *and* looking in surprising places
- Having a culture of experimentation *and* of stretch performance goals

Indeed, a quality associated with innovative organizations is called *"ambidexterity,"* namely the ability to handle the paradox of exploration (innovation) and exploitation (short-term performance).[58] Let us examine these four aspects of ambidexterity.

FIGURE 11-3
From Ideas to
Innovations

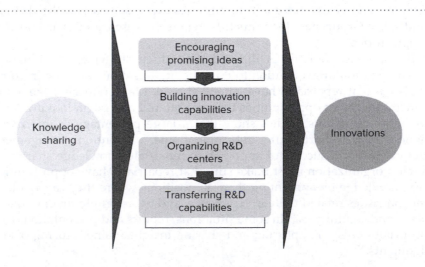

Promoting Unit Diversity and Standardization

Multinational firms, by their very nature, are exposed to a wide variety of different contexts. This diversity can be a source of new innovations if ideas with the potential to be exploited elsewhere can be identified and developed further.

However, with the pressures for standardization in most multinationals today, there is a danger that different organizational units become more alike in terms of their operations. Although this may improve interunit collaboration and facilitate the sharing of knowledge, an unintended consequence is the loss of variety that can be tapped for innovation. This observation builds on a model of evolutionary change, with its parallel to Darwinian evolution. According to this model, a firm should allow for a maximum of variation—natural, unplanned experimentation in its units—out of which will evolve the innovations that allow the firm to adapt in the future.[59] A certain degree of subsidiary autonomy helps combat the natural tendency of organizations to standardize diversity out of the picture. For this reason, knowledge management officers in corporations like Shell see a close relationship with global diversity initiatives, including recruiting outsiders into senior positions.[60]

Rather than trying to standardize everything, good ideas need to be cross-pollinated among units. People need to learn about the ideas of other units and engage in conversations that may spark new ideas. Strong social networks, structural solutions, and corporate-wide communities of practice can help achieve such cross-pollination while simultaneously retaining a reasonable level of subsidiary autonomy.

Encouraging Chance Encounters and Yet Focusing the Search

Innovation sometimes begins with random interpersonal encounters. The weekend meeting in Honolulu is a legitimate way to bring people together, in the expectation that an exchange over coffee or dinner will spark an innovative collective project. One study on the R&D activities of 32 multinational companies shows that the most successful R&D managers are those who meet face to face with their geographically dispersed people at least twice a year.[61]

While some new ideas emerge through fortuitous encounters or by chance, companies such as P&G believe strongly in the value of specifying what they are looking for. Thus, the company produces technology briefs that outline the problem they want to solve, and these are communicated not only within the corporation but also to its network of partner organizations—and sometimes to the world at large.[62]

Another lesson that can be drawn from P&G and other companies that excel at product innovation is the importance of having a profound understanding of customer needs. Input from dissatisfied users can be the source of new ideas, and many multinationals would benefit from improving the ways in which they collect consumer complaints and analyze the data. For example, customer complaints for one major Western airline are handled by a call center in India. A key task of the managers at this center, who are experienced airline generalists, is to assimilate the implications for marketing and operations in a monthly report that emphasizes necessary adaptation in processes and new opportunities for customer differentiation.

Focusing on the Hot Spots of the Industry and Looking in Surprising Places

It is almost a truism that companies need to be present in their industry hotspots where they can observe their competitors' latest moves, where the most competent people tend to congregate, and where the most advanced partner organizations can be found.

Firms naturally tend to focus on following their most important business ventures, on monitoring what their competitors are doing, and on satisfying their largest customers. But learning only from what is important today can make the company myopic. Market leaders may pay so much attention to their "best" customers that they miss ideas from lower-end customers or new competitors.[63] By focusing only on the largest and strategically most important alliances and acquisitions, firms forego the potential novel and useful insights that can be gained from businesses which may be less prominent.[64]

Thailand is rarely seen as a hotbed of new ideas, but in Allianz Ayudhya Thailand (AAT), the Thai subsidiary of Allianz, discussed in Chapter 10, a new management team developed this subsidiary into a highly innovative unit. First, it was able to get local managers to think differently by eliminating much of the hierarchy associated with traditional Thai business culture. Then, asking for more innovative input from employees (encouraging this with rewards and new ways of measuring performance), the company was able to quickly surface and act on fresh new ideas that benefited the business.

For example, AAT launched a brand-building campaign to change customers' perceptions about the industry, crafting a unique competitive position in an otherwise undifferentiated market. Instead of emphasizing the negative side of life insurance—typically associated with sickness, old age, and death—the company adopted the slogan "For the Rhythm of Your Life" and created an entirely different brand image—optimistic, energetic, friendly, and hip. The company achieved not only a business turnaround, but a fundamental transformation. These innovative practices proved so successful that they were also shared with other Allianz subsidiaries, in the context of the company's global innovation initiative.[65]

Having a Culture of Experimentation and of Stretch Performance Goals

A firm's values are important for its innovation. It is crucial to create a culture in which experimentation and entrepreneurship are encouraged, and legitimate mistakes are not frowned upon. The impact of corporate role models is significant. At 3M, a firm renowned for its track record on innovation, virtually all senior line managers have pioneered successful innovations—and also experienced dead ends along the way.

Several companies are famous for their culture of innovativeness. At Google, a "70–20–10 rule" governs the ratio of investment in its core business, adjacent projects, and new ideas. This principle is extended to the way in which technical staff are expected to divide their time: 70 percent on the main task, 20 percent on related projects, and 10 percent on exploratory projects. The rule sends a strong message to employees that they are expected to think outside the box, coming up with solutions to problems that may not even have been recognized yet.

Stretch goals have a different quality to experimentation but they may also support the creation of new ideas. An excessively strong belief in the company's current activities and products can be a formidable enemy of innovation as it often produces a culture of complacency, contributing to a focus solely on how to best exploit the current capabilities of the firm.

For example, when the Chinese telecom company, Huawei, learned in discussion with a Dutch company in China that the customer did not have enough space in the building for a standard network system, they uncovered an underlying need for a small-footprint switch that was not being met—a potential and untouched market niche. However, team members were reluctant to take the risk of moving forward on this idea. Since the industry leader was not in that niche, there must be some reason why it has not been done. This was deeper than an "institutional no," it was a cultural no. "Because people had always been [following the leader] as the status quo," a team member noted, "we always thought we could do what the competitor did, but we never imagined that we could go beyond it." Fortunately, Huawei's innovative leader had ambitious goals and questioned the company's current activities and products. Creating stretch goals to go beyond their existing product base sparked the development of new space-saving equipment that disrupted the market and became the new standard, putting Huawei at the front of the industry.[66]

Building Transnational Innovation Capability

Stretch goals represent the starting point for multinationals interested in moving from ideas to innovation. As companies take a transnational approach to management, they realize that innovative ideas should come from the initiatives of local subsidiaries and then be shared globally to ensure global innovation. Based on research by the authors, building transnational innovation capabilities requires three key behaviors from the subsidiary units inside the multinational.

Go local.   The first, and most vital, unit behavior needed to build innovation capability is to get unit members to go local. Going local means observing the local market context in which potential clients live and work. Many companies lack a deep understanding of customer needs in their various dispersed markets, in part because organizations are reluctant to support knowledge sharing when important intellectual property is involved. This lack of trust creates a barrier to innovation. Even worse, the local leadership does not possess adequate power to do anything about critical knowledge acquired "on the front lines" and therefore lacks innovative presence.

For example, Atlas Copco, the Swedish mining equipment maker, works hard to understand not only the customer but also the unique contexts in which they operate—what type of materials they mine, how the mining is done, and what the weather conditions are under which the equipment will operate. Trust and observation are keys to understanding the contexts of the customer. As a result, units with an innovation capability will be good at identifying and connecting with the customers' concerns, allowing them to understand local problems and latent needs in the market.

Reach out.   But going local is not enough. Understanding the client only helps identify the problem. It does not help develop a solution, and this is where other units have a role. Going local helps see the market gaps, while reaching out to people at headquarters and peer units helps subsidiaries formulate effective, unique, and even lower-cost solutions. Hence, reaching out involves expanding the knowledge search outside of the country domain.

When experiencing stress and pressure at work, the natural human reaction is to turn inward and try to resolve it on our own. Like individuals, subsidiaries often make this mistake by relying solely on their own resources and staying within their country context. We see a general propensity for local subsidiaries to ignore outside help and withdraw inward.

Turning to headquarters and peer units for advice will facilitate the flow of ideas, dismantle preconceived ideas, and empower different units with new capabilities of innovation. Resisting the instinctive reaction, reaching farther outward, and going the distance by investing in rotational programs and developing trusting relationships outside of the local country domain—these are ways to improve the innovation capability of the organization.

Uncover principles.   Most functional work within organizations relies heavily on templates or routines to help subsidiaries make consistent and incremental changes to existing technologies. Templates exemplify the efficiency of operations and teach the "how" of an operation. In predictable and routine operations, templates result in speed and cost savings. However, in an innovation setting where non-routine and uncertainty exist, templates can put true innovation out of reach.[67]

For example, IKEA's international expansion required that they draw upon specific templates spelling out how everything should be done, from greeting the customer to pricing the products. This helped ensure that knowledge of the "IKEA way" was transferred properly. After a number of failed expansion attempts, however, IKEA executives decided that they needed to allow for a more flexible template that permitted stores to adapt the template across areas of pricing, employment, and marketing. As a result, they moved from a template model to a principle model that explained why things were done and allowed individual stores to adapt operations based on these guiding principles (see the box "Focusing on Principles").[68] As explained by one experienced R&D manager, "principles result in very different outcomes than templates. On the one hand, principles create long-term gaps between you and competition. On the other hand, templates create shorter-term leads but are easier to come by."

Most of the innovation-building capabilities in transnational organizations are found within their R&D centers. Today, transnationals are building multiple R&D centers to take advantage of talent and ideas across the world. But how these centers are organized and staffed makes a big difference in whether or not the corporation will be able to build transnational innovation capabilities.

Organizing R&D Centers

The internal R&D organization forms the backbone for innovation in transnational corporations. A distinction is often made between R&D units that focus primarily on developing new technologies and improving existing ones, and those whose main task is product development. The oil giant Shell

Implementing Focus on Principles

Focusing on principles helps employees understand why something works and what the universal principles are behind a product, service, or process. Principles highlight *why* certain tasks are effective. For example, understanding that A leads to B allows you to make the proper connection between those two variables. However, knowing why A leads to B may allow you to know when A can be substituted for something else. Hence, building innovation capability requires that units explore the cause–effect relationships of their products, processes, and services. However, many subsidiary employees hesitate to ask questions to headquarters that help shed light on these relationships, in part because some people fear to "lose face by [appearing to] not know what's going on."[69]

To address this challenge, role modeling has proven successful for many companies. For example, the leader and experienced unit members can begin a discussion with very simple questions. Leaders can encourage their units with statements such as "No question is a dumb question," encouraging subsidiary employees to speak up and understand the principles behind a practice or product. Some leaders hold meetings (known as "knowledge-sharing series") in which participants present knowledge from a field of personal interest and relate that knowledge to the unit's current work. Awareness of the tendency to avoid asking questions, coupled with knowledge of corrective techniques, helps managers encourage questions that lead to a cause–effect understanding of innovation.

makes this distinction. Shell has three central technical centers focusing on innovation and technology development, two in Holland and one in Houston, Texas. The other ten technical centers focus on product development, marketing support, or specific technical assistance for regional operations, located in places ranging from the UK, France, and Canada to India, Qatar, and Singapore. Companies like IBM, Intel, and Shell have invested in developing a 3D virtual reality suite to enhance collaboration between subsidiary R&D units.

E-mail, video-conferencing, computerized databases, and electronic forums have eliminated much of the distance that hindered collaboration and interaction in the past. Or have they? Why are key employees at Microsoft located primarily in the US and, what is more, concentrated in Microsoft's sprawling campus at Redmond, outside Seattle? Why does Cisco still locate some 15,000 people in look-alike buildings in crowded and expensive San José in the heart of Silicon Valley?[70] Why, if distance is "dead", do these leading advocates of virtuality still have a high degree of colocation?

The answer is that while the digital revolution may have reduced distance as an obstacle to information transfer, it has done little for the creative recombination of divergent knowledge. Microsoft, Cisco, and other firms know full well that knowledge, not information, is the source of their competitive strength.[71] Sharing tacit knowledge requires personal interaction; innovation is above all a social process. Thus, in spite of all the technological developments and sophisticated communication tools that now exist, distance is far from dead. Research indicates that while inventors are more linked with other parts of the world through travel and the use of information technology, the clustering of people who work closely together is just as important now as it was in the past.[72]

The importance of close interpersonal collaboration can be seen within Shell's R&D organization. The company has entered into a partnership with the State Key Laboratory of Coal Conversion in Taiyuan, China. The partnership was prompted by Shell's interest in understanding better the challenges facing China, and by China's interest in Shell's coal expertise. Several projects have been chosen for collaboration, with Shell sponsoring doctoral and post-doctoral research. Chinese researchers are also working in Shell's laboratories in Amsterdam, and Shell staff are working in the Chinese facilities.

But where should a multinational establish a particular R&D or product development center? One thesis behind global innovation is that a firm should put the right people where the uncertainties are—where the need for information collection and processing is the greatest.[73] If a company is in an industry where consumer tastes change frequently and are difficult to assess, key people should be located locally, close to the customer. If the firm is in an industry dominated by technological changes that are driven by a "Silicon Valley," the R&D function should be located there.

Most large multinationals today carry out extensive R&D activities outside their home countries. For example, over the past decade China's share of R&D spending has grown by a factor of 15 while the number of China-based companies among the top Global Innovation 1,000 companies jumped from just eight to 114.[74]

Transferring R&D Capabilities

Most multinationals have developed their R&D operations from a strong home country base. Capabilities around innovation are complex bundles of skills, attitudes, and processes,[75] and they can be most carefully nurtured in the parent country before building them in foreign units. P&G had its research labs in the US and Intel's product development capabilities were centered in Silicon Valley. The box "Four stages of capability transfer" describes some of the HRM challenges associated with the transfer of R&D capabilities to foreign units. These challenges are increasingly important as more and more multinationals transfer their R&D capabilities to emerging markets.

R&D capabilities around innovation are difficult to transfer—a capability is a firm-specific, interwoven configuration of skills, in which it is impossible to separate the HRM elements from the technical or managerial elements. As a former director of research for IBM put it, "It is hard to transfer the full complexity of a technology. If the receptor knows very little, he can do very little with even a simple idea, because he cannot generate the mass of detail that is required to put it into execution. On the other hand, if he knows a great deal and is capable of generating the necessary details, then from just a few sentences or pieces of technology he will fill in all the rest. That is why it is hard to transfer technology to emerging markets."[76] Transfer is not a simple technical matter, since it involves learning and adapting knowledge to a new context.[77]

The four-stage model illustrates how a foreign unit may build up its R&D capabilities over time and eventually achieve important worldwide roles in the corporation as a whole. These lead subsidiaries are expected to coordinate their activities with those of other parts of the multinational and to share their knowledge.[80]

Four Stages of Capability Transfer

Below we outline a linear progression of the HRM challenges that come with transferring R&D capabilities from the home country headquarters to a subsidiary.[78]

Stage 1

HRM challenges consist of building foundations—skills training and retention management, managerial and supervisory development, inculcation of basic organizational values such as maintenance ethics, integrity, and safety.

Stage 2

HRM challenges shift to the development of local suppliers' capabilities and performance management. Greater discipline has to be instilled in areas such as quality management, responsibility, cooperation, and weeding out poor performers—if possible also at supplier firms.

Stage 3

HRM challenges move to the local development of complex managerial-technical capacities through advanced education of locals (perhaps at universities outside the host country), projects, sharing best practice, and personnel transfers. Unless the growing sense of local autonomy and initiative is matched with a high degree of normative integration (selection and development based on shared values), it is not certain that this stage will be successful.[79]

Stage 4

HRM challenges climax with global projects that transfer capabilities in reverse (from the subsidiary to the headquarters), developing matrix roles and responsibilities, employee mobility, and building social capital across boundaries. Multinationals tend to be much more skilled at transferring capabilities out from the center: the challenge is to transfer them back from the subsidiary units into the center.

DUALITIES OF EXPLORATION AND EXPLOITATION

The fact is that big, complex global organizations have difficulty with innovation. As one commentator notes, it is like teaching elephants how to dance.[81] The biggest problem is not that multinationals do not know how to be innovative—it is that the properties needed to be innovative are the opposite of those needed to be successful in exploiting what they are doing well today. This is just one of the many paradoxes in the domain of global innovation and knowledge management.

Effective knowledge management is important both to exploit existing capabilities on a global scale and to explore new ideas that can be developed into tomorrow's product and service offerings. While both exploration and exploitation are needed, finding a balance between the two is challenging.[82] Companies easily fall into the trap of focusing too much on one at the expense of the other, one of the many dualities that multinationals are facing.

We have considered many other dualities in this chapter—combining network modes of operating with structural modes, collaboration versus competition with other companies, and inside versus outside orientation. Let us highlight an additional paradox that we have mentioned in passing—the *transfer paradox*. The transfer paradox argues that the most valuable knowledge—complex and contextual tacit knowledge—is also the most sticky. Sticky knowledge is expensive and difficult to transfer within the multinational, requiring linking mechanisms that build on face-to-face relationships. A related paradox, *the evaluation paradox*, holds that this same tacit know-how is also difficult to evaluate and assess. And there are additional paradoxes. For example, it is clear that external contacts in communities of practice can facilitate new knowledge (the bridging of non-connected networks by boundary spanners as described by social capital theory), although research also shows that too strong an orientation to external knowledge sources leads people to miss deadlines.[83]

Organizing for innovation means managing the tensions that underlie such dualities. This is a theme running through this chapter, because "contradiction and nonlinearity may be inherent in most innovative undertakings. As a consequence, the central problem in leading the innovation journey may be ambidexterity, the management of paradox."[84]

The innovation process involves alternating cycles of divergent and convergent behaviors—exploring new directions alternating with focused pursuit of a given direction; building new relationships alternating with execution through established networks;[85] leadership that encourages diversity alternating with focused leadership guided by goals and consensus. Innovation involves exploration; there is a trade-off between a focus on exploration versus exploitation, between tomorrow's profits and those of today.

Many studies have described the overarching quality needed for innovation as the ability to operate "on the edge," between order and chaos. Researchers have found that successful firms in highly competitive computer markets emphasize "semi-structures" as well as improvisation, combining limited structures (priorities, accountability) with extensive interaction and the freedom to improvise.[86] And these firms constantly link time frames, focusing on both present and future. They do not rely on a single plan or scenario, nor are they merely reactive—they constantly use low-cost probes such as experimental products, alliances, consultation with futurists, and incessant feedback to test how the future is emerging.

Strong social capital may promote a climate of cooperation, acting as a defense against opportunism and self-interest. But if the social ties become too strong, the group runs the risk of becoming inward-looking and rigid. Researchers put it well when they observe the tensions that highly adaptive organizations have to balance: "modularity and relatedness, competitiveness and cooperation, and order and disorder . . . the simultaneous presence of competing tensions is an important motor of adaptation within organizations in rapidly changing markets."[87]

The management of knowledge and innovation on a global scale is clearly a tough challenge, with numerous HRM implications. Multinationals need to recruit and select employees bearing in mind the acquisition of valuable external knowledge. They also need to socialize new employees to make sure that this knowledge is shared across units. Training and development should enhance the innovative ability of the firm—as well as the ability of people to deliver on their commitments today. Performance management systems and compensation schemes have to encourage both exploration and exploitation. Firms that can master such human resource management challenges will achieve a competitive advantage that will be difficult to match.

1. Multinational firms need to strike a balance between exploiting existing competitive strengths and exploring new areas of future growth.

2. The ability of the multinational to share knowledge internally is a crucial source of competitiveness. The degree of knowledge sharing depends on the ability and willingness of the providing unit, the motivation and ability of the seeking unit, and the suitability of the mechanisms (levers) used to share the knowledge.

3. Effective worldwide knowledge sharing requires information about where the knowledge is; design of appropriate structural mechanisms and social architecture to support sharing; and reinforcement of a culture of sharing through talent management, performance management and communication.

4. Acquiring new knowledge from external sources demands scanning across borders; partnering with customers, research labs, and other organizations; and accessing the virtual market to identify promising ideas.

5. The tacit knowledge that is embedded in people can be retained by increasing knowledge sharing, through reduction of employee turnover, and by investments in making tacit knowledge explicit.

6. A striking characteristic of global innovation and knowledge management is the need to manage paradoxes such as diversity and standardization, allowing for chance encounters and focused search, and looking for innovation in unlikely places.

7. Driving innovation requires goals that push units and employees to stretch outside of their comfort zones.

8. Increasingly, innovative ideas come from local subsidiaries trying to address local problems and reaching outside the traditional boundaries for input towards a solution.

9. R&D capabilities associated with innovation are not easy to transfer across borders. Such transfers require that multinationals deal with a number of HRM challenges, ranging from building the HRM of the subsidiary to developing the capabilities of local suppliers and educational institutions.

10. Multinationals that spend too much time exploiting existing knowledge will lose their ability to differentiate and create new value. But if they spend too much time exploring new knowledge they may miss the opportunity to leverage ideas they already have.

NOTES

1 Morris, Zhong, and Makhija, 2015.
2 Morris, Oldroyd, and Ramaswami, 2015.
3 Denning, "Storytelling, Knowledge Management & World Bank President Kim," *Forbes*, July 20, 2012, from http://www.forbes.com/sites/stevedenning/2012/07/20/storytelling-knowledge-management-world-bank-president-kim; Kim, 2015; McCormick, J.,"5 Big

companies that got knowledge management right," October 5, 2007—available at May 26, 2015, from http://www.cioinsight.com/c/a/Case-Studies/5-Big-Companies-That-Got-Knowledge-Management-Right; Cho and Pucik, 2005.

4 Kogut and Zander, 1992 and 1993.

5 Morris, Hammond, and Snell, 2015.

6 Morris, Zhong, and Makhija, 2015.

7 Myers and Marquis, 1969.

8 Gupta and Govindarajan, 2000.

9 Welch, J.F., "Timeless Principles," *Executive Excellence*, February 2001, p. 3.

10 The distinction between explicit and tacit knowledge was first made by the epistemologist Polanyi (1966), and developed by Nonaka (Nonaka, 1994; Nonaka and Takeuchi, 1995).

11 Szulanski, 1996.

12 Mäkelä, Andersson, and Seppälä, 2012.

13 Hansen and Nohria, 2004. See also Minbaeva *et al.* (2003) for a discussion of the importance of paying attention to receiver ability and motivation. Their study revealed that the use of HR practices was positively associated with both ability and motivation.

14 Minbaeva and Michailova (2004) use the term "disseminative capacity" to refer to the ability and willingness of organizational members to share knowledge.

15 Hansen, Mors, and Løvås, 2005.

16 Cross and Prusak, 2003.

17 Ibid.

18 Szulanski, 1996. The term "absorptive capacity" (Cohen and Levinthal, 1990) is commonly used in the academic literature to describe the ability of the receiving unit to evaluate, assimilate, and exploit new knowledge from the environment. See Lane, Koka, and Pathak (2006) for a discussion of absorptive capacity.

19 Leonard-Barton, 1995.

20 Ibid.

21 Zahra and George, 2002; Lane, Koka, and Pathak, 2006.

22 Monteiro, Arvidsson, and Birkinshaw, 2008.

23 Dendrell, Arvidsson, and Zander, 2004.

24 Monteiro, Arvidsson, and Birkinshaw, 2008.

25 See Subramanian and Venkatraman (2001) for a study on how cross-national teams contributed to the global product development capabilities of multinationals.

26 See Chapter 4.

27 See Hansen and von Oetinger (2001).

28 Hansen and von Oetinger, 2001; http://www.kmbestpractices.com/bp.html.

29 Probst and Borzillo, 2008; Wegner and Snyder, 2000.

30 "Motivating Workers by Giving Them a Vote," *Wall Street Journal Online*, August 25, 2005; Grant, 2013.

31 Probst and Borzillo, 2008.

32 See Moore and Birkinshaw (1998) for a discussion of centers of excellence in service firms.

33 Three types of centers of excellence have been identified in global service firms—charismatic (formed around an individual); focused (a small group of experts in a single location, e.g., the McKinsey competence units); and virtual (a larger group of specialists in multiple locations, linked by a database and proprietary tools) (Moore and Birkinshaw, 1998).

34 Monteiro, Arvidsson, and Birkinshaw, 2008.

35 Chen, B.X., "Simplifying the Bull: How Picasso Helps to Teach Apple's Style," *New York Times*, August 10, 2014.

36 Åbø *et al.*, 2001.

37 Björkman, Barner-Rasmussen, and Li, 2004.

38 Gupta and Govindarajan, 2008.

39 Support for this conclusion is summarized in Szulanski (1996).

40 Morris and Oldroyd, 2009.

41 The meta-analysis conducted by Van Wijk, Jansen, and Lyles (2008) found that company-internal and -external knowledge sharing/transfers were largely influenced by the same mechanisms.

42 Doz, Santos, and Williamson, 2001.

43 Birkinshaw, 2004.

44 Inkpen and Tsang, 2005.

45 Fleming and Marx, 2006.

46 Doz, Santos, and Williamson, 2001.

47 Reddy, P., "List of top companies in Bangalore. Freshersplane," May 21, 2013. See http://freshersplane.com/company-profiles/list-of-top-companies-in-bangalore-it-companies-in-bangalore/.

48 Munford, M., "With 5,000 Startups, Tel Aviv Is Edging into the Tech Spotlight. Mashable," September 17, 2013. See http://mashable.com/2013/09/17/tel-aviv-tech/.

49 Doz, Santos, and Williamson, 2001.

50 Batson, A., "Not Really 'Made in China,'" *The Wall Street Journal*, December 15, 2010.

51 Tapscott and Williams, 2007.

52 Regalado, A., "23andMe's New Formula: Patient Consent = $," *MIT Technology Review*, January 6, 2015. See http://www.technologyreview.com/view/534006/23andmes-new-formula-patient-consent/.

53 See DeLong (2004) for an analysis on retaining the knowledge of pre-retirees.

54 Nonaka, 1994.

55 See Chapter 9.

56 See Furuya *et al.* (2009) for an analysis of factors affecting individual learning during expatriate assignments; and the application of their competences in new assignments following repatriation. Oddou, Osland, and Blakeney (2009) offer a conceptual model of factors influencing repatriate knowledge sharing.

57 Lazarova and Tarique, 2005.

58 Ancona *et al.*, 2001.

59 Weick, 1979.

60 Åbø *et al.*, 2001.

61 Kummerle's research is reported in "Winning in a World Without Boundaries," *Industry Week*, October 20, 1997.

62 Lafley, 2008.

63 Christensen, 1997.

64 Tsang, 2002.

65 Zalan, Pucik, and Blackburn, 2009.

66 Personal interview from one of the authors with Huawei managers in June, 2014.

67 Govindarajan and Trimble, 2010.

68 Jonsson and Foss, 2011.

69 Morris, S., Chang, H., and Han, J., "Innovation Capabilities in China: Talents, Behaviors, and Processes," 2015 CEIBS-BYU Report on Innovation in China. January, 2015.

70 Johnson, S., "Cisco Systems to Cut 6,000 Jobs," *San Jose Mercury News*, August 13, 2014, http://www.mercurynews.com/business/ci_26330332/ciscos-sales-and-profit-slightly-down-quarter.

71 Thanks to Joe Santos for this observation on Microsoft and Cisco.

72 Fleming and Marx, 2006.

73 Afuah, 1998.

74 Jaruzelski, B., Staack, V., and Goehle, B., "The 2014 Global Innovation 1000: Proven Paths to Innovation Success," 2014. See pwc.com.

75 See the discussion on organizational capabilities in Chapter 1, using among others the examples of Lincoln Electric and Southwest Airlines.

76 Cited by Leonard-Barton (1995, p. 215).

77 For empirical evidence on the difficulty in transferring technology, see Zahra, Ireland, and Hitt (2000).

78 The HP Singapore story is used by Leonard to illustrate the process of transfer of capabilities from the home country abroad (Leonard, 1995; Leonard-Barton and Conner, 1996).

79 Leonard-Barton and Conner, 1996.

80 Gupta, Govindarajan, and Wang, 2008, p. 155.

81 Kanter, 1989.

82 March, 1991.

83 Teigland, 2000.

84 Van de Ven *et al.*, 1999, p. 12. See also Argote (1999) and Dougherty (1996).

85 See McFadyen and Cannella (2004) for an analysis of how the number and strength of relationships are related to knowledge exchange and creation.

86 Brown and Eisenhardt, 1997 and 1998.

87 Galunic and Eisenhardt, 2001.

12

Forging Cross-Border Mergers and Acquisitions

SUMMARY

Challenge

Physical and cultural distance increases the complexity of implementing successful M&As

Analysis

Several organizational capabilities are essential to create value through cross-border acquisitions:

- Understanding cultures at the organizational level
- Capability in managing complex change
- Following a systematic approach to the post-merger integration process

Solutions

- Involve HR early in the M&A planning process
- Include an HR audit and cultural assessment in the due diligence
- Align post-merger integration with the strategic logic of the acquisition
- Empower integration managers and use mixed teams to drive results
- Act quickly to retain key talent.
- Avoid uncertainty—in most cases move with speed

Integrating Global Acquisitions at CEMEX

In September 2004, only a few months after defining its new global governance model and deciding to implement one operating system worldwide, the Mexican building materials company CEMEX announced its intention of acquiring the UK-based Ready Mix Concrete (RMC) group for US $5.8 billion. With this acquisition, CEMEX aimed to consolidate its position as one of the top three global players in the industry.[1]

CEMEX was born in 1906 in Monterrey, Mexico. In 1985, Lorenzo Zambrano, the grandson of the company's founder, became the CEO after working his way up through the organization for 18 years. At that time, the company had five plants and 6,500 employees. Zambrano refused to diversify into other businesses, the route favored by many other Latin American industrialists. Instead he focused on the cement and building materials business he knew well and built up his company through a series of acquisitions, first in Mexico and then in Spain, Latin America, Philippines, and the US.

Most of the newly acquired companies were not efficient and CEMEX saw an opportunity to create value by implementing new processes and instilling new management behavior. The backbone of this strategy was a global operating platform, labeled the CEMEX Way. The aims of the CEMEX Way were to unify global operations, promote the sharing of best practices, streamline and improve the value chain, and allow rapid and simultaneous deployment of strategic initiatives.

To enable faster and smoother acquisitions, CEMEX put in place a systematic post-merger integration (PMI) process to promote the CEMEX Way and learn from previous experiences. Multicountry teams of managers and functional specialists were temporarily assigned to each newly acquired company so that knowledge of best practices would be available to the team responsible for the new acquisition.

A typical PMI process at CEMEX has four stages. During the initial planning stage, pre-assessment teams visit the new subsidiary to analyze the situation and plan next steps. Three execution phases follow. In Phase One, also called "the 100-day plan," transition teams work to identify further synergies through a gap analysis covering all business activities. Phase Two focuses on implementation, with the expectation that the CEMEX Way will be fully operational by the end of this stage. Phase Three marks the return to business as usual—at a higher level of operational efficiency.

The RMC acquisition was bigger, covered more countries (22), and included more diverse cultures and languages than anything CEMEX had encountered previously. The PMI office divided the work between functional teams such as cement operations and back-office; each of these teams was replicated on a country-by-country basis. In total, 600 people from within CEMEX and over 400 RMC managers were involved in the RMC integration. The HR integration was by far the most complex part of the process, and CEMEX spent more than six months defining and building a framework that took staffing and country differences into consideration. At the kickoff of the execution phase Zambrano addressed RMC managers and executives:

> You will quickly discover that CEMEX time seems to have fewer minutes in every hour and more hours in every day. We are highly disciplined and dedicated to consistent, high level performance. We believe in continuous innovation. … Our goal—and our track record—is to out-perform our competitors year in and year out.[2]

The results were impressive. Under its old owners, a large cement plant at Rugby in England often ran at only 70 percent capacity. Two months after the takeover and the implementation of CEMEX Way it was running at 93 percent.

In October 2006, CEMEX announced an unsolicited offer to purchase the Sydney-based Rinker group, with operations in Australia and the US. The target company had well-respected management, so this acquisition was an opportunity to blend the best parts of CEMEX and Rinker to improve overall profitability, rather than to improve operating efficiency, the motive for previous acquisitions. Instead of scrapping what Rinker had, the plan was to start with a thorough evaluation, identify the best practices of both parties, and determine which parts of Rinker's operating system should be incorporated in the CEMEX Way—such as a waste burning initiative common to most Rinker plants.

By December 2007, CEMEX had operations on four continents, with 85 plants in more than 50 countries. The only gaps in its global presence were China and India. CEMEX reported net sales of $21.7 billion and a net income of $2.6 billion—the best in the industry. However, with the onset of global financial crisis in 2008, the competitive conditions changed dramatically—especially in Latin America. Faced with a danger of default on its massive financial obligations, CEMEX had to sell many of its previously acquired assets. Its journey to become a global market leader has been put on hold. Still, CEMEX's approach to implementing acquisitions became the blueprint for the industry consolidation worldwide.[3]

OVERVIEW

Building on the CEMEX case, we start the chapter by reviewing the merger and acquisition (M&A) phenomenon in a global context and then introduce a simple framework for understanding the strategic logic behind the cross-border M&A. This will determine the orientation of the integration process and the role of human resources. We then discuss due diligence, the planning and preparation work necessary before the deal is closed. The assessment of people and cultural factors needs as much attention as the appraisal of strategic and financial factors.

The next section focuses on the PMI process, in which the formula for success combines appropriate speed with careful attention to people processes such as communication, talent retention, and building a shared culture. Firms that make successful acquisitions also recognize that they must capture their learning in order to enhance their ability to execute acquisitions in the future. In this way, M&A capabilities can become an important source of competitive advantage as companies grow across borders.

THE M&A PHENOMENON

What is a merger and what is an acquisition? From a legal point of view, in a *merger* two companies join and create a new entity. In an *acquisition*, one company acquires sufficient shares to gain control of the other organization. We will focus primarily on acquisitions, which represent the large majority of cross-border deals, referring to mergers when appropriate or customary (e.g. *post-merger* integration). However, the actual transaction label also depends on the accounting and tax implications of the deal, as well as public relations and communication strategies. Some mergers may be structured as acquisitions, while many acquisitions are framed as mergers.

Acquisitions can be friendly or hostile. From the perspective of shareholders or top management, most acquisitions are friendly, although the workforce often does not see it that way—there are clear winners and losers since being acquired is perceived as a symbol of failure, and the buyer organization nearly always has more power during the integration process. Cross-border hostile acquisitions are rare, although when they occur they tend to generate strong emotions and a lot of public interest.[4]

Cross-border M&As are popular alternatives to "greenfield" investments (i.e., business units established from scratch) and strategic alliances as vehicles for internationalization. There has been a dramatic growth in cross-border

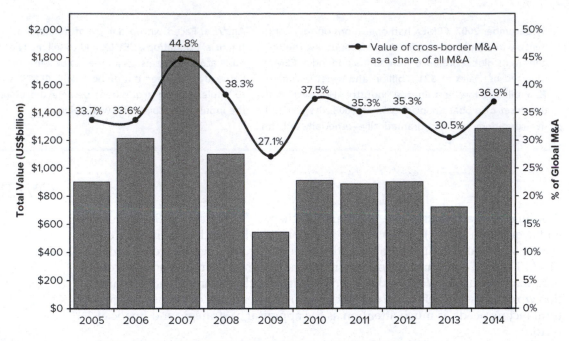

Source: Adapted from Thompson Reuters, Mergers & Acquisition Review, 2014.

FIGURE 12-1
Trends in Global Mergers
and Acquisitions

M&As during the last two decades (reaching US $1.3 trillion in 2014—the second largest M&A volume after the pre-crisis peak of 2007), and the share of cross-border M&As each year is ranging between 35 and 40 percent of the total M&A activity (see Figure 12-1).[5]

While global megadeals continue to grab the headlines, more and more cross-border acquisitions take place among small- and medium-sized firms. Understanding the logic of such strategies for internationalization, their human resource implications, and mastering their implementation is becoming one of the competences required of global managers and HR professionals.

Drivers of Cross-Border Acquisition

There are a number of reasons why companies pursue cross-border M&As:

- Improving competitiveness through economies of scale or scope
- Increasing market share by adding capacity, brands, or distribution channels
- Reducing overcapacity and cost by consolidating operations with competitors
- Gaining quick entry to new geographical markets or segments
- Accessing invisible assets—talent or technology.

Historically, M&A were a domain of North American and European firms, with firms from emerging markets such as CEMEX being an exception. This is changing now—in 2014, nearly 25 percent of the M&A deals (measured by value) involved companies from Asia,[6] spearheaded mainly by investments from China and India.[7] According to some observers, these investments establish a new pattern of cross-border acquisitions (see box "When Chinese Firms Acquire Abroad").

When Chinese Firms Acquire Abroad

With few exceptions, such as the acquisition of the IBM personal computer business by Lenovo, the early cross-border acquisitions that Chinese companies made, including high-profile deals such as TCL's acquisition of France's Thomson or SAIC's takeover of South Korea's Ssangyong Motor Company, ended badly. As a result, many Chinese companies changed course, altering the targets they pursued and their rationale for M&A. Chinese acquirers learned to avoid deals that involve costly turnarounds or tricky integration. Instead of buying brands, sales networks, and goodwill, they now look for hard assets, like mineral deposits and oil reserves, or state-of-the-art technology and R&D. In the past, they tried to buy market share abroad; today they focus on acquisitions in Europe or North America that will help strengthen their capabilities in China. Geely's acquisition of Volvo is perhaps the most visible example.[8]

Though M&As are often the preferred option for businesses seeking to accelerate international growth,[9] they should be evaluated as just one of several strategic options including strategic alliances and greenfield investments. For example, in some situations it may be better to hire a small team with the desired capabilities rather than to acquire an entire firm.

Acquisitions versus Alliances

An alliance can often be a first step toward an acquisition. In countries such as South Korea, where emotional resistance to takeovers from abroad may be strong, or where the regulatory environment restricts full acquisitions, gradual entry through a joint venture with a local partner can be an effective strategy.[10] The alliance may also reduce the risk of entry into an unfamiliar territory. If the partnership is successful, the next step may be acquiring the partner's interest or the partner itself. The timing and conditions for this evolution may even be a part of the initial partnership agreement. On the other hand, the consensual governance process in international alliances slows down decisions and limits the possibilities for rationalization.[11]

From an HR perspective, the most significant difference between an alliance and an acquisition is that the former may restrict influence over people-related decisions. The freedom to select, promote, and compensate people is such an important management tool that it leads many executives to favor acquisitions. On the other hand, retaining talent may be easier in a partnership, and alliances are often better at preserving entrepreneurship in individual units. In a cross-border context, alliances are easier to align with the local environment. When making a strategic decision on whether to build an alliance or pursue an acquisition, it is important for human resource considerations to be on the list.

How Successful Are Cross-Border M&As?

There is no shortage of research on the performance of M&As. Several early surveys suggested that only a minority of the deals achieved the promised financial results.[12] Recent academic studies and consulting reports are more positive, finding that the average contribution of M&As to the value of the acquiring firm is close to zero.[13] In other words, some M&As are successful, some have little effect on the performance of the acquiring firm, and some are disasters for the buyer. The sellers virtually always emerge as winners as the buyer typically pays a significant premium for the target.[14] When the buyer overpays, no amount of skill in post-merger integration can bring back the value lost when such a deal was signed. However, even well-structured and negotiated deals have to face the complexities of merging organizations, and the ability to add value in the merged company depends mostly on what happens after the deal is done. Not surprisingly, high returns go mostly to firms that execute well the *PMI process*.[15] And as integration is essentially a change process, companies that have a *solid HRM foundations* and *good track record in managing change* also tend to be good at managing acquisitions.

There is some evidence that, perhaps surprisingly, the success rate of cross-border deals may be higher than for purely domestic transactions.[16] One explanation is that there tend to be greater complementarities between the parties in international acquisitions.[17] Cross-border acquirers often buy companies in related industries—familiar businesses to which they can add value and, conversely, from which they can gain value. For instance, the acquisition of a foreign competitor can give the buyer access to local markets as well as new products, technologies, and local market knowledge. The target may benefit from similar resources and competences; the increased scale and international experience of the combined organization are additional benefits of such mergers.

Furthermore, it appears that there may be less internal conflict in international M&As, since the degree of integration tends to be more modest compared to domestic acquisitions, leading to less tension between employees. There is also some evidence that a moderate level of integration in international acquisitions is associated with better performance.[18] Finally, the more overt cross-cultural dimensions of such deals may lead buyers to pay more attention to the softer, less tangible, but critical HR aspects of M&A management.[19]

Finally, the ability to learn from past acquisitions, including the mistakes made, is a characteristic that many successful international buyers have in common.[20]

A Framework for Thinking about M&As

In successful M&As, partners share the purpose and accept the terms of their relationship. Therefore, careful and explicit definition of the purpose of the acquisition and the desired end-state is the first step in making the new relationship work. People may well resent and resist change—but they are more likely to adapt if they know the new rules of the game and understand how these will help them to be successful in the future.

The best approach to follow in order to integrate the two organizations will depend on the strategic driver behind the acquisition. A simple framework developed by Killing[21] provides a useful overview of different types of acquisition integration (see Figure 12-2).

Stand-Alone

An announcement of a cross-border deal often contains a section noting that the acquired company will keep its business independence and management autonomy. The aim may be to placate local regulators and/or public opinion. Or a major rationale behind the acquisition may be to get hold of talented management or other soft skills (such as speed of product development) and retain

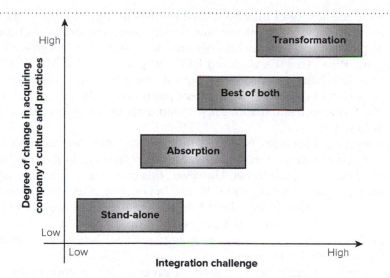

FIGURE 12-2
Four Types of Acquisition Integration

Source: Adapted from J.P. Killing, "Improving Acquisition Integration: Be Clear on What You Intend, and Avoid „Best of Both Deals," Perspectives for Managers, no. 97, 2003, p. 1.

them. Or independence may be appropriate if conformance to the acquiring company rules and systems could be detrimental to the acquired company's competitive advantage.

The "stand-alone" approach—more partnering than acquisition from an integration perspective—is often favored by companies from emerging countries when they acquire firms in developed markets who possess superior product capabilities or a valuable brand.[22] When Tata Motors bought Jaguar Land Rover (JLR), then a loss-making subsidiary of Ford, Tata ownership provided needed capital and strategic stability, allowing JLR to complete a successful turnaround.[23]

If stand-alone acquisition is the objective, the key to success is to protect the new subsidiary from unwarranted and disruptive intrusions on the part of the buyer, though this can be hard to ensure. Even with the best of intentions, there is a danger of creeping assimilation, as the buyer encourages the new unit to adopt its way of working and to develop systems and processes that match those of the parent organization. Therefore, most stand-alone acquisitions do not last.[24]

There is a fundamental question associated with the stand-alone strategy—how can the buyer create value through the acquisition in order to offset the premium that it has paid for the target? A single booster shot of functional knowledge and capabilities soon after the closing is one possible approach to create operational synergies and efficiencies. Also, while the business may appear independent to the outside world, at least some back-office functions are merged with the rest of the organization.[25] Typically "stand-alone" is a temporary phenomenon, lasting until conditions are ready to complete assimilation.

Absorption

This kind of acquisition is straightforward: the acquired company conforms to the acquirer's way of working. Such deals are common when there are differences in size and sophistication between the two partners in the deal, when the target company is performing poorly, or when market conditions force consolidation.

Most of the synergies may be related to cost cutting, usually on the side of the seller, with some from improvements in systems and processes brought in by the acquiring firm. Absorption does not necessarily mean large-scale firings and layoffs. When CEMEX acquired RMC, 80 percent of the identified synergies came from changes in processes, repositioning of business operations, and implementation of common management platforms.[26] The key to success is to choose the target well and to move fast to eliminate uncertainty and capture the available benefits.

The logic of absorption is simple, but as companies are sensitive to public perceptions of being a foreign bully, they are often hesitant to declare their objective of absorbing the target. However, this can create confusion and mistrust that make the process more difficult. In contrast, a local executive of GE operating in Asia offers blunt advice to the management of acquired firms: "If you do not want to change, don't put yourself up for sale." GE makes it very clear that the acquired company must now play by GE's rules and provides an explicit framework for doing so.

Sometimes, assimilation is a gradual process. When companies such as Bosch or ABB first entered China two decades ago, the only path forward was through joint ventures with local firms. As the legal environment changed, most of them were converted into 100 percent owned affiliates, but by the time the conversion occurred, the employees were already fully familiar with the culture and work practices of their Western parent—and could also see the benefits of being a part of an international firm.

Best of Both

The intriguing option of "best of both" is sometimes described as a "merger of equals." This holds out the promise of no pain, since in theory it takes the best practices from both sides and integrates them. There were few genuine mergers of equals, which succeeded over time—AstraZeneca stands out as one such example.[27] However, most were "equal" on paper only, driven by a desire to make the initial idea palatable for various internal and external constituencies.[28]

The scarcity of examples of "best of both" attests to its difficulty. Putting together the "best" parts of both sides risks leading to an inconsistent configuration of organizational practices in the two merging units. Another danger is that the integration approach may become too political and time-consuming, especially when it comes to leadership appointments. A highly visible "merger of equals" in the cement industry between Lafarge from France and Holcim from Switzerland nearly disintegrated within weeks of signing the deal due to disagreements on who should be the CEO of the new entity.[29]

Who decides what is "best" and based on what criteria? During the integration process, and in the absence of explicit criteria and objective evaluation, many employees may view the choice of what constitutes "best" as biased. When the Swedish bank Nordbanken and the Finnish bank Merita agreed on a merger of equals, the Finnish employees coined and used the phrase "Best practices are West practices" ("West" meaning "Swedish," as Sweden is located west of Finland).[30]

CEMEX's integration of Rinker came close to a "best of both" approach, as Rinker's production processes were very advanced in a number of technological areas and geographies. It would be to CEMEX's advantage to leverage this capability within the whole firm. However, without strong mutual respect for the knowledge and skills of each company, this kind of strategy will not work. Saying best of both, without acting accordingly, is likely to backfire, as the target employees will view the buyer as untrustworthy.[31]

A key to success is fair process. On the HR side, this may mean hiring a third party to assess the organizational capabilities and practices of personnel in both organizations. The ability to retain people may be a precondition for a best of both acquisitions, having a balance of management from both firms.

Transformation

In contrast to "best of both" acquisitions, which take existing organizational practices as they come, both companies in a transformation merger hope to use the merger to make a clean break with the past. Merger or acquisition can be the catalyst for doing things differently, or reinventing the organization—the way the company is run, the business it is in, or both. When Novartis emerged through the merger of two Swiss-based pharmaceutical firms, the proposed management style for the new company reflected the desired transformation: "We will listen more than Sandoz, but decide more quickly than Ciba."

For a long time, the creation of ABB through the merger of Asea and Brown Boveri has been an archetype of transformational merger, with its successes and failures. A more recently example is the transformation of Lenovo from Chinese start-up to a global leader, first through the acquisition of IBM's PC business, then by buying from Google what remained of Motorola's handset operation.[32]

This kind of merger is complex and difficult to implement. It requires full commitment, with focus and strong leadership at the top to avoid trapped in endless debates while the ongoing business suffers. Speed is essential, with top management in the merging companies using the time immediately after the merger announcement to carry out major changes. Like the "best-of-both" strategy, the transformation strategy has a better chance of success if key people from both sides are committed to the vision of the merger leading to a new leading company with superior capabilities.[33]

Which Integration Strategy to Choose?

There is no doubt that the purpose of the acquisition should determine the approach to integration. If the objective is to improve the current business model's effectiveness, the resources of the acquired company should be absorbed into the acquirer. In contrast, if the value of the acquired company comes from a distinct business model, then it is better to keep the model intact, by operating it separately.[34] For example, although GE's preference for a quick and full integration is well known, when GE Medical acquired one of their low-cost competitors in China, a "stand-alone" and gradual approach to integration allowed the acquired company to preserve its capability to compete in the local market as well as enter new product segments in the developed world.[35]

A complicating factor in all acquisitions is that there will be parts of the organization where a particular approach to the merger makes sense and others where it does not. Cisco, for example, used to buy companies for their technology and R&D talent; retention of engineers and scientists in the target was an important objective. Therefore, Cisco had typically fully absorbed the support functions of small innovative start-ups that they acquired for their promising product ideas, while the engineers in charge of developing new products retained much more autonomy. Cisco's approach illustrates that many acquisitions have elements of more than one of the (ideal) acquisition types presented in Figure 12-2.

Key Human Resources Issues

There is no shortage of empirical evidence that attention to "soft" factors or people issues is one of the most critical elements in making an acquisition strategy work. In a pioneering McKinsey study of international M&As, the four top-ranked factors identified by responding firms as contributing to acquisition success are all people related:

- Retention of key talent (identified by 76 percent of responding firms)
- Effective communication (71 percent)
- Executive retention (67 percent)
- Cultural integration (51 percent)[36]

According to another consulting report, published nearly a decade later, the problems remained the same. Differences in organizational culture (50 percent) and people integration (35 percent) were top of the list of M&A challenges—in fact, four of the six top issues were people related.[37]

It is hard to find an acquisition where people issues do not matter, though the nature of the people challenges varies with the acquisition intent. When the objective is to establish a new geographic presence, managing cross-cultural, language, and communication issues tops the list of priorities. When the aim is to acquire new technology, or to buy market share or competences, retaining key technical staff or account managers is the principal challenge. When the objective of the deal is consolidation, dealing effectively with redundancies at all levels is the dominant concern.

Based on these observations, it may seem natural that the HR function should play a significant role in all phases of an acquisition. Yet while this tends to be true during PMI, the influence of HR during the acquisition process as a whole is patchy. Many companies have neither the functional resources nor the knowledge to give the HR issues the priority they merit.[38]

According to a Towers Perrin/SHRM study, HR is fully involved in the M&A planning in less than a third of responding firms.[39] HR involvement is marginally higher during the negotiation stage, but it is only after the signing of the deal that 80 percent of firms see HR as fully engaged. It is obviously not easy for HR to ensure the smooth implementation of the deal when it has little or no part in shaping it. US-based companies seem to put rather more emphasis on early HR involvement than their European counterparts.

One reason for keeping HR out of the room is the need for secrecy surrounding most acquisitions before announcement of the bid or agreement. HR is unlikely to be involved if is not already perceived as a valuable contributor to business and strategy development. A determining factor is whether the top HR executive is a member of the senior management team and a full participant in the strategy planning process.

FROM PLANNING TO CLOSING

A typical cross-border acquisition starts with the development of the acquisition strategy and the selection of a target. An integral part of the selection process is the evaluation of the feasibility of the acquisition—due diligence. This examination moves to center stage when formal negotiations begin with the target (or with the launch of a hostile takeover bid). If the negotiations or takeover are successful, the transaction proceeds to closing, as long as the conclusion of the due diligence investigation is positive.

Some multinationals have a special acquisition unit that is involved in the planning and execution of every transaction.[40] Much of the work done during the planning and negotiation stage requires specialized and often highly technical, financial, and legal expertise. However, such units should not work in isolation from the managers who will have the responsibility for implementing the strategy and/or managing the acquisition. In some firms, such as GE, the future business leader and the designated future HR manager are part of the acquisition team from the very beginning.

Planning Acquisitions: The HRM Perspective

The due diligence process should cover all the important HRM considerations, including cultural assessment and a human capital audit. Cultural compatibility or incompatibility is relevant in many domestic acquisitions, and this is probably the most talked-about factor when acquisitions take place across borders. We will come back to this issue in the next section.

Another important component of acquisition planning is making sure that the company has the appropriate leadership team in place. When Renault considered acquiring a 37 percent stake in Nissan, a big factor in the decision-making process was the confidence that it had a team of seasoned managers who could go to Japan to guide the restructuring efforts. In words of then Renault's Chairman Louis Schweitzer: "If I didn't have Mr. Ghosn [sent by Renault to Tokyo to become president of Nissan], I would not have done the deal with Nissan… I had the absolute confidence in his ability."[41]

In international acquisitions, human resource strategy cannot be separated from the cultural and social context. Often the company may not have any expertise in the particular country or geographical area, so advance planning on how to mobilize the necessary resources to guide the firm through unfamiliar territory is important. At this stage, it is also important to provide the necessary orientation to the members of the due diligence team likely selected for their functional and analytical skills, rather than for their familiarity with the culture and environment of the target firm. In CEMEX, more than 300 people received training on what to look for in the RMC environment and cultures in which they would be operating.

Some HRM issues have a direct bearing on the selection of targets. How can a buyer get a quick reading on the quality of human assets and characteristics of the organizational culture before committing resources to full-scale due diligence? No one can expect HR to have all the information readily available, but in the words of an HR manager who participated in planning a number of acquisitions: "Even if you know the industry, each acquisition is different: different culture, legal framework, management team in place.

We are at the table not because we have all the answers, but we certainly know the questions that we have to ask."

The Due Diligence Process

Getting the strategy right depends on doing the homework. Good planning is not possible without good data. There are two aspects to due diligence in an acquisition. The first is to clarify the legal, financial, and business picture. The process for obtaining this information is well developed, as are the analytic methodologies. The second aspect, equally important but often neglected, is learning about the "soft" factors influencing the fit between the two organizations, such as the culture and the people practices in the target organization.

The Art of Being Truly Diligent

In cross-border acquisitions, the due diligence team must be sensitive to the fact that attitudes toward acquisition due diligence vary from country to country.[42] Under Anglo-Saxon practice, lawyers and their clients expect comprehensive due diligence before the acquisition is completed. In other countries, due diligence may be interpreted as intrusive at best, or as a sign of mistrust or bad intentions on the buyer's part. Getting information about the people side of the business, such as the quality of the management team, requires particular care. It is not easy to do this well, even in domestic acquisitions. Less than a third of US HR professionals consider that HR was effective in the due diligence phase of acquisitions.[43]

A list of topics covered by HR due diligence can easily run to several pages, especially if the buyer comes from North America (see Figure 12-3 for broad categories of issues to investigate). [44] As time is short, it is important to start with key priorities rather than becoming lost in technical details. Some items are on the list to protect the company against potential financial exposure,

FIGURE 12-3
Human Resource Due Diligence Checklist

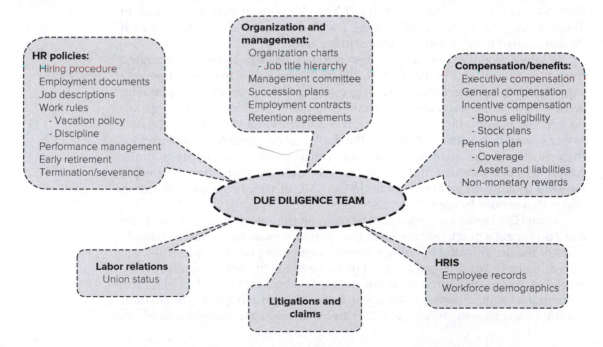

such as pension plan liabilities. Others cover key HR policies, especially those related to the strategic intent of the acquisition, such as identification of key talent, employee rights to technology, and information essential for a successful integration.

Where does this information come from? At an early stage, former employees, industry experts, consultants, executive search firms, and customers who know the company are usually the best sources. Cultivating some of these sources on a longer-term basis helps to mediate the constraints of confidentiality. Some of these data may be in the public domain, and Web-based search engines can speed up finding information. After the initial agreement, HR records and interviews with managers in the target company can supplement and verify the assessment.

However, HR due diligence is not just about collecting reams of data to avoid potential financial landmines or to prepare for harmonizing the policies and practices quickly after the deal. It is equally important to understand how the HR system influences the norms, and behaviors of the target company. When a large German company bought an up-and-coming producer of specialty chemicals near Beijing, the plan was to set up a foothold in the local "good-enough" market—acceptable quality at affordable price. Immediately after the acquisition, the buyer proceeded to revamp local HR system and work practices—in line with its global standards—for example, reducing regular work hours and overtime. Within weeks, most skilled workers left to join local competitors where they could earn more money, and within a year, the plant closed.

The transparency and accessibility of people-related people data vary from country to country. Companies often bemoan lack of soft diligence data abroad. In fact, the real issue is lack of familiarity with local environment and sources. In addition, it is usually not information that is lacking, but discipline and rigor in collecting and analyzing data. Two methodologies can be especially useful here: the human capital audit and culture assessment.

The Human Capital Audit

There are two dimensions to the human capital audit. One dimension supplements the early HR due diligence, focused on employment-related constraints such as pension plan obligations, outstanding grievances, or employee litigation that may affect the acquisition—for example, the cost of anticipated restructuring. It also includes comparing the compensation policies, benefits, and labor contracts of both firms.

The other dimension focuses on talent identification and is probably more critical to the long-term success of the acquisition. Talent identification has a number of important facets: ensuring that the target company has the talent necessary to execute the post-acquisition strategy of the combined units; identifying which individuals are key to sustaining the value of the deal; and assessing any potential weaknesses in the management cadre. It is also important to understand the motivation and incentive structure and to highlight any differences that may affect retention.

Here are some examples of questions to consider:

- What are the unique organizational capabilities of the target firm?
- What competencies do the employees have and how do they compare with those of the buyer?

- What are the sources of talent for the target firm and what is its talent development strategy?
- What is the target's compensation philosophy, for example, the degree of differentiation, and how much pay is at risk at various levels of the firm?
- What influences the social relationships between people in the organization and how important is social capital to performance?
- What will happen if certain members of the management team leave?

Getting access to talent data may take some effort, and many companies ignore the talent question in the early stages of the M&A process. They do not take the time to define the type of skills embedded in people who will be critical to the success of the deal, relying instead on financial performance data as a proxy. However, early assessment can help to pinpoint the potential risk factors so the acquiring company can develop strategies to address them as early as possible. Moreover, this will speed up decisions about who should stay and who should go.[45]

An important component of the human capital audit is the development of action plans to retain key talent (we will revisit this issue again in the next section) to implement immediately after the deal is concluded. The additional costs associated with retaining people, for example, retention bonuses as well as investment in training, must be included in the up-front financial estimates.[46]

At the same time, the audit may uncover weaknesses that call for replacement candidates, external local hires, or expatriates ready to step in immediately after the deal is closed. With each such change, there is also a potential termination, which again has to be carefully prepared based on local rules and practice.

Cultural Due Diligence

Well executed cultural integration is critical for acquisition success, especially in the context of cross-border M&As. Still, culture assessment is often not given much attention *before* the deal is done. In another survey of European executives involved in M&As, assessment of cultural fit came close to the bottom of the list.[47] It is therefore not surprising that culture differences are a source of difficulties during M&A implementation.

When Do Cultural Differences Matter?

A recent survey of executives from around the world identified organizational cultural differences as the most significant issue in cross-border M&As.[48] Not surprisingly, conventional wisdom suggests that companies should avoid any deal where cultural differences might be a problem. This is rooted in the assumption that cultural differences are largely unmanageable and will undermine the success of a deal. However, the empirical evidence suggests that the fear of cultural differences may be exaggerated—cross-border M&As are not less successful then domestic transactions.[49] Still, cultural differences are often the first attribution when a cross-border acquisition fails (see Box "Daimler–Chrysler Fiasco").

The research on this topic offers two important conclusions. First, it is important to distinguish between differences in organizational versus national culture. Organization cultures differ widely within countries—not all American firms

Daimler–Chrysler Fiasco

The poor performance of Daimler–Chrysler, one of the most talked-about cross-border mergers, is frequently attributed to a culture clash that caused major integration problems.[50] Differences between Daimler and Chrysler in management philosophy, compensation systems, and decision-making processes caused friction between members of senior management, while lower level employees fought over issues such as dress code and working hours. Language also became an issue. While most managers on the Daimler side could speak some English, not all were able to do so with the ease and accuracy needed for effective working relationships. Among the Chrysler managers and employees, few had any knowledge of German. However, considering that after a separation from Daimler and acquisition by Fiat, the "new" Chrysler reported record profits, an alternative perspective may be in order. How much were the tensions and conflicts that emerged in the Daimler–Chrysler merger due to cultural differences, and how much was caused by poor execution of PMI, and in particular by neglect of its people-related dimensions?[51]

are like GE, not all German firms are like Daimler. Second, the nature of the deal matters.[52] For example, in an acquisition which needs higher levels of business integration, cultural differences can create tensions that make integration more difficult. However, these differences are more likely to be due to differences in organizational than national culture. In a recent acquisition of a French-owned global business by an American firm, it was the difference between the "Beijing" and "Shanghai" cultures of the two local affiliates that mattered for the integration in China, and not the difference between Americans and French.

In addition, organizational culture differences have been found to be positively associated with post-acquisition performance in M&As that required lower integration (e.g., some recent acquisitions by the emerging market firms), probably due to increased opportunities for mutual learning.[53]

Successful acquirers are not afraid of cultural differences—they learn how to manage them. When Lincoln Electric first attempted to expand abroad through acquisitions, it failed. According to the company's CEO at that time, the lack of understanding of how local norms and values might inhibit implementation of Lincoln's management approach was one of the main obstacles.[54] However, two decades later, cross-border acquisitions have become an integral part of Lincoln's global strategy since the company learnt to adapt its core management practices to local social and institutional environments.[55] In today's global business environment, the proper response to cultural differences between buyer and target is not to avoid deals where there is a risk of culture clash, but to assess and manage the differences.

How to Assess the Culture of the Target Firm

The purpose of cultural assessment is to evaluate factors that may influence organizational fit, to understand the future cultural dynamics as the two organizations merge, and to plan how to address the cultural issues if the deal goes forward. Cultural assessment can be formal or informal, based on a variety of potential sources, such as market intelligence, external data, surveys, and interviews. It is important to have at least a rudimentary framework that helps to organize the issues and draw the proper conclusions.[56]

Assessment questions should look at the leadership of the target company and its view of the business environment, as well as its attitude toward competition, customer, and change:

- What are its core beliefs about what it takes to succeed?
- What drives its business strategy? What worked in the past, or innovation and change?
- Is the company long- or short-term oriented?
- Is the company result oriented or process oriented?
- What is its approach to external partners—competition or collaboration?
- Who are the important stakeholders of the organization?

Other questions examine broader leadership attitudes and evaluate how the company manages internal systems:

- Where is the power? Concentrated at the top, in certain functions, or diffused? Are hierarchical boundaries rigid or flexible?
- How does the management team function?
- How are decisions made—by consensus, consultation, or authority? How is conflict resolved? How much risk is the company willing to take?
- How does the company manage information? Is the flow of information wide or narrow, formal or informal?
- What makes an employee valuable? Getting results, or experience?
- Is the culture oriented to teamwork, individual performance, or both?

Cultural assessment is not just a question of assessing the other company's culture, it also means having a clear culture oneself and understanding it. The "know thyself" adage applies equally well to companies as it does to people. The criteria used in cultural assessment of the target will largely reflect the cultural attributes of the buyer.

Some companies use cultural assessment as an input into a stop/go decision about an acquisition. For example, Cisco avoids buying companies with cultures that are substantially different from its own, recognizing that it would be difficult to retain key staff if they cannot agree how to run a business. On the other hand, GE has been less concerned with retention—cultural assessment is also a "must," but mainly as a tool to plan integration. It is impossible to say that one approach works better than the other, but both companies are clear about what is important and how they want to get there.

Closing the Deal

Until the agreement to acquire is in place, much of the vital HR involvement in the acquisition process will go on behind the scenes. Then, immediately after the deal is sealed, the scope of the HR agenda expands rapidly. Companies often wait until closing before considering HR issues because the period between the signature of the agreement and implementation can be anywhere from several months to a year, depending on the need to obtain shareholder and regulatory approval, but this time should not be wasted.[57]

Pre-closing Action Plans

The first priority is to complete the due diligence, now with full access to data. The extent and conditions of access to managers and employees during this period is often a part of the M&A agreement. This is a sensitive time, and the first impressions of the new foreign owners may last for a long time. For example, when interviewing, it is important to solicit opinions from everyone, not just those who can speak the new owners' language. In many countries, union consent is desirable, if not essential, if the transaction is to go ahead. As with all labor relation issues, honest and open communication with union representatives is most effective.

All of this highlights one of the challenges for HR, namely rapidly acquiring and internalizing new cross-cultural competence, including familiarity with the legal and social context. HR, line, and staff managers involved in cross-border acquisitions have to be able to learn fast. Of course, if the company is already present in the country, the task is much easier. However, most companies require at least some reliance on outside resources, such as local consultants. Assessing and contracting outside resources will require time, so forward planning is essential.

Indeed, the people you hire to work on your behalf may tell local employees a great deal about your intentions and capabilities. A European pharmaceutical firm made a friendly offer to buy one of its large but struggling Japanese distributors. To facilitate the transaction, the company retained a local HR consulting group that, unknown to the potential buyer, had a reputation for a confrontational approach to post-merger integration. The result: Some of the top performers resigned soon after the consultants arrived, while the rest set up a union with the aim of blocking the acquisition. Faced with unexpected resistance, the offer had to be withdrawn.

As discussed before, the acquiring company should have the key components of the HR implementation blueprint in place by the time the acquisition is ready to close. This includes the organizational structure and reporting relationships, the composition of the new team, and the timeline for action on specific HR issues.

The final element of pre-closing activity is the selection of the integration manager and the transition team who will have the responsibility for combining the two organizations. If the team includes expatriates, which is often the case, they may need to receive at least rudimentary cross-cultural orientation and coaching.

THE POST-MERGER INTEGRATION PROCESS

The course of action leading up to closing the deal lays the foundation for next steps but most of the actual creation (or destruction) of shareholder value happens during the PMI phase. Successful acquirers understand well the challenges awaiting the firm as it embarks on the integration journey.

The M&A Integration Agenda

The change in ownership triggers changes in the target and its leadership. Now is the time to put a new organization in place, appoint new leadership, make sure that key talent is retained—and manage the *merger syndrome*. It is critical to be able to turn the uncertainty associated with most M&As into opportunities for employees to become involved in creating value in the new organization.

Recognizing and Managing the Merger Syndrome

Announcing a merger may be fun—for the top management that clinched the deal. It attracts lots of publicity and senior management can enjoy their moment in the spotlight. However, lower down the ranks in the acquired organization, reactions will be different: a merger often comes as a bolt from the blue—the so-called merger syndrome—a strong emotional reaction regardless of whether the bid is friendly or hostile. At a basic level, this simply reflects the fact that any process of change is stressful. To some degree, this merger syndrome is unavoidable, because it reflects the process of human adaptation, but it has to be managed carefully.

People often talk about "the first 100 days" of merger integration process, and what happens during this time sets the tone for later stages of the integration. Those whose company is taken over, invariably feel like losers. The initial responses of disbelief and denial are followed by shock, colored by overreaction ("We're going to lose our jobs"), which may lead to anger, attempts to bargain, or dig in heels. There may be a parallel cycle in the acquiring company, in which the initial reaction is often one of victory ("We did it!" "We'll show them how it's done!"). Attitudes toward the "losers" are often condescending, which will only worsen the PMI problems.

In any merger, there will be some indirect costs. These are measured in lost productivity through distraction (less focus on the here-and-now due to worries or speculation about the future), the upheaval created by departures (some talented people always jump ship and other people will be asked to leave), and drop in employee morale.[58] Whether these negative consequences of change are moderate and transitory, or whether they are debilitating for the integration process, depends on what happens during this period.

During the early stages of the acquisition, it is the responsibility of HR to anticipate people and leadership issues, starting by making sure that the transitional organization and teams are in place on day 1, fully prepared to deal with the complexities of a cross-cultural deal. The next step is staffing—who will stay and who will go? The evaluation of talent initiated before closing the deal continues, but it is not easy to assess people quickly in a foreign setting.[59] However, perhaps the most critical factor is to ensure employee trust because it helps to overcome resistance, gain commitment, and develop a sense of shared identity.[60]

In this respect, researchers suggest that acquirers need to pay attention to the four I's—*insight, information, involvement, and inspiration*—to manage the stress and uncertainty of the first 100 days (see box "The "Four I" Framework").

Managing the PMI Process

As all acquisitions require some degree of integration (even stand-alone deals require integration of financial reporting systems), it is important to tailor integration to the purpose of the acquisition and the characteristics of the companies involved. The integration process requires engaged leadership and often a dedicated integration manager working with a transition team. In most cases, moving with speed is an advantage. A critical part of the process is focusing on the areas where the acquisition can create new value, while maintaining the ongoing business.

The "Four I" Framework[61]

Insight means helping employees to acknowledge that change will be stressful. Pretending that nothing will be different or that there will be no stress only increases tension, undermining the credibility of the acquirer.

Information is never sufficient in the weeks after the merger—and this gap increases with distance. Face-to-face contact is most effective in breaking down feelings of them and us, winners and losers.

Inspiration refers to building positive expectations for the future at the earliest stage. The business plan for the future of the two companies may take time to elaborate, but inspiring (yet realistic) statements can pave the way and lift morale as long as they are genuinely realistic.

Involvement implies that the more people are involved in direct and personal ways, the more they will understand the rationale for the merger and feel committed to its successful implementation.

Leading the Integration

Usually, the signing of the deal means appointment of new leadership for the acquired unit. For most companies, assembling a new leadership team for an international acquisition is not an easy step. Who should head the acquired organization? Ideally, it should be someone familiar with both sides of the deal, for example, a local executive already in a leadership position with the buyer or another foreign company—but these executives are usually in short supply.

As we pointed out earlier, strong and committed leadership is the foundation for the successful execution of integration initiatives. In our research, three capabilities are fundamental to the effectiveness of the top leadership: a credible new vision, a sense of urgency, and an effective communication.[62] In interviews for a study of M&As in Japan, respondents indicated again and again that creating a sense of urgency around implementing the vision and maintaining momentum in driving change are the keys to success.[63] The ability to articulate vision goes hand-in-hand with soliciting feedback and engaging in two-way communication.

While close collaboration and a sense of trust among the top leaders of the merged organizations can also have a positive influence on employees' attitudes toward the merger, we have seen cases where close personal relationships and trust at the top created dangerous complacency. This may lead the leadership team to underestimate the operational obstacles facing the merger, avoiding the necessary but hard decisions that may be seen as rocking the boat.

Finally, another critical factor is getting leadership selection right at the outset. Instability in the top management team increases the likelihood of failed integration. The Daimler merger with Chrysler, which saw three teams of top executives during the first two years after acquisition, is one example of how disruptive leadership discontinuity can be. When Vodafone bought J-Phone (a Tokyo-based mobile operator), the top position was occupied by four executives in three years. Although the business strategy remained nominally the same, expectations changed as the company moved from expatriate to local leadership and back again, leading to confusion and instability within the organization as differences in leadership and communication style between executives aggravated tensions in the organization. After three years, the company—by now deeply in the red—was sold to a local competitor, who brought it to profitability within six months.

The Role of the Integration Manager

The integration of the acquired company with the new parent is a delicate and complicated process. To guide the process immediately after the deal is reached and to avoid a vacuum until the new management team is fully in place, companies are increasingly turning to dedicated integration managers, supported by transition teams.

The role of integration managers is to assure the speed of integration according to the agreed schedule. They help to engineer the short-term successes that are essential to create positive energy around the merger. They should also champion norms and behaviors consistent with new standards, communicate key messages across the new organization, and identify new value-adding opportunities.[64]

An important aspect of the job is helping the acquired company to understand how the new owner operates and what it can offer in terms of capabilities. The integration manager can help the firm take advantage of the buyer's resources, forge social connections, and help with essential but intangible issues, such as interpreting a new language and way-of-doing things. This is important because, outside the acquisition team, few people will be familiar with the target's capabilities.

The integration manager is the information gatekeeper between the two sides. Frustration in many deals stems not so much from what the parent wants the newly acquired unit to do but from ambiguity about what it wants to know. Information requirements expressed in new jargon that is incomprehensible can be overwhelming—indeed, corporate HR is often the guilty party here. The integration manager may be in the best position to decide whether and how the unit should comply with such requests.

What combination of skills does the integration manager need? First, a deep knowledge of the parent company—where to get information, whom to talk to, how the informal system works. Flexible leadership style is another requirement: the integration manager must be tough about deadlines, yet a good listener, and able to relate to people at different levels in the organization. Other traits that go with this role are comfort with ambiguity, emotional and cultural intelligence, and the willingness to take risks.[65] These jobs are often stepping stones into business leadership roles.

The Responsibilities of the Transition Team

In most acquisitions, integration teams and task forces support the integration manager. Since many of these teams are expected to start work on the first day after the acquisition deal is closed, the identification of potential members should be part of the due diligence process. HR professionals are often key members of the team because many of the team's activities will have implications for human resource policies and practices.

The specific charter of the transition teams depends on the integration approaches we discussed earlier. As in the CEMEX case, the key priorities (such as business synergies that can be achieved quickly) should be identified early. Prioritization is critical. Too many task forces slow things down, creating coordination problems, conflict, and confusion. In the ill-fated Daimler–Chrysler merger, the complexity of a transition structure involving over a hundred different projects was one of the reasons why its integration process rapidly came to a standstill.[66] Integration projects should focus on those with high-potential savings at low risk, leaving those with greater risk or lower benefits until later. As one experienced M&A manager stated: "We only attack things that will bring benefits to the business. We do not integrate just for the sake of integrating."

It is important that the transition team have authority. Customers do not like to wait until the team reaches consensus. One of the factors undermining Daimler's (partial) acquisition of Mitsubishi Motors was that local Japanese employees perceived the mostly German integration team members as transients and ignored many of their initiatives. Where did this attitude come from? The locals were keenly aware that the team was not empowered to make independent decisions—most had to be approved in Stuttgart—so there was no need to take them seriously.[67]

Who should be the members of the transition team? Mixing of line responsibility with transition taskforce roles may mean that neither is done well. On the other hand, integration teams are not the place for second-tier managers. The best staffing approach may be to appoint up-and-coming managers, leaving the daily business under the original leadership until the new organization can be put in place.[68] Integration teams are most effective when members come from both the target and acquiring companies. In Air France/KLM mixed integration teams were credited for making the integration more successful than other airline mergers.[69]

People who are suited for a transition team usually have a mix of functional and interpersonal competences (including cross-cultural skills), backed up by strong analytic skills. Having an ability to accept responsibility without full authority and being effective in mobilizing resources across organizational boundaries are especially important. Consequently, these roles provide good development opportunities for those with high potential.

Moving with Speed

When managers are asked what they learnt from their past M&A experiences, they often say: "We should have moved faster, we should have done in nine months what it took us a year to do." GE, for example, has cut the 100-day process back to 60–75 days, because it learnt how to move faster and developed the tools to do so. Speed is essential; if a company takes two to three years to integrate, what counts most tends to be neglected—the customers. According to GE:

> Decisions about management structure, key roles, reporting relationships, layoffs, restructuring, and other career-affecting aspects of the integration should be made, announced, and implemented as soon as possible after the deal is signed, within days if possible. Creeping changes, uncertainty, and anxiety that last for months are debilitating and immediately start to drain value from an acquisition.[70]

The necessity for speed may vary with the institutional and competitive context and considerations of time itself.[71] A survey of European acquisitions of US high-technology firms in Silicon Valley reported that speed of integration was one of the key drivers of successful PMI—but also one of the most problematic.[72] The understanding of European acquirers (usually large, established companies with entrenched routines and procedures) of "fast" was very different from Valley norms. This created confusion, frustration, and ultimately the loss of market opportunities.

A Japanese HR executive with extensive M&A experience with foreign firms in Japan was unambiguous in her assessment. "When you're changing something, you must do it all in one go, as quickly as possible. It becomes much harder to make small changes later on, when you would have to renegotiate every small detail. If you don't compromise, it will be better in the long run."[73]

Restructuring is often an essential step toward the synergies. Restructuring is not integration, but the rule is similar: it should be done *early, fast, and only once*. One problem jeopardizing the success of many acquisitions, perhaps motivated by good intentions, has been a tendency to restructure slowly to avoid excessively painful change. Yet while time is spent helping people to adjust, competitors come along and take away the business.

Sometimes, foreign acquirers' fear of cultural backlash slows down the process. One foreign-owned financial company in Japan suspended the introduction of several key elements of performance-based global HR policies for two years to give employees a chance to adapt. In retrospect, the company's new local CEO believes this may have been a mistake. "I think I may have been a bit too lenient because foreign companies are always criticized for being too harsh, for being vultures."[74]

The other dimension of speed is the focus on delivering quick, visible wins, such as new sales generated through a joint effort, or improvements based on shared practices. A quick win offers tangible proof that the merger or acquisition was a step in the right direction, so it is important to motivate employees by taking time to celebrate success.

Yet speed can also have unintended consequences. Managers take bad decisions made under pressure, without time for a judicious review of the issues. Conversely, good decisions meet resistance when there is not enough time to explain the new business logic. Again, the optimal speed depends on the strategic intent behind the acquisition and the desired end-state for the new organization.[75] Acquirers from emerging economies whose aim is to obtain competencies, technology, and knowledge essential to their global strategies often do not see quick integration as top priority.[76]

Beyond the 100 days

Maintaining momentum in the integration process is another challenge. The 100 days are only the first stage in the integration process. However, even if the early stages are successful, energy typically starts to flag after eight months to a year. Integration fatigue begins to settle in. As we discussed in Chapter 10, one of the biggest challenges in managing change is staying the course.

The pressure remains high since most key individuals have their regular jobs to do while they handle the integration effort. One study points to several dangers at this stage.[77] Divisions in the executive team may begin showing up, slowing down the process. Executives who went along with the fast-paced 100 days, but who were not deeply committed to the vision and ambitions of the process, may now start backtracking. So changes in the executive team may be required, as well as reconfirming and reinforcing the ambition with the new team.

To maintain momentum, HR efforts need to focus on coaching and training people in new behaviors, as well as redesigning measurement, appraisal, and reward systems that will anchor the new culture. If efforts earlier in the integration process focused on "what," attention at the second stage should be on "how," overcoming practical obstacles to change.

People Challenges of Post-Merger Integration

Post-merger integration is a change process. Companies without the experience in managing the people side of organizational change should be wary of tackling complex acquisitions. Often top management falls into the classic change trap of focusing on the content (the financials, the restructuring plans for the functions), and not on its process. All the lessons of change management apply to PMI—the need for communication, the need to establish a vision for the future, the need to restructure to remove resistance and empower champions, and management of the learning process by measuring progress against milestones.[78]

Several people challenges that impact the integration process merit particular attention—communication, retaining talent, and managing the process of culture change.

Communication

Communication is always a vital part of any process of change, but it is critical in cross-border acquisitions, where cultural differences may intensify tensions due to misunderstandings and distance. Furthermore, there are two additional communication objectives, particularly relevant to acquisitions. One aim of PMI communication is to alleviate the anxiety and stress that accompany every acquisition, as discussed earlier, and another is to provide feedback to top management about the progress of integration and any potential roadblocks.

The message to shareholders and the public has to be consistent with the message to employees in both the target and acquiring company. This happens far less often than it should. In the survey of European acquisitions in Silicon Valley cited earlier, every single acquired unit reported lack of clarity about its role in the combined organization.[79] The issues that most employees are anxious about revolved around "What is the intended end state or vision behind the new organization?" Here, consistent and coherent communication helps to build morale and reassure those unsettled by the changes.[80]

It is imperative to communicate a clear vision of how the acquisition or merger will create value. A well-articulated communication campaign conveys to the workforce that the leadership has a clear picture of where to take the acquisition.[81] Being open and honest about difficult issues is another imperative.[82] The hard truth may not go down well, but the consequences are easier to handle than the alienation and mistrust that stem from lack of candor.

Fast and open communication is an element of success in retaining talent. Cisco's and GE integration teams hold small group sessions with all acquired employees on day 1 to discuss expectations and answer questions. Often, members of the integration team were themselves brought into the companies through previous acquisitions. They understand what the newly merged employees are going through, so their messages have credibility.

Effective communication during the integration is a two-way process. Irrespective of the chosen road to integration, it is important to monitor progress in order to surface hidden issues and concerns that may create conflict in the new organization. This is particularly important in cross-border deals where misinterpretations can quickly poison the atmosphere and create confusion. The ability to react when false rumors spread is essential. The intranet and social media are useful tools to receive immediate feedback on how people in the acquired company feel about the integration process so the company can act before unhappy staff walk away.

Retaining Talent

Many acquired businesses lose key employees soon after closing—a major contributing factor to the failure of acquisitions. Research evidence from US acquisitions indicates that the probability of executives leaving increases if the acquisition is by a foreign multinational. About 75 percent of the firms' top management leaves by the fifth year, with a majority departing during the first two years.[83]

Given these statistics, it is not surprising that when the Chinese company Lenovo acquired IBM's PC division, the board of Lenovo allowed the company to proceed with the deal if, and only if, it could retain IBM's senior executives to manage the merged enterprise.[84] However, the talent that Lenovo wanted was not limited to senior executives. When the deal closed, the company offered a job to every IBM employee worldwide, with no obligation to relocate or accept a pay-cut.

Especially if staff cuts are expected, employees often leave unless there is explicit attention paid to retaining talent—and the best will exit first as they have the most opportunities. Retention of key employees is therefore crucial to achieving acquisition goals in both short-term integration tasks and long-term business performance—the key principles are outlined in box "Five Principles of Talent Management in M&As."

Five Principles of Talent Retention in M&As

Find out where your talent is: It is critical to know exactly who the talented people are, and why they are essential to the new organization. The starting point for talent identification is the talent map developed during the due diligence stage.

Attitude matters: In M&As, talent is not only about technical and managerial skill, it is also about attitude and willingness to change. Such talent may be found in unexpected places—perhaps even among employees who may not have been properly recognized in the old organization.

Fast and open two-way communication: Frank conversations about expectations and opportunities help quickly unearth employees' concerns and anxieties so they can be addressed.

Articulate career opportunities: Compensation is important, but high-potential employees expect senior-level attention to their career. They will be more likely to stay if they see opportunities for themselves in the combined firm.

Measure and reward retention: Without retention data, companies have no way of measuring the success of their talent management efforts, and no way of holding managers accountable—and rewarding them—for success in post-merger retention of talent.

The first step is to know exactly who the talented people are and why they are essential to the new organization. This is not easy. The typical top-down talent identification process often yields flawed results, since local managers may not be objective about what their people may offer to the new organization. One of the biggest obstacles in international acquisitions is the difference in performance measures and standards. Even if standards are comparable, many companies are not aware of where their talent is; in one study, only 16 percent of surveyed executives believed their companies could identify high performers.[85]

The initial talent map needs to be refined quickly, through feedback from direct superiors, peers, and subordinates, past performance reviews, personal interviews, formal skill assessments, and direct evaluation of performance during the integration period. While multiple sources of assessment are desirable, the quest for precision may slow down the process too much, increasing uncertainty and the risk of defection. Since the pace of integration may not allow a comprehensive assessment of all individuals, the focus should be on those most critical to the success of the acquisition.[86]

A complementary building block for talent retention is providing inducements for employees to stay. Companies often offer stock options, retention bonuses, or other incentives to employees who stay through the integration or until a specific merger-related project is completed.[87] An important consideration is to highlight the differences between short-term needs (retention incentives for employees not expected to be employed after the integration process) and long-term talent requirements.

For the second group, financial incentives cannot substitute for a one-on-one relationship with executives in the acquiring firm. High-potential employees are used to senior-level attention. Without the same treatment from the acquiring company, they question their future and are more likely to depart. Distance may be an obstacle, but it should not be an excuse. Meetings and informal sessions in the early days of the acquisition, perhaps even before the closing, can go a long way. When BP-Amoco acquired Arco, another international oil major, it quickly organized Key Talent Workshops—two-day events in which senior BP executives networked with Arco's high-potential employees.[88]

Talent retention efforts should not stop after the first 100 days of integration. Junior employees may find the initial impact of the acquisition positive, offering them opportunities for responsibility and higher pay (especially if their seniors leave en masse). However, many of them leave later because of a lack of integration into the leadership development of the new parent company.[89] This may have negative consequences for the company's ability to execute future deals, since its poor record in retaining talent will affect its credibility and reputation for managing acquisitions.

While the link between the retention of talent and acquisition success is widely recognized, it does not automatically translate into support for specific HR initiatives.[90] Frequently, part of the challenge is the lack of management accountability for talent retention. However, many firms have recognized this problem. They not only measure employee turnover, but they also define the retention of key talent as one of the key performance indicators for integration managers and other executives involved in the integration process.

Sometimes, the acquisition may involve only a part of the seller organization, usually as an outcome of divestment strategy on the part of the seller (known as a curve-out). In a recent study by a major consulting firm, 85 percent

FIGURE 12-4
Retention techniques

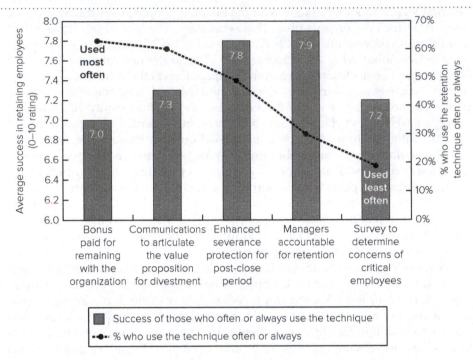

Source: Adapted from Ernst and Young, Human capital curve-out study, 2013.

of the respondents say that employee retention is the biggest driver of the deal success—with manager's accountability for retention as being the most effective method (see Figure 12-4).[91]

Building the New Culture

The process of building a new culture can take a long time; sometimes longing after the old ways can drag on for a decade. In most cases, this does not help the company move forward.

This is the main reason why companies with strong cultures, like GE, AXA, or Haier, do not hesitate to impose their culture onto the company they acquire. Indeed, they see their success as originating from their culture and the practices built on it. However, as acknowledged by CEMEX, while the directions and expectations are clear, there is an understanding that full cultural integration will take longer than changing the operating system.

The focus on creating—or reinforcing—a performance culture seems to be a unifying theme in most successful acquisitions. Rather than focusing on pre-acquisition cultures, the emphasis should now be on the new strategy for the merged firm, the organizational capabilities required to implement that strategy successfully, and on the values, behavior, and organizational practices that are crucial for future performance. Recent research suggests that an explicit *performance contract* should be at the core of the performance culture of the merging units, confirming "a set of mutual understandings of how to run the business, such as: how to manage processes, how to deal with customers and business partners, how to make and follow up decisions."[92] A new culture could take hold surprisingly fast when perceived as beneficial to the employees.[93]

Post-merger culture change is difficult to manage without continuous reinforcement of the organizational values and norms that guide practice and behavior. To build the new culture of ABB after the merger of Asea and Brown Boveri, the founding CEO Percy Barnevik spent three months with the new senior management team defining a policy bible to guide the new organization. This was a manual of "soft" principles, such as speed in decision-making ("Better to be quick and roughly right than slow and completely right"); for conflict management ("You can only kick a conflict upstairs once for arbitration"); as well as "hard" practices, such as the performance measurement system that would apply across all units of the newly merged enterprise.

Values and behavioral norms have no meaning unless translated into action, guiding the process of culture building or cultural assimilation after an acquisition. Take the French company AXA as an example of the latter. In the space of a decade, AXA grew via acquisitions from being a local player in the French insurance industry to becoming a top global financial services institution. It made no pretensions that its acquisitions were mergers of equals, acting quickly to AXA-ize the cultures of the firms it acquired.

Managers from companies brought into AXA commented that one of its most helpful assimilation tools was the company's 360-degree feedback process, encoding AXA values. To accelerate the process of cultural integration all managers and professionals in the acquired company went through 360-degree workshops. For many of the managers, this was the first time that they took part in such a multifaceted assessment, and the rigor of the approach reinforced the credibility of AXA as a highly professional organization. It made the desired culture and values concrete, identified personal needs for improvement, and led to follow up coaching in the AXA way.

M&A AS ORGANIZATIONAL CAPABILITY

An increasing number of global firms across all industries view organizational proficiency at making international acquisitions as one of the supporting pillars of their business strategies.[94] To those mentioned in the chapter we can add Inbev, Reckitt Benckiser, Teva, and Wanxiang, among others. They understand that the ability to execute acquisitions is one of the core competitive capabilities for the future and that the intangible human aspects of an acquisition are just as important as its financial dimensions. From this perspective, multinationals that have *solid foundations in HRM and other functional domains* have an advantage in implementing M&As.

Still, for many companies, implementing international acquisitions is a formidable challenge. The complexity of cross-border deals, with their cultural and physical distance, makes implementation even more difficult. Not surprisingly, probably the best predictor of M&A success is the ability of the acquiring organization to learn from its experience.[95] However, experience is not the same as learning. Previous success may even hurt future M&A performance, if a company believes that it can automatically apply its prior experience to the next case,[96] or stops paying attention to changes in its environment.

Learning from Past Acquisitions

M&As are complex and never identical, and firms need to disentangle what is generic and what works only in specific situations. The more different the acquisitions, the more difficult it is for the company to gain from previous M&A experience. At the same time, as the CEMEX case illustrates well, when learning is built into the acquisition process, different experiences may enhance the quality of learning—and future execution.

A foundation for M&A learning is feedback on progress in managing integration. It starts with a rigorous measurement of key performance indicators:

- **Integration goals:** Reorganization and restructuring targets in terms of schedule and cost, including breakdowns for specific business units or geographical areas.
- **Integration of key HR systems:** Tracking integration objectives in combining systems for human resource information, compensation, talent development, and performance management according to established schedule and budgets.
- **Retention of talent:** Retention of acquired talent, success rates for different retention tools, retention rates for specific business units and functions, and cost-effectiveness indicators such as retention/replacement expenses.
- **Best practices:** Shared and adopted practices compared across organizational units, including estimation of the impact on revenues, cost, or other performance indicators such as customer satisfaction.
- **Employee feedback data:** These include attitude surveys and data from exit interviews.

Building Learning Capability

Some companies create a special acquisition unit that is involved in every transaction. Obviously, this creates a desirable pool of expertise. On the other hand, acquisition competence is increasingly an indispensable generalist skill—having experience with an acquisition is invaluable to all high-potential employees. That is the view of GE, and because HR is one of the functions with a guaranteed seat at any GE acquisition, smart young employees seek out HR jobs to have a chance at joining the acquisition team.

In either case, managers who have developed extensive experience in international acquisitions are valuable resources for the organization. Part of HR's responsibility is to ensure that it knows who and where they are, so they can be mobilized quickly when required. From the employees' point of view, participation in a cross-border acquisition team is a good way to put to use skills accumulated during past international assignments. Indeed, the behavioral competencies of both expatriates and integration team members are similar; both roles demand emotional maturity, cultural empathy, tolerance for ambiguity, and skills in interpersonal communication.

Research shows that the more companies invest in reflecting on their experiences and codifying their M&A learning in due diligence and integration manuals, the better they perform.[97] Still, there is a qualitative difference here regarding learning tools. Acquisition "best practice" books present scenarios and suggest roadmaps for managers to follow. In contrast, acquisition tool kits provide managers with lists of issues and questions to address at each stage in the acquisition, broad guidelines on what to consider, simple and concise instruments, and sources of advice inside and outside the firm. In repetitive acquisitions, the best practice approach may be sufficient, although most international acquisitions are one of a kind. In all cases, a feedback loop recording what worked, what did not, and what can be added is essential.

From Learning to Action

We conclude this chapter by outlining GE's approach to acquisitions (see Figure 12-5), which illustrates well the importance of human resource management in implementing acquisitions.[98] The figure captures the key elements of an acquisition process used successfully in scores of international transactions. It provides detailed guidance on action to take, highlights the key organizational issues and decision points, and provides the methodology and resources. As the company accumulates more experience, it is continuously updated and fine-tuned. However, perhaps the most critical feature is that it allows the people involved in the process find the right answers for themselves. All deals are different, so flexibility in arriving at solutions is important.

The merger implementation process starts well before the deal is out in the open, setting the framework for integration. It begins with an assessment of the target's culture to identify any potential cultural barriers to the success

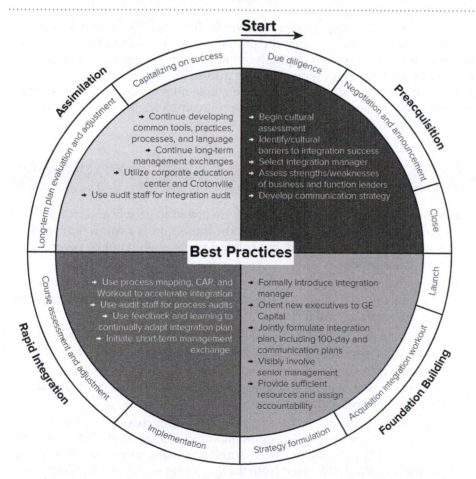

FIGURE 12-5
The Wheel of Fortune at General Electric

Source: R.N. Ashkenas, L.J. DeMonaco, and S.C. Francis, "Making the Deal Real: How GE Capital Integrates Acquisitions," Harvard Business Review, January–February 1998, p. 167.

of the acquisition. As a part of due diligence, the strengths and weaknesses of the business leaders are assessed so that it is clear early who should stay and who may need to be replaced. The integration manager is selected, who then proceeds to assemble the transition team. When the deal is signed, the communication strategy is ready to go into action on the first day.

In the second stage, the integration manager and the transition teams, now expanded to include employees from the target firm, work together to formulate a specific integration plan and to align key processes, including human resources. Through workshops and other communication tools, the new employees are oriented to the acquiring firm's way of doing business. The involvement and visibility of senior management are critical, as is accountability for specific integration tasks. This is also the stage when, if necessary, painful decisions on terminations are made, quickly but fairly, so that the new organization can move forward.

As integration proceeds, process tools and techniques can accelerate integration and to deal with any resistance to change. The transition team helps to identify opportunities to demonstrate success, and these projects receive given high priority. Short-term international exchanges are particularly motivating at this stage. While the integration is managed according to preset guidelines, there are regular learning reviews to allow for adjustment, taking into account feedback from employees.

The process of integration is not over in 100 days. To assimilate the new employees into the parent firm, the development of common tools, practices, and processes continues. Corporate education and long-term management exchanges are two sets of tools that help diffuse the shared culture. In acquisitions, learning never stops. Auditing the whole integration process and incorporating any learning into the core blueprint completes the cycle—so that the next acquisition can be done even faster and better.

TAKEAWAYS

1. Many failures of international M&A are linked to people and cultural challenges during the PMI process. The importance of cultural differences is not to be underestimated, but cultural issues should not be cover for poor management.

2. Merging organizations across boundaries is always a challenging task. The ability to add value in the merged company depends mostly on what happens after the deal is done.

3. Companies that have solid foundations in HRM and a good record in managing change also tend to be good at managing acquisitions.

4. There are different strategic logics guiding mergers—stand-alone, absorption, best of both, and transformational. Each strategic logic has different implications for the nature of the PMI process.

5. The "soft" aspects of the due diligence process, such as culture and people practices, are just as important as financial analysis. HR should be involved early in the acquisition planning, making sure that cultural and people issues are addressed from the beginning of the M&A process.

6. The integration process starts with the creation of a vision and strategy for the combined organization. Clarity in communication about the future strategy is an essential foundation for success.

7. Many acquisition falter because of the loss of key talent. Retention plans should be developed already during the due diligence process. Retention requires leadership commitment to build personal relationships with the newly acquired talent.

8. In most acquisition, it is better to move with speed. Key decisions about management structure, senior appointments, and anything related to people's careers should be made quickly, as any uncertainty and anxiety after the acquisition will drain energy from the organization.

9. Several critical elements in PMI foster success: appointing an integration manager to speed up the process; measuring M&A outcomes and assigning accountability; and securing and celebrating quick wins.

10. Some firms view proficiency in making international acquisitions as one of their core capabilities. For them, the ability to learn from past acquisitions, including from the mistakes made, is a major source of competitive advantage.

NOTES

1 The CEMEX material in this chapter draws mainly on the IMD case of Marchand and Leger (2008).

2 Marchand and Leger, 2008.

3 Zambrano passed away in 2014. In 2015, two leading cement makers, Lafarge and Holcim, agreed to merge to create a new global number one firm.

4 In 2014, less than 8 percent of all global M&A deals were hostile. See Thompson Reuters, *Mergers & Acquisition Review*, 2014, p. 1.

5 Thompson Reuters, *Mergers & Acquisition Review*, 2014, p. 1.

6 Ibid.

7 "Gone Shopping: Chinese firms in Europe," *Economist*, March 28, 2015, pp. 63–64; "India Looks to Invest in Germany's Family Firms," *The Wall Street Journal*, April 13, 2015, p. 18.

8 Kumar, 2009; Williamson and Raman, 2011. In the largest Chinese deal ever, ChinaChem acquired Syngenta in 2016.

9 See Dyer, Kale, and Singh (2004) for an extensive discussion of whether to choose an alliance or an acquisition.

10 In China and in India, two countries with history of restricting foreign acquisitions, the regulatory environment is gradually becoming more open.

11 Garette and Dussauge, 2000.

12 "The case against mergers," *The Economist*, January 1997, pp. 4–7; Kearney, A.T., "Corporate marriage: Blight or bliss—a monograph on post-merger integration," 1999; KPMG, "Mergers and acquisitions: A global research report—unlocking shareholder value," 1999. Most of these and similar studies looked at the financial outcomes of M&A transactions. There are other stakeholders in the acquisition process, including employees, local communities, and customers.

13 King *et al.*, 2004. According to a 2006 KPMG study "The morning after," 31 percent of deals created value, 26 percent reduced value. Dobbs, R., M. Goedhart, and H. Suonio "Are companies getting better at M&A?" *McKinsey Quarterly* (December 2006), www. mckinseyquarterly.com/ (online only) reported a similar positive trend.

14 Sudarsanam, 2012. The premium is the acquisition price minus the stock exchange value of the target before announcement of the deal. The premium tends to vary from a few percent to more than 50 percent.

15 Kearney, A.T., "Corporate marriage: Blight or bliss—a monograph on post-merger integration," 1999; Epstein, 2004.

16 Bleeke *et al.*, 1993, KPMG, "Mergers and acquisitions: A global research report—unlocking shareholder value," 1999; Larsson and Finkelstein, 1999; Bertrand and Zitouna, 2008.

17 Morosini, Shane, and Singh, 1998; Vermeulen and Barkema, 2001; Björkman, Stahl, and Vaara, 2007.

18 Slangen, 2006.

19 Morosini, Shane, and Singh, 1998; Björkman, Stahl, and Vaara, 2007.

20 Zollo and Singh, 2004.

21 Killing, 2003a. Haspeslagh and Jemison (1991) offer a well-known alternative framework for examining different types of M&A integration.

22 Kale, Singh, and Raman, 2009; Kale and Singh, 2012.

23 Tata Motors used this approach in an earlier successful acquisition of the Daewoo truck business (DCVC) in Korea.

24 Killing, 2003a.

25 When Air France acquired KLM, the two companies agreed to maintain separate brands and identities for eight years, but now, while KLM brand remains, many support operations are already fully integrated (Bouchikhi and Kimberly, 2012).

26 See Marchand and Leger (2008).

27 Killing, 2004.

28 The ill-fated merger of the German car manufacturer Daimler and its US competitor Chrysler was publicized as a "merger of equals." In a press interview several years later, Daimler's CEO confirmed what many suspected from the beginning—the plan for integration was a full takeover right from the start.

29 "Holcim-Lafarge tie-up on shaky ground," *Financial Times*, March 17, 2015, p. 17.

30 Vaara, Tienari, and Björkman, 2003. See also Vaara (2003) for a discussion of how cross-border integration issues can easily become political.

31 Killing, 2003a.

32 Stahl and Koester, 2013; Yang, 2014.

33 Killing, 2003a.

34 Christensen *et al.*, 2011.

35 Immelt, Govindarajan, and Trimble, 2009.

36 Kay and Shelton, 2000. A study published by Towers Perrin and SHRM Foundation (Schmidt, 2002) reported similar results.

37 Marsh, Mercer, and Kroll, "M&A beyond borders: Opportunities and risks," 2008, p. 46, www.mercer.com.

38 KPMG, "Mergers and acquisitions: A global research report—unlocking shareholder value," 1999, p. 15.

39 Schmidt, 2002.

40 Hitt, Harrision, and Ireland, 2001, p. 111.

41 "Renault steers forward," *Wall Street Journal Europe*, February 15, 2001, p. 31.

42 Chu, 1996.

43 Schmidt, 2002.

44 For example, acquiring a firm in the US may involve reviewing over 20 categories of benefit plans and policies, going back six years to understand all the potential tax liabilities. See Johnson and Rich (2000).

45 See also Harding and Rouse (2007).

46 For more on integration of knowledge-intensive acquisitions based on an analysis of how Swedish multinationals integrated foreign R&D units with the aim of enhancing knowledge sharing, see Bresman, Birkinshaw, and Nobel (1999).

47 Angwin, 2001.

48 For example, Marsh, Mercer, and Kroll, "M&A beyond borders: Opportunities and risks," 2008, www.mercer.com.

49 For comprehensive reviews of research on this topic, see Schweiger and Goulet (2000), Stahl and Voigt (2008), and Teerikangas *et al.* (2014). See also Chakrabarti, Gupta-Mukherjee, and Jayaraman (2009).

50 Epstein, 2004; Kühlmann and Dowling, 2005; Vlasic and Stertz, 2000.

51 Pucik *et al.*, 2014.

52 Stahl and Voigt, 2008.

53 Ibid.

54 Hastings, 1999.

55 Siegel and Zepp Larson, 2009.

56 One frequently used assessment tool is the Denison Culture Survey. See Denison *et al.* (2012), and Marks and Mirvis (2010, pp. 70–72).

57 During this period people at all levels of the organization speculate about their future in the new organization, some with great expectations, others with fear. It is important that HR plan covers such regulatory contingencies, in particular the impact on retention of talent.

58 According to some estimates, nearly two-thirds of companies lose market share during the quarter following a merger. See Harding and Rouse (2007).

59 Therefore, many companies are turning to outside vendors to assure the fairness and objectivity of this process.

60 Stahl and Sitkin, 2010; Teerikangas *et al.*, 2014.

61 Marks and Mirvis, 2010, pp. 166–171.

62 Sitkin and Pablo, 2005; Fubini, Price, and Zollo, 2006.

63 Pucik, 2008.

64 Ashkenas, DeMonaco, and Francis, 1998; Ashkenas and Francis, 2000; Teerikangas, Very, and Pisano, 2011.

65 Ashkenas and Francis, 2000.

66 For contrasting interpretations of the Daimler-Chrysler post-merger integration, see Morosini and Steger (2004) and Vlasic and Stertz (2000).

67 Froese and Goeritz, 2007.

68 The transition team can also serve as a role model for how the new organization should act. By facilitating personnel exchanges, the transition team can help both sides to develop a better understanding of each other's capabilities.

69 Del Canho and Engelfriet, 2008.

70 Ashkenas, DeMonaco, and Francis, 1998.

71 Angwin, 2004.

72 Inkpen, Sundaram, and Rockwood, 2000.

73 Pucik, 2008.

74 Ibid.

75 Homburg and Bucerius, 2006.

76 Kumar, 2009; Kale and Singh, 2012; Deng and Yang, 2015.

77 Haspeslagh, 2000.

78 See Chapter 10 for a comprehensive discussion of these change management principles.

79 Inkpen, Sundaram, and Rockwood, 2000.

80 Lack of clarity and strategic consistency from top management can have disastrous consequences. In the failed Deutsche–Dresdner banking merger, mixed signals from the leadership about the future of the combined organization's investment banking operations created opposition in both camps, ultimately forcing the cancellation of a deal that looked promising on paper. Because of the high rate of defections during the confused weeks after the initial merger announcement, Dresdner Bank had no choice but to accept a less favorable offer from another financial institution. See "Torch that sent a deal down in flames," *Financial Times*, April 12, 2000, p. 22.

81 Marks and Mirvis, 2010, pp. 77–78.

82 Ellis, Reus, and Lamont, 2009.

83 Krug and Hegerty, 1997.

84 Harding and Rouse, 2007.

85 Michaels, Handfield-Jones, and Axelrod, 2001.

86 Corporate Leadership Council, "M&A talent management: Identification and retention of key talent during mergers and acquisitions," 2000, p. 37.

87 Retention bonus guidelines provide desirable consistency, specifying eligibility, amount, performance criteria, and so on. Their effect depends, however, on employees' expectations as well as on labor and tax legislation in the countries involved.

88 Corporate Leadership Council, 2000.

89 Krug and Hegerty, 2001.

90 For example, in earlier global survey of senior executives, 76 percent of respondents indicated that talent retention was the most critical element of integration success. However, only 8 percent put HRM as their top priority during integration: Watson Wyatt, "Watson Wyatt Worldwide 1998/99 Mergers & Acquisitions Survey," 1999, p. 66.

91 Ernst and Young, *Human capital curve-out study*, 2013, p. 15.

92 Fubini, Price, and Zollo, 2006.

93 Froese, Pak, and Chong (2008) studied three cross-border acquisitions in Korea (one with rapid major change toward more performance-oriented HRM, one with slower change but in the same direction, and one with little change from the traditional Korean system). Employees in the first two cases were significantly more satisfied with the change, because they saw it as necessary to remain competitive and keep their jobs.

94 Hitt, Harrison, and Ireland, 2001; Corporate Research Forum, "HR's role in M&As," 2006.

95 Zollo and Singh, 2004.

96 Barkema and Schijven, 2008.

97 Zollo and Singh, 2004; Fubini, Price, and Zollo, 2006.

98 Ashkenas, DeMonaco, and Francis, 1998.

13

Managing Alliances and Joint Ventures

SUMMARY

Challenge

Many cross-border alliances do not meet expectations, and those involving collaboration with competitors are seen as especially difficult

Analysis

Companies with history of successful alliances exhibit the following capabilities:

- Pro-active management of the alliance process
- Leveraging HR to maintain influence over the partnership
- Maintaining learning parity with the alliance partner

Solutions

- Select alliance partners with compatible strategies and culture
- Design the alliance HRM based on strategic objectives of the partnership
- Ensure that managers in the alliance have high credibility, tolerance for ambiguity, and a desire to learn
- Use career and performance management as alliance control tools
- Align all HR practices with alliance learning objectives

Rebuilding Alliance Strategy at Chemco

Several decades ago, the US-based chemical company Chemco (name disguised) decided to enter the booming Japanese market. However, Japan's foreign investment policies at the time precluded direct entry. Facing the choice between licensing and a minority joint venture (JV), the company decided to establish a 49/51 percent partnership with a well-known Japanese firm to build a local plant and set up distribution. Chemco would contribute technology in exchange for help in market access. Soon after its launch, the joint venture, led entirely by local managers, became the leader in its industry segment.

Later, the US parent decided to take advantage of the liberalization of the Japanese economy to obtain a majority position in the JV. In their opinion, the JV was becoming "too independent," and they wanted more influence on its future direction. After protracted negotiations, the Japanese partner agreed to sell 2 percent of equity to the Americans, and the board composition changed accordingly. The new board instructed the local CEO to streamline the product portfolio and to cut costs by integrating several support functions into the global organization. However, while the local managers never directly questioned the need for more efficiency, most of the integration projects never really got off the ground.

Frustrated by the difficulties in "integrating Japan," the US management decided that additional equity would give it the necessary influence to push through the integration plans. After another round of difficult negotiations, the US parent gained control of 65 percent of the shares. The company name changed, putting its US partner's name first. A senior vice president of finance (who did not speak Japanese) arrived to join the local management team. In spite of these changes, the venture continued to run independently—very much as before. While it was profitable, with nearly US$1 billion of sales, margins were well below corporate expectations. As Japanese customers began to migrate to lower-cost suppliers in China and Southeast Asia, poor coordination with other subsidiaries became a serious business problem.

A third generation of US top management decided to address the problem head-on. They retained a consultant to advise them on what to do next. Should they buy even more equity? Send in more expatriates? Sell the existing business and start again?

It turned out that the company could not sell the plant in the open market because the surrounding infrastructure belonged to the Japanese parent. In addition, the Japanese partner (located right next door) was the legal employer of the vast majority of employees, including virtually all top managers. Even those recruited well after the JV was established were not employees of the joint venture. They were only "dispatched" to the JV—at the discretion of the Japanese partner. Their salaries corresponded to their positions in the Japanese parent company hierarchy. All training, starting with new employee induction, took place jointly with employees of the Japanese parent—and they all belonged to the same company union.

All of this was seen as a "good deal" when the JV was originally set up; it meant that there was no need to worry about any HRM issues in an unknown market. Subsequently, each step in the evolution of the relationship had focused only on the financial aspects of control. What can Chemco do now to change the joint venture direction?

OVERVIEW

Alliances are a useful tool for internationalization, but as they are inherently unstable, they are difficult to implement. The example of Chemco illustrates the complexity of alliances and the dangers of ignoring their management and people dimensions. So first, we review the many motives for entering an international alliance and introduce a framework that helps us to think strategically about alliances, and how they may evolve over time. We then focus on how to plan and negotiate alliances, highlighting the key HRM issues that need attention already at this stage.

Much of the HRM agenda during alliance implementation centers on maintaining influence within the venture. We discuss how HRM can support alliance strategic objectives through carefully calibrated selection, mobility, career development, and performance management practices. The final part of the chapter explores the concept of alliance learning. We describe the human resource processes that can contribute to successful alliance learning, contrasting examples of successful and unsuccessful learning.

THE WHYS AND WHATS OF ALLIANCES

Companies engage in international alliances for many reasons.[1] Understanding *why* a company participates in an international alliance is the first step towards deciding the approach to alliance human resource management.

Cross-Border Alliance Business Drivers

In the early days of globalization, the primary objective of international alliances (usually set up as joint ventures) was to enable firms to secure access to markets restricted by host government regulations—just like in the case of Chemco. Even after several decades of liberalization of global capital flows, many countries including China, India, or Russia limit access of foreign firms in specific sectors deemed critical to national interests.[2]

Entering a restricted market is only one reason explaining alliances. Even when a wholly owned subsidiary may be feasible, there are many arguments in favor of market entry through partnership with a local firm. Such a partnership can reduce the risk of entry into uncharted territories through knowledge of local business conditions, a desirable location and infrastructure, access to the distribution system, contacts with government, supply of qualified labor, and experienced management.[3] For instance, Starbucks entered into a JV with Tata Coffee (part of the global Tata Group based in India) in 2012 to own and operate Starbucks outlets in India. The JV brought together Starbucks' retail concept and international experience with Tata's Indian coffee sourcing organization and local expertise.[4]

Some cross-border alliances are alternatives to mergers, avoiding cost and complexities of integration (the Nissan–Renault alliance is one well-known example[5]) with the objective of achieving economies of scale and scope as discussed in the previous chapter. Alliances often involve direct competitors and emerge in all areas of the value chain—from shared R&D to joint marketing and distribution.[6]

In high-technology industries today, international alliances are the norm, not the exception. Most high-tech firms are engaged in scores of R&D, manufacturing, and marketing alliances. Their objective is to reduce risk in searching for innovations or to leverage their existing knowledge quickly over the broadest possible number of markets with the next generation of breakthrough innovations in mind.

Some firms are heavily involved with alliances; others find them tangential to their global strategy. However, most companies will engage in some form of international alliance as they expand abroad. Consequently, it is important to understand the strategic and management issues relating to international alliances and the role of HRM in alliance planning and implementation.[7]

Understanding Alliances

Choosing the right type of alliance is difficult if the strategy is not clear. What is the business objective of the proposed alliance? What form of alliance should a company choose given its objectives, and what are the HRM implications of such a choice?

Defining Alliance Success

The Chemco case raises the question of what is a successful alliance. Does the mere survival of an international alliance indicate success? Is success measured by the return on the funds originally invested? By current profitability and cash/dividend flow? By transfer of knowledge or creation of new knowledge? Obviously, the choice depends on the specific objectives of the alliance, but these may change as the alliance evolves. From this perspective, the only relevant measure of alliance success is the degree to which it helps the firm to improve the ability to compete.

A desire to get a "win-win" outcome is important, but this does not imply that value creation must be equal or that all alliances should be sustainable for an indefinite period. Most alliances are transitory in nature, reflecting a particular competitive situation at a particular point in time. When the situation changes, so does the need for the alliance. Problematic alliances are a drain on management energy and resources, but they often limp on since shutting them down would imply "failure."

From this perspective, Chemco's alliance in Japan, although growing and profitable, was not as successful as it could have been. This does not mean that the original entry decision was wrong. In fact, in terms of ROI, the deal was the best the company had ever made. However, as the company's internationalization strategy evolved, the alliance in Japan did not follow, largely because of lack of attention to the management and human resource issues involved.

There is ample data showing that many alliances fail to meet expectations, usually because of poor implementation.[8] The complexity of managing a business with international partners is a challenge that few firms seem equipped to handle. When alliances break up, HRM issues are often one of the key factors contributing to "irreconcilable differences."[9]

There is a general agreement that, as one moves through the spectrum of alliances from a "simple" marketing agreement with a foreign distributor to stand-alone joint ventures, the management challenges increase, as does the importance of paying attention to HRM.[10] Even among joint ventures, different strategic drivers may require different HRM strategies.

An Alliance Strategy Framework

An alliance is typically a dynamic phenomenon, as Chemco's case illustrates. The nature of the alliance may change over time, and shifts in the relative bargaining power of the partners and in their expectations about the objectives of the alliance will have corresponding HRM implications.

Two dimensions of alliance strategies require careful consideration from an HRM perspective. One is the strategic intent of the partners, and the other is the expected contribution of the venture to the enhancement or creation of new organizational capabilities.[11] With respect to strategic intent, alliances among firms with competing strategic interests may require different approaches to HRM than those where interests are complementary. With respect to capabilities, while all alliances involve learning, for some learning may be a major purpose. The learning aspect of alliances has major implications for the organizational processes and thus for the management of people.

Figure 13-1 shows the four archetypes of alliance strategies based on these two dimensions: complementary, learning, resource, and competitive alliances. A *complementary* alliance is formed when two (or more) partners with complementary strategic aims join forces to exploit their existing resources or

Alliances can be evaluated on two dimensions. The first reflects the competitive context of the alliance. The second dimension reflects the need and opportunities for knowledge creation.

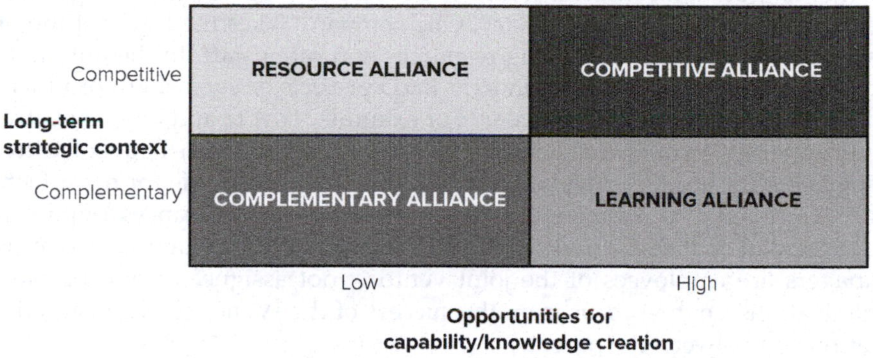

FIGURE 13-1
A Strategic Framework for Understanding International Alliances

	Low	High
Competitive	RESOURCE ALLIANCE	COMPETITIVE ALLIANCE
Complementary	COMPLEMENTARY ALLIANCE	LEARNING ALLIANCE

Long-term strategic context

Opportunities for capability/knowledge creation

Strategic context: competition versus complementarity

The dimension of strategic context positions the alliance with respect to complementarity of interests between the alliance partners. Is the alliance a link with a partner whose long-term strategic interests are in principle complementary (e.g., Airbus), or are they more likely fundamentally competitive?[A]

Capability/knowledge creation context: low versus high capability/knowledge creation opportunities

Some alliances rely exclusively on exploiting existing resources and competencies (partners contribute money, patents, production capacity, and distribution networks); others are designed explicitly to generate new capabilities or knowledge by combining or extending the resources and capabilities of the partners.[B]

[A] It is important to bear in mind that the strategic interests can change over time, and that what was once a collaborative relationship may turn into a fierce competition or conflict. A common experience of many Western firms with their joint ventures in Japan and two decades later in China is often-cited examples in this regard (Reich and Mankin, 1986; Hamel et al., 1989; McGregor, 2005; Hamilton and Zhang, 2008)

[B] In principle, all alliances have the potential to generate new knowledge—at least partners can learn about each other, and how to work together—the difference is in the intensity of the knowledge-creation process.

competencies—say, by linking different elements of the value chain—and where knowledge creation is not a prime objective. A typical complementary alliance is the traditional joint venture where one partner contributes technology and the other facilitates entry into a difficult market. Many of the JVs set up by Western multinationals in China fell into this category. In non-equity alliances, complementary alliance may take the form of a long-term supplier relationship, such as one between Apple and Foxconn—which makes most of Apple's mobile phones.

A complementary alliance may evolve into a *learning alliance* if partners share an interest in enhancing their capabilities. This can happen through the exchange of existing knowledge between the partners or by extracting capabilities newly developed inside the partnership. An example of a learning alliance is the now dissolved Hero Honda joint venture in India. Originally set up to facilitate Honda's penetration of the Indian market, it evolved to become not only a market leader in India but also an export platform to other emerging markets. The JV also allowed Hero to become a major motorcycle company on its own, the Indian Hero Group eventually buying the shares held by Honda.[12] Compared to complementary alliances, learning alliances require much more interaction, including shared work and interface management, which creates demand for HR systems and processes that facilitate effective knowledge creation.

Competitive pressures such as resource constraints, political and business risks, or economies of scale may lead competitors to join forces in a *resource alliance*. Exploration consortia set up to develop and operate oil and gas fields are common in the energy industry. One company takes the lead but the others share the risk by contributing resources and often staff. In the automotive industry, companies cooperate in joint R&D projects or even share production facilities to gain economies of scale.[13] For example, Toyota and Peugeot Citroen jointly operate a small car factory in Czech Republic (with Peugeot Citroen responsible for product development, and Toyota responsible for manufacturing).[14] Compared to complementary alliances, resource alliances require HR practices that reduce frictions limiting collaboration; for example, many key managers are employees of the joint venture, not assignees from the parent organizations, so their focus is on the success of the JV, not on the competitive relationship between the parents.

Finally, there are also learning alliances between partners who are competitors in global markets. In Chapter 3, we have introduced NUMMI—a 50/50 joint venture between General Motors (GM) and Toyota. This venture, which lasted for more than 25 years, supplied both parents with small cars for the North American market, but at the same time, it served as a "learning laboratory" for the two competitors.[15] GM gained insights into Toyota's manufacturing system, and Toyota learned how to operate a US-based manufacturing facility while the parents continued to compete globally. Such partnerships are a *competitive* alliance. Among Western JVs in China, many may fall into this category, if not now, then in the near future.[16] This type of alliance, with its emphasis on knowledge creation in a competitive context, is the most complex to manage and requires the highest level of attention to HRM.

None of these types of alliance is "better" than the others, they all can be successful. However, the management challenges associated with each alliance scenario are fundamentally different, and the HRM strategies, processes, and tools should reflect those differences. Problems occur when the company is not clear about what kind of alliance it needs, or, as in the case of Chemco, when it does not respond appropriately to early signals that the nature of the alliance is changing. For example, in a complementary alliance, it might be possible to rely on the local partner to recruit and train the alliance workforce since there are no risks of divided loyalties—at least in the short term. However, such an approach in a competitive alliance could prove costly in the event of a subsequent conflict between the partners (see the box "Danone–Wahaha: Bitter Taste of Pure Water").[17]

In a complementary alliance, it may make sense to set up the venture as a stand-alone entity to promote internal entrepreneurship. In a resource partnership, there are also benefits to creating an entity with clear boundaries so that the competitive context does not inhibit the performance of the alliance—good fences make good neighbors. However, learning alliances should not be constrained by too many fences, as opportunities for knowledge sharing will be greater when the boundaries between the venture and the parent are thin. HR practices in a learning alliance will therefore focus on facilitating the interface between the parent and the venture to increase the speed and quality of information exchange.

Since it is the speed and effectiveness of learning relative to the partner that counts in a competitive alliance, maintaining learning parity is the key to

Danone–Wahaha: Bitter Taste of Pure Water

In 1996, Danone, the giant French food company, entered into a joint venture for bottled water with Hangzhou Wahaha—a leading Chinese milk-based beverage company originally owned by Hangzhou city government but controlled by a local entrepreneur Zong Qinghou. Wahaha owned 49 percent of the new venture (in exchange for contributing its trademark and four out of ten subsidiaries), with Danone and Peregrine (a Hong-Kong investment company) holding the rest. Following the 1998 Asian financial crisis, Danone bought out Peregrine's share and took control of the JV's board—but Mr. Zong continued to run the JV operations. Within just a few years, Wahaha became the leading bottled water brand in China—but the JV collapsed in 2007 amid unusually bitter recriminations between the two partners.

Danone accused Wahaha of competing with the JV through its other subsidiaries controlled by Zong's family but sharing the same trademark and distribution network. In turn, Wahaha accused Danone of competing against the JV by investing in other local beverage companies, and that Danone's part-time representatives on the board did not understand the reality of business in China. Indeed, when Danone attempted to take a legal action against Zong, it came out that the authorities never approved the original trademark transfer. After Zong resigned from the JV, the employees refused to recognize the authority of the new chairman appointed by Danone. To settle the dispute, Danone sold its interests in what has become nearly $2 billion business back to Wahaha at a substantial discount to its market value.[18]

sustaining such a relationship.[19] The HR approach has to reflect this, as we will discuss later. At the same time, given the competitive context of the alliance, the flow of knowledge may need to be carefully controlled, if not restricted—an approach opposite to what is best for a learning alliance, creating tensions among the partners.

It is important to remember that alliances do not always fit neatly into a simple framework. Some partnerships are complementary in some parts of the value chain, but competitive in others, and need a nuanced approach to HRM. The critical issue is that the character of most alliances changes over time. Successful complementary alliances will become learning alliances, and learning alliances may turn into competitive alliances as the strategic intent of partners change.[20]

Precisely when a complementary alliance becomes a learning or a competitive alliance is a matter of interpretation, but a shift in partnership orientation has to be expected. HR strategy should anticipate such shifts, developing the appropriate tools to moderate any negative impact.

In the Chemco case, the alliance started as complementary, combining the technology of the US partner with the market access capability of the Japanese partner. However, the US partner failed to commit the necessary resources at an early stage to ensure the future integration of the JV into its global network (training, exchange of staff, and so forth). There were no incentives for the Japanese staff to pay attention to global strategy. Their rewards depended solely on local results, and they saw no future for themselves in Chemco's global organization.

One of the few redeeming factors in the Chemco joint venture was that the alliance never migrated into the "competitive" domain, simply because the Japanese partner had no wish to enter this business segment. Had it done so, there was not much leverage left for the US partner to protect its market position. As Danone had learned in China, absentee corporate parents do not retain much influence.

Alliance Is a Process, Not a Deal

There is no best way to structure an alliance. There is no difference between winning and losing alliances on specific configurations of organizing patterns, equity ratios, or reporting relationships.[21] In the case of joint ventures, some argue that fifty-fifty arrangements work best, since the partners must anticipate each other's interest.[22] Others assert that such arrangements lead to paralysis, for example with respect to staffing and compensation issues, and that it is better when one partner has the power to make a decision when there is deadlock.[23] In fact, both types of ventures appear to generate significant but distinct HRM challenges.[24]

It is not the structure of the deal, but the quality of the management process—in planning, negotiating, and implementing the partnership—that makes a difference. In HP and Intel, two firms with a long record of successful alliances, the alliance management process is well defined, highly structured, and institutionalized.[25] On the other hand, Corning, which for a long time derived most of its income from alliances, favors a more informal approach. What successful alliance players have in common is a rigorous and disciplined approach to alliance challenges, including a deep appreciation of the HRM contribution.

PLANNING AND NEGOTIATING ALLIANCES

The HR function should be involved early in exploring, planning, and negotiating alliances because, as we illustrate in the next section, HRM expertise, policies, and practices impact a number of key issues relating to control and influence within the future alliance. Unfortunately, HR often does not participate in the planning process at such an early stage.

HRM Issues in Developing an Alliance Strategy

Successful alliances start with a strategy, not with a partner. This may seem an obvious prescription, but often it is not followed in practice. Companies, or more precisely their chief executives, sometimes "fall in love." However, notwithstanding the importance of personal relationships at the top, it is dangerous to select the partner unless the strategic purpose is clear.

Partner selection starts with identifying long-term objectives for the alliance. For example, Japanese car component manufacturers entered the US because they were following their Japanese customers, for instance Toyota and Honda. These customers expected just-in-time support for their newly transplanted assembly plants, but the component manufacturers knew that they did not have the competence themselves to operate in an alien environment. Given the urgency, the alliance route seemed the most feasible entry strategy, though in the longer run they intended to establish an independent presence.

Consequently, human resource considerations played a major role in partner selection.[26] The Japanese firms searched for local partners situated in rural environments, perceived as having harmonious labor environments conducive to Japanese manufacturing methods. They also preferred partners who were family-owned but with no clear succession. This would give them the opportunity to acquire full control with a friendly bid once the US owner decided to retire.

While the specific strategic and business context frame the alliance HR issues, these considerations are sometimes contradictory, requiring careful analysis. For example, when a firm decides to enter an unfamiliar foreign market, the choice of an experienced local partner may seem to be a smart move that overcomes the existing "liability of foreignness" handicap.[27] Yet, with a strong local partner, there may be less urgency to develop internal market knowledge, and investments in knowledge creation may not be a priority. In a complementary alliance, this may not matter. However, if the alliance ever becomes competitive, this may put the foreign partner at a serious disadvantage.

A well-defined alliance planning process provides an arena for a full consideration of people-related issues.[28] Important HRM decisions regarding the alliance must take place already early on in the implementation stage, such as decisions on negotiation training or selection of an alliance manager. Table 13-1 shows a sketch of the key issues to review. Given the typical uncertainty surrounding alliance creation, such a plan is only a rough guide. It will become more specific when a partner is selected, paving the way for rigorous implementation when the alliance is launched.

HR issues that may influence partner selection:

- Desired competences that a partner should possess
- Need for venture HR support from the partner
- Assessment of HR skills and reputation of potential partners
- Assessment of the organizational culture of potential partners
- Exit options

Venture HR issues that need to be resolved in negotiations:

- Management philosophy, notably concerning HRM
- Staffing: sourcing and criteria
- Performance management and compensation
- Who will provide what HR service support

Desired negotiation outcomes and possible bargaining trade-offs
Specific HRM activities that must be implemented early and resources required:

- Negotiation stage
- Negotiation team selection
- Negotiation training
- Start-up stage
- Staffing decisions
- Alliance management training

Allocation of responsibility:

- Corporate responsibility
- Local management team responsibility
- Partner responsibility

Measurements to evaluate the quality of HR support:

- Recruitment target
- Training delivered
- Skill/knowledge transferred

TABLE 13-1
The HR Alliance Strategy Plan

Partner Selection

There are two main HRM challenges to consider in selecting a partner: the desired contribution of the partner and how much the HR systems of the partners will interface within the alliance.

The first issue refers to the degree to which the partner's HRM capabilities should contribute to the alliance. Will the partner be responsible for staffing the alliance or some of its critical functions? Will the partner provide HR services to the alliance? Does the partner's HR reputation matter? As we will discuss later in this chapter, getting the staffing right is the "make or break" issue for many alliances, and the probability of success can be enhanced by making these questions a part of the selection screen.

The second issue addresses the degree to which the organizational and people processes of the partners connect in the course of the alliance, which is likely if one of the strategic aims is learning. Will there be a clear separation between the alliance and the parents, or will the boundaries between them remain ambiguous? Will there be a lot of mobility between the venture units and the parent companies? Who will evaluate the performance of the venture management and on what criteria?

HR policies and practices have a major impact on the culture of the organization, and research has shown that differences in organizational culture may influence alliance success.[29] In particular, when the partner should contribute significantly to alliance HR management, or when the venture is unlikely to be autonomous because of interfaces with the parents, it is vital to include the partner's HR philosophy, policies, practices, and culture as a factor in partner selection. The process to use is similar to one for assessing the very same issues in merger and acquisitions—discussed in the previous chapter. The point here is not to find a perfect match—a partner who shares the same view on management selection criteria or the role of incentive compensation in the reward package. Rather, the purpose is to identify potential differences and then to determine how these differences might influence the execution of the alliance strategy, whether any differences can be reconciled and whether there are business risks if the gaps cannot be bridged.

A UK company decided to set up a joint venture in Malaysia to assemble its product for the local market. Soon after the results for the first year were in, the UK managing director proposed performance bonuses that differentiated by nearly 40 percent between managers at the same level of responsibility. A row erupted at the JV board meeting; the local partner objected, as the bonus plan would violate the standards of internal equity among managers and hurt morale. The foreign managing director was puzzled. "You told us that bonuses in your company could be up to 40 percent of the total compensation. That is what I believe our best performers deserve." "Yes," came the answer, "but in our company the bonus percentage is the same for everyone."

Selecting Alliance Managers

An alliance manager is usually appointed at the corporate level, responsible for planning, negotiating, and implementing alliances. Ideally, this role should be kept separate from the role of venture manager,[30] who is responsible for managing a specific project, business unit, or joint venture within the alliance (see Table 13-2), though not all firms have the resources to do so.

Alliance Manager Roles and Responsibilities
• **Building interpersonal trust**—unless there is trust and the right chemistry among managers involved in the alliance, it will not go anywhere.
• **Monitoring partner contributions**—how well a firm meets its obligations to an alliance is the most tangible evidence of its commitment.
• **Managing information flow**—drawing the line between information flow that ensures the vitality of the alliance, and unbridled information exchange that could jeopardize competitiveness.
• **Assessing strategic viability/evaluating synergy**—as strategic needs of the firm change over time, what are the implications for the alliance and overall relationship with the partner?
• **Aligning internal relationships**—since an alliance involves many people inside the firm, the alliance manager should mobilize the necessary support across the organization.
Venture Manager Roles and Responsibilities
• **Managing the business**—the venture manager assumes operational responsibility for the success of the venture.
• **Representing venture interest**—the venture manager has to represent without bias the interest of the venture as a business vis-à-vis its parents.
• **Aligning outside resources**—many resources are located outside the venture boundaries in the parent organizations; tapping effectively into those resources is a venture manager's responsibility.
• **Building collaborative culture**—irrespective of the competitive context of the alliance, trust inside the venture is an essential ingredient for success.
• **Developing venture strategy**—successful alliances evolve as any other ongoing business, and this evolution should be guided by solid strategy.

TABLE 13-2
Alliance Manager versus Venture Manager: Roles and Responsibilities

Source: Adapted from Yoshino and Rangan, 1995.

The alliance manager may monitor several existing alliances, or support business units in identifying opportunities where a partnership could create value. When such opportunities emerge, the alliance manager will take the lead in developing the negotiating strategy and framing the partnership contract. After negotiations are completed and a new alliance formed, the manager will oversee the evolution of the alliance and the relationship with the partner. This is like managing a portfolio where new ventures get negotiated, added, and monitored.

A key requirement for the alliance manager's position is a high degree of personal and professional credibility. Mutual trust is the glue that cements alliance relationships, and without credibility, it is difficult to establish trust. The job of an alliance manager also requires a high degree of flexibility and adaptability in coping with different national and organizational cultures, management styles, and individual behaviors. Alliances are by nature unstable and uncertain, so it is difficult to operate under precise rules or to expect that an intended strategy will be followed to the letter. Managers who are not comfortable in working under ambiguity will find it difficult to cope. As one experienced alliance manager put it, "high tolerance for frustration is a must."

In Chapter 4, we indicated that alliance managers are an example of one of the key lateral coordination roles in a multinational firm; much of what alliance managers are required to do involves mobilizing resources across organizational boundaries. They manage laterally in much the same way as a global account manager or an international project leader, but without large budgets or staff and without direct authority over resource allocation.[31] Instead, the manager has to rely on influencing networks of people inside and outside the firm. As one senior executive in a Fortune 500 company put it:

> A leader is one who gets people to do what he wants, but who at the same time makes them think that it was all their idea in the first place. An alliance manager also has to work along the same lines. He has no battalions of his own, yet he has to get the job done. He has to get people to buy into his vision of the alliance, make it part of their own job assignment, and actively work to make the alliance a success.[32]

Individuals involved in alliances face many challenges. They must learn how to manage boundaries, how to deal with ambiguity and conflicting interests, how to mold a culture that balances competing interests, and how to manage the tensions between exploitation (operating results, cash flow, and profit) and exploration (learning). One of the best breeding grounds for transnational managers may be alliance management.

Training for Negotiations

Alliance negotiations resemble other business negotiations, though they tend to be more complex due to the strategic and cross-cultural issues involved. For team members who lack experience in alliance negotiations, properly structured negotiation training could be a worthwhile investment.

An essential part of such preparation is to help the negotiators to become familiar with the business and cultural context of the partner's country. Given the stakes involved, a number of studies suggest that companies underestimate the need to prepare carefully.[33] Without preparation, it is all too easy to fall back on cultural stereotypes. It is also important to sort out the individual roles in a team and to review and practice different negotiation scenarios. HR professionals often have strong process facilitation skills, and they may serve as internal consultants in the alliance negotiations. In complex negotiations, the presence of an experienced facilitator may be beneficial, observing the flow of interactions, interpreting behaviors, and coaching the key actors.

Negotiation Challenges in Joint Venture Formation

When an alliance takes the form of a joint venture, negotiations regarding control and management of the JV should include HR professionals. There are several negotiation challenges where strategy and HRM interact closely. These include issues such as:

- Equity control versus operational influence
- Board composition
- Senior management appointments
- HR policies for the alliance

Equity Control versus Operational Influence

The issue of control is often difficult to resolve in joint venture negotiations. Generally, both parties seek to be the majority owner, considered the best way to protect one's long-term interests, particularly in the context of a competitive alliance. However, in the absence of other supporting mechanisms, equity control is no guarantee that the venture will evolve in line with the intended strategy.

Gaining a majority position may provide a tax or financial reporting advantage. However, it is wrong to assume that equity control equals management control—as the Chemco and Danone–Wahaha cases illustrate. A minority equity position, coupled with effective representation on the JV management team and an influence over the flow of knowledge, may have more impact on how the venture operates than a nominal majority exercised from a distance. Fifty-one percent of the shares may entitle the owner to 51 percent of the dividends, but these are often the last piece of the cash pie to be distributed. Internal transfer pricing, purchasing decisions, the cost of services provided by a local partner, expatriate compensation levels—all have an impact on cash flow long before any dividends are declared.

Not surprisingly, "the last 2 percent" (going from 49 to 51 percent share) is always expensive—the buyer paying the so-called control premium. In many circumstances, a carefully structured human resource strategy that secures influence over key decisions can be less costly and more effective than paying for equity control. Acquiring such influence typically starts with the key appointments— the composition of the board and senior management appointments.

Board Composition

Companies often strive for a majority equity position simply to achieve a majority on the board of directors, thus protecting their voting interests in the event of a dispute between partners. In reality, joint venture boards seldom vote. If the partners have a common interest in maintaining the relationship, disputes are resolved in private, and boards act only to approve such agreements. In addition, the protection of strategic interest can be achieved by other means, such as specific clauses in the agreement or articles of incorporation that stipulate what actions require unanimous or qualified majority consent of the shareholders.

There are several advantages to using the board primarily to oversee rather than to control.[34] Positions on the board may serve for a variety of other purposes. An appointment to the board may recognize an outstanding contribution of an alliance executive. In many countries, "company director" status is the pinnacle of a business career, and such opportunities may help to increase the morale and retention of senior management. Board appointments may expand linkages to outside business circles and the wider community in the local country, broadening learning and business opportunities. A position on the board can also be reserved for an individual who may mediate potential conflicts between the partners.

When setting up the board, there is a natural tendency to appoint alliance champions, people who favored the deal from the outset, who were involved in the negotiations, and who know the partner best. However, it is also useful to appoint at least one "bad cop," who will keep the champions from forgetting that the venture is a business rather than just a relationship.[35]

Appointing Senior Management

In many alliances, senior managers wield far more strategic and operational control and influence than most of the board members.[36] Tasks that determine the venture's success—setting business objectives, interfacing with key customers, monitoring the transfer of knowledge, and developing the organization's culture— are all operational responsibilities of the senior managers inside the venture.

Moreover, it is always preferable to resolve the inevitable conflicts and differences of opinion at the operational level rather than referring disputes to higher levels.

However, there is a paradox here. The shortage of international managers who can implement a market-entry strategy in an unfamiliar environment is often a motive for choosing a joint venture over a wholly owned subsidiary; yet without a pool of suitable candidates, bargaining about positions is a meaningless exercise. Having such a pool ready requires attention to HR from the very early stage of alliance planning, since it takes time to select and groom potential candidates.

The best approach is often to recruit locally and then provide opportunities to learn about the business in the headquarters, or in another country, before joining the alliance team— and this is a long-term effort. The inability of Danone to deploy qualified local managers into its alliance with Wahaha (after twenty years of operating there) was one of the factors behind its failure to influence the evolution of the partnership.

Note however that executive role expectations may vary from one culture to another. In a fifty-fifty French-Swedish joint venture located in France, the Swedish company agreed to the appointment of a senior French executive as chairman in exchange for *de facto* control of the operations. However, in the French organization, the chairman was not the honorary figure that the Swedes expected. He was seen as the ultimate decision-maker in the venture, while the opinions of the Swedish senior managers were ignored. Although the venture continued to make strategic sense, the operational frictions generated so much ill will on both sides that it dissolved a few years later.

The leadership and behavioral demands on JV managers are greater than in wholly owned units, and finding suitable managers is not a simple task. Political skills are indispensable, as top JV managers need to use influence to balance partner priorities and overcome conflicts. Cross-cultural sensitivity and flexibility are particularly important when partners come from different cultures and where JV staff represent two or more nationalities. Having a cooperative disposition, a high tolerance for ambiguity, and an internal locus of control are additional personal traits that help international alliance managers to perform well.[37]

The nomination of the venture general manager can generate intense debate. There is a fine line between representing the best interests of the venture *and* that of the parent company. One can argue that the venture manager must have the goodwill of both parents in order to operate effectively.[38] Installing somebody as venture general manager who only represents the interest of one partner may be counterproductive. However, if the venture activities need to be integrated with those of the parent, then an arm's-length relationship may not be appropriate.

Identifying alliance champions and recognizing their contribution toward implementing the alliance strategy is also important. An alliance is not likely to succeed unless managers and employees believe in the promise of the concept and are willing to invest personal effort to make it happen. Alliance champions, like alliance skeptics, are on both sides of the partnership. Knowing the champions on the "other side"—especially those who have sufficient internal credibility to mobilize resources for the benefit of the alliance—is of great value in the negotiations over managerial appointments.

Human Resource Policies within the Alliance Venture

During the negotiations, it is also important to pay early attention to HR policies and practices, especially when there are likely to be many complex interfaces between the venture and the alliance parents.[39] Some researchers advocate a detailed contract clarifying HR policies inside the alliance in order to reduce the uncertainty and conflict over matters of staffing, transfers, promotion, and compensation.[40] However, detailed contracts do not guarantee compliance. Venture synergy comes from shared business interests, not from legal formulations. A clear statement regarding HR principles is in most cases sufficient, without contractual limit what can or cannot be done.

Sometimes companies take a pragmatic position "when in Rome, do as the Romans" and delegate all responsibility for human resource matters to the local partner. This may make sense provided the "Roman" organization is a paragon of effectiveness, quality, and customer service, or at least close to it. If it does not have solid HR foundations in place, then this attempt to demonstrate cultural sensitivity may only result in replicating the dysfunctional aspects of local practice, not to mention increasing compliance risks.

IMPLEMENTING ALLIANCES

Once the contract is signed and the partnership becomes operational, a new set of people-related issues appear. How to manage the evolution of the partnership? How to ensure that knowledge developed inside the alliance is shared fairly among the partners? How to keep the partnership objectives aligned with those of the parent?

These issues have two major HR implications. The first is managing the interface with the parent, which involves influencing the attitudes and behaviors of staff at home who are in contact with the alliance. The second relates to the management of people inside the venture itself.

Managing the Interfaces with the Parent

An important challenge is to manage the interface between the parent organization and the partnership in order to align the internal processes so they support rather than hinder external collaboration. Often the organizational units that provide resources to the alliance are not those receiving its outputs. The asymmetry in the perceived costs and benefits of collaboration with the venture may cause internal tensions that undermine willingness to support the partnership. The value of collaboration is sometimes not visible in the hustle and bustle of daily operations, so explicit reinforcements of the message may be required.[41]

A rapidly growing US securities firm with global ambitions set up an alliance with a European brokerage to offer their European customers "preferential" access to US financial markets. However, the operational practices at the New York trading desk did not change and the relatively small orders from Europe did not get the same attention as those from large US institutional clients, reducing profit opportunities for the European partner. Why was this happening? The rigid "meet-the-numbers" reward system in the US was incompatible with a strategy that did not yield immediate earnings.

No amount of presentations on the benefits of international expansion could make much difference. In Europe, the initial irritation quickly turned to anger and then to suspicions about the true motives of the American partner. Less than two years later, the much-publicized alliance collapsed. As noted by one of the US HR managers: "If this alliance was important for our future, then perhaps it should have been partly my job to create an environment where phone calls from our partners would be returned without delay."

Top Management Role

The execution of alliance strategy places particular demands on top management, who must "walk their talk," paying attention to the social architecture of the partnership. The box "The Anniversary Speech" illustrates what happens when top management is not involved.

Managing the emotional ties and earning the loyalty of the alliance workforce is only one of the human resource tasks that require the support of top management. Internal communication is another; top management plays an indispensable role in ensuring that the strategic logic of the partnership is clear inside the firm, especially when it comes to balancing the competitive and collaborative aspects of the alliance. Top management must also work closely with HR on the selection of alliance managers, on allocating resource for learning activities, and to ensure alignment of rewards with the partnership strategy.

Human Resource Management Issues in Managing the Alliance

Many of the international HRM issues discussed previously in this book are also relevant to international alliances. Here we will examine those that may have the biggest impact on the success of an alliance strategy:

- Staffing of the alliance
- Mobility between the parent(s) and the venture

The Anniversary Speech

A fifty-fifty joint venture between a Japanese and a US firm celebrated its twenty-fifth anniversary. Over time, the JV had evolved from a small marketing start-up to a fully integrated firm with an independent R&D and manufacturing capability that enjoyed a very profitable leadership position in the Asian market. Given its commercial success, the initial friction between the two partners regarding the future direction of the business has been replaced by a grudging willingness to continue working together. However, on the American side, executives voiced concerns about gradual erosion of their influence as the loyalty of the workforce seemed tilted in favor of the local partner.

On the anniversary date, all employees assembled in one of Tokyo's exhibition halls for an afternoon of celebration. After the company glee club warmed up everyone with songs, the 96-year-old former chairman of the Japanese parent, who signed the original deal—helped onto the stage in a wheelchair—thanked all employees for bringing his dream to life. His speech was short, owing to his failing health, but it was emotional and made a big impact on the audience. Following the speech was a prerecorded video message from the American CEO who, in three years of tenure, had visited the venture once. He said nothing wrong, but the impersonality of the presentation defeated its purpose. Another skirmish in the loyalty battle was lost.

- Competence and capability development
- Performance management
- Rewards and recognition
- Building influence inside the alliance
- Developing a culture of trust

Staffing Alliances

Staffing matters! Inappropriate staffing is one of the major causes of alliance failures.

Some years ago, a European consumer products company assigned a group of its fast-track employees to work on a team with their Chinese partner's colleagues to implement strategies for expansion in China. All assignees had a record of successful postings to wholly owned subsidiaries in the region. However, the added difficulties of working with a partner organization required an adjustment in behavior, communication, and leadership style that several of them could not handle. The project team had to be restructured several times, causing delays and disruptions to the new product launch schedule.

Every strategic plan for an alliance should include a review of staffing requirements. Other HR matters, such as training and compensation, have also an important impact, but problems in those areas can be resolved in a relatively short time. The consequences of bad decisions made by people who are not qualified to meet the challenges of managing an alliance may take years to fix. While the staffing issues will vary from one alliance to another, there are some generic matters to consider:

- What is the number and skill mix of employees required?
- Who is responsible for forecasting competency demands?
- Who will do the recruiting? Each partner individually? Jointly?
- Which positions are to be filled by each parent?
- Which positions are to be filled by expatriates?
- In joint ventures, for whom do the new employees work—for one of the partners or for the new entity?
- How will staffing conflicts be resolved?

On most of these issues, since contractual arrangements may be too rigid for evolving staffing needs, mutual agreement on policies may suffice.

One-way versus Temporary Transfer

There is some evidence that staffing joint ventures with dedicated management teams is more effective than relying on temporary assignments.[42] If employees transfer, they should expect to remain in the venture without a guaranteed ticket back to the parent—their future opportunities depend on the success of the new business. On the other hand, temporary transfers do have merits. They are useful when a venture is evolving rapidly and the required management skills are not available, or as a tool for diffusion of learning.

Transferees are more likely to remember that their task is not to preserve the alliance at all costs. Temporary transfers are also generally the only way in which the foreign partner can insert its employees into the venture. However, any assignments should be of a reasonable duration since new managers will pass through a learning stage before they can contribute fully to the venture. If the value-for-money of the transferee is not readily apparent, resentment and conflict are not far behind. Frequent churn of key venture managers makes it difficult to establish a shared culture.

The foreign partner may experience greater difficulties compared to the local partner in convincing first-class employees from the parent firm to transfer to the JV.[43] In such cases, the personal involvement of top management can make a difference. When Procter & Gamble (P&G) first entered the Chinese market, joint venturing with local partners was the only option. In order to encourage its best candidates to accept these challenging assignments, P&G's top management, including the CEO, took a visible role in candidate selection, acting as a mentor during the assignment and in repatriation. Such leadership commitment to staffing ensured a ready supply of good managers willing to work in China.

Sometimes, a shortage of qualified candidates or cost considerations may persuade foreign partners to limit their representation to a single executive. One person is expected to play the role of corporate ambassador, shadow CEO, chief learning officer, and business developer—quite a challenge! Notably in competitive alliances, this may not be in the best interest of the business.

In most cases, the best strategy is to recruit and develop local talent. If there are a significant number of joint ventures in a strategic market, it may be worthwhile to establish a holding company for all operations in the country. Local managers can then be hired by the holding company, trained, and dispatched to joint ventures to represent the interests of the foreign partner, thus lessening the reliance on expensive expatriates. Many foreign firms investing in joint ventures in China or India, for example ABB and GE, have chosen this route to develop their local management teams.[44]

Developing Capabilities

Strategic objectives of many alliances require developing new knowledge, skills, and competencies. This in turn requires actions to create a learning environment:

- Training employees and managers dispatched to the alliance
- Enhancing collaboration inside the partnership
- Facilitating integration with the parent firm

In companies where alliances are critical to the business strategy, alliance training is an integral part of the implementation process. For example, Hewlett Packard, which is engaged in scores of international partnerships, organizes workshops on a massive scale for managers involved in alliances. The HP alliance management framework, an elaborate knowledge management system presents histories, toolkits and checklists, as well as comparisons of best practice from other firms.[45] As in the case of mergers and acquisitions, codification of prior experiences is helpful, especially in the selection and termination phase.[46]

Estimates suggest that only one third of firms involved in alliances offer alliance training.[47] Part of the problem is that companies may be reluctant to devote resources to alliance training, or even to select potential venture managers, until the partnership is formed. However, once an agreement has been reached, there is seldom time for extensive training. One of the authors has directed alliance management seminars for over 25 years. It is not unusual to see participants subscribing for the course at the last minute and departing for a foreign location virtually as soon as the course ends.[48]

One of the focal areas for management development within the alliance venture itself is helping the venture team to interact and work effectively with each other and with the parents. This process ideally starts when the alliance is launched, helping the staff to get to know each other and learning about each other's company culture and mode of operations. When Corning creates new alliances, venture employees are briefed on the respective organizational cultures and venture strategy and organization in order to minimize confusion and misunderstanding.[49] Other companies organize team-building training, ranging from traditional classroom workshops to outdoor experiential learning.[50] It also pays to follow up the "honeymoon training" with periodic workshops, working jointly through specific business and cultural challenges facing the partnership.

A good and relatively inexpensive way to foster the alliance integration process is to open up in-house training to the staff in the alliance unit and when appropriate to those from the partner. In the Chemco case, the US partner realized that functional training workshops could help to improve coordination in Asia Pacific. Previously, these had been limited to wholly owned subsidiaries. In the new format, the Japanese JV employees were invited and the program was redesigned to facilitate open dialogue. Participants were now able to identify jointly the obstacles to collaboration, suggest actions to remedy the problems, and commit to new joint business initiatives. The bottom line? Profits from joint projects generated by the first three workshops equaled the annual training budget for the whole region.

Defining Performance

During the planning stage, it is generally not difficult for alliance partners to agree that "performance matters." However, for the operating managers dispatched to the JV, it can be much more difficult to agree on what constitutes "performance," how to measure it, and what the consequences of high or low performance should be.[51]

In an oil exploration joint venture created by British, Norwegian (state-owned), and Vietnamese (government) partners, the parties differed in their views about performance management, but the split did not cut along East–West cultural lines. British expatriates and locally recruited young Vietnamese managers were in favor of individually focused, achievement-oriented performance criteria with substantial financial benefits for top performers. The Norwegians and the senior representatives of the Vietnamese partner, concerned with equity and harmonious work relations, preferred to give more emphasis to team goals and process implementation, with less internal differentiation. The net result was confusion, frustration, conflict, and high turnover—the opposite of what a performance management system is supposed to achieve. It was not that one partner was "right" and the other "wrong," the real issue was the lack of a common perspective.

Not surprisingly, resistance to "foreign" ways of managing performance is most pronounced in competitive alliances. This is because managing performance is one of the keys to having an influence inside the venture. The way performance is defined and managed indicates to the alliance staff who is in charge, whose interests have to be taken seriously. Without influence over the performance management process, a partner (especially a distant partner) can expect only nominal control over the direction of the venture. Therefore, performance management issues often become a lightning rod in the latent struggle for influence.

However, the issue is not how much the performance management of the alliance resembles that of the parent but how it supports the parent company's strategy:

- First, this means making sure that the parent's strategic objectives are reflected in the performance targets for the alliance
- Second, achieving these targets has to be measured
- Third, meeting or failing to meet targets should have consequences

In Chemco's case, the first and second requirements for effective performance management processes were met once the US partner attained formal majority control and regional targets were included in the annual objectives set for the local management team. However, target setting was merely a ritual since the results had no consequences, positive or negative—and this would remain the case as long as Chemco had no influence over salaries, bonuses, or promotions. This leads us to the reward aspects of performance management.

Aligning Rewards

One of the first actions Chemco took to increase its influence was to negotiate a gradual transfer of all employees in Japan from the payroll of the Japanese parent to JV employee status. The work conditions offered were more favorable but did not increase the cost as the compensation and benefit system was tailored to the JV workforce. The union and nearly all employees accepted these conditions. As a next step, the management bonus was linked to the achievement of two sets of targets, regional and local, with regional targets being the key objective for senior management. In addition, the variable part of total compensation increased dramatically. Today, the Japanese partner considers its JV as a "human laboratory" where innovative HR practices—novel to the Japanese market—can be tested before being introduced into the parent company.

However, no compensation formula or measurement matrix can overcome a disagreement about strategy. If one partner wants to build market share and the other is interested in cash flow, then developing common performance targets is going to be difficult unless the two partners first agree on priorities.

Another important compensation issue to consider is the tension between external equity with the parent for expatriates and internal equity for venture staff, frequently leading to asymmetry in earnings among different groups of employees within the alliance. For example, expatriate managers often earn many times more than the income of a typical local JV employee (whose pay in turn may be considerably higher than that of a counterpart in a local firm). These differences, while unavoidable in ventures involving companies from countries with widely different standards of living, may lead to motivational problems and conflict unless the added value of staff who receives superior compensation is visible and appreciated. Disparity in compensation sometimes makes it difficult to persuade the local partner to accept expert help even when this could be in the best interest of the venture.[52] One way to reduce such tensions is to place the expatriate staff into a wholly owned entity and support the JV through a service contract.

At the same time, high performers, who tend to have options, may elect to stay clear of difficult alliance assignments since the venture may not be on the traditional ladder of getting ahead in the parent company. Recalibrating compensation does not solve this challenge; other components of the HR system have to be realigned as well. The deliberate positioning of alliance assignments as a key element of long-term career progression is a powerful tool for ensuring a supply of requisite talent, as we saw in the case of P&G's staffing strategy for entering China. Influencing and shaping careers provides stronger leverage over expatriate staffing than short-term financial incentives.[53]

Building and Maintaining Influence

In the Danone–Wahaha case, Danone's top management completely misjudged its ability to exert influence inside the joint venture. When the dispute with its local partner erupted, Chinese employees simply decided to ignore Danone instructions—some because of a grievance against Danone but most because they did not want to be seen as supporting a company that would be a sure loser in the conflict. Danone was caught in a joint venture Catch-22: without credibility, it had no influence, and without influence, it had no credibility.

One of the best ways to gain allegiance among JV employees is to show commitment to their career development. As a sign of commitment to Japan, shortly after transferring Japanese employees to the JV payroll, Chemco offered several young high potential employees the possibility of moving to subsidiaries in Southeast Asia with the assignment of coordinating sales with Japanese customers in the region. The conditions offered were the same as for any other Chemco expatriate. One benefit for Chemco was improved customer service and sales. The other was a dramatic change in how the Japanese staff perceived regional integration. The earlier view that integration was a power game—us versus them—quickly faded. With career opportunities open to all, such initiatives can promote cross-organizational cohesion. However, as with any HRM practice, the execution depends on the alliance's strategic context. In competitive alliances, this need a careful consideration.

The form of the alliance also has implications for career development, and again joint ventures pose most of the challenges.[54] Employees transferred from the parent to a joint venture can feel left behind, especially if the number of expatriates inside the venture is small. The difficulty of managing dual allegiance is one of the arguments in favor of "one-way-transfer" staffing strategies. However, this is often not practical from a staffing perceptive or desirable because of a need to foster knowledge exchange between the venture and the parent.

Developing Shared Culture

In contrast to acquisitions, one has to live with conflicting loyalties in alliances. Whether or not this becomes dysfunctional depends on the type of alliance and the ability of the partners to deal with the contradictions in the alliance relationship. One way to cope is to foster a distinct and shared culture inside the alliance that eases tensions between partners; another is to build strong personal relationships.

The key outcome of a shared culture and strong relationships is trust,[55] which is especially important for organization from different countries. [56] Trust between the partners allows them to concentrate on managing the business rather than on monitoring and control. Creating a shared culture and trust inside an alliance does not mean ignoring differences between the partners' strategic priorities. However, even in a competitive alliance, the partnership will not succeed without trust on an operating level. The best way to build trust is to get to know each other. This can be supported by promoting personnel exchanges and by providing visible examples of commitment to common goals.

SUPPORTING ALLIANCE LEARNING

All alliances include some learning aspects, including how to work effectively with partners.[57] However, some alliances are created with capability development above all in mind, which means that learning and knowledge creation are the focal objectives. Knowledge management is one of the critical features in many international alliances. [58]

In learning and competitive alliances, effective alliance learning is important as a building block for future competitive advantage—for both partners. Successful alliances often focus on gains from mutual learning—contrast the long-term collaboration of Renault and Nissan with the failed partnership between Daimler and Mitsubishi Motors where mutual learning never took off.[59]

Companies that will be good learning partners are probably good learners themselves. In contrast, selecting partners who are poor learners to guard against capability leaks is shortsighted. Weak learning capability is a sign of poor management, and poorly managed firms make poor learning partners.

An organization has many tools to manage the process of learning, but in principle, the learning ability of an organization depends on its ability to transfer and integrate tacit knowledge that is difficult to copy, thereby building organizational capabilities. One objective of HRM in international alliances is therefore to complement business strategy by providing a climate that encourages organizational learning and by installing appropriate tools and processes to guide the process of knowledge transfer and absorption.[60]

We have already discussed some of these issues in Chapter 11, but alliances, particularly competitive alliances, bring particular challenges for HRM. Many of the difficulties in implementing long-term alliance strategies can be traced to the quality of the learning process and the underlying human resource policies and practices.

Obstacles to Alliance Learning

The rapid development of the competitive capabilities of leading Japanese firms in the second half of the twentieth century, as well as the global success of many companies in China and other emerging markets today, can be traced to successful alliance learning through inward technology transfer and capability improvement. By contrast, many European and US firms often struggled to kick start the learning process, even if the intent to do so was there. So what are the obstacles? Some are the consequences of ill-conceived strategies, and others stem from poor HR practices, or a combination of both.[61]

Low Priority of Alliance Learning

Some firms perceive partnerships primarily as a way to reduce risk and minimize the cost of developing new capabilities. They are reluctant to make the necessary learning investments. However, failing to invest in learning will over time result in a deterioration of a firm's competitive position, leading to an asymmetry in the relationship and eventually to a conflict with the partner. Dissolution of the relationship is then the logical next step. In contrast, successful learning alliances are most often driven by a "top-line" orientation where investment in the development of new capabilities is recovered through the growth of business.

Learning through alliances may be faster than learning alone, but it still requires investment. However, activities that are difficult to evaluate in short-term financial terms may be seen as less critical, so learning efforts are given only token support. Also, firms frequently fail to benefit from alliance learning because they do not recognize the benefits of acquiring the "soft" skills of mastering tacit processes underlying product quality, speed of product development, or linkage to key customers.[62]

Decisions on alliance learning strategy are often based on the assumption that the existing balance of contributions to the venture will not change over time. Consider the case of a partnership where one party provides technology and the other secures market access. The executives of the "technology" firm may believe that the partner will have to rely on their technological leadership for the foreseeable future, so they see few incentives to invest in learning about the market. However, if the other partner gradually closes the technology capability gap—after all, technology transfer is often a part of the deal—the basis for the alliance becomes problematic. One partner now has both technology *and* market access, so why share the benefits?

A similarly harmful is the belief that preventing the partner from learning (and thus avoiding asymmetry) may be easier and cheaper than investing in one's own learning. In highly competitive markets, companies that hope to build defensive walls around themselves to prevent knowledge "seeping" to the partner often end up losing customers who are disappointed with the lack of local support.

Inappropriate Staffing

Expatriate staffing is costly, and firms are tempted to reduce alliance costs by limiting the number of expatriate personnel assigned to the foreign venture. As a result, the few expatriates (sometimes only one) are often overwhelmed with routine work, struggling just to get by in an unfamiliar culture. The opportunities for active involvement in knowledge acquisition—for example through relationships with local customers or interactions with the partner—are minimal. However keen the expatriate may be to learn, operational matters prevent them from doing so.

In Chemco's case, company policy for nearly 20 years was to dispatch only one senior-level executive to Japan, occasionally augmented with an experienced engineer bringing knowledge into Japan. In most cases, the expatriates retired after their assignment in Japan was completed. When the company decided to refocus its Japan strategy, the total accumulated experience in the Japanese market among the top management team (Japan was at that time its largest overseas market), including business trips longer than one week, was less than six months. The staffing agenda, however, is not just about how many and where, but about who. If the managers assigned to oversee or manage an alliance are not credible within their own organization and with the partner, learning objectives will be difficult to reach.

Poor Climate for Knowledge Exchange

A characteristic of alliance learning is that partner interactions often take place in a context of competitive collaboration.[63] Not surprisingly, competition and learning commonly go hand in hand in high-technology industries where fast learning is an imperative of the business model. However, principles of equitable exchange, agreed to at the top, do not necessarily translate into same perceptions what is equitable at the operational level.

In a competitive alliance, transfer of knowledge to a competitor will often generate legitimate concern among staff over what will happen to their jobs if their unique knowledge is disseminated to others. When one partner ignores requests for learning support, it may awaken suspicions of duplicity, inviting retaliation. Very soon, the whole atmosphere of partnership is poisoned.

For acquired knowledge to be useful, it has to be assimilated by the parent organization, but internal barriers are often just as formidable as unfriendly actions by the partner. The learning from the outside threatens the status quo. The typical attitude is defensive: "It's a good idea, but it will never work here." Contrast this with the attitude guiding GE approach to alliances: "Stealing with pride" is a message that made it into the company's annual report.

No Accountability or Rewards for Learning

Learning targets are unlikely to be met if there is no accountability. In complex organizations, perceptions of the potential value of learning from an alliance may vary according to the business unit, function, and territory, and the commitment to provide the necessary support will vary accordingly. This can lead to asymmetry, where one unit supplies the resources while another unit expects the learning.

Traditional market-driven reward systems may implicitly encourage the hoarding of critical information, rather than the diffusion of learning. People who have valued knowledge can command higher salaries on the market, so diffusing their knowledge to others (for example by sharing critical alliance contacts) may diminish their market value. Being indispensable is the ultimate in "employability."

HRM Foundations for Effective Alliance Learning

A major role for HR is to help create an organizational context in which alliance learning can flourish (see Table 13-3). Importantly, alliance learning is not about collecting binders of data from the alliance "war room." Rather, effective alliance learning focuses on absorbing knowledge and developing or broadening capabilities.

TABLE 13-3
Core HRM Principles for Alliance Learning

1. Build learning into the alliance agreement
2. Communicate the learning intent inside the parent
3. Assign responsibility for alliance learning
4. Secure early HR function involvement
5. Maintain HRM influence inside the alliance
6. Staff to learn
7. Support learning-driven careers, including repatriation
8. Stimulate learning through training
9. Reward learning activities
10. Monitor your partner's learning

Source: Adapted from V. Pucik, "Strategic Alliances, Organizational Learning, and Competitive Advantage: The HRM Agenda," *Human Resource Management* 27, no. 1 (Spring 1988), pp. 77–93.

In the context of learning and competitive alliances, the need to focus on HRM from an early stage is especially critical. Acquisition of new knowledge and competencies happens only through people, and if the people strategy is not aligned with the learning objectives, the chances of this happening are greatly diminished.

Setting the Learning Strategy

One of the first questions to resolve in developing an alliance learning strategy is the extent to which alliance agreement addresses the learning agenda. Issues to consider may involve practicalities such as freedom to move people across alliance boundaries as necessary and determination of their learning roles and responsibilities. It is difficult—and costly—to renegotiate HR policies for the benefit of one of the partners after the venture is launched.

The best, but probably hardest, way to deal with the competitive collaboration is to accept and be open about the "race to learn." Hiding the learning agenda increases mistrust and encourages opportunistic behavior.[64] Both parties should be explicit about their learning objectives, put forward strategies to accomplish such learning together with their HRM implications, monitor mutual progress, and discuss with each other any important reservations. If the learning objectives are not on the table for open discussion, the merits of the whole alliance may become questionable.[65]

Once the alliance strategy is set, it needs to be communicated clearly and consistently across the organization. Sometimes, companies are reluctant to acknowledge that the alliance is actually competitive in nature, because of the fear that such communication may set a bad tone for the relationship. In fact, the lack of communication does not change the reality; competition does not disappear because it is not talked about, but the result is confusion and disbelief among the employees.

While aligning HR processes to the learning strategy is vital, the responsibility for managing learning belongs to the line, not to HR or any other staff function. In a product development alliance between an American and Japanese high-technology firm, the HR function put itself forward—in good faith—as the champion of alliance learning, one of the explicit objectives for the alliance.[66] Many of the engineers then dismissed the whole activity as another "HR program." For the Japanese partner, the role of the American HR "learning manager" remained a mystery throughout.

Staffing to Learn

The focus on learning starts with appropriate staffing, since the quantity and quality of people involved in the learning effort is fundamental to its credibility and success.[67] The partner's commitment to support the alliance with competent staff is also essential.

The most powerful learning often happens in joint alliance teams where employees from both partners work together on solving business issues. Here it is important to consider the difference between traditional in-company teams discussed in Chapter 4 and alliance teams. A common company culture and above all shared long-term goals facilitate the in-company team process. In alliance teams, these "glue" factors do not exist, introducing additional ambiguity and uncertainty into the learning environment. Selection criteria for alliance learning teams need to take into account the ability of employees to cope with this complexity. They must have the expertise to contribute to executing the business plan as well as a strong learning orientation.

Another critical staffing issue concerns the paradox of staffing for learning and staffing for effective execution. The execution perspective suggests that each partner should field a team in their areas of special expertise, which will foster speed and efficiency in executing the business plan. However, if the partners only focus on what they are good at, how will they acquire new skills? Getting this balance right requires a very clear understanding of the strategic objectives behind the alliance.

Learning to Learn

Different types of training and development activities can stimulate a climate conducive to effective alliance learning. Joint training may be the most effective, but some training is better to conduct internally, with attendance limited to the parent firm so that sensitive issues can be openly discussed. Such training can help employees understand the importance of the learning aims of the alliance, as well as how to learn through collaboration. It should take place early on in the alliance life cycle and it is especially important if the alliance is or is likely to become competitive in nature.

When a US high-tech manufacturer decided to set up a joint new product development project with a Japanese partner, one of the first actions was to conduct a series of alliance management workshops for all key employees who would be directly or indirectly involved. The team discussed in detail the strategic logic of the project, its scope and boundaries, the learning objectives and opportunities as well as ideas on specific learning processes. As an outcome of these discussions, top management decided to redesign the alliance manager role in order to foster clearer accountability for learning and to increase resources allocated to learning.

Managing Careers to Facilitate Learning

The rotation of employees through alliance positions and back to the parent firm facilitates the transfer of knowledge between the venture and the parent.[68] The transfers need to be planned carefully, especially with respect to future career expectations.[69] If the individual knows that the knowledge acquired in the venture will be put to good use on return, this increases their motivation to learn during the assignment.[70]

The need for an explicit strategy to transfer and implement acquired knowledge is well illustrated by the case of NUMMI. GM assigned only a handful of selected managers to the venture in the early years.[71] After two to three years of working with the Japanese, these managers converted to the virtues of Toyota's lean manufacturing system, with a good grasp of its workings. They moved back to different GM locations with the mission of implementing the learning from NUMMI within the GM organization. All these early efforts ended in failure—because there was never a critical mass of ex-NUMMI staff in one location to make a difference.

Asymmetry in personnel transfers is usually a good indication of asymmetry in learning. While GM shuffled individual managers, Toyota trained more than one hundred of its staff (from team leaders to department managers) how to collaborate with NUMMI's American workforce. They were then assigned to Toyota's new wholly-owned plant in Kentucky to replicate the NUMMI experience.

It took GM another ten years before the company decided to leverage the knowledge acquired by its employees in a systematic manner. A team of "alumni" from the ventures at NUMMI and CAMI (GM's JV with Suzuki Motors) took charge of a decrepit East German car plant in Eisenach, and within three years, they turned it into the most advanced car manufacturing facility in Europe at that time.[72] The knowledge that individuals had gained about Toyota's manufacturing system had resulted in a collective action only when there was coherent organizational strategy to apply the learning.

Reinforcing Learning through Performance Management

While successful learning from alliances requires champions of knowledge creation—people who believe in the value of learning and who support the necessary investments—this may not be enough. Thus, alliance learning objectives should be translated into specific measures wherever possible, such as quality or productivity improvement, speed of new product development, or customer expansion.

The climate for learning is best when alliance performance is satisfactory. When the alliance does not meet its expected targets, it may be more difficult to focus attention on the learning agenda, and necessary investments may be cut.[73] But even a failed alliance can be a source of valuable lessons. During its early drive to internationalize, GE organized a workshop in which executives who had been involved in failed alliances presented their experiences at a company forum. No amount of lectures on alliance strategy can match the impact of a high-level manager explaining how his assumptions about the foreign partner's business culture were wrong, resulting in a significant loss to GE. Why were these managers willing to share their painful experiences? Because sharing experience with others, positive or negative, was part of their performance objectives.

There are also alliances designed solely for learning, where the business results are secondary, at least in the short term. However, problems quickly surface if the partners have different priorities in terms of business results versus learning, especially if this issue was not addressed during the formation of the partnership. In the words of a German manager in a Chinese JV: "We pay the tuition and they go to school." Conflicting priorities usually translate into ambiguous performance indicators for managers assigned to the venture, generating tension and disagreements among the executive team.

Successful learning alliances exhibit a bias for action. The best way of learning, sometimes the only way, is to do things together. "Don't just talk about learning and collaboration. Do it!" Such was the advice of a Japanese executive in charge of a highly successful learning alliance in the electronics industry. In this alliance, the approach to stimulating mutual learning was straightforward: focused joint development teams were assigned to specific tasks and then held responsible for achieving results. Those who were unwilling to share their knowledge were quickly moved aside, and those who were not keen to apply what they had learnt did not last much longer. The race to learn lasted three years. With the learning mission accomplished, the alliance was dissolved, and the companies renewed their competition, both of them stronger than before.

THE EVOLVING ROLE OF ALLIANCES

Just as alliances themselves evolve, so the role of alliances as part of corporate strategy is evolving. One increasingly frequent pattern of alliance development is the emergence of alliance networks, where firms engage in multiple linkages and relationships, often across the whole spectrum of the value chain from R&D and manufacturing all the way to distribution and after sales service.[74] Originally limited to the high-technology sector, where multiple alliances were used as a protective device against obsolescence and other technology risks, today they can be found in a number of sectors from airlines to fashion to pharmaceuticals. Such networks pose new challenges for HRM.

Managing Network Boundaries

Alliances among carriers in the airline industry are spreading. Such alliances promise the customer a seamless package of air services around the world. For example, traveling around the world with Star Alliance[75] may involve purchasing a ticket in Asia from Singapore Airlines, flying to Europe via Cape Town with South African Airlines, then on a Lufthansa plane serviced by United to the US, and completing the final leg of the trip with a Japan-based air carrier. If a service complaint on such a journey was met with the response "sorry, but those people were not our employees," then customer loyalty would clearly be compromised. So this raises the question of who the employees work for—their own airline or also for the Star Alliance?

From the time of reservation until the delivery of luggage at the end of the trip, airlines are a people-intensive business. Some argue that people and the service experience they provide is the only differentiator among carriers.[76] Is it possible to deliver a seamless experience without coordinating or perhaps ultimately integrating HR strategies, starting from the profile of who will be hired, to the kind of training they receive, and how they will get paid? How can the airlines share best practices? If at least some amount of coordination of airline HR standards is essential, what kind of process is required to make it happen? Who should lead it, and where is the accountability?

These are new challenges for HRM, particularly since historically the approach for airlines has been strongly domestic in orientation. Most major airlines outside the US are national flag carriers, with close relationships to their home government and strong national unions. Even if the respective management teams in an alliance agree on defining behaviors expected from the employees, the implementation of HR policies influencing these behaviors may be influenced by historic, institutional, and cultural factors.

In the case of Star Alliance, the Lufthansa Business School took a lead, perhaps because it had played an important role in transforming a bankrupt national carrier with a civil service mentality into one of the global leaders in the industry. Participation on its project-oriented programs now include several partner members, with the aim of not just facilitating coordination but also to speed up the internal transfer of learning from one partner to another. Most of the partners bring particular distinctive strengths—Singapore Airlines in customer bonding, United in logistics, and Lufthansa itself in maintenance and managing learning. The HRM vision is that the alliance will become a platform for mutual learning to convert weaknesses on the part of individual partners into collective strengths.

The HR challenge in airline alliances is an indicator of things to come. As one senior HR executive in a European airline put it: "Anybody who delivers value to my customer is my employee." This is a bold statement with broad implications, which go well beyond the airline industry. The density of international alliances is increasing in many sectors as companies engage in a broader variety of relationships across the supply and value chains to the customer. This raises the question of where the boundary of HR's responsibility lies.

The ambiguity of boundaries in an alliance and the need to anticipate future shifts is only one of the tensions in this domain. Alliances are full of tensions between competition and collaboration, between global and local interests, between the venture and its parents, between leveraging and developing capabilities. Ambiguity and complexity are the norm. Bearing in mind that the principal challenge in the international business is learning to manage tension, dilemma, and duality, mastering alliance dilemmas and contradictions, helps firms to learn to manage transnational pressures.

TAKEAWAYS

1. Initially considered only as means of securing market access, alliances are today an integral part of global strategies in all parts of the value chain. Using alliances to generate new knowledge is increasingly important.

2. Alliances are mostly transitional entities; therefore, longevity is a poor measure of success. The aim is not to preserve the alliance at all costs but to contribute to the parents' competitive position.

3. There are four types of alliances: complementary, learning, resource, and competitive. Alliances are dynamic, migrating from one strategic orientation to another. Very few alliances remain complementary for long. Alliances among competitors are increasingly frequent, but they are also the most complex.

4. The approach to alliance HRM depends largely on the strategic objectives of the partnership. It requires a focus on managing the interfaces with the parent companies, as well as managing people inside the alliance itself.

5. The firm's HRM skills and reputation are assets when exploring and negotiating alliances. The greater the expected value from the alliance, the more HR function support is required.

6. Blame for alliance failures is often attributed to cultural differences, even if the real cause may be the lack of attention to HR issues such as appropriate staffing, performance measures, compensation equity, and career management.

7. Equity control is a costly and relatively ineffective form of alliance control, compared to investing in a carefully designed and implemented HRM strategy.

8. Conflicting loyalties, complex relationships, and boundary management issues, coupled with uncertainty and instability, are characteristics of

most alliances. Managers assigned to the alliance need high tolerance for ambiguity.

9. Alliance learning is neither automatic nor free; there must be clear learning targets, sufficient investment in people, and a tight alignment of HR practices with learning objectives.

10. Alliances are full of tensions between competition and collaboration, between global and local interests, between leveraging and developing capabilities. Mastering alliances helps firms to learn to manage transnational pressures.

NOTES

1 Contractor and Lorange (1988, p. 9) identify seven overlapping objectives for the formation of various types of alliances. These include (1) risk reduction, (2) achievement of economies of scale and/or rationalization, (3) technology exchanges, (4) co-opting or blocking competition, (5) overcoming government-mandated trade or investment barriers, (6) facilitating initial international expansion, and (7) linking the complementary contributions of the partners in a "value chain." See also Kogut (1988).

2 In China, all foreign automotive manufactures must have a local partner.

3 Kale and Anand, 2006; Luo, 2001.

4 See http://web.archive.org/web/20120204124053/http://news.starbucks.com/article_display.cfm?article_id=616. Retrieved on July 12, 2015.

5 Founded in 1999, the Renault–Nissan Alliance is the longest-lasting cross-border partnership among major automakers. It sells one in 10 cars globally and employs nearly 450,000 people in nearly 200 countries. Renault and Nissan are separate companies, and the foundation of the alliance is cross-shareholding and joint governance (shared CEO and various coordination teams introduced in Chapter 4).

6 Global airline alliances are one such example—as mergers are not possible due to domestic regulations.

7 Schuler and Tarique, 2012.

8 Kanter, 1994; Morosini, 1998.

9 Pucik, 1988a; Cascio and Serapio, 1991.

10 For a thorough classification of alliances see Yoshino and Rangan (1995) and Salk and Simonin (2003). Cascio and Serapio (1991) and Lorange (1996) reviewed people (HRM) implications of different types of collaborative ventures.

11 Examples of such capabilities could be mastering of a new technology, building a capacity to sell products in new markets or to new customer segments, or increasing effectiveness of existing work processes.

12 "Honda to Sell Hero Stake at Half Market Price," *Wall Street Journal*, March 11, 2011.

13 Yu, Subramaniam, and Cannella, 2013.

14 TPCA (Toyota Peugeot Citroen Automobile) in Kolin, Czech Republic. The factory with over 3,000 employees started production in 2005.

15 O'Reilly, 1998.

16 Moxon, Roehl, and Truitt, 1988.

17 Liu and Liu, 2007. When the Danone and Wahaha alliance in China collapsed, the workforce and managers in the joint ventures overwhelmingly supported the local partner. Danone discovered too late in the game that it had no management capability on the ground to protect its interests.

18 Lu, Tao, and Wei, 2008; Chong, 2013.

19 Hamel, Doz, and Prahalad, 1989.

20 Pucik, 1996.

21 Janger, 1980.

22 Beamish, 1985.

23 Killing, 1982.

24 Zeira and Shenkar, 1990.

25 Thirty-year-old partnership of HP and Canon is one of the oldest competitive alliances in the industry. While HP and Canon compete fiercely in the ink-jet printer business, all HP's laser printers (and some copiers) come from Canon.

26 Cole and Deskins, 1988; Kenney and Florida, 1993.

27 Zaheer, 1995.

28 Pucik, 1988b; Schuler, 2000.

29 Parkhe, 1991.

30 Yoshino and Rangan, 1995.

31 Ibid.

32 Cited by Yoshino and Rangan (1995, p. 146).

33 Weiss, 1994.

34 See Reuer, Klein, and Lioukas (2014) for an overview of research on boards of directors in international joint ventures.

35 Killing, 1997.

36 For a review of strategic control and staffing issues in international joint ventures, see Petrovic and Kakabadse (2003).

37 Adobor, 2004.

38 Killing, 1997.

39 Cascio and Serapio, 1991.

40 Shenkar and Zeira, 1990.

41 During its long-term successful collaboration with Mazda, annual performance review for scores of Ford managers included ratings of their contributions to the alliance success.

42 Killing, 1982.

43 Tung, 1988.

44 Lasserre, 2008.

45 In HP, the core workshop material is a 400-page proprietary manual, supported by an electronic library devoted to alliances. This serves as a repository for the alliance knowledge accumulated by HP over time.

46 Heimeriks, Bingham, and Laamanen, 2015.

47 Findings from Booz Allen's 1997 survey as cited in the Conference Board, 1997, "HR challenges in mergers and acquisitions," *HR Executive Review* 5(2).

48 This is one of the management development areas where Web-based distance learning may create opportunities for greater flexibility—providing access to just-in-time relevant information anywhere, including links to the in-company alliance knowledge base.

49 Conference Board, 1997, "HR challenges in mergers and acquisitions," *HR Executive Review* 5(2).

50 The context of the relationship will determine the most beneficial development applications. However, off-the-shelf cultural training using the traditional "Doing Business with…" approach is probably of limited value—perhaps even dangerous in building stereotypes.

51 See also Chapter 7 where we discussed performance management in general.

52 Sometimes, expatriate cost alone makes a difference between profit and loss. In a dispute between P&G and its Vietnamese partner, the local company alleged that the high cost of expatriates, brought in to deal with unanticipated product launch difficulties, caused the JV to incur major losses. The local partner was ultimately forced to agree with P&G gaining equity control through a recapitalization that the local partner could not match ("P&G plays down Vietnam venture problems," Reuters News Service, 1997).

53 Lorange, 1996.

54 Non-equity alliances are generally temporary and, from a legal perspective, have no "direct" employees. Even those who are assigned abroad to join in an alliance project on a full-time basis usually receive salary directly by parent firm and expect to return to the parent organization. A disciplined career development process, which ensures mentoring and a periodic dialogue with the employee, is generally sufficient to avoid a sense of isolation.

55 Child and Faulkner, 1998; Parkhe, 1993.

56 Krishnan, Martin, and Noorderhaven, 2006; Ertug *et al.*, 2013.

57 Barkema *et al.*, 1997; Westney, 1988.

58 Meier, 2011.

59 In Renault–Nissan case, the leadership of Nissan's CEO Carlos Ghosn was critical in establishing the collaborative learning culture. See C. Gill (2012), and Stahl and Brannen (2013).

60 Pucik, 1996; Pak, Ra, and Lee, 2015.

61 Pucik, 1991.

62 Doz and Hamel, 1998; Tsang, 2002.

63 Hamel, 1991.

64 Ding, Huang, and Liu, 2012.

65 Open discussion about learning needs may result in explicit limitations on knowledge exchange. A clear definition of what is in and what is out is preferable to fuzzy learning boundaries, which only encourage illicit behavior detrimental to trust between the partners.

66 Pucik, Fiorella, and van Weering, 2000.

67 Westney, 1988; Schuler, 2000; Cyr, 1995; Cyr and Schneider, 1996.

68 Harrigan, 1988; Pucik, 1988b.

69 Lei, Slocum, and Pitts, 1997.

70 Conversely, if there is a perceived imbalance in career opportunities, employees may be willing to move to the alliance venture but less willing to return to the parent, or may not want to move to the venture in the first place (Inkpen, 1997).

71 Inkpen, 2005; O'Reilly, 1998.

72 Haasen, 1996.

73 As argued by Inkpen (1998), unexploited learning opportunities may in turn lead to perceptions that the performance of the alliance is not satisfactory.

74 Doz and Hamel, 1998.

75 Star Alliance was established in 1997. It currently links the operations of 27 international airlines, such as United, Lufthansa, and Singapore across 193 countries. The member airlines coordinate schedules, co-market flights, match frequent flyer programs, and align operational activities to benefit from lower costs in areas such as plane maintenance, ground service, and purchasing.

76 Pfeffer, 1998.

Transforming the Global Human Resource Role

SUMMARY

Challenge

In multinational firms, the HR function is expected to make significant contributions toward meeting global business objectives

Analysis

The HR function needs to build the capabilities linked to three roles:

- Providing HR expertise and advice to line managers
- Delivering cost-effective HR services globally
- Contributing to business decisions

Solutions

- Align HR policies, tools and processes with desired organizational capabilities
- Decide on the optimal mix of HR service delivery modes: self-help, shared service centers, and outsourcing
- Make sure that senior leaders internalize people management as a key part of their role
- HR professionals must deliver on business requirements, but they should also be ready to go beyond the traditional boundaries of the function

People management and business development at KONE

Helsinki-based multinational KONE was founded in 1910. Today it is a world leader in the elevator and escalator business, with approximately 50,000 employees in more than 60 countries. The business consists of two elements: selling new equipment and servicing existing equipment. Smooth installation of new elevators and escalators requires a strong local presence. The service business is even more local, with service personnel scattered across small offices worldwide. KONE has grown dramatically above all through a number of acquisitions, mostly of local service companies, though lately also as an outcome of strong organic growth. For a long time the corporation was "a confederation of autonomous units"—a multinational with a strong multidomestic ethos.

People management has always been at the heart of KONE's operations and the head of HR has been a member of the corporate management board for decades. However, the roles and contributions of HR have been changing in line with changes in strategy and priorities over time. At the time when KONE appointed Kerttu Tuomas to become the new executive vice president for HR in 2002, KONE had just begun building a more globally integrated organization. This included tentative efforts to develop global HR policies and processes; until then most people issues were handled locally and in different ways across subsidiaries.

The degree of global integration of HR increased after Matti Alahuhta became president in 2005. Under Alahuhtas's leadership, and with HR involved in the strategy development process and change management work, KONE initiated a comprehensive renewal program. The aim was to make the company more growth- and customer-oriented, enhance global mindset with a strong focus on Asia-Pacific, and increase collaboration across functions and geographic units. The company defined new corporate values, tried to make sure that every KONE employee understood the strategy, and established corporate development programs (referred to as "must-win battles") to be redefined every three years. People management issues were high on the agenda, first with "People leadership," then "Employee engagement" and subsequently "A winning team of true professionals" being among the five corporate must-win battles. Emphasis was also placed on designing and implementing core global HR processes, especially performance and talent management (see the box "Global Talent Management at KONE" on page 244).

In 2014, Henrik Ehrnrooth became the new president and CEO of the company. After taking over the job, Ehrnrooth noted how much time he was spending on people issues—though he found this to be logical and necessary in a fast-growing corporation like KONE. Notably, he spent significant time with the executive vice president for HR, Tuomas, to discuss recruits for key positions and the development of KONE's global leadership supply pipeline. A key capability of the company (and target for continuous improvement) was its ability to supply excellent general managers to several hundred units for which they had full business and financial responsibility. According to Ehrnrooth, "we need to develop general managers who can become country managers and then grow into members of the executive board. Before they get there they should ideally have both experience of running a business and a geographical unit."

Looking forward, Ehrnrooth sees two strategic challenges for KONE. The first challenge is digitalization and how it will change the industry. The company has traditionally done much of the R&D work internally. The challenge is now to collaborate much more with external partners who can supply technological platforms suitable for the elevator and escalator business. "We need to work much more with external parties, learn much more from outside the firm and the industry—this is a huge change project as there are so many white blood cells in the company pushing away ideas coming from the outside!" For the change to take place, in addition to strong commitment and clear communication from the top, new competencies should be brought in from outside. At the same time, it will also be important to rotate people across units, appoint leaders who dare to test new ideas, and build appropriate cross-functional teams.

The second challenge is that the business continues to move toward emerging markets like China where KONE today is the market leader. In fact, China constitutes almost a third of KONE's worldwide sales. Despite progress achieved already, how to find, develop, and retain talent in fast-growing markets will remain a critical issue.

For Tuomas and the others in the HR function, the key question is how HR can help solve the business challenges facing KONE. Moreover, how should the company address the general talent market challenges facing all firms in today's global environment? As Tuomas points out, answering these questions will help KONE improve the way "HR enables customer centricity, business performance and great employee experience."

OVERVIEW

This chapter focuses on how globalization is changing human resource management roles, notably those of the HR function and the HR professional. We begin by examining the unique features of the HR function in transnational firms as described in the previous chapters, summarizing the HRM implications of internationalization; the contribution of HR processes to cross-border coordination; and HR's role in managing change, knowledge, mergers and acquisitions, and strategic alliances. From there we go on to discuss how to organize the global HR function, examining separately the different roles of the HR function introduced in Chapter 1.

The next section focuses on the boundaries of the responsibilities of the HR function. We examine the development of the capabilities of the global HR function and the competencies of HR professionals. We then return to an important task for the HR function, and people management more generally: tension management. We argue that HR has to be a proactive function, fighting for the long-term perspective. In the final section of this chapter, we address broader social issues and conclude the book by asking where human resource management is heading in the era of tension and contradiction.

WHAT IS UNIQUE ABOUT THE GLOBAL HR FUNCTION?

What are the unique features of the global firm, and what are their HRM implications? Much of the book has focused on these issues, and we will summarize here what this means for the HR function.

Chapters 2 and 3 examined the global strategies of multinationals. The local responsiveness strategy (Chapter 2) reflects the need to adapt to the local markets as well as to the cultural, institutional, and social environments in which the multinational corporation operates. Country HR managers need, on the one hand, to demonstrate to headquarters that local ways of managing people lead to superior business results, while on the other hand serving as "translators" of desired global policies so that they fit with local realities.

A global integration strategy (Chapter 3) means that managers take decisions from a global rather than a local perspective. Expatriates play important roles in achieving global integration by acting as corporate agents, enabling control and knowledge transfer. In the past, the domain of international HRM was synonymous with the management of expatriates. Today, however, the corporate HR function has to develop and maintain global HR processes and tools to support integration, while ensuring consistent delivery of HR services worldwide with the highest degree of quality and efficiency.

Coordination becomes an imperative in transnational organizations that attempt to meet both global and local needs. The structural coordination mechanisms examined in Chapter 4 include multidimensional structures, cross-boundary teams, cross-boundary roles and steering groups, and virtual teams. The need to enhance lateral coordination capabilities brings many new challenges for the HR function: how to select and develop managers for lateral coordination roles; how to make sure that global teams contain the right people from different parts of the organization; and how to evaluate performance of individuals who work in "split egg" roles.

The coordination mechanisms of social capital, shared values, and global mindset discussed in Chapter 5 help ensure that employees working in dispersed units act in accordance with corporate objectives. The HR professional who takes on the social architect role will facilitate the development of these mechanisms through cross-border assignments, international training programs, and the support of corporate-wide virtual communities of practice. Technology and new software are extending the realm of social architecture in the multinational; the interface between the IT function and the HR domain is becoming more important.

Four chapters (6–9) dealt with key processes in international HRM: recruitment and selection, performance management, leadership development, and cross-border mobility. These processes are traditionally "owned" by the HR function, though the commitment of senior line management to rigorous implementation of the practices is an imperative. The trend in many multinational firms is toward building integrated global HR tools and processes while maintaining some flexibility for local responsiveness when it comes to implementation. In particular, the need for a comprehensive perspective on global talent management—including making sure that talented employees from any part of the corporation get suitable career development opportunities—is an important reason for establishing an HR organization with a global mandate. Further, steering international mobility requires the expertise of HR specialists.

Chapter 10 addressed one of the most salient and yet neglected domains of international HRM—how to plan and implement complex processes of evolutionary as well as radical change. Building corporate agility is another area where HR must contribute. To fulfill this task, and regardless of whether they have global or local positions, HR managers require extensive knowledge of the people-related dimensions of organizational change, supporting line management in navigating between integration and responsiveness, and continuity and change.

Given the importance of innovation, superior ability to access, share, and recombine knowledge across the world is a hallmark of leading multinationals (see Chapter 11). For the HR function, this means building learning capabilities, contributing to the design of cross-border structural mechanisms to capture and share knowledge such as global committees, task forces, or communities of practice; building an appropriate social architecture to facilitate knowledge building networks; and developing supportive performance management and incentive systems.

Similar challenges of navigating change and enhancing learning confront multinational firms as they expand globally through cross-border mergers and acquisitions (Chapter 12) and international alliances (Chapter 13)—with HR professionals playing major roles in planning the strategy as well as during implementation.

How companies handle these and other global HRM challenges will have a significant impact on how they can compete in global markets. While the HR function cannot be solely responsible for tackling these issues, when the function takes the lead, it can make important contributions. The HRM Wheel (Figure 14-1), first presented in Chapter 1, outlines key elements of HRM in multinational corporations, reminding the reader of underlying guiding principles, core HR practices, HR function roles, and organizational outcomes of HRM.

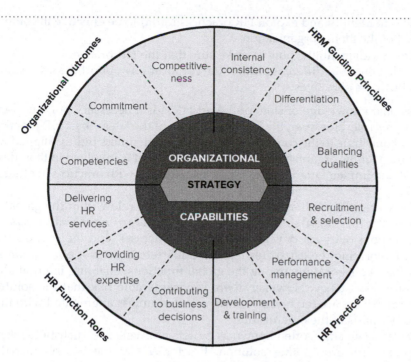

FIGURE 14-1
The HRM Wheel

In multinational firms, the HR function must take a worldwide perspective when configuring these activities. This goes beyond the basics of handling traditional functional processes of recruitment, selection, training, compensation, and the like. Of equal importance is how the HR function succeeds in influencing the way in which top executives and line managers leverage these people management tools when tackling the strategic challenges of international business, often doing this with little formal authority.

ORGANIZING GLOBAL HUMAN RESOURCES

In Chapter 1, we proposed that the HR function has to fulfill three roles: providing HR expertise, delivering HR services, and contributing to business decisions.[1] The way in which HR is organized is significant because it specifies what gets attention—which HRM issues are important, measured, and followed up.[2] The division of the function into three distinct organizational areas also leads to the necessity for coordination between them.

Providing HR Functional Expertise

The "functional expert" role[3] has for many decades been a core task of professional HR departments, though globalization has meant new challenges for this role. Successful development of HRM process and content is a more complex task for the transnational corporation than for multidomestic or home-country-centered firms. The tensions between local responsiveness and global integration discussed throughout this book are at the center of this challenge:

- How to achieve a balance between globally coordinated systems and processes involving some measure of standardization *and* sensitivity to local needs.

- How to identify and exploit HR practices found to be effective in some part of the global organization.
- Most fundamentally, how to make sure that the HR practices implemented in different parts of the corporation support the achievement of business objectives.

Professional knowledge of state-of-the-art HRM is a necessary point of departure for this role. However, the implementation of the latest "best HR practices" will not contribute to the competitiveness of the firm unless tightly aligned with the strategy of the organization; the line management is involved in their development and implementation; and they are consistent with practices in other HR domains.

There are many different ways to organize this role within the global HR function. The traditional solution is to have *functional experts at headquarters* with global responsibility for developing policies, processes, and tools. The advantage of co-locating the expert team at headquarters is deep specialization and face-to-face collaboration among the global functions, enabling internal alignment and consistency. However, there is considerable risk that the solutions of central experts are too home country oriented unless augmented with input from other parts of the organization.

Centers of expertise, often known as centers of excellence, distributed across the global firm are another solution. Proctor & Gamble has organized its HR function into different areas of dispersed expertise, among them recruitment, compensation, learning and development, diversity management, and employee relations. This structure allows the firm to achieve economies of knowledge and skills in its HR function. One of the challenges with this structure is to ensure consistency across HR practices.

A variation of this concept involves using split egg or matrix roles rather than full-time jobs. For example, a firm may have an outstanding expert in recruitment processes located in the German subsidiary that is no longer growing and may not require full-time recruitment support. Why not leverage this expertise across Europe by appointing her to head up a regional recruitment center? She builds a virtual international team of inside and outside resources, while continuing to take responsibility for local recruitment. This setup is appropriate when there is a need for cross-border coordination, but cost of experts at the corporate center would be too high.

Many multinationals use global *functional committees*, regardless of whether they have a centralized HR function or a structure of dispersed centers of expertise. There may also be informal HR *communities of practice* where participation is voluntary; HR professionals participate because they feel that the sharing of knowledge and expertise adds value. These communities also build networks that the participants can draw upon in their daily work.

Irrespective of the structural solution selected, the basic mechanism for developing corporate HR processes and tools is usually the *cross-boundary project group*.[4] Such teams often include members from the businesses and lead countries, line as well as HR managers and experts. The inclusion of line managers helps to ensure the business relevance of HR processes and tools, facilitating their implementation in countries and regions. To the extent that members of the project group have a true global mindset, the team can remain small and manageable.

The use of cross-boundary project groups to develop global HR policies, processes, and tools reflects a deeper reality in transnational organizations; corporate HR managers cannot do the complex work by themselves.[5] The center can no longer be a repository for expertise or a centralized hub where experts tell those in the field what to do. Those at the center must draw upon the expertise out in the subsidiaries, from both the HR function and the line, bringing together the key stakeholders. Doing this effectively requires a different set of skills at the center that we call *network leadership.*

Network leadership involves the following abilities:

1. An awareness of leading-edge trends and developments: The network leader is typically either a functional staff manager or a headquarters coordinator. Such a leader is expected to be at the cutting edge of developments and problem areas. In practice, what this means is that the staff manager must be well networked, both internally and externally, to be aware of relevant trends.

2. The ability to mobilize the appropriate resources: When the network leader senses that a development area is timely, he or she needs to be able to bring together the appropriate people in the form of a project group— those with relevant skills and experience along with key managers from lead application units. This means that the person needs to have a high degree of credibility with units around the world, as well as fine skills in stakeholder analysis. When needed, this also means bringing in outside resources such as consultants and experts.

3. A sense of timing and context: Lastly, the network leader needs an acute sense of timing, a quality that often is lacking. If subsidiaries are besieged by short-term operational imperatives, few things undermine the credibility of the parent more than distracting key people with a long-term corporate or regional initiative, however important it may be.

As with other senior line managers in the transnational who share accountability for coordination, the skills of network leadership require the ability to exercise strong leadership but without authority.

HR Service Delivery

The key output of the HR service delivery role is regular transactional operations connected with HRM, carried out at low cost and with a satisfactory service level. The HR department is under considerable pressure to cut costs as well as improve effectiveness. A typical diagnosis is that the weight of important but nonstrategic transactional tasks is diverting time and attention from more value-added activities focusing on HR expertise and contribution to business decisions. The application of IT to human resource issues, known as e-HR,[6] has opened up new possibilities for service delivery:

1. The automation of transactional processes, which allows *self-help*, shifting the work to the users of e-HR tools

2. Centralization of services through HR *service centers*, often with regional or even global scope, which allows lowering the cost

3. Standardization of HR transactional tasks, so they can be *outsourced*

Examples of transactions that are especially suitable for e-HR are payroll processing; responding to standard employee questions about pensions, benefits, employment rules, and holidays; basic training that is generic; and occupational health. [7] However, e-HR supports a much wider portfolio of HR practices, many of which are more transformational than transactional, including recruitment and selection, training (e-learning), performance management (objective setting, feedback, and appraisal), talent management and succession planning, and real-time employee surveys. Providers of enterprise resource planning (ERP) systems have developed e-HR modules and systems that span a variety of HR practices, and a large majority of the leading multinationals use such systems.

E-HR reinforces the trend to standardization of HR practices across worldwide operations. As HR processes become regional or global, this also accelerates the pressure to adopt a common corporate language (typically English). Further, the use of an integrated HR software package leads to more transparency, as well as the possibility of increased central control over a range of HRM decisions and activities. For example, when data about all new employees must be entered into the global system, the freedom for individual units to hire people in the face of corporate hiring restrictions is curtailed.

Regardless of the solutions that are chosen for service delivery—typically some combination of self-help, shared service centers, and outsourcing—it is crucial to pay close attention to the process of change, building understanding and acceptance for the new behaviors required of employees. Older employees and managers not brought up in the Internet world may still prefer to ask their HR officer. It is important to involve the service users in the design of these HR service solutions, followed up with objective measures and subjective evaluations of user satisfaction.

Self-help

Employees can get the answers online to many of the important but routine questions that they may have about policies, pay, and benefits, and they can also take care of routine issues themselves. For example, if a person needs training in a basic domain such as negotiation skills or quality management, then s/he can access a corporate Web site providing information on certified external courses as well as the names and evaluations of recent attendees. Multinationals are increasingly providing their employees with easy-to-access mobile applications, such as the coaching apps used by GE.

IBM has invested heavily in e-learning technology on generic issues such as the development of basic managerial skills so that staff throughout the world can learn on an anywhere–anytime basis instead of requesting authorization to attend a training seminar. This is guided by a five-step learning model, beginning with basic reading and information, proceeding upward to e-courses, then followed by computer-assisted dialogue sessions, and ultimately a face-to-face workshop with certification that is organized locally. As individuals take more responsibility for managing their own careers, electronically enabled processes can facilitate mentoring, coaching, career track management, and the deployment of people across boundaries to opportunities where their skills are best needed.[8]

Typically, self-help service delivery is hierarchically organized. Automated routine transactional matters allow employees to access information on the intranet. Simple issues needing human response will often be managed by a call center, probably located in a low-cost country (such as India, Costa Rica, or one of the countries in Central or Eastern Europe) or by professionals in a service center.[9] Issues that are not routine—those that require judgment or a decision—are routed for a response to skilled HR professionals or supervisors, and those that raise questions of policy will be worked through in interaction with corporate staff.

Still, there may be a tension between HR benefits and wider costs to the organization. The introduction of self-help based on e-HR can lead to significant cost savings as long as it does not lead employees and/or their superiors to spend unproductive time dealing with issues that would have been resolved faster and more cheaply by local HR professionals. Although e-HR investments may lead to efficiency gains, primarily through reduced HR head count, the gains may sometimes be illusionary since many activities are simply loaded on managers and employees—not to mention more resources spent on IT.[10]

Some executives in high-growth emerging markets like Asia and Latin America have raised concerns that the "global solution" increases their costs without visible benefits. Most major global firms, including Shell and IBM, accept that the underlying investment to deploy e-HR and self-help are high, and they cannot be justified solely by the short-term returns. Yet the potential opportunities that this opens up in the longer term (such as facilitating knowledge transfer and easier deployment of people across boundaries) are such that multinational firms have no option but to forge ahead.

Effective implementation of self-help and its underlying e-HR tools requires acceptance across users located in different contexts. Employee and managers need to internalize a self-help attitude for a comprehensive transition to e-HR to take hold.[11]

Shared Service Centers

Some firms, such as Cisco, have long organized their HR activities in regional or global service centers. Such centers promise economies of scale and a higher level of quality through specialization; see Table 14-1.

Many multinationals began by establishing HR service centers at the country level; others created them for geographical areas. For instance, IBM established an HR service center for its European operations in Portsmouth in the UK, processing 252,000 phone calls and 71,000 e-mails. Most of the questions were routine in nature.[12] Today most large multinationals operate one or multiple HR service centers.[13]

• Cost savings through scale advantages
• Allows "one-stop" solutions for the users
• Improves international learning and sharing of best practices
• More consistent HR service across units
• Deeper functional specialization among HR professionals
• Greater transparency and follow-up of costs and service levels
• Allows other parts of the global HR function to focus more on HR process and content development and contributions to business decisions

TABLE 14-1
Potential Benefits of HR-Shared Service Centers

Source: Partly based on F.L. Cooke, "Modeling an HR shared services center: Experience of an MNC in the United Kingdom," *Human Resource Management* 45, no. 2 (2006).

Such service centers can cover a range of HR processes, often including the responsibility for the e-HR processes that underlie the self-help functions. Professionals will respond to the non-routine inquiries that people cannot answer using the intranet.

Shared service centers appear to have led to lowered costs, reducing the duplication that existed in HR functions organized on a multidomestic basis.[14] However, there are also reports of user dissatisfaction.[15] Employees complain about the loss of face-to-face contact that helps in the discussion of personal and confidential issues, and managers feel that they now have to carry out HR work for which they have neither time nor expertise.[16] Therefore, the focus in many multinationals today is on improving end-user satisfaction with the HR service center rather than further reducing service costs.[17]

Multinationals like Procter & Gamble (P&G) have taken an additional step by consolidating several support functions. P&G decided first to establish a single global business services unit consisting of HR, finance and accounting, facilities management, and later IT. The aim was to achieve synergies by integrating the different functions into one organization, thereby facilitating better workflow management across what previously were different functional silos. The company built three service centers, one in Costa Rica, one in the Philippines, and one in the UK. Later, P&G decided to outsource some of the activities viewed as nonstrategic; IBM was awarded a long-term contract to provide services such as HR data management, payroll processing, compensation and benefits, and expatriate and relocation services. Although P&G reports some positive effects from their consolidation of the global support functions,[18] the jury is still out on whether this will become a common structural solution.

Outsourcing HR

Outsourcing of selected HR practices has been taking place for many decades; firms have relied on executive search and recruitment firms for parts of the hiring and selection process and on business schools for help in developing and delivering management training. The outsourcing of larger parts of the HR function gained momentum around the turn of the century. Today, a number of large multinationals like BP, Unilever, P&G, and Kraft have all signed long-term contracts with HR outsourcing companies like ADP, Paychex, and Aon Hewitt. These companies provide services that range from the recruitment process to retirement. In fact, new tech companies, like Zenefits and Bamboo HR, have begun providing software solutions as an HR service that reduce the outsourcing costs even more by providing software platforms for most HR activities.

Scale advantages on the part of the service providers is one important reason for the increase of HR outsourcing, making it attractive to start-ups and relatively small firms as it allows them to access cost advantages in HR. Also, the service providers may have deeper knowledge in e-HR and shared service center operations, in part drawing on their experience from working with a range of corporate clients.

A key objective when outsourcing HR activities is a reduction in HR service delivery costs.[19] Freeing up time for more strategic HRM is another important goal[20], as is obtaining technologically advanced solutions. Most commonly, firms have outsourced certain HR practices while retaining in-house those viewed as strategically important for its competitiveness.[21]

In a number of firms, HR managers have discovered that when core processes are fully outsourced, they may end up short on the capabilities necessary to play a significant support role for the business (more about this later). As a result, some firms have brought several of the previously outsourced HR services back inside, particularly in the area of recruitment.[22] We, therefore, would advise global firms to think carefully about what they outsource.

Implementing an HR Service Delivery Model

The factors impacting the transformation of HR service delivery vary significantly across regions. Whereas the pressure to reduce corporate costs is strong in North America, the focus on growth in emerging markets like Asia has meant that cutting cost has been less important. Another motivation for the change in the US and increasingly in parts of Western Europe is to free up HR time to provide input to business decisions; but in most of Asia, the concept of the HR function playing a role as "business decision contributor" is a novel idea—far from the reality of an HR function focused on operational tasks such as recruitment.

The implementation of an HR service delivery model in the US is facilitated by the fact that the country has one language, a single legal system, a long history of devolving people management responsibility to the line, and tightly organized professional HR networks for the exchange of experience. Europe is much more varied, with big differences between one country and another; the notion of self-help in the people management area is more deeply rooted in Nordic countries such as Denmark and Finland but meeting resistance in Latin Europe where the HR function is still expected to provide full support. Asia is even more varied, with radically different languages and legal systems, no history of devolution to line managers, and an absence of networks for exchanging ideas and experiences.

Self-help, shared service centers, and HR outsourcing are complementary and are often used in parallel. Companies should carefully analyze the role that each delivery mechanism should play before making the final choice. Changing strategy in midstream is painful—and costly. Doing a great job in terms of HR service delivery is not likely to translate into any sustainable competitive advantage for the firm, but firms that do it poorly will certainly suffer.

Contribution to Business Decisions

The role of *contributing to business decisions* refers to the activities of HR professionals and managers who work in business management teams. This role is generalist in nature, requiring competencies across different functional areas of HR as well as a close understanding of the specific business issues.

One part of this "HR in the Business" role is to contribute to discussions about the people aspects of strategy and organizational capabilities. For instance, at KONE a big question revolved around the people management strategy to adopt when addressing the dramatic influence that digitalization was going to have on the elevator and escalator business. Thus, one of the many tasks of these HR generalists is to work with functional HR specialists to make sure that HR practices are in place to build the intended organizational capabilities. Another particularly important task is paying particular attention to the change management implications. As discussed in Chapter 10, management teams often focus disproportionately on the strategy, plan, or solution (the quality of analysis) at the expense of the necessary change process (building acceptance); and major change will usually involve replacement of key people, adjustment of performance management metrics, as well as training and coaching. Anticipating these requirements is part of the HR business role.

Besides strategy and change, HR professionals working within the line organization are likely to participate in the evaluation of candidates for key positions and to undertake the groundwork for periodic talent reviews. HR managers may work closely with management on specific projects such as organizational redesign. However, there is also a need to be involved in more mundane "how to" HRM issues. HR managers often help resolve employee concerns of various kinds. They are the linking pins between the business units and the centrally located functional expertise centers as well as with the service delivery centers.

During recent years, HR managers and professionals have been strongly encouraged to adopt a role as *strategic partners*,[23] *business partners*,[24] or *strategic players*.[25] A survey of 1,188 practitioners revealed that 56 percent aspired to become strategic business partners, although only 33 percent stated that they performed the role at the time of the research.[26] Another study of more than 700 UK organizations reported that 81 percent had restructured the HR function; by far the most important reason for the reorganization was to enable the function to become more "strategic."[27]

Indeed, the contribution to business decision role is easier if HR managers and professionals have "a seat at the table" when strategy discussions take place—something that is not always the case. One important input is balancing local people considerations with the overall global perspective.[28]

The Responsibilities of Local, Regional, and Global Units

So far, we have discussed the changing roles and tasks of the HR function, but how should these tasks and roles be organized in the multinational firm? In the past, the organization of HR activities in the multinational was driven by a single consideration—what should be centralized (global) and what should be decentralized (local)? Then a middle ground emerged—what should be coordinated and what should be carried out at a regional rather than a local or global level?

Today we recognize that HR activities can be delivered through different sources. This is shown in Figure 14-2, where the two dimensions that guide the organization of HR activities are respectively the requirements of global integration and differentiation by business or geography.

We have argued that the most strategic function of HRM usually is leadership development for key positions and of those with the potential to occupy such roles.[29] This means that leadership or talent development (whatever name is used by the firm) will be tightly integrated at the center, even in multidomestic companies. Local HR business support managers should have a strong dotted line reporting relationship with global HR within their business, and sometimes a regional structure with a focus on talent management may be required. The box "Organization of HR in KONE" describes the organization and corresponding responsibilities in the Finnish multinational.

What activities are integrated globally through corporate HR staff depends on the strategy and the structure of the firm. For example, if the strategy for

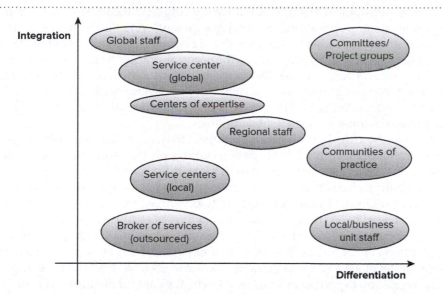

FIGURE 14-2
Organization of HR in a
Multinational Firm

Organization of HR in KONE

The 400 professionals within the KONE HR function work at three different levels—global, regional, and local—each with their own roles. The global HR unit is responsible for developing and supporting globally consistent policies and solutions in areas like talent management, international assignments, and performance management. Mirroring the corporate organizational structure, the geographical areas and the two global business divisions have their own HR managers and organizations chartered with both the implementation of global HR initiatives and contributing to business decision-making. Finally, local HR supports the local business in all people processes, providing functional HR services to employees and managers.

growth calls for international acquisitions, then managing post-merger integration should be part of integrated corporate HR responsibility, as it is at Cisco. Building a boundaryless organization has been a desired capability at GE, and so this is steered by the chief learning officer (CLO), who also overseas its Crotonville management development center. The CLO is responsible for managing the process of collecting, certifying, and transferring best practice knowledge across the complex matrix of GE businesses.[30]

Some HR matters require a high degree of differentiation according to the country or business. Here the locus of decision-making and action should lie with the local unit. In most companies, the recruitment and technical training of the operational workforce falls into this category. Owing to the country specificity of union relations, this also tends to be true of collective bargaining—although that can come into question when there are regional trends such as EU social regulation or union pressure for cross-border negotiation of collective agreements.

In the past, most HR matters in locally responsive companies, aside from senior leadership appointments and development, were the realm of local units. Now, with the shift toward stronger global HR integration in pursuit of HR cost reduction, local subsidiaries must adopt central policies and guidelines—with fewer people. There is a risk that companies may reduce local HR staffing to a point where local units are overwhelmed by operational tasks, losing their ability to adapt corporate HR tools and processes to local needs and leading to suboptimal people management solutions.

It may be clear how to handle activities that are at the extremes—high on either integration or on differentiation but not on the other dimension. However, what about the many activities in the middle zone that require some measure of both global integration and differentiation by country or business?

Here, regional HR staff and regionally-organized service centers and centers of expertise may be useful to cope with activities requiring moderate integration and regional differentiation. For example, companies with global product lines often have a regional structure in emerging markets such as Southeast Asia. In developed Western markets, the businesses have all the necessary HR experience and expertise, but this may not be the case for business units in Thailand or Argentina, for example. There, an overlay of regional HR managers provides guidance and expertise to local management teams on recruitment, resourcing, development, or international mobility.

WHERE ARE THE BOUNDARIES OF HR?

With increasing reliance on external partners to deliver value to the final customer, what are the boundaries of HR's responsibility? Moreover, what is the boundary between the responsibility of line management for people issues and that of the HR function?

Where is the External Boundary of HR's Responsibilities?

Most competent HR professionals would see themselves as customer-focused—but their customers are all internal to the firm. A provocative question for HR professionals is to ask how they add value to the external customer—"Justify your existence in terms of your added value, not to your *internal* customers, but to your *external* customers!"

GE managers have a response to that question. They use GE's mastery of HR foundations as a way of building relationships with their external customers: "If the customers are so impressed by our internal processes that they can learn from them, they'll stick with us as loyal purchasers of our products." The company trains a large number of customers at its Crotonville Learning Center, and the HR function at GE often acts as an advisor or external consultant to client firms on HR and management practices. United Technologies (UT) is another corporation with impressive HR practices. For example, we helped Pratt & Whitney (a company within the UT Group) to organize a conference on HRM for their potential clients in China—the regional airlines and the Chinese civil aviation authority. It achieved what technical partnerships and marketing strategy had not been able to pull off, attracting the participation of most of the

H&M Participates in the Fair Labor Association

H&M is a member of the FLA, a coalition of companies, universities, and NGOs dedicated to protecting workers' rights and improving working conditions. Participation in the FLA involves a commitment to implementing the FLA's workplace code of conduct, along with monitoring and remediation. The FLA's accreditation process requires a company's compliance program to undergo performance reviews over a two–three-year period, including an audit of the company's internal monitoring protocols, training programs, and auditing systems. Companies must also submit to independent monitoring of their supplier facilities (FLA makes unannounced visits to some of H&M's suppliers' factories in China), develop corrective action plans for any problems found, and subject those plans to verification inspections.

Accredited companies commit to continued implementation and independent monitoring, with reviews every three years for reaccreditation. The FLA publishes the results of the independent audits in a yearly report. The association has also provided training to H&M employees in charge of sustainability and production.[31]

airline presidents and party secretaries, who spent the evenings networking with Pratt & Whitney's top executives.

On the other side of the value chain, multinationals have to take some responsibility for how their suppliers conduct their business. Failure to ensure that suppliers follow local labor laws and abide by international labor standards may cost the firm dearly in terms of international reputation. Many multinationals have therefore specified labor as well as health, safety, and environmental standards that their suppliers have to follow. Compliance teams are responsible for making certain that the suppliers abide by these standards. An increasing number of firms are also hiring auditing firms to do supplier audits to ensure that the suppliers follow, among other matters, employee relations agreements.

The box "H&M Participates in the Fair Labor Association" describes how the Swedish clothing retailer H&M has worked with the Fair Labor Association (FLA) in China, joining the ranks of other participating companies such as Adidas, Nike, and Nordstrom.

The Responsibility for HRM: Line Managers or HR?

Who is responsible for human resource management issues in the multinational firm—line management or the HR function? While the HR function obviously has a role in providing expertise and focused attention, the simple answer is that for HRM to be successful, *general managers at different levels* must be involved, and they must at least feel a shared responsibility.[32]

First, general and top managers are responsible for preparing and implementing the strategy of the firm. Although human resources enable and constrain strategy and its execution, senior management would be foolish to delegate such matters entirely to the HR function.[33]

Second, it is difficult to implement any policies and practices in a firm without at least some measure of involvement and visible support by top and line management. Indeed, they should be the drivers of talent management processes, as well as model good performance management practices with their own behavior. In the words of KONE CEO Henrik Ehrnrooth: "The area directors and I have to show how important HR issues are. When we do business reviews of individual countries, we always discuss their employee survey: what are the takeaways and what are their concrete plans? Together with the country manager and the HR manager we also go through their leadership and talent review plan—everybody knows that this is on the agenda and how important it is for us to develop good leaders!"

Third, even in multinationals with disciplined HR policies, clear HR processes, and appropriate HR tools, there are significant differences across units and managers in actual people management practices.[34] While the HR function is responsible for the development of HR policies, tools, and processes, it is the actions and behavior of line managers that counts.[35]

Not surprisingly, firms where HR strategies and policies are decided upon and implemented by HR professionals sitting in ivory towers, detached from the business realities of line managers, are less likely to have an HR function that is seen to contribute significantly to the business results.

In general, there has been a trend toward devolvement of people management responsibilities to the line, but this is also not without problems:

- Line managers may not want the increased responsibility for people management and so are not committed to it.
- Managers may not have time to deal with this role properly.
- They may not have the ability and up-to-date functional knowledge to handle HRM issues effectively.
- On people management issues, line managers have their own units' short-term interests foremost in mind rather than the broader and long-term interdependencies of global integration.[36]
- Countries differ significantly on whether it is common practice for managers to take responsibility for HRM.[37]

Inspiring and helping line managers to carry out successfully their responsibility for people management issues across borders is among the core competencies that HR professionals working in global firms need.

DEVELOPING THE CAPABILITIES OF THE HR FUNCTION

The expanding global scope of the HR function imposes new staffing and skill requirements. What are the competencies that HR professionals and managers need, and how can multinationals develop these competencies?

HR Competencies

A number of competency frameworks exist for people working in the HR function but they all reflect a conviction that HR involves more than just functional knowledge.[38] Based on research by Ulrich and colleagues, a recent model suggests six competency clusters: [39]

- Credible activist (building personal trust through business acumen)
- Strategic positioner (thinking and acting by mastering the business)
- Capacity builder (melding individual competencies into organizational capabilities)

- Change champion (making sure that changes happen)
- HR innovator and integrator
- Technology proponent (using technology to effectively deliver administrative HR and building relationships through social media)

There are other HR competence frameworks—generally anchored in a performance-based view of competencies[40]—that typically encompass a wide range of individual skills, knowledge areas, and personal characteristics.[41] Recently, the ability to use business analytics is also often mentioned as a competence of increasing importance in the future.

People Analytics

With the emergence of standardized databases and new statistical methods, companies have the opportunity to analyze HRM data with greater rigor. The use of advanced analytics to address people management issues is becoming increasingly common in large organizations and today many firms have a separate people analytics unit.[42] Multinationals use analytical tools to address a range of people issues of high importance for business, where the patterns may be specific to the business or culture of the firm rather than generic. For instance, which factors help explain why people in key positions leave the firm; which factors are associated with employee commitment (or "engagement"); or what characterizes the best performers in a certain category of employees?[43] Appropriate analyses can improve HR processes and tools, providing HR managers with stronger data for dialogues with top and line managers.

HR professionals with the skills necessary to engage in people analytics are likely to be in high demand in the years to come. However, while the suppliers of HR software are eager to sell advanced tools as parts of broad packages, there are a number of challenges for HR functions eager to exploit the possibilities. One survey concluded that the existence of multiple sources of data is the biggest barrier to people analytics.[44] There is also a need to standardize people data categories across businesses and locations. Successful people analytics teams are likely to be multi-disciplinary, bringing together professionals with strong statistical skills, behavioral experts, and managers with deep business knowledge.[45] The box "HR Analytics at Shell" describes how one major multinational has developed its people analytics capabilities.

HR Analytics at Shell[46]

Shell's journey toward improved people analytics started in 2005 when the firm began to work on improving the corporate HR data. Following the initial period when the focus was on developing basic HR reports, the company created a global center of excellence for predictive HR analytics. Today, this center consists of four analysts headed by a manager with a background and education in applied mathematics.

The focus of the HR analytics team is on combining HR and business data to address important business

(Continued)

questions. The team carries out predictive analyses of topics identified by HR and line executives. Examples of the topics that the unit is examining include:

- "What are the measurable effects of (variable) pay on performance?
- Should we strive for increased job tenure?
- Do we employ expatriates—our most expensive employees—in places where they add the most value?
- To what extent is management influencing individual employee engagement?

- Can we quantify the effect of our Diversity & Inclusion policies?"[47]

Only some 20 percent of the work is devoted to actual model building. Most of the work relates to data collection, the merging of data from different sources, and the management of key stakeholders. Clear and nontechnical communication of the results, their implications, and the recommended actions to line managers and executives is very important; the creation of a coherent story backed up with good data is a crucial factor in driving change based on the analytic work.

HR Competencies for the Transnational Firm

General competency frameworks can provide a useful starting point for assessing the competency needs of the global HR function, as some competencies are likely to be useful for all professionals and managers working in the function. For instance, it is crucial for functional specialists developing new HR tools and content to understand how to translate the business needs of the firms into appropriate HR processes. HR people in business support roles must be able to provide insightful advice on most functional aspects of people management.

A global mindset helps, also for the heads of HR service centers who must deal with local–regional–global tensions involved in HR service delivery. If senior HR executives do not have international experience, or if they all come from the parent company, it is likely that their policy and operational decisions lack the needed credibility with line managers around the world. HR may be more prone to a lack of global diversity and mindset than other functions since HR professionals in the past seldom pursued international careers.

Given the importance of strategy implementation and the development of new organizational capabilities, executives in senior HR leadership positions require many of the HR change facilitation skills that we outlined in Chapter 10. Moreover, in firms such as IBM, IKEA, and Infosys, values-based leadership provides the binding glue for a talented workforce. HR leadership must help top management make their values explicit and act in accordance.

The competencies of local HR managers will vary significantly according to the strategic orientation of the firm. In multidomestic firms, the skill requirements will tend to mirror the size of the unit, local norms, and the expectations of the general manager. However, this often means that local HR managers in multidomestic firms are ill-equipped to meet the talent management demands that the corporate headquarters may like them to assume. If the multidomestic firm is to move toward becoming a transnational, this may require the creation of a strong regional infrastructure supporting the development of future leaders with a global mindset to minimize the risk of pendulum swings between local and global.[48]

As a meganational corporation moves in a transnational direction, one of the most challenging international HR roles is that of the local or regional HR manager. This requires a combination of strong networking, negotiation, and conflict management skill. When a decision comes from headquarters concerning a headcount reduction or a new reorganization, the local HR person is responsible for facilitating its implementation locally. However, there are likely to be obstacles that the headquarters fails to understand—legal constraints, local competitive circumstances, and resistance of key stakeholders. Without much authority, the local HR manager has to negotiate an acceptable plan, working through his or her network of contacts locally, in other comparable countries, at headquarters, in the line as well as the HR function.

Local and regional HR manager positions are invaluable opportunities for the development of network leadership competencies. Indeed, as people skilled in this art move back to HR leadership positions at the corporate center, the global mindset that is essential for a transnational organization is likely to consolidate.

The competency requirements will obviously vary with the role of any particular HR manager.[49] Deep functional knowledge is the natural basis for the *HR expertise* role. This includes having good connections with professional networks of academics, consultants, and colleagues both within and beyond their own company.

Managers in charge of *HR service delivery* are typically evaluated on cost and service quality measures, and they require a combination of two skill sets. On the one hand, they need "factory management" and process competencies, and on the other hand, they require a high degree of sophistication in HR process and content to manage the exceptions to the standard service norms, identifying those that raise questions of policy (to be worked out with corporate functional experts). Additionally, they should be able to handle tensions between the push for standardization and scale advantages on the one hand and the pull of local responsiveness and individual treatment of internal customers (individuals and business units) on the other.

The role of *contributor to business decisions* has attracted the most attention when it comes to HR competence requirements, at least in Western multinationals. There is general agreement that this role requires a generalist HR competency profile and as well as profound business understanding. As the "HR manager in the line," this person should be a credible activist and have the ability to function as a sparring partner.[50]

Table 14-2 provides some advice from experienced business support executives on what is important in order to play this role. Building strong personal relationships with line management is even more important than in other HR roles in order to influence HRM decision-making. Having work experience outside HR adds great value since it provides an understanding of internal customers' perspectives as well as credibility with line management. According to a UK study, 83 percent of the HR directors of large corporations had indeed experience outside HR, notably in sales or operations.[51]

- Become a *deep generalist.*
- *Listen deeply*—then argue and act.
- On people issues, always make the *business case.*
- *Think and talk straight*—but respect confidences and show deference.
- *Go out on a limb*—but admit mistakes.

Source: Adapted from B. Gandossy and A. Sobel, "Trusted Adviser." *Human Resource Executive* (October 20, 2002).

TABLE 14-2

Playing the Role of "Trusted Adviser" to Senior Line Executives

Personal credibility, global mindset, business acumen, and, as we argue below, international and cross-functional experience are vital for those who advance to the *HR director* level in large multinationals.

Developing HR Managers for the Transnational Firm

The globalization of the HR function requires changes in roles, competencies, and career structures. There are two ways for HR managers to gain the international and cross-functional experience needed in a multinational firm: first, professional competency development; and second, transfers of HR professionals to other functions.

Competence Development

One of the paradoxes we confront is that while HR has a vital role to play in enterprise globalization, the reality is that many HR managers and professionals at headquarters have little international experience. Worse still, because they take a plane from time to time to visit the subsidiaries abroad, managers may *think* that they have a truly international perspective. We joke that there is only one thing more dangerous than the executive who has never been to India—the executive who spent two weeks in India and who is now an India expert!

Many multinational companies make sure that their future line executives acquire international experience, and mobility is essential for those who have the potential to move into senior HR positions. However, there is a particular challenge in finding mobile candidates at the local level. Local HR managers often have highly operational roles focused on recruitment and training, without involvement in strategy. Therefore, in companies such as Schlumberger, talent development and other strategic tasks requiring coordination skills are the responsibility of high potential HR staff recruited by the parent company, working in regional HR roles and thereby acquiring international experience. Many of the HR professionals promoted to top corporate positions within the function do so after having gone through a zigzag pathway. Their career may contain moves both within and, increasingly, outside the function, with participation in global, cross-functional projects as an additional developmental activity.

A subtle but powerful tool, *mentoring relationships,* is increasingly complementing developmental vehicles such as mobility. Many firms pair up HR and line people, headquarters and field people, and HR and IT people. At Cisco, HR staff members have a business mentor; they prepare their personal development plans with this partner, typically someone in sales. *Shadowing* is a related developmental mechanism used by some firms, where junior HR professionals shadow line managers working on international projects. This allows them to get involved in the business, to learn the ropes of coordinating across borders, and to figure out how HR can add value.

HR professionals can get valuable exposure in *formal training programs.*[52] Many corporations are training their middle and senior HR managers in strategic and business knowledge and skills. Such programs will never develop a "business leader," but they can foster the confidence to question line management and to play a more active role as a sparring partner or credible activist. Action learning assignments for cross-national teams of HR professionals with different functional roles are a natural part of HR competence development programs in multinationals. Although there are many advantages to organizing separate programs for the HR function (these can be tailor-made to the needs of the function and used to develop global HR practices through action learning assignments), individual HR professionals can also benefit greatly from participating in regional or global cross-functional management development.

Of course, not everyone working in HR will be able to develop the competencies required for new roles. The following quote from an HR director describes what may happen:

> We've been raising business partners from the basics up…encouraging them to becoming strong business influencers. The move is from that of "helper" to cutting-edge, transformational roles. We started four years ago, and took out half of 50 generalists. We worked on a dozen but only three made it to the end of the assessment and development. It was a painful process.[53]

Cross-functional Transfers

How do you get high potential individuals to request a transfer into the HR function? HR professionals often receive lower salaries than do their colleagues in other functions and many high potential employees do not see the HR function as an interesting career move.

If one accepts that mobility (both cross-functional and international) is the most important tool for leadership development, then HR should be on the career map of high potential individuals. Many companies accept this in principle—"It would be great to give our high potentials experience in an HR staff role." However, companies where this is common practice, like Mars, Schlumberger, or Singapore Airlines, are the exception rather than the rule.

Our experience is that companies are tackling the wrong end of the problem. Rather than trying to attract talented line managers who have a gift for people management *into* the HR function, they should instead tackle the problem of exit routes *out of* the function. There is obvious transformative power in examples such as Schlumberger CEO Paal Kibsgaard who worked as VP for HR on his way toward the top position, and that of Mary Barra who also worked as VP for HR before becoming the CEO of GM.

When companies appoint executives from outside the function directly to senior positions in HR, this may sometimes indicate a perceived lack of business understanding within the HR function. The risk is that the evils of one extreme—excessive professionalism where the means become the end—are replaced by equal evils of another extreme—reinventing the wheel, trying to score quick wins, failing to understand the powerful principles of coherence and consistency. This will further undermine the credibility of the HR function itself, leading to replacement by an HR expert charged to restore professional depth.[54] Avoiding such destructive pendulums requires careful attention to the development of people within the function.

GLOBAL CHALLENGES WORTH STANDING UP FOR

Many line managers see the HR function as an implementer, focusing on the operational role in the bottom of our split egg concept. In our view, the HR function will never be a vital contributor to organizational success unless it constructively fights for perspectives that safeguard both the competitive and the long-term interests of the enterprise. But what should be such "top of the egg" HR agenda? We would like to illustrate this by looking outside of the traditional HR domain at three issues worth fighting for:

- Speaking out for organizational sustainability
- Fighting for the long-term perspective
- Taking into account the social implications of globalization

Organizational Sustainability

In May 1996, five climbers, members of two international climbing expeditions, including two of the best-known Himalayan expedition leaders at the time, perished on the descent from the summit of Mount Everest. The unfolding tragedy was captured in several best-selling books and films, including cases taught in business schools around the world.[55]

A number of incidents—many seemingly irrelevant when they occurred—contributed to the fatal outcome. However, one striking fact keeps coming back. Until the very last day of the climb, all team members were reminded by their leader about the cardinal rule of the Mount Everest ascent: "If you are not at the top at 2 pm, you turn back and come down." Without such a definite rule in place, there was a danger that in pursuit of their lifelong dream, climbers would endanger themselves and their teammates and miss a window to descend safely during daylight.

Yet, on the fateful day, only a handful of climbers from the two teams turned back below summit at the predetermined hour. The rest continued to climb toward the top—including the two leaders who did not turn the team around. When a fierce storm unexpectedly hit the top of the mountain, many of the climbers were caught unprepared, completely exhausted, too high up to come down during the night. At this altitude, most people cannot survive the night.

When we discuss this case in corporate leadership programs, the blame for breaking the rules and the tragic end of the expedition is quickly put squarely on the leaders. They did not walk the talk; they broke the rule they themselves set—so they are responsible for their own death and those of several others. Yet why did so many others follow the leaders beyond the point of no return?

Clearly, some continued to climb because they trusted the judgment of their leaders. After all, they wanted to reach the top, and the concern that they would have to turn back close to the summit was always on their mind. When there was no order to turn back, they did not object.

Yet there were those who knew better—several experienced guides and local Sherpas. They knew very well that by continuing the climb they were putting their own lives at risk and that by not questioning the wrong decision by the leaders, the survival of the whole team was at stake. Yet they all maintained silence.

Following the disaster, some of the survivors were asked why they went along with what they knew was a bad decision. The answers were chilling:

- "I was number three in the team. It was not my job to make the decision."
- "I looked at X, and he said nothing, so I decided to stay quiet."
- "If I questioned my boss, I would not be hired again."

All these would perhaps be reasonable answers in the context of a large bureaucratic organization facing an unpopular truth, but this was a life-and-death situation at the top of the highest mountain in the world—yet people did not speak up even when their own lives were at risk. The simple truth is that challenging how things are done in an organization is a very difficult task.

Unfortunately, there is no shortage of even well-known companies that were caught up in the storm and lost their way. Some survived (Olympus, Shell, and Volkswagen), but others disappeared (Enron, Satyam, and Worldcom)—and billion dollars of shareholder values and thousands of jobs were lost. The "2 pm" rules these companies broke were diverse, yet two factors in all these cases were in common: (1) scores of people were aware that the rules were being broken, and (2) virtually no one spoke up until it was too late. If no one speaks up, the very existence of the organization—its sustainability—can be at risk. Justifiably, society has less and less tolerance for those who break the rules.[56]

Preserving organizational sustainability is an emerging HR domain. In ABB, which has a heavy exposure to markets in some emerging countries where corruption is still rife, the new rules of accountability for living up to the corporate governance rule is simple. Full compliance is the general manager's responsibility—and that of HR. If things are done the wrong way, for whatever reason, either the HR head knows and chooses to remain silent, and there will be consequences, or s/he does not know—but should—which is equally unacceptable. The logic is harsh but simple—if the organization has a climate of openness, someone would speak up—and now HR is accountable.

Fighting for the Long-Term Perspective

Building a healthy sustainable organization requires a long-term perspective. However, while everyone acknowledges the importance of a long-term perspective, all the pressures foster a short-term orientation. Quarterly reports driven by accountability to shareholders are becoming the norm, even in Japan and Germany with their traditionally longer-term horizons. Ideas of long-term employment and careers are increasingly incompatible with the immediate pressure to be flexible and responsive. Not least of all, the future has become quite unpredictable, leading to the demise of long-term planning.

Yet HR must stand for the long-term perspective. Investments in human and social capital take time to yield rewards. Those rewards are rich in providing competitive advantage precisely because it will take others a long time to catch up. We confess to being worried when we see HR executives ceding to the pressures of our times, saying that the bottom line is the only thing that counts. Sure, HR managers must demonstrate a high quality of operational professionalism and keep an eye on efficiency. However, at a time when the long-term perspective is out of fashion, HR wins its credibility both by being highly professional in its day-by-day role *and* by acting as the guardian of the long term. As we argued earlier, HR leaders need to keep future growth in mind when everyone else is taking the axe in the pits of recession and keep the future downturn in mind when people are scrambling to exploit the immediate growth opportunities.

Focusing on the long term means persuading senior managers to think through their values and formalize them. Yes, a business can survive well in the short term without values. But it is questionable whether the powerful coherence of all the elements of organization that provide sustainable competitive advantage can be achieved without the red thread that is provided by a value system.

If layoffs are necessary for the survival of the firm, then acting as a guardian of the long term means making sure that the capabilities that are necessary for future competitiveness are retained, fighting to ensure that necessary layoffs will be undertaken in a humane and socially responsible manner. It is questionable if such a firm will thrive in the future when it has undermined all vestiges of employee trust and commitment. Acting as a guardian means also fighting to ensure that the person who gets a key job in a local subsidiary is not always the best-available local candidate but sometimes a talented employee from another subsidiary who may benefit from an international experience.

What this means is that the HRM role is to put the long-term consequences on the table for debate. HR has little decision-making power, but it has an obligation to foster discussion about underlying dilemmas, dualities, and tensions. Sometimes the outcome will favor the short term and sometimes the long term. This is not simply acting as the social conscience of the firm; it is constructively fighting to ensure that due attention is given to the opposite position that others in the organization may be neglecting.

What does this mean in practice? The future may be unpredictable, and this rules out conventional long-term planning. Still, if one accepts that there is a pattern, which leads from the present to the future, then *anticipation* is the quality that is needed—desperately needed. For example, when decentralization is the norm, the person who ultimately gets ahead is frequently the one who anticipates that the pendulum will one day swing to integration and vice versa. The same is likely to apply to HR in multinational firms. There, leaders must learn to anticipate the need for greater integration when structures are built around local entrepreneurship or anticipating the need for local entrepreneurship when structures focus on global integration. They must learn to organize one way but manage the other. They must learn to build the future into the present.

The Social Implications of Globalization

One of the coauthors was invited by the ILO (the International Labor Office in Geneva that is part of the UN family) to chair a panel of distinguished business leaders discussing the theme of "human resource-based competitive strategies." The panel discussed the war for talent, the importance of localization, and the challenges of leadership and innovation that Western and Japanese companies face in the struggle to be globally competitive. When the panel shared these observations in the plenary session, there was a strong reaction from the representatives of the third world, who constituted a good part of the audience. "What incredibly elitist ideas! In your discussions of talent, in your attempts to develop local management in China and Indonesia, you are focusing on 2 percent, maybe 5 percent of the world's population. The other 95 percent are not worried about talent. They are just worried about keeping their jobs and having enough food for their family to survive."

There is a great deal of truth to the argument. Globalization has brought immense economic benefits to the world's population, including many of the poor. Some countries in Asia, such as Singapore and Korea, have gone in fifty years from third-world to first-world status. Thriving middle classes have emerged in previously poor countries such as Brazil, China, and India with a profound impact on economic and social development.[57] And there has been increasing business attention to those at "the bottom of the pyramid," with the change in thinking about the business opportunities in serving the poor.[58] Yet large parts of the world's population still fall into the category of being below what we would regard a subsistence level of existence. Entire regions such as many parts of Africa suffer from deeper and seemingly intractable economic deprivation, fueling social conflict, and political instability.

Economic progress is a relative matter. The protest against globalization could be safely dismissed if one could show that the world's income distribution has become more equal in the past few decades. Combined with the increase in absolute standards of living, this would be powerful proof for the all-around virtues of globalization. Unfortunately, the evidence does not support this view.[59]

While there has been an undeniable trickle-down effect to growing middle classes in some emerging economies, the net differences between rich and poor within many countries, notably between rural and urban China and India but also within Western countries,[60] have been widening. The rich are getting richer; globalization allows a top performer to capitalize on his or her talents throughout the entire globe rather than just in a single region or country. Why should we be concerned?

In our view, globalization and market competition have brought with them immense benefits. Most leading sociologists, developmental economists, psychologists, and social commentators are supporters of globalization and free market competition. However, some emphasize the need to be conscientious about helping the poor regardless of inequality; others feel that inequality and declining social mobility is the principal challenge.[61] The poor peasants in rural China can watch the well-off middle class in Shanghai on their new television screens. The underprivileged in slums of Latin America or South Africa are only a stone throw away from the rich. If the benefits of economic growth are not shared more equally and if more is not done to eliminate poverty, we risk undermining what has been achieved. As we write, the European refugee dilemma is building up—a consequence of the Mediterranean divide that demographers have long forecasted, the biggest demographic gap in history between rich Europe with its declining population and poor, populous, and disrupted regions in Africa and the Middle East.

History shows that the dynamics of duality and contradiction lead to backlashes that undermine what is virtuous. The historian Arnold Toynbee argued that this was the basic pattern underlying the rise and fall of civilizations.[62] Societies would take their success formula to the extreme, leading to an unraveling of civilizations such as the Roman Empire or the Spanish Empire of the middle ages. Too much of a good thing is bad, as another concerned commentator, Charles Handy, emphasizes.[63]

Handy's major critique is that capitalism and globalization lack a human face. Shareholder value makes no one feel proud, spiraling expectations lead to disenchantment, and the pursuit of another dollar provides no meaning to life once the basics of life maintenance are assured. He points out that even Keynes noted that capitalism was such a soulless philosophy that it was unlikely to be attractive unless it was remarkably successful. Many leading business figures, including Bill Gates and George Soros, share Handy's concerns. In its national economic development strategy, the Singapore government has to balance carefully the attraction and development of talent against the upskilling and protection of its less-privileged population groups.

Why should such matters be of importance to HRM and the HR function? After all, the HR function cannot do anything about such complex issues. Yet, at a minimum, HR professionals need to be cognizant of the vital social debates that will shape the course of our lives in the future. Ideally, HR can be a vital catalyst in building a *responsible culture* in their own organization—a business that pays attention to the triple bottom line of social, environmental, and economic performance[64] and creates sustainable value for all key stakeholders. HRM cannot "solve" this issue, but it can influence it in powerful ways.

The potential backlash against globalization is most likely to be unleashed on the multinational enterprises that are both the principal agents and beneficiaries of this process—the elephants that mate with other elephants, as Handy calls them.[65] These elephants are so necessary to us since they transfer technology, take ideas from throughout the world and develop them, and provide jobs and livelihoods to billions of people. "How can I be confident that these elephants will continue to do good in the world?" asks Handy. His answer is that this depends entirely on the moral values of the people—the *mahouts*—who are riding the elephants.

The media and world opinion will increasingly hold business leaders (the *mahouts* of today's world) accountable for the actions of their corporations. Starting with the US, there are clear trends to holding leaders as personally and indeed criminally liable for their actions. They must grapple on the one hand with the pressures of increasing shareholder value—pressures that come from us, the well-off citizens, since we have invested our future pensions in their success. However, they must also be equally concerned with the still widespread poverty in the world around us, the fragility of the ecosystem, and the potential consequences of increasing inequality.

Therefore, faced with the delicate questions of balance in maintaining and exploiting a global economy, the leaders of tomorrow need to combine business pragmatism with global vision, economic realism with social and environmental conscience, and awareness of the imperatives of the present with awareness of how to shape the future—for the benefit of all of us. HR policies and practices from leadership development to performance management shape, consciously or unconsciously, the orientations and value systems of those entrusted with responsibility to address the challenge.

HRM AS TENSION MANAGEMENT

Contradiction is the defining characteristic of the transnational enterprise. As we have moved into this global era, we have entered a world of visible paradox, contradiction, and duality—and the tensions that these create. These tensions can lead us to frustration, vicious circles, and decline, or they can inspire us with vitality and purpose.

The tensions relating to HRM that we have debated in this book underlie the principles shown in the box "Guidelines for Global Leadership." A duality is present in each of these guidelines, with the tension between its opposite poles. For example, the duality between exploration and exploitation is embedded in the idea that "to innovate you need slack, diversity, flexible budgets, and lots of experimentation … and to make profits from your innovations you need discipline, targets, and deadlines." Other ideas point to the global/local duality, and the reader will find the short-term/long-term, change/continuity, accountability/teamwork, and other dualities. If anything is taken to an extreme, however positive at the moment, it risks creating a pathology.

If we accept that we live in a world of dynamic tensions, then this brings deeper challenges to our ways of thinking. Managers are expected to think in terms of coming up with solutions. However, there are no "solutions" to tensions. The dualities that underlie them cannot be resolved once and for all. Early researchers on duality and tension used the metaphor of the seesaw,[66] though we prefer to the related image of the sailor, the navigator, whose task it is to anticipate the winds ahead. The manager, and particularly the leader, stands with two feet on either side of the fulcrum of the seesaw. The seesaw is never in balance; the very notion of balance is a poor image. The seesaw is in

Guidelines for Global Leadership

Be sensitive to local culture and context	…	but make sure that a person's passport is of no importance.
Understand cultural stereotypes	…	but don't use them in practice.
Make sure that people have clearly defined responsibilities	…	and then focus on building teamwork where it will add value.
Organize one way (for example a globally integrated structure)	…	but manage the other way (to encourage local entrepreneurship).
Benchmark against others, network externally to learn	…	but never forget that superior performance comes only from being different.
Foster constructive debate about your options and alternatives	…	so that there is no need for debate when it comes to action.
The more valuable the know-how that you have in one part of the firm	…	the more you are going to have to invest to transfer it to other parts of the firm.
Tackle "sour" processes like global rationalization and layoffs today	…	with the awareness that you will need teamwork, commitment and loyalty tomorrow.
Be prepared to cannibalize what makes you a market leader today	…	in order to have a chance of being a market leader tomorrow.
Nurture your capabilities by fine-tuning the coherence that lies behind them	…	but don't forget that these strengths can become your biggest liabilities.
Develop your people by giving them more challenge than they think they can handle	…	and train them, coach them, guide them so they won't make big mistakes.
Organizational values and management philosophy provide the consistency underlying great organizational cultures	…	but they can lead to cloning, kill the lifeblood of innovation, and lead to the weakness of strong cultures.
Build face-to-face relationships well	…	so that you can use e-technology to bridge the distance.
Work hard as a professional in your operational job	…	in order to find a maximum of time for your project role.
Matrix everything	…	except the structure.
Embrace market competition	…	but with human values in mind.
Learn locally	…	and act globally.

constant motion, moving from one side to the other, and the role of the leader is to anticipate and counteract with movement in the other direction. This is what we mean by "global mindset"—understanding the nature of this global seesaw.

Where is human resource management heading? The notion of people as resources was born in the minds of scholars and social observers in the last century. Attention at the time was on natural and financial resources, but surely, people should be treated as a resource on a par with other factors generating wealth? What about "human" resources? And this was indeed adopted by the world of practice to cover a host of initiatives that were wider than the technical concerns of personnel management.

Today, fifty years later, the phrase *human resource management* is on everyone's lips. No one can deny its fundamental importance, witness the vast literature on HRM. However, this brings with it new challenges. Is HRM a line responsibility, ultimately of top general management, or a functional role? Should the HR function focus on the vital but ever-changing foundations or basics, or should it also be concerned with bigger issues, such as those discussed above—coping with the tensions of a global society?[67]

Our own stance in this debate is quite predictable for those who have read through our book until this closing section. It is not a question of either/or—HR's role is to face up to *both* of these. One cannot be met without the other, just as the top part of our split egg role (the project role) needs the bottom half of the egg (the operational role). People have to learn to work in split egg ways, and that includes those in the HR function. Unless they have the big picture of dualistic tensions in mind, HR managers will always be followers rather than leaders. And unless they are focused on the tangible practices of operational HRM, they will be out of a job.

What is our scenario for the future of HRM? We ourselves are strong advocates of the role that HRM in general and the HR function in particular can play in the era of tension and paradox. Here we think about the words of Georges Doriot. The late General Doriot was one of those remarkable sages. He was French born but a US citizen, quartermaster general for the American armed forces during World War II, a legendary professor of production management at Harvard Business School, one of the first venture capitalists in the United States, and a cofounder of one of Europe's leading business schools. Like most sages, Doriot was careful with his words. We remember vividly a discussion with him at a time when HRM was in the process of becoming fashionable. "Watch out," he said. "The term 'human resource management' is important but ephemeral. Don't get hung up on the label. People are *not* resources, they are people."

TAKEAWAYS

1. HRM is crucial to how multinationals deal with their global challenges, including how to balance local responsiveness and global integration; how to enhance cross-border coordination; and how to manage change, knowledge, M&A, and strategic alliances.

2. HR functional experts responsible for developing global HR processes and tools have to be skilled at network leadership. This requires

awareness of new trends, the ability to mobilize the appropriate resources, and a good sense of timing.

3. The goal of e-HR is the delivery of standardized, low-cost HR services through a combination of self-help, shared service centers and outsourcing.

4. HR managers and professionals who work "in the line" should contribute to business decisions. This role covers a range of activities, from strategy formulation to facilitating change, but it also includes tasks that are quite operational.

5. Increasingly, the responsibilities of the global HR function go beyond the formal boundaries of the firm. HR needs to work closely with the business, and be able to answer the question "What's the HR value-added to external customers?"

6. There are three reasons why line management must drive HRM: factors such as talent supply greatly constrain strategy; their support is essential for the implementation of HR practices; and they are responsible for people management actions from selection to performance appraisal.

7. Certain competencies—such as business understanding, general functional knowledge, and a global mindset—are useful for all professionals working in global HR.

8. Faced with many important operational tasks, HR leaders need to keep an eye on the "top of the egg" issues; protecting organizational sustainability and proactively fighting for the long-term perspective are two such issues.

9. Globalization and market competition have brought immense benefits to the world's population, including many of the poor. Yet HR has to be aware that widespread poverty combined with widening inequalities increases a risk of a backlash.

10. Contributing to the successful steering among the dualities facing multinationals will be a defining characteristic of HR leaders in the future.

NOTES

1 Lawler, Boudreau, and Mohrman, 2006; Kates, 2006; Caldwell, 2008; Wright, 2008; Lambert, 2009; Ulrich *et al.*, 2013.
2 Caldwell and Storey, 2007.
3 Ulrich and Brockbank, 2005.
4 For a more extended discussion on cross-boundary project groups, see Chapter 4.
5 Some firms have probably gone too far in eliminating headquarters staff, especially in HR, which may result in weakening of support for global coordination.
6 See Stone *et al.* (2015) for an overview of the effectiveness of the use of IT technology in HR.
7 Information systems for the internal use of the HR function are commonly referred to as HRIS (human resource information system).
8 See the discussion of e-HR applied to bottom-up internal labor markets in Chapter 8, with an example of new approaches to self-management that IBM has developed.
9 One of the HR challenges for firms with regional or global call centers is how to find people who can serve employees in their native language, for instance, Danish-, Finnish-, and Dutch-speaking individuals for an HR service center located in Bulgaria.
10 Strohmeier, 2007; Stone *et al.*, 2015.

11 Ruta (2005) provides a theory-based description of the implementation of the @HP Employee Portal.

12 Sparrow, Brewster, and Harris, 2004.

13 Reilly, Tamkin, and Broughton, 2007.

14 Caldwell and Storey, 2007; Caldwell, 2008.

15 Sparrow, Brewster, and Harris, 2004; Cooke, 2006.

16 Cooke, 2006.

17 SharedExpertise and Hewitt (2007) HR Shared Service Centers 2007. Retrieved http://www .hroaeurope.com/file/3991/hr-shared-service-centres-2007-into-the-next-generation.html.

18 The P&G case is described in Bloch and Lempres (2008).

19 Lawler *et al.*, 2004.

20 Reichel and Lazarova (2013) report a positive relationship between outsourcing of noncore HR tasks and the strategic position of the HR department.

21 See for example http://www.cipd.co.uk/hr-resources/factsheets/hr-outsourcing.aspx.

22 Our source for the observation on reintegrating previously outsourced activities is discussions with senior executives from different outsourcing providers. See also Glaister (2014) for a discussion of the impact of HR outsourcing on the HR function itself.

23 Ulrich, 1997.

24 Barney and Wright, 1998.

25 Ulrich and Beatty, 2001.

26 Caldwell and Storey, 2007.

27 CIPD, "The changing HR function. Survey report September 2007," 2007, http://www.cipd. co.uk.

28 Pucik, 1997.

29 See Chapter 8.

30 Hodgetts, 1996.

31 http://www.hm.com/us/corporateresponsibility/independentmonitoring__ independentmonitoring.nhtml; http//www.fairlabor.org/afiiliate/hm-hennes-mauritz-ab.

32 Baron and Kreps, 1999.

33 Ibid.

34 Wright and Nishii, 2013.

35 Guest and Bos-Nehles, 2013; see Sikora and Ferris (2014) for a proposed model of factors influencing line manager implementation of HR practices.

36 Larsen and Brewster, 2003.

37 Brewster, Brookes, and Gollan, 2015.

38 Ulrich *et al.*, 1995.

39 Ibid.

40 See the discussion of three approaches to competence management in Chapter 6— performance-based, strategy-based, and values-based.

41 See, for example, Lambert (2009).

42 A survey of 435 organizations revealed that 46 percent had a dedicated people analytics function (http://www.pwc.com/en_US/us/hr-management/publications/assets/pwc-trends-in-the-workforce-2015.pdf)

43 Fecheyr-Lippens, Schaninger, and Tanner, 2015; Rasmussen and Ulrich, 2015.

44 http://www.pwc.com/en_US/us/hr-management/publications/assets/pwc-trends-in-the-workforce-2015.pdf.

45 Global human capital trends 2015—available at http://www2.deloitte.com/us/en/pages/ human-capital/articles/introduction-human-capital-trends.html.

46 The box is based on http://www.inostix.com/blog/en/the-hr-analytics-journey-at-shell-interview-with-esther-bongenaar/; "Bridging research and practice: The business value of HR analytics"; Presentation by Thomas Rasmussen (VP HR Data & Analytics) and Esther Bongenaar (Manager HR Analytics) at Academy of Management Conference, Vancouver, August 8, 2015.

47 http://www.inostix.com/blog/en/the-hr-analytics-journey-at-shell-interview-with-esther-bongenaar/.

48 See the discussion of the change process leading to transnational management in Chapter 10.

49 Caldwell, 2008.

50 Wright, 2008; Ulrich *et al.*, 2013.

51 See "Power to the people managers," *Financial Times*, October 31, 2005, p. 8. We suspect that the percentage of HR directors with experience outside HR is lower than 83 percent in most other countries.

52 See Ulrich and Brockbank (2005) for a list of principles that can be used when developing HR functional training programs.

53 Lambert, 2009, p. 122.

54 Lambert, 2009.

55 Roberto and Carioggia, 2002.

56 The fundamental purpose of the sustainable organization is to meet the need of the present without compromising the future—thus earning the "license to operate" from society. Sustainable organization lives by its principles and values and pays attention to its economic, ecological, and ethical performance.

57 See "Burgeoning bourgeoisie: A special report on the new middle classes in emerging markets," *The Economist*, February 14, 2009.

58 See Prahalad (2004).

59 For this data and assessment, see R. Wade, "Global inequality: Winners and losers," *The Economist,* April 28, 2001.

60 OECD, "Are we growing unequal? New evidence on changes in poverty and incomes over the past 20 years," 2008, http://www.oecd.org/dataoecd/48/56/41494435.pdf. Piketty's (2014) path-breaking work on long-term income differences across countries has received much attention during recent years.

61 Witness the current debate on rising inequality, centered on Piketty's work (Piketty, 2014) as well as declining social mobility (Putman, 2015).

62 Toynbee, 1946.

63 Handy, 1998.

64 Elkington, 1997. See Dubois and Dubois (2012) for a comprehensive framework on HRM and environmental sustainability.

65 Handy, 1998.

66 Hedberg, Nystrom, and Starbuck, 1976.

67 See also Cleveland, Byrne, and Cavanagh (2015).

REFERENCES

Åbø, E., L. Chipperfield, C. Mottershead, J. Old, R. Prieto, J. Stemke, and R.G. Smith (2001). "Managing knowledge management." *Oilfield Review* 13: 166–83.

Abrahamson, E., and M. Eisenman (2008). "Employee management techniques: Transient fads or trending fashions?" *Administrative Science Quarterly* 53(4): 719–44.

Abrahamson, E., and G. Fairchild (1999). "Management fashion: Lifecycles, triggers, and collective learning processes." *Administrative Science Quarterly* 44(3): 708–40.

Adler, N.J. (1981). "Re-entry: Managing cross-cultural transition." *Group and Organization Studies* 6(3): 341–56.

—— (1984). "Women in international management: Where are they?" *California Management Review* 26(4): 78–89.

—— (1986). "Do MBAs want international careers?" *International Journal of Intercultural Relations* 10: 277–99.

—— (1987). "Pacific Basin manager: A Gaijin, not a woman." *Human Resource Management* 26(2): 169–91.

—— (1991). *International dimensions of organizational behavior.* Boston, MA: Kent.

Adler, N.J., and S. Bartholomew (1992). "Managing globally competent people." *Academy of Management Executive* 6(3): 52–65.

Adler, P.S. (1993). "The learning bureaucracy: New United Motor Manufacturing, Inc." *Research in Organizational Behavior* 15: 111–94.

—— (1999). "Hybridization: Human resource management at two Toyota transplants." In *Remade in America: Transplanting and transforming Japanese management systems*, eds. J.K. Liker, W.M. Fruin, and P.S. Adler. New York: Oxford University Press.

Adler, P.S., and S.-W. Kwon (2002). "Social capital: Prospects for a new concept." *The Academy of Management Review* 27(1): 17–40.

Adobor, H. (2004). "Selecting management talent for joint ventures: A suggested framework." *Human Resource Management Review* 14(2): 161–78.

Afuah, A. (1998). *Innovation management: Strategies, implementation, and profits.* New York: Oxford University Press.

Agrawal, A., and M. Kets de Vries (2006). "The moral compass: Values-based leadership at Infosys." Case study no. 09/2006-5391. INSEAD, Fontainebleau.

Ahlvik, C., and I. Björkman (2015). "Towards explaining subsidiary implementation, integration, and internalization of MNC headquarters HRM practices." *International Business Review* 24: 497–505.

Aiken, C., and S. Keller (2009). "The irrational side of change management." *McKinsey Quarterly* 2: 101–9.

Albert, S., and D.A. Whetten (1985). "Organizational identity." In *Research in organizational behavior*, eds. L.L. Cummings and B.M. Staw. Greenwich, CT: JAI Press.

Allen, D., and S. Alvarez (1998). "Empowering expatriates and organizations to improve repatriation effectiveness." *Human Resource Planning* 21(4): 29–39.

Allen, T.J., and R. Katz (1986). "The dual ladder: Motivational solution or managerial delusion?" *R&D Management* 16(2): 185–97.

Allen, N.J., and J.P. Meyer (1990). "The measurement and antecedents of affective, continuance and normative commitment to the organization." *Journal of Occupational Psychology* 63(1): 1–18.

Almond, P., T. Edwards, and I. Clark (2003). "Multinationals and changing business systems in Europe: Toward the 'Shareholder Value' model?" *Industrial Relations Journal* 34(5): 430–45.

Altman, Y., and S. Shortland (2008). "Women and international assignments: Taking stock—a 25-year review." *Human Resource Management* 47(2): 199–216.

Alvarez, J.L., and S. Svejenova (2005). *Sharing executive power: Roles and relationships at the top.* Cambridge: Cambridge University Press.

Alvesson, M., and H. Willmott (2002). "Identity regulation as organizational control: Producing the appropriate individual." *Journal of Management Studies* 39(5): 619–44.

Amason, A.C. (1996). "Distinguishing the effects of functional and dysfunctional conflict on strategic decision making: Resolving a paradox for top management teams." *Academy of Management Journal* 39(1): 123–48.

Amason, A.C., K.R. Thompson, W.A. Hochwarter, and A.W. Harrison (1995). "Conflict: An important dimension in successful management teams." *Organizational Dynamics* (Autumn): 20–35.

Ancona, D., and H. Bresman (2007). *X-teams: How to build teams that lead, innovate, and succeed.* Boston, MA: Harvard Business School Press.

Ancona, D., and D.F. Caldwell (1992). "Bridging the boundary: External activity and performance in organizational teams." *Administrative Science Quarterly* 37(4): 634–65.

Ancona, D., P. Goodman, B. Lawrence, and M. Tushman (2001). "Time: A new research lens." *Academy of Management Review* 26(4): 645–63.

Angwin, D. (2001). "Mergers and acquisitions across European borders: National perspectives on preacquisition due diligence and the use of professional advisers." *Journal of World Business* 36(1): 32–57.

Angwin, D.N. (2004). "Speed in M&A integration: The first 100 days." *European Management Journal* 22(4): 418–30.

Argote, L. (1999). *Organizational learning: Creating, retaining and transferring knowledge.* Boston, MA: Kluwer.

Argyris, C. (1967). "Today's problems with tomorrow's organizations." *Journal of Management Studies* 4(1): 31–55.

——— (1990). *Overcoming organizational defenses.* Boston, MA: Allyn and Bacon.

Arora, A., A. Jaju, A.G. Kefalas, and T. Perenich (2004). "An exploratory analysis of global managerial mindsets: A case of US textile and apparel industry." *Journal of International Management* 10(3): 393–411.

Arthur, W., and W. Bennet (1995). "The international assignee: The relative importance of factors perceived to contribute to success." *Personnel Psychology* 48(1): 99–113.

Ashby, W.R. (1956). *An introduction to cybernetics.* New York: Wiley.

Ashforth, B.E., S.H. Harrison, and K.G. Corley (2008). "Identification in organizations: An examination of four fundamental questions." *Journal of Management* 34(3): 325–74.

Ashforth, B.E., K.K. Myers, and D.M. Sluss (2012). "Socialization perspectives and positive organizational scholarship." In *The Oxford handbook of positive organizational scholarship*, eds. K.S. Cameron and G.M. Spreitzer. New york: Oxford Unversity Press.

Ashkenas, R.N., L.J. DeMonaco, and S.C. Francis (1998). "Making the deal real: How GE Capital integrates acquisitions." *Harvard Business Review* (January–February): 165–78.

Ashkenas, R.N., and S.C. Francis (2000). "Integration managers: Special leaders for special times." *Harvard Business Review* (November–December): 108–16.

Ashkenas, R.N., D. Ulrich, T. Jick, and S. Kerr (1995). *The boundaryless organization: Breaking the chains of organizational structure.* San Francisco: Jossey-Bass.

Bacon, N. (1999). "The realities of human resource management?" *Human Relations* 52(9): 1179–87.

Bae, J., S. Chen, and J. Lawler (1998). "Variation in human resource management in Asian countries: MNC home-country and host-country effects." *International Journal of Human Resource Management* 9(4): 653–70.

Baker, W. (1994). *Networking smart: How to build relationships for personal and organizational success*. New York: McGraw-Hill.

Baker, J.C., and J.M. Ivancevich (1971). "The assignment of American executives abroad: Systematic, haphazard or chaotic?" *California Management Review* 13(3): 39–44.

Barham, K., and C. Heimer (1998). *ABB: The dancing giant*. London: Financial Times/Pitman.

Baritz, L. (1960). *The servants of power: A history of the use of social science in American industry*. Middletown, CT: Wesleyan University Press.

Barkema, H.G., J.H. Bell, and J.M. Pennings (1996). "Foreign entry, cultural barriers, and learning." *Strategic Management Journal* 17(2): 151–66.

Barkema, H.G., and M. Schijven (2008). "How do firms learn to make acquisitions? A review of past research and an agenda for the future." *Journal of Management* 34(3): 594–634.

Barkema, H.G., O. Shenkar, F. Vermeulen, and J.H.J. Bell (1997). "Working abroad, working with others: How firms learn to operate international joint ventures." *Academy of Management Journal* 40(2): 426–42.

Barley, S.R., and G. Kunda (1992). "Design and devotion: Surges of rational and normative ideologies of control in managerial discourse." *Administrative Science Quarterly* 37(3): 363–99.

Barner-Rasmussen, W., and I. Björkman (2006). "Language fluency, socialization and inter-unit relationships in Chinese and Finnish subsidiaries." *Management and Organization Review* 3(1): 105–28.

Barner-Rasmussen, W., M. Ehrnrooth, A. Koveshnikov, and K. Mäkelä (2014). "Cultural and language skills as resources for boundary spanning within the MNC." *Journal of International Business Studies* 45(7): 886–905.

Barney, J. (1991). "Firm resources and sustained competitive advantage." *Journal of Management* 17(1): 99–120.

Barney, J., and P.W. Wright (1998). "On becoming a strategic partner: The role of human resources in gaining competitive advantage." *Human Resource Management* 37(1): 31–46.

Baron, J.N., M.D. Burton, and M.T. Hannan (1996). "The road taken: Origins and evolution of employment systems in emerging companies." *Industrial and Corporate Change* 5(2): 239–75.

Baron, J.N., and D.M. Kreps (1999). *Strategic human resources: Frameworks for general managers*. New York: Wiley.

Bartlett, C.A. (1996). "McKinsey & Company: Managing knowledge and learning." Case study no. 9-396-357. Harvard Business School, Boston, MA.

Bartlett, C.A., and S. Ghoshal (1989). *Managing across borders: The transnational solution*. Cambridge, MA: Harvard Business School Press.

——— (1990). "Matrix management: Not a structure, a frame of mind." *Harvard Business Review* (July–August): 138–45.

——— (1992). "What is a global manager?" *Harvard Business Review* (September–October): 124–32.

——— (1997). "The myth of the generic manager: New personal competencies for new management roles." *California Management Review* 40(1): 92–116.

——— (1998). *Managing across borders: The transnational solution*, 2nd ed. Boston, MA: Harvard Business School Press.

——— (2000). "Going global: Lessons from late movers." *Harvard Business Review* (March–April): 133–42.

Bartlett, C.A., S. Ghoshal, and J. Birkinshaw (2003). *Transnational management*, 4th ed. New York: McGraw-Hill.

Bartlett, C.A., and A.N. McLean (2006). "GE's Talent Machine: The Making of a CEO." Harvard Business School Case 9-304-049.

Bartlett, C.A., and J. O'Connell (1998). "Lincoln Electric: Venturing abroad." Case study no. 398095. Harvard Business School, Boston.

Bartlett, C.A., and H. Yoshihara (1988). "New challenges for Japanese multinationals: Is organization adaptation their Achilles' heel?" *Human Resource Management* 27(1): 19–43.

Bartolomé, F., and P.A.L. Evans (1980). "Must success cost so much?" *Harvard Business Review* (March–April): 137–49.

Bass, B.M., and R.M. Stogdill (1990). *Handbook of leadership: Theory, research and managerial applications.* New York: Free Press.

Bauer, T., H. Bonin, L. Goette, and U. Sunde (2007). "Real and nominal wage rigidities and the rate of inflation: Evidence from West German micro data." *The Economic Journal* 117(524): F508–29.

Bauer, T.N., E.W. Morrison, and R.R. Callister (1998). "Organizational socialization: A review and directions for future research." *Research in Personnel and Human Resources Management* 16: 149–214.

Beamish, P.W. (1985). "The characteristics of joint ventures in developed and developing countries." *Journal of World Business* 20(3): 13–19.

Beamish, P.W., and N.C. Lupton (2009). "Managing joint ventures." *Academy of Management Perspectives* 23(2): 75–94.

Becker, B., and B. Gerhart (1996). "The impact of human resource management on organizational performance." *Academy of Management Journal* 39(4): 779–801.

Becker, B.E., M.A. Huselid, P.S. Pickus, and M.F. Spratt (1997). "Human resources as a source of shareholder value: Research and recommendations." In *Tomorrow's HR management*, eds. D. Ulrich, M.R. Losey, and G. Lake. New York: Wiley.

Becker, B.E., M.A. Huselid, and D. Ulrich (2001). *The HR scorecard: Linking people, strategy and performance.* Boston, MA: Harvard Business School Press.

Beer, M., R. Eisenstat, and B. Spector (1990). *The critical path to corporate renewal.* Boston, MA: Harvard Business School Press.

Beer, M., and N. Nohria (2000). "Cracking the code of change." *Harvard Business Review* (May–June): 133–41.

Beer, M., and G.C. Rogers (1995). "Human resources at Hewlett-Packard (A) (B)." Case study no. 9-495-051. Harvard Business School, Boston.

Beer, M., B. Spector, P.R. Lawrence, D. Quinn Mills, and R.E. Walton (1984). *Managing human assets.* New York: Free Press.

Begley, T.M., and D.P. Boyd (2003). "The need for a corporate global mind-set." *MIT Sloan Management Review* 44(2): 25–32.

Behfar, K.J., R.S. Peterson, E.A Mannix, and W.M.K. Trochim (2008). "Critical role of conflict resolution in teams: A close look at the links between conflict type, conflict management strategies, and team outcomes." *Journal of Applied Psychology* 93(1): 170–88.

Belbin, R.M. (1981). *Management teams: Why they succeed or fail.* London: Heinemann.
——— (1993). *Team roles at work.* Oxford: Butterworth-Heinemann.

Bennis, W., and B. Nanus (1985). *Leaders: The strategies for taking charge.* New York: Harper & Row.

Benson, J., M. Yuasa, and P. Debroux (2007). "The prospect for gender diversity in Japanese employment." *International Journal of Human Resource Management* 18(5): 890–907.

Berg, N.A., and N.D. Fast (1983). "Lincoln Electric Co." Case study no. 376028. Harvard Business School, Boston.

Bertrand, O., and H. Zitouna (2008). "Domestic versus cross-border acquisitions: Which impact on the target firms' performance?" *Applied Economics* 40(17): 2221–38.

Bettenhausen, K. (1991). "Five years of groups research: What we have learned and what needs to be addressed." *Journal of Management* 17(2): 345–81.

Beugelsdijk, S., R. Maseland, M. Onrust, A. van Hoorn, and S. Slangen (2015). "Cultural distance in international business and management: From mean-based to variance-based measures." *International Journal of Human Resource Management* 26(2): 165–91.

Beyer, D. (2006). "Fixing the talent problem." *Oil & Gas Financial Journal* 3(9).

Bhaskar-Shrinivas, P., D.A. Harrison, M.A. Shaffer, and D.M. Luk (2005). "Input-based and time-based models of international adjustment: Meta-analytic evidence and theoretical extentions." *Academy of Management Journal* 48(2): 257–81.

Bidwell, M. (2011). "Paying more to get less: The effects of external hiring versus internal mobility." *Administrative Science Quarterly* 56(3): 369–407.

Birkinshaw, J. (1999). "Acquiring intellect: Managing the integration of knowledge-intensive acquisitions." *Business Horizons* (May–June): 33–40.

———. (2004). "External sourcing of knowledge in the international firm." In *The Blackwell handbook of global management: A guide to managing complexity*, eds. H.W. Lane, M.L. Maznevski, M.E. Mendenhall, and J. McNett. Oxford: Blackwell Publishing.

Birkinshaw, J., J. Bessant, and R. Delbridge (2007). "Finding, forming, and preforming: Creating networks for discontinuous networks." *California Managment Review* 49(3): 67–84.

Birkinshaw, J., and J. DiStefano (2004). "Global account management: New structures, new tasks." In *The Blackwell handbook of global management: A guide to managing complexity*, eds. H.W. Lane, M.L. Maznevski, M.E. Mendenhall, and J. McNett. Oxford: Blackwell Publishing.

Birkinshaw, J., and C.B. Gibson (2004). "The antecedents, consequences, and mediating role of organizational ambidexterity." *Academy of Management Journal* 47(2): 209–26.

Birkinshaw, J., and K. Gupta (2013). "Clarifying the distinctive contribution of ambidexterity to the field of organization studies." *Academy of Management Perspectives* 27(4): 287–99.

Birkinshaw, J., G. Hamel, and M.J. Mol (2008). "Management innovation." *Academy of Management Review* 33(4): 825–45.

Birkinshaw, J., and N. Hood (1998). "Multinational subsidiary evolution: Capability and charter change in foreign-owned subsidiary companies." *Academy of Management Review* 23(4): 773–95.

——— (2001). "Unleash innovation in foreign subsidiaries." *Harvard Business Review* (March): 131–7.

Biron, M., E. Farndale, and J. Paauwe (2011). "Performance management effectiveness: Lessons from world-leading firms." *International Journal of Human Resource Management* 22(6): 1294–311.

Bjelland, O.M., and R.C. Wood (2008). "An inside view of IBM's innovation jam." *MIT Sloan Management Review* 50(1): 32–40.

Björk, S. (1998). *IKEA: Ingvar Kamprad og hans imperium.* Copenhagen: Børsen.

Björkman, I., W. Barner-Rasmussen., and L. Li (2004). "Managing knowledge transfer in MNCs: The impact of headquarters control mechanisms." *Journal of International Business Studies* 35(5): 443–55.

Björkman, I., P. Budhwar, A. Smale, and J. Sumelius (2008). "Human resource management in foreign-owned subsidiaries: China versus India." *International Journal of Human Resource Management* 19(5): 964–78.

Björkman, I., C. Galunic, and J. Lockard (2015). "Lincoln Electric in China (B)." 05/2015-4850. INSEAD, Fontainebleau.

Björkman, I., and C.D. Galunic (1999). "Lincoln Electric in China." Case study no. 09/1999-4850. INSEAD, Fontainebleau.

Björkman, I., and J. Gertsen (1993). "Selecting and training Scandinavian expatriates: Determinants of corporate practice." *Scandinavian Journal of Management* 9(2): 145–64.

Björkman, I., and J.E. Lervik (2007). "Transferring HR practices within multinational corporations." *Human Resource Management Journal* 17(4): 320–35.

Björkman, I., and Y. Lu (1999). "The management of human resources in Chinese-Western joint ventures." *Journal of World Business* 34(3): 306–24.

——— (2001). "Institutionalization and bargaining power explanations of HRM practices in international joint ventures: The case of Chinese-Western joint ventures." *Organization Studies* 22(3): 491–512.

Björkman, I., and K. Mäkelä (2013). "Are you willing to do what it takes to become a senior global leader? Explaining the willingness to undertake challenging leadership development activities." *European Journal of International Management* 7(5): 570–86.

Björkman, I., G.K. Stahl, and E. Vaara (2007). "Cultural differences and capability transfer in cross-border acquisitions: The mediating roles of capability complementarity, absorptive capacity, and social integration." *Journal of International Business Studies* 38(4): 658–72.

Black, J.S. (1988). "Work role transitions: A study of American expatriate managers in Japan." *Journal of International Business Studies* 19(2): 277–94.

Black, J.S., and H.B. Gregersen (1991a). "When Yankee comes home: Factors related to expatriate and spouse repatriation adjustment." *Journal of International Business Studies* 22(4): 671–94.

——— (1991b). "The other half of the picture: Antecedents of spouse cross-cultural adjustment." *Journal of International Business Studies* 22(3): 461–77.

——— (1991c). "Antecedents to cross-cultural adjustment for expatriates in Pacific Rim assignments." *Human Relations* 44(5): 497–515.

——— (1999). "The right way to manage expats." *Harvard Business Review* (March–April): 52–63.

——— (2008). *It starts with one: Changing individuals changes organizations.* Upper Saddle River, NJ: Wharton School Publishing.

Black, J.S., H.B. Gregersen, and M.E. Mendenhall (1992). *Global assignments: Successfully expatriating and repatriating international managers.* San Francisco: Jossey-Bass.

Black, J.S., H.B. Gregersen, M.E. Mendenhall, and L.K. Stroh (1999). *Globalizing people through international assignments.* Reading, MA: Addison-Wesley.

Black, J.S., H.B. Gregersen, and A. Morrison (1999). *Global explorers: The next generation of leaders.* London: Routledge.

Black, J.S., M. Mendenhall, and G. Oddou (1991). "Toward a comprehensive model of international adjustment: An integration of multiple theoretical perspectives." *Academy of Management Review* 16(2): 291–317.

Black, J.S., and G.K. Stephens (1989). "The influence of the spouse on American expatriate adjustment in overseas assignments." *Journal of Management* 15(4): 529–44.

Blackburn, R., S. Furst, and B. Rosen (2003). "Building a winning virtual team: KSAs, selection, training, and evaluation." In *Virtual teams that work: Creating conditions for virtual team effectiveness*, eds. C.B. Gibson and S.G. Cohen. San Francisco: Jossey-Bass.

Blazejewski, S. (2006). "Transferring value-infused organizational practices in multinational companies." In *Global, national and local practices in multinational companies*, eds. M. Geppert and M. Mayer. Hampshire, UK: Palgrave Macmillan.

Bleeke, J., D. Ernst, J. Isono, and D.D. Weinberg (1993). "Succeeding at cross-border mergers and acquisitions." In *Collaborating to compete: Using strategic alliances and acquisitions in the global marketplace*, eds. J. Bleeke and D. Ernst. New York: Wiley.

Bloch, M., and E.C. Lempres (2008). "From internal service provider to strategic partner: An interview with the head of Global Business Services at P&G." *McKinsey Quarterly* 3: 49–59.

Bloom, N., C. Genakos, R. Sadun, and J. Van Reenen (2012). "Management practices across firms and countries." *Academy of Management Perspectives* 26(1): 12–33.

Bloom, M., and G.T. Milkovich (1999). "A SHRM perspective on international compensation and reward systems." In *Strategic human resources management: Research in personnel and human resources management*, eds. P.M. Wright, L.D. Dyer, J.W. Boudreau, and G.T. Milkovich. Stamford, CT: JAI Press.

Bloom, M., G.T. Milkovich, and A. Mitra (2003). "International compensation: Learning from how managers respond to variations in local host context." *International Journal of Human Resource Management* 14(8): 1350–67.

Blossfeld, H.-P., M. Mills, and F. Bernardi (2008). *Globalization, uncertainty and men's careers: An international comparison*. Northampton, MA: Edward Elgar.

Boam, R., and P. Sparrow (1992). *Designing and achieving competency: A competency-based approach to developing people and organizations*. London: McGraw-Hill.

Boeri, T., H. Brucker, F. Doquier, and H. Rapoport (eds.) (2012). *Brain drain and brain gain: The global competition to attract high-skilled immigrants*. Oxford: Oxford University Press.

Bonache, J., and J. Cervino (1997). "Global integration without expatriates." *Human Resource Management Journal* 7(3): 89–100.

Bonache, J., and C. Zárraga-Oberty (2008). "Determinants of the success of international assignees as knowledge tranferors: A theoretical framework." *International Journal of Human Resource Management* 19(1): 1–18.

Borkowski, S.C. (1999). "International managerial performance evaluation: A five country comparison." *Journal of International Business Studies* 30(3): 533–55.

Boselie, P., G. Dietz, and C. Boon (2005). "Commonalities and contradictions in HRM and performance research." *Human Resource Management Journal* 15(3): 67–94.

Bouchikhi, H., and J. Kimberly (2012). "Making mergers work." *Sloan Management Review* 54(1): 63–70.

Boudreau, J.W., and P.M. Ramstad (2007). *The new science of human capital*. Boston, MA: Harvard Business School Press.

Bowen, D.E., and C. Ostroff (2004). "Understanding HRM-firm performance linkages: The role of the 'strength' of the HRM system." *Academy of Management Review* 29(2): 203–21.

Boxall, P. (1996). "The strategic HRM debate and the resource-based view of the firm." *Human Resource Management Journal* 6(3): 59–75.

Boxall, P., and J. Purcell (2003). "Strategy and human resource management." *Industrial & Labor Relations Review* 57(1): 145–6.

Boxall, P., J. Purcell, and P. Wright (eds.) (2007). *The Oxford handbook of human resource management*. New York: Oxford University Press.

Boyatzis, R., A. McKee, and D. Goleman (2002). "Reawakening your passion for work." *Harvard Business Review* (April): 86–94.

Branham, L. (2005). *The 7 hidden reasons employees leave: How to recognize the subtle signs and react before it's too late*. New York: AMACOM.

Braun, I., K. Pull, D. Alewell, S. Störmer, and K. Thommes (2011). "HR outsourcing and service quality: Theoretical framework and empirical evidence." *Personnel Review* 40(3): 364–82.

Braun, W.H., and M. Warner (2002). "Strategic human resource management in Western multinationals in China." *Personnel Review* 31(5): 553–79.

Breaugh, J.A. (1992). *Recruitment: Science & practice*. Boston, MA: PWS-Kent.

Bresman, H., J.M. Birkinshaw, and R. Nobel (1999). "Knowledge transfer in acquisitions." *Journal of International Business Studies* 30(4): 439–62.

Brett, J., K. Behfar, and M.C. Kern (2012). "Managing multicultural teams." In *International human resources management and organizational behavior*, eds. G.K. Stahl, M.E. Mendenhall, and G.R. Oddou. New York: Routledge.

Brett, J.M., and L.K. Stroh (1995). "Willingness to relocate internationally." *Human Resource Management* 34(3): 405–24.

Brewster, C. (1991). *The management of expatriates*. London: Kogan Page.

——— (1995). "Towards a 'European' model of human resource management." *Journal of International Business Studies* 26(1): 1–21.

——— (2006). "Comparing HRM across Countries." In *Handbook of research in international resource management*, eds. G.K. Stahl and I. Björkman. Cheltenham, UK: Edward Elgar.

——— (2007). "Comparative HRM: European views and perspectives." *International Journal of Human Resource Management* 18(5): 769–87.

Brewster, C., J. Bonache, J.L. Cerdin, and V. Suutari (2014). "Exploring expatriate outcomes." *International Journal of Human Resource Management* 25(14): 1921–37.

Brewster, C., M. Brookes, and P.J. Gollan (2015). "The institutional antecedents of the assignment of HRM responsibilities to line managers." *Human Resource Management* 54(4): 577–97.

Brewster, C., and A. Hegewisch (eds.) (1994). *Policy and practice in European human resource management: The Price Waterhouse Cranfield Survey.* London: Routledge.

Brewster, C., and H.H. Larsen (1992). "Human resource management in Europe: Evidence from ten countries." *International Journal of Human Resource Management* 3(3): 409–34.

Brewster, C., W. Mayrhofer, and M. Morley (2004). *Human resource management in Europe: Evidence of convergence.* Boston, MA: Butterworth-Heinemann.

Brewster, C., and H. Scullion (1997). "A review and agenda for expatriate HRM." *Human Resource Management Journal* 7(3): 32–41.

Brewster, C., P. Sparrow, and G. Vernon (2007). *International human resource management*, 2nd ed. London: Chartered Institute of Personnel and Development.

Brewster, C., and G.T. Wood (2012). "Comparative HRM and international HRM." In *Handbook of research on comparative human resource management*, eds. C. Brewster and W. Mayrhofer. Northampton, MA: Edward Elgar.

Bridges, W. (1980). *Making sense of life's transitions.* New York: Addison-Wesley.

——— (1986). "Managing organizational transitions." *Organizational Dynamics* 15(1): 24–33.

Brim, O.G. (1966). "Socialization through the life cycle." In *Socialization after childhood*, eds. O.G. Brim and S. Wheeler. New York: Wiley.

Briscoe, J.P., and D.T. Hall (1999). "Grooming and picking leaders using competency frameworks: Do they work?" *Organizational Dynamics* 28(2): 37–51.

Brock, D., M.T. Yaffe, and M. Dembovsky (2006). "The global law firm: An initial study of strategy and performance." *International Journal of Business and Economics* 5(2): 161–72.

Broeckx, P.V., and R. Hooijberg (2007). "Nestlé on the move: Evolving human resources approaches from company success." In *Being there even when you are not: Leading through strategy, structures, and systems,* eds. R. Hooijberg, J. Hunt, J. Antonakis, K. Boal, and N. Lane. Amsterdam: Elsevier.

Broekner, J., Y. Chen, E.A. Mannix, K. Leung, and D.P. Skarlicki (2000). "Culture and procedural fairness: When the effects of what you do depend on how you do it." *Administrative Science Quarterly* 45(1): 138–59.

Brown, S.L., and K. Eisenhardt (1997). "The art of continuous change: Linking complexity theory and time-paced evolution in relentlessly shifting organizations." *Administrative Science Quarterly* 42(1): 1–34.

——— (1998). *Competing on the edge: Strategy as structured chaos.* Boston, MA: Harvard Business School Press.

Bruch, H., and S. Ghoshal (2002). "Beware the busy manager." *Harvard Business Review* (February): 62–9.

Bryan, L.L. (2004). "Making a market in knowledge." *McKinsey Quarterly* (3): 100–1.

Bryan, L.L., E. Matson, and L.M. Weiss (2007). "Harnessing the power of informal employee networks." *McKinsey Quarterly* 4: 82–6.

Buckingham, M., and A. Goodall (2015). "Reinventing performance management." *Harvard Business Review* 93(April): 40–50.

Burgelman, R.A., and A.S. Grove (2007). "Let chaos reign, then reign in chaos—repeatedly: Managing strategic dynamic for corporate longevity." *Strategic Management Journal* 28(10): 965–79.

Burt, R.S. (1987). "Social contagion and innovation: Cohesion versus structural equivalence." *American Journal of Sociology* 92(May): 1287–335.

——— (1992). *Structural holes: The social structure of competition.* Cambridge, MA: Harvard University Press.

Burt, R.S., R.M. Hogarth, and C. Michaud (2000). "The social capital of French and American managers." *Organization Science* 11(2): 123–47.

Caldwell, R. (2008). "HR business partner competency models: Re-contextualising effectiveness." *Human Resource Management Journal* 18(3): 275–94.

Caldwell, R., and J. Storey (2007). "The HR function: Integration or fragmentation?" In *Human resource management: A critical text*, 3rd ed., ed. J. Storey. London: Thomson.

Caligiuri, P.M. (2006a). "Developing global leaders." *Human Resource Management Review* 16(2): 219–28.

——— (2006b). "Performance measurement in a cross-national context." In *Performance measurement: Current perspectives and future challenges*, eds. W. Bennet, D. Woehr, and C. Lance. New Jersey: Laurence Erlbaum Associates.

Caligiuri, P., and I. Tarique (2012). "Dynamic cross-cultural competencies and global leadership effectiveness." *Journal of World Business* 47(4): 612–22.

Caligiuri, P., I. Tarique, and R. Jacobs (2009). "Selection for international assignments." *Human Resource Management Review* 19(3): 251–62.

Caligiuri, P.M., and R.L. Tung (1999). "Comparing the success of male and female expatriates from a US-based multinational company." *International Journal of Human Resource Management* 10(5): 763–82.

Cameron, K. (1994). "Strategies for successful organizational downsizing." *Human Resource Management* 33(2): 189–211.

Campbell, A., and M. Goold (1998). *Synergy: Why links between business units often fail and how to make them work.* Oxford: Capstone.

Canney Davison, S., and K. Ward (1999). *Leading international teams.* New York: McGraw-Hill.

Cappelli, P. (1996). "Technology and skill requirements: Implications for establishment wage structures." *New England Economic Review* (Special issue): 139–154.

——— (2008). *Talent on demand: Managing talent in an age of uncertainty.* Boston, MA: Harvard Business School Press.

——— (2015). "Why we love to hate HR… and what HR can do about it." *Harvard Business Review* (July–August): 55–61.

Cappelli, P., and M. Hamori (2005). "The new road to the top." *Harvard Business Review* (January): 25–32.

Cappelli, P., and J.R. Keller (2014). "Talent management: Conceptual approaches and practical challenges." *Annual Review of Organizational Psychology and Organizational Behavior* 1: 305–31.

Carlos, A.M., and S. Nicholas (1988). "Giants of an earlier capitalism: The chartered trading companies as modern multinationals." *Business History Review* 62(3): 398–419.

Caro F., and V. M. de Albéniz (2014). "How Fast Fashion Works: Can It Work for You, Too?" *IESE Insight Review* (21): 58–65.

Carraher, S.M., S.E. Sullivan, and M.M. Crocitto (2008). "Mentoring across global boundaries: An empirical examination of home- and host-country mentors on expatriate career outcomes." *Journal of International Business Studies* 39(8): 1310–26.

Cascio, W.F. (2000). *Costing human resources: The financial impact of behavior in organizations.* Cincinnati, OH: South-Western College Publishing.

——— (2006). "Global performance management systems." In *Handbook of research in international human resource management*, eds. G.K. Stahl, and I. Björkman. Northampton, MA: Edward Elgar.

——— (2012a). "Global performance management systems." In *Handbook of research in international human resource management*, 2nd ed., eds. G.K. Stahl, I. Björkman, and S. Morris. Northampton, MA: Edward Elgar Publishing.

——— (2012b). "Methodological issues in international HR management research." *International Journal of Human Resource Management* 23(12): 2532–45.

Cascio, W.F., and M.G. Serapio, Jr. (1991). "Human resources systems in an international alliance: The undoing of a done deal?" *Organizational Dynamics* 19(3): 63–74.

Castilla, E.J. (2005). "Social networks and employee performance in a call center." *American Journal of Sociology* 110(5): 1243–83.

Cerdin, J.L., and M.L. Le Pargneux (2009). "Career and international assignment fit: Toward an integrative model of success." *Human Resource Management* 48(1): 5–25.

Cerdin, J.-L., and J.-M. Peretti (2000). "Les déterminants de l'adaptation des cadres français expatriés." *Revue Française de Gestion* (July–August): 58–66.

Cerdin, J.L., and J. Selmer (2014). "Who is a self-initiated expatriate? Towards conceptual clarity of a common notion." *International Journal of Human Resource Management* 25(9): 1281–301.

Chakrabarti, R., S. Gupta-Mukherjee, and N. Jayaraman (2009). "Mars-Venus marriages: Culture and cross-border M&A." *Journal of International Business Studies* 40(2): 216–35.

Chambers, E.G., M. Foulon, H. Handfield-Jones, S.M. Hankin, and E.G. Michaels III (1998). "The war for talent." *McKinsey Quarterly* 3: 44–57.

Chandler, A.D. (1962). *Strategy and structure*. Cambridge, MA: MIT Press.

——— (1977). *The visible hand*. Cambridge, MA: Harvard University Press.

——— (1986). "The evolution of modern global competition." In *Competition in global industries*, ed. M. Porter. Cambridge, MA: Harvard University Press.

——— (1990). *Scale and scope: The dynamics of industrial capitalism*. Cambridge, MA: Harvard University Press.

Chang, E., and M.S. Taylor (1999). "Control in multinational corporations (MNCs): The case of Korean manufacturing subsidiaries." *Journal of Management* 25(4): 541–65.

Charan, R., S. Drotter, and J. Noel (2001). *The leadership pipeline: How to build the leadership powered company*. Boston, MA: Harvard Business School Press.

Chatman, J.A. (1991). "Matching people and organizations: Selection and socialization in public accounting firms." *Administrative Science Quarterly* 36(3): 459–84.

Chatman, J., and S.E. Cha (2003). "Leading by leveraging culture." *California Management Review* 45(4): 20–34.

Chatman, J., C. O'Reilly, and V. Chang (2005). "Cisco Systems: Developing a human capital strategy." *California Management Review* 47(2): 137–67.

Chaudhuri, S., and B. Tabrizi (1999). "Capturing the real value in high-tech acquisitions." *Harvard Business Review* (September–October): 123–30.

Chen, C., J. Choi, and S.-C. Chi (2002). "Making justice sense of local-expatriate compensation disparity: Mitigation by local referents, ideological explanations, and interpersonal sensitivity in China-foreign joint ventures." *Academy of Management Journal* 45(4): 807–17.

Cheung, C., and G. Yong (2006). "Job referral in China: The advantage of strong ties." *Human Relations* 59(6): 847–72.

Child, J. (1969). *British management thought: A critical analysis*. London: Allen & Unwin.

——— (2000). "Theorizing about organization cross-nationally." In *Advances in international comparative management*, Vol. 13., eds. J.L.C. Cheng and R.B. Peterson. Stamford, CT: JAI Press.

Child, J., and D. Faulkner (1998). *Strategies of cooperation: Managing alliances, networks, and joint ventures*. New York: Oxford University Press.

Child, J., D. Faulkner, and R. Pitkethly (2001). *The management of international acquisitions*. Oxford: Oxford University Press.

Child, J., D. Faulkner, and S.B. Tallman (2005). *Cooperative strategy: Managing alliances, networks, and joint ventures.* Oxford: Oxford University Press.

Child, J., and G. Möllering (2003). "Contextual confidence and active trust development in the Chinese business environment." *Organization Science* 14(1): 69–80.

Child, J., and Y. Yan (1998). "National and transnational effects in international business: Indications from Sino-foreign joint ventures." Working paper 31/98. Judge Institute of Management Studies, Cambridge.

Cho, H.-J., and V. Pucik (2005). "Relationship between innovativeness, quality, growth, profitability, and market value." *Strategic Management Journal* 26(3): 555–75.

Chong, L.B. (2013). *Managing a Chinese partner: Insights from four global companies.* Basingstoke: Palgrave-Macmillan.

Christensen, C.M. (1997). *The innovator's dilemma: When new technologies cause great firms to fail.* Boston, MA: Harvard Business School Press.

Christensen, C.M., R. Alton, C. Rising, and M. Waldeck (2011). "The new M&A playbook." *Harvard Business Review* 89(March): 44–57.

Chu, W. (1996). "The human side of examining a foreign target." *Mergers and Acquisitions* 30(4): 35–9.

Chua, C.H., H-P. Engeli, and G. Stahl (2005). "Creating a new identity and high performance culture at Novartis: The role of leadership and human resource management." In *Mergers and acquisitions: Managing culture and human resources*, eds. G.K. Stahl and M.E. Mendenhall. Palo Alto, CA: Stanford University Press.

Chung, L.H., P.T. Gibbons, and H.P. Schoch (2006). "The management of information and managers in subsidiaries of multinational corporations." *British Journal of Management* 17(2): 153–65.

Chusmir, L.H., and N.T. Frontczak (1990). "International management opportunities for women: Women and men paint different pictures." *International Journal of Management* 7(3): 295–301.

Cialdini, R.B. (2001). *Influence: Science and practice,* 4th ed. Boston, MA: Allyn & Bacon.

Ciceri, H. (2007). "Transnational firms and cultural diversity." In *The Oxford handbook of human resource management*, eds. P. Boxall, J. Purcell, and P. Wright. New York: Oxford University Press.

Clark, T., and G. Mallory (1996). "The cultural relativity of human resource management: Is there a universal model?" In *European human resource management*, ed. T. Clark. Oxford: Blackwell.

Claus, L., and D. Briscoe (2008). "Employee performance management across borders: A review of relevant academic literature." *International Journal of Management Reviews* 10(2): 175–96.

Cleveland, J.N., Z.S. Byrne, and T.M. Cavanagh (2015). "The future of HR is RH: Respect for humanity at work." *Human Resource Management Review* 25(2): 146–61.

Coase, R.H. (1937). "The nature of the firm." *Economica* 4(November): 386–405.

Coens, T., and M. Jenkins (2000). *Abolishing performance appraisals: Why they backfire and what to do instead.* San Francisco: Berrett-Koehler.

Coff, R.W., D.C. Coff, and R. Eastvold (2006). "The knowledge-leveraging paradox: How to achieve scale without making knowledge imitable." *Academy of Management Review* 31(2): 452–65.

Cohen, J. (1992). "Foreign advisors and capacity building: The case of Kenya." *Public Administration & Development* 12(5): 493–510.

Cohen, W., and D. Levinthal (1990). "Absorptive capacity: A new perspective on learning and innovation." *Administrative Science Quarterly* 35(1): 128–52.

Cole, R.E. (2011). "What really happened to Toyota." *MIT Sloan Management Review* 52(4): 29–35.

Cole, R.E., and D.R. Deskins, Jr. (1988). "Racial factors in site location and employment patterns of Japanese auto firms in America." *California Management Review* 31(1): 9–22.

Collings, D.G., A. McDonnell, and A. McCarter (2014). "Types of international assignees." In *The Routledge companion to international human resource management*, eds. D.G. Collings, G.T. Wood, and P.M. Caligiuri. New York: Routledge.

Collins, J.C. (2001). *Good to great: Why some companies make the leap… and others don't.* New York: Harper Business.

Collings, D., and K. Mellahi (2009). "Strategic talent management: A review and research agenda." *Human Resource Management Review* 19: 304–313.

Collings, D.G., H. Scullion, and M.J. Morley (2007). "Changing patterns of global staffing in the multinational enterprise: Challenges to the conventional expatriate assignment and emerging alternatives." *Journal of World Business* 42(2): 198–213.

Collins, J.C., and J.I. Porras (1994). *Built to last.* New York: HarperBusiness.

Combs, J., Y. Liu, A. Hall, and D. Ketchen (2006). "How much do high-performance work practices matter? A meta-analysis of their effects on organizational performance." *Personnel Psychology* 59(3): 501–28.

Conger, J.A. (1998). "The necessary art of persuasion." *Harvard Business Review* (May–June): 84–95.

Conger, J.A., and B. Benjamin (1999). *Building leaders: How successful companies develop the next generation.* San Francisco: Jossey-Bass.

Conger, J.A., and B. Fishel (2007). "Accelerating leadership performance at the top: Lessons from the Bank of America's executive on-boarding process." *Human Resource Management Review* 17(4): 442–54.

Contractor, F.J., and P. Lorange (1988). "Why should firms cooperate? The strategy and economics basis for cooperative ventures." In *Cooperative strategies in international business*, eds. F.J. Contractor and P. Lorange. Lexington, MA: Lexington Books.

Cook, M. (1999). *Personnel selection: Adding value through people.* Chichester, UK: Wiley.

Cooke, F.L. (2006). "Modeling an HR shared services center: Experience of an MNC in the United Kingdom." *Human Resource Management* 45(2): 211–28.

Correa, C. (2013). *Dream Big: How Jorge Paulo Lemann, Marcel Telles and Beto Sicupira acquired Anheuser-Busch, Burger King and Heinz and revolutionized Brazilian capitalism.* Rio de Janeiro: Sextante.

Crichton, A. (1968). *Personnel management in context.* London: B.T. Batsford.

Cross, R., and L. Prusak (2003). "The political economy of knowledge markets in organizations." In *The Blackwell handbook of organizational learning and knowledge management*, eds. M. Easterby-Smith and M. Lyles. Malden, MA: Blackwell.

Culbert, S.A. (2010). *Get rid of the performance review! How companies can stop intimidating, start managing—and focus on what really matters.* New York: Business Plus.

Currie, G., and M. Kerrin (2003). "Human resource management and knowledge management: Enhancing knowledge sharing in a pharmaceutical company." *International Journal of Human Resource Management* 14(6): 1027–45.

Cyr, D.J. (1995). *The human resource challenge of international joint ventures.* Westport, CT: Quorum Books.

Cyr, D.J., and S.C. Schneider (1996). "Implications for learning: Human resource management in East-West joint ventures." *Organization Studies* 17(2): 207–26.

Darr, E.D., and T.R. Kurtzberg (2000). "An investigation of partner similarity dimensions on knowledge transfer." *Organizational Behavior and Human Decision Processes* 82(1): 28–44.

Davidson Frame, J. (1987). *Managing projects in organizations.* San Francisco: Jossey-Bass.

Davis, S.M., and P.R. Lawrence (1977). *Matrix.* Reading, MA: Addison-Wesley.

De Cieri, H., and P.J. Dowling (1999). "Strategic human resource management in multinational enterprises: Theoretical and empirical developments." In *Strategic human resources management in the twenty-first century*, eds. P.M. Wright, L. Dyer, J.W. Boudreau, and G.T. Milkovich. Stamford, CT: JAI Press.

DeFidelto, C., and I. Slater (2001). "Web-based HR in an international setting." In *Web-based human resources: The technologies that are transforming HR*, ed. A.J. Walker. London: McGraw-Hill.

De Geus, A.P. (1988). "Planning as learning." *Harvard Business Review* (March–April): 70–4.

De Konig, A., P. Verdin, and P. Williamson (1997). "So you want to integrate Europe: How do you manage the process?" *European Management Journal* 15(6): 252–65.

Delany, E. (2000). "Strategic development of the multinational subsidiary through subsidiary initiative-taking." *Long Range Planning* 33(2): 220–44.

Del Canho, D., and J. Engelfriet (2008). "Flying higher together." *Business Strategy Review* 19(1): 34–7.

DeLong, D. (2004). *Lost knowledge: Confronting the threat of an aging workforce*. Oxford: Oxford University Press.

De Meyer, A. (1991). "Tech talk: How managers are stimulating global R&D communication." *MIT Sloan Management Review* 32(3): 49–66.

Deming, W.E. (2000). *Out of the crisis*. Cambridge, MA: MIT Press.

Dendrell, J., N. Arvidsson, and U. Zander (2004). "Managing knowledge in the dark: An empirical study of the reliability of capability evaluation." *Management Science* 50(11): 1491–503.

Deng, P., and M. Yang. (2015). "Cross-border mergers and acquisitions by emerging market firms: A comparative investigation." *International Business Review* 24(1): 157–72.

Denison, D. (1996). "What is the difference between organization culture and organization climate? A native's point of view on a decade of paradigm wars." *Academy of Management Review* 21(3): 619–54.

Denison, D., H.-J. Cho, and J. Young (2000). "Diagnosing organizational cultures: Validating a model and method." Working paper 2000-9. IMD, Lausanne.

Denison, D., R. Hooijberg, N. Lane, and C. Lief (2012). *Leading culture change in global organizations*. San Francisco: Jossey Bass.

Denison, D.R., L.M. Kotrba, and N. Castano (2012). "A cross-cultural perspective on leadership assessment: Comparing 360-degree feedback results from around the world." *Advances in Global Leadership* 7: 205–28.

Denison, D., and C. Lief (2008). "IKEA: Past, present, and future." Case study no. IMD-4-0282. IMD, Lausanne.

Derr, B.C., and G.R. Oddou (1991). "Are U.S. multinationals adequately preparing future American leaders for global competition?" *International Journal of Human Resource Management* 2(2): 227–44.

Dess, G.G., and J.D. Shaw (2001). "Voluntary turnover, social capital, and organizational performance." *Academy of Management Review* 26(3): 446–56.

Dickmann, M., N. Doherty, T. Mills, and C. Brewster (2008). "Why do they go? Individual and corporate perspectives on the factors influencing an international assignment." *International Journal of Human Resource Management* 19(4): 731–51.

Dickmann, M., and H. Harris (2005). "Developing career capital for global careers: The role of international assignments." *Journal of World Business* 40(4): 399–408.

Dierickx, I., and K. Cool (1989). "Asset stock accumulation and competitive advantage." *Management Science* 35(12): 1504–11.

DiMaggio, P.J., and W.W. Powell (1983). "The iron cage revisited: Institutional isomorphism and collective rationality." *American Sociological Review* 38(2): 147–60.

Ding, X.H., R.H. Huang, and D.L. Liu (2012). "Resource allocation for open and hidden learning in learning alliances." *Asia Pacific Journal of Management* 29(1): 103–27.

Dodd, D., and K. Favaro (2007). *The three tensions: Winning the struggle to perform without compromise*. New York: Wiley.

Doh, J.P., S.A. Stumpf, W. Tymon, and M. Haid (2008). "How to manage talent in fast-moving labor markets: Some findings from India." Working paper. Villanova School of Business, Villanova, PA.

Donaldson, L. (1995). *American anti-management theories of organization: A critique of paradigm proliferation*. Cambridge: Cambridge University Press.

Donnelly, T., D. Morris, and T. Donnelly (2005). "Renault-Nissan: A marriage of necessity." *European Business Review* 17(5): 428–40.

Doorewaard, H., and H.E. Meihuizen (2000). "Strategic performance options in professional service organisations." *Human Resource Management Journal* 10(2): 39–57.

Doornik, K., and J. Roberts (2001). "Nokia Corporation: Innovation and efficiency in a high-growth global firm." Case study no. S-IB 23. Graduate School of Business, Stanford University.

Dore, R. (1973). *British factory, Japanese factory: The origins of national diversity in industrial relations.* Berkeley, CA: University of California Press.

Dottlich, D.L., J.L. Noel, and N. Walker (2004). *Leadership passages: The personal and professional transitions that make or break a leader.* San Francisco: Jossey-Bass.

Dougherty, D. (1996). "Organizing for innovation." In *Handbook of organization studies,* eds. S.R. Clegg, C. Hardy, and W.R. Nord. London and Thousand Oaks, CA: Sage.

Dowling, P.J., and R.S. Schuler (1990). *International dimensions of human resource management.* Boston, MA: PWS-Kent.

Dowling, P.J., and D.E. Welch (2005). *International human resource management: Managing people in a multinational context,* 4th ed. Mason, OH: Thomson South-Western College Publishing.

Doz, Y., C.A. Bartlett, and C.K. Prahalad (1981). "Global competitive pressures and host country demands." *California Management Review* 23(3): 63–74.

Doz, Y., and G. Hamel (1998). *Alliance advantage: The art of creating value through partnering.* Boston, MA: Harvard Business School Press.

Doz, Y., and M. Kosonen (2008). *Fast strategy: How strategic agility will help you stay ahead of the game.* Harlow, UK: Wharton School Publishing; New York: Wharton School Publishing/Pearson Education.

Doz, Y., and C.K. Prahalad (1984). "Patterns of strategic control within multinational corporations." *Journal of International Business Studies* 15(2): 55–72.

——— (1986). "Controlled variety: A challenge for human resource management in the MNC." *Human Resource Management* 25(1): 55–71.

——— (1988). "A process model of strategic redirection in large complex firms: The case of multinational corporations." In *The management of strategic change,* ed. A.M. Pettigrew. Oxford: Basil Blackwell.

Doz, Y., J. Santos, and P. Williamson (2001). *From global to metanational: How companies win in the knowledge economy.* Boston, MA: Harvard Business School Press.

Drucker, P. (1996). "Foreword." In *The leader of the future,* eds. F. Hesselbein, M. Goldsmith, and R. Beckhard. San Francisco: Jossey-Bass.

Duarte, D., and N.T. Snyder (2006). *Mastering virtual teams: Strategies, tools and techniques that succeed.* San Francisco: Wiley.

DuBois, C.L.Z., and D.A. DuBois (2012). "Strategic HRM as social design for environmental sustainability in organization." *Human Resource Management* 51(6): 799–826.

Duhaime, I.M., and C.R. Schwenk (1985). "Conjectures on cognitive simplification in acquisition and divestment decision making." *Academy of Management Review* 10(2): 287–95.

Duncan, G.J. (1976). "Earnings functions and nonpecuniary benefits." *Journal of Human Resources* 11(4): 462–83.

Dunning, J.H. (1988). *Explaining international production.* London: Unwin Hyman.

Dyer, J.H., H.B. Gregersen, and C.M. Christensen (2008). "Entrepreneur behaviors, opportunity recognition, and the origins of innovative ventures." *Strategic Entrepreneurship Journal* 2(4): 317–38.

Dyer, J.H., P. Kale, and H. Singh (2004). "When to ally and when to acquire." *Harvard Business Review* (July–August): 108–15.

Easterby-Smith, M., and M.A. Lyles (2003). "The political economy of knowledge markets in organizations." In *The Blackwell handbook of organizational learning and knowledge management*, eds. M. Easterby-Smith and M.A. Lyles. Malden, MA: Blackwell.

Eccles, R.G., and D.B. Crane (1987). *Doing deals: Investment banks at work.* Boston, MA: Harvard Business School Press.

Eddy, J., S. Hall, and S. Robinson (2006). "How global organizations develop local talent." *McKinsey Quarterly* 3: 6–8.

Edström, A., and J.R. Galbraith (1977). "Transfer of managers as a coordination and control strategy in multinational organizations." *Administrative Science Quarterly* 22(2): 248–63.

Egan, M.L., and M. Bendick, Jr. (2003). "Workforce diversity initiatives of U.S. multinational corporations in Europe." *Thunderbird International Business Review* 45(6): 701–27.

Egelhoff, W.G. (1988). "Strategy and structure in multinational corporations: A revision of the Stopford and Wells model." *Strategic Management Journal* 9(1): 1–14.

Eisenhardt, K.M., and D.C. Galunic (2000). "Coevolving: At last, a way to make synergies work." *Harvard Business Review* (January–February): 91–101.

Eisenhardt, K.M., J.L. Kahwajy, and L.J. Bourgeois (1997). "How management teams can have a good fight." *Harvard Business Review* (July–August): 77–85.

Eisenhardt, K.M., and M. Zbaracki (1992). "Strategic decision making." *Strategic Management Journal* 13(Winter Special Issue): 17–37.

Elkington, J. (1997). *Cannibals with forks: The triple bottom line of 21st century business.* Oxford, UK: Capstone.

Ellis, F. (2000). *Rural livelihoods and diversity in developing countries.* Oxford and New York: Oxford University Press.

Ellis, K.M., T.H. Reus, and B.T. Lamont (2009). "The effects of procedural and informational justice in the integration of related firms." *Strategic Management Journal* 30(1): 137–61.

Epstein, M.J. (2004). "The drivers of success in post-merger integration." *Organizational Dynamics* 33(2): 174–89.

Erickson, T.J., and L. Gratton (2007). "What it means to work here." *Harvard Business Review* (March): 104–14.

Ertug, G., I.R. Cuypers, N.G. Noorderhaven, and B.M. Bensaou (2013). "Trust between international joint venture partners: Effects of home countries." *Journal of International Business Studies* 44(3): 263–82.

Evans, P.A.L. (1974). "The price of success: Accommodation to conflicting needs in managerial careers." Unpublished doctoral dissertation. Alfred P. Sloan School of Management, MIT, Boston.

——— (1992). "Developing leaders and managing development." *European Journal of Management* 10(1): 1–9.

——— (1993). "Dosing the Glue: Applying human resource technology to build the global organization." In *Research in personnel and human resources management*, Vol. 3, eds. B. Shaw and P. Kirkbride. Greenwich, CT: JAI Press.

——— (1994). "The paradoxes of a world where solutions are looking for problems." *EFMD Forum* 94(3): 67–74.

——— (2000). "The dualistic leader: Thriving on paradox." In *Management 21C,* ed. S. Chowdhury. London: Financial Times/Prentice Hall.

Evans, P.A.L., and F. Bartolomé (1979). *Must success cost so much?* London: Grant McIntyre; New York: Basic Books.

Evans, P.A.L., and Y. Doz (1989). "The dualistic organization." In *Human resource management in international firms: Change, globalization, innovation*, eds. P.A.L. Evans, Y. Doz, and A. Laurent. London: Macmillan.

——— (1992). "Dualities: A paradigm for human resource and organizational development in complex multinationals." In *Globalizing management: Creating and leading the competitive organization*, eds. V. Pucik, N.M. Tichy, and C.K. Barnett. New York: Wiley.

Evans, P.A.L., and M. Engsbye (2003). "Danmark og danskerne foran den globale udfordring." In *Den Globale Udfordring*, eds. P.A.L. Evans, V. Pucik, J.-L. Barsoux, and M. Engsbye. Copenhagen: JP-Boeger.

Evans, P.A.L., and N. Génadry (1998). "A duality-based prospective for strategic human resource management." In *Research in personnel and human resources management, Supplement 4: Strategic human resources management in the twenty-first century*, eds. L.D. Dyer, P.M. Wright, J.W. Boudreau, and G.T. Milkovich. Stamford, CT: JAI Press.

Evans, P.A.L., and P. Lorange (1989). "The two logics behind human resource management." In *Human resource management in international firms: Change, globalization, innovation*, eds. P.A.L. Evans, Y. Doz, and A. Laurent. London: Macmillan.

Evans, P.A.L., V. Pucik, and I. Björkman (2011). *The global challenge: International human resource management*, 2nd ed. Chicago: McGraw-Hill.

Evans, P.A.L., and A. Wittenberg (1986). "Apple Computers Europe." INSEAD case series, Fontainebleau. Reprinted in *Transnational management: Text, cases, and readings in cross-border management*, eds. C.A. Bartlett and S. Ghoshal. Homewood, IL: Irwin, 1992.

Farndale, E., and J. Paauwe (2007). "Uncovering competitive and institutional drivers of HRM practices in multinational corporations." *Human Resource Management Journal* 17(4): 355–75.

Farrell, D., M. Laboissière, and J. Rosenfeld (2006). "Sizing the merging global labor market: Rational behavior from both companies and countries can help it work more efficiently." *Academy of Management Perspectives* 20(4): 23–34.

Faulkner, D., R. Pitkethly, and J. Child (2002). "International mergers and acquisitions in the UK 1985–94: A comparison of national HRM practices." *International Journal of Human Resource Management* 13(1): 106–22.

Fecheyr-Lippens, B., B. Schaninger, and K. Tanner (2015). "Power to the new people analytics." *McKinsey Quarterly*, March 2015.

Feldman, D.C., and M.C. Bolino (1999). "The impact of on-site mentoring on expatriate socialization: A structural equation modelling approach." *International Journal of Human Resource Management* 10(1): 54–71.

Ferencikova, S., and V. Pucik (1999). "Whirlpool Corporation: Entering Slovakia." Case study no. IMD-3-0796. IMD, Lausanne.

Fernandez, J.A., and L. Underwood (2006). *CEO voices of experience from 20 international business leaders*. Singapore: Wiley.

Ferner, A., and P. Almond (2013). "Performance and reward practices in foreign multinationals in the UK." *Human Resource Management Journal* 23(3): 241–61.

Ferner, A., P. Almond, I. Clark, T. Colling, T. Edwards, L. Holden, and M. Muller-Camen (2004)."The dynamics of central control and subsidiary autonomy in the management of human resources: Case study evidence from US MNCs in the UK." *Organization Studies* 25(3): 363–91.

Ferner, A., P. Almond, and T. Colling (2005). "Institutional theory and the cross-national transfer of employment policy: The case of 'workforce diversity' in US multinationals." *Journal of International Business Studies* 36(3): 304–21.

Ferner, A., and J. Quintanilla (1998). "Multinationals, national business systems and HRM: The enduring influence of national identity or a process of 'Anglo-Saxonization.'" *International Journal of Human Resource Management* 9(4): 710–31.

Ferrazi, K. (2014). "Getting virtual teams right." *Harvard Business Review* 92: 120–3.

Festing, M., J. Eidems, and S. Royer (2007). "Strategic issues and local constraints in transnational compensation strategies: An analysis of cultural, institutional and political influences." *European Management Journal* 25(2): 118–31.

Festing, M., L. Knappert, P.J. Dowling, and A.D. Engle (2012). "Global performance management in MNEs—Conceptualization and profiles of country-specific characteristics in China, Germany, and the United States." *Thunderbird International Business Review* 54(6): 825–43.

Festing, M., L. Knappert, and A. Kornau (2015). "Gender-specific preferences in global performance management: An empirical study of male and female managers in a multinational context." *Human Resource Management* 54(1): 55–79.

Fey, C.F., and P.W. Beamish (2001). "The importance of organizational climate similarity between parent firms and the JV: The case of IJVs in Russia." *Organization Studies* 22(5): 853–82.

Fey, C., P. Engström, and I. Björkman (1999). "Doing business in Russia: Effective human resource management practices for foreign firms in Russia." *Organizational Dynamics* (Autumn): 69–80.

Fine, C.H. (1998). *Clockspeed: Winning industry control in the age of temporary advantage.* Reading, MA: Perseus Books.

Fiol, C.M. (2002). "Capitalizing on paradox: The role of language in transforming organizational identities." *Organization Science* 13(6): 653–66.

Firth, B.M., G. Chen, B.L. Kirkman, and K. Kim (2014). "Newcomers abroad: Expatriate adaptation during early phases of international assignments." *Academy of Management Journal* 57(1): 280–300.

Flamholtz, E.G. (2005). "Human resource accounting, human capital management, and the bottom line." In *The future of human resource management*, eds. M. Losey, S. Meisinger, and D. Ulrich. Hoboken, NJ: Wiley.

Flannery, T.P., D.A. Hofrichter, and P.E. Platten (1996). *People, performance, and pay: Dynamic compensation for changing organizations.* New York: Free Press.

Fleming, M., and M. Marx (2006). "Managing creativity in small worlds." *California Management Review* 48(4): 6–27.

Fombrun, C., N.M. Tichy, and M.A. Devanna (1984). *Strategic human resource management.* New York: Wiley.

Fonti, F., and M. Maoret (2015). "The direct and indirect effects of core and peripheral social capital on organizational performance." *Strategic Management Journal.* DOI: 10.1002/smj.2409.

Ford, R., and W. Randolph (1992). "Cross-functional structures: A review and integration of matrix organization and project management." *Journal of Management* 18(2): 267–94.

Forster, N. (1997). "The persistent myth of high expatriate failure rates: A reappraisal." *International Journal of Human Resource Management* 3(4): 414–34.

Francis, I., V. Pucik, K. Xin, and L. Shengjun (2004). "Michelin China." Case study no. CC-403-021. China Europe International Business School (CEIBS), Shanghai.

Fraser, M., and S. Dutta (2008). *Throwing sheep in the boardroom: How online social networking will transform your life, work and world.* San Francisco: Jossey-Bass.

Freeman, R.B. (2010). "Globalization of scientific and engineering talent: International mobility of students, workers, and ideas in the world economy." *Economics of Innovation and New Technology* 19(5): 393–406.

Friedman, T.L. (2005). *The world is flat: A brief history of the twenty-first century.* New York: Farrar, Straus and Giroux.

Friedmann, J. (2007). "The wealth of cities: Towards an assets-based development of newly urbanizing regions." *Development and Change* 38(6): 987–98.

Froese, F.J., and L.G. Goeritz (2007). "Integration management of Western acquisitions in Japan." *Journal of Asian Business & Management* 6(1): 95–114.

Froese, F.J., Y.S. Pak, and L.C. Chong (2008). "Managing the human side of cross-border acquisitions in South Korea." *Journal of World Business* 43(1): 97–108.

Frost, T.S., J.M. Birkinshaw, and P.C. Ensign (2002). "Centers of excellence in multinational corporations." *Strategic Management Journal* 23(11): 997–1018.

Fryxell, G.E., J. Butler, and A. Choi (2004). "Successful localization programs in China: An important element in strategy implementation." *Journal of World Business* 39(3): 268–82.

Fubini, D., C. Price, and M. Zollo (2006). *Mergers: Leadership, performance and corporate health*. New York: Palgrave Macmillan.

Furuya, N., M.J. Stevens, A. Bird, G. Oddou, and M. Mendenhall (2009). "Managing the learning and transfer of global management compentence: Antecedents and outcomes of Japanese repatriation effectiveness." *Journal of International Business Studies* 40(2): 200–15.

Gabor, A. (1990). *The man who discovered quality*. New York: Times Books.

Galbraith, J.R. (1977). *Organization design*. Reading, MA: Addison-Wesley.

—— (2000). *Designing the global corporation*. San Francisco: Jossey-Bass.

—— (2002). "Organizing to deliver solutions." *Organizational Dynamics* 31(2): 194–207.

—— (2009). *Designing matrix organizations that actually work*. San Francisco: Jossey-Bass.

—— (2011). *Designing the customer-centric organization: A guide to strategy, structure, and process*. New York: John Wiley & Sons.

——. (2014). *Designing organizations: Strategy, structure, and process at the business unit and enterprise levels*. New York: John Wiley & Sons.

Galbraith, J.R., and D.A. Nathanson (1979). "The role of organizational structure and process in strategy implementation." In *Strategic management*, eds. D.E. Schendel, and C.W. Hofer. Boston, MA: Little Brown.

Galunic, C.D., and E. Andersen (2000). "From security to mobility: Generalized investments in human capital and commitment." *Organization Science* 11(1): 1–20.

Galunic, C.D., and K.M. Eisenhardt (2001). "Architectural innovation and modular corporate forms." *Academy of Management Journal* 44(6): 1229–50.

Galunic, C.D., and S. Rodan (1998). "Resource recombinations in the firm: Knowledge structures and the potential for Schumpeterian innovation." *Strategic Management Journal* 19(12): 1193–201.

Garette, B., and P. Dussauge (2000). "Alliances versus acquisitions: Choosing the right option." *European Management Journal* 18(1): 63–9.

Gelens, J., J. Hofmans, N. Dries, and R. Pepermans (2014). "Talent management and organisational justice: Employee reactions to high potential identification." *Human Resource Management Journal* 24(2): 159–75.

Gelfand, M., and J.M. Brett (2004). *The handbook of negotiation and culture*. Stanford, CA: Stanford University Press.

George, C.S. (1968). *The history of management thought*. Englewood Cliffs, NJ: Prentice Hall.

Gerhart, B., and M. Fang (2005). "National culture and human resource management: Assumptions and evidence." *International Journal of Human Resource Management* 16(6): 971–86.

Geringer, M.J., and C.A. Frayne (1990). "Human resource management and international joint venture control: A parent company perspective." *Management International Review* 30(Special Issue): 103–20.

Gerstner, L.V. (2002). *Who says elephants can't dance? Inside IBM's historic turnaround*. New York: Harper Business.

Ghemawat, P. (2007). *Redefining global strategy: Crossing borders in a world where differences still matter*. Boston, MA: Harvard Business School Press.

Ghoshal, S., and C.A. Bartlett (1997). *The individualized corporation*. New York: Harper Business.

—— (1998). *Managing across borders: The transnational solution*, 2nd ed. London: Random House.

—— (2000). "Rebuilding behavioral context: A blueprint for corporate renewal." In *Breaking the code of change*, eds. M. Beer and N. Nohria. Boston, MA: Harvard Business School Press.

Ghoshal, S., and L. Gratton (2002). "Integrating the enterprise." *MIT Sloan Management Review* 44(1): 31–8.

Ghoshal, S., and N. Nohria (1987). "Multinational corporations as differentiated networks." Working paper no. 87/13. INSEAD, Fontainebleau.

Gibbs, J.L., and M. Boyraz (2014). "International HRM's role in managing global teams." In *The Routledge companion to international human resource management*, eds. D.G. Collings, G.T. Wood, and P.M. Caligiuri, London: Routledge.

Gibbs, T., S. Heywood, and L. Weiss (2012). "Organizing for an emerging world." *McKinsey Quarterly* (June).

Gibson, C.B., L. Huang, B.L. Kirkman, and D.L. Shapiro (2014). "Where global and virtual meet: The value of examining the intersection of these elements in twenty-first-century teams." *Annual Review of Organizational Psychology and Organizational Behavior* 1: 217–44.

Gibson, C.B., and B.L. Kirkman (1999). "Our past, present, and future in teams: The role of human resource professionals in managing team performance." In *Evolving practices in human resource management: Responding to the changing world of work*, eds. A.I. Kraut, and A.K. Korman. San Francisco: Jossey-Bass.

Gilbert, J.A., and J.M. Ivancevich (2000). "Valuing diversity: A tale of two organizations." *Academy of Management Executive* 14(1): 93–105.

Gill, C. (2012). "The role of leadership in successful international mergers and acquisitions: Why Renault-Nissan succeeded and DaimlerChrysler-Mitsubishi failed." *Human Resource Management* 51(3): 433–56.

Gittell, J.H. (2000). "Paradox of coordination and control." *California Management Review* 42(3): 101–17.

Gladwell, M. (2000). *The tipping point: How little things can make a big difference*. New York: Little Brown.

Glaister, A.J. (2014). "HR outsourcing: The impact on HR role, competency development and relationships." *Human Resource Management Journal* 24(2): 211–26.

Gluesing, J.G., and C.B. Gibson (2004). "Designing and forming global teams." In *The Blackwell handbook of global management: A guide to managing complexity*, eds. H.W. Lane, M.L. Maznevski, M.E. Mendenhall, and J. McNett. Oxford: Blackwell Publishing.

Godart, F., W. Maddux, A. Shipilov, and A. Galinsky (2015). "Fashion with a foreign flair: Professional experiences abroad facilitate the creative innovations of organizations." *Academy of Management Journal* 58(1): 195–220.

Goffee, R., and G. Jones (1998). *The character of a corporation: How your company's culture can make or break your business*. New York: HarperBusiness.

Golden, K.A., and V. Ramanujam (1985). "Between a dream and a nightmare: On the integration of human resource management and strategic business planning processes." *Human Resource Management* 24(4): 429–52.

Goldsmith, M., L. Lyons, and A. Freas (2000). *Coaching for leadership*. San Francisco: Jossey-Bass/Pfeiffer.

Goleman, D. (1995). *Emotional intelligence*. London: Bloomsbury.

——— (2000). "Leadership that gets results." *Harvard Business Review* (March–April): 78–90.

Goleman, D., R. Boyatzis, and A. McKee (2002a). "The emotional reality of teams." *Journal of Organizational Excellence* 21(2): 55–65.

——— (2002b). *Primal leadership: Learning to lead with emotional intelligence*. Boston, MA: Harvard Business School Press.

Gomes-Casseres, B. (1988). "Joint venture cycles: The evolution of ownership strategies of U.S. MNEs, 1945–75." In *Cooperative strategies in international business*, eds. F.J. Contractor and P. Lorange. Lexington, MA: Lexington Books.

González, S.M., and D.V. Tacorante (2004). "A new approach to the best practices debate: Are best practices applied to all employees in the same way?" *International Journal of Human Resource Management* 15(1): 56–75.

Goodall, K., and M. Warner (1997). "The evolving image of HRM in the Chinese workplace: Comparing Sino-foreign joint ventures and state-owned enterprises in Beijing and Shanghai." Paper presented at the LVMH Conference, February 7–8. INSEAD, Fontainebleau.

Gooderham, P.N., O. Nordhaug, and K. Ringdal (1999). "Institutional and rational determinants of organizational practices: Human resource management in European firms." *Adminstrative Science Quarterly* 44(3): 507–31.

Goold, M., and A. Campbell (1987). *Strategies and styles: The role of the centre in managing diversified corporations.* Oxford: Basil Blackwell.

——— (1998). "Desperately seeking synergy." *Harvard Business Review* (September–October): 131–43.

Goss, T., R. Pascale, and A. Athos (1993). "The reinvention roller coaster: Risking the present for a powerful future." *Harvard Business Review* (November–December): 97–108.

Govindarajan, V., and C. Trimble (2010). *The other side of innovation: Solving the execution challenge.* Boston, MA: Harvard Business School Pub.

Granovetter, M. (1973). "The strength of weak ties." *American Journal of Sociology* 78(6): 1360–80.

Grant, R.M. (1996). "Toward a knowledge-based theory of the firm." *Strategic Management Journal* 17(Winter Special Issue): 109–22.

——— (2013). "The development of knowledge management in the oil and gas industry." *Universia Business Review* 40: 92–125.

Gratton, L. (2000). *Living strategy: Putting people at the heart of corporate purpose.* London: Financial Times Prentice Hall.

Gratton, L., and S. Ghoshal (2002). "Improving the quality of conversations." *Organizational Dynamics* 31(3): 209–24.

——— (2003). "Managing personal human capital: New ethos for the 'volunteer' employee." *European Management Journal* 21(1): 1–10.

Gratton, L., V. Hope-Hailey, P. Stiles, and C. Truss (1999a). *Strategic human resource management.* London : Oxford University Press.

——— (1999b). "Linking individual performance to business strategy: The people process model." *Human Resource Management* 38(1): 17–31.

Gregersen, H.B., and J.S. Black (1992). "Antecedents to commitment to a parent company and a foreign operation." *Academy of Management Journal* 35(1): 65–90.

——— (1995). "Keeping high performers after international assignments: A key to global executive development." *Journal of International Management* 1(1): 3–31.

Gregersen, H.B., J.S. Black, and J.M. Hite (1995). "Expatriate performance appraisal: Principles, practices, and challenges." In *Expatriate management: New ideas for international business*, ed. J. Selmer. Westport, CT: Quorum Books.

Gregersen, H.B., J.M. Hite, and J.S. Black (1996). "Expatriate performance appraisal in U.S. multinational firms." *Journal of International Business Studies* 27(4): 711–38.

Gregersen, H.B., A.J. Morrison, and S. Black (1998). "Developing leaders for the global frontier." *MIT Sloan Management Review* (Fall): 2–32.

Greiner, L.E. (1972). "Evolution and revolution as organizations grow." *Harvard Business Review* (July–August): 37–46.

Greller, M., and D.M. Rousseau (1994). "Guest editors' overview: Psychological contracts and human resource practices." *Human Resource Management* 33(3): 383–4.

Griffeth, R.W., P.W. Hom, and S. Gaertner (2000). "A meta-analysis of antecedents and correlates of employee turnover: Update, moderator tests, and research implications for the next millennium." *Journal of Management* 26(3): 463–8.

Grote, D. (2000). "The secrets of performance appraisal: Best practices from the masters." *Across the Board* (May): 14–20.

Groysberg, B., and R. Abrahams (2006). "Lift outs: How to acquire a high-functioning team." *Harvard Business Review* (December): 133–40.

Guest, D.E. (1990). "Human resource management and the American dream." *Journal of Management Studies* 27(4): 377–97.

Guest, D., and A. Bos-Nehles (2013). "Human resource management and performance: The role of effective implementation." In *Human resource management and performance: Building the evidence base*, eds. D. Guest, J. Paauwe, and P. Wright. San Francisco: Wiley.

Guest, D.E., and N. Conway (2002). "Communicating the psychological contract: An employer perspective." *Human Resource Management Journal* 12(2): 22–38.

Guest, D.E., J. Michie, N. Conway, and M. Sheenan (2003). "Human resource management and corporate performance in the UK." *British Journal of Industrial Relations* 41(2): 291–314.

Guillen, L., and H. Ibarra (2009). "Seasons of a leader's development: Beyond a one-size fits all approach to designing interventions." *Academy of Management Proceedings*: 1–6.

Gulati, R., A.B. Wagonfeld, and L. Silvestri (2014). "Cisco in 2012: Reorganizing for efficiency and flexibility." Harvard Business School Case 9-413-069, Boston.

Gupta, A.K., and V. Govindarajan (2000). "Knowledge flows within multinational corporations." *Strategic Management Journal* 21(4): 473–96.

Gupta, A.K., V. Govindarajan, and H. Wang (1996). "Exploring internal stickiness: Impediments to the transfer of best practice within the firm." *Strategic Management Journal* 17(Winter Special Issue): 27–43.

——— (2008). *The quest for global dominance.* San Francisco: Jossey-Bass.

Gupta, S., and D. Shapiro (2014). "Building and transforming an emerging market global enterprise: Lessons from the Infosys journey." *Business Horizons* 57(2): 169–79.

Guthridge, M., A.B. Komm, and E. Lawson (2008). "Making talent a strategic priority." *McKinsey Quarterly* (1): 49–59.

Guthrie, J.P. (2001). "High-involvement work practices, turnover, and productivity: Evidence from New Zealand." *Academy of Management Journal* 44(1): 180–90.

Haasen, A. (1996). "Opel Eisenach GmbH: Creating a high-productivity workplace." *Organizational Dynamics* 24(4): 80–5.

Hailey, J. (1993). "Localisation and expatriation: The continuing role of expatriates in developing countries." Working paper 18/93. Cranfield School of Management, UK.

——— (1996). "The expatriate myth: Cross-cultural perceptions of expatriate managers." *The International Executive* 38(2): 255–71.

Hailey, J., and W. Harry (2008). "Localization: A strategic response to globalization." In *International human resource management: A European perspective*, eds. M. Dickmann, C. Brewster, and P. Sparrow. London: Routledge.

Hall, E.T., and M.R. Hall (1990). *Understanding cultural differences: Germans, French, and Americans.* Yarmouth, ME: Intercultural Press.

Hamel, G. (1991). "Competition for competence and inter-partner learning within international strategic alliances." *Strategic Management Journal* 12(Summer Special Issue): 83–103.

Hamel, G., Y. Doz, and C.K. Prahalad (1989). "Collaborate with your competitors—and win." *Harvard Business Review* (January–February): 133–9.

Hamel, G., and C.K. Prahalad (1994). *Competing for the future.* Boston, MA: Harvard Business School Press.

Hamilton, S., and J. Zhang (2008). "Danone & Wahaha: A bitter-sweet partnership." Case study no. IMD-3-1949. IMD, Lausanne.

Hampden-Turner, C. (1990a). *Charting the corporate mind: From dilemma to strategy.* Oxford: Basil Blackwell.

———— (1990b). *Corporate culture: From vicious circles to virtuous circles*. London: Hutchinson/Economist Books.

Hampden-Turner, C., and F. Trompenaars (1993). *The seven cultures of capitalism*. New York: Currency Doubleday.

———— (2000). *Building cross-cultural competence*. New Haven: Yale University Press.

Handfield-Jones, H. (2000). "How executives grow." *McKinsey Quarterly* (1): 117–23.

Handy, C. (1998). *The hungry spirit: Beyond capitalism—a quest for purpose in the modern world*. London: Arrow Books.

Hannan, M.T., and J. Freeman (1989). *Organizational ecology*. Cambridge, MA: Harvard University Press.

Hansen, M.T. (2009). *Collaboration: How leaders avoid the traps, create unity, and reap big results*. Boston, MA: Harvard Business School Press.

Hansen, M.T., and J. Birkinshaw (2007). "The innovation value chain." *Harvard Business Review* (June): 121–30.

Hansen, M.T., M.L. Mors, and B. Løvås (2005). "Knowledge sharing in. organizations: Multiple networks, multiple phases." *Academy of Management Journal* 48(5): 776–93.

Hansen, M.T., and N. Nohria (2004). "How to build collaborative advantage." *MIT Sloan Management* Review 46(1): 22–30.

Hansen, M.T., N. Nohria, and T. Tierney (1999). "What's your strategy for managing knowledge?" *Harvard Business Review* (March–April): 106–16.

Hansen, M.T., and B. von Oetinger (2001). "Introducing T-shaped managers: Knowledge management's next generation." *Harvard Business Review* (March): 107–16.

Harding, D., and Rouse, T. (2007). "Human due diligence." *Harvard Business Review* (April): 124–31.

Harrigan, K. (1988). "Strategic alliances and partner asymmetries." *Management International Review* 28(Special Issue): 53–72.

Harris, H. (1999). "Women in international management: Why are they not selected?" In *International HRM: Contemporary issues in Europe*, eds. C. Brewster and H. Harris. London: Routledge.

Harris, H., and C. Brewster (1999). "An integrative framework for pre-departure preparation." In *International HRM: Contemporary issues in Europe*, eds. C. Brewster and H. Harris. London: Routledge.

Hart, S.L., and R.E. Quinn (1993). "Roles executives play: CEOs, behavioral complexity, and firm performance." *Human Relations* 46(5): 543–74.

Harvey, M. (1997). "Dual-career expatriates: Expectations, adjustment and satisfaction with international relocation." *Journal of International Business Studies* 28(3): 627–58.

Harvey, M., C. Speier, and M.M. Novicevic (1999). "The role of inpatriates in a globalization strategy and challenges associated with the inpatriation process." *Human Resource Planning* 22(1): 38–50.

Harzing, A.-W. (1995). "The persistent myth of high expatriate failure rates." *International Journal of Human Resource Management* 6(2): 457–74.

———— (1999). *Managing the multinationals: An international study of control mechanisms*. Cheltenham, UK: Edward Elgar.

———— (2001). "Of bears, bumble-bees, and spiders: The role of expatriates in controlling foreign subsidiaries." *Journal of World Business* 36(4): 366–79.

Harzing, A.-W., and M. Pudelko (2007). "HRM practices in subsidiaries of US, Japanese and German MNCs: Country-of-origin, localization or dominance effect?" *Human Resource Management* 46(4): 535–59.

Haslberger, A., and C. Brewster (2009). "Capital gains: Expatriate adjustment and the psychological contract in international careers." *Human Resource Management* 48(3): 379–97.

Haspeslagh, P. (2000). "Maintaining momentum in mergers." *European Business Forum* 4 (Winter): 53–6.

Haspeslagh, P.C., and D.B. Jemison (1991). *Managing acquisitions: Creating value through corporate renewal*. New York: Free Press.

Hastings, D.F. (1999). "Lincoln Electric's harsh lessons from international expansion." *Harvard Business Review* (May–June): 162–78.

Hatch, M.J. (1993). "The dynamics of organizational culture." *Academy of Management Review* 18(4): 657–93.

Hauschild, P.R. (1993). "Interorganizational imitation: The impact of interlocks on corporate acquisition activity." *Administrative Science Quarterly* 38(4): 564–92.

Hays, R.D. (1974). "Expatriate selection: Insuring success and avoiding failure." *Journal of International Business Studies* 5(1): 25–37.

Hearn, J., B. Metcalfe, and R. Piekkari (2006). "Gender and international human resource management." In *Handbook of research in international human resource management*, eds. G.K. Stahl and I. Björkman. Cheltenham, UK: Edward Elgar.

Hedberg, B.L.T. (1981). "How organizations learn and unlearn." In *Handbook of organizational design*, eds. P.C. Nystrom and W.H. Starbuck. London: Oxford University Press.

Hedberg, B.L.T., P.C. Nystrom, and W.H. Starbuck (1976). "Camping on seesaws: Prescriptions for a self-designing organization." *Administrative Science Quarterly* 21(1): 41–65.

Hedlund, G. (1986). "The hypermodern MNC: A heterarchy?" *Human Resource Management* (Spring): 9–35.

Hedlund, G., and J. Ridderstraale (1995). "International development projects: Key to competitiveness, impossible, or mismanaged?" *International Studies of Management and Organization* 25(1/2): 158–84.

Heenan, D.A., and W. Bennis (1999). *Co-leaders: The power of great partnerships*. New York: Wiley.

Heifetz, R.A. (1994). *Leadership without easy answers*. Cambridge, MA: Belknap Press of Harvard University Press.

Heimeriks, K.H., C.B. Bingham, and T. Laamanen (2015). "Unveiling the temporally contingent role of codification in alliance success." *Strategic Management Journal* 36(3): 462–73.

Held, D., A. McGrew, D. Goldblatt, and J. Perraton (1999). *Global transformations: Politics, economics, and culture*. Cambridge: Polity Press.

Hennart, J.-F. (1991). "Control in multinational firms: The role of price and hierarchy." *Management International Review* 31(Special Issue): 71–96.

Hergert, M., and D. Morris (1988). "Trends in international collaborative agreements." In *Cooperative strategies in international business*, eds. F.J. Contractor and P. Lorange. Lexington, MA: Lexington Books.

Hieronimus, F., K. Schaefer, and J. Schroder (2005). "Using brand to attract talent." *McKinsey Quarterly* (3): 12–14.

Higgins, M.C., and K.E. Kram (2001). "Reconceptualizing mentoring at work: A developmental network perspective." *Academy of Management Review* 26(2): 264–88.

Hill, L.A. (1992). *Becoming a manager: Mastery of a new identity*. Boston, MA: Harvard Business School Press.

Hinds, P., and D. Bailey (2003). "Out of sight, out of sync: Understanding conflict in distributed teams." *Organization Science* 14(6): 615–32.

Hitt, M.A., J.J. Harrison, and R.D. Ireland (2001). *Mergers & acquisitions: A guide to creating value for stakeholders*. New York: Oxford University Press.

Hitt, M.A., R.E. Hoskisson, R.D. Ireland, and J.J. Harrison (1991). "Are acquisitions a poison pill for innovation?" *Academy of Management Executive* 5(4): 22–34.

Hodgetts, R.M. (1996). "A conversation with Steve Kerr." *Organizational Dynamics* 24(2): 68–79.

Hofstede, G. (1980). "Motivation, leadership and organization: Do American theories apply abroad?" *Organizational Dynamics* (Summer): 42–63.

———— (1991). *Cultures and organizations: Software of the mind*. London: McGraw-Hill.

———— (1999). "Problems remain, but theories will change: The universal and the specific in 21st century global management." *Organizational Dynamics* (Summer): 34–44.

———— (2001). *Culture's consequences. Comparing values, behaviors, institutions, and organizations across nations*, 2nd ed. Beverly Hills and London: Sage.

Holden, N., S. Michailova, and S. Tietze (eds.) (2015). *The Routledge companion to cross-cultural management*. New York: Routledge.

Hollenbeck, G.P., and M.W. McCall (2001). "What makes a successful global executive?" *Business Strategy Review* 12(4): 49–56.

Homburg, C., and M. Bucerius (2006). "Is speed of integration really a success factor of mergers and acquisitions? An analysis of the role of internal and external relatedness." *Strategic Management Journal* 27(4): 347–67.

House, R., P.J. Hanges, M. Javidan, P.W. Dorfman, and V. Gupta (2004). *Culture, leadership and organizations: The GLOBE study of 62 societies*. Thousand Oaks, CA: Sage.

House, R., P.J. Hanges, A. Quintanilla, P.W. Dorfman, M.W. Dickson, M. Javidan *et al.* (1999). "Culture, leadership, and organizational practices." In *Advances in global leadership*, ed. W.H. Mobley. Greenwich, CT: JAI Press.

Hsieh, T., J. Lavoie, and R.A.P. Samek (1999). "Are you taking your expatriate talent seriously?" *McKinsey Quarterly* (3): 71–83.

Human Resource Management International Digest (2007). "Employees come first at high-flying Southwest Airlines: Model contrasts with the Ryanair approach to low-cost aviation." *Emerald/Insight* 15(4): 5–7.

Hunt, J., and P. Boxall (1998). "Are top human resource specialists strategic partners? Self perceptions of a corporate elite." *International Journal of Human Resource Management* 9(5): 767–81.

Huselid, M. (1995). "The impact of human resource management practices on turnover, productivity, and corporate financial performance." *Academy of Management Journal* 38(3): 635–72.

Huselid, M.A., R.W. Beatty, and B.E. Becker (2005). "'A' players or 'A' positions?" *Harvard Business Review* (December): 110–17.

Huselid, M.A., B.E. Becker, and R.W. Beatty (2005). *The workforce scorecard: Managing human capital to execute strategy*. Boston, MA: Harvard Business School Press.

Huselid, M., S.E. Jackson, and R.S. Schuler (1997). "Technical and strategic human resource management effectiveness as determinants of firm performance." *Academy of Management Journal* 40(1): 171–88.

Huston, L., and N. Sakkab (2006). "Connect and develop: Inside Procter & Gamble's new model for innovation." *Harvard Business Review* (March): 58–66.

Huy, Q.N. (2002). "Emotional balancing of organizational continuity and radical change: The contribution of middle managers." *Administrative Science Quarterly* 47(1): 31–69.

———— (2004). "Building emotional capital for strategic renewal: Nissan (1999–2002)." Case study. INSEAD, Fontainebleau.

———— (2005). "An emotion-based view of strategic renewal." *Advances in Strategic Management* 22: 3–37.

Ibarra, H. (1992). "Structural alignments, individual strategies, and managerial action: Elements toward a network theory of getting things done." In *Networks and organizations*, eds. N. Nohria and R.G. Eccles. Boston, MA: Harvard Business School Press.

———— (2000). "Making partner: A mentor's guide to the psychological journey." *Harvard Business Review* (March–April): 146–55.

———— (2015). *Act like a leader, think like a leader*. Boston, MA: Harvard Business School Press.

Ibarra, H., and M. Hunter (2007). "How leaders create and use networks." *Harvard Business Review* (January): 40–7.

Ibarra, H., S. Snook, and L.G. Ramo (2008). "Identity change in transition to leadership roles." Working papers, no. 32. INSEAD, Fontainebleau.

Iles, P. (2007). "Employee resourcing and talent management." In *Human resource management: A critical text*, ed. J. Storey, 3rd ed. London: Thomson Learning.

Imai, M. (1986). *Kaizen: The key to Japan's competitive success*. New York: Random House.

Immelt, J.R., V. Govindarajan, and C. Trimble (2009). "How GE is disrupting itself." *Harvard Business Review* 87(September): 56–65.

Ingham, J. (2007). *Strategic human capital management: Creating value through people*. Oxford: Butterworth-Heinemann.

Inkpen, A.C. (1997). "An examination of knowledge management in international joint venture." In *Cooperative strategies: North American perspectives*, eds. P.W. Beamish and J.P. Killing. San Francisco: New Lexington Press.

—— (1998). "Learning and knowledge acquisition through international strategic alliances." *Academy of Management Executive* 12(4): 69–80.

—— (2005). "Learning through alliances: General Motors and NUMMI." *California Management Review* 47(4): 114–36.

Inkpen, A.C., A.K. Sundaram, and K. Rockwood (2000). "Cross-border acquisitions of U.S. technology assets." *California Management Review* 42(3): 50–71.

Inkpen, A.C., and E.W.K. Tsang (2005). "Social capital, networks, and knowledge transfer." *Academy of Management Review* 30(1): 146–65.

Jackson, S.E., and R. Schuler (1999). *Managing human resources*. Cincinnati, OH: South-Western College Publishing.

Jacoby, S.M. (1985). *Employing bureaucracy: Managers, unions and the transformation of work in American industry, 1900–1945*. New York: Columbia University Press.

James, R., and R. Jones (2014). "Transferring the Toyota lean cultural paradigm into India: Implications for human resource management." *International Journal of Human Resource Management* 25(15): 2174–91.

Janger, A.H. (1980). *Organization of international joint ventures*. New York: Conference Board.

Jarvenpaa, S.L., K. Knoll, and D.E. Leidner (1998). "Is anybody out there? Antecedents of trust in global virtual teams." *Journal of Management Information Systems* 14(4): 29–64.

Jarvenpaa, S.L., and D.E. Leidner (1999). "Communication and trust in global virtual teams." *Organization Science* 10(6): 791–815.

Javidan, M., and J.L. Walker (2012). "A whole new global mindset for leadership." *People and Strategy* 35(2): 36–41.

Jay, A. (1967). *Management and Machiavelli: An inquiry into the politics of corporate life*. New York: Holt, Rinehart and Winston.

Jemison, D.B., and S.B. Sitkin (1986). "Corporate acquisitions: A process perspective." *Academy of Management Review* 11(1): 145–63.

Jin, Z., R. Mason, and P. Yim (1998). "Bridging US-China cross-cultural differences using internet and groupware technologies." Paper presented at the 7th International Association for Management of Technology Annual Conference, February, Orlando, FL.

Johansen, R., D. Sibbet, R. Mittman, P. Saffo, and S. Benson (1991). *Leading business teams: How teams can use technology and group process tools to enhance performance*. Reading, MA: Addison-Wesley.

Johanson, J., and J.E. Vahlne (1977). "The internationalization process of the firm: A model of knowledge development and increasing foreign market commitment." *Journal of International Business Studies* 8(1): 23–32.

Johanson, J., and F. Wiedersheim-Paul (1975). "The internationalization of the firm: Four Swedish cases." *Journal of Management Studies* 12(3): 305–23.

Johnson, J.P., T. Lenartowicz, and S. Apud (2006). "Cross-cultural competence in international business: Toward a definition and a model." *Journal of International Business Studies* 37(4): 525–43.

Johnson, L., and J. Rich (2000). "Dealing with employee benefit issues in mergers and acquisitions." *SHRM's Legal Report* (March–April). Arlington, VA: Society for Human Resource Management.

Johnson, G., K. Scholes, and R. Whittington (2005). *Exploring corporate strategy: Text & cases*, 7th ed. Harlow, UK: FT Prentice-Hall.

Jones, C. (1996). "Careers in project networks: The case of the film industry." In *The boundaryless career: A new principle for a new organizational era*, eds. M.B. Arthur and D.M. Rousseau. New York: Oxford University Press.

Jones, G. (1996). *The evolution of international business*. London: Routledge.

Jonsen, K., M. Maznevski, and S.C. Davison (2012). "Global virtual team dynamics and effectiveness." In *Handbook of research in international human resource management*, eds. G.K. Stahl, I. Björkman, and S. Morris. Cheltenham: Edward Elgar.

Jonsson, A., and N.J. Foss (2011). "International expansion through flexible replication: Learning from the internationalization experience of IKEA." *Journal of International Business Studies* 42(9): 1079–102.

Judge, T.A., C.J. Thoresen, V. Pucik, and T.M. Welbourne (1999). "Managerial coping with organizational change: A dispositional perspective." *Journal of Applied Psychology* 84(1): 107–22.

Kale, P., and J. Anand (2006). "The decline of emerging economy joint ventures: The case of India." *California Management Review* 48(3): 62–76.

Kale, P., and H. Singh (2012). "Characteristics of emerging market mergers and acquisitions." In *Handbook of mergers & acquisitions*, eds. D. Faulkner, S. Teerikangas, and R. Joseph. Oxford: Oxford University Press.

Kale, P., H. Singh, and A.P. Raman (2009). "Don't integrate your acquisitions, partner with them." *Harvard Business Review* 87(December): 109–15.

Kamprad, I., and B. Torekull (1999). *Leading by design: The IKEA story*. New York: HarperCollins.

Kang, S.C., Morris, S.S., and S.A. Snell (2007). "Relational archetypes, organizational learning, and value creation: Extending the human resource architecture." *Academy of Management Review* 32(1): 236–56.

Kanter, R.M. (1985). *Change masters: Innovation for productivity in the American workplace*. New York: Simon & Schuster.

—— (1989). *When giants learn to dance: Mastering the challenge of strategy, management, and careers in the 1990s*. New York and Toronto: Simon & Schuster.

—— (1994). "Collaborative advantage: The art of alliances." *Harvard Business Review* (July–August): 96–108.

—— (1995). *World class: Thriving locally in the global economy*. New York: Simon & Schuster.

—— (2009). "IBM in the 21st Century: The Coming of the Globally Integrated Enterprise." Harvard Business School Case 9-308-105, Boston.

Kaplan, A.M., and M. Haelein (2010). "Users of the world unite! The challenges and opportunities of social media." *Business Horizons* 53(1): 59–68.

Kaplan, R.S., and D.P. Norton (1996). *Translating strategy into action: The balanced scorecard*. Boston, MA: Harvard Business School Press.

—— (2001). *The strategy-focused organization: How balanced scorecard companies thrive in the new business environment*. Cambridge, MA: Harvard Business Press.

—— (2008). "Mastering the management system." *Harvard Business Review* (January): 63–7.

Kates, A. (2006). "(Re)Designing the HR organization." *Human Resource Planning* 29(2): 22–30.

Katzenbach, J.R., and D.K. Smith (1993). *The wisdom of teams: Creating the high performance organization*. Boston, MA: Harvard Business School Press.

Kaufman, B. (2007). "The development of HRM in historical and international perspective." In *The Oxford handbook of human resource management*, eds. P. Boxall, J. Purcell, and P. Wright. New York: Oxford University Press.

Kay, I.T., and M. Shelton (2000). "The people problems in mergers." *McKinsey Quarterly* (4): 29–37.

Kelly, J., and J. Gennard (2000). "Getting to the top: Career paths of personnel directors." *Human Resource Management Journal* 10(3): 22–37.

Kennedy, C. (1989). "Xerox charts a new strategic direction." *Long Range Planning* 22(1): 10–17.

Kenney, M., and R. Florida (1993). *Beyond mass production: The Japanese system and its transfer to the U.S.* New York: Oxford University Press.

Kepes, S., and J.E. Delery (2007). "HRM systems and the problem of internal fit." In *The Oxford handbook of human resource management*, eds. P. Boxall, J. Purcell, and P. Wright. New York: Oxford University Press.

Kerr, S. (1995). "An academic classic: On the folly of rewarding A, while hoping for B." *Academy of Management Executive* 9(1): 7–14.

Kerr, S., and S. Landauer (2004). "Using stretch goals to promote organizational effectiveness and personal growth: General Electric and Goldman Sachs." *Academy of Management Executive* 18(4): 134–8.

Kerr, S., and D. LePelley (2013). "Stretch goals: Risks, possibilities, and best practices." In *New developments in goal setting and task performance*, eds. A. Locke and G.P. New York: Routledge, 21–31.

Kets de Vries, M.F.R. (1989). "Leaders who self-destruct: The causes and cures." *Organizational Dynamics* (Spring): 5–17.

——— (1994). "Percy Barnevik and ABB." Case study no. 05/94-4308. INSEAD, Fontainebleau.

Kets de Vries, M.F.R., A. Agrawal, and E. Florent-Treacy (2006). "The moral compass: Values-based leadership at Infosys." Case study no. 806-050-1. INSEAD, Fontainebleau.

Khanna, T., and K.G. Palepu (2006). "Emerging giants: Building world-class companies in developing countries." *Harvard Business Review* (October): 60–9.

Khanna, T., and K.G. Palepu (2010). *Winning in emerging markets: A road map for strategy and execution*. Boston, MA: Harvard Business Press.

Kiesler, S., and J.N. Cummings (2002). "What do we know about proximity and distance in work groups? A legacy of research." In *Distributed work*, eds. P. Hinds and S. Kiesler. Cambridge, MA: MIT Press.

Kilduff, M., and W. Tsai (2003). *Social networks and organizations*. London: Sage.

Killing, J.P. (1982). "How to make a global joint venture work." *Harvard Business Review* (May–June): 120–7.

——— (1997). "International joint ventures: Managing after the deal is signed." *Perspectives for Managers*, no. 1. Lausanne: IMD.

——— (2003a). "Improving acquisition integration: Be clear on what you intend, and avoid 'best of both' deals." *Perspectives for Managers*, no. 97. Lausanne: IMD.

——— (2003b). "Nestlé's Globe Program (A): The early months." Case study no. IMD-3-1336, with video. IMD, Lausanne.

Killing, P. (2004). "Merger of equals: the case of AstraZeneca." In *Managing complex mergers*, eds. P. Morosini and U. Steger. London: Financial Times Prentice Hall.

Kim, C., and R. Mauborgne (1991). "Implementing global strategies: The role of procedural justice." *Strategic Management Journal* 12(Summer Special Issue): 125–43.

——— (1997). "Fair process: Managing in the knowledge economy." *Harvard Business Review* (July–August): 65–75.

———— (1998). "Procedural justice, strategic decision making, and the knowledge economy." *Strategic Management Journal* 19(4): 323–38.

———— (2003). "Tipping point leadership." *Harvard Business Review* (April): 60–69.

Kim, K., J.-H. Park, and J.E. Prescott (2003). "The global integration of business functions: A study of multinational businesses in integrated global industries." *Journal of International Business Studies* 34(4): 327–44.

Kim, Y., R. Williams, W. Rothwell, and P. Penaloza (2014). "A strategic model for technical talent management: A model based on a qualitative case study." *Performance Improvement Quarterly* 26(4): 93–121.

Kimberly, J.R., and H. Bouchikhi (1995). "The dynamics of organizational development and change: How the past shapes the present and constrains the future." *Organization Science* 6(1): 9–18.

King, D.R., D.R. Dalton, C.M. Daily, and J.G. Covin (2004). "Meta-analyses of post-acquisition performance: Indications of unidentified moderators." *Strategic Management Journal* 25(2): 187–200.

Kirkman, B.L., and D.N. den Hartog (2004). "Performance Management in Global Teams." In *The Blackwell handbook of global management: A guide to managing complexity*, eds. H.W. Lane, M.L. Maznevski, M.E. Mendenhall, and J. McNett. Oxford: Blackwell Publishing.

Kirkman, B.L., B. Rosen, C.B. Gibson, P.E. Tesluk, and S.O. McPherson (2002). "Five challenges to virtual team success: Lessons from Sabre, Inc." *Academy of Management Executive* 16(3): 67–79.

Klarner, P., and S. Raisch (2013). "Move to the beat—rhythms of change and firm performance." *Academy of Management Journal* 56(1): 160–84.

Klein, J.A. (2004). *True change: How outsiders on the inside get things done in organizations*. San Francisco: Jossey-Bass.

Kobrin, S.J. (1988). "Expatriate reduction and strategic control in American multinational corporations." *Human Resource Management* 27(1): 63–75.

———— (2015). "Is a global nonmarket strategy possible? Economic integration in a multipolar world order." *Journal of World Business* 50(2): 262–72.

Koen, C.I. (2004). "The dialectics of globalization: What are the effects for management and organization in Germany and Japan?" *Research in International Business and Finance* 18(2): 173–97.

Kogut, B. (1988). "Joint ventures: Theoretical and empirical perspectives." *Strategic Management Journal* 9(4): 319–32.

Kogut, B., and U. Zander (1992). "Knowledge of the firm, combinative capabilities, and the replication of technology." *Organization Science* 3(3): 383–97.

———— (1993). "Knowledge of the firm and the evolutionary theory of the multinational corporation." *Journal of International Business Studies* 24(4): 625–45.

Kolb, D.A. (1984). *Experiential learning: Experience as the source of learning and development*. Englewood Cliffs, NJ: Prentice Hall.

Komin, S. (1990). "Psychology of the Thai people: Values and behavioral patterns." Bangkok Research Centre: National Institute of Development Administration (NIDA).

Kopp, R. (1994). "International human resource policies and practices in Japanese, European, and U.S. multinationals." *Human Resource Management* 33(4): 581–99.

Kostova, T. (1999). "Transnational transfer of strategic organizational practices: A contextual perspective." *Academy of Management Review* 24(2): 308–24.

Kostova, T., and K. Roth (2002). "Adoption of an organizational practice by subsidiaries of multinational corporations: Institutional and relational effects." *Academy of Management Journal* 45(1): 215–33.

———— (2003). "Social capital in multinational corporations and a micro-macro model of its formation." *Academy of Management Review* 28(2): 297–319.

Kotter, J.P. (1982). "What effective general managers really do." *Harvard Business Review* (November–December): 156–67.

———— (1988). "The leadership factor." *McKinsey Quarterly* (Spring).

———— (1990). *A force for change: how leadership differs from management.* New York: Free Press.

———— (1996). *Leading change.* Boston, MA: Harvard Business School Press.

———— (2008). *A sense of urgency.* Boston, MA: Harvard Business School Press.

Kotter, J.P., and J.L. Heskett (1992). *Corporate culture and performance.* New York: Free Press.

Kraatz, M.S. (1998). "Learning by association? Interorganizational networks and adaptation to environmental change." *Academy of Management Journal* 41(6): 621–43.

Kraimer, M.L., M.A. Shaffer, and M.C. Bolino (2009). "The influence of expatriate and repatriate experiences on career advancement and repatriate retention." *Human Resource Management* 48(1): 27–47.

Kram, K.E. (1985). *Mentoring at work.* Glennview, IL: Scott, Foresman.

Krishnan, R., X. Martin, and N.G. Noorderhaven (2006). "When does trust matter to alliance performance?" *Academy of Management Journal* 49(5): 894–917.

Krug, J., and W.H. Hegerty (1997). "Postacquisition turnover among U.S. top management teams: An analysis of the effect of foreign versus domestic acquisition of U.S. targets." *Strategic Management Journal* 18(8): 667–75.

———— (2001). "Predicting who stays and leaves after an acquisition: A study of top managers in multinational firms." *Strategic Management Journal* 22(2): 185–96.

Kühlmann, T., and P.J. Dowling (2005). "DaimlerChrysler: A case study of a cross-border merger." In *Mergers and acquisitions: Managing culture and human resources,* eds. G.K. Stahl and M.E. Mendenhall. Palo Alto, CA: Stanford University Press.

Kuin, P. (1972). "The magic of multinational management." *Harvard Business Review* (November–December): 89–97.

Kulik, C.T., and T.J. Bainbridge (2006). "HR and the line: The distribution of HR activities in Australian organizations." *Asia Pacific Journal of Human Resources* 44(2): 240–56.

Kulik, C.T., and E.L. Perry (2008). "When less is more: The effect of devolution on HR's strategic role and construed image." *Human Resource Management* 47(3): 541–58.

Kulmann, E. (2012). "DuPont's CEO on executing a complex cross-border acquisition." *Harvard Business Review* 90(July–August): 43–46.

Kumar, N. (2009). "How emerging giants are rewriting the rules of M&A." *Harvard Business Review* (May): 115–21.

Kunda, G. (2009). *Engineering culture: Control and commitment in a high-tech corporation.* Philadelphia: Temple University Press.

Kuvaas, B. (2008). "An exploration of how the employee–organization relationship affects the linkage between perception of developmental human resource practices and employee outcomes." *Journal of Management Studies* 45(1): 1–25.

Kwan, C.W., and R. Siow (2013). "Business ecosystems: Developing employable talent to meet Asia's needs." In *The Global Talent Competitiveness Index 2013,* eds. B. Lanvin and P.A.L. Evans. Fontainebleau: INSEAD.

Kwon, S.W., and P.S. Adler (2014). "Social capital: Maturation of a field of research." *Academy of Management Review* 39(4): 412–22.

Lafley, A.G. (2008). "P&G's innovation culture." *Strategy+Business Magazine* 52(3).

Lambert, A. (2009). *Configuring HR for tomorrow's challenges.* London: Corporate Research Forum.

Lane, C. (1989). *Management and labour in Europe: The industrial enterprise in Germany, Britain and France.* Aldershot, UK: Edward Elgar.

Lane, P.J., B.R. Koka, and S. Pathak (2006). "The reification of absorptive capacity: A critical review and rejuvenation of the construct." *Academy of Management Review* 31(4): 833–63.

Lane, H.W., B. Spector, J.S. Osland, and S. Taylor (2014). "Global strategic change: A synthesis of approaches." *Advances in Global Leadership* 8: 229–48.

Lanvin, B., and P.A.L. Evans (2014). *The Global Talent Competitiveness Index: Growing talent for today and tomorrow*. Fontainebleau: INSEAD. http://global-indices.insead.edu/gtci/.

Lanvin, B., P. Evans, and N. Rasheed (2014). "Growing talent for today and tomorrow." In *The Global Talent Competitiveness Index 2014*, eds. B. Lanvin and P. Evans. Fontainebleau: INSEAD. http://global-indices.insead.edu/gtci/.

Larsen, H.H., and C. Brewster (2003). "Line management responsibility for HRM: What is happening in Europe?" *Employee Relations* 25(3): 228–44.

Larsson, R., and S. Finkelstein (1999). "Integrating strategic, organizational, and human resource perspectives on mergers and acquisitions: A case survey of synergy realization." *Organization Science* 10(1): 1–26.

Lasserre, P. (1996). "Regional headquarters: The spearhead for Asia Pacific markets." *Long Range Planning* 29(1): 30–7.

——— (2008). *Global strategic management*. London: Palgrave Macmillan.

Lasserre, P., and P.S. Ching (1997). "Human resources management in China and the localization challenge." *Journal of Asian Business* 13(4): 75–96.

Lasserre, P., and H. Schütte (2006). *Strategies for Asia Pacific*, 3rd ed. London: Palgrave Macmillan.

Latham, G. (2004). "The motivational benefits of goal setting." *Academy of Management Executive* 18(2): 126–9.

Laurent, A. (1983). "The cultural diversity of Western conceptions of management." *International Studies of Management and Organization* 13(1/2): 75–96.

Law, K., C.-S. Wong, and K.D. Wang (2004). "An empirical test of the model on managing the localization of human resources in the People's Republic of China." *International Journal of Human Resource Management* 15(4/5): 635–48.

Lawler, E.E. (1992). *The ultimate advantage: Creating the high involvement organization*. San Francisco: Jossey-Bass.

——— (2002). "The folly of forced ranking." *Strategy+Business* 28(3).

——— (2003a). *Treat people right*. San Francisco: Jossey-Bass.

——— (2003b). "Reward practices and performance management system effectiveness." *Organizational Dynamics* 32(4): 396–404.

——— (2008). *Talent: Making people your competitive advantage*. San Francisco: Jossey-Bass.

Lawler, E.E., J.W. Boudreau, and S.A. Mohrman (2006). *Achieving strategic excellence: An assessment of human resource organizations*. Stanford, CA: Stanford University Press.

Lawler, E.E., D. Ulrich, J. Fitz-Enz, and J.C. Madden (2004). *Human resources business process outsourcing: Transforming how HR gets work done*. San Francisco: Jossey-Bass.

Lawrence, P.R., and J.W. Lorsch (1967). *Organization and environment*. Boston, MA: Harvard Division of Research.

Lazarova, M. (2014). "Taking stock of repatriation research." In *The Routledge companion to international human resource management*, eds. D.G. Collings, G.T. Wood, and P.M. Caligiuri. New York: Routledge.

Lazarova, M., and I. Tarique (2005). "Knowledge transfer upon repatriation." *Journal of World Business* 40(4): 361–73.

Lazonick, W., and M. O'Sullivan (1996). "Organization, finance, and international competition." *Industrial and Corporate Change* 5(1): 1–49.

Leana, C.R., and H.J. Van Buren III (1999). "Organizational social capital and employment practices." *Academy of Management Review* 24(3): 538–55.

Lee, J.Y., D.G. Bachrach, and D.M. Rousseau (2015). "Internal labor markets, firm-specific human capital, and heterogeneity antecedents of employee idiosyncratic deal requests." *Organization Science* 26(3): 794–810.

Legge, K. (1995). *Human resource management: Rhetorics and realities*. London: Macmillan.

——— (1999). "Representing people at work." *Organization* 6(2): 247–64.

Lehmberg, D., W.G. Rowe, and J.R. Philips (2009). "General Electric: An outlier in talent development." *Ivey Business Journal* (January–February).

Lei, D., J.W. Slocum, Jr., and R. Pitts (1997). "Building cooperative advantage: Managing strategic alliances to promote organizational learning." *Journal of World Business* 32(3): 203–23.

Leidner, D., T.R. Kayworth, and M. Mora-Tavarez (1999). "Leadership effectiveness in global virtual teams." Working paper no. 99/68/TM. INSEAD, Fontainebleau.

Lengnick-Hall, M.L., and C.A. Lengnick-Hall (2003). "HR's role in building relationship networks." *Academy of Management Executive* 17(4): 53–63.

——— (2006). "International human resource management and social network/social capital theory." In *Handbook of research in international human resource management*, eds. G.K. Stahl and I. Björkman. Cheltenham, UK: Edward Elgar.

Leonard, D. (1995). *Wellsprings of knowledge: Building and sustaining the sources of innovation.* Boston, MA: Harvard Business School Press.

Leonard, D., and S. Sensiper (1998). "The role of tacit knowledge in group innovation." *California Management Review* 40(3): 112–32.

Leonard-Barton, D. (1992). "Core capabilities and core rigidities: A paradox in managing new product development." *Strategic Management Journal* 13(Summer Special Issue): 111–25.

——— (1995). *Wellsprings of knowledge: Building and sustaining the sources of innovation*. Boston, MA: Harvard Business School Press.

Leonard-Barton, D., and S. Conner (1996). "Hewlett-Packard: Singapore (A), (B), (C)." Case study nos. 694-035, -036, and -037. Harvard Business School, Boston.

Lepak, D.P., and S.A. Snell (1999). "The human resource architecture: Toward a theory of human capital allocation and development." *Academy of Management Review* 24(1): 31–48.

——— (2002). "Examining the human resource architecture: The relationships among human capital, employment, and human resource configurations." *Journal of Management* 28(4): 517–43.

——— (2007). "Employment subsystems and the 'HR architecture.'" In *The Oxford handbook of human resource management*, eds. P. Boxall, J. Purcell, and P. Wright. New York: Oxford University Press.

Lepsinger, R., and D. DeRosa (2010). *Virtual team success: A practical guide for working and leading from a distance.* San Francisco: Wiley.

Lepsinger, R., and A.D. Lucia (1997). *The art and science of 360° feedback.* San Francisco: Pfeiffer.

Lervik, J.E.B. (2005). "Managing matters: Transferring organizational practices within multinational companies." Doctoral thesis. Norwegian School of Management, Oslo.

Leung, A.K., W. Maddux, A. Galinsky, and C. Chiu (2008). "Multicultural experience enhances creativity." *American Psychologist* 63(3): 169–81.

Levitt, B., and J.G. March (1988). "Organizational learning." *Annual Review of Sociology* 14: 319–38.

Levy, O., S. Beechler, S. Taylor, and N.A. Boyacigiller (2007). "What we talk about when we talk about 'global mindset': Managerial cognition in multinational corporations." *Journal of International Business Studies* 38(2): 231–58.

Levy, O., S. Taylor, and N. Boyacigiller (2010). "On the rocky road to strong global culture." *MIT Sloan Management Review* 51(4): 20–2.

Lewin, A.Y., S. Massini, and C. Peeters (2009). "Why are companies offshoring innovation & quest; The emerging global race for talent." *Journal of International Business Studies* 40(6): 901–25.

Lewis, M.W. (2000). "Exploring paradox: Toward a more comprehensive guide." *Academy of Management Review* 25(4): 760–76.

Lewis, M.W., C. Andriopoulos, and W.K. Smith (2014). "Paradoxical leadership to enable strategic agility." *California Management Review* 56(3): 58–77.

Lewis, R.E., and R.J. Heckman (2006). "Talent management: A critical review." *Human Resource Management Review* 16(2): 139–54.

Leydesdorff, L. (2012). "The Triple Helix, Quadruple Helix,…, and an N-tuple of helices: Explanatory models for analyzing the knowledge-based economy?" *Journal of the Knowledge Economy* 3(1): 25–35.

Li, C., and J. Bernoff (2008). *Groundswell*. Boston, MA: Harvard Business School Press.

Lord, R.G., and R.J. Hall (2005). "Identity, deep structure and the development of leadership skills." *Leadership Quarterly* 16(4): 591–615.

Low, J., and T. Siesfield (1998). *Measures that matter*. Boston, MA: Ernst & Young.

Liker, J.K., and M. Hoseus (2008). *Toyota culture: The heart and soul of the Toyota Way*. New York: McGraw-Hill.

Lindholm, N. (1998). *Performance appraisal in MNC subsidiaries: A study of host country employees in China*. EIASM Workshop on Strategic Human Resource Management, Brussels.

Lindqvist, M., O. Sölvell, and I. Zander (2000). "Technological advantage in the international firm: Local and global perspectives on the innovation process." *Management International Review* 40(1): 95–126.

Littrell, L.N., and E. Salas (2005). "A review of cross-cultural training: Best practices, guidelines, and research needs." *Human Resource Development Review* 4(3): 305–34.

Liu, G., and D. Liu (2007). "Danone and Wahaha: China-style divorce (A) and (B)." Case study nos. 207-021-1 & 207-022-1. China Europe International Business School (CEIBS), Shanghai.

Liu, X., and M.A. Shaffer (2005). "An investigation of expatriate adjustment and performance." *International Journal of Cross Cultural Management* 5(3): 235–54.

Locke, E.A., and G.P. Latham (1990). *A theory of goal setting and task performance*. Englewood Cliffs, NJ: Prentice Hall.

——— (2006). "New direction in goal-setting theory." *Current Directions in Psychological Science* 15(5): 265–8.

——— (eds.) (2013). *New developments in goal setting and task performance*. New York: Routledge.

Lombardo, M., and R.W. Eichinger (2000). "High potentials as high learners." *Human Resource Management* 39(4): 321–9.

Lorange, P. (1996). "A strategic human resource perspective applied to multinational cooperative ventures." *International Studies of Management and Organization* 26(1): 87–103.

Lorange, P., and J. Roos (1990). "Formation of cooperative ventures: Competence mix of the management teams." *Management International Review* 30(Special Issue): 69–86.

Lorsch, J.W., and T.J. Tierney (2002). *Aligning the stars: How to succeed when professionals drive results*. Boston, MA: Harvard Business School Press.

Loveridge, R. (1990). "Footfalls of the future: The emergence of strategic frames and formulae." In *The strategic management of technological innovation*, eds. R. Loveridge and M. Pitt. Chichester, UK: Wiley.

Lowe, K.B., M. Downes, and K.G. Kroeck (1999). "The impact of gender and location on the willingness to accept overseas assignments." *International Journal of Human Resource Management* 10(2): 223–34.

Løwendahl, B. (2005). *Strategic management of professional service firms*, 2nd ed. Copenhagen: Handelshojskolens Forlag.

Lu, Y., and I. Björkman (1997). "MNC standardization versus localization: HRM practices in China-Western joint ventures." *International Journal of Human Resource Management* 8(5): 614–28.

Lu, J.Y., Tao, Z., and S. Wei (2008). "*Danone v. Wahaha*: Who is having the last laugh?" Case study HKU 766, Asia Case Research Centre, University of Hong Kong.

Lunnan, R, J.E. Lervik, L.E.M, Traavik, S, Nilsen, R.P. Amdam, and B. Hennestad (2005). "Global transfer of management practice across nations and MNC subcultures." *Academy of Management Executive* 19(2): 77–80.

Luo, Y. (2000). *Partnering with Chinese firms: Lessons for international managers*. Aldershot, UK: Ashgate.

———— (2001). *Strategy, structure, and performance of MNCs in China*. Westport, CT: Greenwood Publishing Group.

Mabey, C., D. Skinner, and T. Clark (eds.) (1998). *Experiencing human resource management*. London: Sage.

MacDuffie, J.P. (1995). "Human resource bundles and manufacturing performance: Organizational logic and flexible production system in the world auto industry." *Industrial and Labor Relations Review* 48: 197–221.

———— (2007). "HRM and distributed work." *Academy of Management Annals* 1: 549–615.

Maddux, W., and A.D. Galinsky (2009). "Cultural borders and mental barriers: The relationship between living abroad and creativity." *Journal of Personality & Social Psychology* 96(5): 1047–61.

Mael, F., and B.E. Ashforth (1992). "Alumni and their alma mater: A partial test of the reformulated model of organizational identification." *Journal of Organizational Behaviour* 13(2): 103–23.

Maerki, H.U. (2008). "The globally integrated enterprise and its role in global governance." *Corporate Governance* 8(4): 368–73.

Maister, D.H. (1993). *Managing the professional service firm*. New York: Free Press.

Mäkelä, K., Andersson, U., and T. Seppälä (2012). "Interpersonal similarity and knowledge sharing within multinational organizations." *International Business Review* 21(3): 439–51.

Mäkelä, K., I. Björkman, and M. Ehrnrooth (2010). "How do MNCs establish their talent pools? Influences on individuals' likelihood of being labeled as talent." *Journal of World Business* 45(2): 134–42.

Manning, S., S. Massini, and A.Y. Lewin (2008). "A dynamic perspective on next-generation offshoring: The global sourcing of science and engineering talent." *Academy of Management Perspectives* 22(3): 35–54.

Mannix, E.A., and H. Sondak (2002). *Research on managing groups and teams*, 4th ed. New York: Elsevier Science.

Manz, C.C., F. Shipper, and G.L. Stewart (2009). "Everyone a team leader: Shared influence at WL Gore & Associates." *Organizational Dynamics* 38(3): 239–44.

Manzoni, J.-F., and J.-L. Barsoux (2007). *The set-up-to-fail syndrome: How good managers cause great people to fail*, 2nd ed. Boston, MA: Harvard Business School Press.

March, J.G. (1991). "Exploration and exploitation in organizational learning." *Organization Science* 2(1): 71–87.

Marchand, D., and K. Leger (2008). "Cemex Way to profitable growth: Leveraging post-merger integration and best-practice innovation." Case study no.IMD-3-1884. IMD, Lausanne.

Marks, M.L., and P.H. Mirvis (1986). "The merger syndrome." *Psychology Today* 20(10): 36–42.

———— (2010). *Joining forces: Making one plus one equal three in mergers, acquisitions, and alliances*. San Francisco: Jossey-Bass.

Marschan-Piekkari, R., D. Welch, and L. Welch (1999). "In the shadow: The impact of language on structure, power and communication in the multinational." *International Business Review* 8(4): 421–40.

Martin, J., and C. Schmidt (2010). "How to keep your top talent." *Harvard Business Review* 88(5): 54–61.

Martinez, J.I., and J.C. Jarillo (1989). "The evolution of research on coordination mechanisms in multinational corporations." *Journal of International Business Studies* 20(3): 489–514.

Maruca, R.F. (1994). "The right way to go global: An interview with Whirlpool CEO David Whitlam." *Harvard Business Review* (March–April): 135–45.

Mayer, M., and R. Whittington (1999). "Euro-elites: Top British, French and German managers in the 1980s and 1990s." *European Management Journal* 17(4): 403–8.

Mayerhofer, W., and C. Brewster (2012). "Comparative human resource management." In *Handbook of research on comparative human resource management*, eds. C. Brewster and W. Mayerhofer. Northampton, MA: Edward Elgar.

Mayrhofer, W., C. Brewster, M.J. Morley, and J. Ledolter (2011). "Hearing a different drummer? Convergence of human resource management in Europe—A longitudinal analysis." *Human Resource Management Review* 21(1): 50–67.

Maznevski, M., S.C. Davison, and K. Jonsen (2006). "Global virtual team dynamics and effectiveness." In *Handbook of research in international resource management*, eds. G.K. Stahl and I. Björkman. Cheltenham, UK: Edward Elgar.

McCall, M.W. (1998). *High flyers: Developing the next generation of leaders*. Boston, MA: Harvard Business School Press.

——— (2004). "Leadership development through experience." *Academy of Management Executive* 18(3): 127–30.

McCall, M.W., and G.P. Hollenbeck (2002). *Developing global executives: The lessons of international experience*. Boston, MA: Harvard Business School Press.

McCall, M.W., and M. Lombardo (1990). *Off the track: Why and how successful executives get derailed*. Greensboro, NC: Center for Creative Leadership.

McCall, M.W., M. Lombardo, and A. Morrison (1988). *The lessons of experience: How successful executives develop on the job*. New York: Free Press.

McFadyen, M.A., and A.A. Cannella, Jr. (2004). "Social capital and knowledge creation: When do marginal costs associated with social capital exceed marginal benefits?" *Academy of Management Journal* 47(5): 735–46.

McGovern, P. (1997). "Human resource management on the line?" *Human Resource Management Journal* 7(4): 12–29.

McGregor, D. (1960). *The human side of enterprise*. New York: McGraw-Hill.

McGregor, J. (2005). *One billion customers: Lessons from the front lines of doing business in China*. London: Nicholas Brealey.

McKinsey Global Institute (2012). "The world at work: Jobs, pay and skills for 3.5 billion people. www.mckinsey.com/mgi.

McNulty, Y. (2014). "Using new approaches in expatriate compensation to improve the effectiveness of talent management programs." In *The compensation handbook*, eds. L. Berger and D. Berger. Columbus, OH: McGraw-Hill Education.

Meier, M. (2011). "Knowledge management in strategic alliances: A review of empirical evidence." *International Journal of Management Reviews* 13(1): 1–23.

Mellahi, K., and D.G. Collings (2010). "The barriers to effective global talent management: The example of corporate elites in MNEs." *Journal of World Business* 45(2): 143–49.

Melvin, S., and K. Sylvester (1997). "Shipping out." *China Business Review* (May–June): 30–34.

Mendenhall, M.E. (2006). "The elusive, yet critical challenge of developing global leaders." *European Management Journal* 24(6): 422–9.

——— (2008). "Leadership and the birth of global leadership." In *Global leadership: Research, practice and development*, eds. M.E. Mendenhall, J.S. Osland, A. Bird, G.R. Oddou, and M.L. Maznevski. London: Routledge.

Mendenhall, M.E., and G. Oddou (1985). "The dimensions of expatriate acculturation: A review." *Academy of Management Review* 10(1): 39–47.

——— (1986). "Acculturation profiles of expatriate managers: Implications for cross-cultural training programs." *Columbia Journal of World Business* 21(4): 73–9.

Mendenhall, M.E., J.S. Osland, A. Bird, G.R. Oddou, and M.L. Maznevski (eds.) (2008). *Global leadership: Research, practice and development*. London: Routledge.

Mendenhall, M.E., B.S. Reiche, A. Bird, and J.S. Osland (2012). "Defining the 'global' in global leadership." *Journal of World Business* 47(4): 493–503.

Mendenhall, M.E., and G.K. Stahl (2000). "Expatriate training and development: Where do we go from here?" *Human Resource Management* 39(2/3): 251–65.

Meyer, E. (2014). *The culture map: Breaking through the invisible boundaries of global business*. Philadelphia: Perseus.

Meyer, J., and B. Rowan (1977). "Institutional organizations: Formal structure as myth and ceremony." *The American Journal of Sociology* 83(2): 340–63.

Meyer, J.P., D.J. Stanley, L. Herscovitch, and L. Topolnyutsky (2002). "Affective, continuance, and normative commitment to the organization: A meta-analysis of antecedents, correlates, and consequences." *Journal of Vocational Behavior* 61(1): 20–52.

Meyerson, D., K.E. Weick, and R.M. Kramer (1996). "Swift trust and temporary groups." In *Trust in organizations: Frontiers of theory and research*, eds. R.M. Kramer and T.R. Tyler. Thousand Oaks, CA: Sage.

Michaels, E.H., H. Handfield-Jones, and B. Axelrod (2001). *The war for talent*. Boston, MA: Harvard Business School Press.

Micklethwait, J., and A. Woolridge (1996). *The witch doctors: Making sense of the management gurus*. New York: Times Books.

Milkovich, G.T., and J.W. Boudreau (1997). *Human resource management*, 8th ed. Chicago: Irwin/McGraw Hill.

Milkovich, G.T., and J.M. Newman (2005). *Compensation*. New York: McGraw-Hill.

Miller, D. (1990). *The Icarus paradox: How exceptional companies bring about their own downfall*. New York: HarperBusiness.

Mills, D.Q. (1994). *The GEM principle: Six steps to creating a high performance organization*. Essex Junction, VT: Oliver Wight.

Mills, M., and H.P. Blossfield (2008). "Globalization, patchwork career and the individualization of inequality? A 12-country comparison of men's mid-career job mobility." In *Globalization, uncertainty and men's careers: An international comparison*, eds. H.-P. Blossfeld, M. Mills, and F. Bernadi. Northampton, MA: Edward Elgar.

Minbaeva, D., and S. Michailova (2004). "Knowledge transfer and expatriation practices in MNCs: The role of disseminative capacity." *Employee Relations* 26(6): 663–79.

Minbaeva, D., T. Pedersen, I. Björkman, C. Fey, and H. Park (2003). "MNC knowledge transfer, subsidiary absorptive capacity and knowledge transfer." *Journal of International Business Studies* 34(6): pp. 586–99.

Mintzberg, H. (1979). *The structuring of organizations: A synthesis of the research*. Englewood Cliffs, NJ: Prentice Hall.

——— (1989). *Mintzberg on management: Inside our strange world of organizations*. New York: Free Press.

——— (1994). *The rise and fall of strategic planning*. Englewood Cliffs, NJ: Prentice Hall.

Mintzberg, H., and J.A. Waters (1985). "Of strategies, deliberate and emergent." *Strategic Management Journal* 6(3): 257–72.

Mintzberg, H., and F. Westley (1992). "Cycles of organizational change." *Strategic Management Journal* 13(Winter Special Issue): 39–59.

Mishra, A.K., K.E. Mishra, and G.M. Spreitzer (2009). "Downsizing the company without downsizing morale." *MIT Sloan Management Review* 50(3): 39–44.

Mitroff, I., and H. Linstone (1993). *The unbounded mind: Breaking the chains of traditional business thinking*. Oxford and New York: Oxford University Press.

Mohr, A.T. (2006). "A multiple constituency approach to IJM performance management." *Journal of World Business* 41(3): 247–60.

Mol, S.T., M.P. Born, M.E. Willemsen, and H.T. Van der Molen (2005). "Predicting expatriate job performance for selection purposes: A quantitative review." *Journal of Cross-Cultural Psychology* 36(5): 590–620.

Monteiro, L.F., L. Arvidsson, and J. Birkinshaw (2008). "Knowledge flows within multinational corporations: Explaining subsidiary isolation and its performance implications." *Organization Science* 19(1): 90–109.

Moore, K., and J. Birkinshaw (1998). "Managing knowledge in global service firms: Centers of excellence." *Academy of Management Executive* 12(4): 81–92.

Moore, K., and D. Lewis (1999). *Birth of the multinational*. Copenhagen: Copenhagen Business Press.

Moran, Stahl, and Boyer Inc. (1988). *Status of American female expatriate employees: Survey results*. Boulder, CO: Moran, Stahl, and Boyer Inc.

Morehart, K.K. (2001). "How to create an employee referral program that works." *HR Focus* 78(1): 3–5.

Morgan, G. (1986). *Images of organization*. Newbury Park, CA: Sage.

Morgan, S. (2007). "National business systems research: Progress and prospects." *Scandinavian Journal of Management* 23(2): 127–45.

Morgan, G., and S. Quack (2005). "Institutional legacies and firm dynamics: The growth and internationalization of UK and German law firms." *Organization Studies* 26(12): 1765–85.

Morgan, G., and R. Ramirez (1983). "Action learning: A holographic metaphor for guiding social change." *Human Relations* 37(1): 1–28.

Moriguchi, C. (2000). "Implicit contracts, the great depression, and institutional change: The evolution of employment relations in US and Japanese manufacturing firms, 1910–1940." Working paper. Harvard Business School, Boston.

Morosini, P. (1998). *Managing cultural differences: Effective strategy and execution across cultures in global corporate alliances*. Oxford and New York: Pergamon.

Morosini, P., S. Shane, and H. Singh (1998). "National cultural distance and cross-border acquisition performance." *Journal of International Business Studies* 29(1): 137–58.

Morosini, P., and U. Steger (2004). "Global mergers and acquisitions: Why do so many fail? How to make them successful." In *Managing complex mergers*, eds. P. Morosini and U. Steger. London: Financial Times Prentice Hall.

Morris, M.A., and C. Robie (2001). "A meta-analysis of the effects of cross-cultural training on expatriate performance and adjustment." *Journal of Management Development* 20(7): 639–49.

Morris, S.S., and R. Calamai (2009). "Dynamic HR: Global applications from IBM." *Human Resource Management* 48(4): 641–48.

Morris, S., R. Hammond, and S. Snell (2014). "A microfoundations approach to transnational capabilities: The role of knowledge search in an ever-changing world." *Journal of International Business Studies* 45: 405–27.

Morris, S., and J. Oldroyd (2009). "To boost knowledge transfer, tell me a story." *Harvard Business Review* 87(5): 23.

Morris, S.S., J.B. Oldroyd, and S. Ramaswami (2015). "Scaling up your story: An experiment in global knowledge sharing at the World Bank." *Long Range Planning*, Available online March 30, 2015.

Morris, S.S., and S.A. Snell (2011). "Intellectual capital configurations and organizational capability: An empirical examination of human resource subunits in the multinational enterprise." *Journal of International Business Studies* 42(6): 805–27.

Morris, S., S. Snell, and I. Björkman (2016). "Toward a global talent management portfolio." *Journal of International Business Studies*, forthcoming.

Morris, S., and E. Vanderson (2015). "Intel's Vietnam War for Talent—Case A." Brigham Young University, Marriott School of Management.

Morris, S.S., B. Zhong, and M. Makhila (2015). "Going the distance: The pros and cons of expanding employees' global knowledge reach." *Journal of International Business Studies* 46(5): 552–73.

Morrison, M. (2007). "The very model of a modern senior manager." *Harvard Business Review* (January): 27–39.

Moxon, R.W., T.W. Roehl, and J. Truitt (1988). "International cooperative ventures in the commercial aircraft industry: Gains, sure, but what's my share?" In *Cooperative strategies in international business*, eds. F.J. Contractor and P. Lorange. Lexington, MA: Lexington Books.

Muller, H. (1970). *The search for qualities essential to advancement in a large industrial group: An exploratory study.* The Hague, Holland: Royal Dutch/Shell publications.

Munford, M. (September 17, 2013). "With 5,000 startups, Tel Aviv is Edging into the tech spotlight." *Mashable.* http://mashable.com/2013/09/17/tel-aviv-tech/.

Murtha, T.P., S.A. Lenway, and R.P. Bagozzi (1998). "Global mind-sets and cognitive shift in a complex multinational corporation." *Strategic Management Journal* 19(2): 97–114.

Muthu Kumar, R., and S.K. Chaudhuri (2005). "Mittal Steel's knowledge management strategy." Case study no. 305-543-1. ICFAI, India.

Myers, S., and D.G. Marquis (1969). *Successful industrial innovations: A study of factors underlying innovation in selected firms. NSF 69-17.* Washington, DC: National Science Foundation.

Myloni, B., A.-W. Harzing, and H. Mirza (2004). "Human resource management in Greece: Have the colours of culture faded away?" *International Journal of Cross Cultural Management* 4(1): 59–76.

Nadkarni, S., and J. Chen (2014). "Bridging yesterday, today, and tomorrow: CEO temporal focus, environmental dynamism, and rate of new product introduction." *Academy of Management Journal* 57(6): 1810–33.

Nadler, D., and M. Tushman (1997). *Competing by design: The power of organizational architecture.* New York: Oxford University Press.

Nahapiet, J., and S. Ghoshal (1998). "Social capital, intellectual capital, and the organizational advantage." *Academy of Management Review* 23(2): 242–66.

Neves, P., and A. Caetano (2006). "Social exchange processes in organizational change: The roles of trust and control." *Journal of Change Management* 6(4): 351–64.

Nicholson, N. (1984). "A theory of work role transitions." *Administrative Science Quarterly* 29(2): 172–91.

Nie, V., K. Xin, and V. Pucik (2007). "Alibaba vs. eBay: Competing in the Chinese C2C Market (A), (B) and (C)." Case studies no.IMD-3-1842-4. IMD, Lausanne.

Nishii, L.H., and M.F. Özbilgin (2007). "Global diversity management: Towards a conceptual framework." *International Journal of Human Resource Management* 18(11): 1883–94.

Noe, R., J. Hollenbeck, P.M. Wright, and B. Gerhart (1999). *Human resource management.* New York: McGraw-Hill/Irwin.

Nohria, N. (1992). "Is a network perspective a useful way of studying organizations?" In *Networks and organizations,* eds. N. Nohria and R.G. Eccles. Boston, MA: Harvard Business School Press.

Nohria, N., and S. Ghoshal (1997). *The differentiated network: Organizing multinational corporations for value creation.* San Francisco: Jossey-Bass.

Nonaka, I. (1988a). "Creating organizational order out of chaos: Self-renewal in Japanese firms." *California Management Review* 30(3): 57–73.

——— (1988b). "Toward middle-up-down management: Accelerating information creation." *MIT Sloan Management Review* 29(3): 9–18.

——— (1994). "A dynamic theory of organizational knowledge creation." *Organization Science* 5(1): 14–37.

Nonaka, I., and H. Takeuchi (1995). *The knowledge-creating company: How Japanese companies create the dynamics of innovation.* New York: Oxford University Press.

Nummela, N., S. Saarenketo, and K. Puumalainen (2004). "Global mindset: A prerequisite for successful internationalization?" *Canadian Journal of Administrative Sciences* 21(1): 51–64.

O'Connor, E. (1999). "Minding the workers: The meaning of 'human' and 'human relations' in Elton Mayo." *Organization* 6(2): 223–46.

Oddou, G.R. (1991). "Managing your expatriates: What the successful firms do." *Human Resource Planning* 14(4): 301–8.

Oddou, G., J.S. Osland, and R.N. Blakeney (2009). "Repatriating knowledge: Variables influencing the 'transfer' process." *Journal of International Business Studies* 40(2): 181–99.

O'Dell, C., and C.J. Grayson (1998). *If only we knew what we know: The transfer of internal knowledge and best practice*. New York: Free Press.

OECD (2013). *OECD Skills Outlook 2013: First Results from the Survey of Adult Skills*. Paris: OECD Publishing.

O'Grady, S., and H.W. Lane (1996). "The psychic distance paradox." *Journal of International Business Studies* 27(2): 309–33.

O'Hara-Devereaux, M., and R. Johansen (1994). *Globalwork: Bridging distance, culture and time*. San Francisco: Jossey-Bass.

Oki, K. (2013). "Why do Japanese companies exploit many expatriates?: Analysis of overseas subsidiaries in Japanese companies." *Annals of Business Administrative Science* 12(3): 139–50.

Oldroyd, J.B., and S.S. Morris (2012). "Catching falling stars: A human resource response to social capital's detrimental effect of information overload on star employees." *Academy of Management Review* 37(3): 396–418.

Orchant, D. (2001). "Expatriate taxation." In *Guide to global compensation and benefits*, ed. C. Reynolds. San Diego: Harcourt.

Ordonez, L.D., M.E. Schweitzer, A.D. Galinsky, and M.H. Bazerman (2009). "Goals gone wild: The systematic side effects of overprescribing goal setting." *Academy of Management Perspectives*. 23(1): 6–16.

O'Reilly, C.A. (1998). "New United Motors Manufacturing, Inc. (NUMMI)." Case study. Stanford Graduate School of Business, Stanford.

O'Reilly, C.A., and J. Chatman (1996). "Culture as social control: Corporations, cults, and commitment." In *Research in organizational behavior*, eds. B. Staw and L. Cummings. Greenwich, CT: JAI Press.

O'Reilly, C.A., and J. Pfeffer (2000). *Hidden value: How great companies achieve extraordinary results with ordinary people*. Boston, MA: Harvard Business School Press.

O'Reilly, C.A., and M.L. Tushman (2004). "The ambidextrous organization." *Harvard Business Review* (April): 74–81.

——— (2013). "Organizational ambidexterity: Past, present, and future." *Academy of Management Perspectives* 27(4): 324–38.

Orlitzky, M. (2007). "Recruitment strategy." In *The Oxford handbook of human resource management*, eds. P. Boxall, J. Purcell, and P. Wright. New York: Oxford University Press.

Orrù, M. (1997). "The institutional analysis of capitalist economies." In *The economic organization of East Asian capitalism*, eds. M. Orrù, N.W. Biggart, and G.G. Hamilton. Thousand Oaks, CA: Sage.

Osland, J.S., A. Bird, M. Mendenhall, and A. Osland (2006). "Developing global leadership capabilities and global mindset: A review." In *Handbook of research in international human resource management*, eds. G.K. Stahl and I. Björkman. Cheltenham, UK: Edward Elgar.

Osono, E., N. Shimizu, and H. Takeuchi (2008). *Extreme Toyota: Radical contradiction that drive success at the world's best manufacturer*. New York: John Wiley.

O'Toole, J. (1985). *Vanguard management*. New York: Doubleday.

Ouchi, W.G. (1981). *Theory Z: How American business can meet the Japanese challenge*. Reading, MA: Addison-Wesley.

——— (1989). "The economics of organization." In *Human resource management in international firms: Change, globalization, innovation*, eds. P.A.L. Evans, Y. Doz, and A. Laurent. London: Macmillan.

Oxley, G.M. (1961). "The personnel manager for international operations." *Personnel* 38(6): 52–8.

Paauwe, J. (2004). *HRM and performance: Achieving long-term viability*. Oxford: Oxford University Press.

———— (2009). "HRM and performance: Achievements, methodological issues and prospects." *Journal of Management Studies* 46(1): 129–42.

Packard, D. (1995). *The HP way: How Bill Hewlett and I built our company.* New York: HarperBusiness.

Paik, Y., and D.Y. Choi (2005). "The shortcomings of a global knowledge management system: The case of Accenture." *Academy of Managent Executive* 19(2): 81–4.

Paik, Y., and C.M. Stage (1996). "The extent of divergence in human resource practice across three Chinese national cultures: Hong Kong, Taiwan and Singapore." *Human Resource Management Journal* 6(2): 20–31.

Pak, Y.S., W. Ra, and J.M. Lee (2015). "An integrated multi-stage model of knowledge management in international joint ventures: Identifying a trigger for knowledge exploration and knowledge harvest." *Journal of World Business* 50(1): 180–91.

Palmisano, S.J. (2006). "The globally integrated enterprise." *Foreign Affairs* 85(May–June): 127–36.

Parkhe, A. (1991). "Interfirm diversity, organizational learning, and longevity in global strategic alliances." *Journal of International Business Studies* 22(4): 579–601.

———— (1993). "Partner nationality and the structure-performance relationship in strategic alliances." *Organization Science* 4(2): 301–24.

Patil, N. (2007). "Managing Talent in the Flat World: An Infosys perspective as practitioner & consultant." Infosys White Paper.

Pauly, L.W., and S. Reich (1997). "National structures and multinational corporate behavior: Enduring differences in the age of globalization." *International Organization* 51(1): 1–30.

Penrose, E. (1959). *The theory of the growth of the firm.* New York: Wiley.

Peretz, H., and Y. Fried (2012). "National cultures, performance appraisal practices, and organizational absenteeism and turnover: A study across 21 countries." *Journal of Applied Psychology* 97(2): 448–59.

Perlmutter, H.V. (1969). "The tortuous evolution of the multinational corporation." *Columbia Journal of World Business* 4(1): 9–18.

Peter, L.J., and R. Hull (1969). *The Peter Principle: Why things always go wrong.* New York: William Morrow.

Peters, T. (1979). "Beyond the matrix organization." *McKinsey Quarterly* (September).

Peters, T.J., and R.H. Waterman (1982). *In search of excellence.* New York: Harper & Row.

Peterson, R.B. (2003). "The use of expatriates and inpatriates in Central and Eastern Europe since the Wall came down." *Journal of World Business* 38(1): 55–69.

Peterson, R., S. Behfar, and K. Jackson (2003). "The dynamic relationship between performance feedback, trust, and conflict in groups: A longitudinal study." *Organizational Behavior & Human Decision Processes* 92(1): 102–12.

Peterson, M.F., T.K. Peng, and P.B. Smith (1999). "Using expatriate supervisors to promote cross-border management practice transfer: The experience of a Japanese electronics company." In *Remade in America: Transplanting and transforming Japanese management systems,* eds. J.K. Liker, W.M. Fruin, and P.S. Adler. New York: Oxford University Press.

Petrovic, J., and N.K. Kakabadse (2003). "Strategic staffing of international joint ventures: An integrative perspective for future research." *Management Decisions* 41(4): 394–406.

Pettigrew, A.M. (1985). *The awakening giant: Continuity and change in organizations.* Oxford: Basil Blackwell.

———— (2000). "Linking change processes to outcomes." In *Breaking the code of change,* eds. M. Beer and N. Nohria. Boston, MA: Harvard Business School Press.

Pfeffer, J. (1994). *Competitive advantage through people.* Boston, MA: Harvard Business School Press.

———— (1998). *The human equation: Building profits by putting people first.* Boston, MA: Harvard Business School Press.

Pfeffer, J., and R.I. Sutton (1999). "Knowing 'what' to do is not enough: Turning knowledge into action." *California Management Review* 42(1): 83–108.

Pieper, R. (1990). *Human resource management: An international comparison*. Berlin and New York: de Gruyter.

Piketty, T. (2014). *Capital in the 21st century*. Boston, MA: Harvard University Press.

Pil, F.K., and J.P. MacDuffie (1999). "What makes transplants thrive: Managing the transfer of 'best practice' at Japanese auto plants in North America." *Journal of World Business* 34(4): 372–91.

Pillai, R., T.A. Scandura, and E. Williams (1999). "Leadership and organizational justice: Similarities and differences across cultures." *Journal of International Business Studies* 30(4): 763–79.

Podsakoff, P.M., S.B. MacKenzie, J.B. Paine, and D.G. Bachrach (2000). "Organizational citizenship behaviors: A critical review of the theoretical and empirical literature and suggestions for future research." *Journal of Management* 26(3): 513–63.

Polanyi, M. (1966). *The tacit dimension*. London: Routledge and Kegan Paul.

Pollitt, D. (2014). "HSBC banks on more women at the top." *Human Resource Management International Digest* 22(6): 18–20.

Porter, M.E. (1980). *Competitive strategy: Techniques for analyzing industries and competitors*. New York: Viking.

——— (1985). *Competitive strategy: Creating and sustaining superior performance*. New York: Free Press.

——— (1986). *Competition in global industries*. Boston, MA: Harvard Business School Press.

Powell, W.W., and P.J. DiMaggio (1991). *The new institutionalism in organizational analysis*. Chicago: University of Chicago Press.

Prahalad, C.K. (2004). *Fortune at the bottom of the pyramid*. Upper Saddle River, NJ: Wharton School Publishing.

Prahalad, C.K., and Y. Doz (1987). *The multinational mission: Balancing local demands and global vision*. New York: Free Press.

Prahalad, C.K., and K. Lieberthal (1998). "The end of corporate imperialism." *Harvard Business Review* (July-August): 69–79.

Prescott, R.K., W.J. Rothwell, and M. Taylor (1999). "Global HR: Transforming HR into a global powerhouse." *HR Focus* 76(3): 7–8.

Price Waterhouse Change Integration Team (1996). *The paradox principles: How high performance companies manage chaos, complexity, and contradiction to achieve superior results*. Chicago: McGraw-Hill/Irwin.

Probst, G., and S. Borzillo (2008). "Why communities of practice succeed and why they fail." *European Management Journal* 26(5): 335–47.

Pucik, V. (1984a). "The international management of human resources." In *Strategic human resource management*, eds. C. Fombrun, N.M. Tichy, and M.A. Devanna. New York: John Wiley.

——— (1984b). "White-collar human resource management in large Japanese manufacturing firms." *Human Resource Management* 23(3): 257–76.

——— (1988a). "Strategic alliances with the Japanese: Implications for human resource management." In *Cooperative strategies in international business*, eds. F.J. Contractor and P. Lorange. Lexington, MA: Lexington Books.

——— (1988b). "Strategic alliances, organizational learning, and competitive advantage: The HRM agenda." *Human Resource Management* 27(1): 77–93.

——— (1991). "Technology transfer in strategic alliances: Competitive collaboration and organizational learning." In *Technology transfer in international business*, eds. T. Agmon and M.A. Von Glinow. New York: Oxford University Press.

——— (1992). "Globalization and human resource management." In *Globalizing management: Creating and leading the competitive organization*, eds. V. Pucik, N.M. Tichy, and C.K. Barnett. New York: Wiley.

————— (1989). "Managerial career progression in large Japanese manufacturing firms." In *Research in personnel and human resources management*, eds. K Rowland and G. Ferris. Greenwich, CT: JAI Press.

————— (1994). "The challenges of globalization: The strategic role of local managers in Japanese-owned US subsidiaries." In *Japanese multinationals: Strategies and management in the global kaisha*, eds. N. Campbell and F. Burton. London: Routledge.

————— (1996). "Strategic alliances, organizational learning and competitive advantage: The HRM agenda." In *Knowledge management and organizational design*, ed. P. Myers. Newton, MA: Butterworth-Heinemann.

————— (1997). "Human resources in the future: An obstacle or a champion of globalization?" *Human Resource Management* 36(1): 163–8.

————— (2003). "Developing global leaders." In *Organization 21C: Someday all organizations will lead this way*, ed. S. Chowdhury. London: Pearson Education.

————— (2005). "Global HR as competitive advantage: Are we ready?" In *The future of human resource management*, eds. M. Losey, S. Meisinger, and D. Ulrich. New York: Wiley.

————— (2006). "Reframing global mindset: From thinking to acting." In *Advances in global leadership*, eds. W.H. Mobley and E. Weldon. Oxford: Elsevier.

————— (2008). "Post-merger integration process in Japanese M&A: The voices from the front-line." In *Advances in mergers and acquisitions*, Vol. 7, eds. G.L. Cooper and S. Finkelstein. Bingley, UK: JAI Press.

Pucik, V., I. Björkman, P. Evans, and G.K. Stahl (2014). "Human resource management in cross-border mergers and acquisitions." In *International human resource management*, eds. A. Harzing and A. Pinnington. London: Sage.

Pucik, V., S. Fiorella, and E. van Weering (2000). "American Diagnostic Systems." Case study no. IMD-3-0870. IMD, Lausanne.

Pucik, V., and N. Govinder (2007). "Canon Europe: Pan-European Transformation (A), (B) and (C)." Case study nos. IMD-3-1074 to 3-1076. IMD, Lausanne.

Pucik, V., M. Hanada, and G. Fifield (1989). *Management culture and the effectiveness of local executives in Japanese-owned U.S. corporations*. Ann Arbor, MI: Egon Zehnder International.

Pucik, V., and N. Hatvany (1981). "An integrated management system: Lessons from the Japanese experience." *Academy of Management Review* 6(3): 469–80.

Pucik, V., and C. Lief (2007). "Leadership at General Electric: A healthy disrespect for history." Case study no. IMD-3-1780. IMD, Lausanne.

Pucik, V., and T. Saba (1998). "Selecting and developing the global versus the expatriate manager: A review of the state-of-the-art." *Human Resource Planning* 21(4): 40–54.

Pucik, V., K. Xin, and D. Everatt (2003). "Managing performance at Haier (A)." Case study no. IMD-3-1332. IMD, Lausanne.

Pudelko, M., and A.-W. Harzing (2007). "How European is management in Europe? An analysis of past, present and future management practices in Europe." *European Journal of International Management* 1(3): 206–24.

Punnett, B.J., and J. Clemens (1999). "Cross-national diversity: Implications for international expansion decisions." *Journal of World Business* 34(2): 128–38.

Putman, R. (2015). *Our kids: The American dream in crisis*. New York: Simon and Schuster.

Quinn, R.E. (1988). *Beyond rational management: Mastering the paradoxes and competing demands of high performance*. San Francisco: Jossey-Bass.

Quinn, R.E., and J. Rohrbaugh (1983). "A spatial model of effectiveness criteria: Towards a competing values approach to organizational analysis." *Management Science* 29(3): 363–77.

Raelin, J.A. (1999). "The design of the action project in work-based learning." *Human Resource Planning* 22(3): 12–28.

Ralston, D.A., D. Holt, R. Tersptra, and Y. Kai-Cheng (2008). "The impact of national culture and economic ideology on managerial work values: A study of the United States. Russia, Japan, and China." *Journal of International Business Studies* 39(1): 8–26.

Ramirez, R. (1983). "Action learning: A strategic approach for organizations facing turbulent conditions." *Human Relations* 36(8): 725–42.

Rangan, S., and A. Drummond (2004). "Explaining outcomes in competition among foreign multinationals in a focal host market." *Strategic Management Journal* 25(3): 285–93.

Rasmussen, T., and D. Ulrich (2015). "Learning from practice: How HR analytics avoids being a management fad." *Organizational Dynamics* 44(3): 236–42.

Rausch, S., and J. Birkinshaw (2008). "Organizational ambidexterity: Antecedents, outcomes, and moderators." *Journal of Management* 34(3): 375–409.

Ravasi, D., and M. Schultz (2006). "Responding to organizational identity threats: Exploring the role of organizational culture." *Academy of Management Journal* 49(3): 433–58.

Reade, C. (2001). "Antecedents of organizational identification in multinational corporations: Fostering psychological attachment to the local subsidiary and the global organization." *International Journal of Human Resource Management* 12(8): 1269–91.

Ready, D., and J. Conger (2007). "Make your company a talent factory." *Harvard Business Review* (June): 68–77.

Ready, D., L. Hill, and J. Conger (2008). "Winning the race for talent in emerging markets." *Harvard Business Review* (November): 63–70.

Redding, G. (2001). "The evolution of business systems." Euro-Asia Centre Report no. 72. INSEAD, Fontainebleau and Singapore.

Regalado, A. (January 6, 2015). "23andMe's New Formula: Patient Consent = $." *MIT Technology Review*. http://www.technologyreview.com/view/534006/23andmes-new-formula-patient-consent/.

Reich, R.B., and E.D. Mankin (1986). "Joint ventures with Japan give away our future." *Harvard Business Review* (March–April): 78–86.

Reiche, B.S. (2009). "Knowledge benefits of social capital upon repatriation: A longitudinal study of international assignees." *Journal of Management Studies* 49(6): 1052–77.

Reiche, B.S., M.L. Kraimer, and A.W. Harzing (2011). "Why do international assignees stay and quest: An organizational embeddedness perspective." *Journal of International Business Studies* 42(4): 521–44.

Reichel, A., and M. Lazarova (2013). "The effect of outsourcing and devolvement on the strategic position of HR departments." *Human Resource Management* 52(6): 923–46.

Reilly, P., P. Tamkin, and A. Broughton (2007). *The changing HR function: Transforming HR?* London: CIPD.

Reuer, J., Klijn, E., and C. Lioukas (2014). "Board involvement in international joint ventures." *Strategic Management Journal* 35: 1626–44.

Revens, R.W. (1980). *Action learning: New techniques for management.* London: Blond and Riggs.

Reynolds, C. (1995). *Compensating globally mobile employees.* Scottsdale, AZ: American Compensation Association.

——— (2001). *Guide to global compensation and benefits.* San Diego: Harcourt.

Rhinesmith, S.H. (1993). *A manager's guide to globalization: Six keys to success in a changing world.* Homewood, IL: ASTD & Business One Irwin.

Rigby, M., R. Smith, and C. Brewster (2004). *Trade unions and democracy: Strategies and perspectives.* Manchester: Manchester University Press.

Riketta, M. (2002). "Attitudinal organizational commitment and job performance: A meta-analysis." *Journal of Organizational Behavior* 23(3): 257–66.

Roberto, M.A., and G.M. Carioggia (2002). "Mount Everest—1996." Case study no. 303061. Harvard Business School, Boston.

Rodrigues, S.B., and J. Child (2008). "The development of corporate identity: A political perspective." *Journal of Management Studies* 45(5): 885–911.

Rogers, P., and M. Blenko (2006). "Who has the D? How clear decision roles enhance organizational performance." *Harvard Business Review* 84(1): 53–61.

Rosenzweig, P. (2006). "The dual logics behind international human resource management: Pressures for global integration and local responsiveness." In *Handbook of research in international human resource management*, eds. G.K. Stahl and I. Björkman. Cheltenham, UK: Edward Elgar.

Rosenzweig, P.M., and N. Nohria (1994). "Influences on human resource management practices in multinational corporations." *Journal of International Business Studies* 25(2): 229–51.

Ross, J.W., and C.M. Beath (2007). "Beyond the business case: New approaches to investment." *MIT Sloan Management Review* 43(2): 51–9.

Rousseau, D.M. (1995). *Psychological contracts in organizations: Understanding written and unwritten agreements*. Thousand Oaks, CA: Sage.

Rousseau, D.M., and S.L. Robinson (1994). "Violating the psychological contract: Not the exception but the norm." *Journal of Organizational Behavior* 15(3): 245–60.

Rowthorn, R. (2008). "The fiscal impact of immigration on the advanced economies." *Oxford Review of Economic Policy* 24(3): 560–80.

Rudlin, P. (2000). *A History of Mitsubishi Corporation in London: 1915 to present day*. London: Routledge.

Rugman, A., and A. Verbeke (2004). "A perspective on regional and global strategies of multinational enterprises." *Journal of International Business Studies* 35(1): 3–18.

——— (2008). "A regional solution to the strategy and structure of multinationals." *European Management Journal* 26(5): 305–13.

Rumelt, R.P. (1974). *Strategy, structure, and economic performance*. Boston, MA: Harvard University Press.

——— (1996). "The many faces of Honda." *California Management Review* 38(4): 103–11.

Russo, J.E., and P.J. Schoemaker (2002). *Winning decisions: Getting it right the first time*. New York: Doubleday/Piatkus.

Ruta, C.D. (2005). "The application of change management theory to HR portal implementation in subsidiaries of multinational corporations." *Human Resource Management* 44(1): 35–53.

Ryan, A.M., D. Wiechmann, and M. Hemingway (2003). "Designing and implementing global staffing systems: Part II-best practices." *Human Resource Management* 42(1): 85–94.

Salk, J.E., and B.L. Simonin (2003). "Beyond alliances: Towards a meta-theory of collaborative learning." In *The Blackwell handbook of organizational learning and knowledge management*, eds. M. Easterby-Smith and M.A. Lyles. Malden, MA: Blackwell.

Sampson, A. (1975). *The seven sisters: The great oil companies and the world they made*. London: Hodder and Stoughton.

Sanchez, F. (2007). "Principles of global integration." *Industrial Management* (September–October): 8–13.

Santos, J. (2001). "Virtual teams and metanational innovation." Working paper. INSEAD, Fontainebleau.

Schein, E.H. (1985). *Organizational culture and leadership: A dynamic view*. San Francisco: Jossey-Bass.

——— (1996). "Kurt Lewin's change theory in the field and in the classroom: Notes toward a model of managed learning." *Systems Practice* 9(1): 27–47.

Schisgall, O. (1981). *Eyes on tomorrow: The evolution of Procter & Gamble*. New York: Doubleday.

Schlesinger, L.A., and J.L. Heskett (1991). "The service-driven company." *Harvard Business Review* (September–October): 71–81.

Schmidt, J.A. (ed.) (2002). *Making mergers work*. Alexandria, VA: Towers Perrin and SHRM Foundation.

Schmidt, F.L., and J.E. Hunter (1998). "The validity and utility of selection methods in personnel psychology: Practical and theoretical implications of 85 years of research findings." *Psychological Bulletin* 124(2): 262–72.

Schneider, S.C. (1988). "National vs. corporate culture: Implications for human resource management." *Human Resource Management* 27(2): 231–46.

Schneider, S.C., and J.-L. Barsoux (2003). *Managing across cultures*, 2nd ed. Harlow, UK: Financial Times Prentice Hall.

Schuler, R.S. (2000). "HR issues in international joint ventures and alliances." In *Human resource management: A critical text*, ed. J. Storey. London: International Thomson.

Schuler, R.S., and I. Tarique (2012). "International joint venture system complexity and human resource management." In *Handbook of research in international human resource management*, eds. G.K. Stahl, I. Björkman, and S. Morris. Northampton, MA: Edward Elger.

Schütte, H. (1998). "Between headquarters and subsidiaries: The RHQ solution." In *Multinational corporate evolution and subsidiary development*, eds. J. Birkinshaw and N. Hood. London: Macmillan.

Schweiger, D.M., and P.K. Goulet (2000). "Integrating mergers and acquisitions: An international research review." *Advances in Mergers and Acquisitions* 1: 61–91.

Scott, W.R. (2001). *Institutions and organizations*, 2nd ed. Thousands Oaks, CA: Sage Publications.

Scott Myers, M. (1970). *Every employee a manager: More meaningful work through job enrichment*. New York: McGraw-Hill.

Scullen, S.E, M.K. Mount, and M. Goff (2000). "Understanding the latent structure of job performance ratings." *Journal of Applied Psychology* 85(6): 956.

Scullion, H. (1994). "Staffing policies and strategic control in British multinationals." *International Studies of Management and Organization* 24(3): 86–104.

——— (1995). "International human resource management." In *Human resource management: A critical text*, ed. J. Storey. London: Routledge.

Scullion, H., and K. Starkey (2000). "In search of the changing role of the corporate human resource function in the international firm." *International Journal of Human Resource Management* 11(6): 1061–81.

Segal-Horn, S., and A. Dean (2008). "Delivering 'effortless experience' across borders: Managing internal consistency in professional service firms." *Journal of World Business* 44(1): 41–50.

Selmer, J. (2001). "Psycological barriers to adjustment and how they affect coping strategies: Western business expatriates in China." *International Journal of Human Resource Management* 12(2): 151–65.

Selmer, J., and C.T. de Leon (2002). "Parent cultural control of foreign subsidiaries through organizational acculturation: A longitudinal study." *International Journal of Human Resource Management* 13(8): 1147–65.

Shadur, M.A., J.J. Rodwell, and G.I. Bamber (1995). "The adoption of international best practices in a Western culture: East meets West." *International Journal of Human Resource Management* 6(3): 735–57.

Shaffer, M.A., D.A. Harrison, and K.M. Gilley (1999). "Dimensions, determinants, and differences in the expatriate adjustment process." *Journal of International Business Studies* 30(3): 557–81.

Shaw, J.D., J.E. Delery, G. Jenkins, and N. Gupta (1998). "An organization-level analysis of voluntary and involuntary turnover." *Academy of Management Review* 41(5): 511–25.

Shen, J. (2004). "International performance appraisals: Policies, practices and determinants in the case of Chinese multinational companies." *International Journal of Manpower* 25(6): 547–63.

Shenkar, O., and Y. Zeira (1990). "International joint ventures: A tough test for HR." *Personnel* 67(1): 26–31.

Shih, H.-A., Y.-H. Chiang, and I.-S. Kim (2005). "Expatriate performance management from MNEs of different national origins." *International Journal of Manpower* 26(2): 157–76.

Shimada, H., and J.P. MacDuffie (1999). "Industrial relations and 'humanware': Japanese investments in automobile manufacturing in the United States." In *The Japanese enterprise*, ed. S. Beechler. London: Routledge.

Shortland, S. (2014). "Women expatriates: A research history." In *Research handbook on women in international management*, eds. K. Hutchings and S. Michailova. Cheltenham: Edward Elgar.

Siegel, J.I. (2007). "Lincoln Electric." Case study no. 707-445. Harvard Business School, Boston.

———— (2008a). "Lincoln Electric." Case study no. 707-445. Harvard Business School, Boston.

———— (2008b). "Global Talent Management at Novartis." Case study no. 708-486. Harvard Business School, Boston.

Siegel, J.I., and B.Z. Larson (2009). "Labor market institutions and global strategic adaptation: Evidence from Lincoln Electric." *Management Science* 55(9): 1527–46.

Sikora, D.M., and G.R. Ferris (2014). "Strategic human resource practice implementation: The critical role of line management." *Human Resource Management Review* 24(3): 271–81.

Simon, H. (1996). *Hidden champions: Lessons from 500 of the world's best unknown companies*. Boston, MA: Harvard Business School Press.

Simonin, B.L. (1999). "Ambiguity and process of knowledge transfer in strategic alliances." *Strategic Management Journal* 20(7): 596–623.

Simons, T.L., R. Peterson, and S. Task (2000). "Task conflict and relationship conflict in top management teams: The pivotal role of intragroup trust." *Journal of Applied Psychology* 85(1): 102–11.

Sippola, A., and A. Smale (2007). "The global integration of diversity management: A longitudinal case study." *International Journal of Human Resource Management* 18(11): 1895–916.

Sisson, K. (1994). "Personnel management: Paradigms, practice and prospects." In *Personnel management*, ed., K. Sisson. 2nd ed. Oxford: Blackwell.

Sitkin, S.B., and A.L. Pablo (2005). "The neglected importance of leadership in M&As." In *Mergers and acquisitions: Managing culture and human resources*, eds. G.K. Stahl and M.E. Mendenhall. Stanford, CA: Stanford University Press.

Sitkin, S.B., K.E. See, C.C. Miller, M.W. Lawless, and A.M. Carton (2011). "The paradox of stretch goals: Organizations in pursuit of the seemingly impossible." *Academy of Management Review* 36(3): 544–66.

Slangen, A.H.L (2006). "National cultural distance and initial foreign acquisition performance: The moderating effect of integration." *Journal of World Business* 41(2): 161–70.

Smale, A., I. Björkman, M. Ehrnrooth, K. Mäkelä, and J. Sumelius (2015). "Organizational identification in MNC subsidiaries: A multi-level study." *Journal of International Business Studies* 46(7): 761–83.

Smith, W.K. (2014). "Dynamic decision making: A model of senior leaders managing strategic paradoxes." *Academy of Management Journal* 57(6): 1592–1623.

Smith, P.B., and M.H. Bond (1999). *Social psychology across cultures*, 2nd ed. Boston, MA: Allyn and Bacon.

Smith, W.K., and M.L. Lewis (2011). "Toward a theory of paradox: A dynamic equilibrium model of organizing." *Academy of Management Review* 36(2): 381–403.

Snell, S.A. (1999). "Social capital and strategic HRM: It's who you know." *Human Resource Planning* 22(3): 62–5.

Snell, S.A., and J.W. Dean (1992). "Integrated manufacturing and human resource management: A human capital perspective." *Academy of Management Journal* 35(3): 467–504.

Snow, C., R.E. Miles, and H. Coleman (1992). "Managing 21st century network organizations." *Organizational Dynamics* (Winter): 5–20.

Snow, C., S.A. Snell, S.C. Davison, and D.C. Hambrick (1996). "Use transnational teams to globalize your company." *Organizational Dynamics* 24(4): 50–67.

Solomon, C.M. (1998). "Today's global mobility." *Workforce* 3(4): 12–17.

Sonnenfeld, J.A., and M.A. Peiperl (1988). "Staffing policy as a strategic response: A typology of career systems." *Academy of Management Review* 13(4): 588–600.

Sorensen, J.B. (2002). "The strength of corporate culture and the reliability of firm performance." *Administrative Science Quarterly* 47(1): 70–91.

Sparrow, P.R. (1999). "International recruitment, selection and assessment." In *The global HR manager: Creating the seamless organisation*, eds. P. Joynt and B. Morton. London: Institute of Personnel and Development.

——— (2007). "Globalization of HR at function level: Four UK-based case studies of the international recruitment and selection process." *International Journal of Human Resource Management* 18(5): 845–67.

Sparrow, P., C. Brewster, and H. Harris (2004). *Globalizing human resource management*. London: Routledge.

Sparrow, P.R., and J.-M. Hiltrop (1994). *European human resource management in transition*. New York: Prentice Hall.

Sparrow, P., and L. Otaye (2015). "Employer branding: From attraction to a core HR strategy." White paper 15/1, Lancaster University School of Management.

Spear, S.J. (2004). "Learning to lead at Toyota." *Harvard Business Review* (May): 78–86.

Spector, B. (1995). *Taking charge and letting go: A breakthrough strategy for creating and managing the horizontal company*. Darby, PA: Diane Publishing.

Spekman, R.E., L. Isabella, T. MacAvoy, and T.M. Forbes III (1998). "Alliance management: A view from the past and a look to the future." *Journal of Management Studies* 35(6): 747–72.

Spreitzer, G.M. (1996). "Social structural characteristics of psychological empowerment." *The Academy of Management Journal* 39(2): 483–504.

Spreitzer, G., M.W. McCall, and J. Mahoney (1997). "The early identification of international leadership potential: Dimensions, measurement and validation." *Journal of Applied Psychology* 82(1): 6–29.

Springer, B., and S. Springer (1990). "Human resource management in the US: Celebration of its centenary." In *Human resource management: An international comparison*, ed. R. Piper. Berlin: de Gruyter.

Staber, U. (2003). "Social capital or strong culture?" *Human Resource Development International* 6(3): 413–20.

Stahl, G.K. (2000). "Between ethnocentrism and assimilation: An exploratory study of the challenges and coping strategies of expatriate managers." Proceedings of the Annual Conference of the Academy of Management, Toronto.

Stahl, G.K., I. Björkman, E. Farndale, S. Morris, J. Paauwe, P. Stiles, J. Trevor, and P. Wright (2007). "Global talent management: How leading multinationals build and sustain their talent pipeline." Working paper no. 2007/34/OB. INSEAD, Fontainebleau.

Stahl, G., I. Björkman, E. Farndale, S.S. Morris, J. Paauwe, P. Stiles, and P. Wright (2012). "Six principles of effective global talent management." *MIT Sloan Management Review* 53(2): 25–42.

Stahl, G.K., and M.Y. Brannen (2013). "Building cross-cultural leadership competence: An interview with Carlos Ghosn." *Academy of Management Learning & Education* 12(3): 494–502.

Stahl, G.K., and J.L. Cerdin (2004). "Global careers in French and German multinational corporations." *Journal of Management Development* 23(9): 885–902.

Stahl, G.K., C.H. Chua, P. Caligiuri, J.-L.E. Cerdin, and M. Taniguchi (2007). "International assignments as a career development tool: Factors affecting turnover intentions among executive talent." Research paper no. 2007/24/OB. INSEAD, Fontainebleau.

——— (2009). "Predictors of turnover intentions in learning-driven and demand-driven international assignments: The role of repatriation concerns, satisfaction with company support, and perceived career advancement opportunities." *Human Resource Management* 48(1): 89–109.

Stahl, G.K., and K. Koester (2013). "Lenovo-IBM: Bridging cultures, languages, and time zones: Integration challenges (B)." WU Case Series, 5. WU Vienna University of Economics and Business, Vienna.

Stahl, G.K., and M.E. Mendenhall (eds.) (2005). *Mergers and acquisitions: Managing culture and human resources.* Stanford, CA: Stanford University Press.

Stahl, G.K., E.L. Miller, and R.L. Tung (2002). "Towards the boundaryless career: A closer look at the expatriate career concept and the perceived implications of an international assignment." *Journal of World Business* 37(3): 216–27.

Stahl, G.K., and S.B. Sitkin (2010). "Trust dynamics in acquisitions: The role of relationship history, interfirm distance, and acquirer's integration approach." *Advances in mergers and acquisitions* 9: 51–82.

Stahl, G.K., and A. Voigt (2008). "Do cultural differences matter in mergers and acquisitions? A tentative model and examination." *Organization Science* 19(1): 160–76.

Stalk, J.G. (1988). "Time: The next source of competitive advantage." *Harvard Business Review* (July–August): 41–53.

Steger, U., and C. Kummer (2004). "Challenges of governance structures in international mergers and acquisitions." In *Managing complex mergers*, eds. P. Morosini and U. Steger. London: Financial Times Prentice Hall.

Stening, B.W., J.E. Everett, and P.A. Longton (1981). "Mutual perception of managerial performance and style in multinational subsidiaries." *Journal of Occupational Psychology* 54(4): 255–63.

Stewart, T.A., and A.P. Raman (2007). "Lessons from Toyota's long drive." *Harvard Business Review* (July–August): 74–83.

Stiglitz, J.E. (2006). *Making globalization work.* New York: Norton.

St. John, C.H., S.T. Young, and J.T. Miller (1999). "Coordinating manufacturing and marketing in international firms." *Journal of World Business* 34(2): 109–27.

Stone, D.L., D.L. Deadrick, K.M. Lukaszewski, and R. Johnson (2015). "The influence of technology on the future of human resource management." *Human Resource Management Review* 25(2): 216–31.

Stopford, J.M., and L.T. Wells (1972). *Managing the multinational enterprise.* London: Longman.

Story, J.S.P., J.E. Barbuto, Jr., F. Luthans, and J.A. Bovaird (2014). "Meeting the challenges of international HRM: Analysis of the antecedents of global mindset." *Human Resource Management* 53(1): 131–55.

Strikwerda, J., and J.W. Stoelhorst (2009). "The emergence and evolution of the multidimensional organization." *California Management Review* 51(4): 11–31.

Stroh, L.K. (1995). "Predicting turnover among repatriates: Can organizations affect retention rates?" *International Journal of Human Resource Management* 6(2): 443–56.

Stroh, L.K., J.S. Black, M.E. Mendenhall, and H. Gregersen (2005). *Global leaders, global assignments: An integration of research and practice*. London: Lawrence Erlbaum.

Stroh, L.K., A. Varma, and S.J. Valy-Durbin (2000). "Why are women left at home: Are they unwilling to go on international assignments?" *Journal of World Business* 35(3): 241–55.

Strohmeier, S. (2007). "Research in e-HRM. Review and implications." *Human Resource Management Review* 17(1): 19–37.

Subramaniam, M., and N. Venkatraman (2001). "Determinants of transnational new product development capability: Testing the influence of transferring and deploying tacit overseas knowledge." *Strategic Management Journal* 22(4): 359–78.

Sudarsanam, S. (2012). "Value creation and value appropriation in M&A deals." In *Handbook of mergers & acquisitions*, eds. D. Faulkner, S. Teerikangas, and R. Joseph. Oxford: Oxford University Press.

Sullivan, J.J., and I. Nonaka (1986). "The application of organizational learning theory to Japanese and American management." *Journal of International Business Studies* 17(3): 127–47.

Sumelius, J., I. Björkman, M. Ehrnrooth, K. Mäkelä, and A. Smale (2014). "What determines employee perceptions of HRM process features? The case of performance appraisal in MNC subsidiaries." *Human Resource Management* 53(4): 569–92.

Sumelius, J., I. Björkman, and A. Smale (2008). "The influence of internal and external social networks on HRM capabilities in MNC subsidiaries in China." *International Journal of Human Resource Management* 19(12): 2294–307.

Suutari, V., and C. Brewster (1999). "International assignments across European borders: No problems?" In *International HRM: Contemporary issues in Europe*, eds. C. Brewster and H. Harris. London: Routledge.

——— (2000). "Making their own way: International experience through self-initiated foreign assignments." *Journal of World Business* 35(4): 417–36.

——— (2003). "Repatriation: Empirical evidence from a longitudinal study of careers and expectations among Finnish expatriates." *International Journal of Human Resource Management* 14(7): 1132–51.

Suutari, V., and M. Tahvanainen (2002). "The antecendents of performance management among Finnish expatriates." *International Journal of Human Resource Management* 13(1): 55–75.

Suutari, V., and C. Tornikoski (2001). "The challenge of expatriate compensation: The sources of satisfaction and dissatisfaction among expatriates." *International Journal of Human Resource Management* 12(3): 389–404.

Szulanski, G. (1996). "Exploring internal stickiness: Impediments to the transfer of best practice within the firm." *Strategic Management Journal* 17(Winter Special Issue): 27–43.

Tahvanainen, M. (2000). "Expatriate performance management: The case of Nokia Telecommunications." *Human Resource Management* 39(2/3): 267–76.

Tahvanainen, M., D. Welch, and V. Worm (2005). "Implications of short-term international assignments." *European Management Journal* 23(6): 663–73.

Tait, E., H. De Cieri, and Y. McNulty (2014). "The opportunity cost of saving money: An exploratory study of permanent transfers and localization of expatriates in Singapore." *International Studies of Management & Organization* 44(3): 80–95.

Takeuchi, H., and I. Nonaka (1986). "The new product development game." *Harvard Business Review* (January–February): 137–46.

Takeuchi, H., E. Osono, and N. Shimizu (2008). "The contradictions that drive Toyota's success." *Harvard Business Review* (June): 96–104.

Tanure, B., P.A.L. Evans, and V. Pucik (2007). *A gestao de pessoas no Brasil*. Rio de Janeiro: Elsevier.

Tapscott, D., and A.D. Williams (2007). *Wikinomics: How mass collaboration changes everything*. New York: Penguin.

Taylor, F.W. (1911). *Principles of scientific management*. New York: Harper.

Taylor, S. (2007). "Creating social capital in MNCs: The international human resource management challenge." *Human Resource Management Journal* 17(4): 336–54.

—— (2015). "Global cultures in MNEs." In *The Routledge companion to international human resource management*, eds. D.G. Collings, G.T. Wood, and P.M. Caligiuri. London: Routledge.

Taylor, S., S. Beechler, and N. Napier (1996). "Toward an integrative model of strategic international human resource management." *Academy of Management Review* 21(4): 959–85.

Taylor, S., and N. Napier (1996). "Working in Japan: Lessons from women expatriates." *MIT Sloan Management Review* 37(3): 76–84.

Tead, O., and H.C. Metcalf (1920). *Personnel administration*. New York: McGraw-Hill.

Teagarden, M.B., J. Meyer, and D. Jones (2008). "Knowledge sharing among high-tech MNCs in China and India: Invisible barriers, best practices, next steps." *Organizational Dynamics* 37(2): 190–202.

Teece, D.J. (1987). *The competitive challenge*. Cambridge, MA: Ballinger.

—— (2014). "The foundations of enterprise performance: Dynamic and ordinary capabilities in an (economic) theory of firms." *Academy of Management Perspectives* 28(4): 328–52.

Teece, D.J., G. Pisano, and A. Shuen (1997). "Dynamic capabilities and strategic management." *Strategic Management Journal* 18(7): 509–33.

Teerikangas, S., G.K. Stahl, I. Björkman, and M.E. Mendenhall (2014). "IHRM issues in mergers and acqusitions." In *The Routledge companion to international human resource management*, eds. D.G. Collings, G.T. Wood, and P.M. Caligiuri. London: Routledge.

Teerikangas, S., P. Very, and V. Pisano (2011). "Integration manager's value-capturing roles and acquisition performance." *Human Resource Management* 50(5): 651–83.

Teigland, R. (2000). "Communities of practice in a high-technology firm." *The flexible firm: Capability management in network organizations*, eds. J. Birkinshaw and P. Hagström. New York: Oxford University Press.

Terpstra, D.E., and E.J. Rozell (1993). "The relationship of staffing practices to organizational level measures of performance." *Personnel Psychology* 46(1): 27–48.

Thibaut, J.W., and L. Walker (1975). *Procedural justice: A psychological analysis*. Hillsdale, NJ: Lawrence Erlbaum.

Thomas, D.A. (2004). "Diversity as strategy." *Harvard Business Review* (September): 98–108.

Thomas, R.J., and W.G. Bennis (2008). *Crucibles of leadership: How to learn from experience to become a great leader*. Boston, MA: Harvard Business School Press.

Thomas, D.C., and M.B. Lazarova (2006). "Expatriate adjustment and performance: A critical review." In *Handbook of research in international human resource management*, eds. G.K. Stahl and I. Björkman. Cheltenham: Edward Elgar.

Thompson, L. (2000). *Making the team: A guide for managers*. Upper Saddle River, NJ: Prentice Hall.

Tian, X., M. Harvey, and J.W. Slocum (2014). "The retention of Chinese managers: The Chinese puzzle box." *Organizational Dynamics* 43(1): 44–52.

Tichy, N.M., M.I. Brimm, R. Charam, and H. Takeuchi (1992). "Leadership development as a lever for global transformation." In *Globalizing management: Creating and leading the competitive organization*, eds. V. Pucik, N.M. Tichy, and C.K. Barnett. New York: Wiley.

Tichy, N.M., and S. Sherman (1993). *Control your destiny or someone else will*. New York: HarperBusiness.

Timming, A.R. (2007). "European Works Councils and the dark side of managing worker voice." *Human Resource Management Journal* 17(3): 248–64.

Toh, S.M., and A.S. DeNisi (2005). "Host country nationals: The missing key to expatriate success and failure?" *Academy of Management Executive* 19(1): 132–46.

Torbiörn, I. (1982). *Living abroad: Personal adjustment and personnel policy in the overseas setting.* New York: Wiley.

——— (1985). "The structure of managerial roles in cross-cultural settings." *International Studies of Management & Organization* 15(1): 52–74.

Tornikoski, C., V. Suutari, and M. Festing (2014). "Compensation package of international assignees." In *The Routledge companion to international human resource management*, eds. D.G. Collings, G.T. Wood, and P.M. Caligiuri. New York: Routledge.

Torrington, D., and L. Hall (1995). *Human resource management.* London: Prentice Hall.

Toynbee, A. (1946). *A study of history*, Vols. 1–6. New York: Oxford University Press.

Trepo, G. (1973). "Management style à la française." *European Business* (Autumn): 71–9.

Trompenaars, F. (1993). *Riding the waves of culture: Understanding cultural diversity in business.* London: Nicholas Brealey.

Tsai, W., and S. Ghoshal (1998). "Social capital and value creation: The role of intrafirm networks." *Academy of Management Journal* 41(4): 464–76.

Tsang, E.W.K. (2002). "Acquiring knowledge by foreign partners from international joint ventures in a transition economy: Learning-by-doing and learning myopia." *Strategic Management Journal* 23(9): 835–54.

Tung, R.L. (1981). "Selection and training of personnel for overseas assignments." *Columbia Journal of World Business* 16(1): 68–78.

——— (1982). "Selection and training procedures of US, European, and Japanese multinationals." *California Management Review* 25(1): 57–71.

Tung, R.L. (1988). "Career issues in international assignments." *Academy of Management Executive* 2(3): 241–44.

——— (1995). "Women in a changing global economy." Paper presented at the Tenth Annual Conference of the Society for Industrial and Organizational Psychology, Orlando, FL.

——— (1997). "Canadian expatriates in Asia-Pacific: An analysis of their attitude toward and experience in international assignments." Paper presented at the meeting of the Society for Industrial and Organizational Psychology, St. Louis, MO.

——— (2004). "Female expatriates: A model for global leaders." *Organizational Dynamics* 33(3): 243–53.

Tungli, Z., and M. Peiperl (2009). "Expatriate practices in German, Japanese, UK, and US multinational companies: A comparative survey of changes." *Human Resource Management* 48(1): 153–71.

Tushman, M.L., W.H. Newman, and E. Romanelli (1986). "Convergence and upheaval: Managing the unsteady pace of organizational evolution." *California Management Review* 29(1): 29–44.

Tushman, M.L., and C.A. O'Reilly (1996). "Ambidextrous organizations: Managing evolutionary and revolutionary change." *California Management Review* 38(4): 8–30.

Ulrich, D. (1997). *Human resource champions: The next agenda for adding value and delivering results.* Boston, MA: Harvard Business School Press.

Ulrich, D., and D. Beatty (2001). "From partners to players: Extending the HR playing field." *Human Resource Management* 40(4): 293–307.

Ulrich, D., and W. Brockbank (2005). *The HR value proposition.* Boston, MA: Harvard Business School Press.

Ulrich, D., W. Brockbank, D. Johnson, K. Sandholtz, and J. Younger (2008). *HR competencies: Mastery at the intersection or people and business.* Alexandria, VA: SHRM.

Ulrich, D., W. Brockbank, A. Yeung, and D. Lake (1995). "Human resource competencies: An empirical assessment." *Human Resource Management* 34(4): 473–95.

Ulrich, D., and J.H. Dulebohn (2015). "Are we there yet? What's next for HR?" *Human Resource Management Review* 25(2): 188–204.

Ulrich, D., and D.G. Lake (1990). *Organizational capability: Competing from the inside out.* New York: Wiley.

Ulrich, D., M.R. Losey, and G. Lake (1997). *Tomorrow's HR management: 48 thought leaders call for change.* New York: Wiley.

Ulrich, D., and N. Smallwood (2007). *Leadership brand: Developing customer-focused leaders to drive performance and build lasting value.* Boston, MA: Harvard Business School Press.

Ulrich, D., J. Younger, and W.B. Brockbank (2008). "The twenty-first-century HR organization." *Human Resource Management* 47(4): 829–50.

Ulrich, D., J. Younger, W. Brockbank, and M.D. Ulrich (2013). "The state of the HR profession." *Human Resource Management* 52(3): 457–71.

Ulrich, D., J. Zenger, and N. Smallwood (1999). *Results-based leadership.* Boston, MA: Harvard Business School Press.

Vaara, E. (2003). "Post-acquisition integration as sensemaking: Glimpses of ambiguity, confusion, hypocrisy, and politicization." *Journal of Management Studies* 40(4): 859–94.

Vaara, E., J. Tienari, and I. Björkman (2003). "Global capitalism meets national spirit." *Journal of Management Inquiry* 12(4): 377–93.

Vaiman, V., and C. Brewster (2015). "How far do cultural differences explain the differences between nations? Implications for HRM." *International Journal of Human Resource Management* 26(2): 151–64.

Vance, C.M. (2006). "Strategic upstream and downstream considerations for effective global performance management." *International Journal of Cross Cultural Management* 6(1): 37–56.

Vance, C.M., S.R. McClaine, D.M. Boje, and D.H. Stage (1992). "An examination of the transferability of traditional performance appraisal principles across cultural boundaries." *Management International Review* 32(4): 313–26.

Van de Ven, A.H., D.E. Polley, R. Garud, and S. Venkataraman (1999). *The innovation journey.* New York: Oxford University Press.

Van der Heyden, L., C. Blondel, and R.S. Carlock (2005). "Fair process: Striving for justice in family business." *Family Business Review* 18(1): 1–22.

Van der Heyden, L., and T. Limberg (2007). "Why fairness matters." *International Commerce Review* 7(2): 93–102.

Van Maanen, J., and E.H. Schein (1979). "Toward a theory of organization socialization." In *Research in organizational behavior*, Vol. 1, ed. B. Staw. Greenwich, CT: JAI Press.

Van Veen, K., and I. Marsman (2008). "How international are executive boards of European MNCs? National diversity in 15 European countries." *European Management Journal* 26(3): 188–98.

Van Wijk, R., J. Jansen, and M.A. Lyles (2008). "Inter- and intra-organizational knowledge transfer: A meta-analytic review and assessment of its antecedents and consequences." *Journal of Management Studies* 45(4): 830–53.

Varma, A., P.S. Budhwar, and A.S. DeNisi (eds.) (2008). *Performance management systems: A global perspective.* London: Routledge.

Varma, A., P. Budhwar, and C. McCusker (2014). "Performance management in the global organization." In *The Routledge companion to international human resource management*, eds. D.G. Collings, G.T. Wood, and P.M. Caligiuri. New York: Routledge.

Vaupel, J.W., and J.P. Curhan (1973). *The world's largest multinational enterprises.* Cambridge, MA: Harvard University Press.

Verbeke, A., and T.P. Kenworthy (2008). "Multidivisional vs. metanational governance of the multinational enterprise." *Journal of International Business Studies* 39(6): 940–56.

Vermeulen, G.A.M., and H.G. Barkema (2001). "Learning through acquisitions." *Academy of Management Journal* 44(3): 457–76.

Vernon, R. (1966). "International investment and international trade in the product cycle." *Quarterly Journal of Economics*. 80(2): 190–207.

——— (1977). *Storm over the multinationals: The real issues*. Cambridge, MA: Harvard University Press.

Vernon, R., L.T. Wells, and S. Rangan (1997). *The manager in the international economy*. Englewood Cliffs, NJ: Prentice Hall.

Visser, J. (2006). "Union membership statistics in 24 countries." *Monthly Labour Review* 129(1): 38–49.

Vlasic, B., and B.A. Stertz (2000). *Taken for a ride: How Daimler-Benz drove off with Chrysler*. New York: Wiley.

Vo, A., and P. Stanton (2011). "The transfer of HRM policies and practices to a transitional business system: The case of performance management practices in the US and Japanese MNEs operating in Vietnam." *International Journal of Human Resource Management* 22(17): 3513–27.

Volberda, H.W. (1998). *Building the flexible firm: How to remain competitive*. New York: Oxford University Press.

Volmer, H.M., and D.L. Mills (1966). *Professionalization*. Englewood Cliffs, NJ: Prentice Hall.

Vora, D., T. Kostova, and K. Roth (2007). "Roles of subsidiary managers in multinational corporations: The effect of dual organizational identification." *Management International Review* 47(4): 595–620.

Vuori, T.O., and Q.N. Huy (2015). "Distributed attention and shared emotions in the innovation process: How Nokia lost the smartphone battle." *Administrative Science Quarterly*. Available online September 18, 2015.

Waddington, J. (2003). "What do representatives think of the practices of European Works Councils? Views from six countries." *European Journal of Industrial Relations* 9(3): 303–25.

Walker, J.W. (1980). *Human resource planning*. New York: McGraw-Hill.

Wang, X., and D.Z. Nayir (2006). "How and when is social networking important? Comparing European expatriate adjustment in China and Turkey." *Journal of International Management* 12(4): 449–72.

Waxin, M., A. Roger, and J.L. Chandon (1997). "L'intégration des expatriés dans leur nouveau poste, une analyse contingente et quantitative, le cas des expatriés français en Norvège." In *GRH face à la crise: GRH en crise?* eds. B. Sire and M. Tremblay. Montreal: Presse HEC.

Weber, Y., and S.Y. Tarba (2014). "Strategic agility: A state of the art." *California Management Review* 56(3): 5–12.

WEF (2014). *Education and Skills 2.0: New targets and innovative approaches*. Geneva: World Economic Forum.

Wegner, E.C., and W.M. Snyder (2000). "Communities of practice: The organizational frontier." *Harvard Business Review* 78(1): 139–45.

Weick, K.E. (1979). *The social psychology of organizing*. Boston, MA: Addison-Wesley.

Weiss, S.E. (1994). "Negotiating with 'Romans'—Part 1." *Sloan Management Review* 35(2): 51–61.

Welch, D.E., and L.S. Welch (2006). "Commitment for hire? The viability of corporate culture as a MNC control mechanism." *International Business Review* 15(1): 14–28.

Welch, D.E., and V. Worm (2006). "International business travellers: Challenge for IHRM." In *Handbook of research in international human resource management*, eds. G.K. Stahl and I. Björkman. Cheltenham, UK: Edward Elgar.

Welch, D.E., V. Worm, and M. Fenwick (2003). "Are virtual international assignments feasible?" *Management International Review* 1(Special Issue): 95–114.

Welch, J. with S. Welch (2005). *Winning*. London: HarperCollins.

Westney, D.E. (1988). "Domestic foreign learning curves in managing international cooperative strategies." In *Cooperative strategies in international business*, eds. F.J. Contractor and P. Lorange. Lexington, MA: Lexington Books.

———— (2014). "The organizational architecture of the multinational corporation." In *Advances in international management*, eds. L. Tihany, T. Pedersen, and T. Devinny. Bingley: Emerald.

Westphal, J.D., R. Gulati, and S.M. Shortell (1997). "Customization or conformity?: An institutional and network perspective on the content and consequences of TQM adoption." *Administrative Science Quarterly* 42(2): 366–94.

Whitley, R.D. (1990). "The societal construction of business systems in East Asia." *Organization Studies* 11(1): 47–74.

———— (1992). *European business systems: Firms and markets in their national contexts*. London and Beverly Hills: Sage.

———— (1999). *Alternative systems of capitalism*. New York: Oxford University Press.

Wiechmann, D., A.M. Ryan, and M. Hemingway (2003). "Designing and implementing global staffing systems: Part I-Leaders in global staffing." *Human Resource Management* 42(1): 71–83.

Wilkins, M. (1970). *The emergence of multinational enterprise*. Cambridge, MA: Harvard University Press.

———— (1988). "European and North American multinationals, 1870–1914: Comparisons and contrasts." *Business History* 30(1): 8–45.

Williamson, O.E. (1975). *Markets and hierarchies: Analysis and antitrust implications*. New York: Free Press.

Williamson, P.J., and A.P. Raman (2011). "How China reset its global acquisition agenda." *Harvard Business Review* (April): 109–14.

Winterton, J. (2007). "Training, development, and competence." In *The Oxford handbook of human resource management*, eds. P. Boxall, J. Purcell, and P. Wright. New York: Oxford University Press.

Womack, J.P., D.T. Jones, and D. Roos (1990). *The machine that changed the world*. New York: Rawson Associates.

Wong, C.S., and K. Law (1999). "Managing localization of human resources in the PRC: A practical model." *Journal of World Business* 34(1): 26–40.

Wood, G., C. Brewster, and M. Brookes (2014). *Human resource management and the institutional perspective*. New York: Routledge.

Wood, G., A. Psychogios, L.T. Szamosi, and D.G. Collings (2012). "Institutional approaches to comparative HRM." In *Handbook of research on comparative human resource management*, eds. C. Brewster and W. Mayerhofer. Northampton, MA: Edward Elgar.

Wren, D.A. (1994). *The evolution of management thought*. London: Wiley.

Wright, C. (2008). "Reinventing human resource management: Business partners, internal consultants and the limits to professionalization." *Human Relations* 61(8): 1063–86.

Wright, P.M., and W.R. Boswell (2002). "Desegregating HRM: A review and synthesis of micro and macro human resource management research." *Journal of Management* 28(3): 247–76.

Wright, P.M., and L.H. Nishii (2013). "Strategic HRM and organizational behavior: Integrating multiple levels of analysis." In *Innovations in HR*, ed. D. Guest. Oxford: Blackwell Publishing.

Wurtz, O. (2014). "An empirical investigation of the effectiveness of pre-departure and in-country cross-cultural training." *International Journal of Human Resource Management* 25(14): 2088–101.

Yamazaki, Y., and D.C. Kayes (2004). "An experiential approach to cross-cultural learning: A review and integration of competencies for successful expatriate adaptation." *Academy of Management Learning and Education* 3(4): 362–79.

Yamin, M., and R.R. Sinkovics (2006). "Online internationalisation, psychic distance reduction and the virtuality trap." *International Business Review* 15(4): 339–60.

Yang, Y. (2014). "I came back because the company needed me." *Harvard Business Review* 92 (July–August): 104–08.

Yanadori, Y. (2011). "Paying both globally and locally: An examination of the compensation management of a US multinational finance firm in the Asia Pacific Region." *International Journal of Human Resource Management* 22(18): 3867–87.

Yip, G.S., and A.J.M. Bink (2007). "Managing global accounts." *Harvard Business Review* (September): 103–11.

Yoo, T., R. Pepper, and J. Garrity (2014). "Talent growth as an equalizer: A view from the ICT industry." In *The Global Talent Competitiveness Index 2014*, eds. B. Lanvin and P. Evans, INSEAD, Fontainebleau. http://global-indices.insead.edu/gtci/.

Yoshihara, H. (1999). "Global operations managed by Japanese." (In Japanese.) Discussion Paper Series No. 108. Research Institute for Economics and Business Administration, Kobe University, Kobe, Japan.

Yoshino, M., and U.S. Rangan (1995). *Strategic alliances: An entrepreneurial approach to globalization*. Cambridge, MA: Harvard Business School Press.

Yu, T., M. Subramaniam, and A.A. Cannella, Jr. (2013). "Competing globally, allying locally: Alliances between global rivals and host-country factors." *Journal of International Business Studies* 44(2): 117–37.

Zaheer, S. (1995). "Overcoming the liability of foreignness." *Academy of Management Journal* 38(2): 341–63.

Zahra, S.A., and G. George (2002). "Absorptive capacity: A review, reconceptualization, and extension." *Academy of Management Review* 27(2): 185–203.

Zahra, S.A., R.D. Ireland, and M.A. Hitt (2000). "International expansion by new venture firms: International diversity, mode of market entry, technological learning, and performance." *Academy of Management Journal* 43(5): 925–50.

Zalan, T., and V. Pucik (2007). "Rebuilding ABB (A)." Case study no. IMD-3-1797. IMD, Lausanne.

Zalan, T., V. Pucik, and W. Blackburn (April 2009). "Corporate entrepreneurship and innovation: The case of Ayudhya Allianz C.P." Paper presented at the Asia Pacific Symposium on Entrepreneurship & Innovation, Sydney.

Zander, L., A.I. Mockaitis, C.L. Butler (2012). "Leading global teams." *Journal of World Business* 47(4): 592–603.

Zander, L., P. Zettinig, and K. Mäkelä (2013). "Leading global virtual teams to success." *Organizational Dynamics* 42(3): 228–37.

Zbaracki, M.J. (1998). "The rhetoric and reality of total quality management." *Administrative Science Quarterly* 43(3): 602–34.

Zeira, Y., and O. Shenkar (1990). "Interactive and specific parent characteristics: Implications for management and human resources in international joint ventures." *Management International Review* 30(Special Issue): 7–22.

Zellmer-Bruhn, M., and C. Gibson (2006). "Multinational organization context: Implications for team learning and performance." *Academy of Management Journal* 49(3): 501–18.

Zeynep, T., E. Corsi, and V. Dessain (2010). *Zara: Managing stores for fast fashion*, Boston: Harvard Business School, 9-610-042.

Zhang, R.M. (2015). "Reflections on managing a Multinational Corporation in China: Business model innovations of the Internet era." *AIB Insights* 15(2): 3–6.

Zhang, Y., D.A. Waldman, Y. Han, and X. Li (2015). "Paradoxical leader behaviors in people management: Antecedents and consequences." *Academy of Management Journal* 58(2): 538–66.

Zohar, D. (1997). *Rewiring the corporate brain: Using the new science to rethink how we structure and lead organizations.* San Francisco: Berrett-Koehler.

Zollo, M., and H. Singh (2004). "Deliberate learning in corporate acquisitions: Post-acquisition strategies and integration capability in U.S. bank mergers." *Strategic Management Journal* 25(13): 1233–56.

Zollo, M., and S.G. Winter (2002). "Deliberate learning and the evolution of dynamic capabilities." *Organization Science* 13(3): 339–51.

Zuboff, S. (1984). *The age of the smart machine.* New York: Basic Books.

INDEX